PREHISTORIC EUROPE

By the same Author

ARCHAEOLOGY AND SOCIETY

PREHISTORIC ENGLAND

THE MESOLITHIC AGE IN BRITAIN

THE MESOLITHIC SETTLEMENT OF
NORTHERN EUROPE

FROM SAVAGERY TO CIVILIZATION

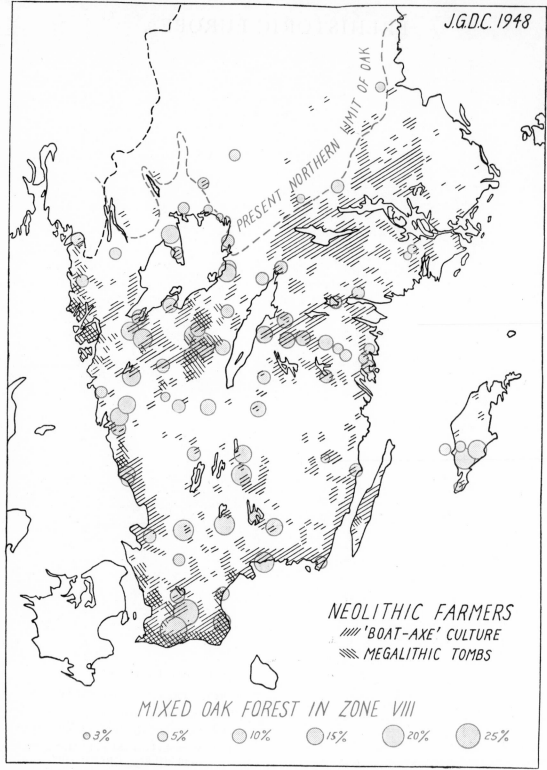

J.G.D.C. 1948

PRESENT NORTHERN LIMIT OF OAK

NEOLITHIC FARMERS
///// 'BOAT-AXE' CULTURE
\\\\\ MEGALITHIC TOMBS

MIXED OAK FOREST IN ZONE VIII

○ 3%   ○ 5%   ○ 10%   ○ 15%   ○ 20%   ○ 25%

Fig. 1   Neolithic settlement and Sub-boreal deciduous forest in south Sweden.

PREHISTORIC EUROPE

The Economic Basis

by

J. G. D. CLARK
M.A., Ph.D., F.B.A., F.S.A.

Fellow of Peterhouse
University Lecturer in Archaeology,
Cambridge

WITH 16 PLATES
AND 180 TEXT ILLUSTRATIONS

STANFORD UNIVERSITY PRESS
Stanford, California

Stanford University Press
Stanford, California
Copyright 1952 by J. G. D. Clark
Library of Congress Catalog Card No. 66-16986
Printed in Great Britain

First published in the United States
in 1952 by Philosophical Library Inc.,
Reissued in 1966 by Stanford University Press

TO FELLOW-PREHISTORIANS

PREFACE

THIS book is concerned with the ways in which early man, in competition with other forms of life, maintained himself on European soil since the end of the Pleistocene Ice Age, and with how he managed not merely to survive but to raise his standards from those of savages to those of peasants ready to support the full weight of urban civilization. An attempt has been made to view this vast subject as it were stereoscopically by bringing into focus two distinct lines of vision, those of the natural scientist and of the historian, the one concerned with the age-long processes of brute nature, the other with human aims and aspirations. It is hoped that the result may prove of interest to geographers, ecologists and historians, as well as to the growing band of prehistoric archaeologists engaged in opening up this great new field of knowledge.

No attempt has been made to assemble more than a small proportion of the information bearing on economic life in prehistoric Europe, evidence which after all includes from one point of view or another every trace of archæological data from this period, as well as a massive weight of biological and geological evidence. The object is indeed less to present definitive results than to stimulate interest in the furtherance of research on lines calculated to yield information at present either lacking or at best lamentably defective. Enough evidence is presented—some of it perhaps unfamiliar to English readers—to show what can be learnt, but the author has been at special pains to point out limitations in existing knowledge.

The late glacial period has been chosen as a point of departure, both because it is from upper palæolithic times that it first becomes possible to recognize human societies rather than mere traditions in the flaking of flint or stone and because it is from the close of this period that Europe began to assume the guise and shape familiar to us. The duration of the prehistoric period of European history has naturally varied in different territories according as these were incorporated early or late within the sphere of literate civilization. In the western Mediterranean and over parts of the temperate zone the prehistoric period was brought to an end by Etruscan, Greek and Punic colonization or by Roman conquest. Over the rest of temperate Europe, the influence of the Empire was so pervasive that the end of the Roman Iron Age marks a convenient limit to our field of study.

Different parts of the continent have had to be treated with unequal emphasis. Soviet Russia and her immediate neighbours are under-represented, since it has been impossible either to visit collections or excavations or to communicate with colleagues in the east and difficult to consult in any systematic manner the literature published there. As regards western Europe, full account has been taken of the character of each of the several zones into which it has been divided by geography, but owing to variations in the standards of research in different territories some are disproportionately represented and others hardly at all. It is only when archæological research has passed the stage of concentrating on establishing the bare cultural and chronological framework that one can begin the task of writing economic prehistory and this has happened in few areas. Again, a real advance can only come through the application of scientific techniques, many of which are of recent origin and few of which

vii

are widely practised. Many of the territories most richly endowed by prehistory, including some with the most honourable places in the earlier history of prehistoric research, are to-day among the chief impediments to the further advance of our studies. If this book does anything to further the extension of techniques developed or perfected in the scientifically most advanced countries to others less fortunate in this respect, it will have served at any rate one of its purposes. It is quite sure that progress in unravelling the prehistory of Europe depends on co-operation between humanists and scientists working in all countries and in full accord.

In writing a book of this kind one inevitably owes much to many individuals and institutions over a period of years. My debt to Cambridge can only be appreciated fully by those who have themselves shared in the life of a great residential university. I would like to acknowledge particularly how much I owe to working in the Department of Archæology and Anthropology, in daily association with colleagues engaged in the study of fossil and living cultures in a museum filled with treasures of human handicraft from all ages. Where close colleagues are concerned it would be invidious to single out names and I prefer to thank them collectively for what they have individually done for me. The atmosphere of Peterhouse, to the Master and Fellows of which I owed my early opportunities for research and to whose society I have recently been more fully admitted, could hardly be more congenial to anyone concerned with history and I would like particularly to acknowledge the stimulus I received from Professor M. Postan's circle of Economic Historians while actually preparing this book. I must also gratefully acknowledge my indebtedness, ever since the active days of the Fenland Research Committee (1932-40), to natural scientists concerned with the ecological setting of early man, and in particular to Dr. Harry Godwin, Director of the Sub-department of Quaternary Research in the University, to whose encouragement I owe so much. I would also like to acknowledge facilities given by the University Library (and particularly the Map Room), the Haddon Library and the libraries of the Museum of Classical Archæology, the Scott Polar Research Institute, the Philosophical Society, the Sedgewick Museum and the Botany School.

I have also to thank friends and colleagues in many other centres in Britain for help in practical ways as well as in many cases through their writings, among them : Mr. M. E. Alexander, Prof. V. G. Childe, Mr. O. G. S. Crawford, Dr. C. Elton, Prof. E. E. Evans, Dr. F. C. Fraser, Dr. T. D. Kendrick, Mr. A. D. Lacaille, Dr. F. J. North, Dr. K. P. Oakley, Miss M. I. Platt, Prof. Stuart Piggott, Dr. R. B. K. Stevenson, Dr. J. F. S. Stone, and Prof. Sulimirski.

The research on which this book is based has involved much travelling and I am deeply indebted to the Trustees of the Leverhulme Research Fellowships for the grant which enabled me to travel extensively in north-western and central Europe during 1947 and 1948. In the course of this I not only gained a vivid impression of the ecology of territories on the northern and southern margins of the temperate zone, but was able to examine numerous museum collections and to visit many prehistoric sites, previously known to me only through the literature. Throughout I was treated with the greatest consideration by European colleagues in the various branches of learning concerned and I would like in particular to thank the following : Dr. C. A. Althin (Lund), Prof. H. Arbman (Lund), Dr. A. Bägge (Stockholm), Dr. C. J. Becker (Copenhagen), Dr. G. Berg (Stockholm), Dr. V. Bodmer-Gessner (Luzern and Zürich), Prof. J. Bøe (Bergen), Dr. M. Degerbøl (Copenhagen), Prof. K. Faegri (Bergen), Prof. G. Gjessing (Oslo), Prof. P. V. Gløb (Aarhus), Dr. J. Granlund (Stockholm), Dr. W. Guyan (Schaffhausen), Dr. T. I. Itkonen (Helsingfors), Prof. S. Lindquist (Uppsala), Dr. E. B. Lundberg (Stockholm), Dr. S. Marstrander

(Oslo, Trondheim), Dr. Therkel Mathiassen (Copenhagen), Dr. Frank Mitchell (Dublin), Dr. N. Nicklasson (Göteborg), Dr. C. A. Nordman (Helsingfors), Prof. J. O. O'Kelly (Cork), Prof. S. P. O'Riordain (Dublin), Prof. R. Pittioni (Vienna), Dr. J. Raftery (Dublin), Dr. H. Rasmussen (Copenhagen), Dr. and Mrs. Sjøvold (Tromsø), Dr. Troels-Smith (Copenhagen), Prof. A. E. van Giffen (Groningen) and Professor E. Vogt (Zürich).

Much of the raw material for this book has been gleaned from published sources, and I am deeply grateful to the many authors, whose works are referred to in the text. I am particularly grateful to the Society of Antiquaries of London, to the Prehistoric Society and to the editors of *Antiquity* for permission to use extracts of material published under my name in their periodicals, and also to many authors, editors and publishers for permission to reproduce illustrations.

I am greatly indebted to my friend Stuart Piggott, Abercromby Professor of Prehistoric Archæology in Edinburgh University, for inviting me to give the Robert Munro Lectures in February, 1949, since it was from these and from their prototypes at Cambridge that the present book took shape.

In the final stages of preparation the text has owed much to my wife's criticisms and patience.

GRAHAME CLARK

Peterhouse, Cambridge
November, 1950

CONTENTS

TEXT ILLUSTRATIONS

PLATES

(a) Mesolithic chisel-ended arrow (*c.* $\frac{2}{3}$), Eising, Ringkøbing, Jutland. (b, c) Tread-traps (*c.* $\frac{1}{8}$), Hinge and Nisset-Nørremose, Lemming, both in Viborg district, Jutland. (d) Resin caulking from Hjortspring boat, Aals, Denmark, showing imprints of bast cords used for sewing (*Nationalmuseet, Copenhagen*). (e) Sterns of dug-out boats from the Trent at Clifton, with grooves for insertion of stern-boards. (f) Mesolithic bow (*c.* $\frac{1}{10}$), Holmegaard, Denmark (*Nationalmuseet, Copenhagen*).

(a) Osier weels used for salmon, Varmland, Sweden (*Photo Nils Keyland*). (b, c) Stone-age traps from Lilla Knabstrup, Holbaek, Jutland (*Nationalmuseet, Copenhagen*).

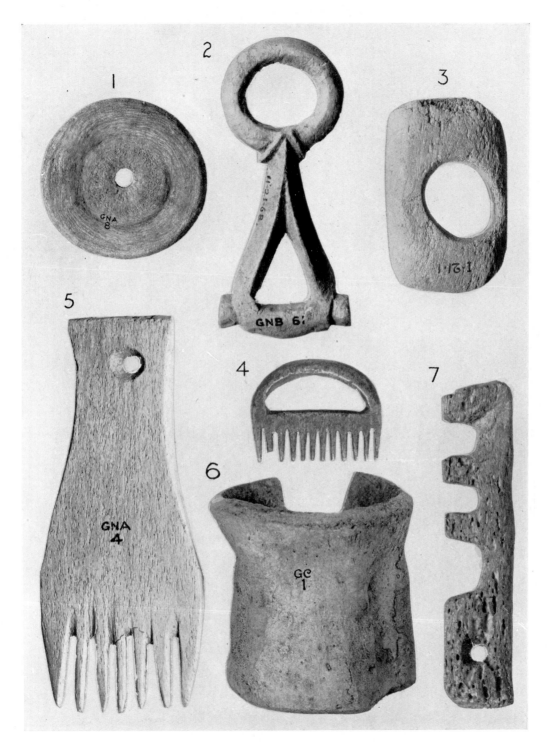

Objects made of whale-bone from Scottish iron age sites (*Nat. Mus. Ant., Edinburgh*).

Scales: no. 1 ($\frac{11}{20}$); nos. 2, 4, 7 ($\frac{1}{1}$); no. 3 ($\frac{2}{3}$); no. 5 ($\frac{9}{10}$): no. 6 ($\frac{9}{20}$)

(a) Miners' picks resting against flint seam, Grimes Graves, Norfolk.

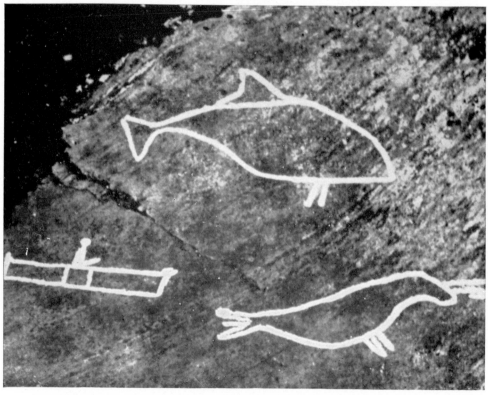

(b) Hunting at sea: Arctic rock-engraving at Rødøy, Nordland, Norway.

a

b

c

(a) Neolithic reaping-knife (*c.* ½), Hitzkirch, Luzern, Switzerland.   (b) Carbonized grain, Itford,
Sussex. (c) 'Burn-beating,' Finland. (*After a painting in the Athenaeum, Helsingfors*).

(a) Modern lakeside settlement, Carelia, with stabilized dug-out canoes in foreground.

(b) Pottery model of plough-scene from the Early Bronze Age, Vounous, Cyprus
(*Nicosia Mus.*).

a

b

(a) Iron age 'long house,' Skørbaek, Jutland. (b) Interior of Neolithic house, Skara Brae, Orkney.

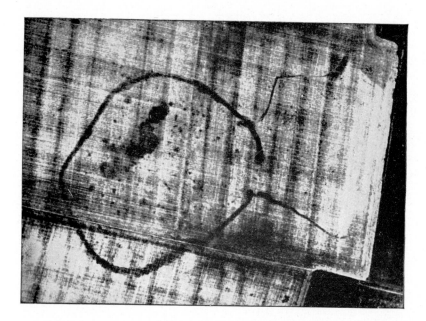

Feet 100 0 100 200 300 400 Feet

b

a

(a) Flint-mines, Harrow-Hill, nr. Worthing,
  Sussex.

(b) Iron age farmstead, Little Woodbury,
  nr. Salisbury, England.

Neolithic adze-mountings, Switzerland (*c.* $\frac{5}{11}$): (a) Lüscherz. (b, c) Greng, Murtensee
(*Photos Landesmuseum, Zürich*).

Lime-bark containers: (a) resin caulking ($\frac{2}{3}$) from iron age burial, N. Kvinneby, Stenasa, Öland I., Sweden (*Statens Hist. Mus., Stockholm*). (b) Modern container, Esthonia (*Nordiska Mus., Stockholm*). (c) Container (*c.* $\frac{1}{2}$) from bronze age oak-coffin burial, Egtved, Denmark (*Nationalmuseet, Copenhagen*). (d) Resin caulking with impression of seam from Iron age burial, Mörbylanga, Öland I. (*Statens Hist. Mus., Stockholm*).

b

a

Prehistoric textiles: (a) bronze age burial, Skrydsrup, Jutland, with woollen garment (*Nationalmuseet, Copenhagen*). (b) reconstruction of neolithic decorated linen textile, Irgenhausen, Switzerland (*Landesmuseum, Zürich*).

XII

Birch-bark: (a) Containers and rolls, modern Finland (*National Museum, Helsingfors*). (b) Finnish peasant removing bark from living birch-tree (*Photo U.T. Sirelius*). (c) Container (*c.* $\frac{1}{2}$) from bronze age oak-coffin burial, Egtved, Denmark (*Nationalmuseet, Copenhagen*). (d) Neolithic roll from Egolzwil, Luzern, Switzerland. (e) Neolithic container from Niederwil, Thurgau, Switzerland (*Landesmuseum, Zürich*).

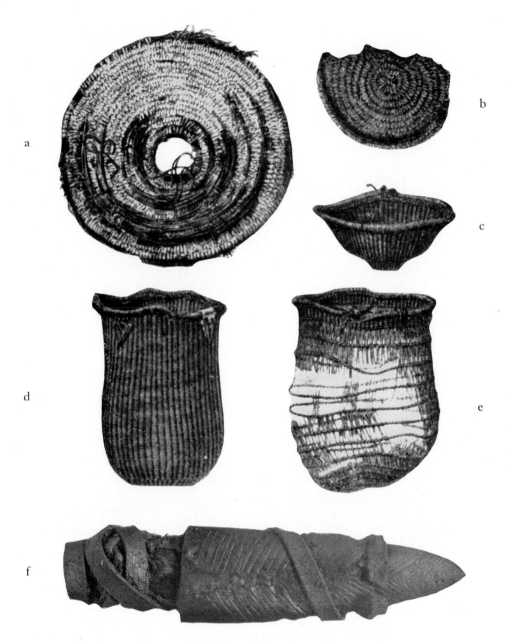

(a-c) Coiled and twined (d, e) basketry from Murciélagos, Spain.
(f) Leather sheath and strap of flint dagger, Wiepenkathen,
Stade, Hanover.

a

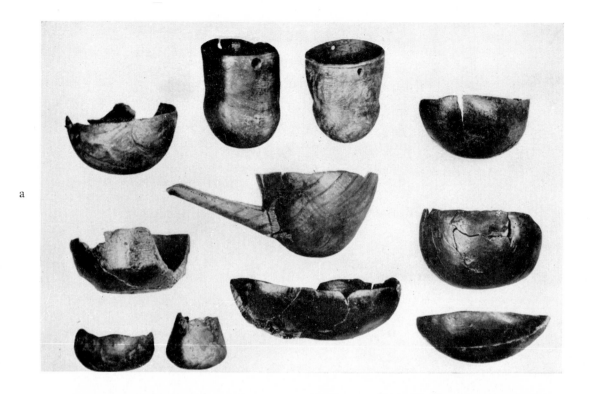

b

c

(a) Bowls and ladle (*c.* ¼) from neolithic settlement, Egolzwil II, Luzern, Switzerland (*Naturhist. Mus. Luzern*). (b) Corner of late bronze age block-house, Wasserburg Buchau, Federseemoor, south Germany (*After Reinerth*). (c) Perforation through pile-shoe from early bronze age settlement of Baldegg, Switzerland, showing axe-marks (*Landesmuseum, Zürich*).

a

b

(a) Stone quarry, Hespriholmen off Bømlo, west Norway. (b) Part of hoard of unused gouges of south Scandinavian flint from Bjürselet, Byske, Västerbotten (*Statens Hist. Mus., Stockholm*).

(a) Hull of dug-out canoe being roughed out from poplar trunk by axe. (b) Inside being hollowed out by adze, Satakunta, Finland (*Photos Eino Nikkilä*). (c, d) Adze-marks on inside of hull of boat 2 and general view of part of boat 1 of the neolithic Verup complex, Aamosen, Denmark (*Photos Troels-Smith*)

INTRODUCTION

" The life of a society is planned on the basis of the traditional arts by which animals, plants, minerals and climate are made to serve the purposes of its existence."[1]

THE principal sources for the reconstruction of economic life during prehistoric times include actual traces of living or working, material embodiments of these activities in the form of artifacts, and contemporary representations of any or all of these. The archæological evidence has survived imperfectly and above all unevenly, according to the substances utilized in antiquity and to the conditions prevailing in the soil where they were found; only too often it is the trivial which has endured, the significant which has perished. Again, it must be admitted that there is still far too wide a range of variation in the standards of archaeological technique in different parts of Europe, since it is upon the competence of excavators that the very possibility of extracting scientific data from vestigial traces in the soil depends. The overwhelming proportion of archaeological evidence has been gathered rather by accident than by design and studied more as an exercise in classification than as a source of history : not only have too many excavations had to be undertaken for reasons extraneous to science, but the whole approach of excavators has too often been perfunctory or at best unimaginative. One may take as an example the " pit-dwellings " consistently reported from early iron age sites in England. Generations of excavators have cleared such pits and accurately recorded their infillings without ever asking themselves what it was they were exploring. Only when Dr Gerhard Bersu undertook the excavation of Little Woodbury, near Salisbury, with the avowed object of learning more about the daily life of a community of iron age farmers was their true function recognized. The transmutation of these pits from dwellings to storage-pits, used for a few seasons and then filled with rubbish, has gone far to alter our appreciation of a whole phase of prehistoric settlement.

Again, too large a part of the material housed in museums or published in the technical literature comprises what may be termed the skeletal structure of prehistoric societies—the flints, bronzes, pots and scraps of iron, which because they survive most frequently are most widely used for classification. The information these are capable of yielding should not be minimized, but the picture they present of the material culture and mode of life of prehistoric man is necessarily limited, since the materials chiefly used by him were perishables like wood, bark, bast, leather, basketry, textiles and matting. If the skeleton is to be clothed with flesh and blood and ultimately inspired with the breath of life, there is need for a shift in emphasis in the sites chosen for excavation from those capable merely of establishing the context of early cultures to those suited to enlarging our knowledge of their content.

---

[1] R. Thurnwald, 1932, 34.

In the meantime the balance can to some extent be rectified by making the most of the exceptional finds where organic materials happen to have survived.

On the credit side there has been a welcome tendency to apply to a widening range of archæological finds the scientific technique best suited to extract the fullest information concerning the materials used and the technique of workmanship. Although an enormous amount remains to be done in this field, significant results have already been obtained. For instance, petrological determination of the stones worked for axes and querns and of the clays used for potting has thrown important light on the extent to which raw materials and finished products were traded at different periods. Again, much has been learnt about the sources of copper and tin ores through chemical and spectrographic analysis of bronzes. Detailed examination of finished or incomplete products, of the moulds used for casting them and of the tools employed in decorating them has revealed much about the ancient bronze smiths and their craft, just as examination of slag has thrown light on early methods of iron-working. There is no limit to what may be learnt as modern technical knowledge is directed to the task of recovering the processes, by which the material objects salvaged by archaeology were made. Particularly fine work has been done in this respect on the prehistoric textiles of Scandinavia and Switzerland.

Another source of information about economic life in prehistoric Europe is representational art, mainly engravings or paintings on rock-surfaces, but including also plastic models in clay or bronze and a few graffiti on clay pots. As with objects of material culture, artistic productions have in the past been studied too exclusively as media for chronology and classification. It must be remembered, though, that as a contemporary record the value of prehistoric art is marred partly by its technical shortcomings—many engravings had to be made on hard rock without the aid of metal—and partly by the more fundamental consideration that the artists rarely even intended to reproduce in naturalistic form the scenes of daily life. The information about economy obtainable from prehistoric art is mainly incidental and is commonly enigmatic. In the matter of publication the position is on the whole not too bad, though it should be appreciated, especially in the case of rock-engravings, many of which are difficult to photograph, that there is a certain subjective element in any modern copy made by hand.

The oldest corpus of material, that from the upper palæolithic caves and rock-shelters of France and Spain, throws precious light on the aims of the hunters and even, despite the rarity of scenes in the former, gives some clues to their methods. The shelter paintings of eastern Spain, the upper palæolithic age of which has recently been confirmed, are particularly valuable in this latter respect. A third art group reflecting the interests of hunters and fishers is that found on the ice-planed boulders of northern Scandinavia, the work of the Arctic dwelling-place people; and to this one should add the rock-engravings round the shores of lake Onega and of the White Sea, studied by Soviet archæologists.

As a rule the art of farming communities was more abstract and less representational and for this reason gives less information about the daily life of its makers. Even so, the late bronze age rock-engravings of Scandinavia and especially of the West Swedish province of Bohuslän, have thrown light on the boats, wheeled vehicles and ploughs of the time, for which only scanty evidence is otherwise available. The practice of making clay models and hardening them in the kiln, which prevailed among many of the earliest peasant groups of south-eastern Europe, has thrown light not only upon livestock for which other evidence is available, but also about houses and even the internal arrangements of these.

In the interpretation of archæological fossils, it is obvious that living societies have much to tell, yet it is very important to remember that the communities with which we are concerned were prehistoric and comparatively primitive. It is impossible, and would in any case be futile, to try and appraise their products in vacuo, but one should be doubly careful to avoid interpreting them in terms of one's own experience in the world of modern technology. Equally to be avoided is the indiscriminate seeking of parallels among cultures far removed in time and space and with which no continuity of tradition can be traced. In truth there is no need to comb the pages of the *Golden Bough*, when the identical activities encountered in prehistoric Europe still survive in the folk culture often of the self-same localities. Professor A. W. Brøgger[2] has gone so far as to claim that :

" To be able to approach any understanding at all of the culture of antiquity, it is absolutely necessary to begin with what we know to-day—to know the elements in the peasant culture still found in Norway and Sweden some 50 to 100 years ago, to know something of life along the coast and at sea, in the forests and amid the mountains, on the land, the fields, the pastures, the hinterland and the mountain farms. Without knowing something of this, one will never attain to the heart of anything comprised within the ancient culture."

To modern prehistorians, concerned with reconstructing rather than with merely classifying the material traces of the past, folk culture is a vital source,[3] but it is one which needs to be used with circumspection, since many elements in peasant life have in fact been devolved from higher strata in the population and may represent comparatively recent emanations from urban civilization.

As might be expected, folk culture has survived longest and most intact in those parts of Europe where the old pattern of economic life has been least disturbed by industrialization, notably in Scandinavia, the western fringes of the old Celtic world, central and south-eastern Europe and the Mediterranean basin. Too many of these areas are ill-provided with resources for large-scale, scientific research. Among the brightest exceptions are the Scandinavian countries and Finland, where splendid research institutions and well-trained scholars are able to work on peculiarly rich material, relating to the economic activities of peasants living on the northern margin of farming and depending to some degree on fishing and on various forms of hunting. The folk culture of these lands as it survived up till the nineteenth century provides rich sources for reconstructing the husbandry and catching activities of the prehistoric peoples of the north. As L. Rütimeyer showed in his *Die Ur-Ethnologie der Schweiz*, Switzerland, also, could show primitive forms of economic activities surviving in remote valleys up till the last century, yet within reach of modern centres of learning and research.

In the more backward parts of Europe there are great and as yet only partly tapped resources, the wealth of which is emphasized from time to time by such a monograph as that by Jankó on Magyar fishing. Owing to the lack of systematic work, however, archæologists have often to explore the possibilities for themselves, as when Werner Buttler travelled through Hungary, Rumania and Yugoslavia to seek data for reconstructing the neolithic granaries and dwellings revealed by excavation at Köln-Lindenthal near Cologne. The

---

[2] A. W. Brøgger, 1940, 166.

[3] J. G. D. Clark, 1951.

relevance of folk-culture in the Mediterranean basin has been well brought out by Stanley Casson[4] who wrote of the Aegean that :

> " the economic condition of peasant and small-town life . . . particularly among the islands, hardly differs in simplicity or complexity from what it was either in the bronze age or in classical Greek times. The average islander and coast-dweller still lives on the same food, and in similar houses to those of his ancestors."

Archæologists working in the Mediterranean area have not been slow to profit from the opportunities around them.

The persistence of elements of culture from prehistoric down to modern times only serves to point the relevance of the historical record. Economic historians have long recognized that the activities of rural society find their origin far back in prehistoric times: the clearance, occupation and cultivation of the soil, the development of stock-raising, fishing, trapping and means of obtaining water, such activities and many others extend far beyond the range of the earliest documents. As Marc Bloch admitted on the opening page of his *Les Caractères originaux de l'histoire rurale française*:

> " Lorsque s'ouvrit la période que nous appelons moyen-âge . . . l'agriculture était déjà, sur notre sol, chose millénaire. Les documents archéologiques l'attestent sans ambages. . . . Cette préhistoire rurale, en elle-même, est hors du sujet que je traite ici ; mais elle le domine."

One reason why historical sources are so valuable is that they help to establish continuity between prehistoric and modern societies, providing the essential link between archæological material and analogies drawn from recent folk-culture. Notable in this respect is the great *Historia de gentibus septentrionalibus* of Olaus Magnus, published in Rome in 1555, the descriptions and woodcuts of which illuminate with wonderful clarity the folk culture of Scandinavia some four hundred years ago. Details of life in the far north from several centuries earlier can be gleaned from the sagas and from such descriptive pieces as those included in King Alfred's edition of the history of Orosius, notably Ohthere's voyage round cape North to the White Sea and Wulfstan's journeyings in the Baltic from Haddeby. Something, also, can be learnt of the mode of life of the Celtic and Teutonic peoples on the threshold of history, whether within or outside the limits of the Empire, from the writings of Strabo, Tacitus and other geographers and historians of the ancient world, vague though these so often are on crucial points of detail. Of the folk culture of Italy in classical times many details can be gathered from the treatises of Varro, Columella and other agronomists, as well as from Vergil, Horace and those who sang of rustic life in their poetry. But the point need hardly be laboured that no record of peasant life should be ignored, whether an elaborate literary description or an incidental reference, or whether depicted in representational arts.

Hardly less enlightening than archaeological or documentary evidence are remains of the animals and plants, on which after all early man subsisted. Since it has long been the practice to publish detailed identifications by experts of the animal and plant remains obtained in excavations, a very substantial body of precise data is already available, though the value of much of this is a good deal less than it might have been. Too often the fauna from caves, bogs or the middens and hearths of open camp-sites has been studied exclusively from a palæontological point of view, its value as a clue to human activities being treated as of

---

[4] *Antiquity*, 1938, 466.

secondary importance, when not entirely ignored. If palæontological interests have been allowed to predominate too exclusively over economic and social ones, this, it must be admitted, is largely due to the narrowly archæological preoccupations of many excavators.

A moment's thought will show how the composition of the fauna from any site can reflect the relative economic importance of hunting and stock-raising. Again it will be evident that the reconstruction of activities such as hunting, fishing and fowling should be based as much on the mammals, fishes and birds, considered as victims, as on the equipment used to catch them. At all times the hunter must adopt his methods and consequently his gear to the anatomy and habits of the creatures he pursues and never more completely than when his weapons were at their least effective. To interpret correctly traces of hunting-gear, at best woefully incomplete, it is essential to establish the proportions in which the various types of quarry are represented, to be sufficiently familiar with the life-cycles and feeding-habits of each species to know their most vulnerable periods and to be aware of the various methods used to catch them by peoples at a comparable level of technical accomplishment. Exceptionally important data have been obtained through the study of individuals which escaped the hunter or the fisherman, bearing in their bodies some portion of the gear intended to secure them. In addition to throwing light on the methods used in hunting and fishing, the faunal remains may be analysed in such a way as to establish the time of the year during which a site has been occupied, a matter of great importance for establishing the seasonal cycle of occupations and the fixity or otherwise of settlements : among the chief clues are seasonal migrants, chiefly birds, foetal or very young individuals and the relative proportions of shed antlers and of specimens broken from the skull.

In the reconstruction of prehistoric farming animal and plant remains have an equally important part to play. Although it is only rarely that an assemblage of faunal remains is large enough for firm conclusions to be drawn about the proportions in which different kinds of livestock were maintained, by combining results from many different sites it is already possible to distinguish broad trends reflecting the development of husbandry during the prehistoric period, as well as regional variations. Considerable attention has been devoted in the past to the origin and diffusion of the various races of cattle, swine, sheep, dogs and horses. A much smaller proportion of the material has been analysed with a view to solving such problems as the age at which different types of livestock were normally slaughtered, but sufficient has been done to yield important clues as to the conditions under which stock-raising was carried on.

As regards plants, it is only to be expected that the evidence should in some respects be less complete. Yet, under certain conditions, notably those obtaining in the beds of ancient lakes, where the deposits are permanently water-logged, plant remains will survive reasonably intact. Although much of the botanical work devoted to the Swiss lake-villages was carried out before the various archæological levels were accurately distinguished, information from this source gives the most complete picture available about the plants collected and cultivated by prehistoric man in central Europe. Similar results can be expected from other areas as more waterlogged sites are excavated. In the meantime carbonized residues and impressions on hand-made pottery and other clay fictiles help to fill out the picture. Indeed, so far as cereals are concerned, one is largely independent of sites where exceptional conditions for the preservation of organic substances prevail : once carbonized, cereal grains and even spikelets and glumes last remarkably well ; incorporated in the walls of pots as they were made and burnt out in the course of firing, their imprints survive as long as pottery itself. By identifying and counting large numbers of such random impressions on hand-made pots it is a simple matter to determine and to express statistically the relative proportions in which the various cereals were cultivated at different times and among different communities.

Much can sometimes be learnt from research carried on independently by natural scientists. The detailed study of ecological change made possible by such a method as pollen analysis is only one example of this. By recording fluctuations in the composition of vegetation, palæobotanists can help, not merely by revealing changes of climate, but even more pointedly by tracing the influence of human activity on the eco-system as a whole. The pollen diagrams allow us to follow not only the effects of climatic amelioration—reflected for instance in the replacement of open vegetation by forest and by the rise to predominance in this of trees requiring progressively warmer temperatures—and of the deterioration which ensued, but also such basic economic processes as the clearance of forest and the extension of cultivation. Variations in the composition of the pollen liberated at successive stages register at the same time ecological and economic change. It is a cardinal thesis of this book that the economic life of early man can most fruitfully be considered in relation to the wider economy of nature.

CHAPTER I

ECOLOGICAL ZONES AND ECONOMIC STAGES

ONE of the principal attractions of prehistory is the opportunity it offers for studying the interplay of social aspirations and environing nature over long periods of time. The economy of any community may be considered as an adjustment to specific physical and biological conditions of certain needs, capacities, aspirations and values. There are thus two sides to the equation—on the one hand the character of the habitat, itself to a greater or less degree influenced or even conditioned by culture, and on the other the kind of life regarded as appropriate by the community and the resources, in the form of knowledge, technical equipment and social organization, available for its realization. The relationship between man and external nature is thus a dynamic one and the development of culture viewed in its economic aspect is indeed one of man's growing knowledge of and control over forces external to himself. The history of man differs from that of any other species precisely in that it has been one of progressive emancipation from the thraldom of instinctive conformity with a pattern imposed by external forces: by every advance in his culture man has enlarged the sphere for the exercise of choice for good or for evil.

Yet it remains true that the economy of any community at any moment of time is necessarily the product of an adjustment between culture and environing nature. Were it possible to visit prehistoric Europe the chances are that one would find stable forms of economy prevailing over wide territories, the result of a more or less perfect adjustment between social appetites, technical capacity and organization and the resources of the several regions. Such a state of equilibrium and stability has at any rate often been observed among modern primitive peoples by anthropologists working in the field. For instance, Evans-Pritchard[1] wrote of the Nuer,

" Oecological relations appear to be in a state of equilibrium. As long as present relations exist cattle husbandry, horticulture, and fishing can be pursued but cannot be improved. Man holds his own in the struggle but does not advance."

Interrelations of culture, biome and habitat in an eco-system.

As the same authority has shown, the Nuer and their culture could well be considered as part of a mature eco-system, itself the product of an interaction between biome (the whole complex of living organisms—plants, animals and men) and habitat (the soil and climate).

---

[1] E. Evans-Pritchard, 1940, 92.

The adjustment between the economic system of the Nuer and their external environment was so perfect that there was no room for any substantial improvement, so long as both these factors remained constant.

Such an equilibrium, with the economic and cultural stability which it implies, was no doubt the normal condition of primitive society. Yet it is equally certain that during prehistoric times there must have been phases of disequilibrium when the pattern of life changed, at times drastically and often quite rapidly. Such periods of change and their underlying causes are obviously a prime concern of economic history, though one should not forget that the tendency must always have been to achieve a new harmony between society and its external environment, so that each phase of disequilibrium invited a fresh adjustment.

The main factors involved in the economic changes whereby the European peoples were ultimately able to reach the stage of recording their own history may be grouped under three main heads. First one should reckon with alterations in the natural environment brought about by processes external to man, changes which were inherent in the natural order of events and over which mankind had no sort of influence, but which enlarged or contracted the range of opportunity open to human societies. The most widespread and comprehensive of these were the climatic changes which marked the transition from late glacial to recent times and are most dramatically exemplified by the retreat of the pleistocene glaciers, by the alterations in land and sea levels due to the melting of the ice-sheets, and by the profound ecological transformations involved in the colonization of open landscape by forest trees and in the successive alterations in the composition of forests brought about by the optimum post-glacial climate and the ensuing deterioration.

Next, and more positively, may be cited changes in the needs and requirements of human societies brought about by a wide range of factors. Some of these, for example the pressure of population on available food supply, were of a purely economic order. Others were primarily cultural, among the most important being the effects of contact between the barbarians of prehistoric Europe and the civilized peoples of the east Mediterranean area. It is indeed axiomatic that the evolution of economic life in prehistoric Europe can only be understood if full account is taken of the influence of the higher forms of economy associated with urban civilization, at first in western Asia and the Nile Valley and later in the Mediterranean. In general it may be urged that once development in any region had gone far enough to give rise to the zoning of societies at varying levels of economy, the mounting needs of the more highly integrated ones affected to an ever-growing degree the history of all the simpler ones within their spheres of influence. So soon as a zoning of societies had been brought about through the attainment of forms of economy more advanced than those based on hunting, fishing and collecting, there was set in motion a process of expansion, whereby the more highly developed spread over the territories of the weaker, less developed communities: farming spread more and more widely over territories formerly given over to food-gathering until it approximated to the limits set by geographical and specifically ecological conditions, and each expansion of the agricultural platform gave more room for enlargements of the urban superstructure. The influence of higher on lower economies was by no means limited to the territories actually incorporated, but through the mechanism of trade spread far beyond these, disturbing the economic—and often the ecological— balance even of distant communities.

Lastly, there are the changes in external environment brought about directly or indirectly by human activities. As a dominant species man must always have affected the balance of nature to some degree, but his importance as an ecological factor grew as he increased in numbers and extended his control over external forces, until he became a principal agent of botanical and zoological change. Each advance in culture increased the ecological dominance of man: the more effectively he was able to intervene in natural processes, the more frequently he must have disturbed by his own activities the adjustment with external nature of his own culture, and the more often in consequence he had to modify his economy to meet the new conditions created by his own exertions. Perhaps the best example of this is deforestation, which is capable not only of altering the character of vegetation and animal life over extensive areas, but also of causing soil-erosion and the formation of mosquito-breeding deltas and even of affecting local climate. Whether as hunter or farmer, the effect of his activities was inevitably to disturb existing relationships between various forms of wild life and between human society and external nature.

The relationships between human society and environing nature were thus reciprocal. The idea that human progress is no more than a product of the inherent dynamism of external nature has only to be formulated for its absurdity to be evident to any whose business it is to observe and classify the manifold diversities of human society. Yet it would be equally wrong, especially when considering societies with a comparatively weak cultural endowment, to minimize the importance of the ecological framework within which all forms of life subsist. As Godwin has recently remarked[2]:

" there is no break in kind between the relationships of the great eco-systems of plant and animal communities, and those which include fewer or more human beings. . . . Since . . . the human agents remain animal in nature, sustain themselves within communities, and subsist on biological materials, they are no less part of the eco-system than were their ancestors."

There is no more faithful indication of regional differences of soil and climate—and few which define more accurately the limits of economic zones at different stages of prehistory —than vegetation. Vegetation is inevitably the main element in the biome of any terrestrial eco-system, since plants " alone have the power of making organic substance from inorganic, of building up living substances from materials like carbon dioxide, water and mineral salts."[3] All other forms of life, including men, even of the most advanced culture, must needs depend for subsistence, directly or indirectly, on vegetation, whether they eat plants or the animals that feed upon them. Since the quest for food is the central fact of economic life, it follows that plant ecology and its development must be of the utmost relevance to economic history.

Geographers have distinguished four main plant-formations which extend at the present day,[4] in broad belts (Fig. 2) across the European continent. From the north to south these comprise:

1. A *treeless zone*, with an arctic or sub-arctic climate too severe to allow the growth of more than tundra or alpine vegetation and comprising: (a) a belt of circumpolar tundra extending across the northernmost territories of Scandinavia and Russia, (b) a contiguous tract of *fjäll* in the Scandinavian mountains, and (c) isolated alpine pockets above the limit of tree-growth in the Alps and Pyrenees and on a smaller scale on the mountain peaks of the British Isles.

---

[2] H. Godwin, *Nature*, 4th October, 1948.

[3] A. G. Tansley, 1946, 15.

[4] The status of the south Russian steppes is uncertain, especially in the marginal areas ; the steppe of the Hungarian Alföld is now considered to date only from the historical period. See A. Garnett, 1945.

2. *Northern coniferous forest*, comprising pine, spruce and silver fir, associated with such trees as birch and willow, capable of flourishing in a moist, cold climate. Although strongly influenced at the present day by scientific forestry, the northern coniferous forest has not suffered deforestation in connection with agriculture or stock-raising to anything like the

Fig. 2.   Main vegetational zones of Europe.

same extent as the deciduous forest. It occupies a broad belt, including much of the Scandinavian peninsula, almost the whole of Finland, and most of European Russia between latitude 60° N. and the circumpolar tundra.

3. *Deciduous summer forest*, adapted to a temperate, sub-oceanic climate, and comprising broad-leaved trees, such as oak, elm, lime, alder and beech, which have their period of growth in summer and shed their leaves in autumn. Immense inroads have been made on

the deciduous forest, which once occupied a broad zone, defined on the north by the northern coniferous forest and on the south by the Mediterranean evergreens. To-day only small patches of deciduous forest survive in what has been transformed into a zone of farmlands interspersed by industrial and urban development.

4. *Mediterranean evergreen forest*, the outcome of a climate of summer drought and winter rains, retains foliage through the winter in order to make growth and is adapted by deep roots and leaves shaped to reduce evaporation to survive the period of enforced rest during the summer heat. At its climax the formation, which is found on the coastal plains and lower mountain slopes of the Mediterranean, was a real forest, though never so dense as those of the temperate and north temperate zones, and comprised such trees as ilex, cypress and olive. To-day it mainly survives in forms to which it has been degraded by human activity, namely maquis (scrub of myrtle, juniper, broom, arbutus, oleander, vine, etc.) and garrigue (including aromatic plants like lavender, thyme and sage, and various bulbs).

Since the final phase of the Pleistocene ice age, the limits of these major ecological zones have shifted within wide limits. Exact and comprehensive information on this point can only be available when the method of pollen-analysis has been applied to the total range of pollen-liberating vegetation over the whole continent and in particular over the pivotal area of France, much of which as regards the late glacial and early post-glacial periods remains virtually unexplored from a palæo-botanical point of view. Yet, provided the limitations are frankly recognized, there is everything to be said for making the attempt to visualize in its broad outlines the course of ecological change. The main sequence of events was determined by climate in which the principal factor was temperature: this rose from the low levels prevailing during most of late glacial times to a peak, constituting the so-called climatic optimum of post-glacial times, from which it fell away during the climatic deterioration marking the closing stages of the prehistoric period. In terms of vegetation this sequence implied, so far as the existing deciduous zone is concerned, a phase of tundra, followed by increasing forest dominance and ultimately by forest revertence and decline. In so far as human activities affected the main course of ecological development during prehistoric times—and they were not sufficient to do so until the third and last phase —they served mainly to speed up and amplify the process of deforestation and to enlarge the areas of open country, whether heath, meadow or cultivated land.

In reviewing the main course of events one should naturally begin with the late glacial period. At the time of the Fenno-Scandian moraines, the retreat from which marks the beginning of the post-glacial period, the ice-sheets, although much reduced in size, still covered a substantial part of the continent including the whole of the zones occupied at the present day by the tundra and northern coniferous formations and even in places the margins of the existing deciduous zone.

Knowledge of the development of vegetation in the ice-free areas of Europe rests to a large extent on material from the beds of late glacial lakes.[5] Wherever these have been investigated over the extensive region from Ireland to East Prussia and from Scandinavia to the Alps the same general sequence has been found to apply, though this naturally varies in detail according to the climatic and topographical features of different territories. The story is best illustrated by reference to the well-explored region of Denmark and Schleswig-Holstein, the main changes in the eco-system of which since the area was uncovered by the ice are set out in Table A. It will be observed that the late glacial period was interrupted

---

[5] F. Firbas, 1935 and 1949; Schütrumpf in A. Rust, 1943, 21–4; M. Degerbøl and J. Iversen. 1945, 52–7; H. Godwin, 1947; K. Jessen, 1949; F. E. Zeuner, 1950, chap. iv.

in this area by two relatively warm oscillations, the second of which, first noted by Hartz and Milthers in 1901 at the Allerød brickworks in north Zealand, has left well-defined traces over the whole of north-western Europe.

	CLIMATE		VEGETATION		FAUNA	POLLEN	ECONOMY		LAND/SEA
POST-GLACIAL	SUB-ATLANTIC Deterioration: wetter, colder — c.500 B.C.	IX	Pine reverlence Beech (Grenz)		Domestic sheep preponderate over swine	FOREST	Settled agriculture, pastoral activities, marine & inland hunting & fishing ← Forest clearance Shifting agriculture, pastoral activities, marine & inland hunting & fishing	IRON / BRONZE / NEOLITHIC	BALTIC SEA
	SUB-BOREAL Drier, more continental — c.2500 B.C.	VIII	Spread of grasses & ling Oak forest Introduction of cereals & weeds of cultivation		Tame horse Red & roe deer, wild pig etc.; domesticated ox, pig, sheep, dog				TRS.4 / TRS.3 (LITORINA SEA)
	ATLANTIC Warmth max.; moist, oceanic — c.5000 B.C.	VII	Mixed-oak forest (oak, elm, lime) and alder		Aurochs, red & roe deer; wild pig etc.; dog		Hunting, gathering, fowling, fishing & strand-looping	MESOLITHIC	TRS.2 / TRS.1
	BOREAL Rising temp., continental	VI	Pine/hazel; beg. mixed-oak forest		Aurochs, elk, red & roe deer; wild pig, beaver, bear; dog				ANCYLUS LAKE
	— c.6800 B.C.	V	Pine/birch forest						
	PRE-BOREAL Slow rise of temperature — c.8000 B.C.	IV	Birch forest		Aurochs, elk Reindeer, bison Wild horse		Hunting, gathering, fowling & fishing	UPPER PALAEOLITHIC	YOLDIA SEA
LATE GLACIAL	YOUNGER DRYAS Sub-arctic	III	Tundra / Park tundra		Reindeer, bison, alpine hare	OPEN VEGETATION			BALTIC ICE-DAMMED LAKE
	ALLERØD Osc. warmer — c.10,000 B.C.	II	Park tundra / Birch forest		Giant Irish deer, elk, beaver, bear				
	OLDER DRYAS Sub-arctic	Ic	Tundra		Reindeer				
	BØLLING Osc. warmer	Ib	Park tundra						
	OLDEST DRYAS Arctic	Ia	Tundra		Reindeer				

JGDC. 1950

Table A.   Transformations of habitat, biome and economy in prehistoric Denmark.

During the cold phases, marked by tundra vegetation with *Dryas octopetala*, arctic birch and dwarf willow, there were no forest trees.   Recent work has shown, though, that the vegetation of the Older Dryas periods was more alpine than arctic in character; in particular ericaceous plants were less common and grasses grew more luxuriantly than in the arctic tundra, to which moreover the plant community typified by *Helianthemum, Hippophae* and *Artemesia,* commonly noted in the Older Dryas deposits, is quite foreign. For certain types of herbivorous animals, and therefore for the human societies which preyed upon them, the late glacial vegetation of the zone beyond the ice-sheets provided ideal conditions of life. During the warmer Allerød stage, forest trees began to encroach on the open tundra : even in marginal territories like Ireland, south-west Norway and Denmark birch forests began to establish themselves ; further south pine trees spread into the birch woods, even penetrating as far north as Holstein. The Younger Dryas period witnessed a substantial return of open tundra conditions, though birch copses may have survived even in Ireland in sheltered localities. Much of north-western Europe seems to have presented at the close of the ice age the appearance of " park tundra," like the zone of transition between tundra and forest which exists to-day in east Russia and Siberia to a depth of several hundred kilometres. The boundary between the forest and park tundra zones would be difficult enough to draw even supposing that the necessary palæobotanical research had been carried out in France, and it may be assumed to have fluctuated considerably in response to climatic change even during the late glacial period. For much of this time it is considered that continental forest extended over south-western France,[6] including the richest areas of upper palæolithic culture. On the other hand there are hints that during the cold spell at the end of late glacial times the Pyrenees may have marked the boundary ; at least it is significant that the numerous antlers of reindeer from Late Magdalenian levels as far south as Isturitz have been referred explicitly to the " barren-ground " rather than to the woodland type.

It would appear that towards the end of the glacial period the areas at present occupied by tundra and northern coniferous forest were still covered by ice-sheets and that the existing zone of deciduous forest then consisted of tundra grading into park tundra, in which the forest element temporarily rose to importance during the warm Allerød oscillation. Beyond the Alps and the Pyrenees forest conditions prevailed, and it may be surmised, though it cannot yet be fully demonstrated, unless from the evidence of fauna, that coniferous and deciduous forests encroached on territories at present occupied by the Mediterranean evergreen formations.

Now just as the temporary increase in warmth during late glacial times, known as the Allerød oscillation, led to an abortive spread of forest over much of the ice-free zones of north-western and central Europe, so the much more marked and enduring rise of temperature during the post-glacial period had commensurately greater ecological effects. Ice-sheets retreated to their mountain refuges, leaving behind them extensive regions for colonization, first by tundra and alpine vegetation and ultimately, apart from the most northerly latitudes and from mountain heights, by birch and coniferous forest. The former area of tundra and park tundra, as far south as the Alps and the Pyrenees, passed through a series of ecological transformations. At first, during the period of Pre-boreal climate, while the rise of temperature was still only slight, the forests which began to consolidate themselves were restricted to trees capable of tolerating cold conditions, including willow, birch and pine; indeed, in marginal territories like Ireland and northern Britain, only the first two species were represented. During the Early Boreal climatic period, the forests responded to increasing warmth; pine increased at the expense of birch and even spread to Ireland, though still only in small proportions, and the first deciduous trees, including oak, elm and lime began to infiltrate. In Later Boreal times the deciduous trees, increased

[6] H. T. U. Smith, 1949, 1504–5.

in importance, though still subservient to pine, but the most striking feature was the abundance of hazel over the whole territory from Ireland, where its pollen reached proportions five, twelve or even seventeen times that of all the forest trees added together, to Esthonia, Transylvania and the Pyrenees. The climax came during the warm, moist Atlantic stage, the period of the post-glacial climatic optimum, when mean annual temperatures in this area reached between $2°-2\frac{1}{2}°$ C. above those now prevailing. The deciduous forests, in which alder was often prominent at this period and into which the beech was beginning to spread from southern France round the western foothills of the Alps, attained their maximum expansion and actually spread into territories such as parts of central Sweden, from which they have since retreated.[7] While the coniferous and deciduous formations were attaining and surpassing their existing areas of distribution the Mediterranean evergreen forest was presumably also advancing to and possibly beyond its present frontiers, though there is little exact information from this zone.

To sum up the situation at the peak of the warm period, it can be said that the major plant formations had occupied their present territories and that the coniferous, deciduous and evergreen forests had even advanced beyond their modern limits. Over the whole territory up to the margins of the tundra, excepting only the windswept islands like the Orkneys, the forests, encouraged by a warm, moist climate and as yet hardly touched by man, spread like a continuous blanket, parted only by rivers and lakes, marshes, sand-dunes, salt-springs and the very sea coasts.

From this point the forests—or at least those of the deciduous and evergreen formations—entered on a period of decline, which led during the historical period to their virtual extermination. This ecological transformation, of such vast significance for the human population of Europe, was the product of climatic and economic forces working together. The spread of farming economy, which first affected Europe at a time when the forests were at their peak, involved inroads on the woodlands which grew as settlement became more dense: not only were trees felled to provide timber for houses, boats, defensive works, fuel and other purposes, but ever-growing tracts of forest were cleared for cultivation (at first temporarily, but later permanently) and domestic livestock grazing on the seedlings and young shoots effectively prevented regeneration. The effects of human interference were particularly catastrophic on the Mediterranean evergreen formation, which at its climax of high forest was notoriously fragile and had but small powers of recuperation[8]; although once " densely forested from snow-line almost to sea-level "[9] the spread of farming soon had the effect of degrading evergreen forest into maquis and garrigue, leaving as the only substantial reserves of timber the deciduous and coniferous forests of the upper mountain slopes. Although the temperate summer forest of north-western and central Europe had greater powers of resistance, the introduction and above all the intensification of farming exerted a profound influence on the biome.

The most significant feature of the vegetation of the Sub-boreal period was the gradual, if at first very slight, replacement of forest by grasslands and heaths. This development, which was particularly noticeable on the poor sandy soils of northern and north-western Germany, has commonly been attributed to the onset of a drier, more continental phase of climate, relatively unfavourable to forest growth. Although it may be questioned whether the climate of Sub-boreal times was drier than that of to-day, the consensus of opinion holds

[7] R. Nordhagen, 1933, 148 ff.

[8] This point has been made admirably by P. George, 1933, 194–5.

[9] J. L. Myres 1930, 6.

that it was substantially so than that of Atlantic or Sub-atlantic times.[10] On the other hand, the influence of climatic change on vegetation was certainly enhanced by the effects of farming, for which direct botanical evidence is forthcoming in the pollen of cereals and of the weeds associated with their cultivation.

The influence of human interference on the natural vegetation of the deciduous zone became more and more marked as the area of primary settlement filled up and agriculture entered upon its settled stage. It was precisely at this time that north-western and central Europe were overtaken by a sustained deterioration of climate. Already during Sub-boreal times there had been recurrent though quite temporary phases of heavy rainfall, but it was not until the Sub-atlantic period that there set in a prolonged phase of heavy rainfall and lowered temperatures. The combined effect of climatic deterioration and of the ever-increasing inroads by man revealed itself clearly in the vegetation: not only did birch trees and conifers—the latter now including spruce and silver fir, which already during Atlantic times had begun to spread from their respective refuges in south-eastern and south-western Europe—regain some importance in the still extensive forests, but the forest area showed further contraction and blanket-bogs spread over the substantial territories subject to excessive rainfall, like the western parts of Ireland and of the Scottish highlands.

Although the major transformations in plant ecology since late glacial times have continually to be born in mind, it is equally true that the evolution of European economy during prehistoric times can only be understood in relation to that of the ancient world as a whole. Much remains to be learnt about the origins of farming and the rise of urban civilization in the Near East, but the general position has been established firmly enough and is sufficiently familiar. Only two salient facts need be recalled, namely that in parts of western Asia and the Nile Valley farming was already practised by the fifth and possibly even by the sixth millennium B.C. and that, in both, urban societies, developed in the course of long ages from peasant communities, had already begun to record their own history before ever a grain of wheat had been sown in European soil: Europe was so marginal to the main originative centres of economic change that, Crete excepted, no part of it came within the sphere of neolithic farming economy until literate civilization had already been established in parts of western Asia and the Nile Valley. An attempt has been made in Table B to portray the time-space relationships of the main forms of economy in the several parts of prehistoric Europe.

From an economic point of view the early history of Europe fell into three main stages : from an age-long and world-wide stage of savagery, under which subsistence was won exclusively by such activities as plant-gathering, hunting, fishing and fowling, it passed by a process of incorporation into the sphere of successively more highly integrated economies, through a stage of barbarism, in which the activities of farming had been added to those of the quest for wild products, to one of urban civilization. Naturally one can trace finer divisions than these: in the field of food-production it is possible to distinguish clearly, at least in the deciduous zone, between the stage of shifting agriculture and that of settled agriculture with fixed fields; or, again, in that of technology, one can point to the transformations wrought by the diffusion from civilized to barbarous societies of copper and bronze metallurgy or iron-working respectively. Yet, the spread of farming, and of the urban civilization based upon it, remain the two chief turning-points in the story and the general pattern of social life in the different parts of Europe during later prehistoric times has been

---

[10] Admirably discussed by J. Iversen, 1941, 38.

determined more by their relationship to the expansion of these economic zones than by any other factor.

The progress of Europe was therefore in broad essentials a consequence of the expansion of economic zones in the ancient world as a whole. The main driving forces were human

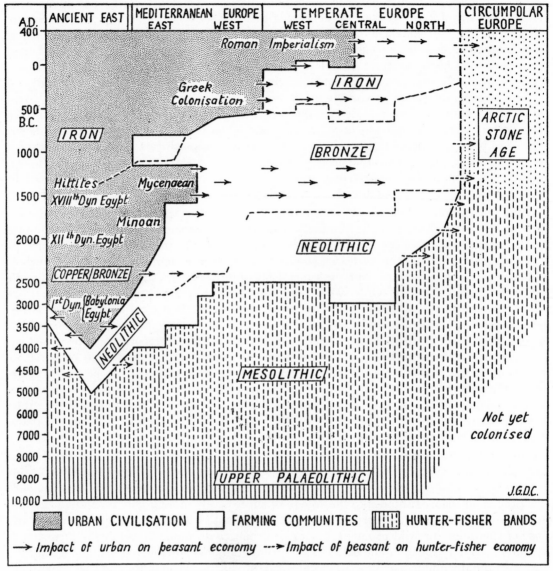

Table B. Time-space relationships of hunter-fisher, farming and urban economy in the several ecological zones of Europe.

needs and aspirations, which in so far as they were economic were inherent in existing forms. The spread of farming was accomplished partly through the gradual appropriation of land by marginal peasants who practised in association with stock-raising an extensive form of agriculture necessitating the continual opening up of new tracts; and partly through the upgrading of indigenous hunter-fishers by a process of acculturation, a process in the course of which higher groups obtained certain economic advantages without the necessity of force and simpler ones assuaged their feelings of inferiority by emulating their more advanced neighbours and adopting in a devolved form their mode of life. The expansion of urban economy was much more deliberate and was normally accompanied by the extension of political authority; yet at bottom the driving impulses were similar and the actual foundation of cities was preceded by a prolonged period of cultural and economic permeation, so that from a comparatively early stage in their history the barbarian communities of Europe were stimulated by the demands of urban societies operating through the medium of trade.

Yet the mere concept of geographical expansion should remind us that the spread of more advanced forms of economy was limited to some degree by the character of the climate, soil and vegetation of the several zones into which Europe has been divided by nature. Thus, the two most northerly zones, those of tundra and northern coniferous forest, were neither of them capable under primitive conditions of supporting societies at any other than a stage of savagery. The frozen sub-soil and arctic-alpine climate of the tundra-*fjäll* regions were—and still are—impassable bars to the practice of agriculture, though not of course to reindeer nomadism. The northern coniferous zone was hardly less favourable: the climate, which was too cold and moist for trees of the oak mixed forest, was no more suited at an early stage in the evolution of agricultural practice to the growth and ripening of cereal crops; equally unpropitious were the prevailing podsols, product of a cool, wet climate, under which the downward movement of water exceeded the upward, leading to extreme leaching and eluviation and to the formation of a hard moorpan and an impoverished topsoil; nor was the coniferous forest itself, with its lack of herbaceous undergrowth and its unpalatable foliage, of much use for the grazing of domestic livestock. At best, therefore, the coniferous forest was of marginal value from the point of view of agriculturalists or stock-raisers. By contrast, conditions prevailing in the deciduous and evergreen zones, although differing in some notable respects and subject in the former case to important qualifications as regards the heavier clay soils, were well suited to the spread of primitive farming economy.

A study of prehistoric settlement shows that in point of fact the sphere of farming economy never expanded northwards of the range of the deciduous forest. In this connection it is worth noting that it was only comparatively late in post-glacial times that deciduous replaced coniferous forest over much of north-western and central Europe and it was not until an advanced stage of Atlantic times that neolithic farming economy spread over these territories formerly unoccupied or sparsely populated by mesolithic hunter-fishers. Although on the conventional chronology this may seem an academic point, it is worth noting that the ecological circumstances requisite to the practice of farming existed much earlier in parts of the Near East and that beyond the northern limits of the deciduous forest they ceased to obtain at all. By the time farming began to spread into Europe the main ecological zones had attained and slightly exceeded their existing northern limits. The new economy spread close up to these within the course of only a few centuries at the turn of the third and second millennia B.C.

Striking confirmation of the role of the northern margin of the deciduous forest as an economic and cultural divide comes from Scandinavia. Here barbarian and savage communities co-existed during the last two thousand years or so B.C. The existence of two distinct provinces has been recognized by Scandinavian archæologists for over a hundred years, ever since Sven Nilsson published his famous book on the primitive inhabitants

of the area.[11] The admirable maps prepared by Oluf Rygh and Oscar Montelius for the
Stockholm Congress of 1874 demonstrated that the distributions of the slate artifacts of
what was already termed the Arctic culture and of megalithic tombs and stone cists were
complementary, and gained acceptance for the view that the later stone age cultures of
northern and southern Scandinavia were at least in some measure contemporary. Investigation of the dwelling-places and their associated fauna and of the rock-engravings emphasized

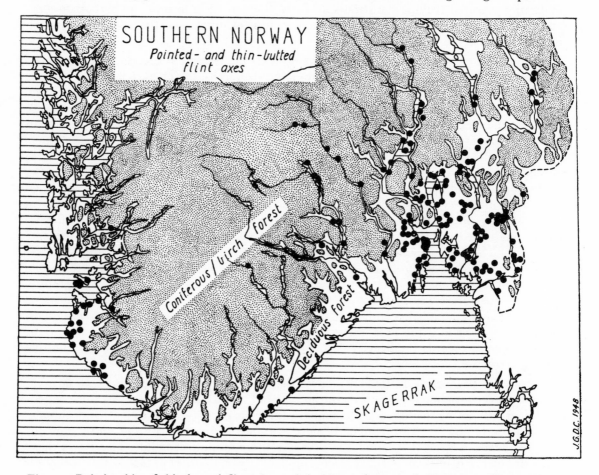

Fig. 3.   Relationship of thin-butted flint axes and deciduous forest in S. Norway.   The deciduous
forest area is shown unshaded.

the contrast and showed that the differences were economic and conceptual as well as
merely formal. As Gutorm Gjessing[12] has brought out so clearly, the Arctic culture of
northern and central Scandinavia is an integral part of an immense circumpolar spread,
embracing hunter-fisher communities right across northern Eurasia to the northern territories of the New World; whereas the farmer cultures of southern Scandinavia shared in
the heritage of central and southern Europe. What no one has yet pointed out, though,
is that the distinction between the two provinces is ecological as well as economic and

[11] Sven Nilsson, 1838–43.
[12] G. Gjessing, 1944.

cultural and that the boundary between them coincides with that which demarcates the deciduous from the coniferous forest. That this was so can be seen by comparing the distribution of features characteristic of each of the two zones.

It may first be shown that the early farmers occupied territories within the deciduous forest. Thus, if one plots the distribution of the battle-axe culture in Sweden, it will be

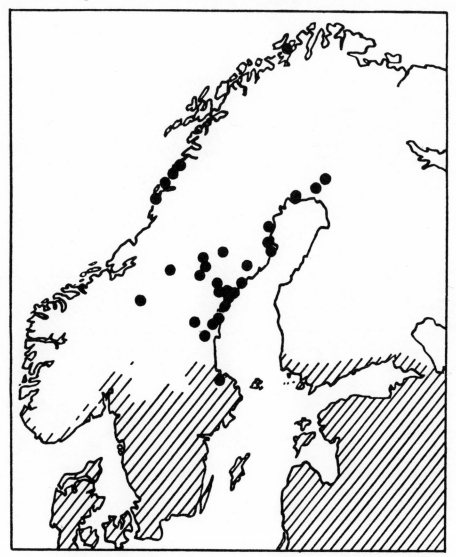

Fig. 4. Relationship of Arctic slate knives with elk-head terminals to the circumpolar zone of tundra and northern coniferous forest. The deciduous forest area is shaded.

found that this broadly coincides with the zone over which the mixed oak forest has been shown by palæo-botanists to have extended during the Sub-boreal period, while that of megalithic tombs falls well within this limit (Fig. 1). Again, in Norway the original colonization by farmers, defined by thin-butted axes of flint and stone, was confined to the deciduous forest zone of the Oslo fjord region, the great valleys into the interior, the coastal strip of southern Norway and the Jaeren region of the south-west (Fig. 3); and the later expansion of farming, which was especially marked at the time of the stone cists, was confined to low-lying patches on the islands and along the western coast as far as the Trondheim region and even beyond, which thanks to the influence of the Gulf Stream once supported small areas of deciduous forest. In Finland, also, one finds that apart from a few strays,

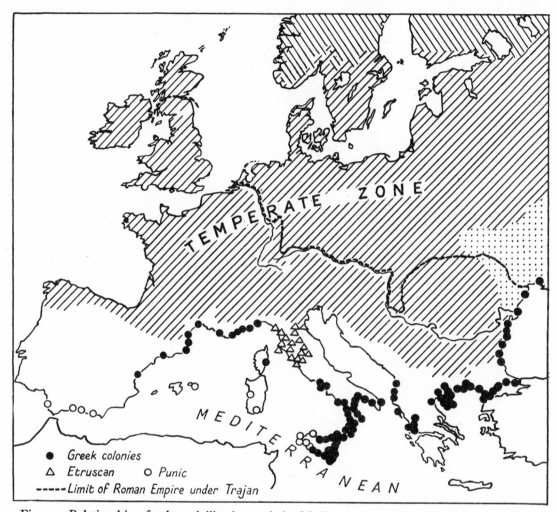

Fig. 5.   Relationship of urban civilization and the Mediterranean zone at the time of Trajan. Distribution of colonies based on *Camb. Anc. Hist.*, vol. III, map 13.

by permission of the Cambridge University Press.

due no doubt to trade with the trappers of the interior and of the northern territories, finds of objects attributable to prehistoric farmers, whether implements of south Scandinavian flint, battle-axes or bronzes, were virtually confined to the narrow zone of deciduous forest in the south and south-west; indeed, down to the end of the prehistoric Iron Age, around 1300 A.D., the territories occupied by farmer cultures had hardly extended beyond this zone unless in certain coastal areas.

If on the other hand the distribution of characteristic Arctic traits, such as animal-headed slate knives (Fig. 4) or wooden skis and sledge-runners (Fig. 160), is examined, it will be found that these coincide substantially with that of the coniferous birch-forest and the open tundra. Now, making all allowances for the fact that there was in reality no rigid divide, either between the ecological areas or between the spheres of the two economies, and that the clarity of the picture is impaired in the case of archæological distributions by the effect of trade, the coincidence of economic and ecological zones is sufficiently marked to justify the hypothesis that the northern margin of the deciduous forest in fact determined the limits of the early spread of farming in the countries of northern Europe.

In conclusion, it is fitting to recall that, as Sir John Myres has taught us,[13] the urban civilization of the Mediterranean represents a remarkably complete and perfect exploitation of the special features of Mediterranean vegetation. Although the primary, barbarian economy, on which several distinctive civilizations were reared, was based on the cultivation of cereals, helped out by fishing and the keeping of livestock, the limited area of cultivable land and the poor conditions for grazing livestock at low altitudes, once the forest had been degraded, set close limits to the potentialities of ordinary mixed farming. The possibility of concentrating substantial numbers of people in cities and of supporting the fabric of civilized existence depended on the cultivation of olive, fig and vine, which in itself involved fixity of settlement. Although all three in their wild forms had been features of the Mediterranean flora since Tertiary times, it would of course be quite wrong to imagine that their domestication took place as it were spontaneously or sporadically at different points within the zone; on the contrary, the domesticated varieties accompanied, as they helped to support, the colonization of the middle and western Mediterranean by civilized peoples. What is true is that this process was immensely facilitated by the perfect adaptation of the three plants to the climate which determined the composition of the natural flora of the Mediterranean zone (Fig. 5). If ecological conditions thus favoured the spread of civilization from the eastern Mediterranean to Italy, the south coast of France and eastern Spain, they also served to limit its diffusion. It needed all the power of Rome to break through the boundaries established by ecology and to incorporate within the sphere of the Empire a substantial area of deciduous forest, a feat which marks for us the conventional end to prehistoric times.

---

[13] Sir John Myres, 1943.

CHAPTER II

CATCHING AND GATHERING: INLAND

FOR the greater part of European prehistory sustenance was drawn entirely from wild life: plants, insects, eggs and shell-fish were gathered; and birds, fish and mammals hunted and caught in a variety of ways. Even when farming and the arts of food-production spread over much of Europe, the old gathering and catching activities continued as important sources of food and raw materials; and this was quite apart from marine catching, from sealing, whaling and off-shore fishing, which, as brought out in the next chapter, first began to develop on a substantial scale at this juncture.

The ecological basis of prehistoric economy is nowhere better defined than in connection with the activities by which early man in effect appropriated to his own use the substance of other organisms from the particular biosystem to which he belonged. This was true, whether as a food-gatherer and hunter he preyed upon the forms of life available in his habitat or whether as a farmer he introduced and protected new species for his own purposes, modifying the biosystem to suit his needs. As a hunter he was mainly interested in herbivorous animals, which existed, so far as he was concerned, to convert vegetation into meat and fat and raw materials, such as hides, sinews, bones and antlers. The kinds of animal hunted, and therefore to some extent the methods and equipment used in hunting, were thus associated more or less directly with the prevailing plant ecology. Carnivorous species were a good deal more independent of their immediate surroundings, but although these were certainly hunted, sometimes on a substantial scale, it is rarely that they entered to a significant extent into the actual subsistence of prehistoric societies.

UPPER PALÆOLITHIC HUNTER-FISHERS

The best-defined human groups to occupy north-western Europe at the end of the late glacial period, the Late Magdalenians of northern Spain, France and Belgium, Switzerland and south and central Germany, and the Hamburgians and Ahrensburgians of north Germany and north Holland, existed mainly by hunting the wild animals of the tundra and park tundra, above all the reindeer.[1] In this respect they resembled the Eskimo of the Barren Grounds, of whom Birket-Smith[2] wrote that "the caribou is the axis on which everything turns," since it provided meat, fat for lamp fuel, skins for clothing and tent-coverings, sinews for thongs and sewing-threads, and antler and bone for implements and weapons. It is at any rate significant, both that remains of reindeer should preponderate over those of other animals among the food debris of the latest upper palæolithic inhabitants of north-western Europe, and that the southern limit of the Late Magdalenian, defined by

---

[1] Certain groups, evidently important in their day, are represented only by their flint industries, as for example the Swiderian industries of Poland (J. G. D. Clark, 1936, 62–6).

[2] K. Birket-Smith, 1929, I, 47.

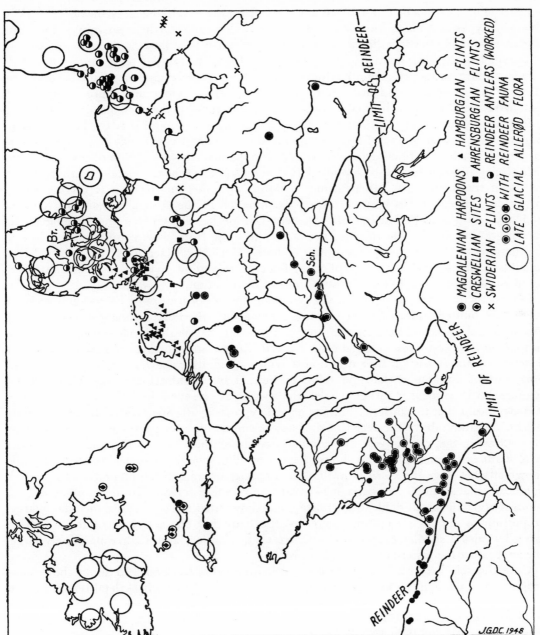

Fig. 6. The extent of the reindeer-hunting cultures of late glacial times in Europe.

barbed harpoon-heads, should coincide so closely with the contemporary margin of the reindeer (Fig. 6); the correspondence is not indeed quite exact—harpoon-heads of slightly divergent types and made from stag antler extend along the northern margin of the Cantabrian mountains beyond the range of reindeer[3]—but it is still sufficiently impressive.

To which of the three main groups of reindeer distinguished to-day on ecological grounds[4] namely tundra or barren-ground reindeer, mountain reindeer and woodland reindeer or caribou, the latter distinguished by its larger size, darker colour and more compact and flattened antlers, did those hunted by the Late Magdalenians[5] and associated groups belong ? It is generally held that the tundra group is the primitive one and that the reindeer is an autochthonous polar animal. The mountain and woodland types may have been differentiated as part of the re-adjustments which accompanied the contraction of the glacial and peri-glacial zones, when it is supposed that some reindeer herds were " marooned " in mountain tracts and that others came to terms with the encroaching forest instead of migrating. However this may be, expert examination of the skeletal remains of reindeer from the late glacial period in north-western Europe has shown that they belong to the barren-ground group. This applies not merely to those from areas comparatively close to the margins of the ice-sheets, like those of north Germany,[6] Denmark[7] or Ireland,[8] but, equally, if Saint-Périer's very explicit statement[9] regarding the antler from Isturitz is accepted, to those close to the southern limit of distribution.

It remains to decide, to which of the two main species of tundra or barren-ground reindeer those hunted during late glacial times belonged, whether to *Rangifer tarandus*, the species found to-day in Scandinavia, in Siberia as far east as the Lena and in Greenland, or to *R. arcticus*, at present inhabiting eastern Siberia and northern Canada. From the skeletal material this is hardly a question to which a definitive answer can be given, but the consensus of opinion is that the reindeer hunted by Hamburgians and Magdalenians belonged to *R. arcticus*,[10] rather than to the species at present found in northern Europe. It is significant that the antlers from late glacial deposits in Europe mostly show the characteristic curvature above the rear tine and this is commonly also portrayed in the cave art; the contrast in this respect with the comparative straightness seen in this part of the antler in *R. tarandus* is marked. One should hasten to add, though, that it is not yet certainly known at what stage the *arcticus* and *tarandus* species became differentiated, and it may be significant that detailed comparison between the reindeer remains from Hamburgian and Ahrensburgian levels in Schleswig-Holstein has shown that the later series includes a larger proportion of antlers with some degree of the flattening characteristic of the woodland form, but also a smaller proportion with arc shaped antlers and a correspondingly larger one approximating towards the *tarandus* profile.[11]

Unfortunately very little information of scientific value has emerged about the relative proportions, in which the various animals were represented by their skeletal remains in the

---

[3] cf. H. Obermaier, 1925 (Spanish edition), 166–7, 171 f. etc.

[4] A. Jacobi, 1931 and refs., see esp. 139–40.

[5] For Spain, see E. Harlé, 1908 and Obermaier, *op. cit.*, *passim* ; for the Riviera, see Boule and Villeneuve, 1927, 41.

[6] K. Gripp in Rust, 1943, 108 and 111–2.

[7] M. Degerbøl, 1935, 24.

[8] G. F. Mitchell, 1941, 188.

[9] R. de Saint-Périer, 1936, 14.

[10] A. Jacobi, 1931, 101 f. cf. Degerbøl, 1935, 24, and Gripp in Rust, 1937, 62–3 and 72.

[11] Gripp in Rust, 1943, 112.

successive levels of the French caves. The impression is all the same definite that the reindeer stood in quite a special relationship to the late Magdalenian culture, the type fossil of which, the barbed harpoon with swollen base, was characteristically made from the antler of this animal.[12] The evidence has been more exactly observed from some of the Late Magdalenian stations of Germany and Switzerland and it is sufficiently striking : at Kesslerloch, for instance, reindeer accounted for *c.* 80 per cent of the fauna, and at Schweizersbild for *c.* 75 per cent[13] ; at Petersfels bei Engen there was evidence for the arctic hare having been caught in exceptional numbers, but excluding this species reindeer accounted for over 70 per cent of the mammalian fauna.[14] At the open stations of the Hamburgian and Ahrensburgian groups of north Germany the proportion of reindeer was even higher : for example at Stellmoor reindeer accounted for 41 out of 42 of the individual mammals represented in the earlier level and for 650 out of 656 in the later one.[15]

The marked gregariousness of reindeer, the large numbers in which they may occur where conditions are favourable and their general all-round utility make them peculiarly suitable for specialized hunting, and the " park tundra " vegetation, which existed over much of north-western Europe during late glacial times, was ideally suited to the reindeer and its associated species. It should be remembered that, although the human groups already mentioned concentrated on reindeer, they by no means neglected the other animals favoured by prevailing conditions. Wild horse, bison and, among smaller game, hare were particularly important for food. Nevertheless, it was the reindeer which largely determined the pattern of life of the western hunters of the late glacial period, just as further east it was the mammoth. Now reindeer are not only gregarious, but strongly migratory. During the winter reindeer herds withdraw to relatively sheltered territories, seeking refuge from bad storms in the fringe of the forest belt, and existing mainly on the lichens and mosses reached by pawing through the snow. With the onset of summer the herds move off instinctively to rich grazings, which may lie hundreds of miles to the north, seeking and returning again and again by familiar routes to their favourite pastures.

How far did the seasonal pattern in the life of the reindeer herds impose itself on the human groups, which depended on them for so large a proportion of their needs ? While a complete answer can hardly be given, there is no question that the Hamburgian and Ahrensburgian sites investigated in Schleswig-Holstein were summer settlements and that many of the Magdalenian caves and rock-shelters were on the contrary occupied, whether exclusively or not, during the winter. The evidence for this is essentially biological. The glacial tunnel-valleys of Schleswig-Holstein provided ideal summer grazing for reindeer: the grasses and sedges, the dwarf birches and willows, the *Dryas*, *Artemesia* and *Rumex* are among favoured foods of the reindeer at the present day [16]; and the ponds and lakes by which the hunters were fond of camping provided, in their surface weeds, another delicacy keenly sought by reindeer. Systematic measurement of sacrum bones, tibia and metatarsal bones from Meiendorf and Stellmoor has shown that a clear gap in size existed between those of calves of one summer and of two summers; this can only be

---

[12] H. Breuil, 1937, 59, observed with his customary penetration that the reindeer attained its maximum distribution in Europe during Magdalenian 5.

[13] K. Lindner, 1937, 173.

[14] Thus, out of 1694 individual mammals from Petersfels, 870 were arctic hares, 640 reindeer 100 wild horses and 45 arctic fox. See E. Peters, 1930, and E. Peters and V. Toepfer, 1932.

[15] W. Krause and W. Kollau in Rust, 1943, 57-8.

[16] L. J. Palmer, 1926, 9 and 21-3.

accounted for by supposing that the series is incomplete and that the calves were elsewhere during the winter months.[17] The marked rarity of shed antlers[18]—only 13 out of 1,276 were present in the Ahrensburg level at Stellmoor and only 6 out of 105 at the Hamburgian site of Meiendorf—suggests that the sites were occupied while the bucks still carried their antlers, which they did until November or December after the breeding-season, but after the hinds had finished shedding theirs following on the birth of their young in May or June.[19] The remains of birds also point to a summer occupation, since at least one crane, a summer visitor, and the young of swan, sea-gulls and geese were represented.[20] In Rust's view the hunting stations in the tunnel-valleys were occupied during a season corresponding roughly with June to September.[21]

On the other hand, analysis of reindeer remains from caves and rock-shelters in the commune of Lespugne, Haute-Garonne by Saint-Périer[22] showed that, whereas the antlers of hinds and young animals had normally been broken from their skulls, those of bucks had invariably been shed. These results have been confirmed in a general way by the Abbé Breuil[23] for the Dordogne, Charente and Poitou and the inference is that the caves of this region were mainly occupied during the months of November to February, though the recovery of foetal bones of reindeer from Petersfels[24] suggests that the south German caves were sometimes occupied until at least May. The conclusion that the Magdalenians sheltered in their caves in the winter and moved off to the summer grazing grounds of the reindeer is supported also by the evidence available about birds and fishes.

A rich avifauna has been recovered from the caves of France, south Germany and Switzerland, but some of the species represented were denizens of the caves and others were introduced by arctic foxes and other predators. Of the others, only two, namely the Arctic willow-grouse (*Lagopus albus*) and to a lesser degree the Ptarmigan (*L. mutus*), occur in sufficiently large numbers to indicate purposive fowling activities. The abundance of the Arctic willow-grouse in the Dordogne caves was already remarked by the ornithologist Milne-Edwards[25] in his contribution to Lartet and Christy's *Reliquiæ Diluvianæ*, and the same authority noted that the bones exhibited clear-cut marks from flint knives, while lacking signs of gnawing by beasts of prey. Both species were present in strength in the Magdalenian deposits of the south German caves, including Schweizersbild, Sirgenstein and Wildscheuer,[26] and white grouse, probably Ptarmigan, accounted for 249-52 out of 280-5 of the individual birds from Petersfels.[27] The interest shown by Magdalenian man in the arctic grouse is displayed in a delicate little representation from Isturitz (Fig. 7), engraved significantly on a piece of reindeer antler.[28] The special relevance of these rich occurrences of arctic grouse in Magdalenian cave deposits is that, where this bird is still

[17] W. Krause in Rust, 1937, 48–9, and W. Kollau, *ibid.*, 72 and in Rust, 1943, 75.
[18] K. Gripp in Rust, 1937, 62–3 and 1943, 106–7.
[19] For connection of antler and sexual cycle, see A. Jacobi, 1931, 236 f.
[20] W. Krause in Rust, 1937, 55–6.
[21] A. Rust, 1937, 115–6; cf. 1943, 135–6.
[22] R. de Saint-Périer, 1920.
[23] *Proc. Prehist. Soc.*, 1939, 268.
[24] E. Peters, 1930, 69, and Peters and Toepfer, 1932, 162.
[25] Lartet and Christy, 1865–75, 226–47.
[26] R. R. Schmidt, 1912, 169, 191 and 207.
[27] E. Peters and V. Toepfer, 1932, 166.
[28] E. Passemard, 1922, 40 and Fig. 38.

caught under primitive conditions, it is taken by snares under snow cover. The method is particularly well adapted to these birds, which prefer to run along an obstacle and seek a hole rather than fly over it. By sticking rows of birch twigs upright in the snow and setting snares in gaps it is easy to catch the birds once they can be attracted, either by scattering berries or, as Ekman has described for the Torne Lapps, by imitating the appropriate sounds.[29]

Fig. 7.   Engraving of Arctic Grouse on piece of
reindeer antler from Isturitz ($\frac{1}{1}$)
(*After Passemard*).

Remains of fish from the French caves are also consistent with the idea of seasonal occupation. Fresh-water species like pike, trout, dace, chub, bream and white-bream might have been taken at different times of the year in the stream flowing close by the caves. On the other hand salmon can only have been caught during the summer, when they came into fresh water for spawning. It is significant, therefore, that so far as one can tell, the salmon were not obtained in the immediate neighbourhood of the caves. In the case of the Vézère it has been argued that rocky obstructions in the Dordogne river a few leagues below the confluence would in any case have prevented the ascent.[30] Of more general application is the observation that, whereas the head bones even of the frailer Cyprinoids are sometimes preserved, salmon is represented exclusively by back bones.[31] From this it is argued that the Magdalenians caught the salmon while occupying summer hunting-grounds lower downstream. It is possible and indeed likely that their seasonal migrations may have included encampments at points where natural obstacles impeded the annual run of the fish. The Indians of British Columbia set up temporary camps at such places, where the salmon, caught in baskets suspended by the falls, could be ripped open, the back bones removed, the heads twisted off and the meat dried for packing in bales for winter use.[32] Evidently the Magdalenians saved some of the vertebræ for beads and it is by these alone that the salmon is represented in the cave deposits. Salmon vertebræ were a main element in the necklace worn by one of the contemporary Grimaldians buried in the Barma Grande,

---

[29] U. T. Sirelius, 1934, 65–6; Ekman, 1910, 182.
[30] C. Rau, 1884, 11.
[31] H. E. Sauvage in Lartet and Christy, 1865–75, 219–25.
[32] J. K. Lord, 1866, 64–75.

near Mentone, and it is amusing to note that pike vertebræ threaded on reindeer gut are still a favourite toy among Lapp children in northern Finland.[33]

The methods used by the hunter necessarily depend largely on the habits of his victim and the more primitive his equipment the closer his dependence is likely to be. Reindeer are shy and hard to approach, unless in herds, and it is significant that these assemble with the appearance of plentiful grazing at the beginning of the brief circumpolar summer. For this reason alone it is only to be expected that the main hunting should have occurred at this time of the year. The material from the caves, though, suggests that individuals were also taken during the winter, despite the fact that there is no evidence that the hunters of the late glacial period had the use of skis or snow-shoes.

It is a matter of extreme difficulty to reconstruct with certainty the methods of hunting in use among the tundra-dwellers and it has to be appreciated that some of the most effective ones might leave no tangible trace. The reindeer's habit of moving into the wind and its keen sense of hearing and smell are strong sources of protection, but its eyesight is not of the best and it is inordinately curious. For both these reasons it can be lured, as the Caribou Eskimo do, for instance, by mounting antlers on the head and trying to attract rival bulls at the mating season,[34] a procedure which may go some way to explain the antler head-dress of the " sorcerer " of Trois Frères. The use of urine as a means of attracting reindeer to fall-traps or pit-falls dug in the snow, another practice of this group of Eskimos, may also have been known to the late glacial hunters.

Certain clues to the methods used in hunting are given by the surviving archæological material. The leading type of the Late Magdalenian culture is the " harpoon-head," with basal swelling and barbs on one (Magd. 5) or both edges (Magd. 6) (Fig. 8)[35] and it is not unreasonable to assume that this was used in catching the reindeer on which the whole culture was based. The fact, already pointed out, that these objects were almost invariably made from reindeer antler, is fully consistent with this ; and, in view of the known influence of sympathetic magic at this time, it strongly reinforces the idea that they were indeed used in hunting reindeer. The shortness of the base and the existence of the swelling below the barbs argue that the head was never intended to be lashed fast to a handle, but rather to be secured to a line, presumably of reindeer sinew, and lightly seated in a shaft from which it would become detached in course of use ; in the case of the Cantabrian specimens, having a loop in place of a swelling, this interpretation is even more straightforward. It should be emphasized, though, that no specimens have been found complete with their mounting and one can hardly dogmatize about the character of weapons from their heads alone. It may prove that these objects really belong to spears with broken heads, the line serving as no more than a flexible hinge between head and shaft. On the other hand there seems no doubt that it was from such that the true harpoon developed and it may well be that some of these Magdalenian pieces were in fact true harpoon-heads. That these weapons were propelled by rigid throwers is suggested by their common association with this form, though it cannot, of course, be excluded that the throwers were used wholly, as they were almost certainly in part, for projecting spears or darts having fixed heads.

Harpoon-heads made from reindeer antler are also found distributed widely in the territories around the Scandinavian ice-sheet, over which various groups of reindeer hunters ranged at least during their summer migrations. In form and style the harpoon-heads

[33] J. G. D. Clark, 1948, 49.
[34] K. Birket-Smith, 1929, I, 107.
[35] H. Breuil, 1937, 46 ff.

associated with the northern cultures differ notably from those from Late Magdalenian levels in the caves. At the same time it is interesting to note that the only Hamburgian specimen available is barbed on one edge,[36] like those of Magdalenian 5, whereas

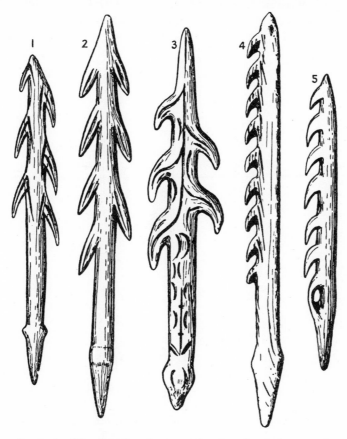

Fig. 8. Late Magdalenian harpoon-heads of reindeer antler ($\frac{2}{3}$).
(*After Breuil*)

many of the Ahrensburgian specimens were biserially barbed[37] as with Magdalenian 6. Again, although differing in style, the basic form of the northern pieces (Fig. 9) was similar, a lateral expansion at the base taking the place of an all-round swelling. In support of the view that the Hamburgians harpooned their reindeer, it has been claimed by Rust that the single point from Meiendorf fits neatly into the keyhole perforations found in a number of

---

[36] A. Rust, 1937, 100, *taf.* 39, abb. 1.

[37] A. Rust, 1943, *taf.* 89. Stray finds of reindeer antler or bone harpoon-heads from the Havel district include uniserially and biserially barbed points; the latter closely resemble some of those from Stellmoor (R. Stimming, 1928). A series of uniserially barbed harpoon-heads, said to be of reindeer antler or bone, has been published from East Prussia by Gross (1940, Nos. 17, 57, 58, 60, 65, 70, 73); one of these, resembling Ahrensburgian forms, though uniserially barbed, from Eckertsdorf, kr. Sensburg, has been dated to the younger Dryas stage (Gross, Zone III). A fine specimen—unfortunately undated—of a biserially barbed harpoon-head of Ahrensburg type comes from Skaftelev, near Slagelse, Denmark (T. Mathiassen, 1941, 126, Fig. 1.)

reindeer shoulder-blades,[38] but until such an object has actually been found in position this should be treated with scepticism, especially in view of the fragility of such bones.

It is particularly difficult to determine how far, if at all, the reindeer hunters used the bow. Representations from the French caves, as for instance those on calcareous pebbles from La Colombière,[39] show beyond any doubt that feathered projectiles were used in Magdalenian times, but it should be remembered that among the Eskimo darts and harpoons

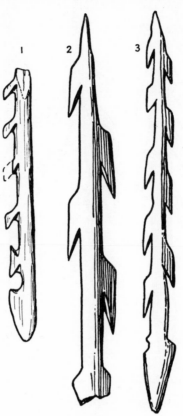

Fig. 9.   Hamburgian and Ahrensburgian harpoon-
heads of reindeer antler.

No. 1.   Meiendorf ($\frac{2}{3}$)
No. 2.   Stellmoor ($\frac{5}{8}$).
No. 3.   Skaftelev ($1\frac{7}{6}$).

may be fletched as well as arrows. Again, it is difficult to be sure whether flint fragments embedded in reindeer, like the fragment of a shouldered point from Meiendorf,[40] were projected by means of bows and not by darts or spears. Evidence for the use of the bow by the Ahrensburgians is a good deal stronger. Upwards of a hundred pine-wood shafts have been recovered from Stellmoor,[41] a few with the broken tangs of microlithic points still

---

[38] Rust, 1937, 124–5; 1943, 132.
[39] L. Mayet and J. Pissot, 1915, Figs. 47, 56 and Pl. XXI, No. 1 and XXII, No. 1.
[40] Rust, 1943, 133, abb. 3 and taf. 35, abb. 1.
[41] Rust, 1943, 188–9.

in place, and their delicacy is such that they can hardly be any other than arrows. A point to be noted about these shafts is that some of them, only 15.5 to 16.5 cm. long, ought probably to be interpreted as foreshafts, and not as complete arrows,[42] the fork at the base articulating with the lower part of the shaft rather than directly with the bow-string. It is further interesting to note the presence of grooved shaft-smoothers,[43] like those associated with later prehistoric archers.

The large numbers in which arctic grouse and hares were occasionally caught by the Magdalenian cave-dwellers makes it possible to infer with fair certainty the use of the snare or noose, which could well have been made from reindeer sinew.[44] The numerous representations of fish in the cave art, including notably pike, trout and salmon,[45] and the presence of fish bones in the deposits suggest that fishing was carried out on in purposive fashion, though actual traces of fishing gear are rare. Line fishing was probably done by means of the double-pointed gorge of wood or bone, examples of which latter come from the Grimaldi caves. The device is used for this purpose down to the present day in the Gironde itself, though also it should be noted both among the Eskimo and also down to recent times on Lake Constance for taking wild fowl.[46] One method of using the fishing-gorge found in modern Finland is illustrated by Fig. 10, which shows the method of mounting a small fish

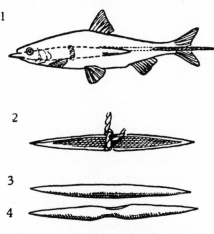

Fig. 10. Double-pointed gorges:
Nos. 1, 2. Modern Finnish.
Nos. 3, 4. From prehistoric lake-
villages, Switzerland. ($\frac{1}{1}$)

as bait for trowling through the water. The recovery from Mas d'Azil of a slender point, barbed on part of one edge and having a long tapered base with oblique scoring to give purchase to the binding,[47] suggests that the fish-spear may already have come into use.

---

[42] As by Rust, 1943, 190.

[43] *ibid.*, 1943, 187, *taf.* 88.

[44] Among the Caribou Eskimo thread for sewing was made from **the spinal sinews of the Caribou**, which were particularly easy to split after drying. For certain purposes threads might be plaited into cords. See Birket-Smith, 1929, I, 247.

[45] H. Breuil and R. de Saint-Périer, 1937.

[46] J. G. D. Clark, 1948, 46–7.

[47] *ibid.*, 45–6, Fig. 1a.

Although plants must have afforded one of the earliest of all sources of food, they are hardly likely to have played as important a role in the diet of dwellers on the tundra and park-tundra of late glacial times as in that of forest dwellers, and it is interesting to note how inconspicuous plant motives are in the cave art.[48] At the same time it was important for heavy meat-eaters to add some vegetable matter to their diet and it is probable that the late glacial people obtained theirs by eating the contents of reindeer stomachs, as is done by some Lapps and Siberians down to the present day. By consuming the " half-digested sour mash in reindeer stomachs " the hunters appropriated in an easy manner the rich supplies of vitamins and iodine from the lichens on which the reindeer grazed.[49] In addition, to judge by analogy with existing peoples living under comparable conditions, they almost certainly gathered some plant food for themselves. The collecting was doubtless carried on during the brief summer and the produce stored for use during the lean season. Among the Chukche of north-east Siberia, who ate substantial quantities of herbs and other vegetation,[50] a favourite food was made by storing the leaves and branches of willow in sealskin sacks, which were left to turn sour during the summer. In the autumn the sour mass froze and could then over the following months be cut into slices and eaten with meat like bread. It is interesting to note also that in Siberia berries of the Swallow-thorn (*Hippophaë*), another element in the late glacial flora of north-western and central Europe, were stored in ice-pits and eaten while frozen.[51]

To the south, beyond the limits of the reindeer and the park tundra, quite different ecological conditions prevailed and the game hunted by upper palæolithic communities in Spain and Italy already comprised forms like red deer, wild pig, roe deer and aurochs, which in the present temperate zone first appeared with forests during the post-glacial period. Before passing on to consider the hunting and gathering activities of mesolithic communities in temperate Europe, for which much more detailed information is available, it is worth emphasizing that during upper palæolithic times in southern Europe the bow seems to have been used to the exclusion of the " harpoon." This is well displayed in the hunting scenes depicted in the Eastern Spanish rock-shelter paintings, the upper palæolithic age of which has recently been vindicated.[52] One of the best of these shows a herd of red deer being driven into a line of bowmen (Fig. 11) ; to judge from the presence of a stag with his hinds, accompanied by a young staggie and some kids, this particular drive seems to have taken place during the rutting season. The bows appear to be of simple type and the shafts are evidently fletched, but it is hardly possible to discern details of the heads. Arrowheads of barbed and tanged form occur down to " Solutrean "—or more properly " Aterian "—levels at Parpalló, near Gandía,[53] and in later levels quantities of microlithic points, manufactured by the notch or micro-burin technique, are found of types which, as argued below, were almost certainly used as arrow armatures. It is significant that microlithic crescents made in this same technique should have occurred down to the base of the *terra bruna* in the cave of Romanelli, Otranto, in the heel of Italy, a deposit

---

[48] One of the few possible exceptions is the Late Magdalenian *bâton* from Veyrier, having what appears to be a branch with leaves engraved on one face (H. Breuil, 1937, Fig. 41, No. 1).

[49] See Baron A. E. Nordenskiöld, 1881, I, 435; cf. G. Lechler, 1945, 501–2.

[50] Nordenskiöld, 1881, I, 110.

[51] A. Erman, 1848, II, 193.

[52] Obermaier, 1925 (English edition), 254 ff., has been proved right by the stylistic affinities with the East Spanish group exhibited by the Lascaux paintings (see *P.P.S.* 1945, 44).

[53] L. Pericot García, 1942, 69–70.

which is contemporary with the peak of the last glaciation and has yielded red deer and fox, as well as alpine-steppe forms, such as ibex, hare and *Equus hydruntinus*.[54] When as a result of climatic change forests and forest animals spread again over temperate Europe, microlithic points of similar type, and made by the same technique, became a leading element also in the flint industries of middle, north-western and northern Europe.

Fig. 11. Deer being driven towards bowmen, upper palaeolithic wall-painting (dark red) in the Cueva de los Caballos, near Albocácer, Castellón.

(After Obermaier).

The rock-paintings of eastern Spain give us the further information that the honey of wild bees was collected already during upper palæolithic times (Fig. 12), in the then temperate zone.

MESOLITHIC HUNTER-FISHERS

Detailed studies of the fate of individual species made possible by the stratigraphical refinements of pollen-analysis have shown clearly enough how drastically the game available to the inhabitants of temperate Europe changed with the onset of post-glacial climate.

---

[54] A. C. Blanc, 1939.

Mitchell's critical studies of the reindeer and giant Irish deer in Ireland[55] have suggested that these barely outlived the late glacial period. Again, the remarkably exact information available from Denmark shows that with the advance of forests the park-tundra fauna faded out of the picture: the occurrence of bison has been established only once for the Pre-boreal period[56]: and mesolithic stations have yielded only a single bone of hare from Mullerup[57] and of horse only a tooth from Aamosen[58] and part of a femur from Kolind.[59] It is only in a few cul-de-sacs, like northernmost Scotland, where the landscape was in any case probably on the open side, that the reindeer survived long into the post-glacial period.[60]

Fig. 12.   Wall-painting at Alpera, E. Spain, showing woman gathering wild honey.

(*After Obermaier*).

The land-mammals hunted by mesolithic man were almost without exception those of the forest. Within this category it is possible to observe a certain progression: for example, elk, which prefer the foliage of trees like willow, sallow and birch, abounded during the Boreal period, but were of comparatively minor importance in Atlantic times. During the time of the mixed oak forest red deer was the leading form, but aurochs—like elk more important in Boreal times—roe deer and wild pig were more or less common. By contrast,

[55] G. F. Mitchell, 1941; Mitchell and Parkes, 1949.
[56] Iversen and Degerbøl, 1945.
[57] H. Winge in G. F. L. Sarauw *et al.*, 1903.
[58] M. Degerbøl in Mathiassen *et al.*, 1943, 165–7.
[59] M. Degerbøl in Mathiassen *et al.*, 1942, 123, 127–8.
[60] Remains of reindeer have been identified from the brochs of Kintradwell, Sutherland, and of Keiss and Yarhouse, Caithness (J. A. Smith, 1869). O. Isberg (1930) argued that reindeer survived rather extensively during the Post-glacial period in Scania, but this has recently been criticized by C. A. Althin *et. al.*, 1949.

species adapted to an open landscape, like horse and hare, are hardly represented among the food debris of mesolithic men in temperate Europe.

There is no reason to doubt that primitive methods of hunting, such as driving over precipices, survived during mesolithic times and it is likely that the noose or hanging snare was used for big game like elk during the forest period, a practice which indeed extended down to modern times in parts of Scandinavia.[61] Of the devices leaving tangible archæological traces the bow was undoubtedly the most important, having apparently displaced

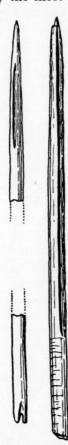

Fig. 13. Maglemosian wooden arrow-shafts. ($\frac{4}{9}$)
(*After Becker*).

the use of the " harpoon " on land except in the territories of the Azilians and Obanians. Recent discoveries at the well-known Maglemosian station of Holmegaard, Zealand, include two elm wood bows of simple type, having well shaped hand-grips (Pl. I, f).[62] There seems little room for doubt that some at least of the flint microliths, which spread over the temperate zone at this time, were used to tip and probably also to barb the arrows used with such bows. It is arguable, though not proven, that the slots near the tips of some of the pointed wooden arrow-shafts found with the Holmegaard bows once held such inserted microliths (Fig. 13). The recovery of a microlithic triangle, embedded for a third of its

[61] J. Granlund, 1940.
[62] C. J. Becker, 1945, 65–9.

length in the vertebra of the skeleton of a young man buried in the Tardenoisian midden on the isle of Téviec off the peninsula of Quiberon in Morbihan,[63] also suggests the use of the bow, and it is furthermore worth pointing out that, if the force of a bow is needed to explain the penetration, it is also evident that this particular microlith must have been hafted at the tip of the shaft and with the point projecting well beyond it. The discovery of two microliths of simple type and of a flint flake in the breast region of an auroch's skeleton from Jyderup, near Vig, in north-west Zealand,[64] suggests that more than one flint was sometimes used, presumably as barbs. The *petit tranchet*, formed from a cross-section of a flint blade, the sides trimmed by secondary flaking, was certainly mounted as an arrow-head, since not only has a specimen been found deeply embedded in a human vertebra from a neolithic chalk-cut grotto in the valley of Petit-Morin, Champagne,[65] but both in Denmark and Germany, as well as in the old culture-lands, examples have been found still affixed to their wooden shafts (Pl. I, a).[66]

It has often been observed that in the mesolithic flint industries both of western and central Europe and also of south Scandinavia and north Germany the predominant form of arrow-head underwent a marked change: whereas the Maglemosians employed pointed or triangular microliths, the Ertebølle people used trapezes to the total exclusion in some cases of other forms of microlith[67]; equally the triangles and battered backs of the Azilian and Sauveterrian cultures gave place progressively in successive stages of the Tardenoisian to trapezes or chisel-end arrow-heads. In other words, during mesolithic times in the temperate zone there was a significant change from pointed to chisel-ended arrow-heads, which must in turn reflect some alteration in the technique of hunting. The most clearly defined evidence for the utilization of chisel-ended arrow-heads in antiquity is to be found in Egypt, where representations on the monuments make it clear that they were used for shooting a variety of game. Thus, an undated rock-engraving in southern Upper Egypt shows an archer shooting a running ostrich with what are undoubted chisel-ended arrows.[68] Even more enlightening in some ways is the painting on the north wall of the tomb of Antefoker, vizier of Sesostris I, which shows the archer shooting down with similar arrows into a netted enclosure crowded with game, among them a bull and a couple of bubale already stricken.[69] The association of chisel-ended arrow-heads with remains of forest game in the Ertebølle middens, and the absence of any other recognizable form of arrow-head, suggests that in prehistoric Europe also they were used for shooting a wide range of quarry.

Already in Boreal times the Maglemosians of Denmark were using blunt-ended wooden arrows[70] (Fig. 14) of a type employed over extensive regions of northern Eurasia and of north America for shooting birds and small furred animals.[71] Bolts of this type were

---

[63] M. and S. -J. Péquart *et al.*, 1937, 52–3.

[64] Hartz and Winge, 1906.

[65] J. de Baye, 1874.

[66] e.g. examples from Tvaermose, Eising, sn., Ringkøping, north Jutland (S. Müller, 1907, 149; J. Brøndsted, 1938, I, 107); from Petersfehner Moor, Oldenburg (G. Kossinna, 1921, 28, abb. 40); and from Schalkholz, Norderdithmarsch (E. Krause, 1904, abb. 262 a, b).

[67] J. G. D. Clark, 1936, 142.

[68] H. Winkler, 1938, Pl. XX, 1.

[69] N. de G. Davies, 1920, Pl. VI and VII.

[70] From Holmegaard IV. See C. J. Becker, 1945, Fig. 4d.

[71] e.g. O. T. Mason, 1893, Pl. LIV.

still used in Finland, for shooting squirrels from crossbows, into the nineteenth century.[72] The advantage of these arrows is that while sufficient to stun small creatures their use avoided damage to pelts or skins.

The evidence for fowling activities is a good deal fuller for mesolithic than for upper palæolithic times in Europe. Much the largest and best studied assemblages are those from Denmark. They fall into two distinct groups, one from inland bogs, associated with the Maglemosian culture and of Boreal age, the other from coastal middens of the Ertebølle culture dating from Atlantic times. The bird remains from the chief Maglemosian sites

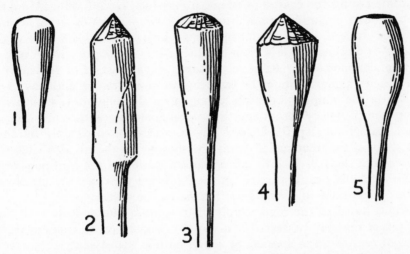

Fig. 14.   Blunt-ended wooden arrow-heads for shooting birds and small game ($\frac{1}{2}$)

Nos. 1, 2.   Maglemosian
Nos. 3–5.   Modern (Burjat, Wogul, Eskimo)

on Zealand[73] agree closely in general composition and differ mainly in the case of species represented only by single individuals. The birds reflect pretty accurately an inland bog habitat, which was not, however, very far distant from the sea, and which was hemmed in by forest. The only ground-birds represented are a few capercailzies, doubtless from the fir woods which covered much of the drier ground. Fresh-water species are by far the commonest and these include the two most abundantly represented, namely wild duck, (*Anas boscas*) and mute swan (*Cygnus olor*), as well as grebe, coot and heron. In addition several species of predominantly sea-birds were taken by the Maglemosian fowlers, including cormorants and gulls and divers of various species ; though none of these, it may be noted, are represented by more than one or two individuals.

In the Ertebølle middens,[74] sea-birds are naturally much more strongly represented. Capercailzie are again the only ground-birds, a reminder that even in Atlantic times pines were not entirely displaced by trees adapted to warmer conditions. Fresh-water species include wild duck and great crested grebe, but sea-birds predominate, including many

---

[72] J. Acerbi, 1802, I, 290, and Pl. opp. 280.

[73] e.g. Mullerup (Winge in Sarauw, 1903, 194–5), Svaerdborg (Winge in Friis Johansen, 1920, 260–4), Holmegaard (Winge in Broholm, 1931, 29–31) and Øgaarde (M. Degerbøl in Mathiassen *et al.*, 1943, 190–1).

[74] H. Winge, 1903, 61–109.

types of duck, auks, cormorants, gannets, gulls—chiefly herring and great black-backed—
and divers. Whooper (*Cygnus cygnus*) and Bewick's (*C. Bewicki*) swans occur on almost
every site, the former often in substantial numbers.

The two assemblages differ markedly in respect of season. The birds from the
Maglemosian sites confirm the generally accepted view that these were occupied only
during the summer months.[75] The presence of cranes and of numerous mute swans, as
well as of young cormorants and sea eagles, indicates occupation during the summer, while
the absence of winter migrants argues for their abandonment during the colder months. The
story is very different for the coastal middens, from which Herluf Winge cited no less than
thirteen winter guests, including, in addition to the two species of swan, several kinds of
divers and ducks. Indeed, it was winter migrants which provided the chief victims for the
coastal fowlers—at Sølager no less than 29 humeri of whooper swan were identified,
57 of eider, 14 of common scoter, 82 of velvet scoter and at least 92 of goldeneye. Arguing
from the bird bones alone, it might be tempting to interpret the middens as exclusively
winter sites, since the summer migrants common on the bog-sites, such a mute swans
and cranes, are conspicuously absent and the sole summer migrants, honey buzzard (*Pernis
apivorus*) from Aamølle and pelican from Havnø, are represented only by single bones.
Yet Winge's study of the mammalian fauna has shown that the midden sites were in fact
occupied throughout the year.[76] The correct interpretation of the bird bones would seem
to be that the Ertebølle people carried on their fowling activities principally during the
winter months, when numerous migrants frequented the coasts.

Sea-birds contributed to the food supply of mesolithic hunter-fishers on the coasts of
many other parts of Europe. In western Norway the rock-shelter of Viste, near Stavanger,[77]
yielded traces of twenty-seven species, of which no less than twenty-three are attributed
to fowling activities by early man. Once again, the only ground-bird is the capercailzie of the
pine forests. Great auk and guillemot are the species represented by the largest number of
individuals, but remains of wild duck, swan, a number of sea-ducks, among them eider
and scoter, three species of grebe and several gulls and divers also occur. Sea-birds were
also pursued by the Obanians of western Scotland, the Snoc Sligeach midden on Oronsay
yielding " great quantities of the bones of marine species," among them great auk, razorbill,
gannet, cormorant and various gulls.[78] The Tardenoisians of Téviec, off the coast of
Morbihan, also took the great auk, as well as a large number of different kinds of bird,
mainly water-fowl, including wild duck and widgeon.[79]

A point, which calls for some explanation, is the presence on many mesolithic sites of
remains of the white-tailed eagle[80]: for instance in Denmark thirteen thigh-bones were
found at Øgaard, and bones have been recognized from the three classic Maglemosian
stations of Mullerup, Svaerdborg and Holmegaard, as well as in many of the Ertebølle
middens; again, one could cite discoveries from as far afield as Téviec and Viste. The
explanation that the eagles were slaughtered as vermin, while it could be advanced for
occurrences on the settlements of farming communities, can hardly apply to these finds
from the middens of hunter-fishers. Again, though the flesh of eagles is said to have been

[75] J. G. D. Clark, 1936, 90.
[76] See A. P. Madsen *et al.*, 1900, 195; cf. V. Nordmann, 1936, 128, and J. G. D. Clark, 1936, 51.
[77] A. W. Brøgger, 1908, 9–11.
[73] *P.S.A.S.*, XLVIII, 105.
[79] M. and S. -J. Péquart, 1937, 101–2.
[80] For detailed references concerning eagles, see J. G. D. Clark, 1948 B, 126–30.

regarded as a delicacy by the Ukrainians and the natives of Kamtchatka during the eighteenth century, it seems hardly likely that mesolithic man caught white-tailed eagles with the primary aim of eating them, when other birds easier to catch were plentifully at hand. Much more probably they were taken on account of their feathers, which have been used for fletching arrows down to recent times over extensive areas of northern Eurasia and of north America; indeed they commanded so high a price in eastern Asia that marginal peoples like the Gilyak and the Kurile islanders reared and fed eagles in captivity in order to sell their feathers, and the province of Manchuria was still rendering tribute to Pekin in eagle feathers towards the end of the nineteenth century. One need only cite Hesiod's description of the arrows of Hercules as being " at the back end covered with the feathers of a dusky eagle " to show that the use of eagle feathers for fletching arrows goes back to an early period in Greece. To judge from Aesop's fable of *The Eagle and the Arrow*, eagles were commonly shot by bow and arrow.

Considered as so much raw material the pinion and tail feathers of eagles are well suited for fletching arrows, but not notably more so than those of geese. Certainly it was not for their physical properties alone that eagle feathers were preferred so long among so many different peoples. Their efficacy was not merely mechanical ; it was also magical. The archer wished to direct the aim and increase the force of his arrow by appropriating something of the eagle's power and keenness of vision. Among modern primitive peoples the potency of eagles is identified not only with the pinions on which it soars in the heaven, but also with the beak and claws by which it secures its prey. The association of bird beaks with hunting luck is quite common—raven beaks for instance are used as amulets by Aleut hunters and the natives of Kamtchatka and the Kuriles wear puffin bills round their necks as talismans—and eagle claws were used for medicinal purposes in some parts of Europe down to the nineteenth century. Again, it is suggestive that a claw-joint of the White-tailed Eagle from the Danish mesolithic site of Hallebygaarde shows distinct cut-marks. More conclusively one may cite four eagle claws from a south Swedish grave dating from the transition from the Stone to the Bronze Age and several distinct finds of falcon beaks, some accompanying burials of bowmen, under bronze age barrows in Yorkshire, Derbyshire and Staffordshire.

It can be assumed that snares were used for taking water-birds in mesolithic and later times, as they had already been for ground birds among upper palæolithic communities. Actual traces of such snares are only liable to survive from prehistoric times very exceptionally, like one from north Sweden of late bronze age date[81] but their widespread use is demonstrated by recent practice (Fig. 15). Martin Martin noticed horse-hair gins in

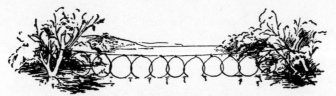

Fig. 15. Siberian duck-snares.
(*After Macpherson*).

use on St. Kilda and the illustrious Linnæus observed and noted lines of snares set for sea-birds on the shores of the Baltic island of Färo.[82] In Finland lines are stretched across

[81] *ibid.*, 121, n. 27.
[82] M. Martin, 1698 (1934 edition, 457); C. von Linné, 1745, 204.

swimming routes leading to the favourite pasturages of wild-fowl and close to the shore in front of nesting-places.[83] The Tungus of the Lena delta set snares across spits of land frequented by wild geese and get a boy or a woman to drive the birds into them.[84] In Siberia snares are even set under water to take swans by the neck when grubbing up the roots of water grasses.[85]

Even more primitive methods suffice for birds like the great auk,[86] which, agile enough on the sea, was quite incapable of flight and could easily be taken during the short breeding season on land. As it is not only easy to catch, but has tasty flesh and useful fat, gullet and stomach, there is no wonder that the great auk has always been a popular quarry. Even the brutish Neanderthalers were able to secure it.[87] Its bones have been recovered from upper palæolithic Grimaldian deposits in Apulia,[88] and what may well be representations of it have been recognized at El Pendo, near Santander.[89] During post-glacial times the great auk no longer reached the Mediterranean, but its bones have been recovered from prehistoric middens from Morbihan and Ireland to the coast of Norway almost to the Arctic Circle (Fig. 16), and it was still breeding in areas so far apart as Antrim, Caithness, Bohuslan and western Norway during the Early Iron Age.[90]

Many kinds of water-bird, including geese, ducks and swans, as well as great auks, are comparatively clumsy during the moulting season and it is then that they could most easily be taken. It is true of the circumpolar people generally, that, as Boas said of the Central Eskimo, " by far the greater number of birds are caught during the moulting season."[91]. It is while the geese are in moult that the Lapps of Finnmark run them down with the help of dogs,[92] just as the natives of Kamtchatka were doing when Krasheninnikov described them two hundred years earlier,[93] and it is at this season that the Eskimo chiefly employ their characteristic bird-dart with side members mounted low down the shaft.[94] Our own English fenmen incurred the wrath of Henry VIII for attacking wildfowl " in the summer season, at such time as (they) be moulted, and not replenished with feathers to fly . . . in such wise that the brood of wild-fowl is almost thereby wasted and consumed . . ."[95] Birds could also be taken at a disadvantage when sitting or before they had left the parental nest as fledglings. The inhabitants of the Westman Islands in the Färoes club young gannets and fulmar petrels to death on the nest just before they are ready to leave and take guillemots and razorbills when sitting by passing nooses round their necks from above.[96] Aleuts and Greenlanders grab cormorants from their nests

[83] U. T. Sirelius, 1934, 66.

[84] H. A. Macpherson, 1897, 222-3.

[85] *ibid.*, 231.

[86] See S. Grieve, 1885, and W. Blasius in Naumann's *Naturgeschichte der Vögel Mitteleuropas*, bd. XII, 169–208. Also J. G. D. Clark, 1948 B, 118–19.

[87] e.g. bones from La Cotte de St. Brelade and from Devil's Tower, Gibraltar (for refs. see J. G. D. Clark, 1948 B, Appendix).

[88] G. A. Blanc, 1920, 79–80.

[89] H. Breuil *et al.*, 1911, 38–9; J. G. D. Clark, 1948 B, Fig. 2.

[90] J. G. D. Clark, 1948 B, 118–19 and Appendix.

[91] F. Boas, 1888, 512.

[92] H. A. Macpherson, 1897, 122.

[93] S. Krasheninnikov, 1764, 158–9.

[94] J. Murdoch, 1892, 210–11.

[95] Quoted from H. C. Darby, 1940, 9.

[96] N. Annandale, 1905, 123.

by night.[97] But it would be superfluous to multiply examples, since the practice of attacking wild-fowl while in moult or on the nest corresponds to basic physiological facts and can

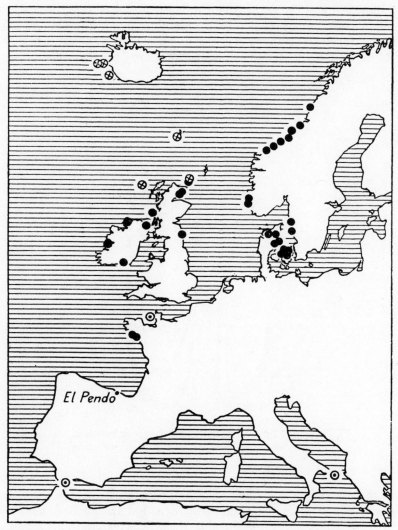

Fig. 16. Finds of Great Auk on sites occupied by Early Man.

⊙ Pleistocene.

● Post-glacial.

⊗ Early 19th century breeding grounds.

reasonably be expected among any people unprovided with firearms. One need hardly be surprised, therefore, that young birds should have been identified among the remains of great auk from sites as far apart as Sejrø in Denmark or Aavik in Norway.[98]

---

[97] W. Jochelson, 1933, 53-4.
[98] J. G. D. Clark, 1948 B, 120 and Appendix.

It may be that some of the devices for fishing, for which the earliest evidence now dates from mesolithic times, were of upper palæolithic origin; what is certain is that most of the principal methods of fishing were already in use some time before the spread of farming. In addition to the spear and the gorge, there appeared in mesolithic times the hook, the net and the funnel-shaped trap or weel—not to mention that important adjunct, the boat. The earliest hooks, for example those of the Maglemosians[99] and Natufians,[100] were almost invariably of U rather than V shape at the base (Fig. 17), which makes it very difficult to

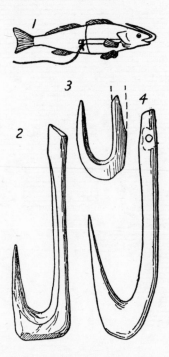

Fig. 17. Bone fish-hooks of the Maglemosian culture, showing possible method of securing bait ($\frac{2}{3}$)

accept the view that they were modelled on natural wooden forks. On the other hand there are chronological difficulties in the alternative idea that the earliest hooks were shaped from copper wire.[101] It is interesting to note that the Maglemosians employed the drill to begin the work of separating the point of the hook from the shank (Fig. 18, Nos. 1–4 and 6–8), a dodge which continued among the neolithic communities in Europe and has parallels as far afield as Ohio, Santa Cruz and New Zealand.[102] V-shaped hooks, of the type which first appeared in Europe at the end of the mesolithic or the beginning of the neolithic period in west Norway (Fig. 18, Nos. 5, 9), were on the other hand made by sawing or cutting. It is an interesting fact that none of these hooks had barbs. This and their large

[99] For references see J. G. D. Clark, 1948, 52, n. 2 and 3.

[100] F. Turville-Petre, 1932, 272 and Pl. XXVIII.

[101] For a discussion on this point, see J. G. D. Clark, 1948, 50–4.

[102] C. Rau, 1884, Figs. 188 and 212. Specimens in varying stages of manufacture from Purakanui, Otago, are exhibited in the Pitt-Rivers Museum, Oxford.

size suggests that they may have been used with live-bait for taking fish like pike; probably they were attached to a *luma* or float, against which the intended victim would tire, as were the very similar hooks used by the Turkomans and Ostiaks in modern times.[103]

Other devices to appear for the first time in the mesolithic period include the plaited trap or weel which still survives in the folk usage of many parts of Europe, even though

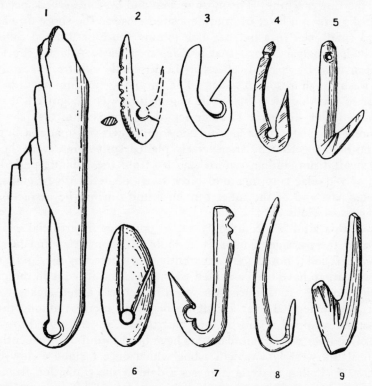

Fig. 18.   Bone fish-hooks from the stone age of northern and central Europe, showing alternative methods of separating the point from the shank ($\frac{2}{3}$, except No. 1, natural scale).

No. 1.   Mullerup, Denmark; No. 2.   Skipshelleren, W. Norway; No. 3.   Visby, Gotland; No. 4.   Mooseedorf, Switzerland; Nos. 5, 8.   Lake Bodman, Switzerland; No. 6.   Gåsen, near Stavanger, W. Norway; No. 7.   Alnäs Västergaard, Östergotland, Sweden; No. 8.   Viste, near Stavanger.

largely replaced by machine-made netting stretched over hoop frames.   The most widespread form, which occurs in many parts of the world and was already depicted on tomb paintings of the Egyptian Old Kingdom,[104] comprises baskets of conical or elongated bell shape, having internal funnels, one of which is commonly placed immediately inside the mouth (Pl. II).   Such traps may be employed individually, set in narrow channels or between weeds and kept in position by stone weights, or they may be fixed at the end of a fence built out from the shore or at the apex of a light V-shaped fence, or again they may be

---

[103] J. Jankó, 1900, Figs. 500–1, 504–5.
[104] G. Steindorff, 1913, *taf.* CXI.

incorporated in the structure of weirs of heavy timber construction. Also, they may be used to catch many different kinds of fish, salt- or fresh-water, with or without bait: in Lake Constance they are even now employed, sometimes at the apex of V-shaped fences, to catch pike, perch, tench, and occasional eels, while in many parts of Europe they are specifically intended for eels, whether in salt-water, as in the Wash or on the Danish coast, or in rivers like the Lower Rhine. The most ancient and best preserved specimen was found in 1940 by peat-diggers in a layer of mud deposited close to the shore of what had been in Litorina times a small islet in a narrow firth joining the now-drained Søborg Lake with the Kattegat. Pollen-analysis shows that it dates from early Atlantic times. Almost certainly it had been used by coast-dwellers of the Ertebølle culture, discarded in damaged condition and washed ashore on the islet. The surviving portion was 2·95 m. long, but, since a metre or so was dug away before its true nature was recognized, it must originally have been about 4 m. or well over 12 ft. in length; its maximum diamater was 0·9 m. or about 3 ft. Among the peat extracted from the trap, which was made of branchlets peeled of their bark and held together by transversely plaited split twigs, were the remains of an internal funnel made from similar materials. Also from the Atlantic period is part of the middle portion of a similar trap, made of birch twigs plaited with fir chips, comprising a piece of the outer part and of the inner funnel, found during the extraction of peat near Nidløse, south-west of Holbaek.

Basket traps of this kind are commonly set in openings in artificial weirs built across streams to obstruct the passage of fish. It is doubtful when weirs first began to be built, but two of the earliest so far noted were apparently constructed by the Arctic dwelling-place people. What appears to have been a ruined weir was found in 1911 in the parish of Kyrkslätt, Nyland, Finland.[105] It comprised a series of vertical aspen stakes with recumbent beams of black alder extended over a distance of c. 13½ metres; among the stakes was a granite weight-stone wrapped round by lime bast thread, possibly used to weight a basket trap. Remains of another weir of similar type have been found more recently in the parish of Høyland, Rogaland, west Norway, in a bog which once formed a slow-flowing stream joining two lakes.[106] Pollen-analysis suggests a date at the transition from the Stone to the Bronze Age in this part of Norway, and associated slate and flint arrow-heads show that the weir was made by people of the Arctic tradition. The only indication of a structure of this class of pre-neolithic date is part of what may have been a fence-like weir from a marine deposit of Atlantic age at Svinninge Vejle, a branch of the Lammefjord, Denmark.[107]

The most effective of all devices for catching fish is the net, and there is ample evidence that this had already been devised by mesolithic times, at least in its most primitive form, the drag, sweep, or seine net, designed to surround and enclose surface-swimming fish, mainly in shallow water. Evidence for the use of such nets might include the floats designed to keep the upper edge on the surface, the weights needed to sink the lower edge, and fragments of the net itself; of these the only elements likely to survive under normal conditions are the weights, which could hardly be recognized as such in isolation unless found as a series in position, although impressions of nets have been found on hand-made pottery. One reasonably complete find from mesolithic times is that recovered from the undisturbed bed of a stone age extension of Lake Ladoga during the draining of some water-meadows near Korpilahti in the parish of Antrea, Viborg, Finland, in 1913, comprising floats,

[105] G. Topelius, 1912.
[106] A. B. Andersen, 1948.
[107] C. J. Becker, 1941, 138–9.

fragments of net, and weights of the seventeen pine-bark floats, each roughly oblong in form and nearly a foot long (30 cm.) with a perforation at one end; four of these covered traces of the actual net, which was made from lime bast or nettle-fibre, and fragments of binding-thread were found under twelve of a number of weight-stones about the size of a man's fist arranged in a group near the floats. There has been some dispute about the exact date of this find; whereas Pälsi relied on the phytopalæontological evidence and assigned it to an early stage of the Ancylus Lake, Ailio, on the strength of the stone axes of Suomusjärvi type found at the same level, referred it to the Litorina Sea stage.[108] On the other hand, the find from Narva Siivertsi in north-east Esthonia, comprising similar net-weights and pine-bark floats of slightly more ovoid form, is firmly dated to the Ancylus-Litorina transition.[109] The seine net, which was equally adapted for inland and inshore coastal waters, where there was a tolerably smooth bottom and a beach for landing, implies a boat and a certain element of team-work. The net could either be worked entirely from a boat, being hauled directly on board, or, after being secured ashore by one wing, it could be rowed out, shot from a boat, and the other wing returned to shore, the catch being landed by parties hauling at both. Whichever course was adopted, the manœuvring and handling of the net would require at least three men, and where a net of any size was used, several more.

The principal fishery for which evidence survives from mesolithic times centred round the pike, a fish widely distributed in the rivers and lakes of Europe and one which at the present day is absent only from the Iberian Peninsula, Greece, and the west coast of Norway, although apparently a modern introduction to Ireland. Essentially fresh-water fish, pike do occur to a certain extent in the Baltic, but there they are concentrated in the island belt and attain no great size. They can be caught all the year round by different means: their voracity makes them easy prey to the hook with live-bait; they are often caught in weels as they penetrate inlets and channels on the way to spawn; and while in shallow water for this purpose they are especially vulnerable to the fish-spear (Fig. 19) and the noose—all methods which could easily have been used by mesolithic man. The spawning season varies according to the size of the fish: in central Sweden the peasants distinguish between " ice pike," the youngest mature fish which arrive before the ice has cleared; " grass pike," the larger fish which often spawn, when spring is far advanced, on the flooded water-meadows; and " leaf pike," the largest fish, compara-tively few in number, which spawn in deeper water during early summer. As a food-fish Isaac Walton opined that pike flesh is " too good for any but anglers, or very honest men " and it has the great merit of preserving well, either salted or dried; in addition, a kind of caviare can be made from the roe.[110]

Fig. 19. Prong of Maglemosian spear from the bed of the North Sea.

[108] S. Pälsi, 1920; J. Ailio, 1922, 7–8.
[109] R. Indreko, 1937, Fig. 3, No. 3; 1948, 325, abb. 79, No. 1.
[110] J. G. D. Clark, 1948, 57.

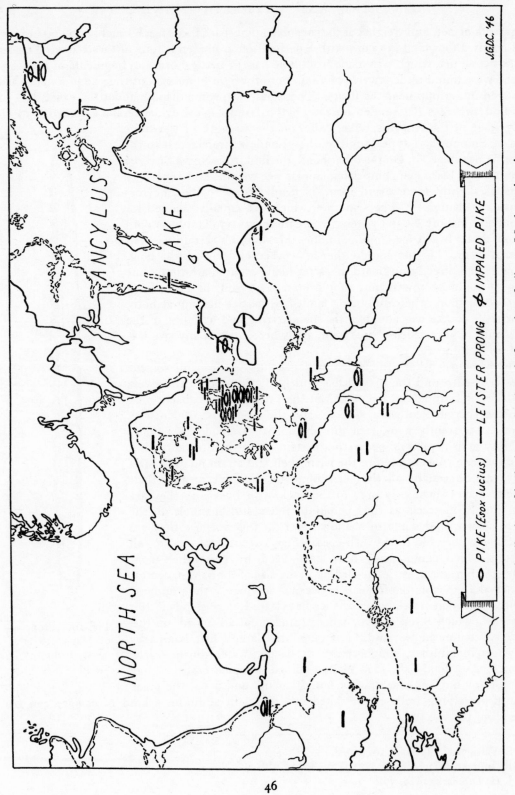

Fig. 20.   Distribution of barbed spear-heads and of remains of pike on Maglemosian sites.

There is some evidence that pike were eaten by the reindeer-hunters of northern Europe in late glacial and earliest post-glacial times,[111] but it was among the Maglemosian people, who occupied the North European Plain during Boreal times, that the fishery was first developed on an extensive scale (Fig. 20). Traces of this may probably be found in the large number of barbed bone points recovered from the bed of the old Boreal lake at Kunda, Esthonia; indeed in two cases such points were found impaling pike skeletons from the bed of this particular lake, one in the back region of a large pike (Fig. 21), the other embedded

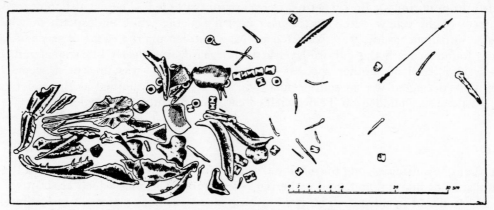

Fig. 21.   Remains of skeleton of pike with a fish-spear prong in the region of the back :
from a mesolithic lake-deposit at Kunda, Esthonia.

(After Indreko).

in a pike's skull. A similar find from southern Sweden helps to support the idea that these points were quite frequently mounted as the prongs of leisters or fish-spears.[112] Detailed study by Danish archæologists of the numerous barbed bone points recovered during recent investigations in the bed of the mesolithic lake at Aamosen in north Zealand has revealed near the tip of many specimens a zone of surface decay. This corresponds approximately with the thickness of a pike and is thought to have been brought about through the decomposition of fish which escaped with a single leister prong in their flesh. The quantity of material found on some sites—for example, 80 upper and 64 left lower jaw-bones of pike and no less than 274 leister prongs and 11 hooks from Svaerdborg—suggests that the pike fishing may even have been a principal reason for the summer occupation of low-lying bog-sites. It is even possible that the preponderance of head-bones from Sværdborg may indicate that pike were dried for storing and use elsewhere at another time of the year. The early summer was particularly favourable for this type of fishing, for it was then the fish lay quiet in still, shallow water. The comparative scarcity of hooks in relation to leister prongs on the summer camping-places is only what might be expected, since live-baiting is normally practised in the colder season. One is reminded irresistibly of Scheffer's description[113] of fishing among the Lapps :

---

[111] Pike remains occurred at the Hamburgian level at Meiendorf (Rust, 1937, 57) and at the Ahrensburgian level at Stellmoor (Rust, 1943, 58), as well as with a broken barbed point from late glacial clay at Abschruten, kr. Pillkallen, E. Prussia (H. Gross, 1937, 77).

[112] J. G. D. Clark, 1948, 58 (with refs.). For modern use of leisters in Scandinavia, see H. Fernholm, 1942.

[113] J. Scheffer, 1674, 107.

" Their way of fishing alters with the season, in the Summer usually with drag nets, between two boats, or else with spears like Tridents, but that they have more teeth. With these they strike pikes, especially when they ly sunning themselves near the top of the Water: they do the same by Night burning dry wood at the prow, by which light the Fish are enticed thither."

Although it can be assumed that plant food entered into the diet of mesolithic man, actual evidence for this is still slight. Hazel-nuts, which abounded in many parts of temperate Europe during the Boreal period, were certainly gathered. There is also some evidence that seeds of the yellow water-lily (*Nuphar luteum L.*), the white endosperm of which is of some nutritional value, were collected by Maglemosian man; a cache of seeds of *c.* 250 c. cm., found beneath the culture layer at Holmegaard, was clearly intentional and, since only a single seed of another species—the white water-lily—was present it seems most likely that the agent was mesolithic man and not some such animal as the water-rat.[114] The Tardenoisian midden on Téviec yielded carbonized fruits of the wild pear.

FARMERS

It would be entirely wrong to imagine that the introduction of farming involved the discontinuance of hunting and food gathering, even among societies which concentrated on the new modes of livelihood. The yield of husbandry was not so great in early times that farmers could afford to neglect other sources of food, and the game which abounded in the forests must also have been welcome for the raw materials it yielded, notably antler and hides. Again, it was necessary in the interests of husbandry to keep wild animals in check and one should not overlook the taste for hunting as a sport, which developed particularly among societies dominated by a warrior class.

The only certain source of information about the extent to which hunting contributed to subsistence is the fauna from prehistoric sites, but reliable information about this can only be forthcoming when really large samples of animal remains are available; again, it is most important that an accurate idea should be given of the proportions in which the various species occur. Unfortunately these conditions are only rarely fulfilled. So far as it goes, the British evidence suggests that, leaving out of account sea mammals, hunting contributed only comparatively slightly to the economy of neolithic and later prehistoric farmers and that during the period of settled agriculture in the south and south-east of England it was quite negligible. Red deer and roe deer must have yielded a certain amount of venison to the earlier farmers, but it is significant that where large number of antlers are available, as when these were used for mining flint or excavating ditches, the great majority prove to be shed ones collected for use, barely one in seven having been removed from the skulls of slain deer (or of individuals dead from natural causes).

		Shed	*Removed from skull*
Grimes Graves flint-mines[115]	..	(166) 84%	(32) 16%
Blackpatch flint-mines[116]	..	(9) 90%	(1) 10%
Avebury ditch[117]	..	(29) 85%	(5) 15%

---

[114] H. C. Broholm, 1931, 19; G. Hatt, 1937, 14.
[115] *Grimes Graves Excavations*, 1914, 143.
[116] *Suss. Arch. Soc. Coll.*, LXV, 27.
[117] *Archaeologia*, LXXXIV, 1935, 149.

It has also been remarked that many of the red and roe deer antlers found in the ditches of the neolithic " camps " and from long barrows in the south of England were shed specimens.[118] On the other hand the number of antlers with portions of skull adhering is still enough, taken in conjunction with bones, to show that, although deer-hunting was only a subsidiary activity, it was still carried on to a perceptible extent. It is interesting to note also the occasional occurrence of fox,[119] no doubt killed as vermin, and in this connection one should mention the necklace of seventeen large wolf canines ground flat on each face found with a burial of the Wessex early bronze age culture at Newton, Wiltshire.[120] Within the sphere of the settled farming cultures of the Early Iron Age in southern Britain the predominance of domestic animals over wild ones was quite overwhelming. So far as the downland sites are concerned, the complete absence or at least the rarity of remains of red deer is particularly striking[121] and confirms that by this time forest clearance in this tract was already very far advanced; on the other hand remains of fox, polecat and badger show that vermin were trapped.[122] The only large assemblages of animal remains available from sites of this stage in the south of England are those from the Glastonbury lake-village[123] and from the three Romano-British farmsteads excavated by Gen. Pitt-Rivers near Farnham, Dorset.[124] These confirm that hunting played a very minor role at this time in this region by comparison with stock-raising.

	Number of bones	Wild (Percentage)	Domesticated (Percentage)
Glastonbury ..	3,426	2·1	97·9
Woodyates ..	3,669	0·2	99·8
Rotherley ..	3,606	0·9	99·1
Woodcuts ..	4,204	3·4	96·6

The Danish evidence is of special interest since it offers the possibility of comparing the respective importance of hunting among hunter-fisher and farmer communities living at comparatively close quarters during the same period. On sites occupied by Stone Age farmers, such as Havnelev, Troldebjerg and Bundsø,[125] the proportion of wild to domestic animals was very low—at the last-named site only 200 out of 10,000 bones belonged to wild species. Quite opposite conditions prevailed at the more or less contemporary sites at Strandegaard and Ordrup Naes[126] occupied by epi-mesolithic hunter-fishers, though at the latter site it is interesting to observe that the proportion of domestic animals rose from 30 per cent in the lower to 60 per cent in the upper levels, indicating the gradual transformation of the older way of life. The picture which emerges is that of hunter-fishers

---

[118] e.g. at Whitehawk Camp, Brighton (*Ant. J.* XIV, 127–8) and Thickthorn Long Barrow, Dorset (*P.P.S.* 1936, 93–4).

[119] e.g. at Windmill Hill, Wilts. (Curwen, 1930, 27).

[120] *Cat. Ant. Mus. Devizes*, Pt. I, No. 206.

[121] Thus in Wiltshire red deer was absent from Fifield Bavant and Swallowcliffe Down and rare at All Cannings Cross; at Meon Hill it was represented only by fragments of antler and from Quarley Hill, also in Hampshire, it was missing.

[122] Fox was present at Meon Hill, All Cannings Cross and Fifield Bavant (?); pole-cat at Meon Hill and Fifield Bavant ; and badger at Swallowcliffe Down.

[123] Bulleid and Gray, 1911, 643.

[124] Pitt-Rivers, 1887–98, III, 233.

[125] Respectively, T. Mathiassen, 1940; J. Winther, 1935; T. Mathiassen *et al.*, 1939.

[126] Mathiassen, 1940, and C. J. Becker, 1939.

and farmers living side by side, the farmers concerning themselves very little with hunting, the hunter-fishers on the other hand gradually adopting the new economy.

In Switzerland hunting seems to have played an enormously greater part in the economy of peoples whose material culture was formally of neolithic or early bronze age character. Owing to the survival of substantial quantities of animal bones from the lake-side settlements and to the careful way in which these have often been identified, one can speak with some assurance and it may be said at once that hunting played a part not always notably inferior to and occasionally even exceeding that of stock-raising. The data from the stratified site of Port-Conthy, St. Aubin, Lake Neuchâtel,[127] is particularly interesting because it seems to show that the proportion varied at different stages, though it was always very much higher than at the sites of formally neolithic people in Denmark or England:

		Wild	*Domesticated*
Late neolithic	..	27·6%	72·4%
Middle neolithic	..	45·1%	54·9%
Lower neolithic	..	29·5%	70·5%

Even more striking is the evidence from sites in the region north and north-west of Luzern, which have yielded the two largest neolithic assemblages from Switzerland:

			Number of individuals	*Wild*	*Domesticated*
Egolzwil[128]	..	..	910	66·6%	33·4%
Wauwyl[129]	..	..	128	40%	60%
Seematte-Gelfingen[130]	..		433	52%	52%

The early bronze age site of Baldegg[131] in the same area showed a rather smaller, though still large proportion of wild species—28 per cent of a total of 145 individuals. From the Zürich area only small assemblages are available from the early period, both of which show that hunting was practised to a substantial extent:

	Number of individuals	*Wild*	*Domesticated*
Obermeilen[132] (neolithic and bronze age)	94	45%	55%
Utoquai[133] (late neolithic)	66	29%	71%

Analysis of the wild animals hunted by the neolithic and early bronze age inhabitants of Switzerland shows that around seven-eighths comprise animals whose flesh is commonly eaten at the present day, including red deer—which comprise some three-eighths of all the wild animals represented—roe deer, wild pig, aurochs, elk and beaver, together with much smaller numbers of wild horse, bison and hare. Of the remaining eighth, which includes fox, wolf, wild cat, badger, otter, lynx, common marten, pole-cat and brown bear,

---

[127] L. Reverdin, 1922 and 1932; P. Vouga, 1934, 57.
[128] Hescheler and Rüeger, 1939, 311–12.
[129] Hescheler, 1920, 286–7.
[130] E. Kuhn, 1947, 42.
[131] *ibid.*
[132] E. Kuhn, 1935, 323.
[133] E. Kuhn, 1932, 666.

some were presumably killed for their skins, others as vermin or both. As might have been expected, an overwhelming proportion of the wild animals killed by the lake-dwellers were inhabitants of the forest, those adapted to life in open country—horse, hare and bison—accounting for hardly more than 3 per cent of the total.

Few large assemblages are available from the later prehistoric periods in Switzerland. The extremely low proportion of wild animals from the middle bronze age site of Crestaulta near Surin in the Grisons[134]—less than 3 per cent—can hardly be compared with results from the lake-side settlements, since it comes from an alpine site well over four thousand feet above sea-level. On the other hand it is surely significant of economic change that from 5,432 bones from the late bronze age pile-settlements of Zürich/Alpenquai only 10·3 per cent were those of wild animals.[135]

The best examples of mixed farming and hunting economies are possibly those on the northern fringes of the temperate zone among coastal communities in south Sweden and Gotland and above all in west Norway. Beyond these, again, there continued to exist in the circumpolar zone communities, like that at Åloppe in Uppland, which depended entirely on the older forms of subsistence. A common feature of many of these groups is that, whether they depended partly on farming, or wholly on gathering and catching, they drew a substantial proportion of their resources from the sea. It will be convenient therefore to defer considering them until the next chapter.

Instead of dilating on the varieties of arrow (Fig. 22) and spear used by the prehistoric farmers—weapons which to an increasing extent were used for war rather than for the chase—attention may be drawn to a type of tread-trap, which, appearing for the first time in the Late Bronze Age and spreading rapidly over the temperate zone, symbolizes the part still played by trapping in the closing stages of European prehistory. The traps consist of heavy wooden frames from two to four feet in length and tapering slightly at the squared ends (Fig. 23). In the middle they have either a single oblong aperture fitted with a wooden flap, or a pair of such (Pl. I, b, c). These flaps are held in a closed position by wooden springs set in grooves cut in the frame and held down by cross pegs. As a rule the frames are made of oak, though one from Hinge in Jutland was of willow. The flaps also are generally of oak, but birch was used in the case of the trap from Auquharney moss, Aberdeenshire.[136] For the springs a more pliable wood was favoured: most often hazel, but sometimes willow (e.g. Auquharney) or beech (e.g. Pindstrup, Jutland).[137]

Although large, complicated and fairly widely distributed, these traps were for long ignored or misinterpreted as among other things musical instruments, machines for making peat-bricks, models of boats or devices for catching pike. Robert Munro addressed himself to this problem with characteristic zest and was not merely the first to demonstrate their distribution from Scotland, Ireland and Wales to Germany, north Italy and Yugo-Slavia, but also to appreciate that they must have been some kind of trap.[138] Basing himself mainly on their occurrence by rivers or in bogs and old lake beds, he argued that they were most probably used for catching otters or beavers. An important advance came with Patrick Gillespie's recognition that one of the deer represented on an Early Christian carved stone from Clonmacnoise in central Ireland had one foot caught in an oblong trap of similar

---

[134] W. Burkart, 1946, 48.

[135] E. Wettstein, 1924, 122; Hescheler, 1924, 105.

[136] *Proc. Soc. Ant. Scot.* LVI (1922), 282–7.

[137] R. W. Reid, 1922; H. Rasmussen, 1940, 114 f.

[138] R. Munro, 1897.

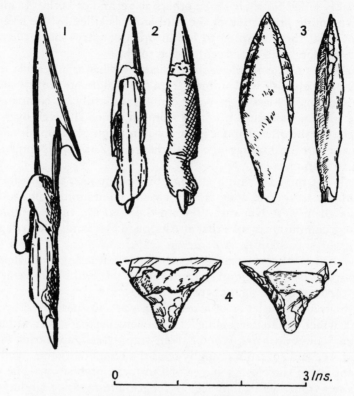

Fig. 22.   Flint and bone arrow-heads from neolithic
Switzerland. The heads were mounted on their wooden
shafts by birch-pitch.

Nos. 1–3 pointed ; no. 4 chisel-ended.

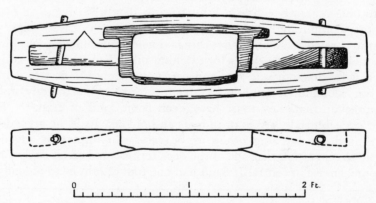

Fig. 23.   Wooden tread trap from Drumacaladerry Bog, Co. Donegal.

(*National Museum of Antiquities, Dublin*)

character.[139]   The matter was not decided definitely, though, until the prehistoric traps were compared by Holger Rasmussen with modern ones (Fig. 24) from the folk culture of western Polesia, Masovia and Galicia for catching red deer, roe deer and even bear[140]. In modern Poland the traps were set in groups on marshy ground near a favourite drinking-place, flap downmost, so that an animal setting its foot in the aperture would release the spring and, plunging through, get firmly caught as well as almost certainly being disabled.

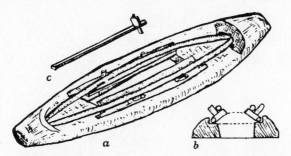

Fig. 24.   Modern tread-traps for deer from Masovia, Poland.
(*After Moszyński*).

This explains not only the situation of the prehistoric finds by rivers and bogs, but also their frequent occurrence in groups: for instance, nine were found stacked together almost upright and evidently out of use in Larkhill bog, Ballyshannon, Co. Fermanagh; groups of five each occurred near Laibach, Yugo-Slavia, and near Vicenza, north Italy; and groups of three and six respectively near Teltow, Brandenburg.[141]

Since Munro's days, knowledge about these traps has also been enlarged both as to date and geographical range.   Thanks to pollen-analysis, examples as far apart as Druma-caladerry bog in northern Donegal[142] and Lake Gölen in Vastergötland[143] can be assigned to the Late Bronze Age of their respective regions, around the middle of the first millennium B.C., and one from near Silkeborg, Denmark, has been dated to the Sub-boreal period, probably to its latter part.[144]   On the other hand, it must be remembered that the type continued in use in Ireland until the Early Christian period and in parts of Poland until modern times.   As regards distribution, the picture has been filled out by the discovery of four new sites in Ireland[145] and, notably, by the extension of finds in Scandinavia—five each in Denmark[146] and south Sweden[147] and one in the extreme south-west of

---

[139] *Proc. Soc. Ant. Scot.* LIII (1919), 166, Fig. 4.

[140] The modern Polish traps were published in 1929 by Moszyński, whose book was translated into Swedish in 1936. Comparison with the prehistoric traps was first made by H. Rasmussen, 1940, 121 f.

[141] All given in Munro, 1897.

[142] F. Mitchell, 1945, 17.

[143] The trap is exhibited in the Nordiska Museet, Stockholm.

[144] Dated by K. Jessen in Rasmussen, 1940, 124–5.

[145] Drumacaladerry bog; nr. Shannonbridge, Co. Offaly; and Townland of Lyranes Lower (all Nat. Mus., Dublin).   Also Dromdaleague par., Derreenacrimig West, Co. Cork (Cork Mus.).

[146] See H. Rasmussen, 1940.   Additional finds have been made at Herning, Jutland, and at Hund-strup bog, Hammer sn., Praestø (inf. H. Rasmussen and G. Berg, respectively).

[147] In addition to the Lake Gölen find, others have been found at Maramö bog, Värnamo sn., Småland; Långamåla, Rödeby sn., Blekinge; Kihult bog, Fagerhults sn., Scania; and Mjälaryd, Norregården, Rogberga sn., Småland (inf. G. Berg).

Norway.[148]   Just as the old finds in north Italy and in the Laibach area emphasized the extension of this form of trap down to the southern margin of the deciduous forest, so the new ones in the north show how they reached up to but not beyond the northern margin of the deciduous forest (Fig. 25).   The absence of finds from the Mediterranean zone should

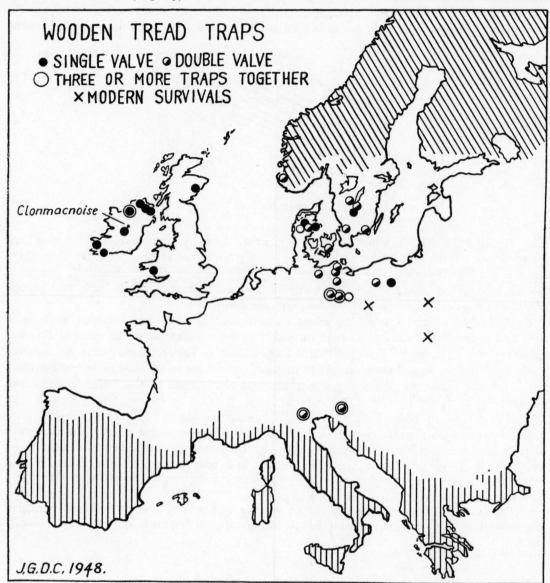

Fig. 25.   Distribution of Prehistoric Tread Traps.

be considered in relation to the fact that by the time this type of trap had come into widespread use the territory had been incorporated within the sphere of civilization.   The fact that the bogs of the circumpolar zone have yielded quantities of prehistoric sledge-runners and skis makes it reasonably certain that, had the traps been used there, examples

[148] E. S. Engelstad, 1934, Pl. XLIII b.

of them would have survived and come to light. The wooden tread-trap with spring valve may be seen as a culture element coterminous with and peculiar to the broad-leafed summer forest of the temperate zone of Europe, a fact all the more impressive in the light of its late date and its association with hunting. From an ecological point of view it is pertinent that the main timber of the traps was almost invariably of oak and that red deer were their principal victims.

Birds were another source of wild food on which the farming communities of prehistoric Europe continued to draw. Naturally the importance of fowling varied very much according to local conditions and it was chiefly among dwellers by marsh, lake and the sea-shore that this activity flourished. The lake-dwellers of Switzerland[149] took large numbers of duck, heron and swan, as well as birds of prey like kites, goshawks, white-tailed and golden eagles and sparrowhawks and the fowlers of the Glastonbury lake-village made a very similar bag.[150] If one turns to a region like the Orkneys the picture is very much the same,[151] except that fresh-water wild-fowl are replaced by cormorants and various species of gull; it is possible that the remains of eagle in a chambered cairn near Midhowe and specifically white-tailed eagle in the iron age level of a stalled cairn on the Calf of Eday, may be connected with the importance of sheep-farming in this region, though it is likely that the use of their feathers for fletching arrows continued to supply a motive for killing eagles down to the end of the prehistoric period.[152] The oil found in some sea-birds may have helped to provide lamp fuel. Again, the long bones of the larger birds served as handles for small tools and among the Peterborough or Neolithic " B " people of Britain the articular ends of some bird-bones were used for impressing patterns on pottery.[153] The methods used in taking birds continued to be of a primitive type and it is noteworthy that the intensive fowling activities on St. Kilda, the Westman Islands and the Faeroes during modern times continued to be based on such methods as snaring or grabbing birds on their nests.[154]

Fishing also persisted[155] and its contribution must have been all the more welcome— as it was indeed throughout the medieval period—before the cultivation of fodder crops had made it possible to feed cattle adequately during the winter and so even out the supply of fresh meat. Although the most striking development was in off-shore fisheries (see Chap. III), rivers and lakes continued to yield a rich harvest.

The most important river-fisheries were devoted to anadromous fish like salmon and sturgeon, which ascend rivers to spawn in fresh water, and to catadromous fish like eels, which go down to the sea to spawn since these can be taken in large numbers during their seasonal runs and smoked or dried for winter use. Such fisheries, indeed, could easily be made to fit into the activities of the farming year, and where conditions were favourable

---

[149] L. Rütimeyer, 1862, 113–15; H. Reinerth, 1926, App. II and 1936, 70.

[150] Bulleid and Gray, 1911, 631–7.

[151] e.g. Midhowe (*P.S.A.S.*, LXVIII, 349), Jarlshof (*P.S.A.S.*, LXVII, 135 and LXVIII, 318) and Eday (*P.S.A.S.*, LXXI, 152–3).

[152] Though the iron age arrow-shafts from Thorsbjerg and Vimose in Denmark show impressions of the threads used for binding on the feathers (C. Englehardt, 1866, 58, Pl. 12, No. 11 ; 1869, 23, P. 14. No. 23), no actual traces of these have survived from prehistoric Europe. With the reduction of eagles resulting from the intensification of farming goose feathers were adopted for fletching.

[153] D. M. Liddell, 1929.

[154] See M. Martin, 1934, edition, 315–16; A. Annandale, 1905, *passim*; K. Williamson, 1948, Chap. 6.

[155] For details and references, see J. G. D. Clark, 1948, 63–73.

their contribution to subsistence must have been out of all proportion to the effort involved. It should be remembered that fish had a much wider range before rivers were fouled by modern cities and industrial development and that salmon, for instance, reached as far inland as Prague and Schaffhausen. Traces of what must have been a seasonal fishery, most probably for salmon, have been investigated at Newferry on the River Bann in northern Ireland[156] : very little occupational rubbish was found, but numerous hearths and great spreads of ash, separated by layers of water-laid diatomite, point to some seasonal activity, which can hardly have been any other than drying fish; the fish were presumably taken in weirs, the construction of which would account for the polished stone axes found on the site, and the sharp flint flakes, often with trimming at the butt-end, which constitute the main bulk of the archæological material, call to mind the sharp knives used by the Indians of British Columbia to rip open salmon previous to drying them over fires.

In certain parts of Europe, and notably in the Danube valley, sturgeon were of particular importance.[157] It may even be that the annual run of this fish was a factor in the colonization of the region by neolithic peasants. Among other sites, Vinča and Starčevo have each yielded bones of sturgeon. It may well be that the stag-antler harpoon heads characteristic of the neolithic cultures of the area were used in the sturgeon fishery. Among the Indians of the Fraser River the harpooner took up his position in the prow of the canoe and felt his way along the bottom until he came into contact with the knobbly back of a sturgeon; then, striking home, he would jerk the head of his harpoon free and play the fish on the line.

Although traces have been recovered from stone age sites in Jutland and Gotland, there is little sign that adult eels were caught on a substantial scale in prehistoric Europe. On the other hand it is possible that large numbers of young ones were taken on the way upstream, an extremely profitable type of fishing, but one which would leave little trace.

The evidence from the Swiss and other lakes indicates active fishing throughout the later prehistoric periods, though no really significant advance in tackle can be demonstrated. To judge from the numerous bark and wooden floats, the fired clay net-weights and the pieces of netting, nets were particularly important for this type of fishing, as indeed they still are. Weels were certainly made during neolithic times[158] and since they survived down to modern times, can be assumed to have continued in use during the Bronze and Iron Ages : rather dubious records from Laibach and from north Italy remind us that this type must have been widespread in prehistoric Europe. Owing to the common survival of fish-hooks, line fishing is more generally represented in the archæological record. The character of the earlier neolithic hooks does not differ from mesolithic ones, but barbed hooks, no doubt inspired by metal prototypes, appeared in the neolithic cultures of Denmark and south Sweden and in the later neolithic levels of central Europe.[159] In the circumpolar zone and on its margins from west Norway into Russia one finds at this time a special type of composite hook, in which shank and point of bone or slate were made as separate members and were lashed together at the base (Fig. 26).[160] Metal hooks, which might be barbed or plain, were first made commonly during the Late Bronze and Early Iron Ages   (Fig. 27).

---

[156] H. J. Movius, 1936, 240 f. and 1942.
[157] Clark, 1948, 73.
[158] C. J. Becker, 1941, 136–7.
[159] Clark, 1948, 65–6.
[160] ibid., 67–8.

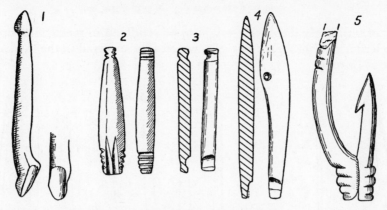

Fig. 26. Parts of composite fish-hooks dating from the stone age in the circumpolar zone of Europe (⅔).

No. 1. Skipshelleren, W. Norway; no. 2. Halsen, Finnmark, N. Norway; nos. 3–4. Finnish dwelling-place culture; no. 5. Volosowa, Russia.

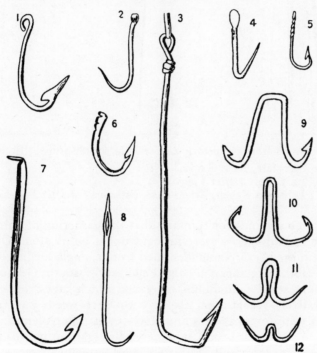

Fig. 27. Metal fish-hooks from late bronze age or early iron age Europe (⅔).

Note.—All are of bronze, except for no. 4, of iron.
Nos. 1, 6. 8. L. Bourget and no. 2 L. Morat, France.
Nos. 3, 4. La Tène, ; no. 9. Corcelettes and no. 10. Cortaillod ; no. 12 unknown, all L. Neuchâtel, Switzerland.
No. 5, Hallstatt, Austria.
Nos. 7, 11, L. Bienne, Switzerland.

Another type of ultimately mesolithic origin to be rendered in metal, first bronze and then iron, was the leister or fish-spear (Fig. 28), which also survived in the modern folk-culture of most parts of Europe.

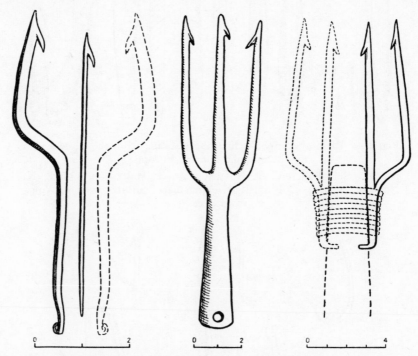

Fig. 28.   Metal leisters from prehistoric and early historic Europe.   Scales in inches.
1.   Peschiera, Lake Garda.   (*After Keller*).
2.   La Tène.   (*After Vouga*).
3.   Lahepera Kabeli, Lake Peipsi, Esthonia.   (*After Indreko*).

Equally, there are no grounds for thinking that the gathering of wild plants came to an end merely because certain species were brought under cultivation. One way of checking this is by reference to the list of plants identified from a single neolithic site. For example, of the 193 species from Sipplingen by the Federsee in south Germany,[161] twenty-nine were more or less domesticated, including seventeen which have dropped out of cultivation during the comparatively recent past; twenty-two were weeds and twenty-five meadow plants; thirty-seven were forest species and sixty-seven water-plants; and thirteen cannot readily be assigned to any single group. One point brought out by this is that the spread of farming, by creating meadows and cultivated land, actually increased the range of wild plants available for gathering. Again, the increased density of population which accompanied the introduction of farming helped to accentuate the pressure on wild foods owing to the uncertain yield of cereal crops, a point most clearly illustrated by the range of wild plant substances used to supplement cereal flour in time of dearth down to historical times. From another aspect also the progress of technology, for example the development of textiles and carpentry, increased the demand on such things as plant-fibres, dye-plants and caulking-moss.

---

[161] G. Lechler, 1945, 506; K. Bertsch, 1932.

The forest was particularly rich in fruits and seeds, including acorns, beech-nuts, hazel-nuts, sloe-plums, rose-haws, elderberries, strawberries, blackberries and raspberries, all of which were identified at Sipplingen. Confirmation that such were in fact eaten is provided by the discovery of around a pint of seeds in the region of the stomach of a contracted burial in the clay of the submerged surface of the Essex coast near Walton-on-Naze, probably of neolithic age; blackberry seeds predominated but rose-haws and *Atriplex* seeds were also present.[162]

In the recent experience of the European peasantries the forest provided several important substitutes for cereal flour in times of dearth. On the northern margins of the farming zone the inner part of the bark of pine, and in case of real need of birch-bark, was scraped down and added to rye meal after this had first been mixed with water. In his journey through Finland in 1873 Retzius saw pine trees robbed of their bark and finely scraped bark-meal in wooden troughs and barrels for daily use and for storage.[163]

In temperate Europe, and still more in the Mediterranean zone, acorns were among the most important substitutes. The value of acorns as food may be illustrated by the following comparison with barley[164] :

Per kilo	Barley	Fresh acorns	Dried and hulled acorns
Digestible albumen ..	65 gr.	24 gr.	45 gr.
Fat	18	18	40
Nitrogen-free matter ..	625	325	610
Fibre	12	40	50

The official hunger-bread of Tsarist Russia consisted of ten parts of acorn flour, two parts of rye flour and two parts of rye bran,[165] and in parts of Poland acorn flour was so usual an ingredient of bread that loaves made purely from cereal flour were virtually unknown.[166] In parts of Norway acorn flour was used for making bread up till the nineteenth century.[167] The monastic mill of Sindersdorf in Upper Bavaria is recorded to have been grinding acorn flour in 1604[168] and William Harrison writing of the state of England in 1586 observed that in times of dearth acorns were used to make bread " of which scourge the poorest doe soonest tast."[169] From such facts as these it has been argued that acorns must have been used for human food during prehistoric times.[170] While it would be rash to assume that the peasants were as badly off in prehistoric times as they were at some later periods in parts of Europe, it is a fair assumption that acorn flour was used as a substitute for cereals during the periods of dearth which must have occurred during the early days of farming. Direct clues are not lacking from prehistoric sites. For instance quantities of acorns found in store-pits at the bronze age settlement of Buch, near Berlin—one such pit a metre in

---

[162] S. Hazzledine Warren, 1911, 201–2.

[163] G. Retzius, 1885.

[164] H. Nietsch, 1939, 112.

[165] H. Brockmann-Jerosch, 1917, 91.

[166] A. Maurizio, 1927, 57.

[167] *ibid.*, 56.

[168] Brockmann-Jerosch, 1917, 90–3.

[169] Quoted from *Elizabethan England* : from " *A Description of England,*" by William Harrison (in " *Holinshed's Chronicles* ") Edited by Lothrop Withington. The Camelot Series, London, 1890, p. 96.

[170] e.g. J. Hoops, 1905, 476.

depth and in diameter was filled to the brim—were seen to have been hulled, split and roasted, which would hardly have been the case had they been intended merely for swine-fodder.[171]

Before the acorns of temperate Europe could be eaten they had first to be boiled, generally after they had been ground into meal, so as to remove some of the unpalatable and indigestible tannin. The acorns of *Quercus esculenta* and of *Quercus Ilex*, var. *Ballota*, found in the Mediterranean area, were a good deal less noxious, though it is significant that the peasants of Sardinia found it necessary to mix the flour of their " sweet " acorns with an iron-bearing clay to counter the tannic acid, before making up the mixture into flat cakes and baking them in oil or fat.[172] In the case of the Mediterranean there is abundant literary evidence—quite apart from the classical legend that acorns formed the original food of mankind—that acorns were eaten in antiquity. One of the most explicit references is Strabo's statement that for two-thirds of the year the mountaineers of Lusitania " feed on the acorn, which they dry, bruise and afterwards grind and make into a kind of bread."[173] Direct evidence in the shape of finds of acorns on prehistoric sites is rare in this region, but this is probably due to physical conditions which generally speaking do not favour the survival of organic materials. Acorns have been recorded from neolithic and middle bronze age sites in Greece[174] without any definite clue as to their status.

Another forest product used as an ingredient of bread in the Mediterranean zone is the chestnut, which in recent times has played a particularly important part in the peasant culture of the south of France, the islands of the west Mediterranean, the Apennines and the southern Alps.[175] Although well established locally as an article of normal diet—after all a kind of cake (*polenta*) made from chestnut and maize flour is the national dish of Corsica—the main rôle of the chestnut in recent peasant culture has been to supplement cereals in bad times ; and in this respect it may be noted that the use of chestnut noticeably revived during the two World Wars.[176] In modern times the chestnuts were dried in the sun or smoked, before being stamped or beaten to break the skin; the kernels were then sifted free, dried and ground to flour. We have it on Pliny's authority[177] that such flour was used as an ingredient of bread in antiquity, particularly among the Sardinians. Discoveries of chestnuts on prehistoric sites are rare, though, together with acorns, they are said to have been found in pots in the Italian terremare and fruits have been reported from an early iron age site on the Lac de Bourget.

As in mesolithic times, water-plants were drawn upon for food. Indeed, several were used to supplement cereal flour among European peasants down to modern times. The root of *Calla palustris* was ground to serve as an ingredient for bread in Sweden during Linnæus' day and Retzius found it still used for this purpose in Finland in the third quarter of the nineteenth century.[178] Dried rhizomes of common reed (*Phragmites*

---

[171] A. Kiekebusch, 1923, 60. According to G. Schwantes (1939, 237–8), masses of roast acorns were found on a site with corded ware in West Prussia.

[172] Brockmann-Jerosch, 1917, 90–3.

[173] Strabo, III, 3, 7.

[174] e.g. Sesklo II (Wace and Thompson, 1912, 73); Vardaróphtsa (A. W. Heurtley, 1939, 93).

[175] L. Rütimeyer, 1924, 236–47.

[176] For 1914–18 war, see Rütimeyer, 1924, 247 ; for 1939–45, see *Daily Telegraph*, 21st April, 1942, p. 4.

[177] Pliny, *Nat. Hist.*, XV, 93.

[178] Brockmann-Jerosch, 1917, 94–5; Retzius, 1885, 113–4.

communis) and of bog bean (*Menyanthes trifoliata*) were also pounded to yield an edible meal.[179] Of greater importance was the water-nut (*Trapa natans*), which during the post-glacial period grew wild over much of central and northern Europe. The kernel, which yields an edible mealy substance,[180] was eaten as a form of dessert by the ancient Egyptians[181] and used for making bread by the Thracians at the time of the elder Pliny.[182] An indication that the water-nut was eaten in prehistoric Europe is given by the accidental discovery in a bog near Lake Vanajavesi in Finland of a mass of specimens, mostly split open, and mixed with charcoal, crackled flints and a piece of two-stranded thread, the whole dating from the beginning of the Late Stone Age.[183] In the northern parts of Europe the geographical range of the water-nut was reduced as a consequence of the deterioration of climate during the Sub-atlantic period, but in earlier times it may well have played an important part near the northern margins of the farming zone ; indeed, Sundelin has shown that in the province of Småland quite a close connection exists between the distribution of stone age settlement and of sub-fossil occurrences of the water-nut.[184] As a last example one may cite the wild grass (*Glyceria fluitans*) which grows in marshy habitats in south Sweden, east Germany, Hungary and parts of Poland and of European Russia.[185] In East Prussia this wild cereal was still gathered by women down to modern times. As a general rule the seeds would be shaken into sieves, dried, unhusked in wooden mortars and stored in bags. Among the Slav peoples in particular the seeds were used to make groats, but occasionally they would be mixed with cultivated cereals for grinding into flour. The importance of *Glyceria fluitans* has been much reduced of recent years through improved drainage and the conversion of marshes into meadows.

---

[179] *ibid.*
[180] J. Hoops, 1905, 335–6; A. Oldeberg, 1932, 229.
[181] F. Hartmann, 1923, 45.
[182] Pliny, *Nat. Hist.*, XXII, 27.
[183] V. Auer, 1924, 131 f.
[184] U. Sundelin, 1920 and 1924.
[185] A. Maurizio, 1927, 44–8.

CHAPTER III

CATCHING AND GATHERING: COASTAL AND MARITIME

IT was emphasized in the last chapter that the shift in the basis of economy in temperate Europe from exclusive dependence on wild products to the exercise of some control over the production of food through farming did not bring to an end the old catching activities, even if it reduced some of them in relative importance. The way in which catching and farming activities complemented each other during the later periods of prehistory, as indeed they have done ever since, is most evident, when one considers the sea. Broadly speaking it seems to be true that the extent to which this vast reservoir of food and raw materials was drawn upon was related directly to the pressure of population on the resources of the dry land. So long as subsistence was based mainly on hunting and gathering and the population remained sparse, the sea was comparatively neglected except for what could easily be gathered on the shore. With the spread of farming a noticeable advance may be noted both in off-shore fishing and in the hunting of sea-mammals, whether among farming communities or among marginal hunter-fishers, who in many cases no doubt supplied a peasant market. It was only the growth of towns which called into being the deep-sea fisheries and large-scale sealing and whaling expeditions of recent centuries. Hand in hand with increased demand for products of the sea went a growing capacity to satify them in the shape of greater capital and improved gear.

In considering how far the resources of the sea were utilized during prehistoric times it is important to bear constantly in mind that the surviving evidence is seriously incomplete. For one thing traces of such activities are almost invariably organic in substance and, even under the most favourable conditions, can only be expected to survive unequally according to the nature of the climate and soil and the character of the site. An even more serious consideration is that vast stretches of the old European coasts are now submerged. This applies, for much of the late glacial and early post-glacial periods, to the whole of the European coat-line outside the isostatically depressed region of Scandinavia. It is all the more unfortunate that, with the saving exception of some caves in west Norway and some middens in south Sweden, organic materials have not survived well on most of the coastal sites of the Scandinavian peninsula. Much of the best evidence comes from middens in Denmark, and from middens and caves on Gotland and neighbouring islands and in parts of Scotland, dating from periods when sea-level was rather higher than it is to-day.

SHELL-FISH

Before considering more genuinely marine catching activities, something may be said about strand-looping, including the gathering of shell-fish and the salvage of whatever might be thrown up upon the shore from flat-fish to whales. The importance of this as a source of food and raw materials is not to be underrated merely because it was common to all societies within reach of the coast. The gathering of limpets and mussels was already being carried on at Devil's Tower, Gibraltar, by Neanderthal man,[1] and so far as one can tell shell-fish have contributed to European subsistence ever since. On the other hand, a diet in which shell-fish are a mainstay is normally associated with a low level of culture, a proposition which is hardly contradicted by the attainments of the Capsians of the Tagus Valley, the Tardenoisians of the islands off Morbihan, the Obanians of Western Scotland or the Ertebølle people of the Litorina coasts of Denmark. It is noticeable that among communities, which pursued hunting and fishing at sea with vigour, shell-fish occupied only a subsidiary place.

WHALES

Much the most valuable creatures stranded on the shores of the Atlantic and of the North and Baltic Seas are whales.[2] The records show for instance that between 1913–26 there were no less than 407 strandings on the shores of Britain, and it is notable that these included on the average four strandings a year of rorquals or finwhales, which generally speaking were beyond the scope of early hunters. There is a wealth of evidence about the strandings of large whales during the historical period (Fig. 29), because so long as the

Fig. 29. Large Rorqual stranded at Tynemouth in August, 1532. (*After Olaus Magnus*).

productivity of farming remained at a low level the accession of meat and fat represented even by a single whale might materially increase the well-being of a whole countryside. In his great book on the history of the northern peoples Olaus Magnus maintained that the proceeds of a single whale might fill between 250 and 300 waggons and yield meat for salting, blubber for lighting and heating, small bones for fuel, large ones for house-building and hide sufficient to clothe forty men.[3] Small wonder that proprietary rights were meticulously defined, as in a charter granted in 1148 by Pope Eugenius III to Hilary, Bishop of Chichester; this confirmed that the bishop was entitled to " any whale found on the land of the church of Chichester, except the tongue, which is the King's," but made it clear that in the case of one stranded elsewhere in the diocese his rights extended to " the right

---

[1] D. A. E. Garrod, 1928, 111–13. Shellfish were also eaten in quantities by the upper palaeolithic Grimaldians.

[2] For bibliography and schedule of finds, together with a full discussion, see J. G. D. Clark, 1947.

[3] Olaus Magnus, 1555, Bk. 21, cap. 20 and 24.

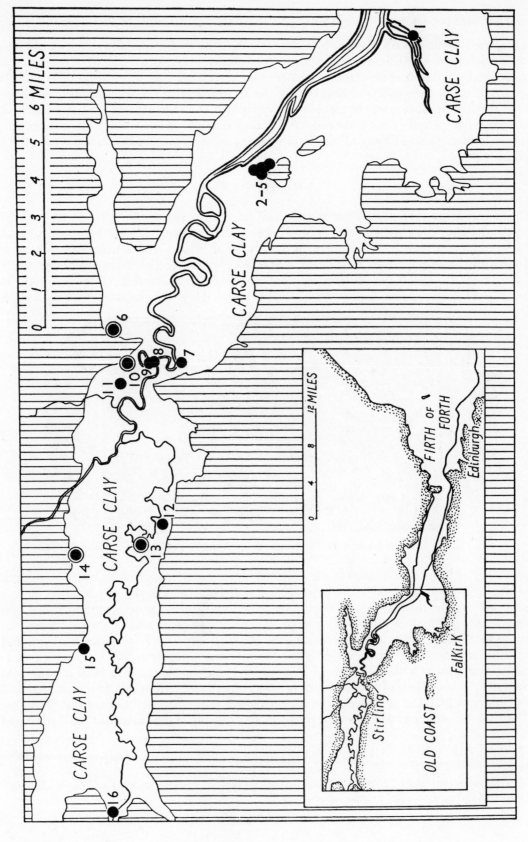

Fig. 30. Finds of whale skeletons stranded on the shores of the Firth of Forth during the Stone Age.

flipper only." It is equally understandable that such rights were commonly flouted by the people and conversely that, before rights were closely defined, strandings must often have been the cause of struggles between rival claimants. A vivid impression of conditions during the early Norse settlement of Iceland is given in the saga of Grettir the Strong, which tells how, when the men of Vik and the men of Kalbak contended for the carcase of a large Rorqual,

> " Hard were the blows which were dealt at Rifsker;
> No weapons they had but steaks of the whale.
> They belaboured each other with rotten blubber,
> Unseemly methinks is such warfare for men."

There is abundant evidence for the stranding of whales during prehistoric times. From Britain one might mention the remains of Greenland right whales, killer whales, bottle-nosed dolphins and porpoises from post-glacial silt deposits in the East Anglian fens, or the still more notable occurrences in the carse clays of the Firth of Forth. Strandings have been recorded in the Firth during historical times; at a time when this extended over the carselands up to twelve miles west of Stirling it must have formed a veritable death trap to the larger whales, which could so easily be caught by a falling tide while far from the open sea. The skeletons, mainly of rorquals and including the great blue whale, found by chance in the carse clays (Fig. 30) doubtless represent only a small fraction of those stranded

Fig. 31. Perforated deer-antler mattock, found with part of its wooden handle against the skull of a Rorqual, Meiklewood, near Stirling.

at the time. The best proof that advantage was taken by mesolithic man is given by the discovery of his perforated antler implements in intimate association with no less than four of the skeletons. The most striking specimen (Fig. 31) is that found, still mounted on its wooden handle, in drainage operations during 1877 on the Meiklewood estate, resting against the skull of a rorqual : it comprises a perforated antler axe blade, which could well have been used for removing meat or blubber from the carcase.

How far whales were hunted during prehistoric times it is far from easy to decide. Since whales of any species can be stranded—and no less than seventeen species were in fact represented among those recorded as stranded on the shores of Britain between 1913–26— it would be wrong to interpret whale-bones from middens as necessarily indicating whale-hunting. As a guide to interpreting such evidence some account may be taken of the extent to which individual species were hunted during the historical period. Thus the hunting of the Greenland right whale did not begin until early in the seventeenth century when whalers began to penetrate the region of pack-ice in which it was at home. On the other hand the Biscay or Atlantic right whale was certainly hunted in the early Middle Ages by the Basques, who attacked the females as they penetrated the Bay of Gascony to bring forth their young in the winter. There is also evidence that whales were hunted off the north-west Norwegian coast from the earliest times recorded by history in that region. In the course of his report to King Alfred on the resources of his native Helgeland, Ohthere[4] described how with five companions he had in the course of two days slain 60 whales, each 48 ells long, the largest 50. What these lengths signify in our measurements is uncertain: Schreiner[5] is inclined to equate an ell with a foot, but Ohthere speaks of walruses, the males of which reach some 14 feet in length, as being not longer than 7 ells. In any case the whales hunted off the coast of Helgeland were certainly large. For reasons which will become apparent, there is no question of their being identified with the larger Rorquals. Equally, as Schreiner noted, the Greenland whale must be ruled out as a species habitually hunted on the Norwegian coast, since it keeps close to the ice-margin. It seems that Ohthere can hardly have been referring to any other than the Biscay right whale. Archæological support for this comes from a stone slab grave at Hundholm, Tysford, in Helgeland, which yielded, in addition to iron weapons dating from the eighth and ninth centuries, an unworked hyoid bone of large whale, referred tentatively by Schreiner to a Biscay right whale.

It is also relevant that, although large, the right whales are comparatively docile and can be taken with quite simple tackle. Murdoch[6] has described how the Eskimo of Point Barrow used to hunt the Greenland whale from skin-covered *umiaks*, a type current in north-west Europe as early as the Late Stone Age. The Eskimo would paddle up to the whale and strike it with a heavy harpoon-head mounted on a detachable shaft and secured to floats. Every time the whale came up to breathe it would be struck again, a fresh harpoon head having in the meantime been mounted in the original shaft and many other *umiaks* and their crews having joined in the fray. Finally when sufficiently wearied, it would be despatched by a heavy lance mounted with a flint head.

As a family the rorquals or finwhales, on the other hand, were mostly neglected by early whalers on account of their speed and lack of buoyancy, combined with their large size. Scoresby's observation that a harpooned rorqual ran out 480 fathoms, or more than half a mile of line, in approximately a minute, gives some idea of their power. Serious pursuit of most species had to wait until the perfection of the harpoon gun in 1865. The only exceptions were the humpback whale, which when inshore could be hunted by common hand harpoons and lances, but which had the grave disadvantage of sinking, necessitating a wait until decomposition had generated enough gas to float the corpse to the surface, and the lesser finwhale, which was only a third the size of the blue whale and even so could only be taken under very special local conditions, such as obtained in two bays in the immediate area of Bergen.[7] The struggle sometimes lasted as many as nine days and nights, which only goes to emphasize the toughness even of the smaller rorquals: as a family and under normal circumstances these must be considered to have been beyond the reach of the prehistoric hunter.

Of the three families of toothed whales commonly found in European waters, only the true dolphins were the object of well established fisheries during early historical times. The hunting of the sperm whale, a dangerous customer, up to 20 metres in length, but capable of jumping clear and of destroying boats, is said to have begun off New England about 1712. The other member of the family *Physeteridæ*, the bottle-nosed whale or

---

[4] A. S. C. Ross, 1940, 21.

[5] 1927, 302.

[6] 1892, 275.

[7] D. F. Eschricht, 1849, 16–17.

dogling, was comparatively easy to catch, but the " Dogling-field," where they concentrate between mid-April and the end of June, is remotely situated north of the Faroes and Shetlands and south of Jan-Mayen; moreover, as Debes commented with reference to individuals caught in the Faroes, " the flesh and fat of these Doglings are not good to eat."[8]

Neither species of the *Delphinapteridæ* family can have played a significant part in pre-historic hunting. The white whale, like the Greenland right whale, is an arctic species, which, though formerly much hunted in the Spitzbergen area by Norwegians and Russians, and though still taken by nets in the White Sea, only rarely occurs further south; for instance schools of white whales appeared in Christiania Fjord in the spring of 1903, following a very severe winter, during which they were hunted in the Bergen area. The narwhal, the long tooth of which so fascinated medieval people, is equally arctic in habit, only rarely penetrating temperate waters.

By contrast with many of the whales so far discussed, several of the eight species included under the family *Delphinidæ* are known to have been hunted in Europe during historical times and none can be deemed to have been beyond the powers of prehistoric man. The pilot or Caa'ing whale, which centres on the Faroes, where it is still taken, used once to be hunted also in the Orkney and Shetland Islands and in the Hebrides.[9] From the many surviving accounts, ranging from Debes up till modern times, it is evident that an extremely primitive method was used: the whales were headed off from the open sea by boats, herded into a chosen inlet and actually driven ashore, a proceeding made possible by the way this species instinctively follows its leader in a blind rush. In this way hundreds of pilot whales might be killed in a single day, and it has been recorded that no fewer than 16,299 were so taken in the Faroes between 1835–44.

The dolphin most abundant in European waters is the Common Porpoise, which habitually moves in small shoals near the coast and penetrates fjords and river estuaries, sometimes venturing considerable distances upstream. As might be expected, records of the catching of porpoises during the historical period are very numerous. For the most part these relate to the accidental entanglement of porpoises in fishermen's nets, but there are nevertheless indications that specialized porpoise fisheries existed in some parts of Europe. Although no regular fishery existed on the Atlantic seaboard of France, there is evidence that one was carried on on the coast of Normandy between the estuaries of the Couesnon and the Bresle and that this was already active by the tenth and remained so into the fourteenth century.[10] Two fisheries were carried on in Danish waters. One of these was devoted to the porpoises, which appear in the Isefjord, Zealand, often in shoals of over a hundred, towards the end of March at the time of the spring herring and remain until the trees turn green ; centred mainly on Jaegerspriis, and carried on by means of nets, this fishery used to yield up to between 300 and 400 porpoises a year. A more prolific fishery was carried on from Middlefart, Fyen. This was aimed at the porpoises which assemble in great shoals to pass through the Little Belt on their way out of the Baltic, a movement beginning in November and substantially complete by Christmas. Up till about 1880 the fishery was controlled between St. Martin's Day (11th November) and Candlemass (2nd February) by a guild of porpoise hunters, which still mustered ten boats of three as late as 1849 and in 1593 had numbered thirty-six members. The hunt was conducted by beating the water so as to head the shoals into bays across which nets had been stretched in

---

[8] 1676, 181.

[9] N. Annandale, 1905, 44; Sir S. F. Harmer, 1927, 36–7; M. Martin, 1934 edtn., 88.

[10] P. Fischer, 1881, 175.

preparation; over a thousand porpoises were often dragged ashore in this way in the course of a year.[11]

There is less information about the pursuit of other species of dolphin in European waters but mention should be made of the hunting well into the nineteenth century of the great shoals of white-sided dolphins and killer whales, which used occasionally to penetrate certain bays in the immediate area of Bergen. One of the largest catches, that made on 31st December, 1834, accounted for some 700.[12]

A review of what is known about the hunting of the main species of whale in European waters during historical times has shown that several can be ruled out as possible quarries of prehistoric man; in this category must be numbered most of the large kinds, including the Greenland right whale, the various members of the rorqual family and the sperm whales. Others, again such as the narwhal, the bottle-nosed whale and the white whale, can have played only a very restricted part during post-glacial times in Europe. On the other hand, it has been shown that Biscay right whales, porpoises, pilot whales and other dolphins have been hunted during historical times by quite primitive methods.

Although remains of whales have been found on many prehistoric sites in the British Isles, these have seldom been more closely identified and the only substantial body of detailed information is that from Scandinavia. The most significant fact which emerges from a consideration of this is that the whales best represented on archæological sites are those known to have been hunted during historical times by comparatively primitive methods. Conversely, only one species of rorqual is represented and that by a skull of a common rorqual, apparently stranded on the Litorina shore and surrounded by stone and flint tools, which could well have been used to despoil the carcase.[13] The single tail vertebra of a Greenland whale from the late bronze age site of Bulbjerg, Thy, was doubtless from a stranded specimen. Sperm whale is represented by a single tooth and white whale by a vertebra. The great bulk of the identifications relate to true dolphins : common porpoises were identified on sixteen sites, killer whale on six, white-beaked dolphin on three, common dolphin, on two, and pilot whale, white-sided dolphin, and bottle-nosed dolphin on one each. Such evidence as this is by no means conclusive and one should remember that the toothed whales are in any case more numerous than baleen ones even among stranded specimens.

There is, however, another and more promising source in the stone age rock-engravings of the west Norwegian coast.[14] Here one sees depicted together with enigmatic signs, boats and human figures, outlines of the beasts on which the hunter depended for his life, among which, in addition to elk, reindeer, bear, water birds, halibut and seals, are no less than twenty-nine representations of whales: of these there is not one example of the species which we have seen to be beyond the reach of primitive hunters ; apart from a possible bottle-nosed whale, all are true dolphins and at least two-thirds are porpoises, though killer whales and a pilot whale (Fig. 32) were also included. As if this were not enough, there is a close association between representations of whales and boats or of quarry, such as seals and halibut, the capture of which implies the use of boats : whales are shown at each of the three sites where skin-covered boats are represented (Rødøy, Forselv and Evenhus), at both those at which seals are depicted (Rødøy and Valle) and at two (Valle

---

[11] D. F. Eschricht, 1849, 15–16; A. Japha, 1909.

[12] D. F. Eschricht, 1849, 16–17.

[13] V. Nordmann, 1936, 127–8.

[14] For details, see Clark, 1947, 97–8 and Appendix II.

and Skogerveien) where halibut are featured. From all this it seems legitimate to conclude that porpoises, killer whales and pilot whales were hunted on the Norwegian coast already during the Stone Age. The fact that the proportions in which the different species are represented in the rock-art agree strikingly with those in which their skeletal remains occur

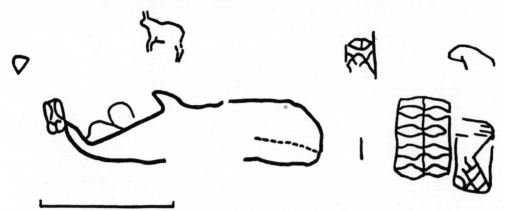

Fig. 32. Stone Age rock-engraving of pilot whale, Strand, S. Trondelag, Norway.
Scale of one metre.

on the Scandinavian sites, helps to strengthen the idea that similar hunting was practised on the coasts of Denmark, West Sweden and Gotland.

What is quite certain is that whales, stranded or caught, were utilized by communities living within reach of the coast (Fig. 33), whether their economy was based primarily on hunting or farming. Among mesolithic groups to make use of whales may be numbered the Tardenoisians of Téviec, the Larnians of Curran Point, the Obanians of Oronsay, and the Ertebølle people of Denmark. The most important finds of whale bones on neolithic sites are those on Gotland, the west coasts of Norway and Sweden, and at Skara Brae on Orkney. Late bronze age finds may be noted at Bulbjerg, Denmark, and Jarlshof, Shetland. Whale bones have been recorded from early iron age sites in Scandinavia and from early iron age levels of Dutch *terpen*; but much the most numerous finds from this time are those from the brochs and wheel-houses of Orkney, Shetland, Caithness and the Hebrides.

Meat and blubber were among the chief substances yielded by whales and some of the sites richest in whale-bone have produced the blades of what may well be the axes or mattocks used for detaching these from the carcases. Mention has already been made of the deer-antler tools used by the mesolithic people of the Firth of Forth for despoiling stranded rorquals. What has been described as " quite the most distinctive tool manufactured " at Skara Brae,[15] made from the distal ends of ox metapodials, could well have served a similar purpose, as could the large heart-shaped perforated blades of schist or slate from late bronze age levels at Jarlshof.[16] Again, very striking analogies exist between certain objects of cetacean bone from Scottish brochs and wheel-houses and the whale-rib mattock-blades from old Eskimo houses from north-west of Hudson's Bay to west Greenland, which to judge from their continued use in recent times were employed to remove blubber from large whales (Fig. 34). The triangular indentations found on both edges were used to secure the thongs by which the handle was secured at right-angles to the blade.

---

[15] Childe, 1931, 124.
[16] A. D. Curle, 1933, 100–1.

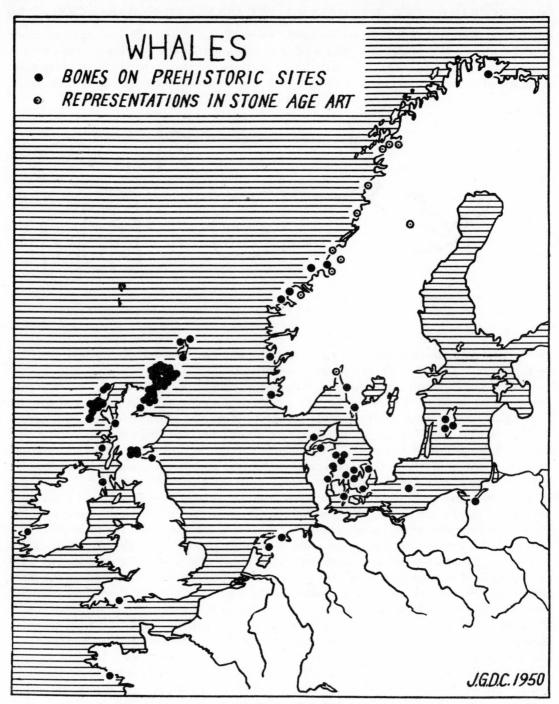

Fig. 33. Indications of whales at prehistoric sites in Europe.

The importance of whale-meat as human food is amply reflected in documentary sources from late Saxon and later times, which on the one hand define proprietary rights and on the other reveal the steps taken by the great to ensure adequate supplies, in particular of porpoise. The use of prepared whale-meat as winter-feed for cattle, noted by Annandale for the Faroes,[17] illustrates the complementary nature of hunting and farming, but there is no way of telling how old this practice was. Blubber was boiled down to yield oil for lighting

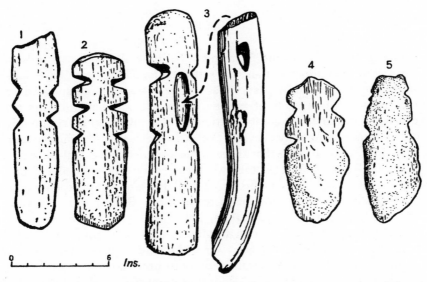

Fig. 34.   Whale-rib mattocks from northern Canada (nos. 1–3) and from
an Iron Age wheel-house at Foshigarry, N. Uist.

and heating certainly as late as the sixteenth century in Scandinavia and in the Faroes down to the twentieth. The hides of certain species were a useful source of leather and as such featured in the annual tribute paid to the Norse by the Lapps in the time of King Alfred.

In their skeletons whales provided a raw material of which the use is amply attested by prehistoric archæology. Where wood was scarce—as it must always have been in the Orkneys and as it must have become during the Sub-atlantic period of climatic deterioration in much of the highland zone of Britain—large whale bones played a certain part in the house-building. At Skara Brae, traces of cetacean bone were found in an aperture, possibly a joist-hole, in the wall of a passage and earlier excavations at the same site revealed the jaw-bones of a large whale lying across the hearth of a hut, as though fallen from above, suggesting that they had formed roof supports.[18] Another use for the bones, particularly the small ones, according to Olaus Magnus, was as fuel, a usage which likewise finds parallels among the mammoth hunters of upper palæolithic times. Fresh cetacean bones were still used as an alternative to peat in the Faroes, certainly up till beginning of the present century, which makes all the more significant Childe's observation that an ash heap, overlying and in front of the fire-place of a Skara Brae hut, " consisted principally of a mass

[17] N. Annandale, 1905, 37 and 47. Annandale (1905, 203) further recalls how he had seen the blades of scythes " removed from the handles and used as fleshing-knives " on a stranded whale.

[18] V. G. Childe, 1931, 48; *P.S.A.S.* VII, 208 and 432.

of charred whale-bones mixed with burnt shells and bones."[19] Again, among the broch-builders of Scotland whale-bone was favoured as a material for making a variety of small objects commonly turned out in metal or deer antler among the other early iron age groups of Britain; for instance, it was used for hair-combs, harness ornaments, keys, knife-handles and weaving combs (Pl. III). Again, the vertebræ of whales lent themselves with compara-tively little improvement for use as containers, from small pigment holders to quite large basins.

SEALS

Positive evidence for seal-hunting[20] during the Stone Age consists primarily of the remains of seals from the middens of ancient settlements, where these have survived above modern sea-level, supplemented by chance discoveries of seal bones associated with harpoon heads and incorporated in deposits of marine origin. It was not until the period of the Litorina Sea that the evidence for coastal settlement is available at all commonly in regions where organic materials commonly survive. Yet it is precisely in Scandinavia, parts of the East Baltic area and North Britain that there is most evidence for seal-hunting in modern times and it is highly probable that the two former saw the main development of this activity during the late Stone Age in Europe. The Baltic and its approaches and to a lesser extent the west coast of Norway and parts of northern Britain were certainly the chief centres of seal-hunting in prehistoric Europe, but there is evidence that the monk seal (*Phoca monachus*) played a certain part in Mediterranean economy. Bones of this species were found in upper palæolithic levels at Grimaldi and there is literary evidence that locally seal-hunting was quite an important activity in pre-Classical Greece.[21]

The earliest evidence available for seal-hunting comprises seal-bones from deposits of upper palæolithic age in the Dordogne, namely the left and right mandibles of the same ringed seal from an Aurignacian level under the rock-shelter of Castanet in the valley of the Vézère, a tooth from a Solutrean level at Altamira, and a single mandible of a harp seal from a Late Magdalenian level in the cave of Raymonden on the Isle, another tributary of the Dordogne river, which itself flows into the Gironde. It is possible that the seals were caught on a distant sea-coast, possibly during a seasonal migration, and carried inland to the caves, but they might in some instances have been slaughtered in the neighbourhood. As was pointed out by the distinguished palæontologist Harlé, there is no reason why this should not have been the case, even though the finds were made some 200 and 190 kilo-metres from the existing coast and, by presumption, even further from the contemporary sea : there are modern records of seals observed in such rivers as the Oder, Rhine and Loire, up which they will often ascend distances of 400 kilometres from the sea in pursuit of salmon.[22] Representations of seals engraved on objects from the cave deposits, like the bear's tooth from the Magdalenian burials at Duruthy, Sordes, and especially the pieces from the rock-shelter of Mège at Tejat, from Montgaudier (Fig. 35), Brassempouy and Gourdan, suggest that the artists were working from life or at least from quite recent impressions. They may well reflect the interest attracted by the occasional seal, which

---

[19] Annandale, 1905, 38; Childe, 1931, 52.

[20] For full references to the stone age finds and to folk culture sources, see the account in J. G. D. Clark, 1946. For references to bronze and iron age finds, see note 27 below

[21] O. Keller, 1909.

[22] E. Harlé, 1913.

found its way into the interior of the country by way of rivers and so intruded into the environment familiar to the reindeer-hunters.

There is no evidence for seal-hunting in the late glacial or Pre-boreal stages in the north and very little from the Boreal time. A single tooth was found in the raised beach at Camp-beltown, Kintyre, with an Early Larnian flint industry, but, since the latter was " apparently derived from (an) old ground surface and washed inland " and no other traces of fauna were

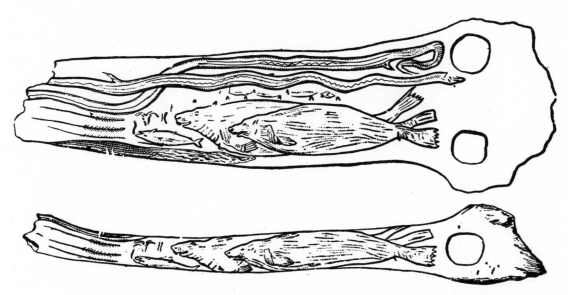

Fig. 35.   Upper palaeolithic engraving of seals, Montgaudier, Dordogne (c. ½)
(*After Cartailhac*).

found, the association is not of much value. The forepart of a lower jaw-bone from the Maglemose site of Svaerdborg, Zealand, which at the time of the Ancylus Lake was more distant from the coast than it is to-day, is regarded by Degerböl as an amulet. Again bones were found at Kunda in northern Esthonia.

From a period contemporary with the Litorina phase of the Baltic there is conclusive evidence that the Obanian people of Argyllshire pursued seals, since bones of two species have been identified from two of their middens on the island of Oronsay (Caisteal-nan-Gillean and Cnoc Sligeach) and from a third on the tiny islet of Risga in Loch Sunnart. The presence of layers of blown sand in the Oronsay middens and the small size of Risga show that these were intermittent settlements, which in the case of Risga at least must have been of a seasonal character and may even have been connected directly with seal-catching. It should be emphasized though, that the evidence for seal hunting during the Stone Age in Scotland is comparatively meagre, even in the area where the old coastal sites are still above water, and there is no suggestion that the activity was developed to anything like the same extent as in the Baltic. The absence of seal remains from Skara Brae is particularly notable.

Approximately half the stone age sites in north-western Europe known to have yielded remains of seal (Fig. 36) are concentrated on the old Litorina shores of northern and eastern Jutland and of the Danish islands. Yet it ought not to be inferred from this that Denmark was the most important focus of seal-hunting during the Litorina time. The concentration of finds is due to the fact that coastal sites from this period happen to be available around much of Denmark and that conditions for the preservation of bone are particularly favourable there. Again, the mammalian fauna from the Ertebølle sites of Denmark is made up predominantly of forest species, and seal remains in no case account for more than a small part. Yet, the fact that seal bones have come from some twenty of their dwelling-places and middens suggests that seal hunting played a definite, if restricted, role in the economy of the Ertebølle people.

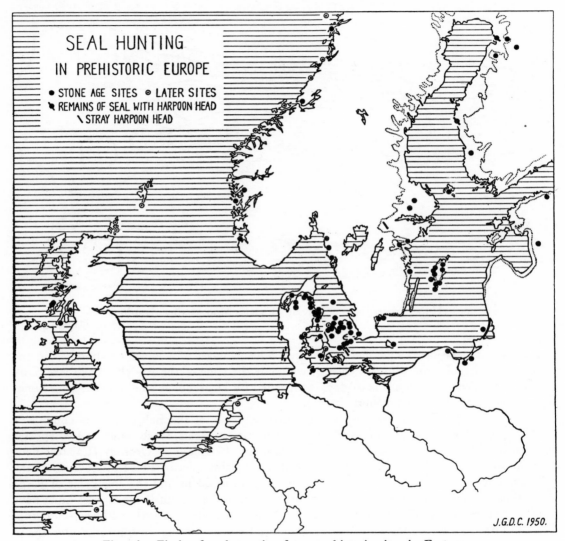

Fig. 36. Finds of seal remains from prehistoric sites in Europe.

Since the majority of the Ertebølle sites were excavated before the successive Litorina transgressions in Denmark had been distinguished, it is seldom possible to decide whether the seal bones related to the period before or after the introduction of farming to that country; in at least one instance, though, where the bones from successive levels were segregated, namely at Langø on Fünen, it was found that traces of seal-hunting were confined to the neolithic levels. Apart from this, evidence of seal-hunting has been found on at

least sixteen sites of neolithic age in Denmark and it is from this period that the first indication of intensive activity appears, notably on the island of Hesselø in the Cattegat, which
has yielded over four hundred corner teeth, among other remains, of the grey seal.

Seal bones have been obtained in some quantity from three stone age rock-shelters in
south-west Norway. Remains of grey seal were common at Viste and the harp seal was also
represented. The status of this site is not yet conclusively settled, though it is probably
mesolithic. Ruskenesset, on the other hand, must date on the evidence of flint daggers and
hollow-based arrow-heads, not to mention some fragments of bronze, from the close of the
local Stone Age. To judge from the presence of bones of domesticated animals and from the
impressions of barley grains on sherds, the seal-hunters of Ruskenesset were farmers, who,
as was common in Norway up till recent times, supplemented their food-supply by seasonal
hunting and fishing. Both at Viste and at Ruskenesset seals were the second most abundant
mammal. Again, at Skipshelleren seal bones occurred freely in the neolithic levels, conspicuous among them those of the spotted seal, including many quite young ones. Further
north, seals are represented on rock-engravings attributed to the Arctic dwelling-place
people at Rødøy and Finnhågen, Valle, both in the province of Nordland.[23] At the former
the seal is accompanied by a porpoise, an elk, and, significantly, a boat (Pl. IV, b).

Evidence relating to seal-hunting during the Stone Age in Sweden has survived very
unequally and the surviving evidence from ancient sites gives no reliable indication of the
relative importance of seal-hunting in different parts of the country. It is for instance,
suggestive that, if one takes into account the number of seals qualifying for government
premiums during the period 1902–6 from different parts of the Swedish coast, one finds that
the provinces north of Uppland, which earned the most premiums, have yielded no finds,
while the return for Gotland, which has produced nearly half the stone age sites, was among
the lowest for any province in Sweden. The great majority of the Gotland finds date from
the farming period. Only at two sites, Limhamn and Gislause, is there any evidence of
mesolithic seal-hunting, and in neither is this impressive. The stone age seal-hunters of
Sweden appear in general to have dwelt on the fringe of the neolithic world, at a period
contemporary with the passage-graves. At such sites as Siretorp, Stora Förvar, Visby and
Västerbjers the bones included domesticated forms, additional to the ubiquitous dog, and
the last two mentioned yielded thick-butted flint axes. At contemporary middens like
Anneröd, Rörvik and Rotekarrslid in Bohuslän, Åloppe and Sotmyra in Uppland and most
of the Gotland dwelling-places, on the other hand, traces of specifically domesticated forms,
other than the dog, are absent, though whether one is dealing here with traces of hunter-
fishers or with the seasonal catching activities of farmers is obscure.

It is often difficult to assess the relative importance of seal-hunting in the chase, but at
Siretorp, despite a number of bones of domestic species, seals accounted for some 84 per
cent of the fauna. Further north, at Vivastemåla in Småland, evidence that quantities of
animal refuse had been discarded by the dwelling-place people was revealed in the high
phosphate-content of the soil, but only four pieces of bone survived; of these, the three
identifiable fragments belonged to seals. Information about the animals hunted by the
neolithic dwelling-place people of Gotland and Karlsö is much fuller and one receives a
livelier impression of the importance of seals: thus, seal bones predominated in the lower
levels of Stora Förvar, at Visborgs Kungsladugård and Gislause, while at Hemmor, Gullrum
and Visby, at which latter they amounted to over a third of the total bones, they formed a
substantial element. In Uppland the fauna from Sotmyra is too meagre to tell much, but

---

[23] G. Gjessing, 1936, Pl. VIIb and 1932, Pl. XXVIII.

from Åloppe more than 10,000 identifiable bones were obtained in the excavations of 1902, three-fifths of which belonged to fish and a number to birds; of the mammals, the ringed seal, represented by over a hundred individuals, was the predominant species, pig being second and elk third in importance. Taken as a whole, one is justified in interpreting the Swedish finds as proof that the neolithic dwelling-place people of that country, and particularly of the Baltic coasts and of Gotland, were keen seal-hunters and that the seal played a role of substantial importance in their economy.

Judging by what is known of later history, this was almost surely true of the dwelling-place people of Finland, but only a few flakes of burnt bone have survived from which to deduce the kinds of animal hunted. It appears that, apart from fish, the commonest species represented were elk, beaver and ringed seal, the latter being identified from four sites on the mainland, Honkala, Nimisjärvi, Pitkäsaa and Uotimäki; in addition, the site of Jettböle in the Aaland Islands has yielded numerous bones of the harp seal. Seal-bones occur at a number of neolithic coastal sites on the East Baltic shore from Esthonia to East Russia,[24] but the Litorina coast-line of North Germany is unhappily submerged, so that the only finds are those dredged from the Ertebølle site off Ellerbek in Kiel Fjord.

The evidence from the Stone Age suggests that, although seals had been hunted since the late glacial period, it was not until farming had spread to northern Europe that the activity was intensified. Among the hunter-fishers who survived alongside the neolithic farmers the activity was doubtless stimulated by the opportunity of effecting exchanges. Just as the islanders of Kihnu and Ruhnu in the Gulf of Riga, among whom seal-hunting survives as a specialized calling, trade seal oil and skins against corn, salt, iron and other goods from the Esthonian mainland,[25] so during neolithic times seal-meat seems to have passed from hunter-fisher groups in Denmark to farmers in exchange for beef and polished flint celts.[26]

Among farmers in coastal territories seal-hunting continued to play a part throughout prehistoric times and numerous finds of seal-bones have been made on late bronze and early iron age sites from the Channel Islands, northern Ireland and northernmost Scotland to Denmark and the north-west coast of Norway.[27] There is indeed no doubt that even from neolithic times seal-hunting, like fishing and other kinds of hunting, was incorporated as a seasonal activity in the peasant economy of the northern territories of the temperate zone of Europe. Rich finds of seal-bones, predominantly from young individuals on small islands, like Hesselø in the Cattegat, suggest that the peasants indulged in seal-hunts at the breeding season. Again, the fauna from the Norwegian rock-shelter of Ruskenesset shows that it was

---

[24] In addition to those mentioned in Clark, 1946, 47, one may add finds from the Kurische Nehrung and Tolkemit, Kr. Elbing, quoted by E. Wahle (1918, 168–73).

[25] F. Leinbock, 1932, 10–12.

[26] Thus the farmers at Havnelev in south-east Zealand imported seal-meat and the contemporary hunter-fishers at Strandegaard, on the old coast some 18 km. to the south-west, obtained beef and, a few polished flint celts. See J. G. D. Clark, 1946, 40.

[27] Channel Islands (Maîtresse Isle), J. Hawkes, 1939, 183–8 ; N. Ireland (Ballintoy Caves), *Irish Nat. J.*, 1936, 34 ; N. Scotland—Brochs of Ayre and Midhowe, Orkney (*P.S.A.S.* XLVIII, 49 and LXVIII, 514), Kettleburn Broch, nr. Wick (J. Anderson, 1883, 215), and Jarlshof (*P.S.A.S.*, LXVII, 135 and LXVIII, 317) ; Denmark (Öster Stigtehaveskov, Langeland : Borrebjerg, Sejerø ; Eltang Vig, Jutland—M. Degerbøl, 1933, 393 and 396) ; Holland (Marsum Terp, nr. Leeuwarden ; A. E. van Giffen, 1914, 95 ff.) ; Norway—Sanda, Traen I. (Gjessing, 1943, 24), Aakvik cave, Dønna (A. Nummedal 1919, 18), Haugshulen, Leka (T. Petersen, 1916, 7), Halmøy caves, Flatanger (Nummedal, 1919), Dalen, Skørn (Rygh, 1911, 15), Hestneshulen, Dolmø, Hitteren (Petersen, 1910), Bjørnerem, Mien (Nummedal, 1912, 21) and Kvaernvig, Jaederen.

occupied during the summer probably during the interval between seed-time and harvest, which included the breeding-season of the spotted seal. It is further of interest that, where seal-hunting has survived in Europe down to modern times, in North Britain, Scandinavia and the East Baltic, the rights over breeding-places have normally been vested in farmers.[28]

Before firearms came into general use for seal-hunting, methods had to be adapted closely to the distinctive habits of the various species, and more particularly in early times, when technical means were limited, hunters must have taken full advantage of fleeting or periodic opportunities. Seals are especially vulnerable at their breeding seasons, particularly the ringed, harp and grey seals which spend the first few weeks of their lives on the ice or the rocks, as the case may be, where their elders will often try to defend them, only too often to share their fate: although well able to elude human enemies when in open water, seals are relatively helpless on land, even though at an earlier stage of their evolution this was their proper element. It also happens that young seals are particularly valuable at the stage immediately before taking to the water, after spending the opening weeks of their lives accumulating resources against the day when they have to fend for themselves. According to observations made off the Frö Islands, near Trondheim, the grey seal cub has fattened to such effect by the age of three weeks that it will yield, in addition to 12–18 kg. of meat, some 20–30 kg.—in rare instances up to 60 kg.—of blubber, much of which it loses in the following months of struggle.[29] There is thus a double motive for pursuing seals at their breeding seasons.

The principal methods, other than shooting, used in modern times for hunting seals on the Atlantic coasts of Europe and in the Baltic basin were clubbing, netting, spearing or piking and harpooning, practised alone or in combination. The choice of method varied according to the species of seal, as well as to the prevailing geographical and climatic conditions and to the season.

The practice of stunning seals by clubbing them is as a rule confined to gregarious species and among these is peculiarly well adapted to the grey seal, which unlike the harp or spotted variety establishes itself for breeding in caves or on rocks well above sea-level.[30] A graphic description of the hunting of grey seals in their caves at the breeding season in the Faroes is given by Debes, who tells how first the adults and then the fat young ones were clubbed and their throats cut by the light of great candles, fifty seals often being taken in this way in a single cave, and the slaughter of this species in the Western Isles of Scotland has often been described. Similar practices obtained at favoured points on the coast of Norway, in the Frö Islands off Trondheim and in Møre. There is also evidence for seal-clubbing in the Baltic: grey seals are surprised as they lie basking on skerries off the coast of Östergotland and Gotland, beaten senseless by iron-shod clubs and despatched by knives; and clubbing is still used especially for young seals by the seal-hunters of the Esthonian islands of Kihnu and Ruhnu in the Gulf of Riga. For ringed seals, the hunters stop up the breathing holes, by means of which this species maintains itself under the fast ice of coastal inlets, by plugging them over a limited area with wooden stakes, so forcing the seals to come to a central hole for breathing: when the seals appear they are clubbed senseless and dragged out of the water.

---

[28] See J. G. D. Clark, 1946, 28–9. In former times resident sub-tenants of Rona are said to have paid part of their rent in seal-oil (Buckley and Harvie-Brown, 1888, XLV).

[29] R. Collett, 1881, 383–4.

[30] Among useful references to the clubbing of grey seals in modern Europe are: Debes, 1676, 170–1; M. Martin, 1934 edtn., 133–4; H. Prichard, 1936, 15–17; R. Collett, 1881, 385; Shetelig and Falk, 1937, 88; Berg and Svensson, 1934, 54; F. Leinbock, 1932, 10; and O. Nordqvist, 1899, 54.

While there is no direct evidence that seals were clubbed on their breeding-grounds in prehistoric times, the frequency with which remains of young ones are represented at many sites suggests that this method was in fact used. Thus at Åloppe it was noted that the majority of the bones of the ringed seal belonged to very young individuals. The abundant remains of grey seals from Hesselø, and also from the lower levels of Stora Förvar, were likewise predominantly those of young individuals; at the latter site Pira observed " a great number of mandibles and other skeletal remains of very young and new-born grey seals." Even the spotted seal, the young of which take to the water a few hours after birth, seems to have been hunted during the breeding season off the west coast of Norway, to judge from the finds of Ruskenesset and Skipshelleren: at the former the bones represented individuals ranging from adults to newly born seals, and at the latter the bones were mostly those of quite young seals. It is likely that several, if not all of these sites were located with direct reference to the breeding-places of the seals and were in fact occupied during the breeding season for the express purpose of securing young ones and their parents.

In modern times seals were caught in nets in north Britain, Scandinavia and Finland, but no evidence for the use of this method has survived from the prehistoric period. Similarly, there is no evidence from early times for the employment of iron traps or pikes, like those used recently in the Baltic area.

The only method of hunting seals of which direct archæological evidence survives is harpooning.[31] Most conclusive are finds of harpoon-heads (Fig. 37), associated with seal skeletons in clays deposited in the Litorina Sea on either side of the present Gulf of Bothnia. The first discovery was made in 1907 during excavations for the foundations of the new city hall of Norrköping. The bones of a fairly young ringed seal, accompanied by a bone harpoon head (Fig. 37, No. 2), were found in the clay bed at approximately the level of the Baltic Sea at the present day; since the Litorina Sea level is estimated to have been approximately 60 metres higher when the clay was deposited, the seal must have sunk in deep water and come to rest on the sea-floor. A second find was made while draining a fen at Närpes in 1935, when a complete harpoon head of elk bone (Fig. 37, No. 5) was recovered from the ribs of a skeleton of a harp seal lying curled up in a deposit formed on the floor of the Litorina Sea, through the waters of which it had evidently sunk, mortally stricken. Thirdly, there is the discovery in a brick-works near Oulu during the winter of 1936–7 of a barbed point of elk bone, unfortunately incomplete at the lower end (Fig. 37, No. 1), amidst a heap of ringed seal bones, dated to a fairly advanced stage of the Litorina Sea; this find may well relate to the comb-ware site at Muhos, a few miles away, which has yielded a few flakes of ringed seal bone. In addition to the specimens with seal skeletons, the Litorina deposits have yielded a certain number of stray harpoon-heads.

The second body of evidence comprises harpoon-heads, barbed on one edge and mostly perforated, though occasionally grooved at the base, for attachment to the line. Particularly rich finds have been made on Stora Karlsö and on Gotland in the Baltic. The cave of Stora Förva has yielded numerous bone harpoon-heads with single barbs and another has come from a dwelling-place at Visby; harpoon heads with two barbs were buried with men at the cemetery of Västerbjers (Fig. 38) and a single one, made from antler, comes from the settlement of Hemmor, also on Gotland. Similar harpoons have been found with seal bones at the neolithic dwelling-site of Möllehausen in the parish of Gualöv, Scania (Fig. 37, No. 4),[32] in the Danish midden of Sølager (Fig. 37, No. 3), and at numerous sites on the

---

[31] E. Lonnberg, 1908; M. Sauramo, 1938.
[32] J. E. Forssander, 1941; H. Berlin, 1941.

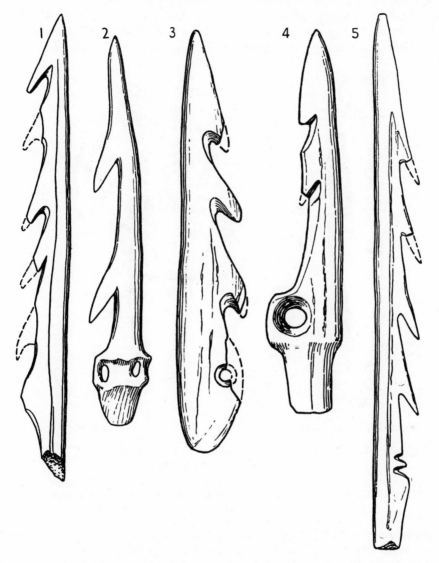

Fig. 37. Harpoon heads used for taking seals during the Stone Age in the Baltic area ($\frac{2}{3}$).

No. 1. Oulu, Österbotten, Finland.

No. 2. Norrköping, Östergotland, Sweden.

No. 3. Sølager, Denmark (Cop. A. 337).

No. 4. Möllehausen, Gualöv, South Sweden (Lund, 28.570).

No. 5. Närpes, Österbotten, Finland.

Norwegian coast from Skipshelleren in the south-west to Kirkhellaren on Sanda, Traen Islands, on the Arctic Circle, and Kjelmøy on the Arctic coast of Finnmark.[33]

The situation of sealing-stations on small islands like Stora Karlsö, Hesselø, Sanda, Risga or the Maîtresse Isle shows that boats must have been used, as indeed one is reminded

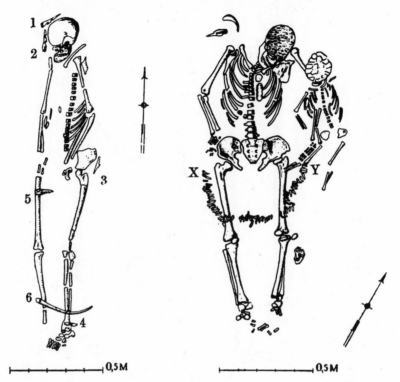

Fig. 38.   Burials of Stone Age seal hunter and woman and child, Västerbjers, Gotland.   (*After Stenberger*).

Note.—Harpoon heads (1–4), leister prong (5) and perforated antler . . . (6) with the man, and cloak fringe of perforated seal teeth (x–y) across the thighs of the woman, who is accompanied by an infant.

by the Norwegian rock-engravings. In the northern parts of the Baltic the grey seal gives birth to its young on ice-floes during February and March, instead of on rock skerries in autumn, as in North Britain or West Norway, and it is known that during the historical period seal-hunters in the Gulf of Bothnia were accustomed to slaughter mother seals and their young on the ice-floes from boats (Fig. 39). It has been suggested that, despite the warmer climate, surface ice may have been more widespread in the Litorina Sea than in the Baltic, owing to the greater salinity of the former and to the existence of a superficial layer of relatively fresh water.[34] Analysis of the proportions, in which the different species of

---

[33] G. Gjessing, 1943, Pl. XXVIII, 4. One from Jørunvåg. Halsa, Sør-Trøndelag, is illustrated by G. Gjessing, 1945, Fig. 48, 3. Among examples from Finnmark may be cited two from Halsen, Kvalsund, said to have been found with slate knives and spearheads (Tromsø Mus.). For Kjelmøy see O. Solberg, 1910, 1911. Opportunity was taken by the present author to examine the objects at the Univ. Oldsaksamling, Oslo.

[34] S. Ekman, 1933, 32–3.

seal were hunted during the Stone Age in the Litorina Sea, has shown that the harp or Greenland seal, which now hardly enters the Baltic, was actually breeding in the area of Gotland and penetrated to the Gulf of Bothnia; indeed, the harpoon-head from Närpes was actually associated with a harp seal, which had presumably been taken from a boat near the ice-margin.   On the other hand, the ringed seals found with the Oulu and Norrköping

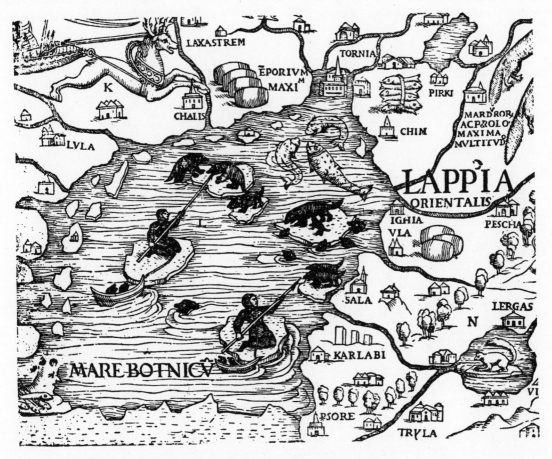

Fig. 39.   Seal-hunting in the Gulf of Bothnia Mid XVIth century.   (*After Olaus Magnus*).

harpoons had probably been caught as they came up to breathe at holes in the ice, as is their habit.   The *Máupoq* method, as the Eskimo term it, was practised in recent times[35] by the Finns and the Swedes and the iron-headed harpoons which they used, resemble fairly closely the Stone Age ones made from bone (Fig. 40).   It is worthy of note, also, that dogs and sledges—both features of the Arctic Stone Age—were used in this type of hunting in the Bothnian region down to modern times, the former, among other purposes, for scenting out the breathing-holes of the ringed seal.

---

[35] For references to the *Máupoq* method in European folk-culture, see Sirelius, 1934, 91 ; Ekman, 1910, 232–3 ; and Berg and Svensson, 1934, 54–5.   Birket-Smith (1936, 80–6) gives an excellent account of Eskimo methods.

Seals were valuable for their blubber, skin, flesh, blood and bones. The blubber, which insulates the seal and adheres to the skin when this is removed from the carcase, is especially important as a source of oil. This might be used for human consumption, for medicinal purposes, for use as fuel or as an illuminant, or for industrial purposes, and it is notable that the decline of the old-style seal-hunting in the Baltic area during the nineteenth century is attributed to a fall in the price of this commodity. Linnæus noted that the fat was eaten fresh instead of butter, as well as being used for cooking omelets, and pancakes baked in the

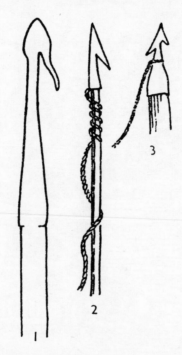

Fig. 40. Iron pike and harpoons used for taking seals in the Baltic during modern times.

oil were considered as delicacies in Gotland down till recent times. As a remedy seal oil has been used both internally and externally from the Celtic fringe of Britain to Finland. Its use for heating and lighting has been especially prominent in the circumpolar zone with its long winter nights and in the Baltic area oil from seal blubber was used for lighting up till modern times. This gives added point to Mathiassen's comparison between Eskimo stone lamps and the oval pottery lamps from the kitchen-middens of the Ertebølle culture of Denmark, analyses of samples of scrapings from the inner surface of one of which has revealed the presence of small quantities of fat. The archæological evidence offers no clue to other subsidiary uses, but it is perhaps worth noting that in Olaus Magnus' time blubber was employed in Scandinavia for greasing ships' planks and working leather.

Although of less importance than blubber in the Baltic area during historic times, seal skins have nevertheless been put to a variety of uses, and it is reasonable to suppose that in earlier times, when alternatives were more restricted, their role was at least as great. Among Eskimo communities seal-skins are used extensively for tents, clothing, dog-harness and boats. The dwelling-place people of Finland and Sweden, who certainly hunted seals, can in some instances be shown to have lived in tent-like structures and it is possible, although not of course established, that they used the skins of seals, as well as of land mammals, for this purpose. The use of seal-skin for clothing is discussed in a later chapter (p. 220). Another function of seal-skins, appreciated alike by the Eskimo and by the fishermen of Donegal, was to cover frame boats, for which they were peculiarly well adapted owing to their toughness. Seals were, indeed, hunted off the Donegal coast primarily for their skins, which were also used for clothing. According to historical sources, seal-skin thongs were used both for maritime transport and for land-haulage. In describing to his lord, King Alfred, what conditions were like in his native Helgeland, Ohthere is reported to have said that ship-ropes were made from whale hide and seal hide and that two ropes, one of each material, sixty ells long, were among the tribute customarily rendered by the Finns. Writing of the Western Isles of Scotland some seven or eight centuries later, Martin Martin noted that seal-skin was " by the natives cut in long pieces, and then made use of instead of ropes to fix the plough to their horses, when they till the ground." According to Debes, the Faroe Islanders used the skins for shoes. In our own day Finnish peasants have been accustomed to use seal-skin for a variety of domestic requirements, including bags and boots.

Seal-meat appears to have been eaten in parts of Europe down to comparatively recent times, especially among the poorer sections of the population, one reason for its survival being that it was regarded as fish and could therefore be eaten on fast days. If seal-meat was eaten in agricultural communities in modern times, one may feel reasonably sure that in similar areas it was consumed on a more substantial scale both before the introduction of farming and during its early days. The occurrence of discarded seal-bones on so many dwelling-places suggests that this was the case during the Stone Age. The common European practice in historical times appears to have been to eat the meat salted or smoked, a useful stand-by in time of need. Martin Martin described how in the Western Isles " the natives salt the seals with the ashes of burnt sea-ware, and say they are good food," slyly adding that " the seal, though esteemed fit only for the vulgar, is also eaten by persons of distinction, though under a different name, to wit, ham . . ." According to Collett the fishermen of the Trondheim area ate the flesh and blubber of young seals salted and found them " to taste tolerably well, as the young ones only subsist on the milk of the mother." Seal flesh used to be salted for human consumption in Gotland, where it may also be noted, front flippers were esteemed an especial delicacy. A liking for seal flippers, hung like game, has been reported from many areas, including Labrador and the territories of the Iglulik Eskimo. The practice of saving seal blood by plugging and sewing up wounds is well known among Eskimos and it is worth noting that up till modern times it was customary for the seal-hunters of Västerbotten to fortify themselves with bags of meal or groats mixed with seal blood.

After stripping the seal of its skin with the inner layer of blubber, removing the meat and storing the blood, the hunter was left with the bones and teeth. The former he used as raw material for implements and weapons. Proof of this has commonly been forthcoming where the bones used by prehistoric seal hunters have been determined by zoologists. Thus, it was found that the majority of the bone harpoon heads from Stora Förvar on Stora Karlsö were made from seal bones, a point of added interest when it is remembered that, so far as one can tell from analogy, these objects were used for hunting seals. More than 60 out of a total of 375 bone awls from the same site were determined as made from seal fibulæ; it may be suggested that many of these were used to perforate seal-skins for sewing.

WALRUSES

Walruses played a much more restricted role in the economy of prehistoric Europe than seals. At the present day *Odobænus rosmarus* is a High Arctic species, which strays as far south as Finnmark, Bear Island, Jan Mayen and Iceland, and only very rarely reaches the North Sea.[36] The only evidence for walrus-hunting in early Europe comes from northern Norway, Shetland and Orkney. According to the account he gave to Alfred, Ohthere visited the land of the Barmians largely on account of the " horse-whales," valued on account of their skins, which shredded and plaited made admirable ships' ropes, and above all for their ivory tusks.[37] Traces of walrus are rare on early sites, but part of a tooth was found at Kjelmøy in Finnmark, dating from the Viking period.[38] Again, a tusk and some beads presumed to have been made from such were found at Skara Brae, Orkney,[39] and walrus bones were recovered from Jarlshof, Shetland.[40] Although they can be dangerous to men in light boats, walruses can be harpooned without much trouble during the moulting-season, when dozing in herds on floating ice or on low islands and rocks.[41]

SEA FISH

In seeking to trace the beginnings of sea-fishing[42] in prehistoric Europe, one is hampered by the rarity of well-preserved fish-bones from coastal sites of late glacial age. Meanwhile investigation of the evidence from the Grimaldi caves suggests that, despite the fact that the inhabitants ate shell-fish from the shore, they caught remarkably few sea fish and these mainly species like wrasses, which could be taken close in to the rocks.[43] The lack of evidence for off-shore fishing may be linked with the absence of any indication that boats were available in upper palæolithic times.

The first tentative beginning of sea-fishing from boats was made towards the end of mesolithic times. The Tardenoisian middens of Téviec and Hoëdic of the south coast of Brittany yielded bones of marine fish in quantities sufficient to show that fishing, although less important than the gathering of shell-fish, yet contributed more to diet than hunting.[44] The abundance of bones of labroids and wrasses shows, though, that the islanders confined their fishing to inshore waters, as their descendants do to this day.

Farther north the middens of the Obanian people on the islands and coasts of western Scotland give further insight into this early stage of inshore fishing and cod bones have been identified from an Early Atlantic level at Cushendun in Northern Ireland. The early inhabitants of Oronsay, as well as catching black sea-bream most probably from the rocks, must surely have fished from boats, since they took conger, haddock, common sea-bream,

---

[36] E. Hentschel, 1937, 40–2.

[37] King Alfred's *Orosius*, Bk. I, Chap. 1, para. 14 (Bosworth, 1855 edtn.).

[38] R. Collett, 1911, 371.

[39] V. G. Childe, 1931, 146. Childe cites early bronze age dagger pommels from a tumulus in Finistère, stated to be of walrus ivory.

[40] *P.S.A.S.*, LXVII, 135.

[41] F. Boas, 1888, 497.

[42] For references to sites mentioned in connection with sea-fishing, see J. G. D. Clark, 1948, especially Appendices II and III.

[43] E. Rivière, 1886.

[44] M. and S. -J. Péquart, 1937, 99–100.

ballan wrasse, thornback ray, skate, and a number of sharks. The occurrence at Caisteal-nan-Gillean and Cnoc Sligeach on Oronsay and at MacArthur's Cave, Oban, of numerous claws of edible crabs, which normally live in relatively deep water, led Henderson Bishop to infer that traps must have been used to catch them, but these could have been taken on shore or in the course of line-fishing.

There is evidence for a line-fishery around the northern and western shores of the British Isles, based mainly on cod, but including also coal-fish, skate, and various rays and accompanied by a certain amount of crab-catching, though it does not appear to have assumed the same importance as in some parts of Scandinavia. Petrie observed that the midden of Skara Brae in Orkney " was thickly studded with fish-bones, chiefly of small fish, apparently the 'sillock,' or coal-fish " and also " repeatedly recognized bones of the cod "; again, the discovery of a stone mortar " nearly filled with fish-bones, which had apparently been pounded into a mass of minute fragments," reminded him forcibly of the practice of the inhabitants of North Ronaldshay, as late as the nineteenth century of supplementing their meal in time of dearth with pounded fish bones.[45] Comparatively few have been found on coastal sites in Britain, though Glenluce yielded two bronze hooks, and in one of the Dark Age caves of Ballintoy, Antrim, an iron fish-hook was associated with " numerous jaws and vertebræ of cod."

The occurrence of remains of large mature haddock and coal-fish, habituated to depths of from 40 to 100 metres, in a number of their middens shows that the Ertebølle people must have caught fish off-shore from boats, but the extent to which this fishery was carried on before or after the introduction of farming to Denmark must remain uncertain, since most of the sites were excavated before the various transgressions of the Litorina sea had been clearly defined. In any case, analysis of the fish remains from the Ertebølle midden on the Litorina shore of Limfjord shows that marine species, including cod, flounder and gar-pike, were balanced by those of fresh-water origin, such as roach and pike. There is strong suggestion that the off-shore fishery was more effectively pursued after farming had been established in the country. Quantities of cod, including 35 middle jaw-bones, and numerous haddock were represented in the Sølager midden, most of which dates from neolithic times, and cod was well represented at the bronze age site of Hasmark on Fyen, and at the iron age one of Borrebjerg on Sejerø.

Important off-shore fisheries were carried on in the Skagerrak by hunter-fisher groups occupying the northern parts of the west coast of Sweden during the period of the passage-graves in southern Scandinavia. To judge from the contents of three of their middens, they mainly caught cod, ling and haddock, together with smaller numbers of ballan wrasse, whiting, and pollack, all of which are bottom feeders, the great majority exclusively so. Analysis of individual fish shows that one of the eight haddock from Rotekärrslid and two of the ninety-seven from Rörvik were larger than the maximum usually met with in these waters and of the ling a large proportion were well grown, a few exceptionally so; on the other hand, only two out of the forty-eight cod from Rörvik were as much as 0·97 m. long, as compared with a present maximum of 1·5 m. A midden at Anneröd also yielded cod and numerous haddock, as well as whiting, pollack, tunny and flounder. It may be assumed that the fish were caught by hook and line from boats during the season when they approached nearest to the shore, much as they are to-day on the same coast. A rock-engraving in the parish of Kville in northern Bohuslän, dating from the Bronze Age, shows two men engaged in this fishery with hook and line from an anchored boat (Fig. 41).[46]

---

[45] G. Petrie, 1866–7, 211, 213.
[46] A. Fredsjö, 1943, 61–71.

The line-fishery, which flourished during neolithic times off the coasts of Gotland, is attested by the discovery of fish-bones—the settlement of Hemmor yielded 5,343 cod bones —and by numerous fish-hooks made from bone or boar's tusk enamel and almost identical in size with those used at the present day for taking codling. At the present day Baltic cod rarely exceed 30–40 cms. in length and are caught in 15 to 30 fathoms, mainly during summer and autumn by men too old for heavy farm work. The burial of a fish-hook with an adult woman in the Västerbjers cemetery[47] suggests that women may have shared in the fishery during the Stone Age.

Fig. 41. Late Bronze Age rock-engraving at Kville, Bohuslän, South Sweden, showing men fishing from a boat. (*After Fredsjö*).

The most considerable sea-fisheries in prehistoric Europe were those of the Norwegian coast, the deep fjords of which brought bottom-feeding fish close in to shore (Fig. 42). The earliest traces are those found in the Svathåla at Viste, near Stavanger, which was occupied by hunter-fishers, probably before farming spread to Norway; each of the eight species represented were adapted to salt-water, the commonest being cod, and ten bone hooks were recovered from the eight cubic metres of deposit investigated. The main fisheries, though, were those carried on by men who combined this activity with farming. During neolithic times the fishery extended northwards to the Trondheim region and along the coasts of mainland and islands up to Nordland and the Lofotens. Down to the present day fishing is combined with farming along this coast and it is notable that the racks used for drying fish, cereals and hay are very similar. Dried fish-heads, indeed, are commonly fed to sheep[48] and in recent times substantial factories have grown up to process fish into cattle-meal.

The fishing was virtually confined to species accustomed to feed on or near the bottom, and of these cod was the one chiefly represented on the prehistoric sites. Every year about the middle of February the cod begin to leave the depths of the Atlantic in great shoals and

---

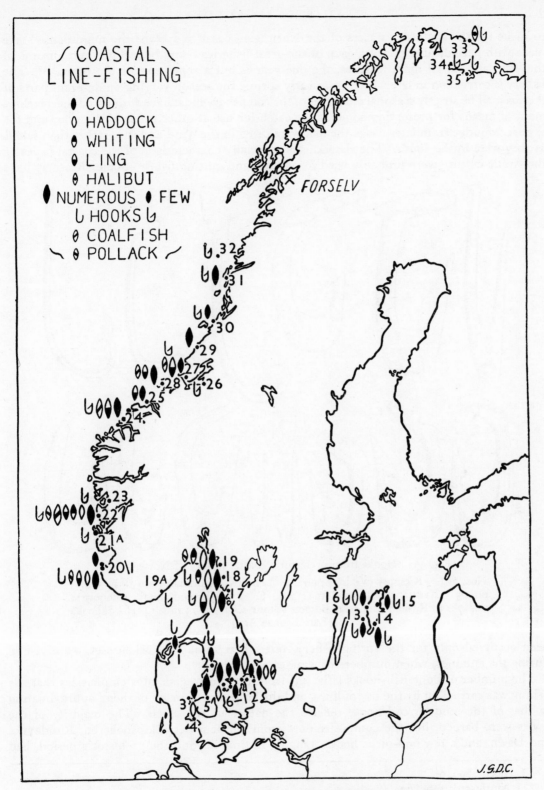

Fig. 42. Extent of the prehistoric coastal fishery of Norway.
Note. For numbered list of sites, see Clark, 1948, 81–84.

to make for the shallower waters of the Norwegian coast to spawn; the migrations " take place with periodical regularity, each of the great fisheries being bound to a certain time of the year, and, in all main features, the one year is but a repetition of the other."[49] The fishery is carried on in late winter or in early spring, the season varying on different parts of the coast. The strictly seasonal character of the cod fishery must have stimulated the development of means for preserving some of the catch for use at other times of the year, and for export; to judge from later usage the fish were dried in the wind and sun, rather than salted as they were in the south. The slate knives especially characteristic of the coastal facies of the Arctic culture were probably used for slitting and gutting fish.[50] Some sites may have

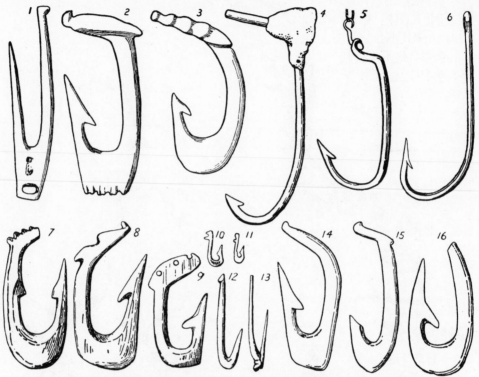

Fig. 43. Hooks from prehistoric coastal fishery of Norway ($\frac{1}{2}$)

Nos. 1–3. Kjelmøy (Viking); no. 4. Lebesby, Finnmark (late 18th cent.);
no. 5. Kristiansund (modern); no. 6. English cod hook (modern);
nos. 7–13. Ruskenesset, near Bergen (Stone Cist per.); nos. 14–16. Skjåvika
(Late Bronze Age).

been occupied only for the spring fishery, but others, notably Ruskenesset, were visited during the summer, when numbers of wrasses were caught.

The number of bone fish-hooks (Fig. 43) from the Norwegian sites emphasizes that the fishing was carried on by the use of lines, and the large size of many of them, approximating to that of the modern cod-hook, reflects the nature of the catch. The majority of the hooks were barbed, but the composite ones from Ruskenesset, Skipshelleren, Rundøyno, and Dalen, and a few one-piece hooks, ranging in time beyond the prehistoric period, had

---

[49] J. Hjort, 1896, 6.
[50] O. Nordgaard, 1908, 67.

plain, barbless points. Many of the larger hooks were marked by a cross-piece projecting forward from the shank towards the point, a feature which first appeared at Ruskenesset from the time of the Stone Cists and which, especially in Finnmark, persisted throughout prehistoric into historical times. According to an early nineteenth-century traveller,[51] the Lapps of this province brought their iron hooks from Bergen, but modified them among other ways by fastening " above the longer arm (i.e. the shank) a heavy piece of tin in a new direction towards the barb "; despite its inefficiency, they adhered " to this ridiculous custom, because it (was) peculiar to themselves, and the opposite of what (was) practised by the hated Norwegians." Occasionally the large bone hooks were provided with devices for securing the bait, either a single external barb as in the case of one from Aavik on Dønna, or by means of grooves or perforations.

The fishing must largely have been carried on from boats, which to judge from representations in the Arctic rock art were skin-covered frame boats of the *Umiak* type. An engraving at Forselv, Skjomen, in Nordland, appears to show a halibut caught on a line from a skin boat.[52] Hand-lines were doubtless generally used in prehistoric times, but a rock-engraving at Kvernevika in the parish of Ytterøy, North Trondelag,[53] showing a dozen halibut, arranged in an arc, all but one head upwards, may possibly indicate the use of a long line. Lines with hundreds or even thousands of hooks were, however, a later development relating to a time when large and sometime distant markets had to be supplied.

Nets do not appear to have been introduced to the Norwegian coast until late in the seventeenth century.[54] Their northward spread was slow; it was only in the middle of the eighteenth century that they reached the province of Nordland and early in the nineteenth century they were still struggling to establish themselves in Finnmark, the high capital outlay and the risk involved in the use of nets of the size needed for this method of fishing no doubt deterring the smaller man from making the change. Conversely, the development of the cod and allied fisheries in modern times into a highly organized industry involved large aggregations of capital and favoured the use of devices beyond the reach of most individual fishermen. Yet, even to-day, the Norwegian and allied line-fisheries are still of great importance, their survival over a period of from four to five millennia being due to the way they are adapted to the feeding-habits of the cod and similar fish, and to the economic potentialities of small communities.

Apart from a few rib-bones from Sølager in Denmark, possibly a by-product of some other fishery, remains of herring are conspicuously absent from the prehistoric settlements of Europe. The herring fishery is notoriously subject to great local fluctuations, but such can hardly be held to account for the absence of herring-bones from so many regions over so lengthy a period. The absence of a fish, which to-day is caught in larger numbers than any other, from early settlements in the whole region from the Baltic to the west coast of Norway and northern Britain, and extending from the Stone Age to the Early Iron Age, can only mean that the fishery was not developed during the prehistoric period. The origins of the herring fisheries, which played so important a rôle in medieval Europe, are lost in the obscurity of the Dark Ages, but such were already flourishing around the shores of Britain before the time of Domesday[55]; the Sound fishery was already productive early in the twelfth

---

[51] L. von Buch, 1813, 289–90.

[52] G. Gjessing, 1932, Pl. XI.

[53] G. Gjessing, 1936, Pl. LXX.

[54] L. von Buch, 1813, 187–9.

[55] J. M. Mitchell, 1864, 95; A. J. Robertson, 1939, documents XCI and CXVII.

century A.D.[56]; and herrings were mentioned more than once in Norse sagas dating from the tenth century. The apparent failure[57] to develop the fishery in prehistoric times can hardly be ascribed to deficiencies in boats, since at the spawning season the fish come in fairly close, and since in recent times such primitive craft as curraghs have been much employed for catching herring around the shores of Ireland.[58] More likely, as with the case of cod nets, manufacture of the drift nets required for herring involved more labour than could be justified by the needs of small communities of farmer-fishers.

SEAWEED

Just as mammals, birds and fish were taken from the sea and its coasts more intensively by farmers and their hunter-fisher contemporaries than by their mesolithic predecessors, so it is likely that seaweed, for which little use had previously been found, was gathered from the foreshore to complement the resources of farming. Direct evidence of this from prehistoric times is lacking, but recent folk-usage suggests strongly that seaweed was utilized for animal fodder under conditions like those which must have obtained during the Sub-atlantic phase of climate in the highland zone of Britain. Martin Martin described how usual it was to feed seaweed to cattle and horses during the difficult winter months in the western isles of Scotland and how the cattle would come down from the hills to feed on the weed exposed at ebb tide.[59] Down the end of the nineteenth century at least the " wild " sheep of North Ronaldshay had to " feed themselves almost exclusively on seaweed, a wall going round the whole island to keep them out of the cultivated ground."[60] Again, Estyn Evans wrote recently of Ireland that " some seaweeds are boiled and fed to cattle, other varieties are considered good for pigs, while several kind are gathered for human consumption."[61] It may be significant in this connection that traces of seaweed (*Ascophyllum nodosum*) were found under the floor of one of the late neolithic dwellings at Rinyo, Rousay, Orkney.[62] Seaweed was also used—and indeed still is used—for manuring the ground, either fresh or in the form of ashes burned in kilns.[63] According to Martin, also, seaweed ash was used in the Western Isles for preserving wild-fowl, seal-meat and cheese.[64]

The extraction of salt from sea-water is discussed in a later chapter (pp. 127-8).

[56] S. Bolin, 1941, 482-3.
[57] J. M. Mitchell, 1864, 131-2.
[58] *ibid.*, 100.
[59] M. Martin, 1934 edtn., 139, 208, 295, 364.
[60] Buckley and Harvie-Brown, 1891, 89.
[61] E. E. Evans, 1942, 150-1.
[62] *P.S.A.S.*, LXXIII, 29.
[63] *ibid.*, Fig. 101.
[64] M. Martin, 1934 edtn., 135, 159, 231, 457.

CHAPTER IV

FARMING: CLEARANCE AND CULTIVATION

THE spread of farming from the old culture-lands opened up vast possibilities of economic advance to the prehistoric inhabitants of Europe. It is important to emphasize, though, that the area affected was limited both by the contemporary margin of the deciduous forest and by the inability of the earliest farmers to cultivate the more difficult soils in the temperate zone. The way in which the boundary between the temperate and circumpolar zones coincided with that between farming and catching economies, once the new economy had spread to its ultimate limits in prehistoric times, has been emphasized in a previous chapter. It may be added here, though, that the extent of the farming zone was by no means constant and that, after a period of expansion during the phase of neolithic colonization, there was a perceptible contraction during the Sub-atlantic phase of climatic deterioration; thus, in Norway the northern limit of farming retreated from Lat. 68° to 60° N., peasant activities being confined during the Early Iron Age to Østfold, Vestfold and the Stavanger district of Jaeren.[1]

As regards soils, the variation in ease of working was far greater in territories which had been subjected to glacial or peri-glacial action than in those of the Mediterranean litoral. In central and north-western Europe the lighter, better drained soils, such as gravel, sand, loess, chalk or limestone, constituted primary areas of settlement and it is on such that finds, at any rate from neolithic times, are concentrated. Of these soils it is not surprising that the early peasants chose the more fertile ones. Thus, in Denmark the early neolithic people preferred the hill-sand to the heath-sand; in Germany the Danubians colonised the loess and neglected the dunes; and in southern England the Windmill Hill people settled the chalk and largely ignored the neighbouring sands. On the other hand, the heavier soils, even when they were richer, were apparently neglected to begin with in favour of those easier to cultivate.

If there is no doubt that the earliest farmers preferred the more pervious soils, it is important to insist that they did so because they were pleasanter to settle and easier to cultivate. The idea that soils like the loess of Central Europe or the " Breckland " of East Anglia were occupied by neolithic man because they were " open " or free from forest can no longer be entertained in view of what the pollen-analysts have been able to learn about the former vegetation of these and similar territores. The all-pervasiveness of the post-glacial forest in temperate Europe has already been sufficiently stressed. Although the mesolithic groups occupying much of the North European Plain worked timber with axes and adzes, there is no evidence that their activities exerted any measurable influence on the natural vegetation, beyond stimulating the *Chenopodiaceae*[2] through the accumulation of organic refuse. If one could have flown over northern Europe during mesolithic

---

[1] R. Nordhagen, 1933, Fig. 77; Shetelig and Falk, 1937, 181–2.

[2] J. Iversen (1941, 39) has shown that high values for pollen of the *Chenopodiaeceae* in the Danish bogs can be used as an indicator of the near-presence of mesolithic man.

times, it is doubtful whether more than an occasional wisp of smoke from some camp fire, or maybe a small cluster of huts or shelters by a river bank or an old lake bed, would have advertised the presence of man: in all essentials the forest would have stretched unbroken, save only by mountain, swamp and water, to the margins of the sea.

The case of the neolithic farmers as, like the pioneers of Ontario or New England of a later age, they penetrated the virgin forests was quite different. Their very mode of life involved the introduction of exotic animals and plants to a strange environment and the upsetting of an age-old equilibrium with the habitat. In the long run they changed the face of the countryside, clearing vast areas of forest and creating in its place extensive regions of cultivated land and meadow; the very domain of farming had to be carved out of primeval forest; at every point economic progress involved ecological change.

The task facing the early farmers varied according to the character of the natural vegetation and in particular there was an important contrast between conditions in the temperate and Mediterranean zones. The Mediterranean evergreen forest was never as formidable as the deciduous forests north of the Pyrenees and the Alps. It was less dense and far more fragile. Not only was the dry atmosphere generally unfavourable to dense forest growth, but for several reasons soil erosion was especially formidable. The soil was thin; glacial deposits such as loess and boulder clay were absent and the growth of soil was slow, due partly to lack of sufficient moisture for vigorous plant growth and partly to the absence of intense cold which might speed up the mechanical disintegration of rocks. The proximity of mountain ranges to the coast meant that during their short season of flow the rivers were torrential. Thus, the first inroads on the forest were liable to result in erosion so severe as to prevent the possibility of regeneration and natural woodland gave way rapidly to *maquis* or *garrigue*.

In the zone of deciduous woodland the struggle was much more intense, although under certain conditions, as on the poorer sands of Jutland or north Holland, the forest had but small power of recuperation and easily reverted to open heath. As a rule, though, the temperate forests were so extensive, so dense and so capable of regeneration that their exploitation formed a chapter of its own in the history of European agriculture,[3] a chapter which did not end with the final clearance of the limited range of soils capable of being cultivated by prehistoric man, but which was reopened with the great deforestations of the Middle Ages, and concluded only in modern times on the northern margins of the agricultural zone. The chief methods of deforestation whether permanent or temporary, have always before the days of bulldozers and similar mechanisms been felling and burning. Among the earliest European farmers there can at first have been no question of initiating systematic, permanent clearance and the formation of settled fields. Their approach was tentative and their agriculture extensive. Patches of forest would be cleared, sown, cropped and after a season or two allowed to revert to the wild, while the farmers took in another tract. In this process burning played a vital role, since it converted timber into ash and so provided a potash dressing for the virgin soil. So long as the forests lasted and until clearance outstripped the capacity of the woodlands to replace themselves, the system of *brandwirtschaft* or burning-economy was capable of supporting the prehistoric peasants at a very tolerable level of well-being.

In modern Europe *brandwirtschaft* survived longest among the Finno-Ougrian peoples, who practised a marginal agriculture on the borders of the birch and coniferous forests (Pl. V, c). There is little doubt that, but for governmental interference in the interests of

---

[3] J. G. D. Clark, 1945, 1945A and 1947A.

forest conservation, it would be widely practised down to this day—as it is still in parts of Carelia—since in this peripheral region it was more profitable to the individual peasant than normal cultivation; according to Manninen the Syrjäns, who practised *brandwirtschaft* down to 1870, were accustomed to obtain a yield of from 50- to 80-fold of rye by this means as against the usual 15- to 20-fold.[4] Yet there is no doubt that the system was appallingly wasteful of timber; in the northernmost provinces of Carelia none of the cleared land yielded more than a single crop and even in the southern parts of the country hardly more than half yielded for two seasons. The methods used to clear the land varied according to circumstances and frequently involved activities spread over a period of time. Among the Wotjaks of the Volga-Kama region the process began in the spring, when small trees would be grubbed up and older ones ringed to prevent the sap rising: the large trees would then be left to dry off before being felled in the following season, but the stumps might be left for some years before being dragged out of the ground. As Linnæus noted on his visit to Öland some two hundred years ago, the actual burning would be done in the summer, but preferably just before rain which served to wash the ash into the soil. The removal of the stumps was certainly not a necessity and it may be doubted whether this was done at all in prehistoric times. According to documentary sources the general practice in East Prussia during the seventeenth to nineteenth centuries was to leave them in the ground[5]; the harrow in normal use—the top of a fir—or pine tree—passed easily over such obstructions and the ploughman had no difficulty in skirting them.

If recent survivals of *brandwirtschaft* on European soil can give much information, it is also instructive to see how the deciduous lands of Southern Ontario were opened up by pioneer farmers in the final decades of the eighteenth century.[6] It appears that the Canadian pioneers, so far from shrinking from the forest, used the trees growing there as indicators of the quality of the soil on which they grew and so were able to clear the best areas for their crops. The larger trees were either felled straight away or ringed and cut down later when dead and dried out. The wood was then burned off and the ashes utilized as a dressing. No immediate attempt was made to remove the stumps, which were allowed to rot in the ground. Indeed, as late as 1880, when Ontario had become one of the granaries of Europe, no less than 46 per cent of the fields in the county of York showed tree stumps. Readers of Dickens may remember how, when crossing the Alleghany mountains on the way to Pittsburg, the novelist was " pained to see the stumps of great trees thickly strewn in every field of wheat," and " how sad and oppressive " he found it " to come upon great tracts where settlers had been burning down the trees, and where their wounded bodies lay about, like those of murdered creatures, while here and there some charred and blackened giant reared aloft two withered arms, and seemed to call down curses on his foes."[7]

Had Dickens been travelling in neolithic Europe he would have found the scene less harrowing, since for a period, probably of some centuries, clearances were temporary and affected only small patches of forest at a time. Yet, in the dry season many columns of smoke must have curled up from the limitless expanse of forest in which the first farmers of temperate Europe sought to practise the new economy. Traces of such a conflagration dating from the neolithic period have recently been studied in the bog of Ordrup, Klampenborg Fjord, Denmark, by Iversen,[8] who has been able to show that the charcoal level left from

[4] I. Manninen, 1932, 274-5.
[5] G. Schwantes, 1939, 462-3 and C. Schott, 1935, 86 f.
[6] C. Schott, 1935.
[7] C. Dickins, *American Notes*, p. 165.
[8] J. Iversen, 1941.

the burning coincides with a steep decline in the proportion of forest trees and a corresponding increase in that of herbs and grasses (Fig. 44). He has further identified at this level the pollen of weeds which commonly accompany agriculture, including *Rumex*, *Artemesia* and *Plantago*, as well as of cultivated cereals. A fascinating detail is that, when the forest re-established itself on the neolithic clearing, the birch, owing to its greater speed of movement,

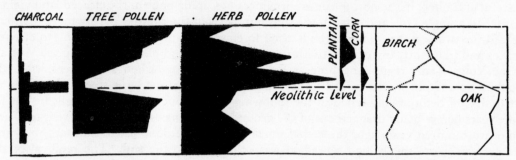

Fig. 44. Fluctuation in the frequencies of charcoal and fossil pollen brought about by neolithic colonisation : Ordrup Mose, Denmark. (*After Iversen*).

arrived first, being represented in the pollen diagram by a distinct secondary peak above the charcoal layer. When Dr. F. J. North was travelling in Finland just before the war he noted that birch trees made up " a large part of the forest where burn-beating has been practised."[9] As is so often the case one can gain an insight into a vital process of the remote past by observing its repetition in our own day.

Although, therefore, there can be no doubt that burning played a part in the early forest farming, it is equally sure that the axe must have been an essential agent in the process of clearance in neolithic Europe as it was in Ontario or Finland during recent generations. There is ample evidence of neolithic man's capabilities as a lumberman and worker in wood. He used the timber which he felled for the construction of dwellings, earthworks and tombs, and he hollowed out oak trunks for boats. Where the actual marks of his flint and stone tools can be studied, they reveal a sureness which speaks of a well-established tradition of working in wood, but also of the effectiveness of the axes and adzes used.

This has indeed been tested more than once by experiment. Many years ago Vicomte Lepic cut down a small oak some eight inches in diameter using " a polished Danish flint hatchet eight inches long " without injury to the blade.[10] More recently Dr Jacob-Friesen experimented with chipped and polished flint axes to test their relative effectiveness : briefly, he found that whereas he needed seven minutes to fell a pine stem 17 cm. in diameter using a chipped axe, he could manage a similar stem in five minutes with a polished one.[11] The polished axe is thus no chance element in the material equipment of neolithic man : it not only reflects his capacity to shape timber to his needs for houses, boats and other purposes, but symbolizes his activities as a lumberman, activities without which he could not have practised the new form of economy in the deciduous zone of Europe.

The significance of the polished axe for neolithic man is not implied only by its ubiquitous occurrence, but also by the immense pains he took to secure the most suitable material for the blade, whether by trading stone of particular toughness and tractability or by

[9] F. J. North, *Finland in Summer*, 92–3, Cambridge, 1937.
[10] Sir J. Evans, 1897, 162.
[11] Quoted by H. Nietsch, 1939, 70.

mining the most perfect flint available. The flint-mines at Grimes Graves, near Brandon, Norfolk, are doubly significant in this respect, since they are situated in the midst of one of the most notable areas of neolithic forest-clearance in Britain. The fauna recovered from the shafts and galleries gives a clear indication that at the time of the workings forests were close at hand. No less than 323 red deer antlers were recovered from the three galleried pits excavated up till 1914 and at least 346 of these pits are visible on the surface. In addition, quantities of red deer bones were found as well as the bones of beaver and, even more significantly, of Bechstein's bat (*Myotis Bechsteini*), a forest-haunting species now extinct in Britain.[12]

Microscopic examination of a vertical series of samples through some thirty feet of organic mud and peat in the bed of Hockham Mere on the northern fringe of Breckland has recently revealed the main lines of development of vegetation in this area since the late glacial period.[13] The fossil pollen at the bottom of the deposit showed a high proportion of species indicating an open landscape; of the tree pollen present the overwhelming proportion was birch. Higher up in the section grasses and herbs declined as the forest closed in and covered the whole landscape. In this forest, pine and hazel rose first to leadership, then as the temperature reached its peak deciduous trees came into their own, at first oak and elm and then lime and alder predominating. A crucial point came with the fairly sudden decline of elm, which both in the Cambridgeshire and Somerset Fens and again in Denmark and south Sweden is correlated with the beginning of neolithic culture; at this juncture, coinciding with the spread of farming economy, there set in a sharp increase in the pollen and spores of vegetation which flourishes in the open—grasses, ericoids (including *Calluna*), *Sphagnum* moss, ferns (possibly bracken) and miscellaneous herbs. In other words, precisely at the point when neolithic man made his appearance, heath and grasslands began to replace forest. The inference that this change was brought about by the clearance needed for the practice of farming is strengthened by the occurrence among the miscellaneous herbs of the rib-wort plantain (*Plantago lanceolata*), a species commonly associated with farming and regarded by the American Indian as marking " the white man's trail."[14] It has been shown, in fact, that the open heaths, characteristic of Breckland before the Forestry Commissioners began to replant the woodland, only began with the appearance of neolithic man and the suggestion is strong that the neolithic farmers initiated the deforestation of a region, which, when they first arrived, was covered with deciduous forest.

The best known exponents of the extensive, shifting agriculture of neolithic times were the Danubian peasants who colonized the loess of Central Europe, a formation once hailed as an open corridor through the hostile forest, but now recognized as itself supporting a friendly mixed oak forest.[15] The fact that this forest admitted sufficient light to allow the growth of foliage on which cattle and swine could feed was one attraction, but it was mainly preferred for combining a high degree of fertility with exceptional ease of working. As is well known the Danubians worked their way rapidly over the loess in more than one wave.[16] From Moravia they spread on the one hand eastwards into Galicia and over Poland as far as the lower Vistula, and on the other, northwards and westwards, over

---

[12] *Grimes Graves Report*, 1914, 218.

[13] H. Godwin, 1944; cf. the work especially of J. Iversen, 1941, and of K. Faegri, 1944.

[14] For a study of the ecological effects of *brandtwirtschaft* and tillage during modern times in eastern Finland see K. Linkola, 1916, 73–6, 216–20.

[15] J. G. D. Clark, 1945, 57 and 62; K. Tüxen, 1931, 77 and 88–9; A. Garnett, 1945.

[16] e.g. V. G. Childe, 1929, Chap. IV–V.

Germany, following the Oder into Silesia, the Elbe into Saxony and the Danube into Bavaria, and ultimately settling the loess lands of the Main, the Neckar and the Rhine, and reaching the Hesbaye and north-west France by way of the Meuse valley. The rapidity of the movements and the fact that several different groups, characterized by distinct pottery wares, were involved are consistent with the notion of peasants clearing small patches of forest, taking a few easy crops, and passing on to fresh ground (Fig. 45).

Such a way of life must have involved frequent change of settlement: when all the available ground within easy reach had been exploited in this way, it would be necessary to abandon the village and move to a fresh region, leaving the natural vegetation to reform. On the

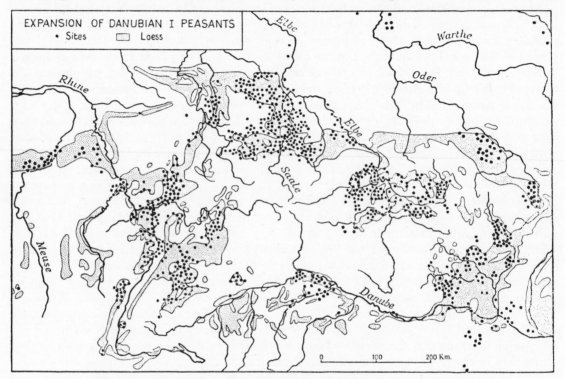

Fig. 45.   Colonisation of the loess by neolithic Danubian peasants.
(*Based on Grahmann and Buttler*).

northern margins of farming, among the Finno-Ougrians of north-east Europe, who practised forest-burning down to modern times, it was common to move the place of settlement so as to be in a position to exploit new tracts of forest, even though land was sometimes cultivated in the Dvina-Kama region at distances up to 70 versts (*c.* 46 miles) from the villages;[17] thus, we are told that among the Wotjaks it was customary, either to abandon their villages, leaving the wooden houses intact, or to dismantle the buildings and transport them to a new site.[18] That the Danubian peasants behaved in a similar way is suggested both by the speed with which they spread and by the evidence that their sites, like Köln-Lindenthal on the loess south-west of Cologne[19] or Brześć Kujawski, some 60 km.

---

[17] I. Manninen, 1932, 274.

[18] *ibid.*, 236.

[19] W. Buttler and W. Haberey, 1936, 162–3.

south-east of Torun in Poland,[20] were abandoned, sometimes on as many as three separate occasions during a life of a few centuries.

So long as sufficient virgin forest remained on the light, easily worked soils, which constituted the area of primary settlement, the primitive regime of shifting agriculture, associated with burning and felling, was capable of maintaining the pioneer peasantries in reasonable comfort. The duration of this happy state of affairs depended partly on the capacity of the woodland to regenerate itself and partly on the pressure of population. The evidence brought forward by palæobotanists shows that regeneration of woodland certainly did occur and that the passing of shifting cultivators was often followed by the reforming of the forest; indeed, the succession of events noted at Köln-Lindenthal and elsewhere suggests that the cycle may sometimes have been repeated several times. On the other hand, since at first there was land and to spare, new communities must continually have hived off from old ones, so that ultimately the point was reached when clearance outstripped the capacity of the woodlands to regenerate themselves. The effect of this was doubtless enhanced by the depredations of grazing animals, which must have been a principal agent in making permanent the temporary clearances of shifting agriculturalists by eating off the seedlings and preventing replenishment of the forest. The breakdown seems to have occurred earlier in countries like Denmark on the poorer, sandier soils, on which the recuperative power of the forest was low, than upon the richer soils of the younger moraines. On the other hand, it must be remembered that the pressure of population was greatest on the more desirable soils, such as the loess of central Europe, so that it might be expected that the crisis made itself felt within a fairly short period over the whole area of primary settlement in temperate Europe.

Exact information about the growing extent of open country and heaths is liable to increase as more is learnt about the local development of vegetation in different parts of prehistoric Europe. Meanwhile useful information can be gained from the materials used to build round barrows and above all from the nature of the old ground surfaces on which they were raised. It appears that during neolithic times corded-ware battle-axe people were already beginning to construct their burial-mounds over heathlands, at least in Jutland,[21] Schleswig-Holstein and north-west Germany,[22] though it is noticeable that in north Holland the neolithic mounds were normally made of sand, whereas the bronze age additions—and separate mounds—were commonly built from heath sods.[23] There is thus little doubt that, although heath country was more widespread during the Bronze Age, the crisis had come to a head, particularly on some of the poorer soils, already before the end of neolithic times.

Indeed, in the light of what is known from purely archæological sources, one might well put the matter a good deal more strongly. It has long been appreciated that the closing stage of the neolithic phase was an uneasy one over temperate Europe as a whole: instead of peaceful peasants, whether Danubians, makers of painted pottery, westerners or funnel-neck beaker folk, moving quietly forward over the waste, pioneering the new economy, one finds warriors, some equipped with battle-axes, others relying on their bows, but all intent on commerce, war and domination, moving at times rapidly, and themselves depending more on pastoral activities and rapine than on agriculture, a veritable scourge to the older

[20] K. Jaźdźewski, 1938, Tabl. II.
[21] G.F.L. Sarauw, 1898 and 1901.
[22] G. Schwantes, 1939, 457.
[23] e.g. A. E. van Giffen, 1930, abb. 7 and 31.

peasantries into whose territories they irrupted. Prehistorians have indeed vied in emphasizing the contrast between the early peasants and the later warriors, without, however, offering any very satisfying explanation. Yet, surely one is dealing here with the effects upon human history of an immense ecological change wrought unthinkingly by the neolithic farmers and their livestock. The crisis when it came extended far beyond the sphere of animals and plants and involved not merely the economic basis, but the whole outlook of large segments of the population of prehistoric Europe. In many parts at least the fat times of forest farming were over for good and all. The stored up fertility of the virgin soil had been taken and the potash from the burnt woodlands had been absorbed.

For a period of several centuries between the breakdown of *brandwirtschaft* and the spread of settled farming with fixed fields, little or nothing is known of what was going forward in the settlement of temperate Europe. The absence of more than a few traces of bronze age habitations, and even in a country so well explored as Denmark and from a period so rich in funerary monuments and grave goods, has not merely provided one of the problems of prehistory, but has deprived us of the chief sources from which a firm answer might have been obtained. It is possible that the commonly received opinion that pastoral activities had increased in importance may prove correct, but it seems equally sure from the number of impressions of cereal grains on the funerary pottery[24] that agriculture must also have been carried on actively at this time. Again, recent investigations suggest that new land was being taken up in the midlands of England during the period when collared cinerary urns were being made.[25] It may tentatively be concluded that the population was larger during the Bronze Age than it had been in neolithic times and that this was maintained by exploiting the whole area of primary settlement : over large tracts pastoral activities, including sheep-rearing, were of more importance than agriculture : yet, agriculture was not only carried on, but extended into new lands, some of which belonged to the richer intermediate soil-group.

The methods of cultivation employed in modern times by communities practising *brandwirtschaft* were often of the most primitive description. Manninen tells how among the Finno-Ougrians it was customary to do no more than harrow the seed in among the burnt ashes.[26] Again, according to Schott, the early colonists of southern Ontario were able to raise crops by merely scratching the surface of freshly cleared ground with rake or harrow and scattering in the seed; indeed, it appears that the plough was not always used until after five or six years of this elementary procedure.[27] By analogy it may be supposed that the prehistoric pioneers, appropriating the first richness of the soil from a few seasons' cropping, would find no need to engage in elaborate methods of cultivation. Certainly no good evidence has yet been advanced for the use of ploughs among the earlier neolithic peasantries of Europe.

The spread of settled agriculture with fixed fields is extremely difficult to trace owing to the nature of the evidence. To begin with remains of prehistoric fields can hardly be expected to survive except on soils beyond the margin of cultivation during the historical period. As a test it is instructive to compare the distribution of iron age fields with that of settlements, burials and stray finds from the Pre-Roman Iron Age in Denmark (Fig. 46) : the two patterns are so far from coinciding that hardly any fields survive in the richest areas

[24] Jessen and Helback, 1944, 27.

[25] T. G. E. Powell, *Proc. Prehist. Soc.*, 1950.

[26] I. Manninen, 1932, 30.

[27] C. Schott, 1935, 98–9.

of settlement and conversely the areas most prolific in traces of early agriculture were among those most sparsely settled at that time. From nearer home one might quote the example of East Anglia, which though an important centre of population during the Early Iron Age is almost destitute of traces of prehistoric agriculture. It is sufficiently evident that the existing distribution of prehistoric fields gives no reliable indication of the extent of early agriculture. Moreover, it is likely that the better soils in the primary area of settlement

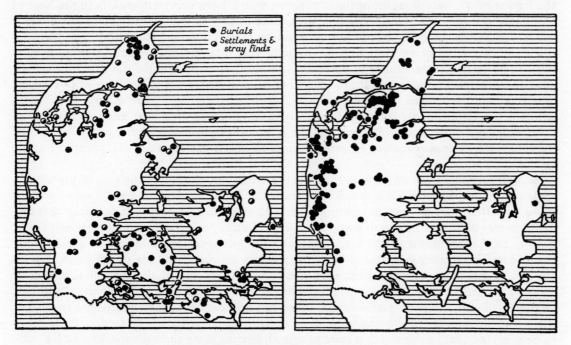

Fig. 46. Comparative maps illustrating marginal survival of Celtic fields in Denmark.
(*left*): burials and other finds from the Celtic Iron Age. (*After Brøndsted*)
(*right*): finds of Celtic fields. (*After Hatt*).

would be among the first to be taken up and that in other words the prehistoric fields which survive to-day were marginal even in prehistoric antiquity. Settled agriculture may in fact be substantially older than the earliest traces of " Celtic fields."

As a general rule, indeed, the prehistoric fields of which superficial traces survive, notably on the chalk of southern England[28] and on the sands and heaths of north Holland[29] and of Jutland,[30] belong to the Pre-Roman or Roman Iron Ages, though a few occurrences on the Sussex Downs have been referred to the closing stages of the Bronze Age in that area.[31] On the other hand, traces of tillage, in the form of old plough-soil, sometimes with marks of criss-cross cultivation, buried under and preserved by burial-mounds, can in several instances be referred back to the Bronze Age, as with those found by Hatt at Vesterlund, Jutland,[32] or those uncovered by van Giffen while excavating three round

[28] O. G. S. Crawford and A. Keiller, 1928, *passim*; E. C. Curwen, 1938, 38–40 and 1938 B.
[29] A. E. van Giffen, 1928.
[30] G. Hatt, 1931, 1937, 1949.
[31] e.g. New Barn Down, near Worthing, Holleyman and Curwen, 1935 ; E. C. Curwen, 1938, Fig. 5.
[32] G. Hatt, 1931, 161 f.

barrows near Zwaagdijk, North Holland, dating from the Middle or Late Bronze Age.[33] Indeed, van Giffen has assigned such traces under a barrow near Gasteren, Drenthe, to the close of the neolithic phase in Holland.[34]

As for ploughs,[35] it must be remembered that these were normally made of wood and that where metal was used at all, as in some cases for shares and coulters, it is hazardous to reconstruct the form of the plough from these alone. This makes all the more important the frames of wooden ploughs, or parts of these, which have survived, mainly in the bogs of temperate Europe. The chief difficulty with these is how to date them. The most obvious method is pollen analysis, but it is important to remember that such finds are normally made in the course of peat-digging or draining and that the exact circumstances usually have to be reconstructed through cross-examination, often long after the event. Further, since the overlying deposit has almost certainly been dug away, it is hardly ever possible to determine the circumstances under which the plough originally reached the position in which it was found. Only where pollen-analysis has been applied critically to a number of cases with consistent results can the dating be accepted as a firm one. It is equally dangerous, though, to argue from negative evidence, where so much has certainly disappeared leaving no trace.

Some information can be gathered from representations, though in the case of prehistoric rock-engravings, like the bronze age ones from the Ligurian Alps or from south Sweden, these are often obscure on vital points of detail; one has to remember not only that the medium was by nature intractable and the tools defective, but that grave uncertainties exist both as to the intentions of the artists and as to the conventions followed in giving these expression. References in classical literature are less helpful than they might be in view of the lack of direct knowledge on the part of certain authors and of the corrupt character of some of the vital texts. Indications from existing folk culture and from medieval sources, including illuminations on manuscripts, tapestries and carvings, may contribute in certain ways, but the dangers of arguing backwards in time need hardly be stressed. The fact has to be accepted that in the existing state of knowledge no more than the most tentative conclusions are justified either about ancient fields or the ploughs used to cultivate them. The need, as in most branches of prehistory, is for much more intensive and purposeful research.

In considering the early history of agriculture in prehistoric Europe one should remember first and foremost that its underlying concepts and the material appliances used in its practice originated in the ancient east, and were first established in Europe in the eastern part of the Mediterranean zone. The agricultural technique which spread over temperate Europe was basically Mediterranean in character. The dominating factor in Mediterranean tillage was the need to guard against evaporation during the summer drought, a need which was all the more pressing owing to the comparatively minor role played by livestock and the consequent lack of moisture-holding manure. The remedy, as in the dry-farming of north America, was frequent ploughing, which by pulverizing the soil prevented moisture from rising to the surface by capillary attraction.[36] Such pulverization could of course be achieved by means of mattocks, hoes and other hand tools, but it was made easier by the frequent use of the traction plough.

Strictly speaking the Mediterranean peoples used the ard (*aratrum, araire*) an implement admirably adapted for the pulverizing process so necessary to the regime of the area, rather

---

[33] A. E. van Giffen, 1944.
[34] A. E. van Giffen, 1941, 30 and abb. 31.
[35] For early references, see P. Leser, 1931. For classical ploughs, A. S. F. Gow, 1914.
[36] E. C. Semple, 1932, 285 ff.; C. E. Stevens, 1941, 93.

than the plough proper (*caruca, charrue*). The ard itself existed from early times in two varieties, the crook-ard and the spade-ard, each of which had spread to the northern limits of the temperate zone before the end of the Bronze Age. The crook-ard resembled a hoe dragged through the soil, the blade of which functioned as a sole, and the handle as a beam. The principal member of the spade-ard was shaped at one end into a handle and at the other into a sole, the beam, a separate piece of timber, being attached fairly low down.

Despite the wild claims advanced for the ard found in a bog at Walle, Hanover,[37] and the more plausible but still not convincing plea that certain perforated shoe-last celts should be interpreted as shares,[38] there is no good evidence for the use of the plough in neolithic Europe, unless one accepts as such the scratches under the Gasteren barrow, which dates at earliest from the very end of the period in the Low Countries. The oldest representations from barbarian Europe comprise the rock-engravings of the Alpes Maritimes studied by Bicknell and referred to the Early Bronze Age of the Ligurian region.[39] The precise form

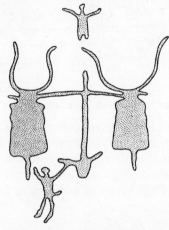

Fig. 47. Bronze Age plough-team engraved on a
rock in the Alpes Maritimes.

of ard employed is very often difficult to determine owing to the habit of the artists of depicting plough-scenes more or less from above. In the great majority of instances—in eighteen out of twenty-two of those illustrated by Bicknell—the ards are shown drawn by pairs of yoked oxen (Fig. 47). It has recently been claimed by Payne that the Ligurians also depicted three-, four-, five- and six-ox teams, but, bearing in mind what was earlier said about the interpretation of prehistoric rock-engravings, appearances may well prove deceptive.[40] As Payne himself admits, the three-ox team " is unsatisfactory ; in practice it would be found well-nigh impossible to yoke it to the plough in the formation shown,"

---

[37] Found in digging peat in 1927 ; it was not until after some months that peat samples were taken from the level at which a peat-digger remembered making the discovery. Originally attributed to the beginning of the neolithic period and hailed as the oldest plough in the world, the object was later referred to the Atlantic—Sub-boreal transition (G. Görz, 1928 ; K. H. Jacob-Friesen, 1934 ; W. Rytz, 1935 ; G. Hatt, 1937, 56–9). In reality, as Gløb (1942, 265) points out, the dating of this find (cf. J. Troels-Smith, 1942) cannot be accepted as of critical value.

[38] P. V. Gløb, 1939.   These were almost certainly adze-blades (see *Prähist. Z.* xxxiv-xxxv (1950), 230–232).   [39] C. Bicknell, 1913.

[40] F. G. Payne, 1948. In one case Payne seems to have omitted the foot of the second of a pair of ards in line ahead ; cf. Payne's Pl. V, 7, with Bicknell's Pl. III, 12.

nor does the team of five depicted with three one side and two the other of the beam commend itself as any more practical. Again, in the case of the representations interpreted as teams of two or three pairs of oxen in line ahead, the possibility can hardly be excluded, to put it at its mildest, that the artists in fact depicted two or three separate teams working one immediately in front of the other, as in the famous clay model from Vounous, Cyprus,[41] dating from the Bronze Age (Pl. VI, b). While, though, the standard Mediterranean plough team undoubtedly comprised two oxen, it is hardly to be expected that this was rigidly adhered to or that larger teams were not used when local conditions demanded this. As regards the human complement of the plough-team, it is notable that in addition to the ploughman at the handle a man is commonly represented walking backwards in front of the team apparently urging on the oxen and probably equipped with a goad.

Fig. 48.   Spade ard and crook-ard depicted on Bronze Age
rock engravings from south Sweden.   (*After Brøndsted*).

For the temperate zone the well-known rock-engravings of south Sweden, referred to periods V and VI of the Northern Bronze Age, form one of the leading sources of information, all the more valuable in that they depict plough-scenes from the side.[42] Both crook- and spade-ard may be distinguished (Fig. 48) and it is notable that these are invariably drawn by yoked two-ox teams. Both types of ard, again, are represented by the wooden

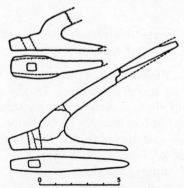

Fig. 49.   Soles of crook-ards from Sejbaek (upper) and
Hvorslev (lower), North Jutland.   (*After Glob*).
. Scale of decimetres

frames recovered from bogs in Denmark, south Sweden, north Germany and Poland. All the crook-ards belong to the primitive natural form, and at least three of those from north Jutland—the finds from Vebbestrup, Sejbaek and Hvorslev (Fig. 49)—have been reliably

---

[41] Dikaios (1933). Payne himself (Pl. VII) shows a similar scene in the Himalayas.

[42] A. Steensberg (1936A, 248) rates the engravings highly as sources, see Baltzer, 1919, Pl. 23–4 and Pl. 55–6, No. 4.

dated to the Early Iron Age by means of pollen-analysis.[43] In most cases the beam has been broken off short, but the engravings invariably show yoked ox-teams and the hook for securing a yoke was recovered with the ard from Walle; what may well have been a plough yoke was recovered from an allegedly chalcolithic site at Vinelz on lake Switzerland (see p. 309n.). On the other hand, the Vebbestrup ard (Fig. 50) was accompanied by what

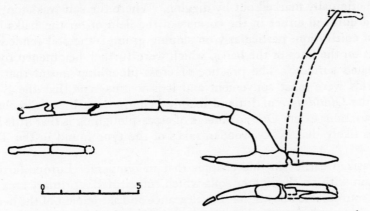

Fig. 50.   Crook-ard with swingle-tree from Vebbestrup, north
Jutland.   (*After Steensberg*).
Scale in decimetres

Steensberg has interpreted as a swingle tree, indicative of harnessing by means of traces. A remarkably complete specimen of a spade-ard (Fig. 51) from a bog at Døstrup, Jutland,

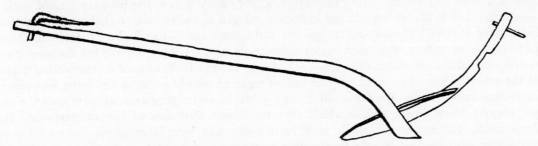

Fig. 51.   Spade-ard from Døstrup, Jutland.   Length of beam 10 ft.   (*After Curwen*).

has been referred to the beginning of the Early Iron Age by Jessen on the basis of a sample taken from a cavity in the beam.[44] In no instance has the frame of a prehistoric ard been found with an iron share,[45] but wooden ones occurred with the Døstrup ard and with an undated crook-ard from Dabergotz, north Germany.[46]

The indications are that ards were employed in northern Europe for cross-ploughing. Proof that this was carried on during prehistoric times in this area was first obtained by

---

[43] P. Gløb, 1942; A. Steensberg, 1945.

[44] S. Müller, 1907, abb. 1; A. Steensberg, 1936A, 251–2.

[45] Conversely, it is often dangerous to infer the type of plough from the character of detached iron shares.

[46] P. Leser, 1931, 138 ff., taf. 5, abb. c.

Hatt while excavating a house of the Pre-Roman Iron Age at Alrum, Jutland[47]; series of scratch-like marks crossing one another at right-angles were found in the soil underlying the floor, which had evidently been laid directly on cultivated ground. As already mentioned, similar markings have since been found under barrows dating from the Bronze Age in the same area and in parts of Holland. According to Hatt's observations,[48] the ancient fields of Jutland were originally marked out by digging. Where the soil was stony, stones might be collected and dumped either in the corners of the field or on the balks between them. In the course of cultivation, particularly on sloping ground, the soil tended to form quite marked lynchets on the lines of the balks, which were further heightened by dust blowing from the cultivated surface. The practice of cross-ploughing meant that comparatively short, broad fields were most convenient and it is to this type that the " Celtic fields " of Britain and the *Oldtidsagre* of Jutland mainly belong, though both in shape and size a wide range of variations exist. One advantage of cross-ploughing is that little harrowing was needed and it is likely that heavy wooden rakes of the type found in the Thorsbjerg bog sufficed.

It was emphasized earlier in this chapter that in temperate Europe farming was concentrated to begin with on the lighter soils which constituted a primary area of settlement. From historical sources it is known that the clearance and settlement of the heavier claylands was particularly active during the later Dark Ages and that in many parts of Europe this process had still not worked itself out until centuries later. The problem is to what extent, if at all, the movement from lighter to heavier soils had already begun before the end of prehistoric times.

The initial stages of this are even more difficult to trace than was the original transition from shifting to settled agriculture, since the soils occupied in the process were among those most attractive to farmers during the historical period. Whereas the primary area of settlement extended in places beyond the historical margin of cultivation so that traces of actual fields have survived at least on the poorer soils, such could hardly be expected in those parts of the secondary area taken under cultivation first, since these have for the most part remained under cultivation ever since. There is indeed little chance of recovering plans of the actual fields. The most fruitful line of research would seem to lie in the systematic investigation of soil samples from old ground-surfaces underlying ancient earthworks, more particularly those linear dykes which traverse broad stretches of the countryside. By determining the extent to which such earthworks had been erected on cultivated soil, pasture or woodland, it should be possible to reconstruct something in the nature of soil utilization maps of certain areas as these existed in early times.

Archæological distributions are of less help than might be expected, since these relate substantially to areas of burial or settlement as the case may be. It is true that in the long run changes in the extent or distribution of tillage must be reflected in the pattern of settlement, so that within certain limits the distribution of material like pottery can be used to give some indication of the territories farmed. Yet there is room for quite a marked extension of tillage without any significant change in the pattern of settlement becoming apparent. From the earliest times pervious soils have been preferred for settlement and this preference still operates: it must be evident, though, that the mere disposition of settlements on gravels and sands by no means precludes the cultivation of neighbouring claylands, particularly in regions where such are traversed by river valleys. Thus, detailed examination of the

---

[47] G. Hatt, 1941, 155 ff.
[48] G. Hatt, 1949, 150–1.

distribution of Domesday vills in the Cambridge region shows that the great majority are sited either on the margin of claylands or on the gravels and sands of the river valleys,[49] even though by this time substantial tracts of claylands were being cultivated. Examination of the one-inch survey of the boulder-clay capped heights of East Anglia will show that settlement is still to this day concentrated on the porous soils of the river valleys.

It follows that any extension of settlement from the primary to the secondary zone can be accepted as an indication that heavier soils had been taken into cultivation. At the same time it must be remembered that, as Wooldridge and Linton emphasized,[50] the distinction between pervious and impervious soils is not as clear-cut as one might imagine from the drift geology maps, the " relatively simple age nomenclature " of which may mask wide variations in cultivability. In particular, they obscure the loams and brick-earths, to which the lands opened up by the Belgae at the end of the prehistoric period in south-eastern Britain belong.[51] There are indeed signs that some of the heavier, richer soils were already being taken into cultivation before the end of prehistoric times in certain parts of temperate Europe. In his recent study of the early settlement of an area of north-western Jutland,[52] Dr Therkel Mathiassen has been able to show that, whereas finds from the beginning of the neolithic period are twice as dense on the heath-sand and three and a half times as dense on the hill-sand as on the morainic clay, by the Early Iron Age finds were almost evenly distributed over all three formations with a slightly greater density on the clay.

The Mediterranean method of pulverizing the soil by means of frequent cross-ploughing was adapted well enough to the cultivation of light soils in the temperate zone, but was quite unsuited to the loams and clays which were already beginning to be taken under cultivation during the Early Iron Age. As it happens, the heavier soils began to be taken over at a time of climatic change, when the relatively dry Sub-boreal climate was giving way to the Sub-atlantic period of heavy rainfall. The combination of these two factors necessitated a radical change in the technique of cultivation. The aim of the ploughman was no longer to conserve moisture in the sub-soil, but on the contrary to achieve adequate drainage. This was done by ploughing in one direction, cutting a sod and turning a furrow. As is only to be expected, this fundamental change of practice resulted in important modifications both in the implements of tillage and in the shape of the cultivated fields.

There seems little doubt that the plough with four-sided frame, comprising sole, handle, beam and sheath, was evolved to work heavy soils as these were taken under cultivation, though precisely at what stage still remains uncertain. Such ploughs were commonly fitted with broad socketed shares and iron coulters to cut the furrow slice vertically ; they might also be provided with mould-boards or analogous devices for turning the sod and with wheels for supporting the frame, though each of these ends could be served in other ways. Direct evidence for the use of the four-sided plough during prehistoric times is still dubious. So far as actual ploughs are concerned, the only find to merit consideration is that from Tømmerby, Jutland,[53] comprising the sole and sheath in one piece, the landside of the former set with guard-stones, mainly of quartz and quartzite. Although recovered two generations ago, the fragment yielded pollen samples from both faces and these dated without doubt from the beginning of the Early Iron Age in Denmark; on the other hand, as Steensberg

---

[49] C. Fox, 1923, Map V.
[50] S. W. Wooldridge and D. L. Linton, 1933.
[51] cf. C. Fox, 1932, 73–4 and 1933, 162; R. E. M. Wheeler, 1936, 13–14.
[52] T. Mathiassen, 1948, 138–43.
[53] A. Steensberg, 1936 and 1936A, 252–5; G. Hatt, 1937, 60–2.

has admitted, it is possible, since only quite a small part of the plough is present, that
this had been pushed into a hole in the peat at a much later date and it is significant in this
connection that the use of guard-stones was customary in Jutland down to the beginning
of the nineteenth century. The Tømmerby find is poor evidence indeed for the early use of
the four-sided plough. More satisfactory in some respects is the testimony of iron coulters,[54]
like those from south-eastern England, notably from Great Chesterford and Silchester,
and from the Rhineland and Switzerland. On the other hand, evidence for the use of
coulters in pre-Roman times is still inadequate, despite suggestive occurrences like those at
Bigbury[55] and Twyford Down, Winchester.[56] Even if these are accepted at their face value,

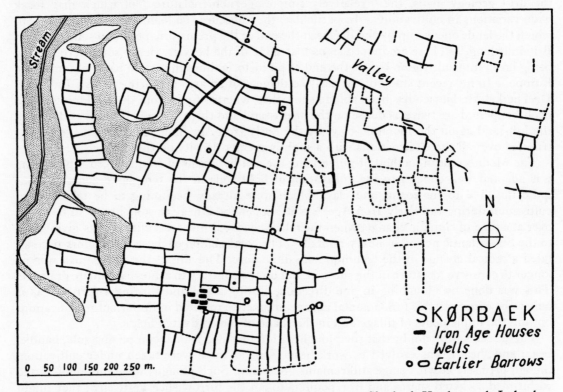

Fig. 52. Plan of Celtic fields round Iron Age settlement on Skørbaek Heath, north Jutland.
The stippled area indicates marsh. (*Based on Hatt*).

they tell us no more than that the plough was in use among the Belgic inhabitants of south-
eastern Britain at the very end of the prehistoric period and on the very margin of the
Roman world.

Plenty of evidence is available from Jutland, notably on Byrsted Heath,[57] but also
on Skørbaek Heath (Fig. 52) and elsewhere, that broad, short fields were sub-divided for
inheritance among heirs and cultivated in strips. It should not be inferred, though, that

---

[54] J. B. P. Karslake, 1933.
[55] *Arch. J.*, LIX, 213–15.
[56] J. D. M. Stuart and J. M. Birckbeck, 1936.
[57] G. Hatt, 1949, Pl. II. On the sub-division of fields for inheritance, see further G. Hatt, 1939.

these strips were necessarily ploughed by means of a true four-sided plough, since the ard fitted with the right kind of share and handled in the proper manner was quite capable of performing the job. On the other hand the chance of finding the earliest strip fields on the intermediate soils is slender for reasons already emphasized. The heavier claylands were not taken into cultivation at any rate on an important scale until the early medieval period and the social and technological changes which accompanied this great expansion must be left to the historian.

CHAPTER V

FARMING: CROPS AND LIVESTOCK

THE agriculture which spread over much of prehistoric Europe was based pre-dominantly on the cultivation of cereals and it was still possible for Tacitus[1] to remark of German husbandry that " grain is the only harvest required of the land. . . ." So soon as fixed fields were established, these were cultivated under the two-field régime[2] in which crops alternated with fallow, a régime sung by Pindar and Virgil, but imposed by the dry summer of the Mediterranean and the difficulty of raising any other than winter-wheat. The three-field regime, which came to dominate the temperate zone during historical times, depended on summer rains and the feasibility of growing spring as well as autumn sown wheat. Like strip cultivation and the four-sided plough, it grew out of conditions peculiar to the temperate zone and like these its early history is still obscure.

Since wheat and barley were the staple crops of the earliest farmers of western Asia and the Nile Valley, it is only to be expected that they should have spread to Greece and ultimately over the whole territory occupied by farming economy in prehistoric Europe.[3] The species of wheat most abundantly cultivated was Emmer (*Triticum dicoccum*), though Einkorn or Small Spelt (*T. monococcum*) was still common in neolithic Europe; neither Bread Wheat (*T. vulgare*) nor Dwarf or Club Wheat (*T. compactum*)—varieties which can hardly be distinguished from one another from the grains alone—were nearly as important, according to Jessen and Helbaek, as they were once thought to have been. The leading kind of six-rowed Barley during the Stone and Bronze Ages was the erect, hexagonal form (*Hordeum hexastichum*), but the nodding, quadrangular type (*H. vulgare*) gradually prevailed in the later periods. Significant fluctuations in the relative importance of wheat and barley have been noted on the basis of identifications of grains and of systematic counts of impressions on hand-made pottery from successive periods. Wheat was much the most important grain during neolithic times, whether in the British Isles, Denmark or Central Europe. On the other hand in each of these territories barley rose to predominance during the bronze age. Wheat regained some of its former importance during the early iron age in southern England, but in Denmark it remained quite secondary to barley.

	Neolithic		Bronze Age		Pre-Roman Iron Age	
	Wheat	Barley	Wheat	Barley	Wheat	Barley
Britain[4]	17	9	23	223	19	15
Denmark[5]	355	54	22	214	1	30

Table showing numbers of impressions of wheat and barley on prehistoric pottery from Britain and Denmark.

---

[1] *Germania*, cap. 26.   [2] M. Bloch, 1931, 31–5; 1934, 479–80.
[3] For details see : J. Hoops, 1905 ; E. Neuweiler, 1905, 1919, 1935, 1946 ; F. Netolitzky, 1931 ; G. Hatt, 1937; K. Bertsch, 1939; J. Percival, 1943; K. Jessen and H. Helbaek, 1944.
[4] Jessen and Helbaek, 1944, 27.
[5] G. Hatt, 1937, 20–2. Further evidence for the predominance of wheat in neolithic Denmark comes from the settlement of Bundsø, where Jessen (in Mathiassen, 1939) was able to count a total of 515 grains as against only 51 of barley, including carbonised grain impressions on pottery and daub.

The presence on neolithic sites of millet, cultivated intensively at the present day in a broad belt from the Danube delta across south Russia to central Asia and north China, suggests that the Mediterranean was not the only source contributing to the rise of agriculture in temperate Europe. That this cereal spread into Europe from the east is shown by its presence during neolithic times in the eastern and central parts of the continent and by its absence from the north and west. Millet[6] has been identified on sites of the Tripolye, Boian, Vardar and Thessalian cultures of the Ukraine, Rumania, Macedonia and central Greece; in Hungary it has been found in a Bükk level in the Aggtelek cave and, in an uncertain context, at the Danubian II site of Lengyel; and it is present at a number of neolithic sites in Switzerland and south Germany. Millet was commonly used by the Lausitz people of central Europe and it was thence that its cultivation spread by way of north Germany to Denmark, where it was never of more than subsidiary importance; it contributed no more than five out of 273 grain impressions from the Late Bronze Age counted by Sarauw and died out completely during the Early Iron Age, due probably to the onset of Sub-atlantic climate. There is no evidence that it reached Britain during prehistoric times. It may be added that of the two main varieties of millet, Club Millet (*Panicum miliaceum*) and Panicle Millet (*P. italicum*), only the former, which ripens more rapidly in a cool climate, was cultivated north of the Danube during prehistoric times.[7]

Among the younger cereals may be numbered spelt (*Triticum spelta*)[8], which is unknown in the wild state and is thought to have originated as a cross between different cultivated wheats. During the Bronze Age spelt was confined to Switzerland and south Germany, and though it appeared already at Baldegg, it was not until the Late Bronze Age that it became at all common, as at Mörigen, Zürich-Alpenquai and Buchau. There is no record from Denmark and it did not reach southern England until the Early Iron Age.

Oats (*Avena sativa*) and rye (*Secale cereale*) seem to have originated from mimics growing in crops of emmer and of wheat or barley respectively, such as are found still growing in Persia and Asia Minor. No doubt the prototypes spread into Europe with wheat and barley, but it was only with the worsening of climate during Sub-atlantic times that, owing to their greater tolerance of cold, they were able in parts of the temperate zone to strangle their parent crops and emerge in their own right as cultivated cereals.[9] Oats were first cultivated during the Late Bronze Age, both in Switzerland and to a slight extent in Denmark, but in the last-mentioned it was not until the Roman Iron Age that they played a part of any importance. Rye[10] appears first to have been domesticated in north central Germany during the Hallstatt phase of the Iron Age, but it was not until the Roman Iron Age that it became at all common in south Germany, Switzerland or Hungary or that it spread to Denmark. Neither oats nor rye have yet been recorded from the prehistoric period in Britain.

The harvesting of grain, its storage and its preparation, were all activities commensurate in importance with the part played by cereal cultivation in economic life. The earliest harvesting tools were reaping-knives with cutting-edges formed by a number of small flakes inset into a straight grooved handle, such as mesolithic hunter-fishers had already

---

[6] J. Hoops, 1905, *passim* ; Wace and Thompson, 1912, 54 ; F. Netolitzky, 1931, 20 f. ; G. Hatt, 1937, 23, 28, 34–6; E. Werth, 1937; H. Reinerth, 1938, 96; A. W. Heurtley, 1939, 79; J. H. Gaul, 1948, 67, 86, etc. Childe's reference (1947, 218) to millet in a Portuguese Beaker seems to be based on a misreading of his authority.

[7] See Netolitzky's map (1931, 21, abb. 1).

[8] Jessen and Helbaek, 1944, 41.

[9] For a good summary see G. Hatt, 1937, 41–2.

[10] K. Bertsch, 1939, abb. 10, gives a useful diagrammatic map of prehistoric occurrences.

devised, presumably for gathering wild grasses, and early farmers from Egypt to Iran had taken into use.[11] Among the most primitive specimens found in Europe are those associated with the neolithic painted pottery culture of west Bulgaria,[12] which had deer antler handles, grooved to receive overlapping primary flakes of flint, but to judge from a find at Murcié- lagos[13] an analogous form with wooden handle was used in Spain. The old find from Polada in north Italy[14] and the recently excavated reaping-knives from Cortaillod sites in Switzerland (Pl. V, a)[15] are provided with ear-hooks for holding a bunch of stalks in prepara- tion for grasping them in the left hand and severing them by a saw-like motion with the right. As Steensberg has pointed out[16], the stalks can hardly have been cut near the ground, since in the process of reaping the hook of the reaping-knife turned downwards ; to judge from harvesting-scenes on Egyptian tomb-paintings and medieval illuminations, it is likely that the stalks were severed not far below the heads.

The sickle proper, having a handle at an angle with the blade, appeared in Europe at about the same time as the use of metal (Fig. 53). To judge from examples found at Solferino in north Italy and at Acebuchal, Spain,[17] the jaw-like form with a reaping edge formed from

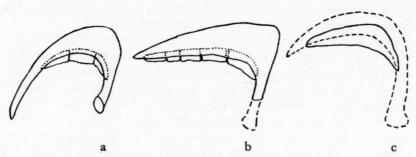

a   b   c

Fig. 53. Jaw-shaped sickles with flint teeth.
a. Kahun, Egypt (XIIth dyn.).
b. Solferino, N. Italy.
c. Suggested method of hafting crescentic flint sickles of the northern Stone Cist period.

a number of flint teeth spread from the Near East into Mediterranean Europe. On the other hand, at the end of neolithic times in much of northern and parts of central Europe sickle blades made from a single piece of flint came into use among peoples unable to afford to use much metal. Although none of the crescentic blades have been found actually mounted, it has been noted that traces of resin were still visible on some Swedish examples, arguing that they were set in slots cut into the inner arc of curved wooden handles.[18] The treat- ment of the butt-ends of certain single-piece flint sickle blades from Britain suggests rather

---

[11] E. C. Curwen, 1941 and 1946, 87–8.

[12] J. H. Gaul, 1948, 40–1, 43–5, Pl. XVI, 8, Pl. XVII, 7.

[13] A. Vayson, 1920, Fig. 12. In this case the flint insets comprised overlapping triangular pieces.

[14] Well illustrated in R. Munro, 1912, frontispiece.

[15] e.g. from Seematte, near Luzern (Landesmuseum Z. 38924) and Egolzwil II (Luzern Mus.). See V. von Gonzenbach, 1949, 48 and Taf. 10, No. 3 and 7.

[16] A. Steensberg, 1943, 129.

[17] A. Vayson, 1920.

[18] A. Oldeberg, 1932, 212.

that these were hafted at right-angles to straight handles,[19] probably resembling that found at Stenild, near Aalborg, Jutland,[20] with its blade, in this case a flint primary flake, wedged into a socket by means of two wooden pegs. The handle of the Stenild sickle shows signs of having been shaped by a metal tool and it is likely that sickles of this type were substitutes

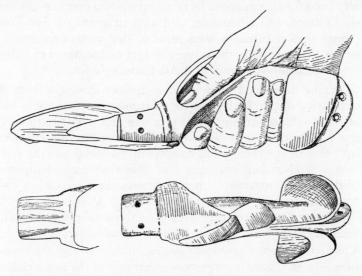

Fig. 54. Late Bronze Age sickle from Mörigen, Switzerland, illustrating how the handle has been shaped to give a firm grip and at the same time protect the user ($\frac{1}{3}$)

for bronze ones. In the few cases where the wooden handles of unbalanced bronze or iron sickles have survived, such as those from Mörigen (Fig. 54) or Vimose, they exhibit the careful workmanship needed to give a first-class grip.

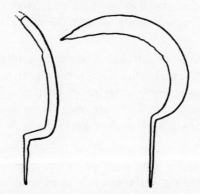

Fig. 55. Balanced iron sickles from La Tène, Switzerland.

The idea of bending the blade rearwards from the handle, to produce a balanced sickle was not apparently developed until La Tène times (Fig. 55).[21] This made possible a simpler handle and a longer blade and in time gave rise to the scythe.

---

[19] J. G. D. Clark, 1932, 67.
[20] G. Hatt, 1937, 66 and Fig. 31; A. Steensberg, 1943, 74.
[21] Steensberg, 1943, 209 f.

The deterioration of climate, which brought about a certain contraction in the zone of cultivation in Scandinavia during the Early Iron Age, made it necessary over extensive areas of north-western Europe to harvest cereal crops before they were fully ripe. In marginal territories, where the sun is insufficient to ripen grain, artificial drying is still practised: kilns were normally used for this purpose in Donegal up to a century ago and are still in the Hebrides, Faroes, Orkneys and Shetlands, and also in parts of Scandinavia.[22] During Romano-British times similar furnaces were used to dry corn as far south as Wessex and Sussex,[23] and there is evidence that these were in fact elaborations of cob-ovens found on early iron age sites like Little Woodbury and All Canning's Cross.[24]

This process of drying unripened grain is quite distinct in origin from the old Mediterranean practice of roasting or parching grain for storage or preparatory to milling, the object of which was partly to facilitate threshing and grinding and partly to impart a sweet flavour by converting some of the starch into dextrin, though in northern territories the two might in practice overlap. One of the recognized dangers of parching was the risk of burning the grain itself and there is abundant evidence that this frequently happened in temperate Europe from neolithic times onwards. It is significant that more or less complete heads of cereal are often found in deposits of carbonized grain (Pl. V, b), showing that the burning had taken place before and not after threshing. Analysis of coarsely ground barley meal from a pot excavated by Hatt from an iron age house at Solbjerg, Mors, has shown many sharply fractured particles among the coarser pieces, such as would arise when roasted grain was ground on the quern.[25] There is no evidence that any of the more elaborate methods of threshing were carried on in temperate Europe during prehistoric times: climatic conditions were not particularly favourable to the ancient Egyptian method of treading out the grain on an earthen floor; the tribulum, though apparently introduced by the Romans to temperate Europe, was at home in the Mediterranean area; and the origin of the flail, characteristic of Eurasia and of central Europe, though also found in the north-west, is still undated. It seems likely that the processes of threshing, winnowing, and on occasion of drying as well were combined, as in the graddan method practised during modern times in the Western Isles of Scotland. Extracts from Martin Martin's vivid account of this may be quoted[26]:

"A woman sitting down takes a handful of corn, holding it by the stalks in her left hand, and then sets fire to the ears, which are presently in a flame. She has a stick in her right hand, which she manages very dexterously, beating off the grain at the very instant when the husk is quite burnt. . . . The corn may be so dressed, winnowed, ground and baked within an hour after reaping from the ground. . . ."

Grinding or milling is inevitably an activity of some importance in communities based to any degree on corn growing.[27] The most primitive contrivance, the hammer or pestle and mortar, which like the reaping-knife was inherited from mesolithic sources, continued

---

[22] E. E. Evans, 1939, 217–18; A. Roussell, 1934, 11–12, 48, 60–2.

[23] *Archæologia*, LXXI, 151–8; E. C. Curwen, 1946, 102–3; R. G. Goodchild, 1943.

[24] G. Bersu, 1940, 61–2.

[25] G. Hatt, 1937, 122–4.

[26] M. Martin, 1934 edtn., 243–4.

[27] For a general summary, see E. C. Curwen, 1946, 105–10; see also Curwen, 1937A and 1941A and V. G. Childe, 1943.

in use among neolithic peoples,[27a] survived for grinding corn among Roman bakers down to the first century A.D. and could actually be photographed in use on the Isle of Foula, Shetland, in the twentieth century.[28]   As a rule, though, the prehistoric farmers used saddle-querns, in which an upper rubber was moved backwards and forwards on a lower stone, a device invented somewhere in the ancient east (Fig. 56) and diffused to Europe with other basic elements of agricultural practice.   Such querns were generally made

Fig. 56.   Method of using the saddle quern :
Egyptian (5th Dynasty) statuette.
(*After Bennett and Elton*).

from some such rock as sarsen, quartzite or tufa, but flint was sometimes used where these were not easily available.[29] The discovery of pieces of lava from the eastern slopes of the Eifel at Niedermendig in a post-hole of the Sanctuary on Overton Hill near Avebury, suggests that a quern made from this material was brought into the country with Beaker immigrants ;[30] where possible, though, querns would be made from local materials.   The milling surfaces were probably prepared by bouncing hammerstones on them from a height of about a foot.[31]   Although, to judge from tests made among the Bemba of Northern Rhodesia, it probably took about an hour a day to prepare the grain for one family by this primitive means,[32] the saddle quern remained in use down to near the end of the pre-historic period in most of Europe.   The rotary querns which replaced them were apparently derived from large donkey or slave driven revolving mills developed in the urban economy of the Græco-Roman world by way of the small portable versions used by the Roman

[27a] e.g. Pestles and mortars occurred in a Thessalian A level at Tsangli (Wace and Thompson, 1912, Fig. 70) and in a site of the Bulgarian mound culture at Rusé (Gaul, 1948, Pl. XXXVI, 2).

[28] E. C. Curwen, 1937, 134 and Pl. I.   The mesolithic Natufians of Palestine used stone pestles and mortars cut out of the living rock, but they also made portable mortars (Turville-Petre, 1932, 276) such as were used by early farmers in the Near East, e.g. at Sialk, but also in prehistoric Europe, e.g. in the Mound Culture of Bulgaria (J. H. Gaul, 1948, Pl. XXXVI, 2).

[29] J. G. D. Clark, 1935, 44.

[30] M. E. Cunnington, 1931, 332.

[31] M. E. Cunnington, 1923, 24–6.

[32] Audrey I. Richards, 1939, 103–4.

armies ; they thus provide a good example of the process of cultural devolution (Fig. 57).
Appearing first in the zone of La Tène culture during the second century B.C., they crossed
the English Channel around 100 B.C. ; among the Germans and Scandinavians on the other
hand the new principle was not applied to milling until the third century A.D.[33]

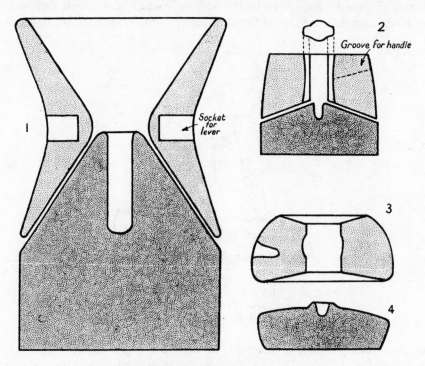

Fig. 57.   Rotary Mills.   (*After Curwen*).
No. 1.   Donkey-mill from Pompeii.
No. 2.   The Trundle hill-fort, Sussex (*c.* $\frac{1}{12}$).
Nos. 3, 4.   Glastonbury lake-village, Somerset (*c.* $\frac{1}{12}$).

Among the chief food crops other than cereals were podded plants, such as beans, lentils
and peas. The Celtic Bean (*Vicia faba* var. *celtica*) appeared in south-eastern Europe already
in neolithic contexts, as in a Dimini level at Rakhmani, Thessaly,[34] and in the Bükk cave
of Aggtelek and at Lengyel in Hungary.[35] Similar small beans have also been noted from
the Tarxien temples in Malta,[36] from Spain [37] and from a chalcolithic level at the Pinnacle,
Jersey.[38] On the other hand, they first appeared in Switzerland during the Middle Bronze
Age,[39] in Britain at a late stage of the Early Iron Age[40] and in Denmark not until the

---

[33] V. G. Childe, 1943, 19; G. Hatt, 1937, 125 f.
[34] Wace and Thompson, 1912, 53.
[35] E. Neuweiler, 1905, 85.
[36] T. Zammit, 1930, 55.
[37] E. Neuweiler, 1905, 85.
[38] E. Neuweiler, 1935, 114; J. Hawkes, 1937, 169.
[39] E. Neuweiler, 1946, 130.
[40] e.g. at Glastonbury and Meare lake-villages and at Worlebury Camp (Jessen and Helbaek, 1944,
13 and 59).

Migration Period.[41] The story is much the same with the lentil (*Lens esculenta* or *Ervum lens*)[42] and the pea (*Pisum sativum*).[43] Flax was cultivated for its oil-bearing seeds in some areas earlier than for textile fibres (see p. 233). Cameline (*Camelina linicola*), which grew as a weed with flax, and the seeds of which may yield up to 30 per cent oil, was not only utilized, but probably cultivated with flax, especially during the Iron Age in Germany[44] and Denmark, where Hatt found seeds mixed with those of flax and barley in the same pots, and where they were used as an ingredient of bread down to the nineteenth century.[45] The poppy (*Papaver somniferum*) was already domesticated for its seeds during neolithic times in Switzerland, where the cultivation is still carried on ; the find at Murciélagos shows that it was also being grown in Spain at a time when metal was coming into use.[46]

Although many of the fodder plants needed for winter-feed for livestock and of the vegetables used to vary human diet in modern times were then lacking, it is certain that prehistoric man had partially domesticated many plants which have since been relegated to a wild state, including the ruderals which accompanied his settlement and cultivation of the soil. As Brockman-Jerosch has so well argued,[47] under primitive conditions the distinction between " wild " and " domesticated " plants is often slight and a multitude of gradations in status may exist between wild, protected and fully domesticated species. As illustrated by the case of the cameline, no clear division was recognized between " weeds " and the main crop. Among other weeds associated with human settlement and used as sources of food, may be mentioned *Chenopodium album*, the seeds of which contain fat and albumen, and various species of *Polygonum*.[48]

It is likely also that an incipient form of cultivation, extending at least to protecting or improving the conditions of life of wild trees, was practised in relation to some of the fruit trees growing in the temperate forest. For example, it was early observed that the remains of apples from the Swiss lake-villages belonged to two kinds, one evidently wild, the other rather larger, though still very small,[49] a situation later paralleled from the Swedish neolithic site of Alvastra.[50] In the following table the range of diameters of the two grades of apple are shown :

	Alvastra	*Robenhausen*
Small wild apples	22/4 × 20/5 mm.	18/27 × 15/24 mm.
Larger apples	32/4 × 28/30 mm.	36 × 29/32 mm.

From this it has been argued that certain trees must have been protected or possibly even

---

41 *ibid.*, 59.

42 It occurred for instance at Aggtelek and Butmir (J. Hoops, 1905, 338), but not until the Late Bronze Age in Switzerland, e.g. at Mörigen.

43 Neolithic occurrences include finds in Greece, Bulgaria, Rumania, and Hungary. It was also present at the Swiss neolithic site of Pfyn, where is was notably smaller than from later prehistoric sites in Switzerland (E. Neuweiler, 1946, 130). Peas did not reach north Germany until the Early Iron Age or Denmark until the local Late Bronze Age (F. Netolitzky, 1931, 49–50 ; G. Hatt, 1937, 22).

44 F. Netolitzky, 1931, 56; E. Neuweiler, 1935, 112.

45 G. Hatt, 1937, 30–1 and 1938, 224–5.

46 Netolitzky, 1931, 59–61; Neuweiler, 1935, 108 f.

47 J. Brockman-Jerosch, 1917, 85 f.

48 G. Hatt, 1937, 26–7; Jessen and Helbaek, 1944, 60.

49 O. Heer, 1865, 24 f.

50 Wulff in O. Frödin, 1910, 65–70.

transplanted. The situation probably resembled that in the early medieval woodland described by Parain[51] :

" . . . wild fruits gathered in the forest were the mainstay of consumption. Not all were wild in the sense of self-grown. On the edges and even in the heart of the woods rough fruit trees bearing small fruit were planted. . . ."

On the other hand no real advance in the cultivation of fruit trees was made in temperate Europe until the Middle Ages were well advanced.

Although grape seeds have been identified in early pile-settlements in Switzerland and north Italy,[52] there is no reason to think that the vine was domesticated in temperate Europe during prehistoric times. In the east Mediterranean vineyards were certainly established by Homeric times[53] and several finds from archaeological sites—including grape pips from a pithos at Hagios Kosmos in Attica[54]—suggest that the vine was domesticated there during the Bronze Age. On the other hand, viticulture was not established in Italy and the south of France until after these areas had been drawn within the orbit of urban civilization.[55] Similarly the few olive stones from a bronze age settlement near Peschiera, north Italy,[56] and from El Garcel in Spain, may be attributed with fair certainty to the wild form (*Olea europæa* var. *Oleaster*).[57] The cultivated form (*O. eur.* var. *sativa*) originated in the east Mediterranean area and was first brought to Italy, the south of France and Iberia by colonisers from the east during the last half of the first millennium B.C.[58] To judge from numerous occurrences, including a number of fruits an inch and a half long from a pot in a Dimini level at Rahkmani, it would seem that the fig may have been cultivated in Macedonia and Thessaly already during neolithic times.[59] Here again, though, the domesticated fig was first introduced to the central and western Mediterranean as these became incorporated into the sphere of Classical or Punic civilization.

Attention has been concentrated so far on agriculture, but it is important to remember that generally speaking the prehistoric farmers of Europe were essentially mixed farmers and that stock-raising played an important, sometimes maybe a predominant part in their economic activities. The relative importance of each in the economy of prehistoric communities is difficult to determine with any exactitude: where the evidence survives one can tell fairly easily whether or not corn-growing or stock-raising was practised and often with some accuracy in what proportions the various species were raised; but there is no obvious method of comparing quantitatively the extent to which food-production was based on domesticated animals or cultivated plants. A point to be remembered is that generally speaking, agriculture is far more productive of archæological fossils than pastoral economy and that in consequence it is liable to be over-represented in the archæological record. It is reasonably certain for example that pastoralism was the dominant form of economy over

---

[51] C. Parain, 1941, 157.

[52] E. Neuweiler, 1905, 95–8.

[53] *Iliad*, XVIII, 563–6.

[54] *Am. J. Archæology*, XXXVIII (1934), 266.

[55] J. Hoops, 1905, 559 f., M. Rikli, 1946, 750.

[56] E. Neuweiler, 1905, 103.

[57] *Pace* V. G. Childe, *Dawn* (1939 edtn.), 251.

[58] M. Rikli, 1943, 52–7. See also To. Fischer, 1904.

[59] A. W. Heurtley, 1939, 79; Wace and Thompson, 1912, 53, 73 and Fig. 28b. According to M. Rikli, 1946, 727–8, the wild fig yields no edible fruit. See also E. Werth, 1932.

much of the highland zone of Britain during the Early Iron Age, but very little positive
archæological evidence can be advanced to support this view.

Sources of direct information about the livestock kept by prehistoric farmers are so
uneven that conclusions based on comparisons have to be made with circumspection. This
unevenness in the evidence is due in part to the varying extent to which animal remains
survive in different areas, in part to the restricted sampling due to the small size of most
archæological excavations and in part to defective analysis of the material obtained. Indeed,
it is only exceptionally that the remains of domesticated animals have been recovered in
sufficient quantities or studied in sufficient detail to give adequate information even about
the composition of the livestock maintained by different communities. Yet, if the evidence
is defective, it is consistent enough to sustain some discussion of the causes underlying
certain changes in the flocks and herds of prehistoric man.

The most significant change in temperate Europe was the decline of the pig and the rise
to importance of the sheep and horse, a change which, it may be argued, reflects the progress
of forest clearance in the primary area of settlement.[60] Although woefully incomplete
the evidence is at least consistent. One may begin by considering assemblages of animal
remains from the geologically homogeneous chalk downs of southern England, ranging
in date from neolithic to Romano-British times. The position is most clearly exemplified at
the Trundle, Goodwood, Sussex, since here the fauna from neolithic and iron age occupations can be compared directly. The significant fact, to which Professor D. M. S. Watson
drew attention at the time, is that in the earlier levels remains of pig outnumbered those of
sheep or goat, whereas in the later ones the proportions were reversed. Evidence from other
sites shows that this change was general. Whether one looks to " camps " like Whitehawk,
Brighton, Maiden Castle, Dorset, or Windmill Hill, near Avebury, or to sacred sites of the
character of Woodhenge, Amesbury, or the Sanctuary on Overton Hill, sheep are rare or
absent and swine second only to cattle on neolithic sites. Conversely, at early iron age sites
like All Cannings Cross, Fifield Bavant or Swallowcliffe Down, Wiltshire, or Meon Hill
and Quarley Hill, Hampshire, sheep ranked next to cattle. On Romano-British sites on
Cranborne Chase, Dorset, sheep predominated over swine and in one case exceeded cattle,
though not to anything like the extent noted at the Glastonbury lake village dating from late
in the native Iron Age[61] :

	Glastonbury	Woodyates	Rotherley	Woodcuts
Ox	5%	37%	33%	39%
Sheep	88	33	40	29
Pig	2	2	3	13
Horse	2	26	18	10
Dog	1	2	4	6
Wild	2	trace	1	3
Specimens	3,426	3,669	3,606	4,204

The scarcity of settlement material from the Bronze Age makes it very difficult to be sure
just when the change in emphasis from swine to sheep occurred in the chalk country, but
animal remains from the ditches of enclosures of South Lodge type on the Dorset and
Wiltshire Downs suggest that it was already under way by the Late Bronze Age.

---

[60] J. G. D. Clark, 1947B. References quoted in this paper will not in general be repeated here.
[61] Data from Gen. Pitt-Rivers, 1892, 233, and from Bulleid and Gray, 1911, 643.

Analysis of the remains of domestic animals from Swiss sites shows conclusively that swine were more important than sheep or goats in neolithic times, as the following table[62] illustrates:

	Port-Conthy		Wauwyl	Ossingen	Obermeilen
	Early Neo.	Middle Neo.			
Ox	50%	44%	42%	58%	40%
Pig	18	36	38	36	31
Sheep/goat	11	13	15	—	14
Dog	21	7	4	6	15
Minimum No. of individuals	151	45	78	36	52

The position was quite different in the Late Bronze Age. As long ago as 1883 Studer had contrasted the position of sheep in the economy of the neolithic and late bronze age lake-dwellers of the Bielersee, noting that, whereas at Schaffis they were subsidiary to swine and cattle, at Mörigen they were actually predominant. At Alpenquai, Zürich, the position was much the same, as shown by the following table[63] :

	Specimens	Proportion of domestic animals
Ox	1,550	32%
Pig	1,253	26
Sheep or goat	1,651	33
Horse	195	4
Dog	252	5

Sheep and goats were numerically inferior to swine also on neolithic sites in Denmark and south Sweden, though here a distinction should be drawn between material from coastal settlements and that from the settlements of communities based more completely on farming. Among the former swine outnumbered not only sheep and goat but also cattle[64] :

	Shoulder-blades from Danish kitchen-middens of neolithic age: average for Aalborg, Leire Aa and Ørum Aa middens	Remains from coastal dwelling-places of neolithic age on Gotland:		
		Visby	Hemmor	Västerb-jers
Ox	11·5%	10·9%	—	3·9%
Pig	76·3	87·3	100	91·9
Sheep and goat	12·2	1·8	—	4·2
Total specimens	137	276	4,582	1,373

[62] Data from L. Reverdin, 1922 and 1932; K. Hescheler, 1920; E. Kuhn, 1932 and 1935.
[63] K. Hescheler, 1924, 105.
[64] A. P. Madsen et al., 1900, 145–6, 158–61, 172; J. Nihlén, 1927, 192; M. Stenberger, 1943, 107.

On the other hand, cattle appear to have been the leading element, with swine as the second most important, in the livestock maintained by the farmers of Havnelev, Zealand, and of Blandebjerg, Lindø and Troldebjerg, Langeland.

Although the evidence is quantitatively meagre, the fauna from later prehistoric sites in Denmark reflects a definite growth in the importance of sheep in relation to swine, and this process appears to have begun already during the local Late Bronze Age. Such evidence as Hatt obtained from the iron age settlements of Jutland confirms this trend and it is interesting that in each case the animal remains identified by Winge from cinerary urns of the Roman Iron Age and the Migration Period were assigned to sheep.

From this survey of the remains of domestic animals from prehistoric sites in northern, north-western and central Europe, it is apparent first that cattle and swine were predominant in neolithic times and second that by the Late Bronze and Early Iron Ages sheep or goat. frequently, though not by any means always, came to play a part of increasing and sometimes of predominating importance. It would seem that one is here confronted with ecological factors which transcend the influence of individual, communal or even cultural predeliction. Since livestock depend for their existence on plant food, it can be assumed that, before the introduction of fodder crops in comparatively modern times, a particularly intimate relationship must always have existed between the composition of flocks and herds and the character of the vegetation prevailing in and around the area of settlement. This in turn must have been the product of interaction between such factors as soil and climate and the effects of human activities like forest clearance, cultivation of the soil and the grazing of livestock. It follows that livestock ought to be considered in the light of contemporary vegetation and that explanations for alterations in the proportions in which different animals were maintained should first be sought in changes in plant ecology.

One may begin by pointing out that the type of vegetation most congenial to cattle and swine under primitive conditions differs from that favoured by sheep. Just as the aurochs and the wild pig were essentially forest animals, so their domesticated forms continued down to modern times to depend to a large extent upon woodland resources, a dependence which must have been all the greater during prehistoric times when the distinction between " domesticated " and " wild " forms was much less clearly defined. The association between swine-herding and certain types of foliaceous forest has been reflected in historical records since classical times and is well known to have formed one of the principal bases of Anglo-Saxon economy. The number of swine which a given area of woodland was capable of carrying was commonly noted in pre-Conquest charters and formed one of the stock entries in Domesday. Indeed, historians have not hesitated to measure the progress of deforestation between the conquest and the survey in terms of the diminution in pannage between the two dates.[65]

Although not linked with woodland in the narrow sense that swine were in early times, oxen nevertheless benefited from the leaves and branches of foliaceous trees, notably of the elm and the lime, for winter fodder, and this applied with especial force to the period before hay-making was developed during the Early Iron Age.[66] The practice of feeding leaves and branches to cattle was well known to the ancients[67] and undoubtedly reached back into prehistoric times. Lopping-knives of a type used for gathering the leaf harvest certainly go back to the Pre-Roman Iron Age in central and north-western Europe,[68] and some

---

[65] J. H. Round, *V.C.H. Essex*, I (1903), 333; H. C. Darby, 1934, 211–15.

[66] M. Sjöbeck, 1932; A. W. Brøgger, 1940, 172; A. Steensberg, 1943, 100.

[67] A. Steensberg, 1943, 180.   [68] *ibid.*, 100.

authors interpret as such the pressure-flaked flint " saws " of lunate form dating from the
end of the Stone Age.[69] During the summer, also, in parts of Scandinavia, cattle are still
turned loose in leafy meadows, artificial and more open versions of the former forest glades.
It may be that Strabo was referring to something in the nature of the Norwegian *sætter*
when he wrote of the Britons that[70] :

> " Forests are their cities, for having enclosed an ample space with felled trees, they
> make themselves huts therein, and lodge their cattle, though not for any long con-
> tinuance."

The relationship of sheep and goats to forest was very different. Describing the wild
forebears of the domestic sheep, Lydekker wrote that, although preferring open country
to the rugged and often precipitous ground favoured by their close relative, the goat, they
are " essentially mountain-animals," which " shun forest, and feed entirely by grazing, or
by nibbling the shoots of herbaceous plants."[71] As for domesticated sheep, it is well
known that these flourish on moorland and hill-country and not least on the downlands of
southern England, on which they first became abundant towards the end of prehistoric
times. The contrast ought not to be overdrawn, since, just as cattle adapted themselves
to open pastures when these became available, so did sheep avail themselves of foliage in
a forest habitat; indeed in marginal areas both cattle and sheep even adapted themselves
to a diet of seaweed in times of dearth. Still, it remains true that, by and large, sheep would
have found a forested landscape less congenial than either oxen or pigs.

If the comparatively minor role of sheep-breeding in the earliest husbandry of much of
north-western Europe is to be associated with the general prevalence of forest at the time
of the neolithic settlement, then it is only reasonable to suggest that its later rise to importance may have been due to a reduction in the extent of woodland. That such must have
occurred as an inevitable accompaniment of the progress of agriculture hardly needs
emphasis. During the phase of shifting agriculture it is true that much clearance must
have been of a transient character, the forest regenerating as the peasant farmers moved on
to new lands, burning and felling as they went; yet, even at this stage, it is unlikely that
regeneration was everywhere complete and it is known that on some of the poorer soils,
such as those of central Jutland, stretches of heathland had come into being even at the time
of the colonisation by battle-axe people. Progressively, under pressure of increasing density
of settlement, the forest must have ceased to hold its own even on the richer soils and, within
the area of primary settlement, permanently cleared zones must have increased in size.
At the same time the system of shifting agriculture itself would gradually have broken down,
leading by the end of the Bronze Age to the establishment of settled agriculture with fixed
fields.

It is only to be expected that an intimate connection should exist between cereal-growing
and stock-raising, since each involved interference with a common ecological background.
As prehistoric agriculture grew more intensive, the forest was driven back and the area of
more or less open country increased. This in itself created conditions favourable to the
increase of sheep and less congenial to swine, although it must be remembered that throughout prehistoric times the area of primary settlement was often closely environed by untouched forest in which livestock could be fed. Even more important in some respects was

---

[69] A. Sandklef, 1934.
[70] Strabo, 4.5.2. Hamilton and Falconer transl., 1854.
[71] R. Lydekker, 1912, 27 and 43.

the general institution of a fixed agricultural régime: the fallow must have made an ideal feeding-ground for flocks of sheep, and sheep in themselves would have been invaluable for maintaining the richness of the soil. Sheep-breeding, then, fitted neatly into the pattern of settled farming and it is significant that both rose to importance over much of north-western Europe at the same time.

In support of an ecological interpretation, it may be emphasized that in the few parts of Europe where the deciduous forest was absent or relatively unimportant, as on the Orkneys or the rocky islets off Morbihan, sheep-breeding was strongly developed already during neolithic times and swine were either absent or of slight importance. Professor Watson attributed the scarcity of pig remains and the comparative abundance of sheep at Skara Brae specifically to the lack of deciduous woodland on Orkney[72] and it was doubtless for this reason that the proportion of cattle killed off before the first winter was exceptionally large even for prehistoric times. It may be added that in the case of a settlement site on Rousay and of a burial chamber near Midhowe on the same island swine were found to be quite absent and sheep or goat present. At a neolithic midden on Er Yoh off the coast of Morbihan sheep were twice as numerous even as cattle[73]:

	Number of specimens	Individuals represented
Ox	274	12 (28·5 per cent)
Pig	31	4 (9·5 per cent)
Sheep	327	26 (62·0 per cent)

The history of the horse, whether as a wild or as a domestic animal is equally illuminating. Like other elements in the late glacial fauna it was reduced to comparative insignificance by the spread of forest during the Post-glacial period[74] and it did not begin to revive—this time as a domesticated species—until forest clearance got under way. There is some evidence (see p. 302) that nomadic groups characterized by the use of battle-axes and cord-impressed pottery, who were on the move in parts of central Europe during late neolithic times, possessed tame horses, but it is certain that the domesticated horse played only a very minor role among the European peasantries during the period of shifting agriculture. Remains of horses are excessively rare among the rich fauna from neolithic stations in Switzerland and such as do occur are generally attributed to wild ones[75]; it was not until the Late Bronze Age that the tame horse made a definite appearance in Switzerland, accounting for around 4 per cent of the remains of domesticated animals at Alpenquai.[76] No remains of horse were found in the " camps " of the western neolithic people of southern Britain, nor is it at all certain that the horses represented at Peterborough were tamed. There is no doubt, though, that a small, slender breed of domestic horse reached Britain by the end of neolithic times,[77] though it was not until the Late Bronze Age that it began to be at all

---

[72] Watson in V. G. Childe, 1931, 204.

[73] *Rev. anthropologique*, XXXVI, 1926, 206–11; L. Reverdin, 1931.

[74] Horse was virtually absent from the classic Maglemosian and Ertebølle finds (Degerbøl, 1933, 383). Part of a femur has since been found in the lowest level of Kolind, Jutland (Mathiassen *et al.*, 1942, 123, 127–8), and one tooth has come down from Vinde-Helsinge, the oldest of the dwelling-places of Aamosen on Zealand (Mathiassen *et al.*, 1943, 165, 167).

[75] Hescheler, 1933, 207–8.

[76] Hescheler, 1924, 105.

[77] For a convenient summary of the evidence, see J. Wilfrid Jackson in R. E. M. Wheeler, 1943, 366–7.

significant quantitatively.[78] In Denmark, also, the domestic horse first appeared in numbers at sites like Voldtofte and Hasmark, dating from the Late Bronze Age.[79]

A considerable literature has grown up round the dog, the earliest domestic animal kept by prehistoric man.[80] Much of this is concerned with distinguishing races and with tracing these to their respective origins, but until much longer series of skeletal remains have been recovered and systematically studied it is unlikely that conclusions of more than local validity will be reached. It is generally agreed that the dog, which appeared already in mesolithic contexts in Denmark and was kept by hunter-fishers as far afield as Téviec off Morbihan,[81], Denmark[82], and Viste near Stavanger, south-west Norway,[83] was originally domesticated as a companion and watch-dog and that its use for hunting and herding, leading ultimately to the appearance of breeds specialized to these functions, came comparatively late. The earliest European dogs belonged to the small race *Canis familiaris palustris*, first identified by Rütimeyer from the Swiss lake-villages.[84] The characteristic dog of neolithic Britain has been described as a " medium-sized, powerful, rather thick-set beast agreeing in its proportions and general character more closely with a chow than with any other breed," an animal which was in fact " just dog," a primitive and unspecialized animal, from which it is conceivable that all other breeds could have been derived by selective breeding.[85] A second and heavier type, *Canis familiaris inostranzewi*, seems first to have become important in central Europe and Britain in later prehistoric times, though originally noted on a stone age site near Lake Ladoga and appearing in Denmark already in middle neolithic times at Bundsø in association with the smaller kind.[86] The most probable source of both races is the wolf, and it may well be that the process of domestication was gone through more than once. In this connection Pira's investigations of cranial fragments of wolf from the neolithic seal-hunters' cave at Stora Forva, off Gotland, are relevant, since he found clear evidence in the dentition that certain wolves had been reared in captivity.[87]

The chief races of cattle kept by the prehistoric farmers of western Europe fall into two main groups, the *Primigenius* group with large horns and the *Longifrons* group with short ones.[88] It is generally recognized that both were derived from the same parent stock, the Aurochs or Urus (*Bos primigenius*). Where, for instance, at the middle neolithic site of

---

[78] e.g. to a slight extent at Boscombe Down, Wilts. (*W.A.M.* XLVII, 659) ; Minnis Bay, Bridlington (*P.P.S.*, 1943, 41 f.) ; Handley Down and Martin Down, Dorset (Pitt-Rivers, 1898, 134–5 and 208–14). The small Celtic pony is normally present, though not in large numbers, at early iron age sites. At the Romano-British farmsteads of Woodyates, Rotherley and Woodcuts it formed a substantial element in the fauna (see table, p. 117).

[79] H. Winge, 1919.

[80] For a useful account with references, see Ebert, Vol. V, 403–10.

[81] M. and S. J. Péquart, 1937, 101.

[82] e.g. at the Maglemosian stations of Mullerup (G. F. L. Sarauw, 1903, 195–6), Holmegaard (H. C. Broholm, 1931, 30) and Svaerdborg (K. Friis Johansen, 1920, 261) and from the Ertebølle kitchen middens (H. Winge in Madsen *et al.*, 1900, 84–6).

[83] A. W. Brøgger, 1908, 12.

[84] L. Rütimeyer, 1861, 119.

[85] For the material from southern England see Jackson in Wheeler, 1943, 364–6 ; *Country Life*, 17th September, 1932 ; *W.A.M.* XLVII, 1935, 76–8.

[86] M. Degerbøl in Mathiassen, 1939, 168–95.

[87] A. Pira, 1926, 139–49.

[88] For the best recent account see M. Degerbøl in Mathiassen, 1939, 99–133.

Bundsø in Denmark, it is possible to detect a wide gap in the dimensions of the aurochs and the largest domestic race, one can be sure that the latter was introduced. On the other hand the extremely wide distribution of the wild prototype in antiquity, over Europe, north Africa and western Asia means that the problem of tracing particular races or breeds to their sources can only be tackled when much more is known about the distribution of these in time and space. The three races of *Primigenius* type commonly recognized in Europe can be distinguished among other things by the profile of the frontal bone between the horns : in *Bos taurus primigenius* this is more or less straight, in *B. t. frontosus* convex and in *B. t. trochoceros* concave. The absence of the *Frontosus* race from the rich Swiss material shows clearly enough that the appearance of domestic cattle in different parts of Europe can hardly be thought of in terms of a single spread. Further one has to reckon in the temperate forests with the effects of crossing with wild stock.

The short-horned *Bos taurus longifrons* is generally recognized to represent a more advanced stage in the domestication of the wild prototype. It appeared in Denmark and Switzerland already during neolithic times, though it does not seem to have been introduced to Britain until the Late Bronze Age. Its ultimate origin is still obscure, but it is worth noting that a similar duality of long and short-horned types of cattle existed in different parts of western Asia. Describing remains of both from Anau, Duerst wrote that " it was not in Anau alone that through unfavourable conditions of life the originally large and stately ox was changed into the short-horned form. . . . The same change took place in Mesopotamia."[89] The contrast between the prodigious oxen running wild in the German forests and the tiny ones bred in captivity, noted by Tacitus,[90] reflects the influence of domestication. The more completely the ox was tamed and deprived of its natural food, the more drastically, under primitive conditions of farming, it diminished in size.

The commonest type of domestic pig found in prehistoric Europe is that originally recognized by Rütimeyer from the Swiss lake-village (*Sus scrofa palustris*). Although at first thought to have been domesticated from the wild pig of India and the Far East (*Sus vittatus ferus*), it is commonly accepted to-day as a stunted version of the wild pig of Europe, western Asia and north Africa (*Sus scrofa ferus*), the body being smaller, the head shorter and the tusks weaker. This makes it very difficult to say where or even how often the process of taming and stunting took place. Where a clear gap exists between the skeletal structure of wild and domesticated forms, as is normally the case, one is entitled to assume that the latter were introduced in a tame state. On the other hand, since Nehring begun to publish the results of his investigations on sub-fossil swine from north Germany, it has become evident that the process of domestication was continued at any rate locally in northern Europe. In studying the pig remains from Stora Forvar on Karlsö near Gotland, for example, Pira found a continuous series morphologically between the wild pig of the region and the tame marsh-pig, intermediate stages corresponding with progressive intensification of domestication.[91] The occurrence of intermediate forms in other parts of Sweden, in north Germany and even in Switzerland[92] suggests that wild swine were tamed and incorporated into domestic livestock in different parts of temperate Europe.

---

[89] J. N. Duerst in Pumpelly, 1904, 440.

[90] Tacitus, *Annals*, IV, 72.

[91] A. Pira, 1909.

[92] Thus Dr. Uhlmann (in F. Keller, 1878, 288) noted, in addition to wild pig and domestic marsh pig, " a quantity of swine's bones intermediate in size but belonging to tamed pig."

Although, to begin with, sheep played only a restricted role in temperate Europe, they everywhere accompanied cattle and swine in the spread of farming economy. It was once thought that two distinct races, both small and frail, were concerned, namely the turbary sheep (*Ovis aries palustris*) with goat-like horns and the copper sheep (*O. a. studeri*) with stout out-turned horns, but recent research has made it evident that these were in fact the female and male respectively of the same breed.[93] The best impression of the appearance of the turbary is given by the short-tailed sheep living under almost wild conditions in Iceland, the Faroes, Shetlands, Orkneys and Outer Hebrides, particularly on the island of Soa or Soay, St. Kilda.[94] Their slightness and the character of the females' horns are also indicated by the difficulty encountered in distinguishing their remains from those of the domestic goat (*Capra hircus*). More than usual uncertainty exists about the origins of the European domestic sheep, which remained unaltered at any rate in skeletal structure down to the end of the prehistoric period. Of the four main groups of wild sheep, only two, the urial (*Ovis vignei*) of the Elburz—Tibet region and the mouflon, are in question and expert opinion has recently tended to favour the latter.[95] At the present day the European race (*Ovis musimon*) is confined to Sardinia, Corsica and Sicily, but it was once more widespread and there is a suggestion that it was present in the Alps during later prehistoric times.[96] As an alternative preference is often given to the red mouflon of Cyprus, Asia Minor and Persia (*Ovis orientalis*). In any case the sheep was certainly introduced to many parts of temperate Europe, for instance southern Britain and Denmark, in its domestic form, since no possible wild prototypes existed there.

Less is known about the conditions under which pastoral activities were carried on than about the character of the livestock. It has already been pointed out, though, that in temperate Europe livestock found much of their nourishment in the forest in the form of foliage, branches, bark, shoots and mast. For a large part of the year domesticated animals obtained their own food under much the same conditions as wild ones. The difficult period was during the winter and, before the introduction of cultivated fodder crops in comparatively modern times, the gathering of forage for the winter imposed a severe burden.[97] In describing the methods used among Swedish peasants, in some parts of the country down to the present day, Axel Olsson[98] has given an insight into activities which stretch far back into the prehistoric period. The impression one receives is that of a succession of harvests of natural vegetation, among which in some regions and among certain societies the corn harvest was relatively inconspicuous, a point which has continually to be borne in mind when attempting to infer economic activities from finds of sickle blades. Bark would be stripped in the spring and dried for winter use, being fed to cattle either as it was, ground to powder or boiled in water. Foliage was as a rule gathered immediately after the hay-harvest and stacked in the form of complete twigs and branches. There is no doubt that originally these forest crops were the main ones and the gathering of these, together with constant browsing, particularly of seedlings, was an important factor in reducing the area of forest. It has been estimated by Sjöbeck[99] that the average prehistoric cow, weighing no more than 150 kilograms or so,

---

[93] M. Hilzheimer, 1936; Degerbøl in Mathiassen, 1939, 143–66.

[94] R. Lydekker, 1912, 59.

[95] R. Lydekker, 1912, 55; Hilzheimer, 1936, 205.

[96] J. W. Amschler, 1949, 42 and 64.

[97] C. Orwin, 1938, 52–6.

[98] M. Olsson, 1938.

[99] M. Sjöbeck, 1933, 289.

would have needed approximately 1,000 leaf sheaves, each of 1 kilogram, during the winter. The harvesting of hay on an extensive scale, symbolized by the appearance of the balanced iron sickle and, during the Roman Iron Age, of the scythe,[100] dates from the closing stages of the prehistoric period and is itself a telling reflection of the retreat of forests and the enlargement of bogs and grasslands under the influence of clearance for agriculture, of grazing by livestock and of climatic deterioration.

Despite the efforts of the early farmers, it was barely possible to get sufficient livestock through the winter. In medieval Denmark, for instance, cattle were so emaciated by the spring that it was common to carry them from the byre and in the Western Isles of Scotland at the close of the seventeenth century the cows were " mere skeletons in the spring, many of them not being able to rise from the ground without help,"[101] and this in a region where seaweed, not to mention fish, afforded a valuable additional source of fodder. Even this bare minimum was only achieved by killing off a substantial part of the stock before winter set in. Analysis of remains of cattle from Skara Brae[102] showed that nearly three-fifths were slaughtered at less than six months and that less than a fifth reached maturity ; and it is significant that the remainder were killed off either between twelve and eighteen or between thirty and thirty-six months, suggesting seasonal killings. The indications are that they were pole-axed in the middle of the forehead. On balance forage was easier to come by in Switzerland, the forest more than compensating for seaweed, and at the neolithic sites of Ossingen and Storren rather more than two-fifths of the cattle were killed at three years or more. Since cows and ewes provided milk as well as meat, and the latter gave wool as well, every effort was made to bring as large a proportion as possible through the winter, and in Switzerland this met with greater success in later prehistoric and Roman times. On the other hand around three-quarters of the pigs from the Swiss sites of these latter periods analysed by Kuhn were killed off between one and two years and only those needed for breeding were allowed to grow to full maturity.

	Under 1 year	Intermediate	Adult
Cattle	8·3%	34·7%	57%
Sheep	8	43	49
Swine	18	69	13

Table illustrating the average age at which livestock was slaughtered at Utoquai (LBA), Engelhalbinsel and Alpnach (Roman IA) Switzerland.[103]

There is no evidence that cattle were stalled as a general rule during the phase of shifting agriculture. It is true that beds of excrement of " cows, pigs, sheep or goats, together with the remains of the litter they had used . . ." were observed " between the huts " at Robenhausen, [104] but one can hardly generalize from sites of a special and still largely unknown character, and the fact remains that the first certain traces of stables date from the Early Iron Age. The introduction of the traction plough and of fixed fields—and the consequent need to shelter the plough-ox and to obtain manure—and above all the deterioration of climate during Sub-atlantic times combined to make the stalling of cattle general at least during the winter months (see p. 159). Presumably also the folding of sheep as a method of

---

[100] A. W. Brøgger, 1940, 172; A. Steensberg, 1943, 194.

[101] M. Martin, 1934 edtn., 207.

[102] Watson in V. G. Childe, 1931, 200–1.

[103] Based on E. Kuhn, 1932.

[104] F. Keller, 1878, 50–1.

enriching the land, followed the introduction of fixed fields and for this purpose hurdles were available already from the Late Bronze Age,[105] if not before. So far as the general management of livestock is concerned, it may be noted that there is evidence for the castration of cattle and sheep already during neolithic times from Skara Brae and Bundsø respectively,[106] and that cattle were polled by the Early Iron Age.[107]

Domestic livestock yielded a substantial proportion of the organic substances needed for industrial crafts, notably hides, hair, wool, horn and bone, and in addition their dung was useful for fuel, where timber was short, as well as for manure. Their main value though was, of course, for food. As a corollary of seasonal killing it is probable that, as in Norway a hundred years ago, very little meat was eaten during the summer while the beasts were fattening, and conversely that steps were taken to preserve meat from the main killing for winter use. To judge from the practice of primitive communities, meat and fish were preserved by burying in pits or by drying in the wind, before salt was sufficiently cheap to use for this purpose. The earliest salted meat recorded from temperate Europe is the pork made by the Gauls and praised by Strabo.[108]

Classical writers agree that milk played an important part in the diet of the iron age Britons, Gauls and Germans and it is reasonably certain that ewes as well as cows were milked. Although Strabo[109] averred of the Britons that some of them, though possessing plenty of milk, had not skill enough to make cheese, Caesar[110] wrote of the Germans that milk, cheese and meat formed the main part of their diet. It has been suggested that certain colander-like pots dating from the Late Bronze and Early Iron Ages were used to drain off the whey in cheese-making, but it is just as possible that in many cases they were used for straining honey.[111] The early history of seasonal transhumance of the type which still survives, though on a much reduced scale in parts of Scandinavia, in the Alps and in Spain, and which until recently prevailed in the highland zone of Britain,[112] is one of those numerous fields of economic prehistory on which little systematic work has yet been done. Under the system of maintaining livestock which prevailed in early times dairying activities must have been concentrated during the season when forage was plentiful, and so soon as settled agriculture became established it might be expected that cattle and sheep would be grazed away from the immediate area of the settlement. Where it was necessary to move considerable distances away from permanent farms beyond the forest margin, up in the mountains or on the bogs and moors which developed increasingly in north-western Europe during Sub-atlantic times, shielings or booleys would have to be set up for those tending the flocks and herds and carrying on the dairying.

---

[105] e.g. Minnis Bay, Kent (*P.P.S.*, 1943, Pl. IX).

[106] Watson in Childe, 1931, 198–200 and Degerbøl in Mathiassen, 1939, 147.

[107] M.E. Cunnington, 1923, 44 and 46.

[108] Strabo, 4.3.2.

[109] Strabo, 4.5.2.

[110] Caesar, *de bello Gallico*, VI, 22, Strabo, 4.4.3, emphasized the importance of milk in the diet of the Gauls.

[111] Such occurred at late bronze age settlements at Buch, near Berlin (A. Kiekebusch, 1923, 86, Taf. XIV b) ; Abbetred, near Lejre Vig, Denmark (G. Hatt, 1937, 52, Fig. 18) ; and Lac de Bourget (F. Keller, 1866, Pl. LVII, 2). Pots with perforated bases have been noted at English early iron age sites, as for instance, All Cannings Cross (M. E. Cunnington, 1923, 32–3) and Glastonbury, those from the latter site having been interpreted as honey-strainers (Bulleid and Gray, 1911, 517).

[112] e.g. E. C. Curwen, 1938, 273; E. E. Evans, 1942, 50–55.

It would be wrong to conclude these chapters on subsistence without a word each on salt and sugar. People who live largely on an animal diet obtain the salt they need in their meat. On the other hand the appetite for free salt grew with every increase in the part played by plant food,[113] and it is notable that in prehistoric Europe ostensible indications of salt-working first appear with the establishment of settled agriculture. Salt was obtained either by mining rock-salt or by evaporating salt from brine-springs or from the sea. The salt-mines of the eastern Alps, at Salzburg, Hallstatt, and at Dürrnberg, Hallein, were worked on a scale far transcending local needs, the shuttered galleries reaching on occasion as far as 350 metres into the mountain.[114] The tools discarded in the mines, notably the handles of winged axes and the socketed bronze picks, show that they were operated during the Late Bronze Age. The rich cemetery at Hallstatt dates from the full Early Iron Age and it is con-sidered by some authorities that the mining of rock-salt had already been given up by that time in favour of brine-springs.[115]

The extraction of salt from brine-springs was in fact carried on during the Early Iron Age on the Dammwiese within an hour's journey of Hallstatt itself[116] and the activity was one which flourished in suitable localities over the whole territory of the Hallstatt culture.[117] Where rocks of sufficient toughness were available, as appears to have been the case in the Dammwiese itself and at different points in north-eastern Württemburg,[118] it was only necessary to heat these and pour on the brine. Elsewhere, though, artificial structures built up from fired clay bars and pedestals, were erected over fires and the brine allowed to trickle down from clay troughs. Notable traces of this activity, in the form of burning and accumulations of briquetage, have been found in the valley of the Saale in central Germany, particularly in the neighbourhoods of Halle and Magdeburg,[119] and in that of the Seille in Lorraine east-north-east of Nancy at Vic and Bourthecourt.[120] There are many references to salt springs among classical authors and it was presumably to this method of mining salt that Pliny referred when he spoke of the practice among Gauls, Germans and Iberians of pouring salt water over burning firewood.[121]

At the present day salt is evaporated from sea water by the direct power of the sun on the Atlantic and Mediterranean coasts of France, as well as on those of Iberia and Italy, and it is likely that this has been carried on from remote times. Further north, where the sum-mer was shorter and some rainfall usual, the process had to be carried to a conclusion by the use of artificial heat. The most extensive traces take the form of great volumes of reddish burnt soil and quantities of briquetage like that associated with the brine springs. The red-hills, as they are sometimes called, are associated with the Hallstatt-inspired Iron Age A culture of south-east England : good examples are known from the estuaries of the Essex coast between Clacton and the Thames,[122] on the fenland margin of north-west Norfolk[123]

---

[113] I. Manninen, 1932, 307–8; T. A. Rickard, 1932, 74–5.

[114] J. Andree, 1922, 57 ff. Also G. Kyrle, 1916, 50–70 and H. W. Sanders, 1910, 120–1.

[115] Kyrle, 1916, 70; Andree, 1922, 63; L. Franz, 1929, 73 ff.

[116] Andree, 1922, 61.

[117] R. A. Smith, 1918.

[118] A. Schliz, 1903, 646 ff.

[119] ibid.; also W. A. von Brunn, 1939.

[120] Déchelette, III (1927 edtn.), 202–4.

[121] Pliny, XXXI, 82–3; cf. Tacitus, Annals, XIII, 57.

[122] F. W. Reader, 1908 and 1910.

[123] e.g. at Runcton Holme (P.P.S.E.A. VII (1933), 258–60).

and on the Lincolnshire coast between Ingoldmells and Chapel St. Leonards.[124] Similar salt-workings of early iron age date flourished on the coast of Belgium, notably at La Panne, and there are some indications from the west coast of Brittany.[125] Where salt could be evaporated from the sea, it must have been comparatively cheap and it was on such workings that the early salted fish industries of western Iberia[126] and the Dnieper estuary[127] and the pork industry of Gaul[128] were based.

The consumption of sugar on a great scale is quite a recent phenomenon, but, though it is true that down to modern times peasant diet was predominantly sour, the taste for sweetness is a primitive one.[129] The most obvious source was honey and there is evidence already from upper palæolithic times that early man went to a good deal of trouble to collect the honey of wild bees (see p. 33). Tomb-paintings show that apiculture was carried on intensively among the Egyptians of the dynastic period, who not only ate honey and mixed it with their wine, but also used the wax for sealing the nose, eyes and mouth of mummies and also for modelling the mask of the departed. When and to what extent a knowledge of bee-keeping spread into prehistoric Europe is unknown. It has been established that honey was added to the cranberry wine deposited in a birch-bark pail in the bronze age oak-coffin buried in the Danish Guldhøj, but this could easily have been of wild origin. The abundance of wax suggested by the prevalence of the *cire perdue* method of bronze-casting reflects the importance of bees, but does not of itself allow us to infer domestication. Yet it may be that in prehistoric Europe the relations between men and bees were as various as they remained among the Finno-Ougrians of the Volga-Kama region down to modern times[130] and that in Mediterranean and possibly in temperate Europe a quasi-domestication was practised already during the Bronze Age.

[124] *Ant. J.* XII, 239 and 254; *Arch. J.* XCI, 97–8.
[125] *P.S.A.* 2nd ser. XXII, 207–14.
[126] Strabo, 3.2.6.
[127] Herodotus, IV, 53.
[128] Strabo, 4.3.2.
[129] For a general account with references, see J. G. D. Clark, 1942.
[130] I. Manninen, 1932, 215–17 and 243–4.

CHAPTER VI

HOUSES AND SETTLEMENTS

SHELTER from the elements is one of the basic economic needs of man. No doubt this could most easily be met in some areas by taking refuge in natural caves or rock-shelters. Yet it would be quite wrong to regard cave-dwelling as marking in any sense a universal stage in the history of human settlement. Geological formations, notably limestones, in which caves naturally occur are of restricted occurrence. Again, though no evidence for this survives from the remotest periods of prehistory, it can be assumed in view of the elaborate structures built by quite lowly animals that the most primitive men were capable of building artificial structures for themselves. On the other hand, under certain conditions caves and rock-shelters have remained in use even in Europe down to modern times.

By no means all caves were occupied by early man—many for instance in the Alpine region were left to the cave bear[1]—but a large proportion of the more suitable ones were inhabited, often at several periods. Caves must have been particularly welcome with the onset of the last glaciation, especially during the winter months, but they continued to be used freely by the food-gathering groups of post-glacial times. Many of the caves occupied by the Late Magdalenians in northern Spain and south-western France were used by the Azilians and many of those of central France, south Germany, Belgium and Britain were occupied by Tardenoisians. Beyond the northern limit of upper palæolithic settlement, also, mesolithic or epi-mesolithic groups were accustomed to occupy caves and shelters at least seasonally, as among the Obanians of western Scotland[2] or the hunter-fishers of Viste near Stavanger.[3]

Over extensive parts of Europe caves were occupied by groups whose economy was based to a greater or less degree on farming. They were admirably adapted for temporary shelter away from permanent settlements, such as would be needed during seasonal activities like fishing and sealing carried on at intervals in the farmers' year. Examples which immediately suggest themselves from neolithic times include Ruskenesset and Skipshelleren near Bergen[4] and Stora Förvar on Stora Karlsö off Gotland.[5] As late as the close of the seventeenth century, Martin Martin wrote[6] of the isle of Raasay in the Western Isles that " there is an abundance of caves on the west side, which serve to lodge several families, who for their convenience in grazing, fishing, etc., resort thither in the summer." Caves also served for general occupation. Sometimes, as with the Iberian cave-dwellers, the people

---

[1] S. Brodar, 1930.

[2] e.g. the Oban caves, see H. J. Movius, 1942, 181.

[3] A. W. Brøgger, 1908.

[4] Brinkmann and Shetelig, 1920; J. Bøe, 1934.

[5] H. Rydh, 1931; Schnittger and Rydh, 1940.

[6] M. Martin, 1934 edtn., 214.

concerned, though formally neolithic, seem to have subsisted mainly by hunting.[7] On the other hand, there is no reason for thinking that the Cortaillod people who lived in caves in the south of France, particularly in the department of Gard,[8] were any less addicted to husbandry than those who in Switzerland settled the margins of lakes. At Arene Candide in Liguria the neolithic occupants at successive stages of the later occupation of the cave belonged to three distinct traditions.[9] Again, the caves of the Bükk mountains of northern Hungary sheltered neolithic communities whose material culture and mode of subsistence compared quite favourably with those of other Danubian groups of the same period. The Bükkien people occupied open settlements as well as caves and there is no suggestion of any difference in the economic level represented at the two classes of site. Indeed, the Aggtelek cave provided one of the classic assemblages of evidence relating to neolithic farming: the Bükkien cave-dwellers not only maintained the usual domestic livestock, but also harvested three kinds of wheat, as well as millet, beans, lentils and peas.[10]

During the period of settled farming caves were chiefly important as refuges during the periods of stress occasioned by ethnic movements : thus the famous late bronze age hoard from Heathery Burn Cave, Co. Durham, is thought to represent the worldly wealth of refugees fleeing from the La Tène invaders,[11] and the considerable occupation of the Mendip caves by Celtic people of the Glastonbury culture may very well reflect the Belgic invasion of the south-west towards the close of the prehistoric period.[12] Caves were often situated in remote districts, they were there for the taking and sometimes they were easily defensible.[13] It has been said of Britain that the troglodyte population reached its peak during the Romano-British period.[14] In France, Spain and the Alpine area, in particular, cave-dwellings survived down to modern times and locally still continue in use, if not for human occupation, at least for stables.[15] Generally the fronts of inhabited caves are closed by dry-stone or other walling in which a door and windows could be set and it is not unlikely that even in upper palæolithic times some kind of screen, probably of skins, was set up before rock-shelters or cave-mouths. It should not be forgotten also that among more advanced peoples, where the rock was sufficiently soft, artificial cave-dwellings might be excavated from the living rock and down to modern times over three thousand inhabitants of a suburb of the little town of Gaudix in Spain occupied dwellings cut out of a Pliocene conglomerate.[16] On the other hand, as Oelmann has stressed,[17] such artificial caves contributed nothing essential to the history of the house, since they reproduced within the limits imposed by the material the plans of structures built above ground.

In the case of artificial dwellings one is confronted with a wide range of variation and it is worth considering how far these were due to purely geographical factors. Local topography exerted an obvious influence on the choice of a particular site for habitation, notably

---

[7] V. G. Childe, 1947, 262.   [8] For a useful map, see V. von Gonzenbach, 1949, 3.

[9] L. B. Brea, 1946.   [10] V. G. Childe, 1929, 62.

[11] F. Elgee, 1930, 172–3 and 192.   [12] Kendrick and Hawkes, 1932, 180.

[13] M. Martin (1934 edtn., 205) tells how a certain cave on the east side of Portree, Skye, though capable of holding eighty people and provided with a well, had so narrow an entrance that it could be held by a single man with a staff.

[14] F. Haverfield in *V.C.H. Derbyshire*, I, 201 and 233–42; J. G. D. Clark, 1940, 28.

[15] J. Brunhes, 1925, 107–8; L. Rütimeyer, 1924, 315–16 and Fig. 157.

[16] J. Brunhes, 1925, Figs. 22–4.

[17] F. Oelmann, 1927, 11–12.

through surface relief, sub-soil and water-supply. Climate, including the amount and character of sunshine and precipitation and also the direction and intensity of prevailing winds, must be considered in relation to the design of the roof, the build of the walls and the disposition of the entrance. Most important of all were the raw materials available for building, since for the purposes of daily life—though not of course where structures of magical or religious function were concerned—the materials used in prehistoric Europe would be those immediately at hand, and the use of such would impose certain structural limitations.

Yet, all along, one has to take account of the factor of culturally and socially determined choice. Geographical factors may influence the location of a house or settlement, but the choice is determined ultimately by the economic and social needs of human communities and by cultural traditions which may have arisen in quite different geographical milieus. Again, if, for example, heavy rainfall necessitates some form of pitched roof, such may be achieved by a variety of means. The cultural factor is even more important in relation to the use of raw materials. Thus, the same mud might be used unprocessed, either alone or as a rendering to a wall made from organic materials: if the climate allowed it might be dried in the sun, but, only if the economy was more advanced than that which prevailed in prehistoric Europe, would it be made into kiln-dried bricks or tiles. Stone could be employed undressed or shaped in a great variety of ways, with or without any kind of mortar, and its influence on the form and character of structures would vary accordingly. With organic materials there is an even wider range from which selection might be made and an even greater diversity in use; in certain instances, as with cereal straw, the very possibility of using them depends upon the attainment of a certain form of economy. The range of animal materials used—bones for roofs and frames, skins for coverings, guts for windows, dung for plaster and so on—will depend in part on natural ecology, but also on the degree to which hunting and stock-raising are carried on. As a working rule it seems to be true, as Oelmann stated,[18] that where within any single geographical zone one can trace any progressive change in the raw materials utilized for building, it will commonly be found that inorganic are substituted for organic substances and that this process begins with the foundations and works up to the roof. In temperate Europe and more particularly on its Atlantic fringes ecological changes, brought about by forest clearance and by the effects by climatic deterioration during the Sub-atlantic period, favoured the replacement of timber by earth and stone. On the other hand, as Oelmann has emphasized, the adoption of more permanent building materials, in a region where organic substances are equally abundant, is commonly only an aspect of general progress in material civilization.

Concern with narrowly economic and geographical factors should not be allowed, though, to obscure the importance of quite different ones. The house after all exists to provide shelter for a family and its plan and build must to some extent be determined by the structure of the family. In the same way the manner in which houses are aggregated in settlements, or alternatively occupied as isolated units, must be connected with the larger organization of social communities. More than this, the character of early settlements and their sites is more or less strongly influenced by the nature of relationships existing between different communities: above all there are questions of security and these involve not merely general political considerations, but also the actual methods of warfare in use among neighbouring peoples. Although these and other social forces will not be considered in detail, it is in practice neither desirable nor even practicable to disassociate them from

18 *ibid.*, 8.

specifically economic ones. There is thus an obvious connection between the organization of the family group and the basic mode of subsistence. Again, the competition between communities which engenders the need for defence is commonly economic in its basis. One may here recall (see p. 97) the contrast between the relatively peaceful conditions which prevailed during the opening stages of the neolithic colonization of temperate Europe, when almost limitless and often unoccupied tracts of loess and other easily worked soils opened up before the pioneer peasants, and the period of storm and stress which marked the beginning of the breakdown of the initial phase of extensive farming. Again, as a general proposition it seems to be true that competition between groups became more intense with each increase in the density of population and with every advance in social cohesion, material well-being and the means of waging war. Thus it is hardly surprising that as a general rule considerations of defence came to play a progressively greater part in determining the location and planning of settlements.

It needs to be stressed that information about the houses and even more about the settlements of prehistoric Europe is still scanty and unevenly spread. This is partly because it is only comparatively recently that their importance as sources of information about economic and social conditions in the remote past has been widely recognized, or indeed that prehistorians have regarded these conditions as a proper subject for investigation. It is true that caves and lake-villages have been investigated with ardour, after a manner, over a long period, but it is only during the last twenty or thirty years that really purposive efforts have been made to locate and investigate other types of houses and settlements. It is only fair to add, though, that the difficulties inherent in this research are formidable. To begin with, outside the limited areas of Europe—mainly in the south-east—where tells or settlement mounds exist, houses are a great deal more difficult to find than graves, except in areas where stone was used for building. Thus in Britain it is only in the highland zone, where the older rocks provide plentiful building material of a kind liable to survive, that any considerable body of information about prehistoric houses exists. Where, as in lowland Britain and over much of the temperate zone of Europe, houses were built largely of timber and other perishable materials, they are not only harder to find but much more difficult to excavate: here indeed the amount of information available depends very largely on the standard of archæological technique prevailing in each particular region. Even where something is known of single houses, it is only rarely that whole settlements have been excavated and information obtained about the size and social organization of prehistoric communities, other than what can be learnt from burials. Lastly, it has to be recognized how extremely difficult it often is to reconstruct buildings from their ground plans. The roof can commonly be " restored " in several different ways from the same arrangement of post-holes, and it has conversely to be remembered that quite elaborate houses can be constructed without driving a single post into the sub-soil. So far as walls are concerned, there is the difficulty of establishing their character and former height, since these were commonly made from materials like earth, turf and wattle, which soon disintegrate. In the existing state of knowledge it would therefore be most misleading to attempt to systematize what are evidently little more than random fragments of the evidence. The results obtained during recent years, though, warrant great hopes from further research in the field.

The earliest artificial dwellings, of which traces have so far been recovered, are those of south Russia. Here caves are restricted to the Crimea and the Caucasus, and the upper palæolithic mammoth hunters had to make houses for themselves. As a rule the dwellings were situated on the banks of a great river. Some were tent-like structures, but others were

were true earth houses. The dwelling at Gagarino[19] on a terrace of the Don a few miles below Lipsetsk was irregularly oval in plan ($4\frac{1}{2} \times 5\frac{1}{2}$ m.) and the floor was sunk only $\frac{1}{2}$ m. below ground level. Mammoth tusks and limestone slabs were disposed round the edge and it may be suggested that these served to weight down a tent-like covering made from animal skins. What has been interpreted by Ephimenko as a substantially larger dwelling 15 m. long and likewise belonging to the first phase of the upper palæolithic culture of the region, has been found at Kostenki[20] some 35 km. south of Voronesh on the same river. Post-holes are claimed to have been set into the semi-subterranean floor, presumably to support the roof. To judge from the ash in the hearths, mammoth bones had been used as fuel. Of quite different type is the settlement comprising at least six dwellings of elongated rectangular form $11\frac{1}{2}$ to 12 m. long and 3 to $3\frac{1}{2}$ m. wide, at Timonovka[21] on the river Desna, some 4 km. below Briansk. The floors were much lower than those at Gagarino and Kostenki, being sunk as much as from $2\frac{1}{2}$ to 3 m. below ground level. Some of the dwellings were entered from the narrow end, others from the middle of the long side. In one example there were traces of a conical chimney made of bark covered with clay to carry off smoke from the fire ; in others hearths were found near the entrance. The roofs were evidently made by logs laid across the excavation and covered by spoil and by kitchen refuse. The dwelling was evidently lighted by lamps cut from soft stone. Associated with the dwelling were four basin-shaped pits, which may have served for storage.

In general the Timonovka dwellings resemble winter houses in the contemporary circumpolar region like those of the Kamchadals of north-east Siberia,[22] strung out along river banks, of oblong rectangular plan, ranging up to 30 feet in length, and having the floor sunk about 3 feet below ground level with timber walls and the roof heaped over by spoil.

The Gagarino type on the other hand recalls more the summer tents of certain north Canadian Eskimo made from the skins of caribou or seals stretched over a few poles and weighted round the edge by a ring of stones. When such tents are moved the stones are left behind to form the stone rings so familiar to travellers in the far north.[22a]

Closely similar stone rings, sometimes with annexes giving a pear-shaped plan, have been found by Rust[23] in Schleswig-Holstein, dating from the late glacial period and associated with flint industries of Hamburgian character. There can be no doubt that these belong to tents of reindeer skin, in which the hunters lived during their summer migrations in the periglacial zone. Such tents are entirely what one might expect of migratory reindeer-hunters in a treeless landscape.

No traces of artificial dwellings have been found from the upper palæolithic period in south-western Europe, where caves and rock-shelters were frequently available. It is possible that traces of huts or tents, particularly those used during the summer, await discovery. Meanwhile, certain tectiform designs of Magdalenian age, painted on the walls of Font-de-Gaume in the Dordogne, have been accepted by Breuil and others as representations of artificial dwellings like the summer houses of the Navaho Indians of north-east

[19] S. Zamiatnine, 1934.

[20] E. A. Golomshtok, 1938, 308–24.

[21] *ibid.*, 395–401.

[22] W. Jochelson, 1928A, Chap. IX.

[22a] e.g. T. Mathiassen, *Material Culture of the Iglulik Eskimos*, 131f. Copenhagen, 1928.

[23] At Ahrensburg-Bornwisch, see *Hammaburg*, I, 33–38.

Arizona.[24] It is only fair to add, though, that the same designs have been interpreted by others as fall-traps.

From mesolithic Europe there are abundant traces of huts, but few completely satisfactory plans. Part of the plan of an irregularly oval hut, brought to light on a low terrace of the Lopau river at Bockum, kr. Lüneburg, Hanover, seems to have been made from branches set in the sub-soil and pulled together at the top ; in this case it could be seen that the wall was doubled on the eastern side.[25]

Where the floor of the hut was scooped out of the sub-soil there is a greater chance of its being found during casual excavation in sand—and gravel—pits, and in fact several examples have been noted in Britain, Belgium and western and southern Germany.[26] In many of the older discoveries, like those at Glen Wyllan in the Isle of Man and in the Colne Valley of Essex, or at Sougné and Roche-aux-Faucons in Belgium, little is known beyond the association of flints of mesolithic type, and often of hearth material, with depressions in the sub-soil, which all too often have been assumed to be saucer-shaped on the evidence of an occasional section. Where the top-soil has been removed and the plan revealed, the depressions have generally been found to be irregular in form, like those at Farnham, Surrey,[27] at Königsforst, Cologne,[28] and at Tannstock on an old shore of the Federsee, Württemburg.[29] In no case has convincing evidence been found of the superstructure, though at Farnham one of the depressions was provided with a single post-hole at the entrance, and there appears to have been at least one definite post-hole among the otherwise doubtful patches round one of the Königsforst examples. It has frequently been found that such hut-emplacements occur in groupings—no less than thirty-eight were observed at Tannstock—but it can hardly be assumed that all were occupied at once, in view of the custom of returning on more than one season to the same camping-place.

From the remotest times the margins of lakes have attracted human settlement and it is hardly to be wondered at that Hamburgian and Ahrensburgian hunting-bands should have chosen to camp during the summer by the lakes and ponds formed by the melting of subterranean ice in the glacial tunnel valleys of Schleswig-Holstein.[30] With these reindeer hunters, though, there was no question of actually settling or camping on a bog; they occupied the margins of the tunnel-valleys and it was merely their refuse which accumulated in the lake basins. It was not until post-glacial times that extensive bogs were formed around the margins of lakes, themselves vestiges of the old ice-sheets, and that one meets for the first time with structures specifically adapted to camping on these. Recent excavations at Star Carr, Seamer, have shown that the early Maglemosian elk and deer hunters of eastern Yorkshire laid down a rough flooring of birch brushwood directly on the reed swamp bordering a lake, so as to be able to camp in relative comfort.[31] Again, at Duvensee, near Lübeck, Maglemosian hunters occupied a low knoll in the bog and on this they spread successive floors of birch bark, each marking presumably a summer's occupation[32] ; patches of sand were laid over these so that fires could be lit in safety, but neither here nor at

---

[24] H. Breuil, 1910, 226–246.

[25] H. Piesker, 1937.

[26] ibid., 105.

[27] ibid., 66–70. To this may be added the recently discovered site at Abinger Common, Surrey.

[28] W. Lung, 1942.

[29] H. Reinerth, 1929, 50–7.

[30] A. Rust, 1934 and 1937.

[31] J. G. D. Clark, 1949.

[32] G. Schwantes, 1928.

Seamer have traces yet been found of any shelter. Investigations, as yet unpublished, in the great bog of Aamosen on Sjaelland, however, have brought to light traces of a type of hut square in plan, but with rounded corners, having a floor made from sheets of birch and pine bark, round which slender uprights were set in the sub-soil and presumably pulled together to form a roof.[33]

Such floors and huts relate to seasonal camps rather than to permanent habitations, yet it is permissible to see in them an early stage of that adaptation to bogs, which later gave rise to permanent settlements on platforms like that near Alvastra, in Östergötland, Sweden,[34] contemporary with the middle neolithic period in Denmark, to the pile and moor settlements of the Alpine area, and to the iron age crannogs of the British Isles. On the other hand, it must be admitted that the artificial dwellings of the hunter-fisher peoples are unimpressive and consist at most of nothing more than clusters of huts or tents. By contrast the houses and settlements of communities of farmers were already during the stone age not so different from those of European peasants down to modern times (Pl. VI, a).

In the Mediterranean, as also in the temperate zone of Europe, houses of oblong and more or less rectangular form have predominated since the first beginnings of farming. The round house or hut, though present, seems to have played an essentially subsidiary role in this area. The only evidence for round buildings, other than tombs, in early Crete comprises votive " hut-urns " from Knossos and Phaistos, dating from the end of the Minoan period (LM IIIb) and representing small circular structures with low conical roof, probably thatched.[35] Although these have been interpreted as dwellings,[36] it seems more likely from the character of the door fastening, which could be closed only from the outside, that they were really used for storage, just as Oelmann has shown[37] to have been the case with the prototypes of analogous " hut-urns " from north Germany. Although Pendlebury[38] has argued that the plan of the oval house of Middle Minoan I age from Khamazi (Fig. 58, a) was " fortuitous and determined by the lie of the land," one can hardly avoid seeing in it some influence from a tradition of building in round houses. Childe has noted the general agreement in function with the courtyard houses of Britain.[39] On the Greek mainland the great majority of the prehistoric houses were oblong : among the few exceptions may be noted a round hut with pottery from the earliest neolithic period of Thessaly, near the main settlement at Sesklo,[40] and a number, ranging in diameter from 2.1 to 6 metres, from the earliest occupation at Orchomenos.[41] It may well be that in accordance with Oelmann's thesis, the apsidal and double-apsidal houses from early and middle Helladic contexts in Thessaly—the former at Rakhmani II/IV and Orchomenos II and the latter at Rini (Fig. 58, b)[42]—reflect the influence of rectangular on round houses and it is suggestive that this fusion did not occur until the Bronze Age.

---

[33] Information obtained in the field and from Dr. Mathiassen.

[34] O. Frödin, 1910.

[35] Evans, *Palace*, II, 129–30, Figs. 63 and 65.

[36] e.g. by Childe, 1947, 24.

[37] F. Oelmann, 1929.

[38] Pendlebury, 1939, 100; Evans, *Palace*, I, Fig. 108.

[39] Childe, 1947, 22–3.

[40] Wace and Thompson, 1912, 74.

[41] *ibid.*, 195.

[42] *ibid.*, Fig. 17; p. 195; Fig. 80.

Further west the neolithic peasants of the Foggia plain in Apulia dug circular or pen-nanular ditches within larger enclosures, but no evidence has yet been found of their actual houses.[43] Neolithic round houses have been claimed, though not yet adequately documented, for Iberia.[44] On the other hand, numerous round huts with thick walls faced with stones are known from Languedoc. One may cite the rich find at Fontbuisse in the

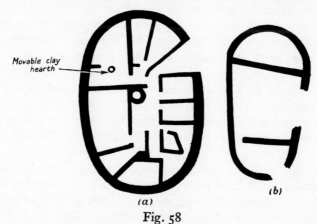

Movable clay hearth

(a)   *(b)*

Fig. 58

(a) Oval House from Khamazi, Crete (MM I) 1 : 220.
(*After Pendlebury*).

(b) Apsidal House from Rini, Thessaly (MH) 1 : 100.
(*After Wace and Thompson*)

commune of Villevieille, Gard,[45] where round huts having internal diameters of only $2\frac{1}{2}$ to 3 metres were associated with irregularly quadrangular ones; the finds, comprising a rich flint industry, copper objects including dagger-blades and round-based " neolithic " pottery, suggest a date in the second millenium B.C. Round huts also proliferate on some of the west Mediterranean islands, though when they began to be built is uncertain; those which cluster round the nuraghic towers of Sardinia[46] (Fig. 59) are the product of a provincial Late Bronze Age lasting down to the end of the prehistoric period.

The houses of the first peasantries, like those of the first townsmen, of the Aegean area were almost exlusively oblong and, when cultures based on metallurgy spread as far west as Iberia, the houses associated with them were of this character. No house-plans have been recovered from early or middle neolithic levels, but the late neolithic structures under the central court at Knossos (Fig. 60) comprised houses of " but and ben " type with an entrance-lobby and an inner living-room knit together by accretions of smaller rooms.[47] Of the walls only the bases survive, made from undressed limestone blocks bedded on clay and pebbles, but it may be surmised that the upper portions were built from sun-dried bricks. The plans of these cellular aggregations of rooms, as of the later Minoan palatial and other structures, suggest that the roofs were flat, as they are indeed shown in the " town mosaic " from Knossos.[48] In much of the Mediterranean, as of western Asia, the

[43] J. Bradford, 1949, 60–4.
[44] e.g. Childe, 1947, 259.
[45] M. Louis, *et al.*, 1947.
[46] A. Taramelli, 1916.
[47] J. D. S. Pendlebury, 1939, 39–40.
[48] *ibid.*, 132 and Pl. XXI, 1.

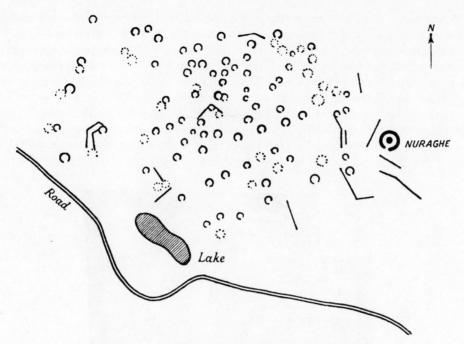

Fig. 59. Nuraghic village of Serrucci, Sardinia.

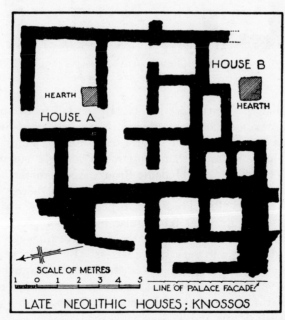

Fig. 60. Neolithic houses, Knossos. (*After Pendlebury*).

137

problem was not to drain off rain-water by ridging the roof, but rather to catch and store it.

On the Greek mainland[49] houses were normally made from sun-dried bricks of mud mixed with grass or straw, based on a foundation course of flat stone slabs or more commonly of small stones set in mud plaster, though wattle and daub applied to wooden frames seems also to have been used. The commonest plan to which the early neolithic Thessalian A people built their houses, was a simple oblong with an entrance asymmetrically set in one of the long walls. At Tsangli some of the houses were nearly square in plan and were provided with internal buttresses in opposite pairs, evidently designed to carry cross-beams (Fig. 61). Unlike those of Crete it is fairly certain that the houses of the Greek mainland were provided with ridged roofs. Already from the beginning of the neolithic

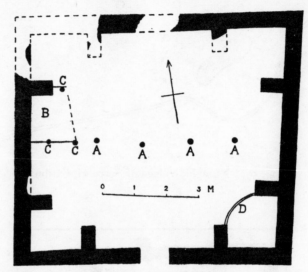

Fig. 61. Neolithic (Thessalian A) house, Tsangli, Greece.
(*After Wace and Thompson*)

settlement the Thessalian peasants were sufficiently settled to occupy their villages permanently, a fact which, taken in conjunction with their use of mud-brick, led to the formation of regular mounds resembling west Asiatic tells. Such a mound, locally known as a *maghula* or *tumba*, might be no more than 3 metres or so high, but where settlement continued with little or no break into the Helladic Bronze Age it might be more substantial : for instance, the mound of Tsangli attained a height of 10 metres and was around 200 metres in length and breadth. The Thessalian B people had already brought into use the megaron type (Fig. 62) with its great rectangular living room, opening out by way of a portico into a courtyard and surrounded—with an intervening gap to contain rainwater from the eaves[50]—by sleeping and servants' quarters. By this time, also, considerations of security made it necessary, as at Dimini itself, to defend the inner courtyard and it was between the concentric walls of the defences that the lesser dwellings of the settlement were packed. By Mycenæan times an urban architecture had grown up on the mainland, as on the islands, complete with drains and wells.

---

[49] Wace and Thompson, 1912, *passim*.
[50] J. L. Myres, 1930, 273.

The researches of the brothers Siret have shown that the earliest metallurgists of south-eastern Spain lived either in concentrated settlements, like that of Los Millares itself, situated on the tip of a steep promontory between the Andarax river and the Huechar stream and defended by a rampart and ditch, or in small mining camps like Parazuelos or El

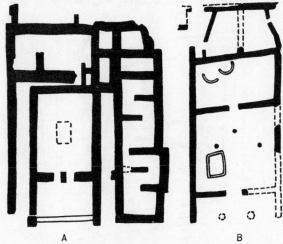

Fig. 62.   Megara from Phylakopi III (Mycenaean) and Sesklo II (Thessalian B).

Scale *c.* 1 : 2000

Officio (Fig. 63), consisting of aggregations of a few rooms, generally on isolated promontories or hillocks. Unfortunately, although the Sirets published lavish illustrations of such

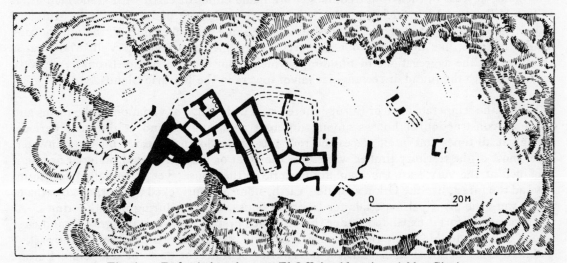

Fig. 63.   Defended settlement, El Officio, Almeria.   (*After Siret*).

things as flints, stone implements, metal objects and sherds, they were vague about settlements and structures.[51]   One of the very few illustrated from Los Millares comprises

---

[51] L. Siret, 1887, *passim*; also *L'Anthropologie*, III, 388.

an irregularly oblong building (Fig. 64) having pairs of slots in the inner walls, presumably to contain wooden uprights for carrying roof supports. In plan this resembles the early Thessalian one at Tsangli already mentioned, though in the Greek structure the roof beams were carried instead by pairs of wall buttresses. The Iberian buildings resemble those of parts of the east Mediterranean in their general angularity of plan, though it should be

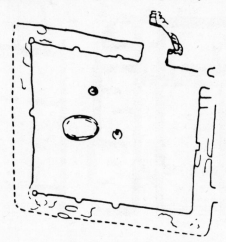

Fig. 64.   Oblong building at Los Millares, Almeria.
(*After Leisner*).

emphasized that in the west Mediterranean little attempt seems to have been made to keep to a rectangular plan and oblique or even curved walls were freely used where convenient. The walls, at least in their lower courses, were made either of earth with stone facings, as at Los Millares and Parazuelos, or, as at the bronze settlement of La Bastida in Murcia,[52] of undressed stones set in clay. Architecture of the same general character, though showing insular features, like the stone roof-supports, exemplified at Capocorp Vell, Mallorca, is exhibited by the aggregations of buildings, which from the end of the Bronze Age were associated with the round or rectangular talyot towers in the Balearic islands.[53]

Within the temperate zone of Europe there was a wide range of variation in the forms and mode of construction of houses among different communities and at different periods, though at all times and in all places the roof was made sloping to carry off the rainwater. Over most of the territory timber was either the chief or only structural material or else it provided at the very least the main framework of the house; yet in marginal territories beyond the forest, like the Orkney islands, earth, stone and turf, eked out perhaps by whale-bone, were the principal materials for building houses already during neolithic times. As the area free of forest expanded under the influence first of clearance and grazing and later also of climatic deterioration, these materials came to play an increasingly important part.

There is no doubt that the earliest peasantries of different parts of temperate Europe occupied nucleated settlements or villages. Yet, though their buildings were often quite large, it was only south-east of the Middle Danube area that their sites were occupied sufficiently permanently to give rise to settlement mounds, like that of Vinča on the south

---

[52] J. M. Santa-Olalla, 1946, Pl. XXIII.
[53] Ebert, Bd., 2, 272–3 and Taf. 128b.

bank of the Danube a little below Belgrade, which grew to a height of over 9 metres, more than half during neolithic times.[54]

It was long thought that the earliest " Danubian " peasants, who introduced farming to the loess lands of middle Europe, lived in some form of pit-dwelling. Even the excavators of Köln-Lindenthal, the great settlement on the western outskirts of Cologne, imagined that irregular hollows, filled with rubbish and often surrounded by traces of some form of light fencing, served as dwellings.[55] The great buildings associated with these, from 10 to as much as 35 metres in length and from 5 to 7 metres wide, were rather perversely assigned to some alternative but unknown function. Critical examination of the plans of Köln-Lindenthal and particularly of the settlement at Arnsbach near Borken, Kassel,[56] has shown fairly conclusively that these long buildings were in fact houses and that the attendant hollows were in origin no more than quarries, from which material was obtained for plastering the walls.[57] The lack of internal " domestic " features in the long buildings

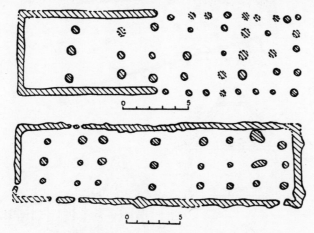

Fig. 65.   Long buildings from Köln-Lindenthal. (Danubian II).

(*After Buttler and Haberey*).

Scale in metres.

can be explained from the fact that the floor, presumably of wood, was apparently raised up on three rows of stilts, and partly from the fact that rubbish was shot into the disused hollows. The fencing round these latter may well have been designed to prevent people falling in or alternatively to contain pigs feeding on the garbage; it would be strange indeed if men capable of constructing " economic " buildings on this scale should have crouched in these miserable quarters. The few " pit-dwellings " which can be established were of quite minor status, like the conical hut from Frauenberg near Marburg,[58] comprising a central hollow within a setting of eight posts sunk obliquely into the sub-soil.

The walls of the long buildings (Fig. 65) were in some cases formed entirely of timbers set into slots cut in the sub-soil, but often these were restricted to one end only, the rest

[54] Vassits, 1910, 1932; Childe, 1929.
[55] Buttler and Haberey, 1936.
[56] E. Sangmeister, 1937, 215, abb. 2.
[57] O. Paret, 1942 and 1946, Ch. II.
[58] G. Wolff, 1917.

being defined by a single or double row of posts.[59] This apparent differentiation of many of the long houses into two halves, together with their great size, suggests that in addition to sheltering the family they also served some other function. What this may have been it is difficult to say. If the floors were in fact raised, the buildings can hardly have been used as byres. Again, so far as is known, the Danubians had no bulky gear such as ploughs or waggons. The only obvious alternative is that parts of the long buildings were used for storing produce, though it is known that at Köln-Lindenthal at least the Danubian peasants also had small separate store-houses mounted on piles, possibly for keeping seed-grain.

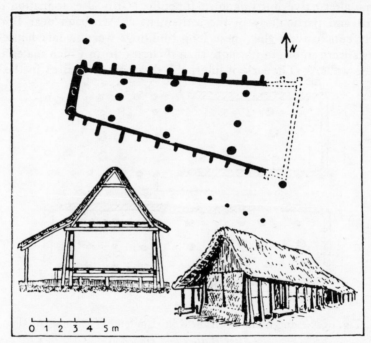

Fig. 66. Plan and reconstruction of trapeze-shaped Rössen house at
Deiringsen-Ruploh, Westphalia. (*After Buttler*).
Scale in metres.

A variation of the basic Danubian form is the trapeze-shaped house, with one end substantially broader than the other. An example, attributable to the Rössen people of Danubian II age, $7\frac{1}{2}$ metres broad at one end against only 5 metres at the other, has been explored at Deiringsen-Ruploh, kr. Soest, Westphalia,[60] (Fig. 66). In this case three rows of postholes were also found between the wall-slots. Similar houses, in which no internal postholes have yet been observed, occur in Poland associated with late Danubian II groups, notably at the great settlement of Brześć Kujawski[61] (Fig. 67) and at Dobre, kr. Nieszawa.[62] At the former site the houses varied from 15 to as much as 39 metres in length and the wall

---

[59] Double rows of wall posts were present at Harth, Zwenkau, near Leipzig (K. Tackenberg, 1937, 219, abb. 1).

[60] W. Buttler, 1938, abb. 12.

[61] K. Jaźdźewski, 1938, 93. Jaźdźewski specifically disagrees with Buttler's interpretation of the Köln-Lindenthal structures (pp. 104–5).

[62] *ibid.*, 102.

slots were 2 metres deep. It may be noted that both at Köln-Lindenthal and at Brześć Kujawski there was evidence for at least three intervals in the occupation of the settlement, a consequence of the extensive system of agriculture pursued.

The earliest peasants of the Black Earth of Roumania and the Ukraine, makers of the painted and grooved Cucuteni and Tripolje wares, also occupied houses which might be 20 metres or more long. Extensive excavations at Kolomysczina near the village of Khalépjé,

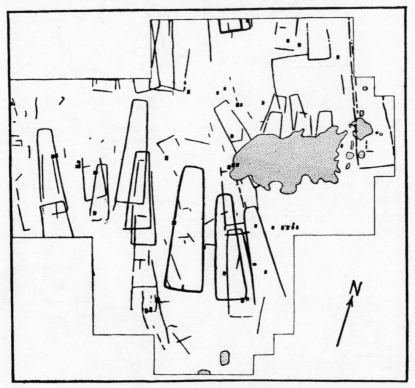

Fig. 67. Superimposed plans of trapeze-shaped neolithic houses, Brześć Kujawski, Poland. 1 : 1000. (*After Jaźdźewski*).

Oboukhov, Kiev province, have revealed a complete village plan, comprising between 26 and 31 such houses set radially in a great circle with two, and traces of more houses in the middle.[63] Some of these houses (Fig. 68) were no more than 30 square metres in area, but there were several of 90 and some of 140 square metres. Disappointingly little is known of details of their construction. It has been noted, though, from a study of the floors, which were commonly made from layers of baked clay slabs and clods of coarse clay bearing impressions of timbers, that some of the houses had been enlarged and the number of hearths increased, as though the original family had expanded through children marrying and setting up house under the parental roof. Post-holes or charred stumps have sometimes been noted round the margins of the clay floors, as at Kolomysczina (house 24) and more convincingly at Bely Kamen, but no firm conclusions have been reached about the character of the walls or roofing. As one can see from the well-known clay model from Popudnia in

---

[63] E. Kričevsky, 1940.

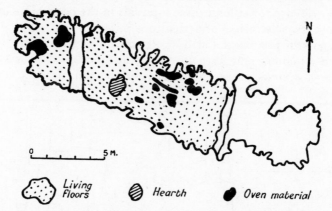

Fig. 68.   Plan of long house of the Tripolje people, Kolomysczina,
Khalépjé, prov. Kiev.   (*After Kričevsky*).
Scale in metres.

the Ukraine—rather perversely interpreted by Buttler as a pile-dwelling[64]—the interior
of a Tripolje house was furnished with a low bench on which store jars were set, a saddle-
quern near the door and a great domed oven (Fig. 69).   Traces of such ovens are a common
feature of Tripolje house-ruins and their use went hand in hand with the domed kilns used

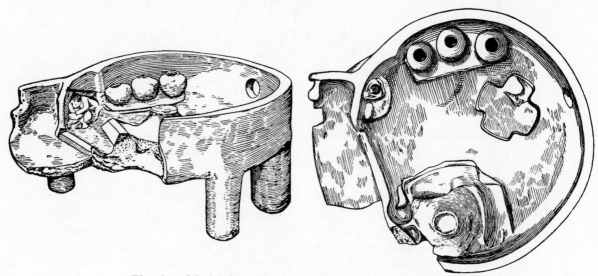

Fig. 69.   Model from Popudnia showing internal features of a
house of the Tripolje culture.   (*After Childe*).

for firing storage jars and other pots and of which models were found at Erösd, type-station
of the allied painted pottery culture of the Alt valley the other side of the Carpathian
mountains.

---

[64] Buttler and Haberey, 1936, 68.   The feet on which the model house rests may be compared
with those attached to the plough scene from Vounous.

The Erösd people occupied rectangular and almost certainly gabled houses grouped in village communities. At Erösd itself the settlement was sited on a loess spur cut off by a defensive ditch.[65] Within the area excavated a row of seven houses was found and there was room for up to another fourteen in the unexplored portion. The houses were built of wattle and clay daub supported on a frame of wooden posts, and consisted of an inner room and an outer porch, roofed but probably open at one side as well as in front. Rectangular

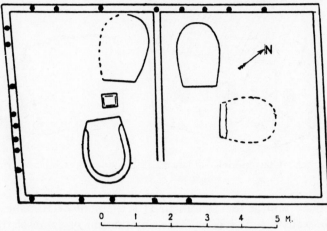

Fig. 70. Late Neolithic house at Vinča, near Belgrade. (*After Vassits*).

houses of the same general character and likewise a good deal smaller than the Danubian I form were found in the upper neolithic level at Vinča[66] (Fig. 70), as well as on the western

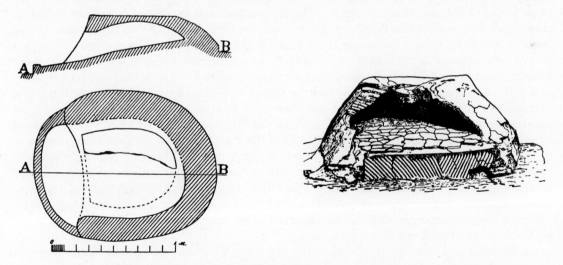

Fig. 71. Clay oven from late neolithic level, Vinča, near Belgrade. (*After Vassits*).

margins of the Danubian II territory in south Germany. Over this whole region, also, clay ovens (Fig. 71) were a marked feature of the internal arrangements.

---

[65] V. G. Childe, 1929, 98–9.
[66] M. M. Vassits, 1910 and 1932.

Before considering these further, it may be worth recalling that rectangular plans do not of themselves necessarily imply a very elaborate type of house. Among the clay hut models from Kodža Dermen, a site of the late neolithic mound-culture of Bulgaria, there was a tent-like form in which the ridged roof was carried down to the ground, as well as a gabled one with side walls (Fig. 72).[67]   Whether correctly or not, Banner considered that the

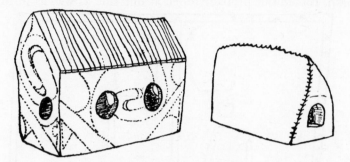

Fig. 72.   Clay models of late neolithic houses, Kodža Dermen, Bulgaria.   (*After Childe*).

oblong floors found by him at the Danubian II settlement of Kopancs in Hungary were roofed without side walls[68] and Reinerth's reconstruction of some of the tomb houses of corded-ware people under the Sarmenstorf round barrows followed rather similar lines.[69]

The best traces of Danubian II houses are those round the shores of the Federsee in Württemburg and referable to the Aichbühl people.[70]   At the name site twenty-two rect-angular houses and two other buildings were arranged in irregular rows along the shore of an outlet of the lake (Figs. 73, 74).   The houses themselves, although varying in detail, conformed with remarkable fidelity to a common plan (Fig. 75).   Built on a frame of vertical posts arranged to form a rectangle from 7 to 10 metres long, they were provided with a row of central posts to support the gabled roof and an internal division separating an inner from an outer room.   The walls were most commonly made from split timbers, set vertically and with the convex face outermost, and the floors from planks with a loam covering.   The entrance set in the middle of one of the narrow ends of the house was approached by a planked forecourt, unsheltered save possibly by the overhang of the roof and by the forward extension of the side walls.   On the right hand of the door as one entered the front room was the hearth and the clay oven, resting on sheets of birch-bark and built of daub on a founda-tion of wattle.   By placing ashes from the hearth in the oven the vaulted clay roof could be heated sufficiently to bake cakes of flat bread laid upon it.[71]   Although certain features, like the timbered forecourt, may have been adapted to lakeside settlement, the same general plan and cooking-arrangements can be observed in the traces of Aichbühl houses recovered by Bersu on the Goldberg.[72]

On the opposite bank of the same outlet from the Federsee, but at the point where it debouched into the lake, the Aichbühl settlement of Riedschachen has the special interest

---

[67] J. H. Gaul, 1948, 91 and Pl. XXXI, 2 and 4.
[68] J. Banner, 1929 and 1930.
[69] H. Reinerth, 1928.
[70] R. R. Schmidt, 1930–6.
[71] H. Reinerth, 1929.
[72] G. Bersu, 1936.

of exhibiting two phases.[73] The houses of the earlier stage were from 9 to 10 metres in length and from 4 to 5 metres in width and were built on piles, either over the edge of the lake or, more likely, on the shores within the area liable to flooding. Between the two phases of occupation peat had time to grow over the abandoned pile settlement, so that the

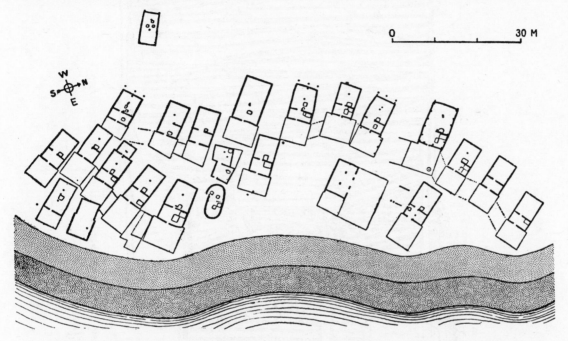

Fig. 73. Plan of neolithic (Danubian II) village of Aichbühl, Federsee, Württemburg. (*After Schmidt*).

Fig. 74. Reconstruction of neolithic lakeside village, Aichbühl, Württemburg. (*After Schmidt*).

later houses could be erected on frames laid directly on the bog. The houses of this second phase were notably smaller, being from 7 to 8 metres long and from 3 to 4 metres wide, and either lacked the forecourt entirely or were provided at most with a few planks before the entrance. Again, they were bunched closely together, so that no less than ten were found in the same area as two of the underlying pile-dwellings.

[73] H. Reinerth, 1936, 71–8; 100–5.

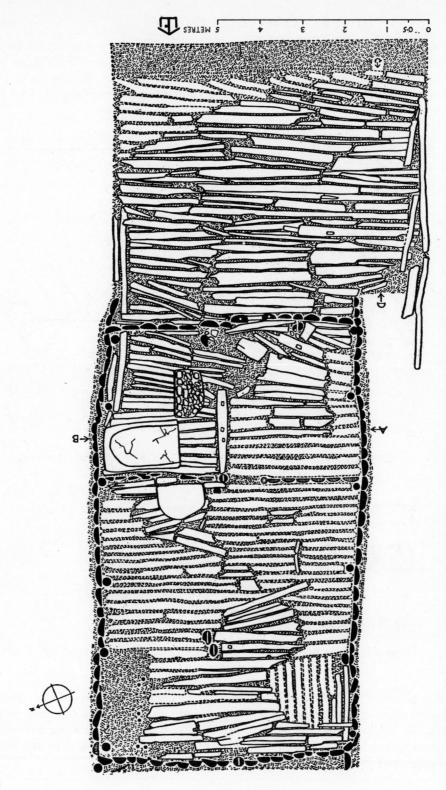

0 0·5 1 2 3 4 5 METRES

Fig. 75. Ground floor of house from the Aichbühl settlement, Württemburg.
(*After Schmidt*).

148

As Childe has noted,[74] there was indeed a progressive trend towards a reduction in the size of the house in the Danubian territories from the great long houses of Danubian I to the oblong structures of Danubian II and the relatively small ones of Danubian III. The houses of the late neolithic Altheim culture on the Goldberg,[75] for instance, were not more than 4 to 5 metres square (Fig. 76). The floors were sunk up to a foot or so below the surface, a hearth and pit were situated near the middle, and the walls were made from thin and fairly closely set saplings which must presumably have been drawn together at the

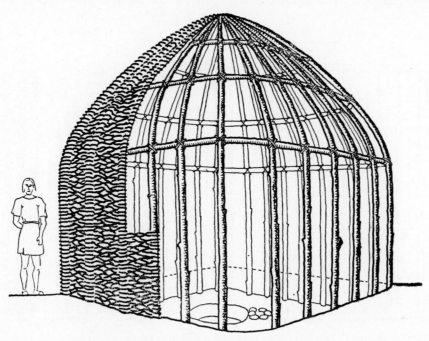

Fig. 76. Reconstruction of house of the Altheim (Danubian III) culture, Goldberg, Württemburg. (*After Bersu*).

top to form a roof. Small squarish houses with slightly sunken floors have also been noted in later neolithic contexts at Mulheim, near Koblentz,[76] and at Mayen on the Eifel, some two kilometres north-west of the famous earthwork.[77] Somewhat analogous houses were associated with the contemporary Baden culture at Praha-Bubenec and Homolka in central Europe.[78]

Apart from some humbler structures at Dullenried on the Federsee, the dwellings associated with the Western and hybrid cultures of the Alpine and Swabian lakes have all proved to be of the rectangular gabled type. Many of the houses of the Alpine area were certainly of Danubian origin, as Childe has recently emphasized, and, in view of the fact that Danubian influence, in the form of Rössen pottery, has been detected even in the earlier Cortaillod culture, it would be rash to accept any as exemplifying a specifically western building

---

[74] V. G. Childe, 1949.
[75] G. Bersu, 1937.
[76] *Bonner Jahrbücher*, Hft. 143/4, 355–7.
[77] K. H. Wagner, 1938, 254–8.
[78] V. G. Childe, 1949, 82.

tradition. Excavations at Schötz I and at Egolzwil II in the Wauwilermoos near Luzern[79] show that the younger Cortaillod peasants occupied substantial houses, frequently around 8 metres long and 4 metres broad. Those at the Michelsberg settlement of Weiher near Thayngen were single-roomed and noticeably smaller, ranging down to 5·3 by 3·2 metres; a detail of construction worth noting is that the wall uprights of the narrow ends were mortised into the cross beams defining either end of the floor (Fig. 77).[80] Lastly one can point to a number of houses associated with the Horgen ware, which followed the Michelsberg pottery in eastern Switzerland and the younger Cortaillod in the west. At Sipplingen

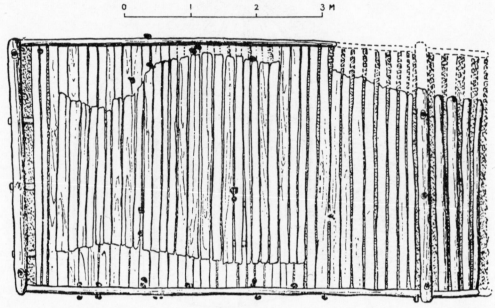

Fig. 77. Ground floor of house occupied by Michelsberg people, Weiher near Thayngen, Switzerland. (*After Reinerth*).

Scale in metres.

on lake Constance[81] the houses from the upper level of the settlement, which yielded Horgen pottery in quantities, resembled in scale and plan those from Weiher. The houses from the lower level on the other hand were of typical Aichbühl type with two rooms and a porch, though the few sherds from this level were also of Horgen type. The settlement at Dullenried,[82] assigned by Reinerth to an early phase of the Western tradition, but in fact yielding exclusively Horgen pottery, comprised a cluster of huts with approximately oblong timber flooring: the superstructures were made from light branches arched over to form roof and walls and thatched with bundles of reeds tied on by bast cords (Fig. 78). It is possible that these huts may have been occupied seasonally for hunting and fishing, or that their inhabitants were lower in the social scale than those who lived in timber frame houses.

---

[79] J. Heierli and P. E. Scherer, 1924, abb. 7, 8.
[80] R. Sulzberger, 1924, 163 f.; H. Reinerth, 1926, abb. 20.
[81] H. Reinerth, 1938.
[82] H. Reinerth, 1936, 60–70.

In the sphere of scientific research into prehistoric houses northern France remains a regrettable blank[83] and the position in the lowland zone of the British Isles is little more satisfactory for the earlier stages of prehistoric farming. Apart from traces of what appears to have been a rectangular house disturbed by subsequent occupation of the site at the Easton Down flint-mines, Wiltshire,[84] the only house attributable to the Western neolithic tradition of England is that uncovered on Haldon Hill, near Exeter,[85] and represented

Fig. 78.   Reconstruction of Horgen hut, Dullenried, Federsee, Württemburg.   (*After Reinerth*).

by a rectangular arrangement of post-holes, set in the midst of the stone footings of a turf or wattle wall; a couple of central posts may have helped to support a gabled roof (Fig. 79).

Thanks to O'Riordain's excavations at Knockadoon on the shore of Lough Gur in county Limerick,[86] rather more is known from Ireland. Among the neolithic houses at this site is a rectangular one having internal dimensions of 9½ by 4½ to 5 metres (Fig. 80). The walls, possibly of turf, were defined by a stone footing and by a double row of post-holes, in which were set the uprights of the wooden frame; the hearth was central and two rows of posts dividing the house into aisles presumably helped to support the roof. But Knockadoon can also boast round houses[87] defined by concentric rows of post-holes and apparently also dating from a time when Western neolithic pottery was current in this part of Ireland.

---

[83] Traces of neolithic houses have from time to time been uncovered by French excavators, but all uncomprehendingly. In this, as in so many fields of later prehistoric research, France could be made to yield rich, one might dare say fabulous, returns. Only modern technique is needed.

[84] J. F. S. Stone, 1933, Pl. IX.

[85] E. H. Willock, 1937; *P.P.S.* 1938, 222–3.

[86] O'Riordain, 1946, 147–8.

[87] *ibid.*, Pl. IX, 3.

Rather more is known of the dwellings of neolithic groups outside the western tradition in northern Britain. At Ronaldsway in the Isle of Man a single long house has been found with the floor sunk into slightly rising ground to a depth of from $1\frac{1}{2}$ to $2\frac{1}{2}$ feet below the contemporary ground-level. The rectangular frame was defined by post-holes, others of which may have been designed to support a smoke-hole over the central hearth.[88] The late neolithic settlements explored mainly by Childe at Skara Brae[89] and Rinyo[90] on Orkney represent adaptations to a windswept and virtually treeless landscape on the

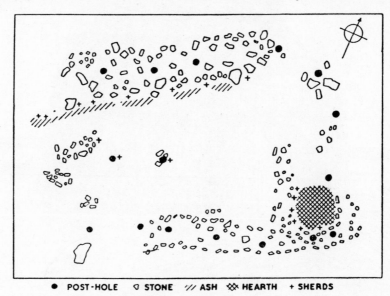

● POST-HOLE   ◁ STONE   ⁄⁄⁄ ASH   ⧆ HEARTH   + SHERDS

Fig. 79.   Ground-plan of neolithic house on Haldon Hill, Devon.   (*After Piggott*).
Scale : 9 feet to 1 inch.

margin of the temperate zone, a landscape, it will be remembered, that supported sheep rather than swine at this period (see p. 121). The houses were basically squarish or oblong in plan, though with rounded corners, ranging in size from 21 to 20 feet to 15 by 11 feet internally. The walls were built of local flagstone laid horizontally two courses deep. This mode of construction lent itself to corbelling and even from the surviving walls it is evident that this method was in fact used. Though an overhang of as much as $2\frac{3}{4}$ feet was achieved at a height of $9\frac{1}{2}$ feet from the floor, there is no sign that the houses were completely roofed over by lofty corbelled vaults; the probability is that the aperture was appreciably reduced by corbelling and then spanned by whale bones or timbers, heaped over with turf. The inclemency of the climate is reflected in the lowness of the doors and by the way in which the houses at Skara were clustered together. Indeed, in the course of time the whole settlement coagulated into a low mound, in which the individual houses, linked together by low covered passages or tunnels, were heaped around with ash, excrement and sand (Fig. 81). Protected thus against the winds and provided with drains to carry off superfluous rainwater—all the more necessary at Rinyo, situated as it was at the foot of a steep brae—

---

[88] Bruce and Megaw, 1947, 143–6.
[89] V. G. Childe, 1931.
[90] Childe and Grant, 1939 and 1947.

these more or less subterranean villages must have given snug protection to the predominantly pastoral communities inhabiting them. Owing to the rarity of wood and the ease with which the local stone could be worked, the internal furnishings of these Orcadian houses are exceptionally well preserved (Pl. VII, b). The degree of uniformity is striking. In the middle of the floor, covered with clay helped out by a few stone slabs, was set the stone-lined hearth, and at Rinyo an oven, consisting of a clay dome set on a slate base, was placed

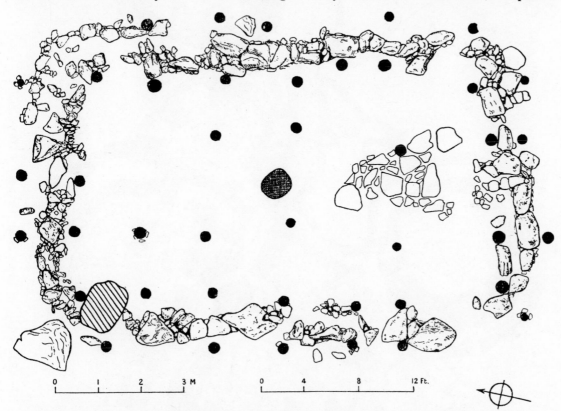

Fig. 80. Ground-plan of rectangular neolithic house, Knockadoon, Lough Gur, Co. Limerick. Post-holes are shown in black and central hearth by cross-hatching. (*After O'Riordain*).

immediately next to this. On either side were the beds and over these ambries or keeping-places were set in the thickness of the wall. Stone dressers, comprising two tiers of stone shelves, were built against the rear wall and three slate-lined boxes, possibly for keeping limpets, were commonly let into the floor at one or more corners.

No traces of the houses of the earliest farmer immigrants to Denmark have been recovered, unless one can accept as such the rectangular house-plan, approximately 10 by 4 metres, defined by stone wall-footings, found at Strandegaard in south-east Zaelland[91] and occupied by Ertebølle hunter-fishers, who nevertheless, seem to have lived alongside the immigrant farmers and borrowed elements of culture from them. Of much greater interest, though, is the settlement of Barkaer in Djursland[92] occupied by peasants of

---

[91] Broholm and Rasmussen, 1931; J. Brøndsted, 1938, I, Fig. 87.

[92] P. V. Gløb, 1949. I have to thank Professor Gløb for his great kindness in allowing me to see a photograph of his as yet unpublished plan.

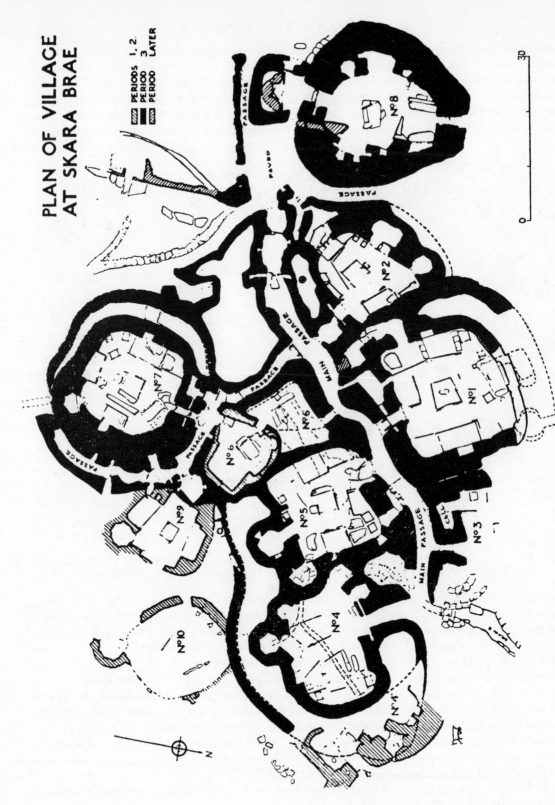

PLAN OF VILLAGE
AT SKARA BRAE

PERIODS 1. 2.
PERIOD 3
PERIOD LATER

Fig. 81. Neolithic village of Skara Brae, Orkney. (After Childe).

154

the third and last phase of the early neolithic period of Denmark. Here, situated on a low knoll, which during neolithic times was yet a small island, was the settlement of people, who supported themselves by cultivating the soil and maintaining livestock on the neigh-bouring mainland. Traces of the structures have survived owing to their having been sealed early on by sand; it is to be noted that this was blown up from the area cleared by the prehistoric farmers, traces of whose burning and tillage activities have been recovered by Iversen from the bed of the neighbouring Korup lake.[93] Two ranges of building were found, separated by a road some 10 metres wide. Of these the southern range has survived the more intact, but, except in that the northern one was a metre or so broader, they appear from the surviving traces to have resembled each other closely. It can be seen that the southern range was built in two sections. At first a structure 67.5 metres long and 6.5 metres broad was built and sub-divided into compartments each about 3 metres wide. Later, presumably when young people married and set up house, another 17·5 metres was added on a slightly different alignment and on a slightly broader plan. If this interpretation is correct, the smallness of the extension argues for a comparatively brief occupation of the site. In the original building there were twenty-two compartments, each of which seems to have served as a family dwelling, and in the extension another six, giving a total for both ranges of between fifty and sixty families. The general impression given by the Barkaer settlement is one of rigid organization and discipline, such as one might expect of immigrant pioneers of a new form of economy in a territory strongly occupied by hunter-fishers. An obvious and significant parallel is given by the rows of houses, each covered by a common gabled roof, packed within the defences of the early iron age fortress of Biskupin in northern Poland.

Of the several middle neolithic settlements investigated in Denmark none have yielded adequate house-plans, but there are clear indications at Troldebjerg on Langeland island [94] of two distinct types of structure. On the lower slope of the morainic hillock there is a range of buildings close to the margin of the bog extending over some 71 metres, though bent slightly out of alignment near the middle. The outer margin is marked by a well-defined wall-slot, and in the interior there is a single line of stone-packed post-holes rein-forced at the northern end by a second and in places by a third parallel row. Although evidently incomplete, this lay-out reminds one strongly of that of the Danubian long house, and it is significant that the excavator of Troldebjerg should have noted a difference of usage as between the two ends of each of the main units, indicated by the presence or absence of occupational rubbish. Immediately east of the long range traces were found of at least two and probably more buildings of horseshoe form, which resemble in a general way a group of middle neolithic structures with low walls of loam and stones excavated early in the century at Klein-Meinsdorf, in Schleswig-Holstein.[95]

One of the most striking facts to emerge from this cursory survey of the houses of the neolithic peasantries in temperate Europe has been the overwhelming predominance of rectangular plans. In central and northern Europe the oblong house was to persist during the Bronze and Iron Ages, albeit with modifications in form and mode of construction. On the other hand, in the British Isles these later periods were marked by outstanding develop-ments of the round house.

---

[93] J. Iversen, 1941.
[94] J. Winther, 1935.
[95] K. Kersten, 1936A, 77 and abb. 18.

As pointed out in a previous chapter, much less is known about human settlement in temperate Europe during most of the Bronze Age than during neolithic times. For instance, the best clues to the houses built during the great period of the Northern Bronze Age are those given by the funerary houses under round barrows in Schleswig-Holstein: examples at Sottorf, kr. Harburg, and Grünhof-Tesperhude, kr. Lauenburg (Fig. 82), dating from periods II and III respectively, were based on rectangular settings of stout posts; another, at Baven, kr. Celle, had in addition a roofed porch.[96]

Fig. 82.   Reconstruction of mortuary house under Bronze Age barrow at Grünhof-Tesperhude, Schleswig-Holstein.   (*After Kersten*).

Rather more evidence is available from the Late Bronze Age. At both the settlements excavated by Kiekebusch[97] in north central Germany—Hasenfelde, kr. Lebus, and Buch near Berlin—the houses were substantial, up to 10 by 5 metres, and of magaron type with a hearth in the inner room. The best preserved site from this time, though, is Wasserburg Buchau in the Federsee Moor, south Germany.[98] Here were two successive settlements on what was then an island in the lake, defended by a multiple palisade (Fig. 83). Although some of the houses from the earlier phase were made with walls of wattle mounted on a frame of vertical timber posts, some, and all of those from the latter phase, were built on the log-house principle, by which the component timbers interlocked by means of notches cut near either extremity of each (Pl. XIV, b). In the first settlement all the thirty-eight houses but one were single-roomed and rectangular in plan. By contrast the later settlers occupied nine farmsteads (Fig. 84), each comprising aggregations of three rooms with hearths, together with ancillary buildings and granaries of short rectangular form. The most likely explanation of this alteration of plan is that it reflects an economic change, probably a trend towards a more markedly agricultural type of farming. Traces of another block-house

---

[96] *ibid.*, 56–70 and 82.
[97] A. Kiekebusch, 1911 and 1923.
[98] H. Reinerth, 1936, 119–50.

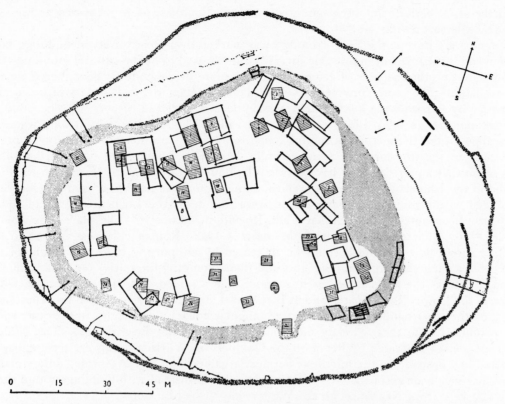

Fig. 83. General plan of Late Bronze Age settlement of Wasserburg Buchau, Federsee, Württemburg. (*After Reinerth*).

Fig. 84. Reconstruction of farmstead at Wasserburg Buchau. (*After Reinerth*).

157

from the same period, this time mounted on stone boulders, were recovered at Riesi on lake Hallwilersee, Switzerland.[99]

In temperate Europe the Early Iron Age was marked by a great variety in building, both in plan and structure, but before this diversity can be used to define cultural groupings and throw light on other aspects of economic life far more evidence must be gathered than is yet available. The most convincing house plan referable to the Hallstatt phase is that recovered by Bersu on the Lochenstein plateau near Balingen in Swabia.[100] The building was rectangular, 19 metres long and 7 metres wide. The house was built on a frame of vertical posts, but the method of roofing remains obscure, since neither the marginal posts, nor those in the interior were symmetrically disposed. There were two hearths and a suggestion that a partition may have divided the house into two parts. From the La Tène period in the Rhineland rounded as well as oblong structures have been found. Oval huts attributed to the middle La Tène period were found on the Lochenstein[101] and round huts have been noted in the Neckar Valley[102] and in Alsace[103]. The plan of an oblong house, $8\frac{1}{2}$ by 7 metres, brought to light under a Gallo-Roman villa near Mayen in the Eifel,[104] shows how the width could be increased by supporting the main weight of the roof on an arrangement of main uprights and then extending the rafters outwards; in such aisled structures the walls served as little more than a screen. At Bruckhausen, kr. Dinslaken, in the Lower Rhenish area and at Barkhauser Berg, Oerlinghausen in the Teutoburg Wald, on the other hand, one encounters rectangular houses with hearths in the inner room and porches,[105] like those already mentioned from the Late Bronze Age. The Middle La Tène houses excavated by Bersu on the Goldberg in Württemburg were rectangular in plan and had posts down the middle to support a gabled roof.[106] As a rule, only isolated structures have been reconstructed, but the plan of a farmstead with buildings round three sides of a yard from Neuhäusel on the Westerwald[107] may be noted.

Favourable conditions of preservation and large-scale excavation have gained fuller knowledge about the settlements of the West Friesians in the marshlands between the Zuider Zee and the estuary of the Elbe during the Iron Age. A good idea of their character can be gained from the terp at Ezinge near Groningen (Fig. 85) explored by van Giffen.[108] To judge from the traces found on the original ground surface (VI), the Friesians who colonized the marshlands around the fourth century B.C. settled in very small groups, probably no more than enlarged families. About 200 B.C. a mound of turf (V) about a metre high and 35 metres across was thrown up and on this another small group of buildings was erected (Fig. 86). When it became necessary a hundred years or so later to heighten the mound, so as to counter the effects of flooding, the chief material used was dung (IV). Further additions were made by throwing on loads of clay (III) and in due course, around 200 A.D., a second layer of dung (II). When a further clay capping (I) was added, with the arrival

---

[99] R. Bosch, 1924.

[100] Bersu and Goessler, 1924, Taf. III.

[101] *ibid.*, Taf. IV.

[102] Ebert, V, 195b.

[103] *S.G.U.*, 1947, 50, Fig. 9.

[104] *Bonner Jahrbücher*, Hft. 133, 1928, Taf. VIII.

[105] R. Stampfuss, 1938, 221 ff. and 234 ff.

[106] G. Bersu, 1930, Taf. XV.

[107] *Deutscher Kulturatlas*, Bd. 1, 22b.

[108] A. E. van Giffen, 1936.

of the Saxons around 400 A.D., the mound stood to a height of 5 metres and its maximum diameter was around a quarter of a mile. Throughout the whole period of the Friesian settlement the same fundamental type of structure persisted (Fig. 87), the ancestor of the Lower Saxon peasant house. Although the corners were sometimes rounded through the bending of the wattle and dung-plastered walls, the structures were fundamentally rectangular in plan. The main weight of the rafters was carried on pairs of uprights set at

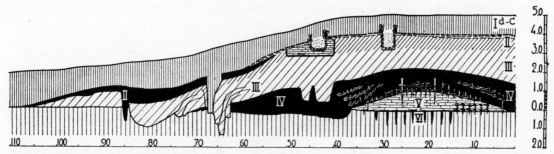

Fig. 85. Section through the Ezinge terp, near Groningen. Scales in metres. (*After van Giffen*).

intervals in the interior, but the roof was carried over the walls and supported on either side by rows of small external posts. The buildings were entered either at the narrow end or from the side or occasionally from both and the hearth was placed in the middle between two pairs of main uprights. Some of the buildings were constructed with a broader roof span so as to provide room for stalls along the side aisles, each partitioned off by wicker-work between the main posts and the walls. It is surmised that the cattle were stalled

Fig. 86. Reconstruction of iron age settlement on the original 'terp' at Ezinge, near Groningen. (*After van Giffen*).

with their heads towards the central gangway, on either side of which wicker-work pavements were laid down, doubtless to save wear when feeding the stock. Occasionally complete buildings were given up to cattle, but sometimes these were stalled at one end of the dwelling. Although cattle were the principal wealth of the terp dwellers, they also kept horses, sheep and swine and cultivated barley, flax and beans.

Quite a different style of house construction is found at the great fortified site of Bis-kupin,[109] near Znin, some 65 kilometres north-east of Poznan on the northern marches of the territory of the Lusation Urnfield people. The situation of the settlement on a peninsula jutting out into an old lake and the elaborate rampart of cellular timber construction emphasize its essentially military character. The settlement comprised rows of identical dwellings, each row having a gabled roof in common and being separated from its neighbour by no more than a narrow corduroy timber track. The houses themselves were built on frames of vertical posts, round pine stems at the corners and rectangular oak

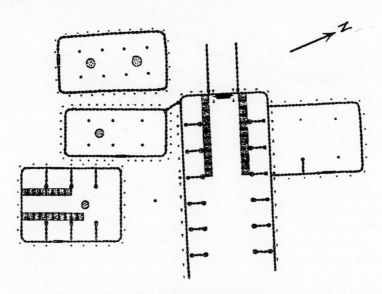

Fig. 87.　Plan of structures on the original 'terp' at Ezinge (level V),
near Groningen.　(*After van Giffen*).

ones between. The walls were filled in by short transverse planks cut into a wedge-shape at either end and inserted into grooves cut into the uprights (Fig. 88), a method still used in parts of Poland and one which calls for a high standard of wood-working. In order to prevent the main uprights from sinking too far into the soft subsoil small transverse timbers were placed underneath them recalling the " pile-shoes " devised by the early bronze age lake-dwellers of Switzerland.[110]

The iron age houses of the north were invariably more or less oblong with gabled roof. In Jutland[111] the houses of the Celtic and Roman Iron Ages were mostly from 14 to 16 metres long, though a few shorter ones were no more than 10 metres; both long and short ones had parallel rows of upright roof-supports half a metre or more inside the side walls (Pl. VII, a). The houses were grouped in small agglomerations closely hemmed in by the cultivated fields (Fig. 89). Evidence for the frequent reconstruction of individual houses shows that such villages were occupied at least for some generations. The iron age houses were designed to shelter cattle as well as men, just as the long houses of Jutland—or for that matter of parts of the British Isles—still do. The living-quarters were generally at the

---

[109] J. Kostrzewski, 1936 and 1938.
[110] e.g. at Baldegg (*S.G.U.* 1939, 40 f.) and at Bleiche-Arbon, Thurgau (*S.G.U.* 1945, 20).
[111] H. Kjaer, 1928 and 1930; G. Hatt, 1928, 1930, 1935 and 1935A, 1937A and 1938.

eastern end, the byre being down-wind and often on a lower slope: in house A at Østerbølle the floor of the byre was indeed lowered artificially as much as 25 cms. Again, whereas the byre had an earthen floor, that of the living-end was commonly covered with clay. The entrance was set in the side, commonly near the middle and the approach to the threshold was frequently paved with stones. The walls were made either from earth or sods plastered on the inner face with clay, or from wattle and daub supported by vertical posts set at

Fig. 88. Corner of Iron Age house at the fortified site of Biskupin, Poland, showing mode of construction

intervals of around half a metre. Some rainwater doubtless drained into the thickness of the earth walls, but as in the case of the Hebridean black-house water was liable to run down both faces during heavy rain; it was doubtless to catch the drip that stones were commonly placed along the wall footings of the Jutland houses. Cooking was evidently carried on over open fires, which were generally placed near the middle of the residential end of the house. Only too often the houses were burnt down and it is from such that most has been learnt about internal details; at Ginderup for instance there survived even the charred remains of what appears to have been a halter of the kind used for tethering cattle in their stalls. Water was obtained from shallow hollows sunk into the subsoil with stone packing or an old tree-stump at the base to catch the water.[112]

As research is extended it is becoming clearer that within the category of long gabled houses many subsidiary groups can be distinguished in northern Europe during the Iron Age. Even within Denmark, for instance, the houses on Fyen[113] were predominantly

[112] e.g. stone-lined wells from Skøbaek Heath and Osterbølle, Jutland (G. Hatt, 1935, Fig. 30–1 and 73–5) and tree-stump well from Lundsgaard, Fyen (A. Albrectsen, 1946, Fig. 10–11). For early wells and springs, see Clark, 1944, with refs.

[113] A. Albrectsen, 1946.

short by contrast with those of Jutland. Again, no iron age houses found on Fyen had earth or turf walls nor did any of them have rows of posts inside the walls; instead the wall posts were sufficiently strong to carry the roof and withstand its lateral thrust, though in a few cases posts were set up along the middle line of the house to carry some of the weight of the gable.

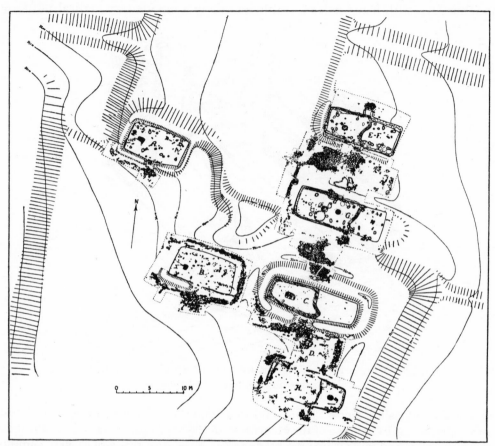

Fig. 89.   Plan of iron age settlement on Skørbaek Heath, north Jutland.   (*After Hatt*).

From the Migration Period and later long houses are known in large numbers in Scandinavia, due to the use of stone for wall-footings. This applies particularly to the Baltic islands of Gotland and Öland,[114] from the former of which around 1,100 have been identified. As a rule they occur with ancillary buildings in loose agglomerations knit together by drystone walls. How far cattle were housed in the same buildings as men is uncertain, though it seems that subsidiary byres were used at least occasionally. The houses were commonly 40 and occasionally more than 50 metres long and from 5 to 9 metres wide. As with many of the Jutland houses the main weight of the roof was borne on two rows of uprights arranged in opposite pairs on either side of a central aisle (Fig. 90). The walls, which had little structural importance, were made from a core of earth, gravel or stone rubble with stone facings and were generally between one and two metres thick. The

---

[114] M. Stenberger, 1931, 1933; A. Roussell, 1934; J. Nihlén and G. Boëthius, 1933.

main entrance was set at one end of the house, though a subsidiary one might be made in the side, as when it was desired to give access to a yard between two houses. In plan the walls, unlike the settings of roof posts, tapered at either end and the corners were somewhat rounded. The floors were commonly sunk slightly and covered with stamped clay, broken in places by stone paving. Long houses, dating from the same period have been studied in Jaeren and Lista, in south-west Norway.[115] Although resembling in some ways the Baltic examples they agree with the Jutland ones of the Celtic and Roman Iron Ages, in that they were invariably entered from the side and gave shelter to cattle as well as men.

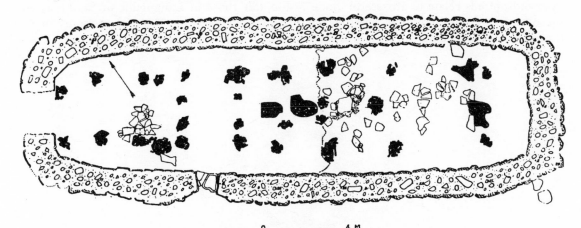

0   4 M

Fig. 90. Iron Age long house, Brostorp, Öland. (*After Stenberger*).
Scale in metres.

In the British Isles, on the contrary, there is little evidence for any other than round or at least curvilinear houses during the Early Iron Age.[116] The evidence already cited from Knockadoon suggests that round houses were being built alongside oblong ones already during neolithic times in southern Ireland.[117] Many of the hut-circles on Dartmoor and some no doubt in other parts of the highland zone[118] relate to a native bronze age, if not to a still older tradition. The Dartmoor huts occur both in isolation and in groups which may be surrounded by irregular curvilinear enclosures or pounds. Grimspound,[119]

---

[115] H. Shetelig, 1909; J. Petersen, 1933 and 1936; A. Roussell, 1934; S. Grieg, 1934.

[116] Indications of rectilinear houses have been claimed at Maiden Castle, Dorset, but the settings of post-holes at site B could more easily be explained as relating to drying-frames and those at site L reveal no certainly rectilinear plan (see R. E. M. Wheeler, 1943, 36, 90, 124–5 and Pl. VII and Fig. 22). A rectilinear house has been claimed, but not certainly validated, at Park Brow, Sussex (*Archæologia* LXXVI, 26 and 34).

[117] S. P. O'Riordain, 1946, 147–8 and Pl. IX, 1 and 2.

[118] e.g. F. Elgee, 1930, 134 ff. Elgee's evidence, while suggestive, is hardly satisfying in detail. The supposed hut-circles, associated with beaker pottery, in the parish of Muirkirk, Ayrshire, published by J. G. A. Baird (*P.S.A.S.* XLVIII, 1914, 373–81) are surely better interpreted as cairn circles. As regards the group on Carrowkeel Mountain, Co. Sligo, comprising at least 47 and probably more circles with thick stone-faced walls, no datable material has ever been found in any of these and there is therefore no proof that they were associated with the cemetery of chambered tombs, which nevertheless surrounded them on three sides (*P.R.I.A.* XXIX (1912), Sect. C, 331–2 and 344–5).

[119] S. Baring Gould *et al.*, 1894.

one of the best preserved of these, contained some twenty-four huts, of which about half seem to have served as dwellings. The walls of the huts were up to six feet thick and were made of turf and loose stones with dry-stone facings. The internal diameters ranged from $6\frac{1}{2}$ to $15\frac{1}{2}$ feet, but the great majority were between 9 and 12 feet across. The entrances, formed of stone uprights and lintels, were low and narrow and sometimes screened by a projecting wall (Fig. 91). Each dwelling normally contained a hearth, stone-lined cooking-hole and low stone bench, presumably for sleeping. The nature of the country in which they are found, and such indications as the absence of grinding-stones, suggest that these huts and pounds relate to a pastoral mode of life, like those of Languedoc or Sardinia; on the other hand it is unknown whether they relate to whole-time pastoral economy or to transhumance on the part of people who cultivated the soil in the valleys.

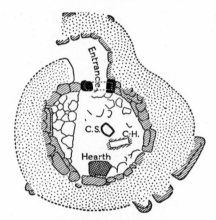

Fig. 91. Hut circle, Grimspound, Devon.

The antiquity of the round-house in lowland Britain is still shrouded in a gloom which only excavation can illuminate. At the same time, the erection of henge monuments and of timber structures in round barrows, like the one observed in barrow 23 on Calais Wold in the East Riding of Yorkshire,[120] argues that already, early in the second millennium B.C., a tradition of building circular constructions of house-like character was firmly rooted in the lowland zone. Until more work has been done on domestic sites of the period, both in south-eastern England and on contiguous parts of the continent, it is hardly possible though to estimate the part played by indigenous bronze age traditions in the development of the early iron age architecture of Britain. The earliest round houses, of which the existence can be proved in the lowland zone, are those associated with late bronze age immigrants on the Sussex Downs. Generally they were built on a framework of vertical posts set at intervals round the perimeter and sometimes encircling a central post. At Plumpton Plain and kindred sites they are found in small groups of oblong enclosures with rounded corners and were associated more or less certainly with Celtic fields, through which they were approached by tracks.[121]

Many of the most characteristic types of early iron age settlement—hill- and promontory-forts, crannogs, brochs and the like—were the product of political insecurity rather than of

---

[120] J. R. Mortimer, 1905, 155 and Figs. 397 and 400. Cf. the structure revealed by Fox in Sheepley's barrow, 279, Llantwit Major, Glam., *Ant. J.*, 1941. 111, 114, 123.

[121] E. C. Curwen, 1937, 186–98.

strictly economic necessity. Apart from these, though, several distinct forms can be recognized. First there are small agglomerations of dwellings of the kind which existed in parts of Britain already from the Stone Age; thus, at Chysauster,[122] the buildings were arranged in four pairs on either side of a road to form a long hamlet (Fig. 92). Then, there is evidence, mainly inferential, for more substantial villages; thus, although considerations

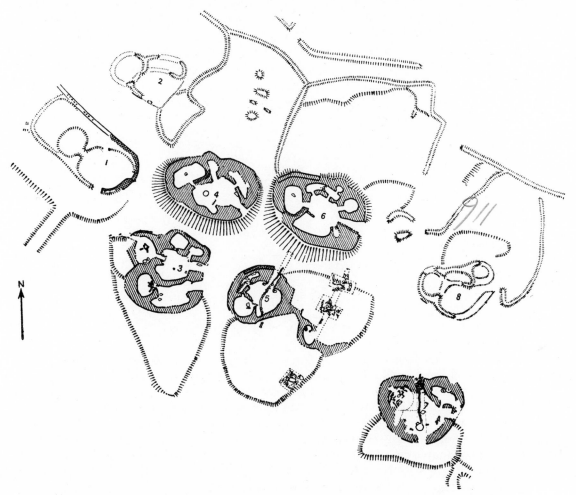

Fig. 92. Hamlet of courtyard houses, Chysauster, Cornwall. (*After Hencken*).
Scale: 90 feet to 1 inch.

of security may have determined the site of the Glastonbury and Meare marsh-settlements, the intensity with which they were occupied—more than sixty of the Glastonbury mounds were provided with hearths, most of which had been several times reconstructed—and their character as centres of leather-working, wood-turning and weaving makes it reasonable to regard them as real villages rather than as mere refuges (Fig. 93). [123] Thirdly, there

---

[122] H. O'N. Hencken, 1933.
[123] Bulleid and Gray, 1911; V. G. Childe, 1940, 234 f.

is evidence for the existence during the Early Iron Age of more or less isolated, farm-steads; and this applies not only to the north-western parts of the highland zone, where mixed farming gave way to a specialized pastoral mode of life with the onset of the wet Sub-atlantic climate, but equally to lowland Britain where stock-raising was combined with cereal cultivation. Bersu's excavation of Ballacagen on the Isle of Man[124] has revealed a circular homestead designed to shelter livestock as well as men, an exemplar of the single homestead unit of Celtic pastoral society during the first centuries of our era. Of the lowland sites Little Woodbury, near Salisbury,[125] may serve as an example (Pl. VIII, b). To judge from the loose finds and from the amount of reconstruction, the home-stead seems to have been occupied for around two or three centuries. At any one moment it

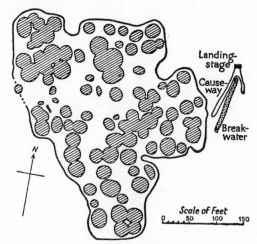

Fig. 93. Plan of marsh village of Glastonbury.

is improbable that there was more than a single dwelling; this was accompanied by drying-racks, storage-pits lined no doubt with some such material as basketry or leather, store-houses mounted on piles and hollows used in connection with preparing grain, the whole being enclosed within a timber palisade. The ditches, which were begun in the course of the occupation and never completed, played no part in the life of the farmstead.

So far as the houses themselves were concerned, those built in early iron age Britain included many of simple circular form built either on a framework of vertical posts or from earth and stone.[126] It is likely, indeed, that the dwellings erected on the circular platforms at Glastonbury (Fig. 94) were in effect little more than wigwams, though even so the floors sank so badly in the bog that they and the hearths with them had to be renewed at frequent intervals.

In the highland zone the simple round house was sometimes incorporated, together with ancillary buildings, within the thickness of a massive wall of earth and stones with dry-stone facings enclosing an open courtyard. Courtyard houses of this kind began to be made during the Late Bronze Age in Shetland, as Curle has shown for instance in the case of Jarlshof (Fig. 95).[127] On the other hand some at least of those in north Wales, where

---

[124] G. Bersu, 1946.

[125] G. Bersu, 1940; see also *P.P.S.* 1948, 1–23 and 1949, 156–68.

[126] Thus the majority of the houses occupied by the native population of northern England during the Roman occupation were of this form. See A. H. A. Hogg, 1943.   [127] A. O. Curle, 1932-4.

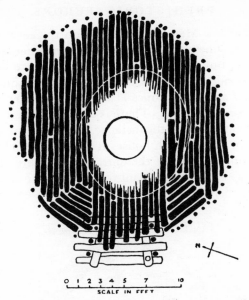

Fig. 94.   Floor of hut at Glastonbury marsh-village.

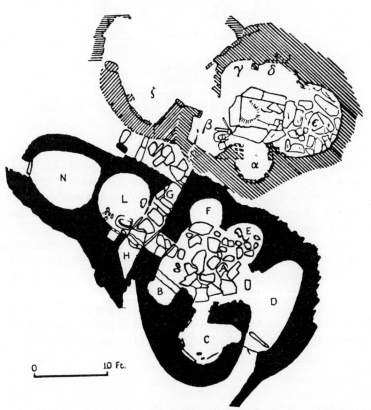

Fig. 95.   Houses I (lower) and V (upper) at Jarlshof, Shetland.
(*After Curle*).

167

they occur on either side of the Menai Straits and on the coast of Merioneth, date from the mid-Roman period.[127a]   There is evidence that Chysauster dates from near the close of the prehistoric Iron Age, but courtyard houses continued to be built in west Cornwall down to the late Roman period.[128]   The common presence of querns in courtyard houses —saddle-querns at Jarlshof and rotary ones at Chysauster—emphasizes that their inhabitants lived to a certain degree on cereals.   There is also evidence that they kept at least some of their cattle under cover: at Jarlshof, for instance, the rear room of house V seems to have been used as a stable and in the Cornish houses it is usual to find an elongated chamber in the thickness of the wall on the right of the entrance, destitute of settlement material but capable of housing two beasts.   It is important to note that the courtyards were open to the sky and that where hearths have been detected these have been set in the dwelling-house itself.

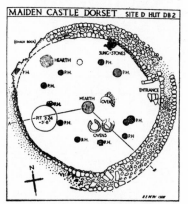

Fig. 96.   Iron Age B house at Maiden Castle, Dorset.
(*After R. E. M. Wheeler*).
Scale 15 feet to 1 inch.

The commonest way of enlarging round houses was to support the roof on a continuous lintel mounted on a ring of powerful uprights.   If the roof was allowed to rest directly on the ground, as may well have happened at the early iron age settlements of East Harling, Norfolk,[129] and Castle Dore, Cornwall,[130] the general form might be conical.   More often the outer span of the roof rested on side walls and these might be made either from earth or stone or built on a frame of timber uprights.   As a rule the former were commoner in the highland, the latter in the lowland zone, though local factors affected the supply of timber and the traditional requirements of intruders might further complicate the pattern, as illustrated for example by the chalk-walled house with inner circle of posts from Maiden Castle, Dorset (Fig. 96). [131]   Where timber was very scarce, as it was in parts of the highland zone during the Early Iron Age, radial stone piers might replace timber posts (Fig. 97), a method well seen in the so-called wheel-houses of Orkney, Shetland and the Hebrides.[132]

[127a] B. H. St. J. O'Neil, 1936.

[128] e.g. Porthmeor, Zennor.

[129] Excavations conducted by the author for the Norfolk Research Committee and the Prehistoric Society (1948).

[130] Information from Mr. C. A. Ralegh Radford.

[131] R. E. M. Wheeler, 1943, 94, Fig. 18.

[132] Sir Lindsay Scott, 1947, 21–5 and 1948.

The scale on which round houses with inner circles of uprights were sometimes built
might be considerable. For instance the earlier of the two Little Woodbury houses was
nearly 15 metres in diameter (Fig. 98). The roof was contrived with a break to admit

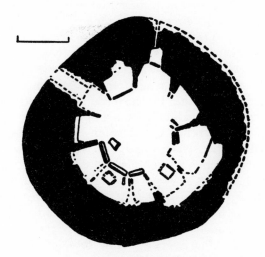

Fig. 97.   Early wheel-house, Calf of Eday, Orkney.
(*After Scott*)
Scale of 10 ft.

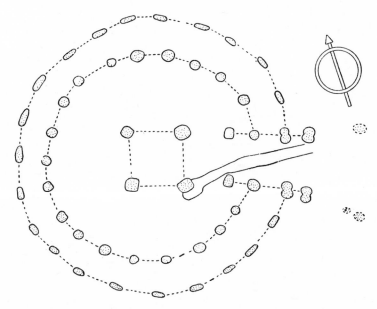

Fig. 98.   Plan of the original iron age house at the Little Woodbury
farmstead, near Salisbury, Wilts. (*After Bersu*).

light and allow the escape of smoke, the loftiest part being carried on a square setting of four exceptionally powerful posts, and a well-made porch was provided to give easy access through the roof-slope.

Little evidence has yet been obtained about the artificial shelters made by the Arctic hunter-fishers over much of the circumpolar zone. The stone age dwelling-places of Finland,[133] for example, are marked by nothing more than scatters of artifacts and charcoal and an occasional hearth, but it is fair to assume that tents of bark or skins or conical huts of pine stems were used. More substantial houses were built on the coast of Norway where sea fishing made for greater fixity of settlement along the stone age strands. Intensive work by Gjessing[134] on Sanda in the Traena Islands off north-west Norway has shown that the mesolithic Nøstvet people made oval huts, but that their successors living about the time of the passage-graves and stone cists of south Scandinavia occupied oblong houses. These Arctic houses had earthen walls faced with stone and usually $2\frac{1}{2}$ or more metres thick, a mode of construction encountered already during the Stone Age on the treeless margins of the temperate forest, as at Skara Brae, and more widespread in highland Britain and southern Scandinavia during the Early Iron Age. To give some idea of the scale of the Sanda houses, No. XXI was over 12 metres long inside and from $2\frac{3}{4}$ to $3\frac{1}{2}$ meters across. The entrance passage was normally driven through one of the side walls near one end. The hearth was placed inside near the doorway. The roof, presumably made from wood or whale-bone heaped over with earth or turf, was supported by rows of posts set some distance in from each side wall recalling the aisled houses of the Baltic farmers.

---

[133] J. Ailio, 1909, 6–7.
[134] G. Gjessing, 1943, e.g. Pl. VI and IX; also 1944, 46 f.

CHAPTER VII

TECHNOLOGY: STONE, BRONZE AND IRON

IF we are to arrive at any clear understanding of economic life in prehistoric times, close attention must be paid to technology, since it was through this that early man adjusted his relationship to external nature and so modified his way of life. Whatever the ultimate inspiration or the intermediate cause, it was by their hands that the early Europeans dragged themselves out of the primeval mire of savagery, struggled up the long and undulating slopes of barbarism and ultimately attained to some kind of civilized existence. Many of the material objects which form the principal documents of archæology were in themselves the means whereby prehistoric man augmented his limbs in the struggle to satisfy his needs. They were at once the tools and the products of handicrafts through which early man transmitted his stock of technical knowledge and brought it to bear on the habitat and biome of the eco-systems of which he formed part.

FLINT AND STONE

Any consideration of the crafts of prehistoric man should logically begin with the working of flint and stone and with metallurgy, since these have not only produced the objects on which the fundamental classification of prehistoric cultures has long been based, but have themselves set well-defined limits to human achievement in the whole sphere of technology and indeed of economic life. As Professor Childe has recently shown,[1] there is a very real sense in which Thomsen's ages of Stone, Bronze and Iron can in fact be equated with significant stages in the control exercised by human societies over their external environment, or rather, as one may prefer to put it, in the role played by these societies in their respective eco-systems. This is true, even though communities at the same stage as regards the chief material used for tools, may in other respects appear to stand in quite distinct categories. It may be admitted for instance that the most significant change in the mode of subsistence, the transition from food-gathering to food-production, took place within the same technological stage and that in this sense the concept of a Stone Age masks a fundamential turning-point in economic history. Yet this very instance in reality helps to emphasze the importance of the technological factor. The revolutionary implications of the change in the basis of subsistence have too often obscured the slightness of the alteration it immediately involved in the standard of living of prehistoric societies. There was in reality a far closer community between the earliest peasants and the mesolithic hunter-fishers of temperate Europe than is generally admitted. The change in subsistence itself can hardly have been so very abrupt, but the important fact is that both neolithic and mesolithic communities were alike subject to the same limitations imposed by their common stone age technology ; it was because of this, for example, that the Danubian farmers were

---

[1] V. G. Childe, 1944.

no further advanced in many matters than the Maglemosian hunter-fishers of the North European Plain.

A point to which full weight has not always been given is that in the sphere of stone-working itself practically every form and every technique available to neolithic man had already been anticipated or even perfected by craftsmen at a food-gathering stage of subsistence. The striking of flakes from elaborately prepared cores in the Levallois technique, which survived, even if in somewhat specialized form, in the manufactories of Grimes Graves till the end of neolithic times, had already been developed at an early stage of the Old Stone Age. The scraper, awl, spokeshave, saw and even the leaf-shaped and the barbed and tanged arrowhead[2] with delicate surface flaking had already appeared among certain upper palæolithic cultures, but on the other hand the many kinds of burin or graver characteristic of the latter failed to survive in other than degenerate from among the neolithic farmers of Europe. The flint axe and adze which played so great a part in neolithic economy, both in the clearance of forest and the working of timber, first appeared in Europe among communities of hunter-fishers at an early stage of the forest period, and the polishing of the flint blades, which marks one of the few neolithic innovations in this sphere and may well reflect the increased importance of forest-clearance due to the needs of agriculture, itself represents no more than the transference of a technique applied since upper palæolithic times to bone and antler and already extended by mesolithic hunter-fishers to the shaping of stone blades.[3] The technique of shaping stone by pecking was applied by mesolithic, as well as by neolithic man, to the production of axes from coarse-grained rocks.[4] The cutting of fine-grained rock by means of saws, either of sandstone or of wood or bone used with an abrasive, to form flat axes and chisels, marks another extension of a technique applied much earlier to antler and bone, and it is significant that identical methods appear to have been used in central and in circumpolar Europe, for instance among the farmers of the Swiss lake-villages[5] and among the hunter-fishers of the Finnish dwelling-places.[6] Some advance can be noted in the direct perforation of stone axes by means of a tubular drill,[7] since mesolithic man perforated sandstone and quartzite by the clumsy method of sinking hollows from opposed faces resulting in holes of hour-glass[8] form ;

---

[2] The barbed and tanged arrowheads found by Pericot García in the cave of Parpallo, near Gandia in E. Spain, below a Magdalenian level. See Pericot García, 1942, Figs. 21–6, and Fig. 38.

[3] e.g. the perforated adze of fine-grained gneiss with ground cutting-edge from the Maglemosian station Holmegaard (H. C. Broholm, 1931, 40–2 and J. G. D. Clark, 1936, 105). Although chipped and polished stone axes of Limhamn type first appeared at a late stage of the Ertebølle culture in Denmark (E. Westerby, 1927, 44) at a time when farming was beginning to spread into Denmark and south Sweden, they were nevertheless made by hunter-fishers.

[4] Pebble axes, comprising natural forms regularised by pecking and having the cutting-edge ground smooth, were found at the mesolithic station of Sandarna, near Gothenburg, Sweden (Alin, Niklasson and Thomasson, 1934, 86–9). Stump-butted axes pecked into shape and with ground cutting edge goes back to the earliest stage of the Ertebølle culture (T. Mathiassen et al., 1942, 71).

[5] H. Reinerth, 1926, 100–1.

[6] J. Ailio, 1909, I, 57–8 and abb. 53–5 ; II, 56, abb. 32 and Taf. 16, 3.

[7] The technique goes back to Danubian I times in south-east Europe ; see V. G. Childe, 1929, Fig. 22 and p. 40. For illustrations of incomplete perforations by this method, see inter alia H. Reinerth, 1926, abb. 28 ; Ailio, 1909, I, abb. 33 and II, abb. 6 and 53.

[8] For Danish Maglemosian occurrences, see Broholm, 1931, 85–6 and Clark, 1936, 145 and Fig. 53, 2. A sandstone sinker with hour-glass perforation from Kunda is illustrated by Indreko, 1948, abb. 79, No. 5. Similar maces were used by the Finnish dwelling-place people, as shown by Ailio, 1909, I, 29 and abb. 24. For English examples, see W. F. Rankine, 1949.

on the other hand the method of direct perforation was commonly applied to bone and antler axes and adzes in mesolithic times.[9] Two of the most characteristic elements in the equipment of European farmers up to well into the Bronze Age, the flint-bladed reaping knife and the sickle, incorporate the mesolithic innovation of insetting flint flakes into slots to form a sharp edge: among the mesolithic Maglemosians of northern Europe and among hunter-fisher communities extending far into Siberia the device was used for knives and for the points of hunting weapons,[10] and it is significant that it was already brought into use among the Natufians of Palestine for reaping-knives presumed to have been used for harvesting wild grasses.[11] Thus, one is justified in concluding that the neolithic farmers of Europe made no fundamental advances in the technology of flint and stone, though, in common to a large extent with contemporary hunter-fishers in the circumpolar zone, they extended the application of certain techniques originally acquired by palæolithic or meso-lithic man to new materials, and to new uses.

The kinds of stone available to the prehistoric Europeans varied widely in different localities and, since a close relation existed between the properties of the raw material and the techniques most suitable for working it, this meant that the geological structure of different parts of the continent influenced to a greater or less extent the character of the prevailing lithic industries. An obvious example of this may be found in the contrast between the slate industries of northern Scandinavia and the flint industries of much of temperate Europe. On the other hand cultural traditions, once these had taken root, effectively determined the choice of materials. As G. Gjessing has pointed out,[12] the dolomitic flint available in limited quantities in parts of northern Norway, which were eagerly exploited by the earliest inhabitants of Finmark with their tradition of flaking, were on the other hand virtually ignored by the later Arctic people of the circumpolar slate tradition. In so far as traditions of working in flint and stone were originally formed by utilizing the inherent and sometimes peculiar properties of different raw materials, it is only to be expected that the stone age peoples should continue to choose where possible the kinds of flint or stone best suited to their traditional techniques. Thus, when flint-using peoples penetrated an area where this material was scarce, they either continued, as in parts of northern Britain, to seek it out and use it down to the smallest fragments, even though this severely cramped their style of work and limited the size of their tools, or where available they might turn to some substitute, such as the fine-grained, tractable and tough augite-granophyre of north Wales or the greenstone of west Norway. The relationship between the availability of raw materials in nature and the character of stone industries was thus a complex one, since it involved the factor of cultural choice, and this complexity was of course greatly increased by the possibility of consciously modifying the geological distribu-tion by means of trade.

Stones adapted for pecking, sawing and rubbing into shape occurred profusely in regions where these techniques were at home, and except in so far as certain local varieties were preferred to others, there was no problem of supply; suitable pieces had only to be selected from beaches, stream beds or mountain slopes. Although flint and certain kinds of stone

---

[9] For mesolithic uses, see Clark, 1936, 112 and Fig. 40, Nos. 1-4.

[10] The device is found in mesolithic contexts as far west as western Norway, Denmark and Belgium. Small slotted wooden handles inset with flint knives are found in the Swiss lakeside settlements (Reinerth, 1926, abb. 30).

[11] D. A. E. Garrod, 1937, 37–8, Pl. XIII, I. For discussion see E. C. Curwen, 1941, 331 f.

[12] G. Gjessing, 1942, 24–5.

suitable for flaking are also widely distributed in nature and could be collected from surface deposits, the supply of the best varieties was much more restricted or difficult to obtain, and could only be achieved either by mining or quarrying or by working intensively local surface deposits by means of more or less complex economic organization, involving a comparatively advanced degree of specialization and sub-division of labour. Activities of this kind centred particularly, although not exclusively on the supply of axe and adze blades. It has been claimed that flint was already being mined in parts of Poland[13] during mesolithic times. Certainly the Nøstvet hunter-fishers of Norway had begun to organize the supply of a particularly effective and easily flaked greenstone, found only on the tiny islet of Hespriholmen (Pl. XV, a), off the extreme west coast, before farming economy had spread into the area. Supplies were quarried from the solid rock along a front of some thirty metres. The floor of the working was barely a metre above sea-level at the time and the material could conveniently have been removed by boat to the factories on the much larger island of Bømlo.[14]

The great increase in the demand for axes of the finest quality associated with the need for clearing forest for agriculture, led to an enlargement and intensification of activities concerned with their supply during neolithic times. One of the most striking manifestations of this was a great development in the mining of flint.[15] The principal centres were situated in the cretaceous areas of south-eastern England, north-eastern France, and the Belgian provinces of Hainaut and Liége, but flint-mines have been found in the Charente and the south Auvergne, in an isolated cretaceous area at Rocio, Lisbon, in the Tertiary lime-stone of Monte Tabuto, Sicily, and sunk into small chalk rafts at Kvarnby and Tullstorp near Malmo in south Sweden. Since the technical means available to the miners were so limited, the methods adopted to win the flint depended to a large extent upon such factors as the depth at which the veins occurred, the character of the parent rock and the thickness of overlying deposits. Where the vein of flint which it was desired to work outcropped on or close to the surface, the material could often be obtained most easily by numerous open workings. Otherwise it was necessary to reach the flint either by tunnelling, as was done at Monte Tabuto, or as most often happened in the chalk by means of vertical shafts. Since this involved arduous, unproductive work, the miners sought in each case to tap as large an area of flint as possible, either by undercutting the base of the shaft or by sending out a radiating series of horizontal galleries. To some extent the choice was determined by the depth at which the flint occurred: only where the shaft was really deep and the amount of dead work commensurately great was it economic to drive galleries from the bottom, as at Spiennes for example (Fig. 99), the deepest shafts of which were over 50 feet deep ; where, as at Easton Down or Stoke Down, the flint was only a few metres deep, it paid to sink a larger number of shafts and to rest content with enlarging the bases of these. Investigations at Spiennes[16] and later at Grimes Graves[17] suggest that new mine-fields were first opened up by working outcrops and that shafts were not sunk until it became necessary to follow the vein underground : in this way one can understand how the ancients came to penetrate

---

[13] Information from Professor Sulimirski.

[14] Excavations at Sokkemyra on Bömlo have shown that the axe-factories were most active during the Nøstvet stage, though the industry was also carried on by the Vepestad farmers. See K. Faegri, 1943, 51–68.

[15] References to most of the main sites will be found in Clark & Piggott, 1933, 183.

[16] Briart et al., 1868, 1872 and 1889 ; de Loë and Munck, 1889 ; Baron A. de Loë, 1928, I, 184–94.

[17] Grimes Graves Report, 1914; A. L. Armstrong, 1926, 125.

depths of up to thirty feet of overlying deposits, and then to pass through veins of inferior flint in the chalk, at Grimes Graves two and at Spiennes as many as ten, before being in a position to obtain the flint they sought. Another factor to be considered was safety. Although the stone age miners sometimes sustained fatal accidents—the man of Obourg, crushed by a fall of roof while still grasping his antler pick in one hand, is a well-known example[18]—their judgment, based as it was on practical and professional experience of the work in hand, was generally sound and can be judged by the skill with which they

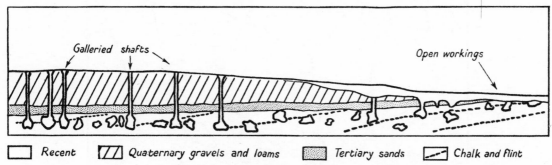

| Recent | Quaternary gravels and loams | Tertiary sands | Chalk and flint |

Fig. 99.   Diagrammatic section through the flint-mining area at Spiennes, Hainaut, Belgium. (*After Cornet and Briart*).

cut the galleries at such sites as Grimes Graves (Fig. 100), Cissbury, Champignolles and Spiennes, leaving pillars just sufficient to support the roof. Indeed, their wisdom has since been confirmed rather strikingly at La Petite-Garenne, where they prudently refrained from driving galleries, since modern road-builders tunnelling the site for road-metal met with a fatal accident.[19]

As regards the implements used in the mining it is interesting to note how important was the part played at many centres by red deer antler, a wild product of the forest background. The commonest tool of this material was the so-called pick (Fig. 101), which consisted of the main beam of an antler cut short above the trez tine and from which all others than the brow tine were removed.[20] As well as being widely distributed the antler pick sometimes occurred in great numbers, no less than 244 coming from the galleries of two of the pits at Grimes Graves, Norfolk (Pl. IV, a).   It is evident that implements of this material could hardly have been used to hew the chalk with a swinging blow as one might wield a metal pick. It has sometimes been argued from the occurrence at the back immediately behind the brow tine of abrasions and cut-marks, sometimes accompanied by minute spicules of flint, that the picks were used for hammering the flint nodules, either to detach them or to break them into smaller pieces.[21] Yet, the fact that this feature occurs on so large a proportion and that in most cases the projecting burr is undamaged, makes it seem more likely that the marks were caused by hammering the antler with a flint nodule and not the other way round. That the brow tines were functional is shown by the signs of wear which they normally exhibit, when indeed they have not been damaged or broken off in use, by the number of holes in the chalk made by them and by the fact that examples have

[18] Baron A. de Loë, 1928, I, 216–17.

[19] Clark and Piggott, 1933, 181.

[20] H. W. Sanders, 1910; *Grimes Graves Report*, 1914, 142 f.

[21] *Grimes Graves Report*, 144.

been found embedded in the walls of the mine at Mur-de-Barrez.[22] The most satisfactory explanation is that given by Curwen,[23] who supposes that the brow tines were hammered

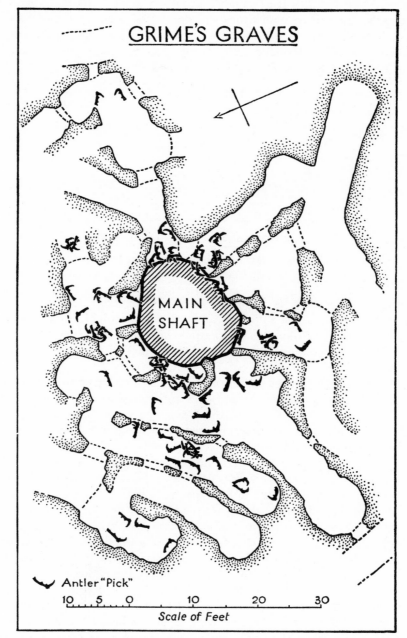

Fig. 100.   Flint mine galleries radiating from shaft : Grime's Graves, Norfolk.

at intervals into natural lines of fracture in the chalk and that intervening and adjacent slabs were then levered out by exerting pressure on the handles of one or more picks at a

---

[22] *ibid.*, 27.   [23] E. C. Curwen, 1937, 112–13.

time. In an uncompleted operation of this kind, of which traces were found in one of the galleries at Blackpatch,[24] seven picks appear to have been used. This helps to account for the very large numbers in which the antler picks commonly occur.

At Spiennes the chief mining tool was the rough flint pick, the marks of which were visible on the chalk walls and many hundreds of specimens of which were found discarded in the workings.[25] There is evidence that flint was occasionally used to cut the galleries

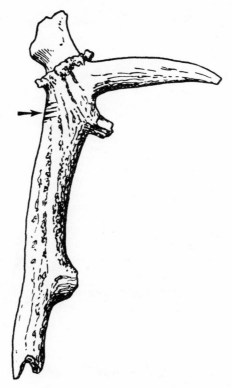

Fig. 101. Deer antler "pick," Grime's Graves, Norfolk. The arrow points to abrasions and cuts.

at Grimes Graves,[26] perhaps at points where the rock was particularly tough, and there is no doubt that polished stone axes were also used for the same purpose.[27] Fire was used to dislodge or break the flint at Mur-de-Barrez,[28] but no signs of this have been noted in the English mines. Two-pronged rakes (Fig. 102, 1) made from antler have been found at several sites on both sides of the Channel[29]; other antler tools include hammers

---

[24] *ibid.*, Pl. IX; also *Sussex Arch. Soc. Coll.* LXV, 1924, 79.

[25] de Loë, 1928, I, Figs. 59 and 60.

[26] *Report*, 1914, 59.

[27] Canon Greenwell found a basalt axe while excavating a gallery at Grimes Graves (Clark and Piggott, 1933, Fig. 4). Marks of such an axe were noted both during Greenwell's own excavations (*J. Ethn. Soc.*, London, Ser. 2, Vol. II, 429) and during the 1914 excavations (*Report*, 43 and 84; A. L. Armstrong, 1926, 99).

[28] *Grimes Graves Report*, 1914, 27.

[29] e.g. at Grimes Graves, Blackpatch, Harrow Hill, Champignolles and Spiennes.

or mallets,[30] wedges made from single tines[31] and a perforated axe-hammer from Mur-de-Barrez.[32]   Shovels made from the shoulder-blades of ox, deer or pig by chopping off the spine were used at Cissbury and Harrow Hill (Fig. 102, 2–5).   In the galleried mines at least some form of artificial lighting must have been necessary, and in some of the English mines, including Grimes Graves and Cissbury, this was provided by lamps hollowed

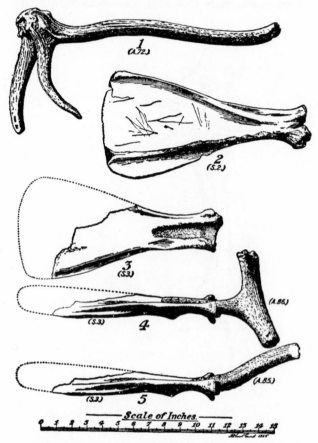

Fig. 102.   Antler rake (1) and shoulder-blade shovels (2–5), from the
Harrow Hill flint-mines, near Worthing, Sussex.   (*After Curwen*).

out of chalk blocks, of the type also found in the neolithic " camps " of Sussex and Wessex.[33] An alternative form of lighting would have been by faggot or taper, such as was used in the late bronze age copper mines of the eastern Alps.   Access to the mines at Spiennes was given by wooden steps, the sockets of which were noted in the chalk walls of the shafts.[34] Much of the spoil from the galleries was disposed of by packing worked-out portions, but the material excavated from the shafts and the flint itself all had to be evacuated

[30] e.g. at Harrow Hill and Spiennes.
[31] e.g. at Harrow Hill.
[32] Clark and Piggott, 1933, Fig. 2, No. 3.
[33] *ibid.*, Figs. 5 and 9.
[34] *Grimes Graves Rep.*, 1914, 22.

presumably in baskets or leather sacks ; indications of wear by ropes both on the walls of the pit shaft and on the soffits of the gallery adits at Grimes Graves[35] suggest that these were sometimes hauled to the surface, though there is no evidence for the use of the windlass in stone age Europe.

It is hardly possible yet to reach detailed conclusions about the economic organization implied by the prehistoric flint-mines (Pl. VIII, a), few of which have been investigated systematically and none with any approach to completeness.   Yet one is entitled to assume from the technical difficulties encountered and from the way in which these were overcome that the miners were professionals.   That they lived exclusively by mining and by working up the product or not can only be determined when it has been established whether the mines and factories operated all the year round or merely during slack seasons in the farming year, something which could be settled if a sufficiently large body of biological fossils was collected and studied from this point of view.   Our knowledge would also be much more soundly based if more attention had been paid to indications of settlement in connection with the mines ; the discoveries at Easton Down, Wiltshire,[36] only emphasize the need for more extensive excavations of a similar character.   The fact that pottery belonging to more than one ceramic tradition is sometimes found on mining sites—Windmill Hill and Peterborough ware occurred at Grimes Grave and at Easton Down beakers as well—suggests that expeditions may have come from different communities to replenish supplies of axe blades, possibly camping in the vicinity of the factories as did the stone age people of central Australia down to modern times.[37]

An approximate idea of the scale of the mining operations can be gained from their extent at the few sites where this has been established. At Grimes Graves for example the total mined area covered at least 34 acres : just under half of this was exploited by means of comparatively deep galleried mines leaving surface hollows and of these some 366 have been counted; the remaining $17\frac{1}{2}$ acres were worked by shallow pits, invisible on the surface, but whose presence is inferred from excavation at various points.[38]   The investigations at Grimes Graves have made it quite clear that more than one of the deep pits, the subterranean galleries of which interconnect, must have been open at the same time,[39] though how many pits were worked at once is unknown, nor can it be told how long the mining lasted.   Some idea of the labour involved can be gained by considering the volume of material removed.   At Grimes Graves it has been calculated that the galleries of one of the deep pits involved nearly 5,000 cubic feet of quarrying : the same amount was removed from the shaft of one of the pits cleared in 1914, and it is interesting to recall that pit I at Grimes Graves was evacuated by a gang of three men, two digging, one barrowing, using simple tackle, in twenty working days.[40]   In estimating the effort involved for the stone age miners, it has to be appreciated that removing loose material is a good deal easier than quarrying undisturbed rock and, even allowing for the overlay of boulder clay and sand and the batter of the sides, at least two-thirds of the shaft was solid chalk; in addition one has to allow for the quarrying of an equivalent volume of material, all of it chalk or flint, from the galleries, and for the fact that equipment was poorer.   Yet, it may not be extravagant

---

[35] *ibid.*, 72 and 82.

[36] J. F. S. Stone, 1931–5.

[37] A. W. Howitt, 1904, 311–12.

[38] A. L. Armstrong, 1926, 91.

[39] *Report*, 1914, 63.

[40] *ibid.*, 92.

to assert that a gang of three men—and there were indications at Grimes Graves that only a few workers operated each pit—could have exhausted a deep mine and coped with the product within say half a year. Assuming for the sake of argument that three pits were operated at the same time and that work at the mines was carried on during only six months in the year, this would allow a hundred and twenty years or so to exhaust the deep mining area at Grimes Graves, with a total of nine men working at any one time. It need hardly be added that these figures are given by way of illustration and are not intended as a serious estimate, for which the basis hardly yet exists.

Whatever may ultimately be proved about the tempo of activity at the flint-mines, there can be no doubt about their object, which was to supply material for manufacture into objects for trading or exchange. The mines were centres of flint-working on a commercial scale far transcending the needs of the mining communities or their immediate neighbours, and the miners, in so far as they devoted their time to mining or knapping, lived by what they received in exchange, supplemented by the labour and production of their families. The reason for working the flint as close as possible to the sources of raw material lay in its weight and in the high proportion of waste involved in the manufacture of tools ; the reduction of the weight of material for carriage brought about by manufacturing on the spot was a matter of special importance to people limited by the exigencies of stone age transport. Evidence for the trade which called into being the axe factories will be dealt with in a later chapter, but it is worth saying something more here about the salient features of the industry.

It should first be emphasized that the axe factories at the flint-mining centres differ in no significant way from those associated with surface supplies of flint or stone of special quality and commercial value; each was called into being by similar economic forces and shared the same essential characteristics. The material found on the flaking-floors, whether at the mines, at surface spreads of flint like those on Rügen[41] or in the Stevns district of Zealand,[42] or at exposures of tough but easily worked and keenly sought after stone, like those explored at Langdale in the English Lake District,[43] at Graig Lwyd, Caernarvonshire[44] or at Teivebulliagh, near Cushendall, Antrim,[45] comprises in the main the mass of waste and by-products of knapping, together with axes discarded at various stages of manufacture, from rough-outs resembling palæolithic " hand-axes "[46] to tools damaged at the point of completion (Fig. 103). The early stages of manufacture varied according to the nature of the material, the flint workers starting from nodules, the stone-workers either from scree or from flakes struck off large blocks ; but the types of thinning-flake and rough-out recur at widely separated sites. In certain cases, notably in the Danish area, the flint was merely roughed out into bars before being traded, but as a rule the axes were finished up to the point at which they were ready for grinding and polishing.

Polished axes are either absent from the workshops, as they were at Langdale, or else, like the few used and broken specimens from Graig Lwyd, are best interpreted as personal

---

[41] Ebert, *Reallexikon*, VIII, 466.

[42] J. G. D. Clark, 1948A, 219.

[43] B. Bunch and Clare I. Fell, 1949.

[44] S. H. Warren, 1919, 1921, 1922.

[45] W. J. Knowles, 1903, 1906. Also information from Professor E. E. Evans, and Mr Frank Mitchell.

[46] It was these that led Mr R. A. Smith to classify the industry as palaeolithic (*Archæologia*, LXIII, 109 f., and *Grimes Graves Report*, 1914, 147 f.).

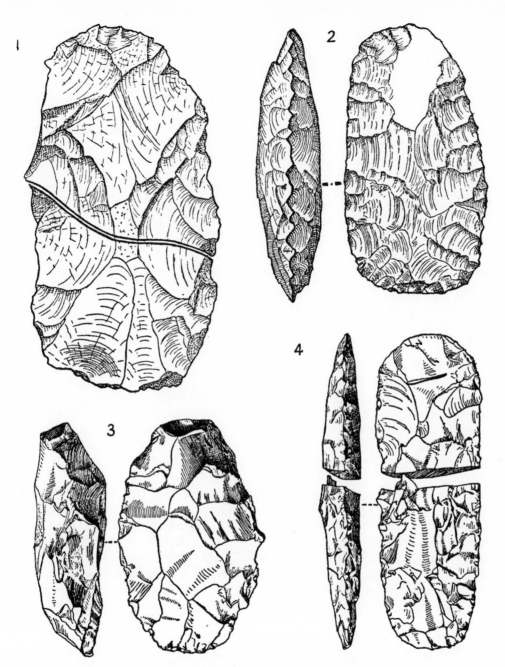

Fig. 103. Incomplete and broken axe-blades from factory-sites ($\frac{1}{2}$).
Nos. 1, 2.   Craig Lwyd Quarry. (*After Hazzledine Warren*).
Nos. 3, 4.   Blackpatch flint-mine. (*After Curwen*).

equipment of the people engaged in the quarrying or knapping. The loss of weight occasioned by grinding and polishing was too slight to necessitate the operation being carried out in the immediate neighbourhood of the source of the material. On the other hand there is evidence in the case of Langdale that the axes were polished at various points within the Lake District away from the axe factories, before being traded to more distant areas for use.[47].

To sum up, the need to make flint and stone axes and adzes represents in the final analysis a response to an ecological situation and marks the determination of prehistoric man to utilize and ultimately to tame his forest environment. The spread of farming into the deciduous forest, by emphasizing the importance of effective tools for felling trees, stimulated the quest for the most effective raw materials. This led in turn to a great increase in the mining of flint and in the exploitation of stones of appropriate toughness and tractability even when these occurred on remote mountain slopes. The weight and bulk of the raw material, the high proportion of waste involved in the shaping of implements and the limited facilities available for transport combined to promote the rise of large-scale manufactories by professional knappers and the organization of widespread trade in finished products.

Although axes were the principle objects of industrial production, they were not the only ones. The most prolific of all the European flint factories, those of Grand Pressigny, which extend over twelve kilometres in the valleys of the Claise and the Creuse near the frontiers of Indre-et-Loire and Vienne in south Touraine, were devoted principally to the production of long blades and of the various types of artifact made from these.[48] The properties of the honey-coloured flint were indeed already appreciated by palæolithic man,[49] but the first signs of a large-scale industry supplying a more or less extensive market did not appear until much later and in fact the activity did not reach its zenith until the end of neolithic times. The process of making the characteristic blades, which attained lengths of up to 30 cm., involved the preparation of elaborate cores, known locally from their shape as *livres de beurre* (Fig. 104). After removal of the blades these cores were discarded and together with preparatory flakes and rejects form the bulk of the debris on the factory sites.

Evidence that they were extensively traded, together with the extremely high standard of workmanship which they display, suggests that many of the flint daggers and lunate saw or sickle-flints of the west Baltic area were manufactured as a specialized activity by skilled and practised artificers. Indeed, flint-mines recently discovered at Aalborg, Jutland, appeared to have been called into existence to provide the raw material needed for manufacturing such daggers for trading.[49a] On the other hand, finds of half-made arrowheads on settlements in association with debris of other activities should warn us not to forget that skill in flint working must have been widely diffused among communities dependent on flint or stone or among which metal was still too costly for normal use. It is at any rate certain that implements which required no special skill and for which local materials were normally adequate, viz. scrapers, awls, rough cutting implements and the like, were made locally, and to judge from the widespread occurrence of the debris of flint knapping by

---

[47] Bunch and Fell, 1949, 14.

[48] J. de Saint-Venant, 1911.

[49] *B.M. Guide to Stone Age Collections*, 1926, p. 150. Professor D. A. E. Garrod tells me that the availability of this exceptional material had a distorting effect on the Magdalenian industry from Angles-sur-l'Anglin.

[49a] Verbal information from Dr C. J. Becker.

most if not all households. When metal first became available for tools in substantial quantities towards the end of the Bronze Age and particularly during the Early Iron Age, it was at this domestic level that flint-working alone survived.

COPPER AND ITS ALLOYS

Although, as was pointed out earlier in this chapter, all the stone age peoples of Europe, whether farmers or hunter-fishers, were subject to the same broad limitations inherent in

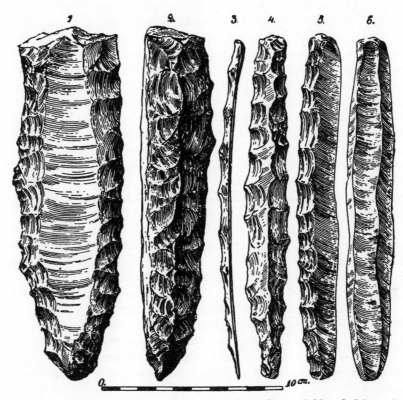

Fig. 104.   Core and blades: Grand Pressigny flint.   (*After de Morgan*).

the materials used for their tools, it is equally true that the advance from food-gathering to food-production itself created the possibility of technological advance through the use of metals. A more stable food-supply, the possibility of larger social groups and of a finer sub-division of labour were necessary prerequisites for the spread of metallurgy. With the origins of metal-working as such we are hardly concerned here, except to emphasize that the working of copper and of its alloys first developed in the Near East among communities based securely on farming subsistence at a time when Europe was still inhabited by meso-lithic hunter-fishers, and that it spread over that continent from the old culture lands only when farming had reached a certain stage of development there. Yet, if the processes and consequently the equipment used in metallurgy, and for a time at least also the main products of metallurgical industry, reflected clearly enough the alien origin of the craft, it is equally true that the development of the new technology was bound up intimately with the general course of economic history in the different regions of Europe and with the disposition and accessibility of European mineral resources. The intimate connection between trade and the rise of European metallurgy is discussed later in this book (p. 256).

The advantages of working copper and its alloys, the possibility of producing keener, tougher edges and of multiplying the varieties of tool available to the craftsman were only realized gradually in prehistoric Europe; moreover, there were certain regional differences in what Childe has usefully termed modes in the utilization of metal.[50] In effect, this is only another way of saying that flint and stone were not immediately displaced by copper and its alloys and that the degree and the speed with which this happened varied in different zones of Europe. The mere hammering of native copper into beads and trinkets hardly affected technology and had no serious economic significance. On the other hand there is no theoretical reason why, in regions where native copper was sufficiently abundant and accessible, tools of real influence in transforming economic life should not have been produced by cold hammering without the use of any distinctively metallurgical process. One of the areas where this is most likely to have happened is Hungary; nuggets of native copper weighing up to 15 kilos have been found up to recent times on the Matra mountains and copper tools, including adzes or hoes with tubular sockets have been found in this and neighbouring lands in Danubian III contexts.[51] It may be emphasized though that no proof has been offered that the objects in question were in fact made by hammering.[52]

Again, there is no doubt that copper ornaments, and what is more interesting copper axes, were traded fairly extensively in central and northern Europe among communities at a neolithic stage of culture. Although in Vouga's classical sequence for the western lakes of Switzerland copper is shown as making its appearance in the final stage marked by Corded Ware,[53] flat axes of this material have in fact been found associated with the Michelsburg and even with the younger Cortaillod cultures.[54] Again, an earth-grave at Salten, near Silkeborg, Jutland, has yielded part of an embossed copper disc of a type found in a Danubian III burial at the Polish site of Brześć Kujawski, together with thin-butted flint axes and other objects assigned to the last phase of the early neolithic of Denmark.[55] The famous find at Bygholm, near Horsens, Jutland, of four flat axes, a dagger and three spiral arm-bands of copper in a pot of Becker's class D shows that copper tools, as well as ornaments, were entering Denmark at the beginning of the middle neolithic times in that country.[56] Numerous stray finds—around fifty for Denmark alone—and a few hoards show that similar objects were being imported into the northern area from the south in substantial numbers.[57]

For a large part of the European Bronze Age flint and stone continued to play an important part as materials for tools, even though metal was used for ornaments and increasingly

---

[50] V. G. Childe, 1944, 3–4.

[51] V. G. Childe, 1929, Ch. XI.

[52] It is equally true that Childe has recently stated (1947, III) that as regards the copper industry of the Danubian III Bodrogkeresztur culture, "none of its products has been demonstrably cast . . ."

[53] P. Vouga, 1929, 25.

[54] e.g. at Weiher, Thayngen (Michelsberg) and at Seematte, Hitzkirch, Luzern (younger Cortaillod). Schaffhausen and Hitzkirch Museums.

[55] C. J. Becker, 1947, 249–54.

[56] C. A. Nordman, 1935, 131 f.; J. E. Forssander, 1936, 7 ff.; G. Schwantes, 1939, 214 f.; H. C. Broholm, 1944, 13–14.

[57] Forssander, 1936, 9 f., abb. I.

for weapons; indeed, the prestige and high cost of metal objects, by stimulating the production of analogous forms in cheaper materials, actually led to local advances in the flaking of
flint.[58] There were, however, as Professor Childe has recently emphasized, significant
regional differences in the relative importance of metal as a material for tools during the
Early Bronze Age. In particular he has shown[59] that the earliest metallurgists of Iberia
and the Balkan peninsula made a conspicuously broader range of tools from copper and its
alloys than did those of northern Italy and of Cis-alpine Europe, including knives, a variety
of chisels and carpenter's saws, this last of special importance in relation to wheeled transport. From an ecological point of view the matter can be put quite simply by saying that
metallurgy was able to spread into the Mediterranean zone of Europe, after all a mere
prolongation of that which gave birth to the whole technique, in a more advanced mode
(Childe's mode 2) than it could into the temperate zone, which was not only more remote
but also differed as a biome.

There was only one metal tool of importance common to both the main zones of Europe
in which early bronze age metallurgy was practised and that was the axe, which absorbed
a large part of the copper or bronze in use. It is quite true that axes and kindred tools
continued in many areas to be made in stone, but it is equally the case that axes flaked from
flint or fine-grained stone declined in standing very rapidly as native metallurgy established
itself in different regions. It is particularly significant that, although the great flint and
stone axe manufactories languished, the Grand Pressigny workshops, concentrating on
such forms as daggers and knives, continued to flourish well into the Bronze Age. The
supreme ecological importance of the axe, which led neolithic communities to undertake
deep-mining and to organize large-scale manufactories, also ensured that when metal
became available a substantial proportion should be devoted to the fabrication of this type
of tool. If anyone should doubt whether the early bronze age axes of temperate Europe
were used as tools, let him examine the marks on the pile-shoes or the pointed piles of
Baldegg (Pl. XIV, c) and admire the deftness and mastery with which the woodworker
wielded his bright axe. Even in the temperate zone of Europe, therefore, the introduction
of metallurgy was from its early days technologically and ecologically significant, since it
materially enhanced man's control over the trees of the forest, still a dominant factor in
the biome.

The final mode in the use of copper alloys for tools—Childe's mode 3—was distinguished
by a great increase in the weight of metal, and by a significant extension of the sphere of
activities within which metal tools were applied; it was also accompanied by a comparable
decline in the status of flint and stone work. Among the most characteristic features
was the employment of metal tools for farming, notably for sickles, several varieties of
which occurred in different parts of Europe. Metal was also used for miners' picks and
mauls, for a wide range of smithing equipment, e.g. anvils, hammers, files and punches,
and for such carpenter's tools as chisels and gouges. Obviously there was a close connection
between the extent to which metal was used for tools and the amount of metal available.
So long as copper remained expensive it was naturally restricted in use and for many
purposes was unable to compete with older and cheaper, if sometimes less efficient,
materials. The great widening in the range of metal tools characteristic of mode 3 was

---

[58] e.g. the flint daggers of the Grand Pressigny factories, of the Stone Cist period in Denmark,
of the A Beaker culture of Britain and of the Remedello culture of Italy.

[59] V. G. Childe, 1944, 9.

accompanied by an expansion in the supply of metal made possible by an intensification of mining.

The earliest metallurgists of Europe depended principally upon limited finds of native copper and upon the oxides, silicates and carbonates of this metal in the form of surface ores. The precise sources of these can only be determined by the diligent application of modern scientific techniques. Little can be deduced from modern data about the distribution of minerals, since ease of access and working were of more importance to early man than the scale or potential wealth of deposits and, conversely, some of the most accessible supplies may be supposed to have been exhausted in antiquity. Further, in view of the possibilities of trade it is dangerous to infer that early copper industries were necessarily supported from local sources. Finds of slag, especially substantial ones, are more reliable, since in early times smelting was normally carried on as close as possible to the source of the ore. The most promising source of information lies in the identification of impurities in artifacts and ores by means of chemical or spectrographic analysis, but these techniques have been applied very unevenly to the material and it is difficult to know how much reliance to place on results obtained from limited areas.

Although precise information is commonly lacking, it may still be worth reviewing the main sources of copper likely to have been available to the earliest European metallurgists. The traditional source of copper in the east Mediterranean was Cyprus and, although there are no specific indications that copper ores were worked there before Mycenæan times,[60] the wealth of the island in previous stages of the Bronze Age is suggestive. Little copper is found on the Greek mainland and though mines in the Othrys mountains were worked during Hellenistic and early Roman times, traces of prehistoric settlement are slight in that neighbourhood.[61] Small deposits were apparently worked in the Cyclades; prehistoric slag has been recovered from Syra and Paros and on the latter island Davies identified an exhausted malachite working.[62] A small worked-out mine and some slag have been noted at Chrysokamino near Gournia in Crete, but there are no signs that the copper deposits in the western part of the island were attacked in Minoan times.[63] Although there is no direct proof that the rich copper deposits of Etruria began to be worked for the Minoan market, it is suggestive that the earliest metal equipment of Italy should show Early Minoan influence, notably in the daggers with mid-rib and rivetted tang found in cemeteries of the Remedello culture of the Po Valley and in the central Italian Rinaldoni culture.[64] The reported discovery of a flat copper axe in old workings at Montanto also points to an early beginning.[65] The copper deposits of Sardinia, which later supported the insular nuraghic Bronze Age, may also have been tapped earlier.[66] The copper deposits of Iberia were of outstanding importance, at first more particularly those of the territory extending from Algarve and Alemtejo to the Sierra Morena, Almeria and the coastal zone of Murcia.[67] The close agreement in the distributions of cupola tombs and the early

---

[60] O. Davies, 1932.

[61] O. Davies, 1935, 242.

[62] *ibid.*, 264.

[63] *ibid.*, 266.

[64] Forssander, 1936, 40 f.; Childe, 1947, 239, Fig. 116a and 266.

[65] J. Andree, 1922, 46–7.

[66] O. Davies (1935, 70–1) interpreted the Mycenæan ingots from Serra Ilixi as signs that east Mediterranean copper was being imported to Sardinia; it is possible, though, that they really mark Mycenæan exploitation of Sardinian copper.

[67] L. Siret, 1887; O. Davies, 1935, 110–19; *Historia de España*, I, 582–4. Madrid, 1937.

sources of copper in this area—closer even than would appear from Leisner's map[68], which omits the small but in early times significant deposits of Murcia—together with the wealth of metal implements and weapons in the finest tombs, suggests a close connection between the spread of the east Mediterranean burial-rite and the rise of the earliest metallurgy of south-western Europe. Other very important copper deposits centred on Asturias[69] and combined with the tin of the north-west to support the Atlantic Bronze Age.

Many sources of copper are known in central Europe, but it is not always easy to be sure when all these began to be worked. As already noted, there is some evidence that native Hungarian copper was already being used in Danubian III times and analysis of objects from the contemporary cemetery at Jordansmühl in Silesia suggest that these were probably made from silver-free Hungarian ores.[70] Other sources of copper ore were the Slovakian, Transylvanian, Slovenian and Bosnian mountains. The metallurgical researches of Wilhelm Witter have shown that the central German ores played a much greater part than has hitherto been realized, though it must be admitted that his book is marred by extravagant claims. There is good evidence, also, that the copper deposits of the East Alpine area began to be exploited at an early date. Much's view[71] that the flat axes, dagger-blades and armlets of the " late neolithic " and " chalcolithic " cultures of the Alpine area were made from local ores is supported by the fact that the Mondsee potters mixed pounded copper slag with their clay, since it can be assumed that smelting was done close to the source of the ore. Similar observations have been made by M. Hell[72] in respect of pottery, mostly of the Reinecke B stage, from the Götschenberg, a defended height near Bischofshofen, and from other sites in the Salzburg area. Again, an early bronze age exploitation of East Alpine copper has been argued by Reinecke[73] from the distribution of ingot torcs in the south German area.

Southern Ireland may well have been one of the main sources of copper in the west and it is only to be regretted that so little modern research should have been devoted either to the early workings or to the diffusion by trade of their products. The information available is sufficiently suggestive to be worth summarizing, even if it rests on reports which by modern standards are vague and imprecise.[74] The most important workings appear to have been in the Avoca valley of Wicklow, on the coast of Waterford between Dungarvan and Tramore bays, and at numerous points between Skibereen, Co. Cork, and Kenmare and Killarney in Kerry. Native copper, as well as copper ores, outcrops on the cliffs around Bonmahon in the Waterford area, and " stone hammers and chisels, and wooden shovels " have been reported[75] from old but undated workings. Stone mauls have been recovered from mining sites on Ross Island in the largest of the Killarney lakes,[76] and from Mount Gabriel near

---

[68] G. and V. Leisner, 1943.

[69] e.g. the Aramo, Old Riner and Milagro mines. H. W. Sanders, 1910, 119–20 ; J. Serra Vilaró, 23 ; O. Davies, 1935, 110

[70] W. Witter, 1938, I, 199.

[71] M. Much, 1893, 249 f.; cf. Forssander, 1936, 16 ff.

[72] M. Hell, 1927.

[73] P. Reinecke, 1930.

[74] A. Mahr., 1937, 365–7. An admirable survey for the time was given by R. Kane, 1845, 181 ff. See also G. A. J. Cole, 1922. The connection between copper deposits and passage-graves in Ireland has recently been discussed by Daniel and Powell, 1949, 178–9.

[75] Kane, 1845, 189.

[76] W. R. Wilde, 1857–62, I, 86.

Schull in south-west Cork[77] and it may be added that rude stone implements have been recorded from " beneath six feet of peat in an old copper mine, in the townland of Boulysallagh " in the parish of Kielmore, near Skibereen.[78]　Further north copper ore occurs inland in the Silvermine region south of Lough Derg; there are many occurrences in the west coastal area around lake Corrib, Galway, on the coasts of Connemara and northern Mayo and at Pollboy, near Leitrim; and in the east it is known from Loughshinny near Dublin, from Beauparc[79] and Brownstown,[80] Meath, and from as far north as county Tyrone where it is said by Kane to have been found as " masses of grey sulphurate of copper " near Dungannon.[81]

Elsewhere in the British Isles copper ores are known from widely separated parts of Scotland and Childe has argued from the concentration of antiquities in the immediate area of the Crinan lode in Argyllshire that this was worked in prehistoric times.[82]　The best-known English localities for early workings are situated on the north-eastern flanks of Alderley Edge, north-west of Macclesfield, Cheshire, where numbers of grooved hammerstones have been found[83]; but these objects, although identical in form with others dating from the Bronze Age in Austria and Spain, cannot be narrowly dated, since they continued in use in parts of the Roman world down to the first century A.D.[84]　It is possible that native copper found in the neighbourhood of Mullion on the Lizard may have been worked in early antiquity,[85] but the Cornish copper ores occur as a rule at deep levels.　Early copper workings at Orme's Head, near Llandudno, Wales, may be prehistoric in origin, since they have yielded bronze picks, resembling those from the Austrian mines, as well as horn ones and stone wedges.[86]　What is even more significant than the meagre indications of early working in the highland zone of Britain is the complete absence of copper resources from the lowlands.

Few traces of prehistoric exploitation are known from France, despite the occurrence of copper ores at different points, and it is significant that during the Early Bronze Age copper seems to have been imported from the central German ore-field in the form of double-axe ingots at least as far west as Indre.　Even more striking is the complete absence of copper resources from the Scandinavian area, apart from certain Swedish ores, which however do not seem to have been exploited until the Middle Ages.[87]

During the earlier part of the Bronze Age, when metal was employed only for a comparatively limited range of tools and was still supplemented largely by flint and stone, surface ores were generally sufficient to meet the need.　The extended use of metal characteristic of mode 3 necessitated, and was at the same time permitted by, the more intensive mining of deeper deposits.　Although mines were certainly worked during the Bronze Age in

---

[77] A. Mahr, 1937, 366.

[78] W. R. Wilde, 1857–62, I, 86.

[79] G. A. J. Cole, 1922, 28.

[80] R. Kane, 1845, 200.

[81] *ibid.*

[82] V. G. Childe, 1935, 6, 60 and 181.　For a full account, see Sir Lindsay Scott, *P.P.S.*, 1951.

[83] C. Roeder, 1901.

[84] O. Davies, 1935, 38.

[85] H. O'N. Hencken, 1932, 179.

[86] O. Davies, 1935, 154, 157.

[87] W. Witter, 1938, II, 16–17.

Iberia[88] and Italy,[89] the most elaborate ones yet discovered were those of Salzburg[90] and the Tyrol.[91] More investigation in the field is needed before we shall know for certain when mining as distinct from superficial working began in the East Alpine area. On the other hand there is evidence that many at least of the known mines and working-places belong to the Late Bronze Age and specifically to the Hötting culture.[92] The scale of the mines is such that Childe[93] has sought to explain them in terms of Mycenæan markets and even of Mycenæan capital and enterprise. It may be emphasized, though, that copper ingots of Alpine metal have yet to be traced in the east Mediterranean. In any case it is common ground that the mines continued to be operated to supply the needs of the peoples of central Europe after the Mycenæan power had gone into eclipse.

The character and size of the mines varied greatly. Those investigated by Kyrle near Viehofen on the Saalach[94] were comparatively small oval workings entered by shafts from above (Fig. 105). In both those investigated the original shaft was vertical and the work was pressed forward from north to south at gradually decreasing depths so that the

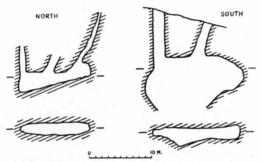

Fig. 105. Sections of prehistoric copper-mines at Viehofen, Salzburg. (*After Kyrle*).

part first excavated could serve as a sump to contain the water which invaded the workings. Thick layers of soot on the walls of the galleries and deposits of fine rock debris show that fire-setting was used and it was doubtless to carry off smoke and provide ventilation that sloping shafts were cut to the surface as the galleries advanced. The lodes in the Mühlbach-Bischofshofen area were attacked on a far more ambitious scale. The workings on the Mitterberg for instance were driven up to 100 metres into the hillside at intervals along a front of some 1,600 metres. Their object was to exploit a 2-metre vein of copper pyrites, which shelved into the mountain at an angle of between 20° and 30°. Although the miners used square-socketed bronze picks up to 28 cm. long,[95] they depended mainly on fire

---

[88] H. W. Sandars, 1910, 119–20; J. Andree, 1922, 44 f., Fig. 18; J. Serra Vilaró, 1923.

[89] J. Andree, 1922, 46–7.

[90] e.g. the mines of Mitterberg, Einöden and Buchberg in the Mühlbach-Bischofshofen region (Zschocke and Preuschen, 1932) and those at Viehofen on the Saalach (G. Kyrle, 1916, 27–37).

[91] e.g. the ore sorting-places on the Kelchalpe near Kitzbühel (Preuschen and Pittioni, 1937; Pittioni, 1947); also sites mentioned by L. Franz, 1929, 59–60.

[92] G. Kyrle, 1912 and 1932; R. Pittioni in Zschocke and Preuschen, 1932, 155–72; Preuschen and Pittioni, 1937, 70 f.; and Pittioni, 1947, 71 f.

[93] V. G. Childe, 1948 A, 189.

[94] G. Kyrle, 1916, 27–37.

[95] *ibid.*, 3 and Fig. 2.

and water as at Viehofen. The method was particularly effective on the crystalline rock of the region and it is one that had already long been used in prehistoric Europe. Its value may be judged from the fact that in some parts of Europe it survived the introduction of gunpowder; when discarded in the silvermines of Kongsberg, Sweden, between the sixties and eighties of the nineteenth century,[96] this was not because it was ineffective, but merely that once steel drills and dynamite came into common use the older method was by comparison too expensive of labour. One of the drawbacks of fire-setting was that it fouled the atmosphere and it is supposed that the Mitterberg miners allowed the fires to burn at night and extinguished them before beginning work in the morning.

According to Zschocke and Preuschen's invaluable account, the development of each mine began with working the vein where it outcropped on the surface (Fig. 106). At first the fire

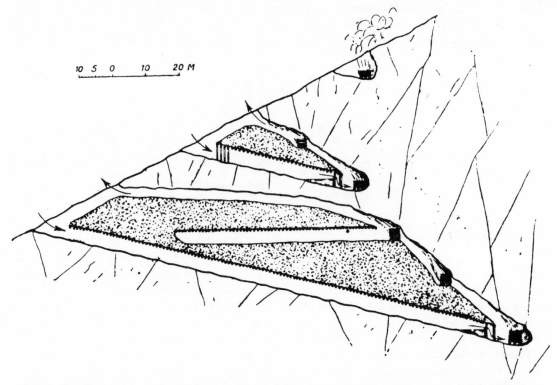

Fig. 106. Supposed method of operating prehistoric copper-mines by means of fire-setting. Mitterberg, Mühlbach-Bischofshofen, Salzburg. (*After Zschocke and Preuschen*).

could only be brought to bear on the face of the working, but as soon as the miners succeeded in tunnelling into the hillside it could be applied to the roof of the working as well as to driving forward. As the gallery advanced wooden staging was set up, to carry rock waste and to serve as a platform, from which fires could be brought to bear on the roof. The floor and roof passages under and over the staging and its overburden not only gave access to the workings, but also allowed free circulation of air. By damming the lower one a sump was formed for ground water, which could easily be collected in buckets. As the vein was followed more deeply into the mountain, an intermediate blind passage was introduced to

---

[96] A. L. Collins, 1893, 87.

prevent the overburden from becoming too heavy for the staging underneath. So the mines grew until the sloping wall passage reached as much as 160 metres in length and the total height of the gallery at the opening attained up to 30 metres, at which point it would be abandoned.

The magnitude of the operations can be judged by the amount of labour they consumed and by the quantity of crude copper produced. It is estimated for example that each of the thirty-two mines on the Mitterberg main lode took about seven years to exhaust, allowing a continuous activity spread over two or three centuries and assuming that they were worked without intermission and consecutively. The labour force needed to operate and maintain each mine must have varied according to the stage of its development, but at the peak it is estimated[97] that some 180 men would be needed. Of those, more were employed on getting the timber needed for the fire-setting and staging than for working underground, as brought out by the following hypothetical roll :

Miners	40
Lumbermen	60[98]
Ore workers	20
Smelters	30
Porters	10
Cowmen	10
Supervisors and Guards ..	10

The total quantity of crude copper produced in the Mühlbach-Bischofshofen area has been estimated by the same experts at 20,000 metric tons,[99] two-thirds of which is supposed to have come from the Mitterberg lode. It is instructive to compare this huge production with, say, the quantity of copper contained in the axes, daggers and ornaments from the thousand graves of El Argar in Spain,[100] one of the richest early bronze age cemeteries of Europe. The figures are as follows :

Mühlbach-Bischofshofen production	..	20,000,000,000 gr.
El Argar cemetery (c. 1,000 burials)	..	34,611 gr.

Even if Zschocke and Preuschen's estimate is heavily discounted, it is evident that the Alpine mines were capable in themselves of supporting a more advanced mode in the use of copper over a substantial part of Central Europe.

As with the flint-mines, preparation of the raw material was carried on in the immediate vicinity of the mines (Fig. 107) up to the point at which it could be transported without loss from dead weight, in this case to the stage of cake metal ready for the foundry. The ore was first drawn out of the workings on wooden sleds (Fig. 108, 3) and then sorted and prepared for smelting. The places where this was done (*Scheideplätze*) were generally sited close to watercourses, but where more convenient water was sometimes conducted to them by means of channels or wooden conduits.[101] Concentrated ore was first picked out by

---

[97] Zschocke and Preuschen, 1932, 66.

[98] According to Collins, the method of fire-setting employed in the Kongsberg mine involved the burning of 9 cubic yards of wood for each cubic yard of rock.

[99] Zschocke and Preuschen, 1932, 135.

[100] L. Siret, 1887, 410 f.

[101] At one point on the Mitterberg water was conducted for 200 metres from a mountain pool to a convenient sorting-place. Traces of wooden conduits associated with sorting-places on the Kelchalpe are illustrated by Preuschen and Pittioni, 1937, Taf. XIV, 2.

hand and worthless rock discarded. The residue containing a mixture of ore and gangue would then be pulverised by stone hammers or even rubbed down on querns like grain[102] and ultimately washed in wooden troughs (Fig. 108, 2). In winning the metal from the concentrated ore two processes were used, roasting to expel volatile matter such as sulphur and smelting to reduce the ore to copper, and these might be repeated several times.

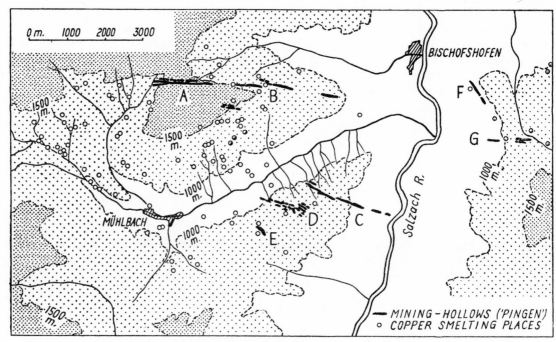

Fig. 107. Map showing relationship between mining and smelting in the Mühlbach-
Bischofshofen area, Salzburg. (*After Zschocke and Preuschen*).

A, B. Mitterberg lodes.
C–E. Einödberg lodes.
F, G. Buchberg lodes.

Plans of stone-walled roasting-beds recovered on the Mitterberg[103] show these were substantial affairs up to $12\frac{1}{2}$ metres long and $1\frac{1}{2}$ metres wide; associated with these were batteries of ovens. So far as can be seen from the rather meagre domestic activity in the mining areas of Salzburg and the Tyrol,[104] the miners camped by the workings, rather than living there in settled communities. It has been suggested, very plausibly in view of conditions high up on the mountains, that the miners had already adopted something like the *Wochenberg* system known from the historical period,[105] whereby they put in spells of

---

[102] M. Much, 1893, 262–3, Figs. 98–9.

[103] Zschocke and Preuschen, 1932, 76 f., Taf. III.

[104] A long terrace house was found on a ledge close to the entrance of one of the Einödberg mines. It yielded a considerable amount of gear used in extracting ore from mined rock, including stone hammers and rubbing-stones, as well as pottery, pins, etc. Zschocke and Preuschen, 1932, II, 4 ff., Taf. XV.

[105] *Ibid.*, 108–9.

hard work under camp conditions, coming down at intervals to join their families in permanent settlements in the valleys.

Although copper was the basic raw material for metallurgy before the spread of iron-working, it was subject to grave disadvantages when used alone, since it was not merely soft, but also difficult to cast in any but open moulds: only in combination with substances like tin, antimony, arsenic, zinc, nickel or lead could copper easily be cast in valve moulds and so used for the wider range of tools, which this made possible.[106] In areas such as the

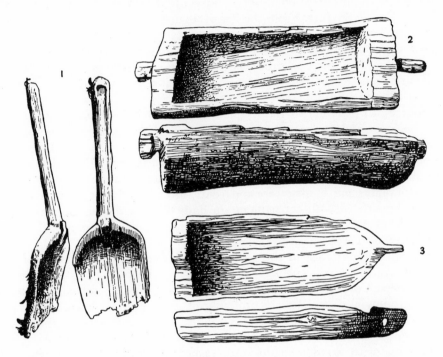

Fig. 108.   Wooden gear from prehistoric salt and copper mines, Austrian Alps.
(*After Andree*).

No. 1.   Dürrnberg, Hallein (45 cm. l.)

No. 2.   Mitterberg (115 cm. l.)

No. 3.   Viehofen (84 cm. l.)

Vogtland and Saalfeld in Saxo-Thuringia, some of the copper ores contained sufficient tin to make a natural tin-bronze on smelting, but the ratio was usually too low for the alloy to be fully effective and it was also variable. It may have been in such a region, where natural bronze and the constituents of artificial bronze existed side by side, that the production of artificial tin-bronze first developed. However that may be, it is certain that over the greater part of Europe the manufacture of bronze depended on the organized trading of one and often of both the main constituents. Thus the extent to which communities used copper, natural alloys or artificial alloys depended partly on the character of the ores locally

---

[106] See W. Gowland, 1912, 30 ; T. A. Rickard, 1932, 132–7. Another advantage of adding tin was that it lowered the temperature at which the metal could be liquefied. According to Witter (1938, I, 40), the addition of 8 per cent tin reduced the required temperature from 1085°C. to 1020°C.

available to them, but in the long run upon the extent and character of their trade connections.

The tin needed for bronze founding was a scarce commodity for which there were comparatively few sources in prehistoric Europe, and one of the most important of these was Cornwall.[107]   Evidence for trade relations with Ireland suggests that the Cornish tin-deposits may have been worked as early as the beginning of the Bronze Age, but it is not until near the end of this period that we have a more definite indication in a piece of tin and two bronzes with an exceptionally high tin-content ($16\frac{1}{2}$ and 17 per cent) in a hoard from Kenidjack Castle, St. Just. From the Pre-Roman Iron Age there is direct evidence for tin-smelting in a small stone smelting-furnace and slag from Chûn Castle and a hearth with pieces of slag found with a La Tène brooch at Redmore, St. Austell. It is probable that a certain amount of tin was produced in Ireland, since it occurred " disseminated through the auriferous soil of Wicklow "[108] and must almost certainly have been recovered when washing alluvial gold.

Another source of tin lay across the English Channel in the Breton peninsula.[109]   Signs of placers, open-cast and underground workings have been noted in the Josselin massif of Morbihan and there are placers at Piriac on the west coast of the Loire Inférieure, as well as possible open-cast workings in the same department. The other main sources of tin in France were centred on the departments of Haute-Vienne and Creuse, where the workings at Montebras and Vaulry were apparently already active at the time of the Roman conquest. The poverty of both departments in finds of bronze hoards, on the other hand, suggested to Déchelette[110] that the tin deposits of central France were probably not opened up until the Early Iron Age.

Of much greater importance in the ancient world were the tin deposits of north-west Iberia, most of which are concentrated in a broad belt, following the junction of granite and schist, between Coruña and Zamora.[111]   Open-cast workings of some antiquity have been noted, but alluvial deposits were probably of greater importance during prehistoric times. The geographer Strabo quotes Posidonius, who wrote during the first century B.C., for the report that the Artabri, who dwelt at the extreme north-west of Galicia, scraped up the soil with wooden spades and washed it in sieves " woven after the fashion of baskets."[112] Although it is almost certain that the tin bought by the Greeks at Tartessus during the early part of the sixth century B.C. came from the north-western territories, it is not possible to date specific workings. There can thus be no direct proof that·the tin deposits were exploited during the Bronze Age, but the fact that a distinctive bronze industry, typified by the double-looped palstave (Fig. 147), arose precisely in this area makes it almost certain.

As regards possible sources of tin within the Mediterranean area itself, Davies has argued that it was probably obtained in Greece from the open-cast mines on the Cirsæan Plain north of the mound of Cirrha (Crisa), supposedly worked out during the Bronze Age.[113] Another and in the long run more important source of Mediterranean tin was the mining

[107] For an admirable survey with full references, see H. O'N Hencken, 1932, Chap. V.

[108] R. Kane, 1845, 222.

[109] For early tin-working in France generally, see O. Davies, 1935, 83–4 and 91–3.

[110] J. Déchelette, II (1924), 95, n. 3.

[111] W. C. Borlase, 1897; O. Davies, 1935, 103–5.

[112] Strabo, 3.2.9. (Hamilton and Falconer, 1854 transl.) ;   cf. Pliny, *Nat. Hist.* XXXIV, Chap. 47.

[113] O. Davies, 1929.

area of south-west Tuscany,[114] where the Etruscans are known to have worked deposits at Cento Camerelle and Monte Valerio. Direct proof that the Tuscan tin was won already during the Bronze Age is lacking, though there are strong indications that it was. In particular, the occurrence of V-perforated buttons made of tin in a cave-burial of the Rinaldoni culture, in association with a metal dagger of Early Minoan form, suggests exploitation of the deposits under east Mediterranean influence. Again, the fact that north Italy was the seat of a distinctive and influential metallurgical industry at such an early stage of the Bronze Age is easier to explain, if it is allowed that native sources of tin were available.

Lastly, there is the difficult question of central European sources. The tin-stone of the Fichtelgebirge and the adjacent Erzgebirge has enjoyed such wide renown in archæological literature that it may be salutary to quote Childe's cautious comment that this was " neither plentiful nor easily worked, but the weathered surfaces may once have contained alluvial ' pipes ' now exhausted."[115] On the other hand the early rise of bronze metallurgy in central Europe argues in favour of a source of tin somewhere in the region and Witter[116] has recently drawn attention to the occurrence of tin ores side by side with copper in the neighbourhood of Olsnitz in the Vogtland, immediately north of the western end of the Erzgebirge.

While the tin lodes themselves were sometimes attacked directly, the main sources of supply in prehistoric Europe were undoubtedly alluvial placer deposits. The principal of working these was to concentrate the heavy tin by washing away the lighter waste in sluices or baskets. The tin-stone could be further concentrated by grinding on querns and further washing. For general purposes the proportion of tin to copper was early standardized at around one to nine[117] for general purposes, but for special uses such as anvils the ratio could be much higher.[118] As an alloy for copper, tin thus played a rôle of crucial importance in bronze age technology ; on its own account its uses were merely decorative.[119]

Antimony was one of the less common components of bronze, though it was used in Germany, Slovakia, western Hungary and the Caucasus.[120] As a free metal it is extremely rare in nature,[121] but it is found more commonly as antimony sulphide and also as an impurity in copper. The high proportion of antimony sometimes found in copper ores—a sample from Kamsdorf near Saalfeld showed as much as 15.05 per cent[122]—makes it difficult to decide whether in any specific instance it was added intentionally. At the Velem St. Vid foundry site in Hungary there seems little doubt that it was sometimes used consciously as a substitute for tin, since as a rule metal cakes and ingots with high values for

---

[114] O. Davies, 1935, 67; V. G. Childe, 1947, 235.

[115] V. G. Childe, 1929, 5.

[116] W. Witter, 1938, I, 185.

[117] e.g. the mean tin content of thirty bronzes from El Argar was found to be 9·17 per cent by L. Siret (1887, 218–19).

[118] e.g. an anvil recently published by Childe (1946, 9) yielded c. 30 per cent tin.

[119] It was used, for example, for making V-perforated buttons by the Rinaldoni people (V. G. Childe, 1947, 235) and tin nails were driven into wooden cups during the great period of the Danish Bronze Age so as to form patterns (J. Brøndsted, 1938, III, Fig. 56a). See also A. Oldeberg, 1942, I, 235.

[120] Ebert, *Reallexikon*, I, 196.

[121] A. Lucas, 1948, 222.

[122] W. Witter, 1938, I, 135 f.

antimony (up to 18 per cent) are free from tin and vice versa; in only a few instances are the two alloys associated in the same piece.[123]

Another alloy of some importance was lead-bronze. Although lead was rare in its native state, it must in the form of its sulphide, galena, have attracted notice on account of its lustre. Both lead, and the silver with which it is commonly associated in nature, were used at a comparatively early date in the eastern Mediterranean, though the lead used at Mycenæ may well have come from Anatolia.[124] In Iberia lead appeared only in small quantities at El Argar and El Officio.[125] The deposits of Sardinia were certainly being worked in the Late Bronze Age [126] and the metal was exploited in Italy by the Etruscans, if not by their predecessors. In temperate Europe the use of lead appears to have been an innovation of the Late Bronze Age, though rich deposits were available in England, France, the Eifel district of western Germany and parts of Yugoslavia. When present in bronze only in small quantities, lead is best explained as an impurity of the tin alloy,[127] but there is no doubt that it was on occasion employed as an intentional alloy on its own account ; some of the cake metal from Velem St. Vid contained around one third of lead and an ingot was composed of two parts lead, one of copper and one of tin[128] ; or, again, one might cite a trumpet from the Dowris hoard made of bronze containing 9 per cent lead.[129] In its own right lead was appreciated by urban societies on account of the fact that it neither rusts nor taints water and it was already used for water-tanks by the Mycenæans.[130] Lead was used for weights among barbarians, as well as by the late Minoans[131] and a number have been found in the late bronze age lake villages of Switzerland.[132] Doubtless it was on account of its weight also that it was used to fill bronze sword hilts.[133] It was employed for beads during the Late Bronze Age in Sweden.[134] By the end of the prehistoric period it was sufficiently cheap in the Mendip area for use as net-weights by the Glastonbury lake villagers.[135] Of greater technological interest was the use of lead for making dummy socketed axes, on which clay valve-moulds could be shaped.[136]

---

[123] Von Miske, 1908, 33, Table XI.

[124] O. Davies (1935, 249) points out that there is no evidence for the mining of silver at Laurium during the Bronze Age. Small votive axes of lead were found already in an Early Minoan II tomb at Mokhlos (J. D. S. Pendlebury, 1939, 71).

[125] L. Siret, 1887.

[126] Cakes of lead weighing up to 2 kilos were found in the Teti hoard (J. Déchelette, II (2nd edt.). 367).

[127] W. Witter, 1938, I, 132 and 135.

[128] Von Miske, 1908, Tables XI–XII.

[129] Sir John Evans, 1881, 360.

[130] Circular water-containers of lead were found in the Shaft-graves at Mycenae (G. Karo, 1930, 160, 231, abb. 78).

[131] Lead weights were found with remains of weighing-scales in a Late Minoan III context at Mavrospelio (J. D. S. Pendlebury, 1939, 254).

[132] J. Déchelette, II (2nd edtn.), 400 f., gives many examples.

[133] A. Oldberg, 1942, I, Pl. I.

[134] ibid., 82, Fig. 70.

[135] Bulleid and Gray, 1911, 243.

[136] These dummies were themselves made in bronze moulds, as is shown by examples with part of the lead casting in position, e.g. from the Harty hoard (Sir John Evans, 1881, 442), from Southall, Middlesex (B.M. Guide to Bronze Age Coll., 2nd edtn., 114), and from New Street, Cambridge (Camb. Mus., No. 1905, 6).

An enormous amount of work has been devoted to the stylistic appreciation and typological classification of the products of bronze-smithing and there have latterly been considerable advances in our knowledge of the technical processes involved in the practice of the craft.[137] Much less is known about the way in which bronze working was organized, a fact which is perhaps less surprising when one reflects on our ignorance of bronze age settlement in general and of the communities whose needs were served by the early smiths. One of the few facts which does emerge fairly clearly is that a well defined division of labour existed between those who produced the raw materials and those who fabricated from these the tools, weapons and ornaments of bronze age Europe. This division existed even in the case of comparatively simple metallurgical industries like those of south-east Spain, where the brothers Siret found on the one hand small mining camps like Parazuelos,[138] in which those who worked nearby veins of copper and smelted the ore sheltered in small agglomerations of stone huts, and on the other townships such as El Argar, where finds of crude copper, crucibles, moulds and finished metal products betray the practice of smithing.[139] The contrast is even more striking when one compares large-scale centres of copper production like those of Salzburg and the Tyrol, in which as a general rule metal working stopped short at the smelting of crude copper, and extensive and flourishing provinces of bronze-smithing like those of southern Scandinavia and north Germany, in which metallurgical activities began with the alloying of crude copper in the cakes or ingots in which it was imported, often from hundreds of miles distant.

Theoretically the production of bronze could have been accomplished by smelting the ores of copper and the chosen alloy together, but the two are only rarely found in close conjunction in nature and there is no evidence that tin for example was traded to the mining centres. In any case the practice would have been incompatible with anything approaching a standard or regular alloy.[140] A closer approximation could have been obtained by adding concentrated tin ore to crude copper, but really accurate results could only be achieved by fusing together carefully weighed quantities of the metals concerned. It seems likely that the lead weights already mentioned from the late bronze age lake settlements of Switzerland were used for this purpose and it is significant that other indications of smithing activity in the form of crucibles and moulds have been recovered from such sites. There is indeed no reasonable doubt that the production of bronze as distinct from its component metals fell within the province of smithing.

Something more can be learned by considering the distribution of such objects as crucibles and above all moulds. The most striking conclusion is that, unlike mining and the reduction of ore by smelting associated with it, smithing was carried on over the whole territory within the sphere of bronze age farming economy, a fact brought out admirably by Oldeberg's map (Fig. 109), which shows moulds and smithing-places widely distributed over the deciduous zone of southern Scandinavia.[141] This does not of itself imply resident smiths,

---

[137] See H. Maryon, 1936, 1938, 1938A; A. Oldeberg, 1942.

[138] At Parazuelos the nearest copper outcropped about 2 km. from the site. The finds included c. 10 kilos. of copper ore, some copper slag from defective smelting (over 12 per cent copper content) and a few lumps and rods of copper. The miners themselves apparently used flint and stone tools. L. Siret, 1887, Pl. VI, VII.

[139] ibid., Pl. XXVII.

[140] W. Witter, 1938, II, 2.

[141] A. Oldeberg, 1942, Pl. IX. It should be noted that on his map Oldeberg does not distinguish between moulds of the Nordic Bronze Age and those of the Arctic or Lappish smiths, for which see A. M. Tallgren, 1937. Only moulds of Nordic type are shown on our Fig. 109.

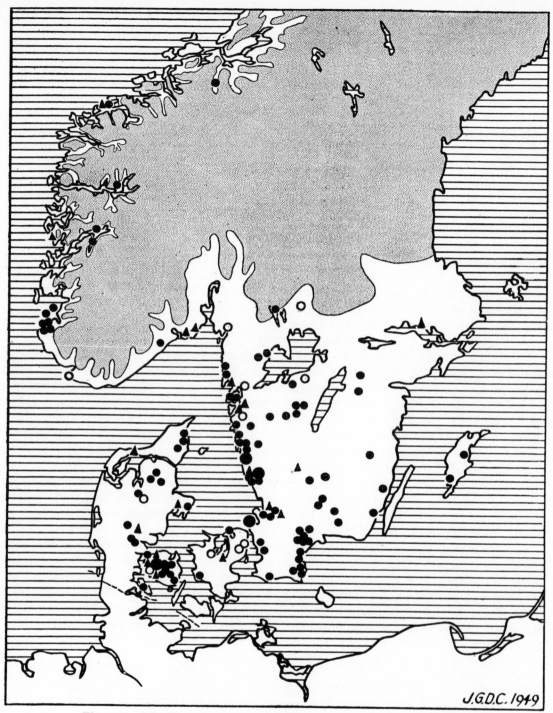

Fig. 109. Metallurgy in the Nordic Bronze Age. (*Based on Oldeberg*).

○ Early Bronze Age moulds.　　●● Late Bronze Age mould or moulds.

▲ Late Bronze Age smithing sites (crucibles, etc.).

Note.—German sites not shown ; stippled area shows birch, pine and fjäll.

since the needs of isolated farms and small communities might easily have been satisfied by itinerant smiths or tinkers. On the other hand there are signs, for example at the late bronze age village of Jarlshof, Shetland,[142] that smiths at least sojourned for considerable periods, even if it cannot be proved that they were permanent members of settled communities. What is at any rate sure is that smithing was not centralized at a comparatively few points. On the other hand there are indications that during the prevalence of mode 3 in the use of copper and bronze, smithing did become more highly organized and that, in addition to local or itinerant production, metal objects were turned out at workshops catering for extensive markets. Evidence for this will be discussed more fully in connection with bronze age trade (p. 257), but it is worth noting that traces of what may well have been such centres have actually been found. A well-known, though poorly investigated example is Velem St. Vid,[143] a promontory site on an eastern spur of the Köszeg mountains in western Hungary, which yielded, among other traces of metallurgical industry, cakes and ingots of metal, bronze scrap, clay nozzles for bellows, socket cores, a clay crucible, at least fifty-one stone moulds (mostly for socketed axes and pins, but also for several other forms) and a whole series of smithing tools, including anvils, hammers, punches and rasps.

IRON

At first sight it might seem strange that a metal, of which the ores were as widespread as were those of iron and as easily reduced,[144] should not have supervened directly on the working of flint and stone instead of following a stage of copper and bronze-working, which in most parts of Mediterranean and temperate Europe lasted for around a thousand years and in certain territories of the ancient world more than twice as long. Sporadic occurrences of iron objects in very early contexts in the Ancient East—and one can point to undoubted instances of forged iron of telluric origin[145] as well as to the use of meteoric iron[146]—only serve to throw into relief the broad fact that metallurgy was practised for a long period before iron was used systematically for weapons or tools; only in parts of the circumpolar zone beyond the contemporary limits of farming economy did iron directly succeed flint and stone, as this vast territory passed within the economic hegemony of the later iron age peoples of the northern temperate zone, though even among the Arctic hunter-fishers some bronze-working was carried on, notably for the production of socketed axes.[146a] The explanation is of course that until a technique had been devised for toughening the forged metal by repeated hammering of the bloom at red heat in contact with charcoal, so introducing the carbon needed for carburization, it was too soft to be of practical use.

Although there is still some room for conjecture, there is wide agreement among archæologists that this was probably achieved by the Hittites as early as the fifteenth century B.C.[147] The secret, which was, after all, one of the most direct military significance, was jealously

[142] A. O. Curle, 1932–4; V. G. Childe, 1935, 184 f.

[143] Von Miske, 1908.

[144] Thus it needs no more than 800–900° C. to reduce iron ore to a malleable metal, as against c. 1085° C. to melt copper.

[145] G. A. Wainwright, 1936.

[146] T. A. Rickard, 1941.

[146a] A. M. Tallgren, 1937; G. Gjessing, 1942, 256–7.

[147] T. A. Rickard, 1932, 870.

guarded[148] somewhere in the traditional homeland of iron-working in the lands bordering the south shores of the Black Sea,[149] until the breakdown of the Hittite empire some two centuries later. At least it is certain that, so far as Europe is concerned, iron-working was first established in Greece and the Aegæan during the troubled centuries between the eclipse of Mycenæan civilization and the beginning of the Geometric period proper around 900 B.C. Knowledge of iron-working was brought to Tuscany from the east Mediterranean by Etruscan immigrants, and to south Italy by Greek colonists, in the former case possibly as early as *c.* 800 B.C. Iron-working was first established in temperate Europe in and around the eastern Alps, probably around 640 B.C., and was carried thence over a large part of central and western Europe in the course of Hallstatt migration.

It is very important to remember, though, that iron still played a comparatively limited part in the economic life of the Hallstatt peoples and of the territories which fell under their influence. The spread of iron-working, like that of copper and bronze-working before it, did not immediately result in significant advances in the range of tools or in any substantial increase in the control exercised over their environment by prehistoric communities.[150] A realization that iron was capable of giving a keener edge than bronze is of course implicit in the very nature of the discovery of carburization, but it was some time before the possibilities of the new metal as a medium for tool-making were fully appreciated. To begin with iron was used to reproduce more or less faithfully forms previously rendered in bronze, a fact which is even more eloquent of human inertia when it is remembered that, whereas the bronzes were cast in moulds, the iron reproductions had to be wrought often laboriously by the early smiths. For obvious reasons weapons, notably swords, daggers and spears, were among the first objects to be rendered in the sharper metal, but axes of socketed and trunnion type were also commonly made of iron,[151] and on the margin of the Hallstatt world one can point to the well-known iron sickle from Llyn Fawr in south Wales, which follows closely the pattern of others fabricated in the final mode of the Bronze Age and associated with it in the same hoard.[152]

The peculiar properties of iron as a material for tools were first utilized in Europe by craftsmen working within the sphere of literate civilization, which by the end of the sixth century B.C. had established itself round the shores of the Mediterranean as far west as Spain. By this time Greek craftsmen (Fig. 110) were already using devices like hinged tongs, frame saws, specialized forms of hammer and the rotary lathe, and before the end of the fourth century B.C. the hinged compass and paired shears had been added.[153] The utilization of iron was carried to a new pitch in the Hellenistic and Imperial periods, when metal bladed spades, scythes, many kinds of specialized agricultural tool and a whole range of craftsman's tools, including planes, augers, draw-blocks for wire and nail-heading anvils came into use. A visit to the museum at the *limes* fort of Saalburg on the Taunus[154] or even to the Silchester collection at Reading will emphasize the justice of Childe's claim[155]

---

[148] Only a few royal presents and such-like were sent out, as with the presents of the King of the Mitanni to the Pharaohs Amenhotep III (1411–1375 B.C.) and Akhenaton (*c.* 1375–1359 B.C.).

[149] C. Blinkenberg, 1925, 204-5.

[150] V. G. Childe, 1944, 13.

[151] *B.M. Guide to Early Iron Age Antiquities*, 2nd edtn. (1925), Fig. 32.

[152] Crawford and Wheeler, 1921; Sir C. Fox and H. A. Hyde, 1939.

[153] V. G. Childe, 1944, 13.

[154] L. Jacobi, 1897.

[155] V. G. Childe, 1944, 14.

that, apart from screws and scissors, "all the main species of manual tools employed in handicraft or husbandry to-day were already in vogue" by the beginning of our era. The technological revolution brought about by the extended use of iron, a revolution of which the repercussions were felt far beyond the range of mere handicrafts and which profoundly affected the ecological situation of societies which shared in it, was thus accomplished by the civilized peoples occupying the Mediterranean zone, and it was from them that the new methods and appliances spread by trade and ultimately in part by conquest among the barbarians of the temperate zone.

As compared with those of copper or tin, iron ores are both abundant and widespread in nature. It was for this reason that, having once learnt the technical possibilities of iron as a raw material, the La Tène smiths were able to supply metal tools and gear on a scale never

Fig. 110. Greek smithy : representation on a black-figured vase. (*After Childe*).

previously attained, so that flint and stone, although not wholly abandoned, were now depressed finally into a role of quite subsidiary importance, and bronze, commonly in the form of hammered sheets or even of surface sheathing for the cheaper metal, survived mainly for objects of display or parade, such as shields, helmets, greaves, scabbards, horse and chariot trappings, mirrors and a multitude of small objects of personal adornment or toilet.

For the same reason it was unnecessary to mine iron ore with the intensity of copper, or even of the better class of flint. In some of the richest iron-bearing regions, like our own Forest of Dean, the ore had only to be picked up or at most gained from surface diggings[156] and it is significant that the ores for the historic Wealden industry were obtained from bell-shaped pits, about six feet in diameter at the top, generally shallow and "rarely more than twenty feet deep."[157] It follows as a corollary that direct evidence for prehistoric iron-mining is difficult to establish, all the more so when regard is paid to the widespread and destructive character of modern ironstone quarrying, and to the fact that ancient slags were so rich in iron, owing to the low level of extraction possible by the bloomery process, that they were commonly smelted in modern times.

---

[156] Fox and Hyde, 1939, 387.
[157] E. Straker, 1931, 101 f.

Iron ore was nowhere more widespread than in the northern territories of the temperate zone, where climatic conditions, more particularly during the Sub-atlantic phase of heavy rainfall, favoured the formation of bog ore. In such regions iron compounds formed in the soil were concentrated in still pools of water—hence the reference in the Kalevala epic to the blacksmiths seeking iron " in the wolf-tracks of the marshes "—and ultimately precipitated in the form of small lumps of ore, such as are found to-day under the peat. Since the working of bog-iron survived down to modern times as a peasant industry in the northern countries, it has attracted a good deal of attention from Scandinavian researchers[158] and in Denmark at least has been shown to date back to the beginning of the local Iron Age. It is virtually certain that bog-ore similarly provided the main, if not the only, source of iron during early times in northern Britain. Martin Martin's remark on Skye in the late seventeenth century[159] that, " The fuel here is peats dug out of the heaths. There are cakes of iron found in the ashes of some of them," is a reminder that bog-ore was readily available to the occupiers of the brochs, wheel houses, forts and crannogs of prehistoric Scotland and to the iron age inhabitants of other parts of the highland zone of Britain. Indeed the indications are that haematite and other sources of the mineral only began to be worked in Scotland, at any rate on an appreciable scale, during the eighteenth century.[160]

As regards the organization of the industry, it seems probable that within the territories in which bog-ores were exploited iron-working was carried on locally as a domestic industry during slack periods of the farming year.[161] So true was this of the industry as it survived into the historical period in Scandinavia, that up till about 1600 A.D. the peasants of certain parts of Jutland continued to pay their feudal dues in lumps (*kloder*) of iron,[162] while in the Swedish province of Småland iron was paid as a form of taxation to the Crown.[163] Although gradually swamped by the cheaper iron which began to be produced in Germany during the fifteenth and sixteenth centuries, the peasant industry was sufficiently virile to continue in parts of Norway down to the nineteenth century.[164] The earlier history of the industry has been particularly well attested by archæology in Jutland, where Hatt[165] has finally traced it back to the Pre-Roman Iron Age, by discovering plentiful slag on " Celtic fields " and by uncovering the slightly concave clay hearths on which the ore was reduced on charcoal fires.

It is likely that the industry was mainly local over the whole of the temperate zone, although in regions of nucleated settlement it may well be that, at least by the last phase of the prehistoric Iron Age, professional blacksmiths had already begun to operate. There is no doubt that iron-using immigrants tended to settle in localities particularly rich in ore, as witness the close agreement between the Hallstatt settlement and iron deposits of France noted by Déchelette.[166] Equally it is possible to recall individual sites—Hunsbury,[167]

---

[158] N. Nielsen, 1925, 434 ; A. W. Brøgger, 1926, 151 f. ; G. Hatt, 1936 ; Shetelig and Falk, 1937, 177–9 ; T. D. Hauge, 1946.
[159] M. Martin, 1934, edtn., 207.
[160] M. Macgregor *et. al.*, 1920, I.
[161] A. W. Brøgger, 1940, 171.
[162] N. Nielsen, 1925, 339 ff., 427.
[163] S. Bolin, 1941, 484.
[164] N. Nielsen, 1925, 434.
[165] G. Hatt, 1936.
[166] J. Déchelette, II (1924), 549.
[167] C. I. Fell, 1937, 95 f.

which has yielded quantities of slag and the richest iron finds of any prehistoric site in England, is as good an example as any—whose position has evidently been determined by the presence of iron ore ; in this particular instance, indeed, the hill-fort actually overlies iron-stone. But the point one would prefer to emphasize is that iron ore was seldom far off an early settlement. The gulf between iron and the constituents of bronze in this respect was admirably brought out by Wheeler when he pointed out that, while the early iron age farmers of Maiden Castle, Dorset, were unable to buy the imported metal, " iron lay to hand, and the Wessex yeoman used it in season and out."[168]   The picture of small-scale local production is admirably reflected at All Cannings Cross in Wiltshire, which yielded slag and iron ore, some of it partly calcined, of a kind available within a radius of ten miles on the Lower Greensand near Seend.[169] Yet there are signs that, as iron came into use for a broader range of equipment, its production came to be centred, in part at least, on localities where the ore was particularly rich and accessible. Recent consideration of the iron " currency bars " from Britain, for example, suggests that they were made from iron from the Forest of Dean.[170] No physical proof of this is yet available, but it is notable that out of the thousand or so examples known some four-fifths were found within a radius of forty miles of the ore-field. In any case the size of some of the hoards—one of 394 from Meon Hill, Gloucestershire, two of 150 each from Malvern, Worcestershire, and one of c. 140 from Salmondsbury Camp, Bourton-on-the-Water, Gloucestershire, may be noted—suggests that whether we chose to interpret the bars as sword-moods, currency, or both, they represent production on a scale too substantial to meet mere local needs. On the continent similar indications are given by the four-sided ingots, tapered at either end, which are found concentrated in south Germany, but which extend to central and western France and up to northern Jutland : in this case, though, it is clear that large-scale production was brought into being to meet Roman needs and it is significant that the great majority of the ingots have been found within the lines of the Empire.[171]

Until the invention of the blowing-engine in fourteenth-century Europe, the temperature (c. 1,535°C.) needed to liquefy iron and so render it capable of being cast was unattainable.[172] Consequently in early times all iron artifacts had to be wrought directly from blooms or lumps of malleable iron reduced immediately from the ore, a process for which a temperature of no more than 800–900° C. was needed. Production was achieved by heating the ore sufficiently to cause its siliceous content to separate and combine with ferrous oxide so as to form a fusible silicate, or slag. As Weiershausen and others have shown,[173] the furnaces in which this was carried on varied in construction, even though some supposed variations may be due in reality to the loss of the superstructure ; but even the most elaborate like those in the Engsbachtal, kr. Siegen, in south-west Westphalia,[174] were small and easily worked. From the earliest times, long before the use of water-power to operate

---

[168] R. E. M. Wheeler, 1943, 382.

[169] M. E. Cunnington, 1923, 53.

[170] R. A. Smith and W. Gowland, 1905 ; Bulleid and Gray, 1911, 395–403 ; E. W. Hulme, 1933 ; C. Fox, 1940 ; R. E. M. Wheeler, 1943, 383–5 ; C. Fox, 1945, 32–3. On the haematite deposits of the Forest of Dean, see T. F. Sibly, 1919.

[171] G. Kossinna, 1915, 117–25 and 1919–20, 412–13 ; N. Nielsen, 1925, 42–5 ; P. Weiershausen, 1939, 194–202.

[172] T. A. Rickard, 1932, 860–1.

[173] P. Weiershausen, 1939, passim.

[174] A. Stieren, 1935.

blast-furnaces was thought of, it was usual to construct furnaces close to running streams —the Engsbachtal furnaces are a case in point—so that water might be available for cooling iron tools and for quenching the thirst of those engaged on the work.[175] The commonest fuel used to heat the furnaces was charcoal, which may well have been prepared by burning wood stacked in conical piles heaped over with turf, as was still done in parts of western and central Jutland down to the present day. One advantage of this method was that by the simple expedient of lifting the necessary turves the draft could be regulated to secure sufficient, but not too complete, carbonization. In regions where timber was scarce —and this must have applied to extensive territories on the north-western margins of the temperate zone under the influence of climatic deterioration—carbonized peat may have been used either alone or in combination with charcoal, as it still was in parts of Jutland down to around 1870.[176] To bring the furnace up to the temperature required, it was necessary to use bellows, a device already established during the Bronze Age, and which to judge from the multiple nozzle-sockets in the Engsbachtal furnaces were sometimes at least operated in batteries. Even so the process of extracting the iron was only partly completed and it was necessary to expel the slag and unreduced ore remaining in the bloom by hammering. A high proportion of iron was admittedly lost in this way, but it would be senseless to brand as uneconomic a process perfectly attuned to and in fact an outcome of the form of economy then prevailing in the temperate zone of Europe; and once again it must be remembered that iron ore was not in itself a precious substance.

From the perspective of world history the harnessing of iron was assuredly " the most portentous event in the development of human industry,"[177] in the sense that it provided the material framework for modern civilization. So far as prehistoric Europe is concerned, though, one must remember that it was only in the last few centuries, and particularly within the sphere of influence of La Tène culture, that iron began to play a really significant rôle as a material for tools, and further that all the decisive steps by which technology was enriched by applications of its distinctive properties were taken by civilized, literate communities. Ecologically the influence of iron was immense, since not only did its production involve the use of charcoal and by consequence the clearing of woodland, but the iron axe itself was the most effective agent of deforestation. Here again, though, one has to remember that the process of enlarging the sphere of human settlement by clearing the heavier soils had barely begun before the temperate zone had been brought under the domination or at least the influence of imperial Rome. In more ways than one the Early Iron Age bridged the gap between prehistoric Europe and the Europe of recorded history.

---

[175] E. Straker, 1931, 20.
[176] N. Nielsen, 1925, 383 f.
[177] T. A. Rickard, 1932, 832.

CHAPTER VIII

TECHNOLOGY: OTHER HANDICRAFTS

IF the principal tools through which early man exercised control over his environment were made of flint and stone or metal, the materials which served most purposes of his daily life were organic and to an overwhelming extent local in origin. One of the obvious exceptions was clay, from which were fabricated such things as spindle-whorls, bobbins, loom- and net-weights, lamps and ladles, as well as a broad range of pots and pans.

POTTING

The significance of pottery for the understanding of prehistoric society can easily be overrated, though the variety in which it can be fashioned and its great durability, when compared with many other categories of material equipment, makes it peculiarly suitable for classification. It must always be remembered that pottery was only one of many substances used to make containers and that even when it had come into use it was not everywhere the most important of these. Potting is traditionally associated with farming, but pastoralists often made little or no pottery and not all communities in which pottery was made practised any form of farming. Recent work has shown that the Ertebølle midden people of the Danish coasts were making pottery back to the time of the first Litorina transgression,[1] substantially earlier than the spread of neolithic economy into any part of temperate Europe. Again, in the Later Stone Age of Scandinavia, potting was found among the Arctic hunter-fishers of the northern territories up to Finnmark itself,[2] as well as among the farmers of the south. Incidentally, the dwelling-place people of Ångermanland and Romsdal can claim to have pioneered the use of asbestos,[3] which they mixed with clay for their pots.

Among the prehistoric Europeans potting was essentially a domestic hand industry. There is no evidence that pottery was made for a distant market[4] and such trade as can be proved took the form of importing pots from the civilized Mediterranean world. The potter's wheel, which first came into use among communities at the level of urban civilization was used in Crete at least by the beginning of Middle Minoan times, but was only spread over the Mediterranean as a whole by Greek, Etruscan and Punic colonization. In

---

[1] T. Matthiassen *et al.*, 1942, 62.

[2] G. Gjessing, 1942, 257 f., 460 f.

[3] Ebert, I, 173 ; G. Gjessing, 1942, 268 f. Asbestos fibre from Karystos, Euboea, was used by the ancient Greeks for textiles, particularly in connection with burial clothing. See *Paulys Real.— Encyclopädie*, I, 2, 1830 (under Amiantus).

[4] Trade in pottery has been claimed for neolithic groups by W. Buttler (1938A, 29 f.), but the facts are interpreted differently in the present work, see p. 251.

temperate Europe it arrived during Middle La Tène times, but even at the close of the pre-historic period coarse pottery continued to be made by hand. It is further significant that in the one early European culture, in which potters' kilns are found, these are " so numerous that they must belong to individual families rather than to a single professional."[5]

It is somewhat ironical that the shapes and to some extent the decoration of prehistoric pottery preserve the memory of prototypes, which though often of great importance in their own day have failed to survive the processes of decay. The very plasticity of clay, which allowed the potter to achieve smooth and graceful profiles seems also to have deprived her under the conditions of primitive society of any large measure of initiative, so that her products may often be most important for what they can tell us of the cognate crafts from which she drew so much of her inspiration. The very process used in building the pot may give information of this kind. For instance, the fact that Ertebølle pottery was built in coils suggests that coiled basketry goes back at least to late mesolithic times, even though the earliest tangible specimens are neolithic in age. Whether Schuchardt's[6] celebrated deriva-tion of the main families of neolithic pottery in Europe from pre-ceramic prototypes is any longer accepted in detail, his general hypothesis remains attractive. It is significant that details of the decoration of British neolithic A2 or Abingdon ware, notably oblique strokes or stabs on the shoulder and thickened rim and vertical furrows on the hollow neck, have been satisfyingly explained[7] in terms of the sewing and puckering of a leather vessel with inserted hoops, though the ware in question was unknown when Schuchardt first suggested leather prototypes for the whole class of western neolithic pottery.

The influence of basketry has been a good deal discussed, particularly in connection with bell beaker pottery and with the northern " passage-grave " wares.[8] Rather less attention has been paid to wooden vessels as a source of ceramic forms. Many of the hand-cut wooden bowls of the Swiss lake-villages resemble Cortaillod pots just as closely as do the hypo-thetical leather prototypes, but it could easily be in this case that the wooden forms were modelled on the ceramic. More convincing examples of pottery vessels based on wooden prototypes are the straight-sided handled beakers from the Cambridge region, most notably the specimen from Bottisham with concentric circles on the base recalling the growth-rings of trees.[9] These pottery vessels, the tankards of their day, provide the only memorial of a school of wood craftsmen working at the dawn of the Bronze Age. Again, the fret-work or *kerbschnitt* decoration, found on pottery of the middle bronze age tumulus culture of south Germany, as well as on many food-vessels from the highland zone of Britain, and executed by excising small triangles and lozenges from the surface of the pot before firing, is pretty clearly borrowed from the wood carver. Closely similar decoration is found on the carved woodwork of many primitive peoples as well as on that of modern European folk cultures.[10]

Particularly during the Early Iron Age, also, the potters reproduced in clay the forms of metal vessels too precious for ordinary use. It is common doctrine[11] that the dominant form of the Iron Age A ceramic of Britain is derived from the Hallstatt urn of sheet bronze,

---

[5] V. G. Childe, 1947, 133–4.

[6] C. Schuchardt, 1909–10.

[7] S. Piggott, 1931, 81.

[8] e.g. Schuchardt, 1910, 145 f.

[9] S. Piggott, *Antiquity*, 1935, 348.

[10] L. Rütimeyer, 1924, 342, fig. 172.

[11] For discussion, see Hawkes and Dunning, 1930, 165–8.

though it must of course be admitted that a ceramic tradition once in being might spread far beyond the sphere in which its prototype was current in time and space. Again, the origin of the bead-rim bowls of the Wessex hill-fort B culture has been sought[12] in metal vessels, the rims of which were rolled over for strength; bronze bowls close to the ideal prototype have indeed been found in south-western England at Glastonbury and Spettisbury.[13] The prestige of exotic vessels of metal often prompted the potter to make a clay version, as did that of bronze beaked flagons of Italian origin among more than one La Tène community.[14] This may sometimes yield a priceless clue to contacts with higher cultures, as in the clay cup from Nienhagen, the handle of which has been interpreted as a copy of that of the Minoan Vapheio cup.[15]

It has long been recognized, also, that many schemes of decoration, particularly those found on pottery, were inspired by the arrangement of cords or slings, by which the vessels were carried or suspended. This is well shown by the multiple chevron decoration often seen on stroke-ornamented Danubian pottery, especially when lugs are present. Again, the decoration of the earliest cord-ornamented ware, comprising a series of horizontal lines encircling the neck, often with pendant fringes, clearly reproduces the carrier or sling: in this case, indeed, it is not merely the arrangement, but also the very character of the decoration impressed on the clay, which reveals its origin.[16]

BARK-WORK

One of the organic materials which came most readily to the hand of prehistoric man was tree bark. Easily removed at spring or autumn, it needed comparatively little preparation and by means of plaiting or sewing certain kinds could be fashioned into a broad range of useful objects. Among the purposes for which bark has been used among the peasants and hunter-fishers of temperate and circumpolar Europe down to the present day (Pl. XII, b), may be mentioned the construction of tent-like shelters, roofs and flooring, the lining of fish store-pits,[17] tapers and torches, shoes, cradles, beehives,[18] net-floats, holsters and a wide

---

[12] R. E. M. Wheeler, 1943, 206–7.   [13] Bulleid and Gray, 1911, 179–82.

[14] P. Jacobsthal, 1929, 60–1.

[15] H. Mötefindet, *Sächsische Jahresschrift*, X (1911), 76 f.; G. Neumann, *Prähist. Z.*, XX (1929), 135-6; Evans, *Palace*, II, 175; V. G. Childe, 1929, 238.

[16] As to the material used to make the cords for decorating cord-impressed pottery, experiments made in Scotland (*P.S.A.S.*, 4th Ser., III, 551–2) and Germany (W. von Stockar, 1938, 43–4) have shown that wool is too elastic and gives much too indefinite impressions. Cords made from hair-moss have been shown to be equally unsatisfactory. The suggestion that the cords were made from flax is hardly acceptable, at least as a general rule, since flax cultivation did not reach Denmark until at earliest the Late Bronze Age. The suggestion may be made that the Jutland cord-breakers were decorated by cords made from bast. The manufacture of bast cords goes well back into the Boreal period in the Baltic area and there is evidence from a Sjaelland bog of an early neolithic pot being wrapped or contained in a twined plait of lime bast (C. J. Becker, 1948, 10 f.). The crisp impression made by bast cords can be judged from the imprints of the bast ties on the caulking of the Hjortspring boat (Pl. I, d).

[17] For an excellent account of the manifold uses of birch-bark among the Finno-Ougrians see I. Manninen (1932). It is worth recalling that some of the Viking ships burials of Valsgärde and Vendel were covered by shelters made from sheets of birch-bark sewn together (G. Arwidsson, 1942, 106–9, abb. 76).

[18] Pliny, XXI, 80, says that the best beehives are made from bark smeared with cow-dung and Virgil (*Georgics*, IV, 33–4) also refers to bark beehives.

range of boxes and containers (Pl. XII, a). There is no doubt that the working of bark, like that of skins, was part of the heritage derived by the European peoples from the Old Stone Age.

As it happens, the most useful bark of all was that of the birch, which dominated the first forests to colonise the open spaces at the dawn of the post-glacial period. Evidence of its use already at this early period has recently come to light at Star Carr in north-east Yorkshire, in the shape of tightly rolled strips of birch bark varying in width from one to eight inches and up to thirty inches in length.[19] The Lapps of the modern birch zone store the bark for use in precisely this way, and similar rolls were found at the original Maglemosian site of Mullerup in Denmark,[20] dating from rather later in the post-glacial period. Although no finished articles made from birch bark have yet been recovered from mesolithic sites, it can hardly be doubted that this will sooner or later happen. The peculiar aptitude of a light material like birch bark for the needs of nomadic hunter-fishers need hardly be emphasized, and the technique of sewing bark would come easily to people well used to working skins in the same way.

A mesolithic, if not a still earlier origin, for the use of birch bark has indeed been inferred by Emil Vogt[21] merely on account of the advanced standards attained in its working in neolithic Switzerland. Particularly fine workmanship is shown in part of a delicately sewn box from Niederwil, Thurgau (Pl. XII, e),[22] but it is perhaps equally significant that a rougher specimen from Port, near Bienne[23] should have been used to contain fish-scales. The vigour of the tradition of working birch-bark is sufficiently well shown by the influence it was able to exert on the younger craft of potting. Examination of Cortaillod pottery from lake-side settlements in the Neuchâtel and Luzern regions has shown that this was sometimes overlaid by chevrons and other patterns cut out in silhouette from birch-bark and applied to the surface on bands painted with tacky birch-pitch.[24] The fact that this effective method of decoration has not yet been found on any other group of western neolithic pottery may of course be due to the exceptional conditions for survival which obtain at many Swiss sites. On the other hand, it is significant that it has so far been confined to the younger Cortaillod pottery, as though it was only after the passage of some years that the indigenous craft was able to impose itself on the one introduced from outside.

Evidence may also be cited for the use of birch-bark for containers during the Northern Bronze Age. A particularly well-preserved vessel of birch-bark sewn with lime bast was found in the oak-coffin burial of Egtved, Denmark (Pl. XII, c)[25] and this contained the solidified dregs of a fermented drink mixed with honey. Birch-bark was also used to fashion holsters for the fragile bronze trumpets (*lurer*) of Denmark, if one is to judge from the find at Påarp Mose.[26] Finds of birch-bark from the bronze-age barrows of Barkåkra, Scania,[27] include a covering for a cist burial and wrapping for a bronze dagger deposited in its leather sheath.

---

[19] J. G. D. Clark, 1949, 63.

[20] G. F. L. Sarauw, 1903, 191.

[21] E. Vogt, 1949, 5.

[22] Landesmuseum, Zürich (Z.834). This was misinterpreted by H. Messikomer (1913, 76) as part of a girdle. Its true character was recognized by Vogt.

[23] O. Tschumi, 1940, abb. 17 and Taf. III, 1.

[24] E. Vogt, 1949, Pls. VI, VII.

[25] T. Thomsen, 1929, 184, Fig. 16.

[26] J. Brøndsted, II, 188.

[27] R. Rausing, 1949, 170.

The neolithic inhabitants of Switzerland and south Germany also used spools of birch-bark as tapers or torches, the charred stumps of which have been recognized at a number of sites (Pl. XII, d).[28] It is interesting to note that a similar use of birch-bark persisted in certain Alpine valleys into the present century and still survives in the birch zone of northern Europe.[29] Birch-bark was also used in neolithic times for wrapping round the stumps of combs as a handle.[30] Its incorporation in building—for example, sheets were placed under clay ovens at Taubried, Federsee,[31] to prevent damp rising from the peaty sub-soil—and its use for matting, noted at Riedsachen, Federsee,[32] and at the Swiss site of Moosseedorf,[33] may well point back to a time when the material was more generally used for dwellings.[34]

The properties of the resin or pitch (*Birkenteer*)[35] contained in birch-bark was appreciated in very early times, and the substance was certainly extracted, presumably by some process of dry distillation, during neolithic times in the alpine area. Stone pebbles used in the preparation have been found together with lumps of the pitch in Liechtenstein,[36] and many finds have been confirmed from the Swiss lake-villages. As already noted, it was used for applying birch-bark patterns to pottery and it also served for repairing cracks or even for plugging holes.[37] Its main use, though, was for fixing flint sickle or knife blades in their handles and for securing arrow-heads of flint or bone to their shafts (Fig. 22). It is highly probable that the resins used in northern Europe during mesolithic times for hafting implements were of the same origin. Indeed, pebbles, resembling those from Liechtenstein already mentioned, have been recognized in an early mesolithic context at Star Carr, Yorkshire.[38]

Another kind of bark available during Boreal times was pine-bark. Slabs of this were used by the Maglemosians for flooring[39] and small pieces were shaped for net-floats during mesolithic times in the Baltic area, but apart from its buoyancy pine bark had few useful qualities and was used only for limited purposes.

The most valuable accession brought by the rise of temperature during post-glacial times was beyond doubt lime-bark, which down to modern times has played a considerable part as a material for containers, particularly in the east Baltic lands (Pl. X, b) and in the territories of the Tscheremiss on the Volga.[40] The earliest find available is a box, about 11 cm. in diameter and half as high, made from lime-bark sewn with bast, from the early

---

[28] e.g. Weiher bei Thayngen and Robenhausen; also noted by Reinerth at the Federsee.

[29] For a detailed account, see L. Rütimeyer, 1924, 80–94.

[30] e.g. one from Auvernier, Neuchâtel, in the Landesmuseum, Zürich (Z.36007).

[31] H. Reinerth, 1936, 94.

[32] *ibid.*, 101.

[33] Berne Hist. Mus. No. 2326.

[34] Successive floors of birch-bark were for instance noted by G. Schwantes (1928, 201–12) at the Maglemosian station of Duvensee, near Lübeck.

[35] According to Merck's *Warenlexikon* (5th edtn., 54), birch-pitch was used in preparing Russian leather and in folk medicine as a cure for skin complaints.

[36] Information from Professor Vogt.

[37] e.g. in the case of the circular clay lamp from Egolzwil, 2 (V. von Gonzenbach, 1949, abb. 7, No. 9). It was also used to plug the bases of small cups made from deer antler found at Seematte, Hitzkirch, Luzern (Landesmuseum, Zürich, Z.38050). For decoration, see E. Vogt, 1949.

[38] J. G. D. Clark, 1949, Pl. XX, f and g.

[39] e.g. at Amosen, Denmark, in 1947.

[40] I. Manninen, 1932, 218; J. Granlund, 1939, 264.

bronze age coffin-burial of Egtved, Denmark (Pl. X, c)[41] ; the box contained some cord, two burnt bones and a metal awl and its wooden handle, the latter of which may well have been used to perforate the bark for sewing. Much of our knowledge, though, is based on reconstructions. For example, Granlund has been able to show[42] that pieces of resin found with cremation burials from the Roman and Pre-Roman Iron Age in southern Sweden belonged to circular boxes made from this material (Pl. X, a and d). Two types

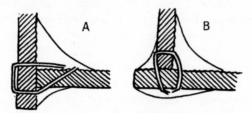

Fig. 111. Methods of sewing bases to the walls of lime-bark containers from the Iron Age in South Sweden. (*After Granlund*).

have been distinguished, type A in which the floor has been sewn onto the wall of the container and type B in which the wall has been sewn onto the floor (Fig. 111). There is also considerable variation in the arrangement of the stitching, by which the band forming the wall of the vessels was joined (Fig. 112). If vessels of this type were used almost up to

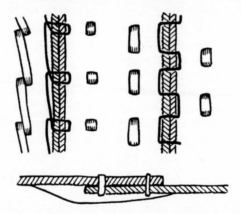

Fig. 112. Methods of sewing seams of lime-bark containers from the Iron Age of South Sweden. (*After Granlund*).

the northern limit of the lime tree (Fig. 113), we may feel all the more confident that lime-bark played its part over wide territories of temperate, though not of course of circumpolar Europe.

There is little doubt that the tradition of making containers for fluids with wooden bases and bark walls, a tradition which still survives in the folk-culture of the Great Russians,[43]

---

[41] T. Thomsen, 1929, 183 and Fig. 12.
[42] *op cit., passim.*
[43] cf. D. Zelenin, 1927, 109 and abb. 71.

dates back to the Stone Age. From the neolithic level of the lake-side settlement of Roben-hausen in Switzerland there comes a flat circular base cut with a flange, into the side of which four horizontal wooden pegs or nails have been driven, evidently to secure some walling material whether bark or thin wood.[44] A more sophisticated version of the same basic type was found at the late bronze age pile-settlement of Zürich-Alpenquai in the same country, but in this case the upper surface of the base was dished and the pegs, eight in

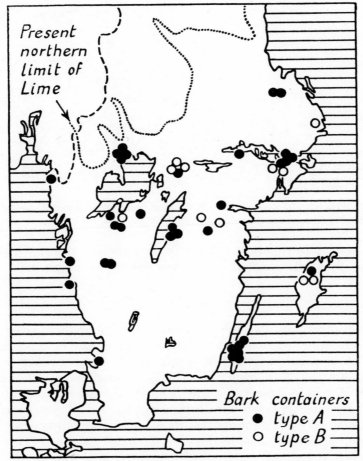

Fig. 113. Distribution of resin caulking of lime-bark containers from Iron Age burials in Sweden. (*Based on Granlund*).

number, had been driven into the flange alternately horizontally and obliquely, the latter coming right through to the flat base (Fig. 114).[45] Small objects like these were held in the hand without the need of any handle. There were two main difficulties in making any-thing of this kind with a greater capacity, namely how to keep the flimsy sides sufficiently rigid and how to secure a handle. These problems were ingeniously solved by the late

---

[44] I have to thank Professor E. Vogt for allowing me to examine this at Zürich and for his help by correspondence.

[45] Examined in the Landesmuseum, Zürich, See *Mitt. d. Ant. Ges. in Zürich*, XXIX, h. 4, Taf. V, 7.

bronze age copper-miners of Salzburg and the Tyrol,[46] who set handles consisting of two tapered uprights, joined at the top by a cross-piece, into sockets cut into the wooden bottom: the lower ends of the handle uprights being thicker than the upper, the handle became more firmly fixed the heavier the load and so far from straining the walls of the container only served to lend it support. The bottom edge of the walls of such vessels,

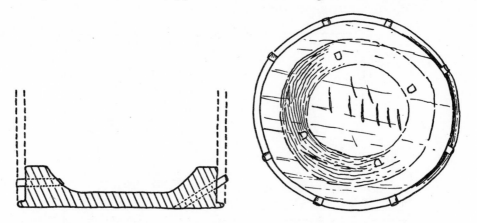

Fig. 114.   Wooden base of container with wooden nails for securing side-walls from the Late Bronze Age lake settlement at Zürich-Alpenquai, Switzerland.

whether of bark or of splinter-thin wood, was set in a groove cut into the thickness of the base and anchored by wooden pegs or nails driven obliquely through both.

WOOD-WORKING

The most ample opportunities for the craftsman in wood were those given by the deciduous forest of the temperate zone and it is from here that the main evidence for the development of wood-working must necessarily be drawn, whether one considers houses, boats or the handicrafts dealt with in this chapter. It is likely that during the earlier stages of settled occupation the Mediterranean zone supported a more vigorous tradition of wood-working than that known from later times when the natural woodlands had been degraded by human activity, but it is only very exceptionally that traces of organic substances other than bone or antler survive on prehistoric sites in this climatic zone. As the numerous finds of skis and sledge-runners have testified, conditions for the survival of wooden objects are as good in much of the circumpolar zone as they are locally in temperate Europe, but only a limited range of timber, predominantly birch and pine, was available and it would seem that bark and skin were frequently used where wood was employed further south.

So long as the craftsman had to make do with tools of flint or stone, his mastery over wood was limited, though he might if he so willed produce highly finished articles within this range. Flint knives and scrapers, supplemented where necessary by awls and adzes (Pl. IX), were capable of producing a variety of equipment needed for hunting, fishing, farming and domestic life, including such things as bows with admirably shaped hand-grips (Pl. I, f), a variety of axe and adze handles, sickle hafts, ladles, and the like. Splitting by means of wedges along the grain of the wood and smoothing by abrasion were other simple

---

[46] See Preuschen and Pittioni, 1937, 82 f., Taf. 27.

processes involved in the production of objects like the long toothed combs favoured by the Cortaillod and Lagozza people of Switzerland and north Italy.[47] Possibly the best way of following the effect of improvements in tools is to trace the history of a single product such as wooden containers. The vessels made by neolithic man—and up to the present no trace of wooden containers has been found at any mesolithic site—were cut out of the solid by hand. To judge by an unfinished lugged bowl from Zürich-Utoquai,[48] the hollowing of such vessels, as indeed of wooden ladles, was done by means of the adze, but as a rule traces of workmanship were removed by polishing. Although such vessels were small and primitive in form (Pl. XIV, a)[49], it is easy to see that for many purposes they must have been at least as attractive as hand-made pottery. The introduction of bronze metallurgy in its earliest mode (mode 1) had no apparent effect in this particular sphere of wood-working; for instance, the gold-encrusted bowl from Caergwrle, Flintshire[50] and the handled bowls from the Danish oak-coffin burials, decorated in some instances with precious tin nails,[51] were similarly cut from the solid by hand.

This primitive form of course survived for certain purposes alongside the new types of container associated with the spread of mode 3 of bronze metallurgy. During the Late Bronze Age, for instance, the copper-miners of the Tyrol[52] continued to eat their food out of bowls cut by hand from one piece and the earliest crannog-dwellers of Ballinderry[53] used similar vessels.

The general use of metal gouges and chisels at this time, though, made it easy to cut grooves with sufficient accuracy to make wooden containers with inserted bases. These were of two main kinds, a typologically more primitive one, having the walls cut from one piece, and a more complex one, in which the walls were built up from a number of staves, but both made their appearance in certain parts of temperate Europe at the same stage. The lower part of a bucket of the former type was found at Stuntney, near Ely, Cambridgeshire,[54] containing a founder's hoard dating from the second phase of the Late Bronze Age in Britain and weighing approximately 43 lb. The body which had an external diameter of about one foot, was hollowed out of an alder trunk, the walls being reduced to two-thirds or three-quarters of an inch except for the bottom two or three inches, where they were left thicker to contain the groove. The depth and strength of the flanges formed by the groove must have been related to the volume of the bucket and the consequent weight of the milk or water it was designed to carry, and it is noticeable that these were much less prominent on some of the smaller buckets of the same type from Glastonbury (Fig. 115).[55]

---

[47] e.g. the greater part of a yew wood comb from Egolzwil 2 in the Naturhist. Mus., Luzern, and an almost complete one from Lagozza in the Como Museum. A smaller comb of yew wood with two rows each of twenty-five teeth from the Murtensee, Greng, is in the Berne Hist. Mus. (No. 18711).

[48] Landesmuseum, Zürich. Z.37849.

[49] A broken example from Ehenside Tarn, W. Cumberland (*Arch.* XLIV, 289) shows that similar wooden bowls were made in neolithic Britain.

[50] W. F. Grimes, 1939, 83–4, Fig. 27.

[51] e.g. Brøndsted, 1938, II, Fig. 56a.

[52] See Preuschen and Pittioni, 1937, 81, Taf. 26.

[53] H. O'N. Hencken, 1942, Fig. 7. Prof. S. P. O'Riordain has recorded a handled cup, *c.* 8 inches in diameter, cut from one piece from a late bronze age level in a bog at Oldtown, Kilcachel, co. Roscommon (*Galway Arch. and Hist. Soc.*, XVIII, 40–2).

[54] J. G. D. Clark, 1940, 53 f.

[55] e.g. the decorated oak bucket, having a maximum interior diameter of *c.* $5\frac{1}{2}$ inches, illustrated by Bulleid and Gray, 1911, Fig. 98.

In the case of these solid-walled buckets the base must presumably have been inserted into the groove after the vessel itself had been expanded by prolonged soaking in water and retained in position by the shrinking which occurred as the walls dried out. The effectiveness of buckets of this kind, which were doubtless carried by handles passed through ears projecting from the rim and often suspended in turn from hooks at either end of a yoke, is proved by their long survival at any rate in Ireland and Scotland, where they were used to store bog butter down to a comparatively recent period.[56]

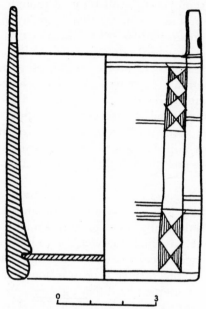

Fig. 115. Reconstruction of wooden bucket, cut from the solid, but with inserted base, from Glastonbury marsh-village.

Scale in inches.

There is as yet no evidence that stave-built buckets with inserted bases reached Britain until a late stage of the Early Iron Age, when they are met with for instance at Glastonbury[57], but in Switzerland they appeared already during the Late Bronze Age, as at Zürich-Alpenquai (Fig. 116).[58] In view of the antiquity of the wooden nail, noted in connection with bark or splinter vessels having wooden bases, it is hardly surprising that the staves of the late bronze age buckets should already have been dowelled. Such vessels were also strengthened by enclosing them with hoops. For ordinary purposes these were made of withes, but metal bands were apparently used at Glastonbury[59] and for purposes of social ostentation these might be made, as with the Belgic buckets from Aylesford[60] and Marlborough, to carry more or less elaborate embossed decoration.

---

[56] See *Proc. Roy. Soc. Ant. Ireland*, 5th Ser., II, 285–6.
[57] e.g. Bulleid and Gray, 1911, Fig. 65.
[58] Landesmuseum, Zürich. Z.32027.
[59] Bulleid and Gray, 1911, 315 and Fig. 65.
[60] e.g. *B.M.G. Early Iron Age Collections*, 124–5, Fig. 135.

The final stage was reached with the spread of the lathe, which made it possible to turn thin-walled vessels, of graceful form and decorated with a variety of cordons and grooves, with precision and dispatch. Like the wheel and the rotary-quern, the lathe spread from the Mediterranean to the temperate, though not to the circumpolar zone, of Europe during prehistoric times. There is still some room for discussion about when the device first appeared. It has been argued, largely on the basis of a shallow dish of cypress wood from Shaft Grave V at Mycenæ,[61] that the lathe was used in Greece as early as the middle of the second millenium B.C. The profile of the dish, but above all the hole at the centre with its wooden stopper, suggest that this can hardly be brushed on one side, as Rieth has recently done,[62] though more conclusive evidence is required before the Mycenæans

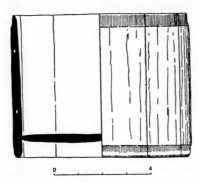

Fig. 116.   Stave-built tub with inserted base,
Zürich-Alpenquai.
Scale of inches.

can be credited with the lathe. The point is not quite an academic one, since the only objects from the Bronze Age of the temperate zone seriously claimed as having been turned on the lathe—the amber and shale cups from southern England brought forward by Evans and more recently by Newall[63]—belong to the Wessex culture, which was linked by commerce, if indirectly, with Mycenæ. It should be noted, however, that the cups in question have been so well polished that no traces of working are visible, that although the grooved decoration is consistent with the use of the lathe, it is not of the regularity one might expect if it had in fact been made by this means, and that the presence of a handle, though compatible with the use of a reciprocal bow lathe,[64] precludes the use of a rotary one. In any case, even if the possibility is allowed that the Mycenæans used the lathe and that knowledge of it spread as far as Wessex, it is certain that it was no longer in use during the Late Bronze Age in temperate Europe,[65] all the wooden vessels, of which were either cut out by hand or built up from staves.

Although direct evidence in Greece itself is lacking for some centuries after the Shaft Graves, and despite a certain element of doubt which still lingers about the use of the lathe

---

[61] G. Karo, 1930–3, 153, Taf., CXLVII.

[62] A. Rieth, 1941.

[63] R. S. Newall, 1929, 112.

[64] Wooden cups were made in Ireland by this means down to modern times. The handle was left solid and cut out later with a sharp knife.

[65] This was first pointed out by Reith, 1941, 91, but the present writer confirmed this for himself, particularly by examining the museum material from the Swiss lakes.

by the Mycenæans, Rieth was right to conclude that the device was not in common use, if indeed it was used at all, until iron cutting-tools were available.[66] The oldest wooden vessels, of which we can rightly say that they were turned at any rate on a rotary lathe, come from the Etruscan Warrior's Tomb at Corneto.[67] When the Etruscans colonised northern Italy they brought the device with them and we find for example a shallow cordoned dish of turned wood in one of the cremation burials at Certosa, Bologna.[68] From northern Italy the rotary lathe appears to have spread into south-western Germany during a late stage of the Hallstatt culture, as testified by a number of turned wheel-naves and amber-headed pins. It is to this period also that the oldest turned wooden vessel from north of the Alps belongs, namely the beautifully moulded kylix from inside a bronze situla in a barrow at Uffing, near the Staffelsee, northern Bavaria[69]; one may agree with Rieth, though, that this masterpiece of turnery based on a Greek prototype was an import from Italy rather than, as was claimed by Naue, a south German product.

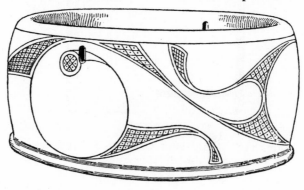

0   4

Fig. 117. Lathe-turned wooden tub, Glastonbury marsh-village.
(*After Bulleid and Gray*).
Scale of inches.

There is no evidence, as yet, that wood-turning was practised on any scale in temperate Europe before the middle La Tène culture. The pedestalled boxes with lids and the small bowl from the Hjortspring boat on Aals, Denmark,[70] dating probably from the third century B.C., may well have been imported from the south, but it may be accepted that the numerous turned wooden vessels, wheel-hubs and spokes from La Tène[71] were made in the region of the site. It is pretty certain that the lathe was not among the elements of culture introduced by the earlier iron age immigrants to Britain. One of the earliest assemblages of wooden objects turned on the lathe in this country must be that from the Glastonbury lake-village,[72] comprising wheel-hubs and a range of bead-rim vessels and tubs, some incised with curvilinear decoration (Fig. 117) and others having fine moulding. The lathe

[66] *op. cit.*, 105.
[67] *ibid.*, 86–7.
[68] *ibid.*, 93.
[69] J. Naue, 1887, 142–4, Taf. XXXV.
[70] G. Rosenberg, 1937, Fig. 34.
[71] P. Vouga, 1923, Pl. XXIX.
[72] Bulleid and Gray, 1911, 310 ff.

was also applied to shale in southern England and it is interesting to note that, whereas bracelets made by the Iron Age A people were cut out by hand, as at All Cannings Cross, Wiltshire,[73] the Glastonbury lake-village yielded one of the cores, which result from turning these objects on the lathe.[74] There is no doubt that the Belgic invaders of south-eastern England were well accustomed to using the rotary lathe, material evidence of which may be cited in such vessels as the cordoned urns from Old Warden, Bedfordshire,[75] and the tazza from Barnwell, Cambridgeshire,[76] turned from shale with an assurance speaking of much practice. Naturally it was used mainly for vessels for personal use or for furnishing graves and did not displace so much as supplement older methods. For instance, the Glastonbury lake-villagers were content to cut out rough troughs by hand and to make buckets and tubs for dairying and other purposes by means of staves and coopering. A wooden tankard from Shapwick, Somerset,[77] dating from the fourth century A.D., but native made and embodying a prehistoric tradition, was built from wooden staves with bronze sheathing and handle, but the wooden base with its concentric cordons had evidently been turned on the lathe.

LEATHER AND SKINS

Some knowledge of the properties of animal skins and of the methods used in preparing them must be among the oldest elements in the heritage of European society. Among communities of hunters, lacking any knowledge of textiles, animal skins must have been the most obvious material for clothing and under the conditions prevailing in the tundra of late glacial times some form of covering would have been essential at any rate in the open. Although no actual traces of hides or leather can be expected from the remotest periods of prehistory, and although their survival from later times is local and capricious, certain of the tools used in their preparation have come down to us and help to emphasize the important part played by these materials in daily life. It is true that flint " scrapers " may have been mounted in some cases as planes and that they were pretty certainly used for working other materials, but the conventional view that many of them were designed for dressing skins is probably sound.[78] The amount of preparation needed to prepare skins and the long period over which they were used helps to explain the ubiquity of flint scrapers in prehistoric Europe and their persistence with comparatively little change from upper palæolithic times down to the Early Iron Age. On the other hand, analogy with modern primitive peoples suggests that tools of other materials were also used and a number of more or less close parallels may be quoted between European neolithic antler tools and implements employed by the Eskimo for working skins. For instance, as Vogt has pointed out, some small triangular blades, made from deer antler and provided with two perforations for securing the grip (Fig. 118), from the Michelsberg site at Weiher near Thayngen in Switzerland, are so similar to the Eskimo skin scraper or *ulu* that it is difficult not to think

---

[73] M. E. Cunnington, 1923, 141, Pl. 26, Nos. 1–5. Reference should also be made to Henrietta F. Davies' description (1937) of waste material from the shale bracelet manufactories of the Kimmeridge district, Dorset.

[74] Bulleid and Gray, 1911, 260, Fig. 54.

[75] C. Fox, 1923, 96, Pl. XV, 3.

[76] *ibid.*, 97.

[77] *J.R.S.*, XXX (1490), 175.

[78] Sir John Evans, 1897, Chap. XIII.

that they were used for the same purpose.[79] Again, one might compare other Swiss neolithic tools, cut with a rounded scraping-edge from a section of deer antler (Fig. 119).[80] with analogues from musk-ox shoulder-blades used by the Eskimo for removing meat and tissue from the inner surface of hides.[81] Of special interest to British archæologists are the deer antler combs (Fig. 120) characteristic of the neolithic " causewayed camps "

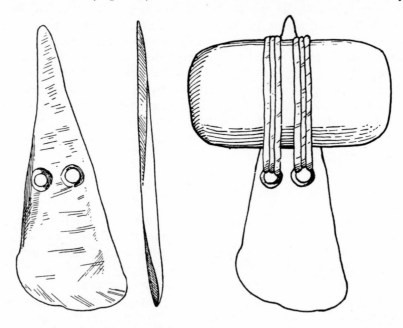

Fig. 118.   Skin-scraper made from deer antler, showing probable method of
mounting : Weiher, near Thayngen, Switzerland.   (*Schaffhausen Museum*).

of southern England,[82] and also met with in Belgium[83] and Schleswig-Holstein.[84] Although these bear a superficial resemblance to the stumps from which pins and needles might have been cut, the worn condition of the tips of the teeth, up to nine in number, shows that the objects were complete tools in themselves. As such they resemble very closely combs used by the Eskimo of the Point Barrow area for removing hairs from skins.[85]

Although the evidence is hard to come by, it may be assumed that chemical, as well as mechanical means, were used in the preparation of leather. After removing the hair—not a difficult task if the hide was first soaked—the skin might be tanned by immersion in a concoction, which to judge by medieval and recent practice might have been made from

---

[79] E. Vogt, 1947 A, 47 f., Taf. I. Vogt illustrates similar objects, but lacking the perforations, from Robenhausen, Obermeilen and Lüscherz.

[80] e.g. from Egolzwil 2 (Luzern Mus.), Ossingen (Zürich No. 28091–3), Lattrigen and Lüscherz (Berne Hist. Mus.). The same type occurs in the " terremare " of Toscanella Imolese (Bologna Museum).

[81] e.g. Birket-Smith, 1929, I, 240–5, Fig. 92 h.

[82] e.g. Windmill Hill, Wilts, Abingdon, Berks, and Whitehawk, Sussex.

[83] e.g. from Spiennes, see V. G. Childe, 1931A, Pl. VIII.

[84] e.g. from a bog at Heikendorf, near Kiel, see Schwantes, 1939, abb. 143.

[85] J. Murdoch, 1892, Fig. 301.

bark, oak-galls or roots.[86] On the other hand, it has been claimed by Olshausen[87] that samples of bronze age leather from Denmark examined by him showed evidence of having been tawed by immersion in clay-salts, no doubt in order to soften the hide for use as sandals.

The use of leather and skins for boats and dwellings is discussed elsewhere. For garments, skins must have been important, not only among hunter fishers, but also among the neolithic farmers of northern and parts of north-western Europe, including Britain. The fine-eyed

Fig. 119. Probable skin-scraper made from deer antler, Switzerland ($\frac{1}{3}$)

Fig. 120. Antler comb, probably used for dehairing skins, from Windmill Hill, Wilts. ($\frac{1}{3}$)

needles made by the Magdalenians[88] suggest that skins were sewn during late glacial times, presumably with animal sinew, and there are hints of skin coverings in the cave art.[89] More circumstantial evidence is available from the late stone age cemetery of Västerbjers on Gotland, belonging to a community of seal-hunters; fringes of seals' teeth lying across the thighs of female skeletons (Fig. 38) suggest that the women wore seal-skin garments

---

[86] Oak bark was commonly used in medieval England. According to Manninen (1932, 314–15) the Lapps use birch and willow bark for the same purpose. Oak galls were also useful on account of their high content of tannic acid. M. Martin (1934 edtn., 364) recorded during the late seventeenth century that "the common people dress their leather with the roots of tormentil instead of bark" and N. Annandale (1905, 196–7) noted much more recently that the Faroe islanders used the same roots for tanning sheep-skins. The roots were gathered by the women who prepared them for use by grinding them in natural depressions in the rocks by means of stone pestles. The powder was mixed with water to form a paste, which was rubbed into the hairy side of the skin after the wool had first been removed. After a couple of days or so the skins were washed in sea-water and dried.

[87] Ebert, bd. VII, 264–5.

[88] e.g. Lartet and Christy, 1875, 127–41, Pl. XVII.

[89] e.g. on the early Magdalenian man recently discovered by Professor D. A. E. Garrod at Angles-sur-l'Anglin, Vienne, France.

hanging down in front in pendant arcs, like those worn by the Eskimo.[90] When Tacitus[91] was describing the habits of the barbarians of Germany, he noted that the tribes distant from the Rhine wore the " skins of wild beasts " and that these included " the pied skins of the creatures native to the outer ocean and its unknown waters," creatures which can only have been seals. Leather was particularly well-suited for rough work and it is interesting to note that leather jerkins were worn by late bronze age copper-miners in the Austrian Tyrol.[92] The use of leather for footgear during the Bronze Age is proved by the presence of primitive shoes, secured to the foot by thongs threaded through holes along the upper margin and passed round the foot or ankle, in the Danish oak-coffin burials of Skrydstrup and Jels.[93] From the Early Iron Age we have a calf-skin shoe (Fig. 121) from the salt-mines of Dürrnberg, near Hallein in Austria,[94] and one with elaborate triangular excisions

Fig. 121. Calf skin shoe from salt-mine of Dürrnberg, Hallein, Austria. (*After Andree*).

for the lacing from a Danish bog in Amitlund, Vedsted parish.[95] The Dürrnberg mines also yielded a goat-skin cap[96], and a particularly neat conical cap, made from six pieces of skin with the hairy side innermost and a tassel of fine thongs hanging from the crown, (Fig. 122), came from Hallstatt.[97]

Whatever may be thought of Schuchardt's theory about the derivation of western neolithic pottery, there is little doubt that leather containers were used for carrying liquids in pre-historic, as they were certainly in proto-historic times[98] and as they still are in the folk-culture

---

[90] M. Stenberger, 1943, 96. One may compare with this the fringe of animal teeth, evidently bordering a mantle, from a grave in Weimar associated with the corded-ware culture. See W. von Stokar, 1938, 41 and abb. 59.

[91] *Germania*, cap. 17.

[92] An example was found at Kelchalpe, near Kitzbühel (Preuschen and Pittioni, 1937, abb. 2).

[93] Broholm and Hald, 1939, 84–9.

[94] G. Kyrle, 1916, Fig. 65; J. Andree, 1922, Taf. XI, 165.

[95] Broholm and Hald, 1939, Fig. 81.

[96] G. Kyrle, 1916, Fig. 62; J. Andree, 1922, Taf. XI, 162.

[97] F. Morton, 1942.

[98] e.g. leather vessels with silver handles were found in the Anglo-Saxon ship-burial at Sutton Hoo, Suffolk (C. W. Phillips, 1940, 170 f.).

of backward parts of Europe.[99] Skin bags were used by the salt-miners of Dürrnberg[100]; an elaborate rucksack with wooden stiffeners and laced thong decoration (Fig. 123) was

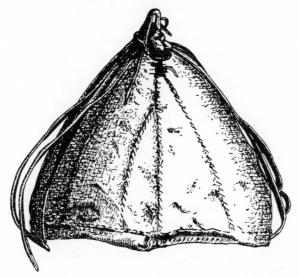

Fig. 122.   Leather cap from salt-mine at Hallstatt, Austria ($\frac{1}{3}$)
(*After Marton*).

Fig. 123.   Leather ruck-sack from salt-mine at
Hallstatt, Austria ($\frac{2}{25}$).   *After Andree*)

found in the Hallstatt mines[101] and a leather tool bag survived from La Tène.[102] Leather also played an important part in armament. A leather shield of late bronze age form was

---

[99] e.g. the skin containers used for raising water from Bulgarian wells. According to C. Wakarelski (1939, Fig. 14b) sheep-skin bags were used for hand-operated wells and ox-skin ones of up to 50 litres capacity for horse-operated ones.

[100] G. Kyrle, 1916, Fig. 63; J. Andree, 1922, Taf. XII, No. 168.

[101] J. Andree, 1922, Taf. XI, No. 163; L. Franz, 1929, Taf. 22.

[102] P. Vouga, 1923. 116, Taf. XLVI.

found at Clonbrin, County Longford, Ireland,[103] and what was almost certainly a wooden form on which similar ones were moulded comes from Churchfield, Knock, County Mayo.[104] The oldest leather object to survive from Europe is the scabbard of a flint dagger of early stone cist type from a bog near Wiepenkathen, Hanover,[105] made from sheep's skin and consisting of a narrow guard for the edge of the blade, an outer sheath decorated on the outer face and a thong for securing to the belt (Pl. XIII, f). Leather was commonly used during the Bronze Age for covering the wooden sheaths of swords and daggers[106] and for making the necessary webbing. With the introduction of chariots and later of riding, leather must have played an important role in the manufacture of harness. Among the industrial uses of leather should be numbered the bellows needed by smiths.

ANTLER, BONE AND HORN

In antler and bone, the natural armament and skeletal structure of their victims, the upper palæolithic and mesolithic peoples of Europe found materials admirably suited for the heads of harpoons, spears and arrows, and which could readily be shaped by simple flint tools. Indeed, there can be few other materials, of which it can be truthfully said that some of the finest products were made, not merely in the Stone Age, but by people at a hunter-fisher level of economy.

Among the reindeer hunters of the European tundra, it is noteworthy that antler was favoured at the expense of bone as a raw material,[107] whereas the Maglemosians of the forest period preferred bone for much of their equipment. That these preferences were the result of choice and not of the inherent needs of certain types of gear or weapon is neatly illustrated by recent discoveries at a camping place of an early mesolithic group at Star Carr, Yorkshire[108]; although the Yorkshire hunters concentrated on antler to the virtual exclusion of bone and used a technique of working closely resembling that of the Hamburgians, the barbed points which they produced were typically Maglemosian in form.

Examination of the quantities of antler discarded by reindeer-hunters at Meiendorf[109] and Stellmoor[110] in Schleswig-Holstein has shown very clearly how the Hamburgian craftsmen set to work. Parallel grooves were cut through the hard outer walling of the antler by means of flint burins; then by working a pronged flint in these it was not difficult to cut away the spongy interior, so that the intervening splinter could be prized off by antler wedges.[111] From splinters formed in this way the Hamburgians shaped the heads of their harpoons and arrows. A similar technique was applied by the mesolithic community at Star Carr to red deer antler, though here the worker was able to do without the pronged flints; despite this he succeeded in removing splinters right down to the burr of the antler, instead of stopping short as the Hamburgians had done at the brow tine.[112] Deer antler

---

[103] G. Coffey, 1913, 76; A. Mahr, 1937, 383.

[104] S. P. O'Riordain, 1946, 161, Pl. XIV, 2.

[105] A. Cassau, 1935, 109; *P.P.S.* 1937, 178 f.

[106] e.g. J. Brøndsted, 1938, II, Fig. 85d; G. Schwantes, 1939, Figs. 515–16.

[107] A. Rust, 1937, 106.

[108] J. G. D. Clark, 1949, 60-3.

[109] A. Rust, 1937, 92–6.

[110] A. Rust, 1943, 141–4.

[111] A. Rust, 1937, *Taf.* 32.

[112] J. G. D. Clark 1949, 62–3.

was worked in similar fashion in neolithic Switzerland[113] though the coarse harpoons commonly found in the lakeside settlements were apparently shaped while still attached to the parent antler, as shown by an unfinished example from the Baldegersee (Fig. 124).[114]

Another way of using reindeer antler, well demonstrated by the Ahrensburgians of north Germany during the younger Dryas period, was to remove the crown and bez and trez tines from the main branch and to shape part of the brow tine into an axe- or adze-like club.[115] When axes and adzes came into general use over the whole extent of the Maglemosian territory during the forest period, elk and deer antler were commonly used to

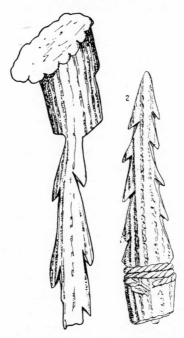

Fig. 124. Harpoon-head of deer-antler (with part of line) and unfinished specimen from neolithic Switzerland ($\frac{1}{3}$). (Luzern Museum).

make them, supplemented by flint and stone and to a certain extent by bone. The ingenuity with which quite primitive people could turn their knowledge of materials to practical use is well seen in the way the early Maglemosians handled elk antler for this purpose. In removing the palmated crown, just sufficient was left to accommodate the perforation needed for the wooden handle ; the burr was then cut away and the pedicle and part of the adhering frontal bone converted into a tough blade, the whole being smoothed down by abrasion.[116] With red deer the process was simpler. The burr was generally removed and the antler cut through a few inches above this, so as to form a blade parallel to or at right-angles with the handle, which was inserted through a hole near the base.[117] During the

---

[113] e.g. examples from the Michelsberg settlement " Weiher," near Thayngen, in the Schaffhausen Museum.

[114] Naturhist. Museum, Luzern.

[115] J. G. D. Clark, 1936, 81 f., Fig. 27.

[116] J. G. D. Clark, 1949, 62.

[117] J. G. D Clark, 1936, 112 and Fig. 40, Nos. 1, 2.

final stage of the mesolithic settlement of northern Europe the hafting was improved by retaining a few inches of the brow tine and driving the perforation through at this point, so as to make a socket.[118] Axe and adze heads of stag antler were also made by the neolithic and bronze age peasantries of some parts of Europe with little or nor change.[119] Rather less frequently the Maglemosians made axe- or adze-blades from antler[120] and delicate versions of the latter, almost as smooth and well-finished as blades of polished stone, are known from neolithic settlements in Switzerland.[121]

The continued use of antler axes, adzes and blades thereof, at a time when finely polished flint and stone blades were available, suggests that these possessed certain advantages or at least that they were sufficiently effective for certain purposes to withstand the competition of more expensive materials. In view of their physical character, it seems hardly reasonable to suppose that they were used for working wood. The suggestion is worth considering that one primary use was for chopping meat off carcases, as we can reasonably infer was the case with those found with the skeletons of whales stranded in the Firth of Forth during late mesolithic times.[122] If this is correct we need look no further for an explanation of the persistence of the type, since farmers, especially those of the Alpine area, continued to hunt,[123] quite apart from the need to deal with the meat of domestic livestock. Another suggestion would be that they served as the blades of mattocks for grubbing up roots or making holes in the ground for traps or other purposes, activities by no means restricted to whole-time hunter-fishers.

Another mesolithic antler form to persist was the holder or sleeve, which held the flint blade and itself received the wooden handle.[124] The natural resilience of the antler absorbed some of the shock and so lessened the strain on the wooden handle. The device was practical and efficient, but it is important to note that it did not, despite this, survive in its original homeland. Again, although some of the antler sleeves from the Swiss lakes resemble closely their mesolithic prototypes,[125] the majority were made on quite a different principle, the sleeve being inserted into, rather than being perforated by, the handle.

The Maglemosians made great use of bone, not merely for the barbed points which are so characteristic of their material equipment, but also among other things for axes, netting-needles, fish-hooks, bodkins and leather polishers. So far as fish-hooks and bodkins are concerned, bone was the normal material used in neolithic times over the whole of Europe.[126]

Although bone and antler were replaced for many purposes by metal in most parts of Europe, they were made to serve many new purposes as economic life developed. Their persistence is best brought out by considering the material equipment of a peasant community near the end of prehistoric times, for example the lake-villagers of Glastonbury.

---

[118] *ibid.*, 150 and Fig. 55, No. 1.

[119] e.g. the fine series from Egolzwil in Luzern Museum. Evidence for the persistence of the type into the Late Bronze Age may be cited from Zürich-Alpenquai, see D. Viollier *et al.*, 1924, Taf. IV, 18.

[120] J. G. D. Clark, 1936, 111.

[121] e.g. an example from Lüscherz, Erlach, Bern, mounted on a wooden handle. In private possession, but photographs in the Landesmuseum, Zürich (neg. nos. 9264–5). See Pl. IX, a.

[122] See p. 65.

[123] See p. 48.

[124] J. G. D. Clark, 1936, 112.

[125] e.g. Basle Museum, No. I.13955. From the western Swiss lakes, provenance unknown.

[126] For bone fish-hooks, see pp. 42, 56.

Apart from objects of display and adornment and things made from fired clay and wood, the finds included 201 objects of antler and 233 of bone against only 65 of flint (mostly scrapers), 12 of bronze (5 needles, 4 awls and punches and 3 terret-rings) and 81 of iron. If the uses to which antler and bone were put are analysed, the following result is obtained[127] :

	Antler	Bone
Leather-working	—	25 polishers
Weaving	81 combs	8 combs, 152 bobbins
Sewing	1 needle	40 needles, 5 awls
Potting	4	3
Hammers	14	—
Handles and ferrules	52	—
Horse-harness	45 cheek-pieces	—
Doubtful	4	—

Of these, the bone needles are ultimately of upper palæolithic ancestry and the leather polishers made from metapodial bones are of mesolithic origin,[128] but antler bridle cheek-pieces and handles for metal tools first became common in the Late Bronze Age, and weaving-combs and bobbins from sheep metapodials seem to have come into use late in the Early Iron Age. The use of antler or bone as a substitute for new metal forms, exemplified by the antler cheek-pieces, carries on a process which began in territories marginal to the first spread of bronze-working, as when the passage-grave and stone-cist people of Denmark copied Aunjetitz pins in bone,[129] and continued down to the end of the prehistoric period in peripheral regions, as evidenced by the whale-bone rendering of Celtic metal-work found in the Scottish brochs (Pl. III).[130] It may be noted that, although the use of metal tools must have eased the labour of shaping antler and bone, there is no sign that they sensibly enlarged the control over these already exerted in upper palæolithic and meso-lithic times by hunter-fishers equipped with tools of flint and stone.

Finally, the point is just worth making that the domestication of animals broadened the sources of material or at any rate compensated for the loss or diminution of supplies obtained by hunting. One might for example quote the sheep metapodials used for bobbins by the Glastonbury lake-villagers. The domestication of cattle, again, provided an easy and prolific source of horn, which was used during the Bronze Age among other purposes for dagger hilts,[131] combs,[132] ladles[133] drinking vessels,[134] and trumpets.[135] As we are reminded though, by the stone relief from Laussel in the Dordogne, showing a woman holding a bison horn

---

[127] Bulleid and Gray, 1911, *passim*. Waste and unidentifiable fragments have been excluded.

[128] G. F. L. Sarauw, 1903, 225; K. Friis Johansen, 1920, 338; H. C. Broholm, 1931, 65.

[129] C. A. Nordman, 1935, 117 ff., Figs. 52–4.

[130] J. G. D. Clark, 1947, 99 and Pl. 11.

[131] e.g. the solid ox-horn hilt of an early bronze age riveted dagger from a grave at Wester Mains of Auchterhouse, Angus, in the National Museum of Antiquities, Edinburgh (No. EQ. 255).

[132] e.g. the beautifully cut combs found attached to women's girdles in the Danish oak-coffin burials (Brøndsted, 1938, II, Fig. 51a).

[133] e.g. an ox-horn ladle found hanging over the rim of a beaker pot in a stone cist at Broomend, nr. Inverurie, Aberdeenshire (*P.S.A.S.* VIII, 116).

[134] e.g. cow-horns, evidently intended for drinking-horns, have been found in a number of the Danish oak-coffin burials. Brøndsted, 1938, II, 61.

[135] The bronze mountings from what has been conjectured to have been a horn trumpet were found in a bog at Wismar, Mecklenburg (Brøndsted, 1938, II, 61, Fig. 57).

in her right hand, this material had already been known at least from late Aurignacian times.[136]

PLAITING : NETS, BASKETS AND MATS

The materials used for plaiting are so perishable and the tools so simple that it is more than usually difficult to recover its history. The ultimate origin of both plaiting and weaving is probably, as van Reesema has argued,[137] to be found in the processes of binding and sewing, each of palæolithic origin. For example, in binding the heads of his arrows and spears to their shafts and so at once lengthening, strengthening and solidifying by a spiral motion, and in sewing skins by threads of gut, the upper palæolithic hunter and his wife were all unconsciously elaborating the two processes which went to the making of coiled basketry. It is highly unlikely that plaiting originated on the late glacial tundra in view of the character of the raw materials normally used. On the other hand it does not necessarily follow that the indications found in mesolithic contexts in the temperate zone are the earliest, since equally favourable ecological conditions prevailed at an earlier date in regions further south. A palæolithic origin for plaiting cannot therefore be excluded, and there are hints that netting at least dates from this period.

The harvesting and preparation of the necessary raw materials must always have been of more than usual importance in a craft like basket-making,[137a] and it can be assumed that the prehistoric Europeans, like modern primitive peoples, had a remarkably exact knowledge of the correct times and places for gathering the materials they needed. Although little evidence has survived from the Mediterranean zone, we know, from the great find in the burial cave of Murciélagos,[138] and from a number of traces at sites of the Argaric bronze age culture of Almeria,[139] that esparto grass was utilized for plaiting baskets, sandles and cords in prehistoric Spain. In the temperate zone marshes and forest provided reeds, osiers, bast and even bark. A material of more limited importance, but which must have become of special value in territories like north-western Britain during the sub-Atlantic phase of climate, was the cleaned core of the stem of hair-moss (*Polytrichum commune*), a member of the *Sphagnetum* community. This was used down to recent times in Britain for making baskets, brooms and hassocks. An unfinished basket (or hat?) of hair-moss was found at the bottom of the ditch of the early fort (*c*. 80 A.D.) at Newstead, near Melrose,[140] and a tapered plait of this material came from the Lochlee crannog. For certain purposes horsehair was used during the Bronze Age ; for instance the woman in the Skrydstrup burial wore a net of this material over her blonde hair and a kind of tasselled girdle, found in a bog in the parish of Armoy, County Antrim, and dating from the Late Bronze Age, was also made from horsehair.[140a]

Netting. Of the various forms of plaiting, netting, composed as it is of a single element plaited in an open mesh, has some *a priori* claims to be regarded as the most primitive.[141]

---

[136] H. Obermaier, 1925, Pl. IX.
[137] E. S. van Reesema, 1926, 57.
[137a] T. Okey, 1932, 16; O. T. Mason, 1904.
[138] M. de Góngora, 1868, 24 ff.
[139] e.g. Campos (Siret, 1887, 59 and Pl. 10, Nos. 66–7) ; Fuente Vermeja (*ibid*., Pl. 14a, 14d) ; Lugarico Viejo (*ibid*., Pl. 16, No. 70).
[140] J. Curle, 1911, 358 and Pl. XV.
[140a] G. Coffey, *P.R.I.A.* XXVI (1906–7) 119–124.
[141] E. S. van Reesema, 1926, 68; M. Hald, 1942, 39–40.

The oldest specimen to survive, that from Antrea in Finland, was part of a seine net used by Maglemosian fishermen in the waters of the Ancylus lake; it was made from a two-thread cord, almost certainly of willow bast,[142] and it was knotted. The rather younger, but still mesolithic net, of which traces were found at Siivertsi,[143] Esthonia, was made from similar cord, probably of lime bast. The caps or hair-nets mounted with shells worn by some of the burials in the Grottes de Grimaldi, allow one to assume with reasonable certainty, as Vogt was the first to point out, that knotted nets were already being made during upper palæolithic times on the Riviera.[144] Of the numerous finds of netting from neolithic deposits in the Alpine area all but one were knotted and always the knots have been made in the same simple fashion (Fig. 125A).[145] The only knotless net from neolithic Switzerland

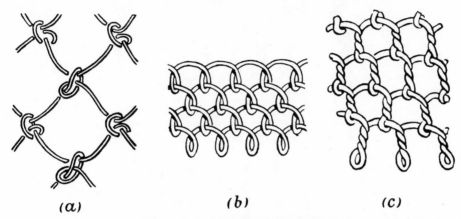

(a)   (b)   (c)

Fig. 125. Samples of neolithic knotted and knotless netting from Switzerland and Denmark. (*After Vogt*).

(a) Diagram of " lake-dwelling knot."

(b) Knotless net from Schötz, Luzern.

(c) Twisted knotless net of lime-bast thread, Ordrup Mose, Denmark.

cited by Vogt was of the simplest type (Fig. 125B). A more complicated form of bast, having three twists to each loop, comes from a neolithic level in the bog of Ordrup, near Copenhagen (Fig. 125C).[146] A special variety of net-like plait, known in Norwegian as *sprang* and which still survives in parts of Norway, Galicia and Croatia, was already practised during the Nordic Bronze Age (Fig. 126), notably for making woollen hair-nets.[147]

Coiled Work. Baskets and mats built from a continuous coil, arranged spiral-wise and sewn together in a variety of ways, are almost certainly, like nets, pre-neolithic in origin. Coiled basketry was extremely popular in early and pre-dynastic Egypt[148] and it was in this technique that the formally neolithic Fayumis wove their silos from reeds and

---

[142] V. Kujala, 1948.

[143] R. Indreko, 1948, 325.

[144] J. Déchelette, I (1924), 207; E. Vogt, 1937, 37.

[145] E. Vogt, 1937, 35.

[146] Broholm and Hald, 1939, 54 and Fig. 40.

[147] e.g. from Borum-Eshøj burial near Aarhus, Jutland. See Broholm and Hald, 1935, 276–8, figs. 61–2. E. Vogt, 1947, 1952–3.

[148] See Flinders Petrie, 1927, 48–9; M. Schmidle, 1928; G. Brunton, 1928, 63 and 67.

straw.[149] Little is known about early basketry in western Asia, apart from Palestine, where the impressions of coiled mats have been recognised on the bases of pots from chalco- lithic levels at Jericho and other sites,[150] but some of the earliest painted pottery from Sumer recalls in its decoration patterns which so easily arise when coloured strands are introduced during the plaiting of baskets.[151]

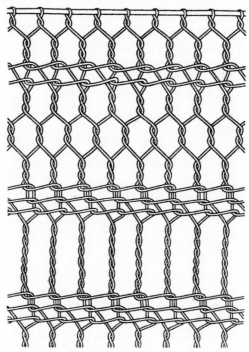

Fig. 126. *Sprang* plait from bronze age burial, Borum, Aeshog, Denmark. (*After Hald*).

It has already been pointed out that the earliest Ertebølle pottery of Denmark was built by the coil-process, as was that of many of the later hunter-fishers and farmers of Europe. The oldest actual traces of coiled basketry from this continent are those from neolithic lake-side settlements in Switzerland (Fig. 127A),[152] and south Germany,[153] and from the Murciélagos cave in south Spain (Pl. XIII, a-c).[154] In addition, impressions of coiled work appear on pot-bases from areas as widely separated as Orkney[155] and Greece.[156] The

[149] G. Caton-Thompson, 1935, 42 and 53.

[150] G. M. Crowfoot, 1938.

[151] Traces of patterns formed by the introduction of red and blue-green strands have been noted on early coiled basketry from Egypt, see Schmidle, 1928, 649, and G. Caton-Thompson, 1935, 44.

[152] e.g. St. Aubin, Neuchâtel; Schötz, Luzern; Murtensee, Freiburg. See E. Vogt, 1937, 9-11.

[153] e.g. Schussenried, Federsee, Württemberg. See *ibid.*, 12.

[154] M. de Góngora, 1868, 24 ff.; Ebert, II, 338, Taf. 169-70.

[155] Impression on a pot-base from Rinyo. Nat. Mus. Ant., Edin., No. HDA.198. I am grateful to the Director, Mr Robert Stevenson, for pointing this out to me.

[156] On Minyan (Middle Bronze Age) pottery from Llianokladhi III. See Wace and Thompson, 1912, 187-8 and Fig. 136.

antiquity of the process in Egypt, its use in the pre-neolithic pottery of Denmark, and its occurrence on the settlements of early farming communities at widely separated points over the whole extent of the Mediterranean and temperate zones suggest that in coiled plaiting we have yet another element in what, so far at least as Europe is concerned, was a pre-neolithic spread.

Twined Plaits. Twined plaiting, in which the parallel elements are joined by cross-elements twined in and out in a variety of ways, was used to make fish-traps at least as early as late mesolithic times in Denmark (see p. 44) and, like netting and coiled plaiting, ante-dates the introduction of farming into Europe. The earliest assemblage of twined basketry is that from early and middle neolithic levels in the lake-side settlements of Switzerland.[157] Much of this has U-shaped twists of unspun flax incorporated in the twine, giving a fleece-like texture to the finished product (Fig. 127C).[158] Much the most complete specimens of

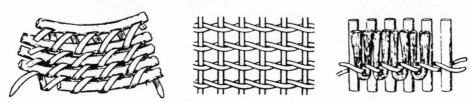

Fig. 127.   Examples of coiled, twined, and twined-fleecy plaitwork from neolithic Europe.

(*a*) Lake Morat, Switzerland.

(*b*) Tulstorp, Denmark.

(*c*) Murtensee, Switzerland.

(*After Vogt and Becker*).

twined baskets (Pl. XIII, d, e) from this early period are those associated with coiled baskets in the burial cave of Murciélagos in south Spain.[159] From Denmark may be cited a twined basket, which apparently contained an early neolithic pot (Fig. 127B); microscopic examination of the bast fibres, of which it had been made, showed that they had been used with little preparation.[160] The earliest finds from Britain are of bronze age date, including part of the rim of a container with the cremated remains of a child under an inverted cinerary urn of native type in a Dorset barrow,[161] and the remains of what is said to have been a covering over the contracted skeleton of a woman from an Orkney stone cist.[162] To these may now be added a particularly clear impression on the base of an urn recently excavated from a late chambered-tomb at Knockeboy, Scilly Isles.[162a]

Plaited Matting : Plain (chequered) and Twill. Plaiting, in which the main elements ran parallel to the margins of the finished article, was chiefly used for matting. How far back these methods go is uncertain, but, although apparently a late feature in Egypt,[163]

---

[157] e.g. Robenhausen, Niederwil and Weiher bei Thayngen. See E. Vogt, 1937, 12 f.

[158] e.g. Robenhausen, Murtensee, Auvernier, Port and Wangen. See E. Vogt, 1937, 20 ff.

[159] See n. 154.

[160] From Tulstorp bog, Graested sn., north Sjaelland. See C. J. Becker, 1947, 11–13.

[161] Barr. 3, Martinsdown. See *Proc. Dorset F.C.*, XXVI 28–30.

[162] Stone Cist opened on 6th May, 1911, at Stromness, Orkney. Information from the Director, Nat. Mus. of Ant., Edinburgh.

[162a] I have to thank Mrs B. H. O'Neil for allowing me to see an impression of this.

[163] The earliest examples given by Petrie (1917, 162–3, 168, and Pl. XLII) date from the Roman period.

impressions of plaited mats have recently been found on the floors of huts at Qalat Jarmo, in the Kurdish foot-hills of northern Mesopotamia[164] occupied by extremely primitive farmers to whom pottery was apparently unknown. Impression of twill-plaited mats, in which the weft is passed over and under two or more warp elements at a time, have been recognized

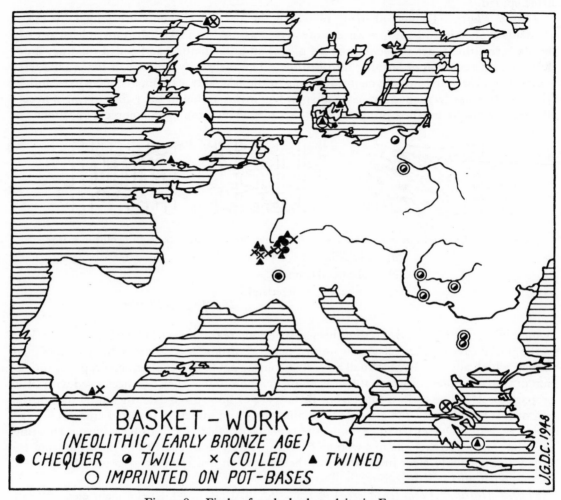

Fig. 128. Finds of early basket plaits in Europe.

on the bases of pots from chalcolithic levels at Jericho.[165] Twill-plaiting spread into Europe from the south-east during neolithic times (Fig. 128), traces having been found from Bulgaria,[166] through Rumania,[167] Yugo-Slavia,[168] Hungary[169] and northern Poland,[170]

[164] Information kindly supplied by Mr. Robert J. Braidwood of the Oriental Institute, Chicago.

[165] G. M. Crowfoot, 1938, Pl. 1, 5, 7 and Pl. IV, 3, 4.

[166] Gorni Bogorov and Čelopečne. See V. Mikov, 1933, Fig. 12 and J. H. Gaul, 1948, 57–8 and .Pl. XX.

[167] Tordos, Siebenbürgen. See E. Vogt, 1937, 8.

[168] Aradac, nr. Veliki Bečkerek. *ibid.*, abb. 2, 3.

[169] Kökénydomb. See J. Banner, 1930, Taf. VII, 9–12.

[170] Brześć Kujawski, kr. Włocławek. See K. Jaźdźewski, 1938, 80, 102 and Tab. XXXVII, 1, 2

but its absence from the Swiss lake sites emphasizes that this was essentially an east European trait. Most of the evidence consists of impressions on pot-bases, but the twill-plaited mats found in a bog at Łaczyńska Huta, kr. Kartuzy, west of Danzig, were made from strands of common reed and lime bast.[171]

By contrast, the only indications from neolithic Europe, of plain plaited matting, in which a chequer pattern was formed by strands crossing at right-angles and passing alternately over and under one another, come from the lake-side settlements in Switzerland[172] and north Italy.[173]

Various Rare Plaits. In addition to a wealth of coiled and twined plaits, the cave of Murciélagos yielded a specimen of pig-tail plaiting resembling that met with in west Africa, but otherwise unknown in early contexts in Europe.[174] Another type, a simple plait with oblique strands, is represented only by a single fragment from the neolithic site of Wangen on Lake Constance.[175] Such finds as these emphasize both the vigour of the craft of plaiting in neolithic Europe and the scanty basis of existing knowledge.

Wicker-Work. Wicker-work, in which the general form of the basket is determined by a warp composed of stiff rods, seems by comparison to have been a much later introduction at any rate to temperate Europe. It is particularly significant that wicker-work is quite absent from the neolithic levels of the Swiss lake-side sites, which have been so prolific in other kinds of plaited work, but yet appears in quantity in late bronze age sites in the same territory.[176] The earliest traces of wicker-work baskets in Britain seem to be those from the Glastonbury lake-village.[177]

TEXTILES

Whereas the fibres used for plaiting were derived mainly from wild plants, the most important of those employed in weaving textiles were obtained from plants cultivated for the purpose or from the wool of domesticated sheep.

Nettle Fibre. An exception was the fibre of the common nettle (*Urtica dioica*), which was doubtless used also for food and for medical purposes over the extensive territories of northern and central Europe, where damp woodlands afforded a congenial habitat. For the preparation and use of nettle fibre there is ample evidence from among the more primitive groups of northern Europe and Eurasia. Manninen gives a good idea of how the Ob-Ougrians gathered the crops of nettles, which throve during the summer months round about the winter houses, during the autumn, pulling them up by the roots and suspending them in bundles from the wall to dry.[178] The thread was obtained from the outer skin of the stalks, which after being moistened were peeled by means of bone or wooden chisels. The fibres were then broken down by beating or by pounding in a trough, and after being rubbed in the palms of the hands or swingled by a wooden knife were spun on a wooden

---

[171] Several mats were found by peat-diggers. Fossil pollen from one of them gave 49.5 per cent alder and mixed oak forest, including 17 per cent lime (*ibid*).

[172] e.g. Weiher bei Thayngen (E. Vogt, 1937, abb. 1).

[173] Isola Virginia, L. Varese (R. Munro, 1912, 352, Pl. XLII, 29).

[174] E. Vogt, 1937, 38–9, abb. 67.

[175] *ibid.*, 40–1, abb. 70–1.

[176] E. Vogt, 1947, 1952. It was common e.g. at Zürich-Alpenquai.

[177] Bulleid and Gray, 1911, I, 340 and Pl. LVII.

[178] I. Manninen, 1932, 185, and 352–3.

spinning-stick. An earlier observer[179] has told how the people of Kamtchatka, in preparing the fibre for the fishing-nets on which they largely depended, first split the stalks
of the nettles between their teeth, then peeled off the skins, beat them, combed them with
the wing-bones of cormorants, spun them between their hands and wound them onto
spindles. But, as M. Hald has shown,[180] nettle fibre was also capable of being spun and
woven into fabrics, which were famous in many parts of northern and central Europe towards
the end of the eighteenth century for their fine, gauze-like qualities and which in the middle
of the nineteenth century were still being recommended for sifting flour and filtering honey.
The use of nettle fibre in prehistoric times—the earliest historical reference dates from the
thirteenth century[181]—was first demonstrated as recently as 1941 by Mogens Køie, who
identified fragments of textile used to enclose cremated bones in a cinerary urn from
Voldtofte, Flemlose parish, Denmark, dating from the closing stage of the Bronze Age, as
" of pure nettle fibres."[182]

Flax. The only cultivated textile plant to play an important part in prehistoric Europe
was flax. Hemp was certainly known to the Romans,[183] but there is no evidence for its
cultivation in western Europe during prehistoric times.[184] Flax on the other hand was a
very important source of textile fibre during early times in the Near East[185] and it can be
accepted that its cultivation spread into temperate Europe from the Mediterranean zone.

The main stages in the harvesting and preparation of flax and the chief implements
employed have come down with very little change from the remotest times of which pictorial
records survive. The problem of extracting fibres from flax stalks and preparing threads
for spinning was and still is posed by the physical constitution of flax itself. It has always
been important to keep the stalks straight and even and from the earliest times it has therefore been customary to pull the flax by hand; even to-day much of the flax grown in northern
Ireland is hand-pulled and a good worker can harvest a quarter of an acre a day in this way.
As the flax is pulled, it is bound into beets and put up into stooks to dry. Next comes the
business of removing the bolls from the stalks by passing them through a big-toothed
comb, often fixed to a bench, a process known as rippling; seed for future use can then easily
be obtained by rolling the capsules. After rippling, the beets of flax are placed in water
and held down by stones for the vital process of retting, by which the fibres are detached
from the woody cores by bacteriological decomposition. In northern Ireland to-day the
retting may take anything from five to fifteen days according to the hardness of the water

---

[179] Krasheninnikov (J. Grieve's transl. 1774, 94 and 155).

[180] M. Hald, 1942, 28–49.

[181] Albertus Magnus (1193–1280) ascribed to nettle fabrics qualities distinct from those made
from hemp or flax. cf. K. Jessen in H. Shetelig and F. Johannessen, 1929, 25.

[182] M. Hald, 1942, 40; M. Køie, 1943.

[183] Several lengths of hemp rope were found at Bar Hill.

[184] According to Hoops, 1905, 472–3, the cultivation of hemp began in Asia or south Russia and
spread thence to eastern and central Europe.

[185] Most authorities agree that domesticated flax (*Linum usitatissimum L.*) was derived from a
wild form (*L. angustifolium*), which has a smaller seed and a more open capsule and grows over a wide
territory from the Canaries to the Black Sea and from the Caucasus to Palestine. Seeds of domesticated
flax and pieces of linen from the Fayum (G. Caton-Thompson, 1935, 49) show that flax was cultivated
at least by the earliest dynastic period in Egypt. Since the wild form is absent from Egypt, it can be
assumed that the cultivated variety was introduced from western Asia. Although evidence for the
early cultivation of flax in Asia is still slight, it may be recalled that de Morgan found impressions of
linen on copper axes from Susa (*Mém. de la délégation en Perse*, XIII (1912), 163 and Pl. XLIII.)

and the temperature, so the work is usually done in late August or early September while the water retains its summer warmth. After another drying, the flax is broken by being drawn over the edge of a stone or being beaten by a wooden mallet. Then follows the process of skutching, by which the woody parts of the stalks, already pulverized, are beaten out of the fibres against a wooden board, over which hunks of flax are held in position by one hand, leaving the other free to wield the wooden skutching-blade. Finally, the fibres are prepared for spinning by successive processes of roughing and hackling, by which they are progressively refined.

It is known from the tomb-paintings that the ancient Egyptians already went through a similar routine in preparing their fibres and Vogt's researches on the material from the Swiss Lakes show that the neolithic peasants of the Alpine region did much the same. Implements closely resembling those used down to our own day in several of the processes have come from neolithic deposits with balls of flax thread and pieces of linen textile. Particularly notable are a wooden skutching-blade,[186] roughing-combs made from bundles of pointed deer ribs bound together at one end,[187] or from forked bones,[188] and a broken hackling-board, shaped like a square-headed racket with some 270 thorns set into small holes and, on the same face, a raised beading at the square end to give clearance to the threads.[189]

Although the material evidence has not survived elsewhere, it may be assumed that a similar routine was practised wherever the craft of making linen spread in prehistoric Europe.

Comparatively little is known yet about the spread of flax-cultivation and linen-weaving into the parts of Europe nearest to the early centres, but it is significant that one of the burials in a stone slab grave under a kurgan in the Tsárskaya (now Svobodnaya) cemetery in the Kuban should have been wearing a linen garment under his furs.[190] When flax cultivation first reached Iberia, near the western end of the range of the wild plant, can hardly be determined, though it was certainly established in Almeria before the end of the Argaric Bronze Age.[191] The richest finds from prehistoric Europe have been made in and around the lakes of the Alpine area, where flax-cultivation and linen-weaving were certainly established among the early neolithic communities of the region.[192] North of the Alps the cultivation of flax spread among neolithic communities as far as the Halle region of central Germany[193] and by way of the Rhine—a lump of carbonized seeds was found at Köln-Lindenthal[194]—to the Dutch province of Drenthe.[195] The evidence from Britain is meagre enough, but though comprising no more than a few seed impressions on native

---

[186] From Robenhausen. Originally identified as a weaving sword, but correctly interpreted by Vogt (1937, 46).

[187] e.g. from Lüscherz, kt. Bern (*ibid.*, abb. 72, 4 and 5).

[188] e.g. from Weiher bei Thayngen (Schaffhausen Mus.).

[189] From Lattrigen (Vogt. 1937, 46 and abb. 72, 6 and 7).

[190] M. Rostovtzeff, 1922, 21–2.

[191] L. Siret, 1887, 103, 143, 154, 191, etc.

[192] E. Vogt, 1937. Linen was also used by the Lagozza people of north Italy.

[193] Flax seeds, found with traces of textile and typical Bernburg pottery from the Latdorf barrow, near Bernburg, were noted by Vogt (1937, 43) in the Univ. Museum at Jena.

[194] Buttler and Haberey, 1936, 149.

[195] On sherds of hun's bed pottery from Drouwen (Jessen and Helbaek, 1944, 57).

cinerary urns[196] and some dubious references to linen textiles,[197] it is enough to show that flax was cultivated in Britain before the end of the Bronze Age. Despite the fact that Danish prehistoric pottery has been intensively investigated for seed impressions, not a single trace of flax seed has been found on sherds earlier than the pre-Roman Iron Age and they first become common in the full Roman Iron Age.[198] It is true that some seeds from Trelleborg[199] have recently been assigned by Jessen to the end of the Sub-boreal period, but it would seem that before the Roman period flax can only have been cultivated on a very small scale. Again, it is by no means certain when it was first used for textiles. The oldest linen textile recovered from Denmark dates from the Migration Period and the single piece in question showed some admixture with wool fibres.[200] The circumstances under which flax seeds have been found mixed with barley and cameline seeds suggests that the crop may well have been raised primarily for food in prehistoric Denmark.[201]

Wool. In striking contrast with linen, no traces of wool have yet been found in neolithic contexts. The earliest finds seem to be those from northern and north-western Europe. Quantities of woollen textiles, constituting much the largest aggregation of fabrics from prehistoric Europe, have survived in the oak-coffin burials (Pl. XI, a), mainly dating from period II of the Nordic Bronze Age (*c.* 1300–1000 B.C.).[202] On the other hand, traces have been found on the copper oxide formed on a socketed spearhead from northern Jutland, which can be dated on typological grounds to period I[203] of the Nordic Bronze Age. A small quantity of woollen fabric was found in the sheath of the flint dagger from Wiepenkathen, Hanover, which dates from the time of overlap between stone and bronze in north Germany.[204] In Holland two finds have been made from period II, namely a fragment from a decayed oak-coffin burial near Groningen[205] and a hank of wool and pieces of textile found with a horn comb, an amber necklace and the top of a bronze palstave near Roswinkel, Drenthe.[206] Little can be said yet about the first appearance of wool in Britain, although two widths of plain woven woollen cloth, each about 18 inches wide and

---

[196] e.g. urns from Westwood, Fife (Nat. Mus. Ant. Edinb. E.A. 62) and Agfarell, Co. Dublin (Nat. Mus. Ant. Ireland).

[197] Of barrow No. 69 near Stonehenge, opened in 1803, Cunnington said, " We discovered a considerable quantity of decayed linen cloth (and some pieces which I conceived to be woollen), but although we could see enough to remark on the coarseness and thinness of the texture, it would not bear exposure to the rough wind we had that day " (*Wilts. Arch. Mag.*, XXI, 260–1). Again, in a barrow at Ringwold in Kent there were found " a few fragments of some burnt substance resembling linen," with cremated bones in a cinerary urn, *Arch. Cant.*, IX, 24. As well as digging away the structure of barrows without noticing its significance, the old barrow diggers destroyed much of the earliest history of textiles in Britain.

[198] G. Hatt, 1937, 33 ff.

[199] K. Jessen in P. Nørlund, 1948, 169.

[200] *Aarbøger*, 1900, 263 and 274.

[201] A mass of carbonised flax seed from a house at Œsterbølle in Himmerland, dating from the Roman Iron Age, contained not merely the seeds of weeds of cultivation and a few cereal grains, but such large quantities of cameline seed that this must have been cultivated side by side with the flax. Both flax and cameline seed yield oil. See G. Hatt, 1938, 221–4.

[202] e.g. Broholm and Hald, 1935 and 1939.

[203] Tumulus of Stubdrup, Øster Brønderslev, Vendsyssel (Broholm, 1938, 81).

[204] A. Cassau, 1935.

[205] F. C. Bursch, 1936, 55, afb. 38, 3.

[206] *van Giffen Festschrift*, 84, Pl. 76.

30 inches long with borders on the sides and at one end, were found with a late bronze age hoard in an Antrim bog[207] and it is on record that among the ashes from an urn excavated from a barrow on Banniside Moor, Coniston, was a charred piece of soft, fine, loosely woven, all-wool fabric.[208] In the Alpine area woollen fabrics do not make their appearance in the archæological record until near the end of the Bronze Age, from which time they have survived in the prehistoric mines of the Salzburg area.[209]

It might be argued in the case of the Alpine region that this state of affairs is really due to an accident of survival, that the alkaline lake-chalk (*seekreide*) which preserved linen was fatal to wool,[210] and that only when salt-mining began in the Late Bronze Age did conditions obtain in this area which made it possible for wool textiles to survive. The fact remains, though, that in the north, where acid ground-water provided almost ideal conditions for wool and where some remarkably complete wool textiles have survived from the Bronze Age, there are no signs that wool was used in neolithic times. It seems reasonable therefore to accept as a fact that woollen textiles were first made in temperate Europe at the close of neolithic times and during the course of the Bronze Age, a conclusion which fits very well with what we have learnt about the comparative unimportance of sheep in earlier times.

Close examination of the wool from the oak-coffin burials of Denmark has indeed shown that the breeding of sheep, at least as regards the fleece, was still at a very elementary stage. So poor were the samples of wool from this source that many authorities, from Gram in 1891 to Broholm and Hald[211] as late as 1935, believed that sheep wool must have been mixed with deer hair. More recently, though, microscopic examination of hairs from the bronze age textiles by Geijer and Ljungh,[212] and also by von Schlabow,[213] has shown that the hairs in question differed from those of red deer and compared with those of wild sheep. It is now generally agreed by the leading authorities[214] that the hairiness of the bronze age wool textiles was due to the character of the sheep of the time, which were evidently deer-like, resembling the now extinct Faerö sheep. By the Roman Iron Age a marked improvement must have taken place in respect of the fleece, since, whereas Gram found that 31 out of 37 samples of bronze age material contained " deer's hair,"[215] Thomsen was only able to detect this in two out of twelve samples from the later period and in neither case were more than a very few hairs involved.[216] Again, it is noteworthy that, whereas the bronze age wool was predominantly brown, a progressively larger proportion of white fleece is found from the Roman Iron Age and Viking periods.

Weaving. The linen textiles of stone age Switzerland and the woollen ones of bronze age Denmark have been particularly well studied by specialists and the reader is referred to the published works of Vogt and of Broholm and Hald for detailed information.[217]

---

[207] G. Coffey, 1907, Fig. 2.

[208] Although the piece of fabric measured only five-eighths by seven-sixteenths of an inch, the account is more circumstantial than most earlier ones from Britain. See *Cumb. and Westm. Arch. and Ant. Soc.*, *N.S.* X, 1910, 350.

[209] G. Kyrle (1916, 57) identified the materials as linen, but see O. Klose (1926).

[210] W. von Stockar, 1938, 100.

[211] Broholm and Hald, 1935, 338.

[212] Geijer and Ljungh, 1937.

[213] K. von Schlabow, 1939, 120–1.

[214] Including Broholm and Hald, 1939, 37–42.

[215] B. Gram, 1891, 119.

[216] T. Thomsen, 1900, 215.

[217] E. Vogt, 1937 and 1947; Broholm and Hald, 1935 and 1939.

No more will be aimed at here than to give some idea of the immense richness of the material as an expression of prehistoric culture and as a means of helping to enlarge our knowledge of prehistoric peoples. Textiles were used for decorative hangings as well as for clothing. A good idea of the appearance of the interior wall of a late neolithic house is given by an engraving on a megalithic slab of a gallery-grave at Göhlitzsch, Merseburg (Fig. 129): what appears to be patterned hangings are suspended on the walls and immediately above this and below the roof can be seen the bow with a quiver of arrows at one end.

Fig. 129. Engraving on slab of megalithic gallery-grave, Göhlitzsch, Merseburg, Germany, showing interior wall of house. (*After Ebert*).

The stone age fabrics were evidently woven in quite small pieces instead of being made in lengths to be cut up before use. It is possible to be sure of this because, despite the small size of the surviving fragments, so many of them display a portion of selvedge or border. Originally no doubt the main purpose of the initial selvedge was to arrange the warp threads of the fabric and that of the terminal one to dispose of their hanging ends, but the decorative possibilities of these borders, many of which were worked independently, were early appreciated. Their contrivance, particularly that of the stone age linens, was often of amazing intricacy and lent itself to variations immensely greater than those seen in the conventional materials of archæology, such as bronzes or ceramics.

Another feature of the textiles, most marked in those of the Stone Age, but also common on the late bronze age ones of the Salzburg salt-mines, is their decoration. The simplest way of making a patterned fabric was to introduce a number of coloured threads into the weave either as warp or weft. It is not possible to estimate how far coloured threads were used in the Stone Age, since all the surviving textiles are carbonized, but the plain-weave woollen cloths from the Dürrnberg mines[218] have broad and narrow stripes in blue and violet-brown colour. The more complicated technique of brocading, by interlacing threads into the warp of a plain woven fabric so as to produce a pattern standing out from the ground, was already highly developed during the Stone Age and, in fact, to judge from the surviving material, reached its peak in prehistoric Europe during this time. A reproduction of a restored version of a particularly fine example from Irgenhausen (Pl. XI, b) will give some idea of the effects obtained. The carbonization of this brocaded work is really tragic, because

[218] E. Vogt, 1947, 1964.

much of its virtue must have been in the colouring of the different threads. At least half a dozen stripe patterns, some with variants, were made in stone age Switzerland by lacing extra weft threads in by hand (Fig. 130); there can be no doubt that these also were coloured. Although unfortunately of a rather simple design, some brocading of late bronze age date survives from the Dürrnburg salt-mines with its colours intact, showing that dark brown and green threads were laced into the buff-coloured ground fabric.[219] Embroidery done by a needle and independent of the ground fabric seems to have been little used, though it has been argued that the decoration at the neck and sleeves of a tunic in the Skrydstrup oak coffin burial was made in this way.[220]

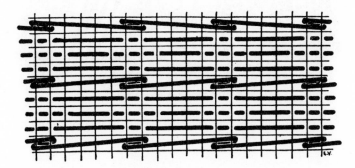

Fig. 130.   Stripe pattern laced into neolithic linen fabric by hand.
Irgenhausen, kt. Zürich.   (*After Vogt*).

Despite the detailed information available about textile fabrics, very little indeed is known about the character of the weaving apparatus used in neolithic or bronze age Europe. Although the use of an upright loom with weights has been inferred from a study of the Danish bronze age fabrics,[221] the first definitive evidence survives from Hallstatt times, when the looms in use resembled those depicted on Greek vases of the Classical period.[222] The representations on the well-known Hallstatt urns from Ödenburg, Hungary, are highly schematic (Fig. 131), but there is no doubt that on one of them there is depicted a scene of spinning and weaving, and that the loom in use is of the vertical type with warp threads hanging from a cross-bar and kept taut by weights at the bottom.[223]   Again, the plans of Hallstatt weaving-huts recovered by Bersu on the Goldberg, near Neresheim, Württemberg,

[219] O. Klose, 1926, abb. 1.
[220] Broholm and Hald, 1939, 52–4; but see E. Vogt, 1947, 1964.
[221] Broholm and Hald, 1935, 299–307.
[222] e.g. the well-known painting of Penelope's loom reproduced in von Stockar, 1939, abb. 105.
[223] See S. Gallus, 1934. Our reproduction is taken from M. Hoernes, 1898, Taf. XXIX.

were clearly designed for upright looms, broken or intact weights from which were found in each.[224]   The use of fired clay for loom-weights among the Celtic peoples is a useful pointer to the presence of the upright weighted loom, and variations in the form of weights may on occasion be of cultural significance.[225]   It should be remembered, though, that not all clay weights were used for looms—net and thatch-weights have to be taken into account—and that the absence of clay weights is no evidence of itself that the weighted

Fig. 131.   Women spinning and weaving depicted on Hallstatt urn from Ödenburg, Hungary.
(*After Hoernes*).

loom was not in use, since unworked stones, for example, have normally been used for this purpose in Scandinavia during modern times.[226]   Further, it should not be forgotten that by no means all upright looms were weighted: in many, like those of the Egyptian New Kingdom, the fabric was woven from the ground-level upwards, and wound onto a wooden roller at the bottom of the frame.[227]   It is logical to assume that the loom, like the cultivation and preparation of flax itself, was introduced into Europe from the centres of higher civilization.   As regards Egypt, it is generally accepted that the looms of the Old and Middle Kingdoms were all horizontal and that the new vertical loom with rollers first appeared during the New Kingdom.[228]   Unfortunately very little is known either about textiles or the instruments used in fabricating them during the earliest stages of settled life in western Asia.   Much the most promising sources of information about the weaving apparatus used in neolithic and bronze age Europe are the bogs and waterlogged sites of the temperate zone, from which one might reasonably hope to obtain parts of the looms

---

[224] E. Vogt, 1937, 112–13, abb. 152–4.
[225] e.g. V. G. Childe, *Communities*, 2nd edtn. (1947), 193 and 201.
[226] For illustration, see Shetelig and Falk, 1937, Pl. 55.
[227] e.g. Vogt, 1937, 102, abb. 151 (right).
[228] H. Ling Roth, 1918; Vogt, 1937, 98–9.

themselves.[229] An item of equipment connected with weaving peculiar to Britain is the long-handled comb, generally of deer-antler, but sometimes of bone, which appeared in the Early Iron Age and is thought to have been used for closing the weft threads on an upright loom.[230]

For making such things as selvedge borders or girdles, the technique of tablet-weaving[231] had come into use before the end of the prehistoric period at least in parts of the temperate zone of Europe, though precisely when is still an open question. It was certainly practised during the later Pre-Roman Iron Age in Denmark and southern England, as shown by the occurrence of a couple of wooden tablets, one broken, the other with four holed, in a pot forming part of the great bog-find of Dejbjerg[232] and of triangular three-holed ones of bone at Meare and Wookey Hole.[233] It has been argued by Broholm and Hald that tablets of a more primitive kind, having only two holes, were probably used to make some of the borders and girdles found in the bronze age burials of Denmark, though they admit that such could have been accomplished by a finger weave.[234]

COLOUR

The drabness of much of the material evidence in its existing state should not be allowed to obscure the role of colour in prehistoric society. Already in upper palæolithic times one is confronted with an aptitude and taste for colour which can hardly have been limited to the cave art. In later times mineral pigments were used to decorate pottery, particularly among communities under the influence of higher culture, such as the neolithic peoples of south-eastern Europe and the Celts of the early and middle La Tène period. For display or personal decoration colourful effects were also obtained by the use of materials such as amber, faience, coral or enamel, and by overlaying sheets of bright gold or bronze over baser and duller substances.

No doubt patterns were brought out in basketry and textiles by selecting materials of varying natural hues, but the comments of classical writers would alone be sufficient to indicate that the barbarian peoples also used artificial dyes, and Pliny's remark[235] that

---

[229] Parts of looms appear to be represented among the wooden objects from the Glastonbury lake-village (e.g. Bulleid and Gray, 1911, Pl. LII), even if it be allowed that some of the pieces belong to leather-working frames (Ling Roth, 1918, 140–1).

[230] Bulleid and Gray, 1911, 269. Ling Roth's objections (1918, 130 f.) lose much of their force when it is appreciated that many of these combs are more or less flat.

[231] M. Lehman-Filhés, 1901; M. Hald, 1932 and 1934; M. W. Peach, 1934; G. M. Crowfoot, 1939, 72–4; von Stockar, 1939, 75–8; M. Hald, 1950, 453 f.

[232] M. Hald, 1934, 391–3, Fig. 3.

[233] The author is indebted to Professor Stuart Piggott for these references. For the Wookey Hole specimen, see *Arch.* LXII, Pl. LXXVIII, 3. Triangular tablets are also known from modern Swedish folk culture and from Roman levels at Vienne.

[234] M. Hald, 1934, 396–408; Broholm and Hald, 1935, 318–20; Broholm, 1944, bd. 2, 288; cf. G. M. Crowfoot, 1939, 73, n. 1.

[235] *Hist. nat.* XX, 3. Tacitus (*Germania*, cap. 17) noted that German women often wore " trailing garments, striped with purple."

the Gauls "imitate with herbs all colours, including Tyrian purple "[236] indicates the main source. Knowledge of vegetable pigments must indeed have been acquired at an early stage of human experience through gathering plants for food. Although it is only under very special conditions, such as those which obtained at the Dürrnberg salt-mines, that the colouring of prehistoric fabrics remains evident to the naked eye, von Stockar claims to have made them visible in many cases by chemical treatment, and to have shown that blue was the colour most frequently used.[237] This could well have been obtained from the dwarf-elder (*Sambucus ebulus*), which is frequently represented in the plant remains from neolithic and later prehistoric settlements in Switzerland.[238] Woad (*Isatis tinctoria*) is conspicuously absent from the Swiss sites and, though it was certainly known to the iron age Britons of Caesar's day,[239] it is doubtful when dye from this substance was first used in temperate Europe.[240] It is worth remembering in this connection that dye was not obtained very simply from woad; not only did the leaves have to be fermented in water, but the blue colour only appeared through oxidization in the air after the dye had been exposed for some time. Lilac dye may have been got from bilberry or whortleberry (*Vaccinium Myrtilus*), though this was rare on the Swiss neolithic sites. Reds and golden-reds were probably obtained from *Chenopodium album* and *Galium palustre*, both very commonly represented. Weld (*Reseda luteola*), which used to be cultivated as a source of yellow dye, was gathered, presumably for the same purpose, by the stone age inhabitants of the Swiss lakes. No doubt the plants used to produce colours varied to some extent in different parts of the continent, but whatever the precise sources there can be no doubt that it was from the vegetation of his home area that prehistoric man obtained most of the colours which brightened his daily life.

---

[236] Tyre was a main centre for the extraction of purple dye from shell-fish (mostly *Murex* and *Purpura*). This source of dye was already known to the Middle Minoans of Crete and knowledge of it must have spread to the western Mediterranean at least by the time of Greek and Punic colonisation. To what extent the prehistoric peoples of temperate Europe obtained purple dye from shell-fish is not known, but dye was obtained from this source in Britain at the time of Bede. See J. W. Jackson 1917, Chap. I; Evans, *Palace*, IV, 111, n. 5; Bosanquet, *J.H.S.*, XXIV, 321; Bede, *Ecclesiastical History of the English Nation*, Bk. I, Chap. I.

[237] W. von Stockar, 1938, 59–62.

[238] E. Neuweiler, 1924, 117; cf. von Stockar, 1938, 36 and 61 and Vogt, 1947, 1967.

[239] See his well-known reference to the iron age Britons using woad as "war-paint." *De Bello Gallico*, V, 14.

[240] As J. Holmboe (1927, 35–44) has pointed out, although at present found in a wild state over a vast territory from Madeira, Portugal and Ireland to Russia, Persia and India, and from North Africa to Norway, Sweden and Finland, it is likely that in the more northerly parts it was introduced as a cultivated plant in antiquity. Philologically there is evidence (J. Hoops, 1905, 473–4) that woad was known earlier in southern than in northern Europe, and there are references to its use in classical literature. Several authors have referred to the reported occurrence of woad in a neolithic deposit in the cave of Adaouste in France, but this needs confirmation. The oldest actual trace from Britain is the imprint of a fruit on an Anglo-Saxon pot from Somersham (Jessen and Helbaek, 1944, 58). The oldest find from Denmark comes from the Roman iron age site of Ginderup (G. Hatt, 1937, 32).

CHAPTER IX

TRADE

THE ultimate origin of trade may well lie in the selection of localized raw materials during the seasonal movements of food-gatherers—and here one should recall that the detailed knowledge of their habitat and its resources so often remarked by anthropologists applies quite as much to the raw materials needed for ornaments and tools as to sources of food. When such peoples changed their hunting-grounds, owing to movements of game or to some other cause, they might be expected to maintain supplies of materials integral to their traditional way of life. This might be achieved up to a point by occasional journeys, but sooner or later it would be necessary to enter into trade relations with those who occupied their former habitat. For example, the Eskimos who migrated from the Hudson's Bay area to their present home in western Alaska continue to obtain the soapstone needed for their blubber lamps from quarries by the Tree River in Coronation Bay, now some 1,400 miles to the east.[1] The habit of using this particular kind of stone was acquired when this group occupied territories, which either included these quarries or at least were within easy reach of them.

The distribution of ornaments made from shells of *Spondylus Gaederopus* in south-eastern and middle Europe (Fig. 132) affords one of the clearest examples of such trade developing as a result of migration.[2] Since this mussel is native to the Black Sea, the Sea of Marmora and the Aegean, it can only have been through human agency that specimens were distributed from the extreme south-east as far north and west as Poland and the Rhineland over the whole territory occupied by the Danubian peasants. Up to a point the facts might be explained by supposing that the shells were carried by the neolithic colonists themselves, but the occurrences are so ubiquitous in the Danube Valley and over the loess of central Europe and the distances so great that trade alone meets the case. Although complete shells were sometimes worn perforated, the commonest ornaments made from this material were beads or pendants cut from the thick part of the shell or bracelets made from the rim (Fig. 133). A hoard of twenty such bracelets found at Kozludža in eastern Bulgaria[3] suggests that trade may sometimes have been carried on in the form of finished ornaments. There is no difficulty in accounting for the demand which drew *Spondylus* shells from the Aegean area to the lower Oder, the Rhineland or the Ligurian coast. The Danubians were merely satisfying a need which had become established in their traditional culture during an earlier stage of their history. As they moved away from their old homelands where the shells were close at hand, they were constrained to ensure a supply by means of trade.

---

[1] Chapple and Coon, 1947, 256 f.

[2] W. Buttler, 1938 A, 27 f., Taf. 12 ; J. F. Gellert and Fr. Garscha, 1930 ; J. H. Gaul, 1948, 95 ; K. Jaźdźewski, 1948, 95.

[3] Gellert and Garscha, 1930; M. Vassits, 1910, 34.

Shells and other objects of personal adornment are indeed among the earliest trade objects represented in the archæological record, but in interpreting such evidence it is important to remember the distances over which hunter-fisher groups were accustomed to move during the year. For instance the salmon vertebrae in the Dordogne caves beyond the annual run

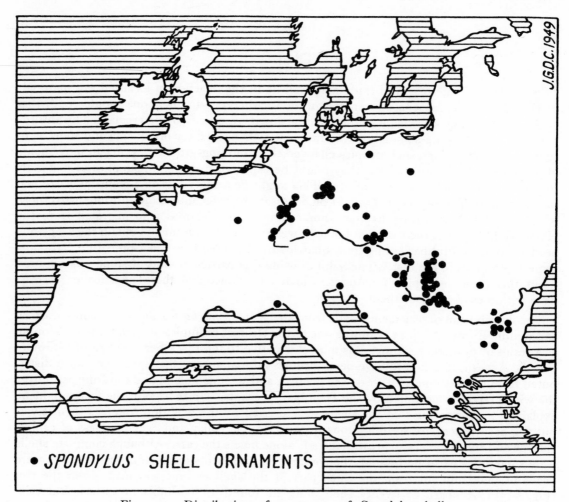

• *SPONDYLUS* SHELL ORNAMENTS

Fig. 132. Distribution of ornaments of *Spondylus* shell.

of these fish could be explained as having been brought back from seasonal fisheries lower downstream.[4] On the other hand, specimens worn as beads by an individual buried in the Barma Grande at Grimaldi, near Mentone,[5] can hardly be accounted for in any other terms than trade, since they must have come from the Atlantic watershed and so crossed from the territory of the Magdalenians to that of the Grimaldians.

Trade was also carried on from an early period in the materials needed for making implements and weapons. So far as food-gathering groups are concerned, evidence relating

[4] H. E. Sauvage in Lartet and Christy, 1865–75, 223.
[5] E. Rivière, 1886.

to the distribution of such materials is often ambiguous. For instance, although it is well-known that the Tardenoisians in parts of Belgium and Holland, used a pale chocolate-coloured-quartzite from a certain outcrop near the church of Wommersom, east of Tirlemont,[6] the possibility can hardly be excluded that the material was gathered during the seasonal wanderings of a single group or of two or more contiguous ones without the necessity of any exchange. Again, while it is certain that Antrim flint was brought by human agency across the water to Scotland, either in the form of blocks like those from Campbeltown, Kintyre[7] or as parcels of flakes, like the hoards of 77 and 156 found under peat near Portpatrick Luce Bay, Wigtownshire,[8] it is not proved that trade was involved. The blocks from Campbeltown were actually found with an industry of Early Larnian character and it is possible that the flint was brought over during a comparatively brief visit.

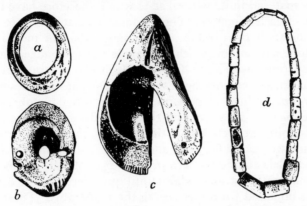

Fig. 133. Use of mussel *Spondylus Gaederopus* for ornaments ($\frac{2}{9}$)
(*After Buttler*).

There seems to be fairly definite evidence for a trade in obsidian in parts of central and south-eastern Europe. In central Europe some of the chief sources were found in the Hargita and Hegyala mountains and it has been suggested that the neolithic Bükk people of northern Hungary owed their prosperity to their control of obsidian from the latter.[9] It is interesting to note that the material was diffused among several different groups of neolithic peasants, including the painted and crusted pottery people of the Upper Maros and Alt valleys and the Danubian peasants of lower Austria and eastern Moravia. Blocks of obsidian weighing up to 36 kilograms from the Bükk site at Kenézlö show that in the homeland the material was sometimes distributed in untouched natural lumps.[10] On the other hand the Nyirlugos hoard[11] contained twelve nodules, from 11 to 19 cm. long and from 7.2 to 22 kilograms in weight, ready dressed for the removal of flakes, and it is interesting to note that Melian obsidian was traded in this form during the East Mediterranean Bronze Age.[12]

---

[6] L. Dursin, 1931, 391–2; J. G. D. Clark, 1936, 207.
[7] J. G. Callander, 1917, 120–1; H. J. Movius, 1942, 177.
[8] J. G. Callander, 1917, 121; *ibid.*
[9] F. von Tompa, 1937, 35–6.
[10] J. Hillebrand, 1928.
[11] *ibid.*
[12] A. C. Bosanquet, 1904.

By far the most important trading activity of the Stone Age in north-western Europe to leave traces in the archæological record was the commerce in finished or partly finished tools, most commonly axe and adze blades, made from raw materials of superior quality and limited distribution. Although based fundamentally on the virtues of certain materials, it should be stressed that this was nevertheless a trade in more or less completely manufactured objects. The precise stage to which the work was carried varied. Sometimes, as in Denmark, one finds hoards of bars of flint—for instance those from Alslev, near Logumkloster, and Purland, Vallo[13]—evidently roughed out at such surface spreads of flint as that in the Stevns district ; but more often the blades were finished up to the point at which they were ready for polishing. A moment's reflection will show why trade took this form. No one who has watched flint or stone being flaked need be reminded of the high proportion of waste. Transport of the raw material in its natural state would therefore have involved the carriage of a large proportion of useless matter. The obvious alternative was to remove the waste at the mine or quarry and trade the product. This implies that the most important single tool among most later stone age communities, the blade of axe or adze, was not produced on a domestic basis, unless from cheap and inferior kinds of flint or stone, but was manufactured in bulk by professional knappers working at the sources of the most desirable raw materials.[14] These knappers were maintained in part no doubt by other members of their immediate families, but in some measure they lived on the proceeds of exchange.

One of the most significant facts about this trade is that it was carried on by hunter-fishers in just the same way as by farmers, and indeed it sometimes passed from one to the other. The closest parallels among modern primitive peoples are to be sought among food-gathering groups in parts of Australia, where until quite recently the tougher stones needed for ground axes were obtained from quarries in the mountains. These would generally be owned and operated by the tribe in whose territories they were situated or by a family within the tribe. The quarry for axe-blades at Mt. William, near Lancefield, south-east Australia, was owned by one Billi-billeri, who lived with his family on the site and split the rock needed for the whole Wurunjeni community.[15] When a neighbouring tribe needed a fresh supply of stone, messages would be sent offering articles in exchange for a stipulated quantity of the material and later a party would be sent to camp near the quarry. Anyone caught stealing the stone was liable to get involved in a fight with Billi-billeri and his family, but as a rule a barter transaction would be arranged and so trade in this essential raw material would eventuate.

Some of the most interesting stone axe factories in prehistoric Europe, those on the island of Bømlo off the south-west coast of Norway, were certainly active in pre-neolithic times in that part of the world; indeed the indications are that, although the neolithic Vepestad people continued to make stone axes on the island, the main trade, which extended over much of Jaeren on the mainland, was conducted by the mesolithic Nøstvet people.[16] In this case quarry and factory were separated by the open sea, the raw material having to be quarried from the side of a small rocky islet called Hespriholmen (Pl. XV, a), and carried by

---

[13] See T. Mathiassen, 1934; J. Brøndsted, 1934, 6–8.

[14] From the point of view of interpreting the archæological evidence, this is very important since it allows one to discount the various natural agencies capable of scattering nodules over extensive areas. Large-scale manufacture could only be carried on in conjunction with mines, quarries or surface concentrations of material.

[15] A. W. Howitt, 1904, 311-312, 340-341.

[16] K. Faegri, 1943.

boat to the factories on Bømlo, which are situated at the head of a small fjord still used as a port for shipping from the mainland. The Bømlo industry illustrates in a very striking fashion that the sea, so far from being an obstacle to prehistoric trade, served to link quarry, factory and market.

Further evidence that trade in objects made from localized but keenly sought after stone was carried on among hunter-fishers is to be found in Finland and the East Baltic area. The material from which the traded adzes, gouges, chisels and ornaments were made, the so-called Olonetz green slate, was apparently roughed out close to the village of Suoju, near Petrosavodsk in Eastern Carelia, where great quantities of splinters and waste have been found.[17] As the map shows (Fig. 134), finished objects made from this material abound in contiguous parts of Carelia and of south-west Finland and isolated finds occur both in Esthonia and over the greater part of Finland up to beyond the Arctic Circle. It is particularly to be noted that no finds have been made in the region south-east of Lake Onega, over which erratics of the "green slate" were deposited by the Pleistocene ice-sheet. This only goes to confirm that one is here concerned with the export of finished objects from workshops in the Petrosavodsk area.

Over much of north-western Europe the trade in axe and adze blades of stone was carried on by neolithic farmers. Where flint of good quality was available in the chalk or in residual deposits, this might also be traded in the form of more or less completed tools. Although one can often recognize flint axes or adzes in lowland Britain as the products of mine-factories, it has not yet proved possible to verify this by objective means, still less to determine the actual mine involved. Style of workmanship, distinctiveness of raw material and absence of native sources of supply, though, are all clues, which in combination can give fairly sure results. Examples of such include thick-butted axes from south Germany and Switzerland[18] and gouges from northern Scandinavia, all of grey flint from the west Baltic area. The colour and texture of the flint of Grand Pressigny, combined with the technique by which blades were struck from long prepared cores, makes it comparatively easy to recognize products of the factories. Another easily recognizable material is the conspicuously banded flint from eastern Galicia[19] and southern Kielce in Poland.[20] As a rule it was traded in the form of thick-butted axes, but it was also used for sickle-blades, knives and scrapers. The flint was traded over the territories of the semi-nomadic herdsmen, whose culture is defined by their characteristic globular amphoræ, from the Carpathians to the Baltic and from the Niemen to the Elbe and the Saale (Fig. 135). Since Baltic amber is distributed fairly widely over the same territory and is commonly associated with the banded flint in graves, it may well be that the two commodities were exchanged.[21]

In the case of stone, petrological determinations have already yielded important results, even though the method is still only in process of being applied and in some countries has hardly been used. Mention has already been made of the trade between certain west Norwegian islands and the mainland of Jaeren, which flourished mainly in mesolithic times. In addition it has long been known that axes made from grorudite, a material from the immediate area of Oslo, were traded over much of the eastern part of the country,[22] and

---

[17] J. Ailio, 1920, 6; V. Luho, 1948, Kuva 114; and information from Professor C. A. Nordman.

[18] R. Ströbel, 1939, 36.

[19] G. Kossinna, 1917, 143–150; and 1918.

[20] J. Kostrzewski in *Ebert*, IV, 181–2.

[21] V. G. Childe, 1947, 188. W. Gaerte, in *Ebert*, IX, 254, argued that amber was exchanged for banded flint.   [22] Shetelig and Falk, 1937, 76.

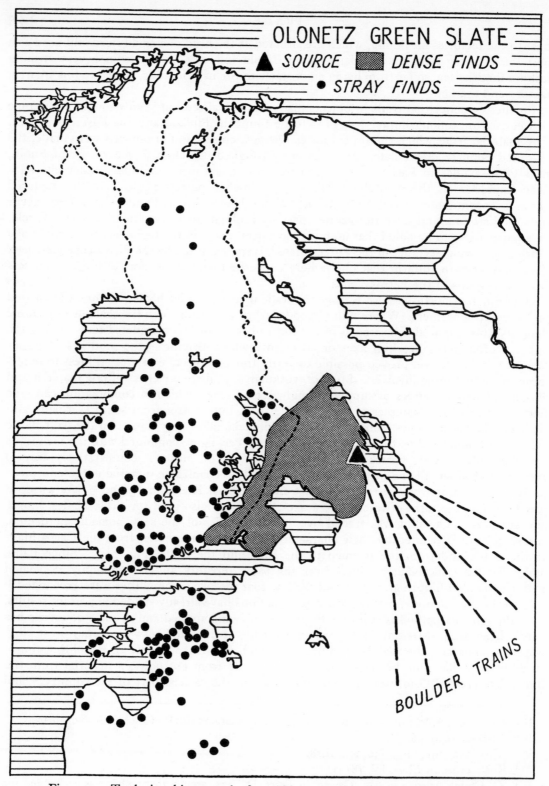

Fig. 134. Trade in objects made from Olonetz green slate. (*Based on Luho*).

246

quite recently it has been shown that axes of Vestland type made from west Norwegian schist were traded across the Skagerrak to Vendsyssel in northern Jutland.[23]   Evidence is cited in a later paragraph for the trading of stone axes from the Taunus to the Cologne area, and instances might be multiplied.

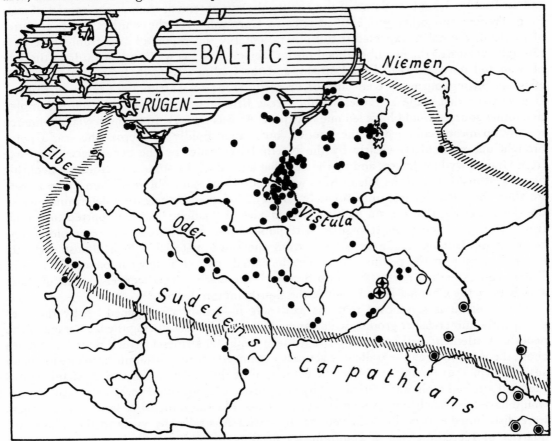

Fig. 135. · Trade in banded flint from eastern Galicia and southern Kielce.
(*Based on Kossinna and Krukowski*).

O Galician sources.   ⊕ Kielce sources.   ● Thick-butted axes of banded flint.

\\\\ Limits of globular amphora culture.

The most thorough investigations so far undertaken are those now in progress in Britain.[24] The first step was the identification at Windmill Hill, Avebury, and at other sites, mostly in Wessex, of axes made of augite granophyre from the workshops of Graig Lwyd in North Wales, a type of stone which can often be recognized at a glance, particularly when fractured.[25]   Systematic investigation by petrologists of slices cut from a large number

[23] P. V. Gløb, 1939.
[24] See especially the activities of the Sub-committee of the S.W. Group of Museums and Art Galleries on the Petrological Identification of Stone Axes reported in *Proc. Prehist. Soc.* 1941, 50–72 and 1947, 47–55.
[25] T. A. Glenn, 1935.

of prehistoric axes has not only extended the range of the Graig Lwyd trade to Cambridge-shire and northwards to East Lothian (Fig. 136), but has revealed the presence up and down the country of the products of a number of axe factories including the well-known ones at Stake Pass,[26] Langdale, Cumberland and at Tievebulliagh[27] near Cushendall, Antrim, and on Rathlin Island.[28] Some of the results already obtained, such as the spread of axes from Trenow and other unidentified sites in Cornwall over the south-western counties of England, are not unexpected,[29] but others, notably the export of axes from Stake Pass through Wessex to the neighbourhood of the Dorset coast, as well as westwards to the Isle of Man and northwards to East Lothian, and the trading of North Irish products as far afield as Sittingbourne in Kent and of Prescelly stone to Antrim[30] are more surprising. It is evident that trade activities within Great Britain were a good deal more complex than other sources would have led one to expect. As was the case in Scandinavia, commerce was by no means confined to the interior, but struck boldly out across the sea, a point brought out particularly clearly by the North Irish trade, by the occurrence of an axe from Graig Lwyd on Jersey, and by the fact that a third of the stone axes from the neolithic house at Ronaldsway in the Isle of Man were made from stone obtained from Stake Pass.[31] Further, there is evidence, unfortunately not yet confirmed by scientific determinations of the raw materials, that certain highly polished axes of " jadeite " were imported to Britain from Brittany. Their form, triangular, with pointed butt and thin section, resembles a type common in Brittany, made apparently from the same material, which almost certainly occurs naturally in the peninsula. It may be noted that, although comparatively rare in Britain and extending northwards into Scotland, there are marked concentrations of these axes both in the Channel Islands and in the Southampton district.[32]

Historically it is significant that the axe-trade in Britain was opened up by the pre-dominantly hunter-fisher groups, which spread in from the east during the later stage of the neolithic settlement, rather than by the western neolithic farmers. Much remains obscure about the way in which the trade was actually organized. Strong grounds have already been advanced (p. 179) for thinking that the extraction of the raw material and its shaping into axes and kindred tools was carried out by specialists, who for some part of the year at least would have been solely engaged on these activities. The question arises how their products were distributed. Was this achieved, as in central Australia, by visits to the mines and quarries of representatives of communities needing to replenish their stores ? To what extent was the trade carried on through a number of intermediaries, the axes passing from hand to hand through many different territories before being taken into use by some remote community ? And how far was the commerce in the hands of merchants, who, drawing their supplies from the workshops, travelled around and disposed of them direct to consumers ?

As will be shown later, there is little doubt that in so far as it extended into the coniferous zone, over territories occupied by hunter-fishers, the axe trade was organized by merchants

---

[26] B. Bunch and Clare I. Fell, 1949.

[27] W. J. Knowles, 1903.

[28] Professor Estyn Evans and Mr Frank Mitchell have each warned me that axes made from the rock on Rathlin Island and at Tievebulliagh are not yet to be distinguished.

[29] The appearance of the " trumpet-lug " of Hembury type at Maiden Castle, Dorset, suggested links in neolithic times between the south-west and Wessex.

[30] A. Keiller, 1936, 220. For the movement of Prescelly stone to Wessex, see H. M. Thomas, 1923.

[31] Information by letter from Mr. B. R. S. Megaw, Curator of the Manx Museum, Douglas.

[32] C. Fox, 1933, Fig. 6B.

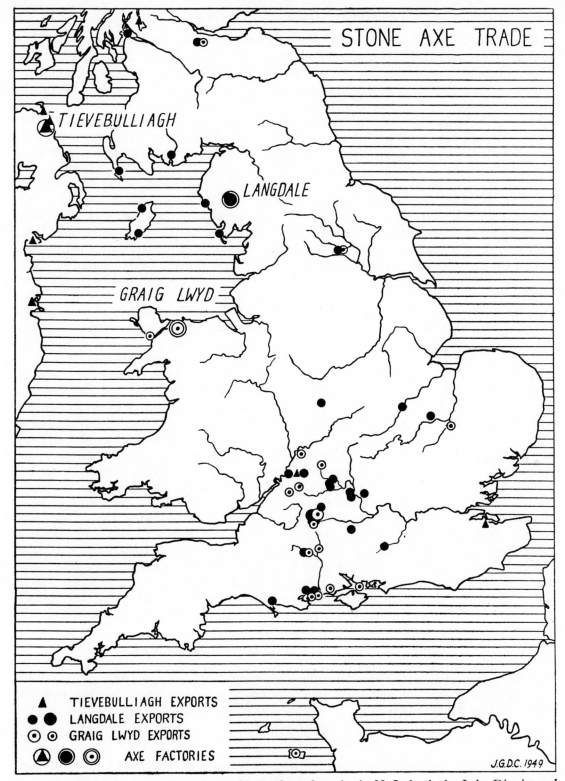

STONE AXE TRADE

TIEVEBULLIAGH

LANGDALE

GRAIG LWYD

▲ TIEVEBULLIAGH EXPORTS
● ● LANGDALE EXPORTS
⊙ ⊙ GRAIG LWYD EXPORTS
◬ ◉ ◉ AXE FACTORIES

J.G.D.C. 1949

Fig. 136. Trade in stone axe and adze blades from factories in N. Ireland, the Lake District and N. Wales.

249

who maintained trading posts well beyond their own homeland. On the other hand, it is difficult to believe that the circulation of axes among farming communities at a similar level of culture could have provided a sufficient livelihood to merchants and it is significant that, apart from Scandinavia, one does not find large concentrations of merchandise buried in the soil. Numerous small hoards of unused and often unpolished flint axes are of course common,[33] but these are rightly interpreted as personal possessions buried for safety, votive offerings, or in the case of those buried with the dead as provision for the next world. Such hoards do, on the other hand, show that unused axes were regarded as a form of wealth and it is conceivable that among peoples to whom they were almost a technological necessity they would have formed a convenient medium of exchange. It may well be, therefore, that axes were distributed over extensive areas in the ordinary course of barter. The great distances over which the axes travelled, particularly in the case of those from Langdale and Tievebulliagh or Rathlin Island, show that the distribution can hardly be explained alone in terms of visits to the workshops by representatives of the consumers, though such visits must have occurred and may help to explain the rather flimsy traces of settlement on the part of several different groups at such a site as Easton Down in Wiltshire.[34]

Trade in the well-known yellow wax-coloured flint from Grand-Pressigny in southern Touraine falls into the same category as the axe-trade in the sense that it comprised artefacts rather than unworked blocks of raw material.[35] This is shown by the absence in the export areas of cores and by the presence over the whole area of distribution of traits, such as shallow, oblique, parallel flake-scars, characteristic of the Grand-Pressigny workshops. The most specialized type, and one that was also widely diffused, is a blade having one face pressure-flaked and subsequently polished over part of its surface. A great part in the diffusion of the flint was evidently played by rivers : from Touraine the trade spread downstream to Morbihan and upstream, across to the Paris basin and so by way of the Aisne and the Oise, into Belgium and Holland,[36] and further, round the bend of the river into the Bourbonnais, eastwards to the Saône and on through the Belfort gap into Switzerland[37] as far as Lake Constance. The sea played a much less important role than in the axe trade, and though Grand-Pressigny flint reached Jersey and even Guernsey, it is doubtful whether it crossed the English Channel.[38] As might be expected of trade objects, blades and other forms of Grand-Pressigny flint penetrated the territories of several distinct cultures. It is found on the settlements of the people who made decorated Chassey pottery and it was also current among the Seine-Oise-Marne neolithic people, who buried it with their dead in the characteristic gallery graves and chalk-cut grottoes. The trade reached its greatest extent at the end of neolithic times and during an early stage of the Bronze Age : Grand -Pressigny flint seems first to have entered Switzerland in any quantity, with corded ware[39] ; in Jersey

---

[33] e.g. England: Kendrick and Hawkes, 1932, 72; Belgium: M. de Puydt *et al.*, 25–6.

[34] J. F. S. Stone, 1931–5.

[35] There is no modern study of the French material available and I have relied on V. de St.-Venant, 1911. Mr Gale Sieveking of King's College, Cambridge, is at present engaged on research on this problem and his results are awaited.

[36] F. C. Bursch, 1928; M. E. Marien, 1948, 41–4.

[37] R. Ströbel, 1939, 36–7, Map 4. A middle Rhenish find has recently been published by R. Giessler, 1948.

[38] The status of the honey-coloured flint from West Grimstead in the Blackmoor Coll. at Salisbury (Clark and Piggott, 1933, 166, n.i.) is now under investigation.

[39] P. Vouga, 1929, 24.

it was common at the Pinnacle site, which also yielded bell beaker pottery and a flat copper axe[40]; and a typical blade, with one face flaked and polished, from a secondary burial in barrow III at Emmen in Gelderland, dates from the Early Bronze Age.[41]

There is some evidence in south-eastern Europe of trade in small well-polished bowls, sometimes provided with feet, made of alabaster or white or golden coloured marble. Stone vessels of this kind from Parţa in the Banat, from Vinča near Belgrade and from Larissa in Thessaly were probably of Mediterranean origin and seem to have been traded among different cultural groups.[42] On the other hand, claims for a trade in pottery in these regions and as far west as the middle Rhineland are less plausible. It is true that among large assemblages of pottery from neolithic settlements exotic sherds can often be recognized and that petrographic analysis of samples from such will sometimes show that they were made from clay foreign to the neighbourhood in which they were found. Buttler,[43] for instance, has cited sherds from a binocular vase of Tripolje type from level IIA of the mound of Vidra near Bucharest, some 500 kilometres from its probable source of origin, as well as Theiss sherds from Vinča, the clay of which has been shown to be foreign to the neighbourhood of that site. Again, Bersu[44] found Aichbühl sherds in Rössen levels at the settlement on the Goldberg, near Nordlingen, and Schussenried ones in Michelsberg levels. Even more striking results were obtained by Buttler and Haberey[45] at Köln-Lindenthal, where foreign sherds from at least five different sources were revealed by analysis of the clays used, one group being identified on stylistic grounds with Plaidt ware from the neighbourhood of Coblentz, another with Hinkelstein ware from near Worms and a third with a ware known in Belgium. Discoveries like these are certainly consistent with the view that the foreign wares were traded, but there is no evidence for the manufacture of pottery for export in neolithic Europe and the facts could be explained more economically by supposing that the exotic sherds represent the domestic waste of visitors, possibly traders in some other commodity. It is significant that it was only in the fourth phase at Köln-Lindenthal that exotic sherds occurred and that at the same time there should have appeared the first evidence of trade in stone axes.[46]

Something has been said of trade within the territories of hunter-fishers and of farmers respectively. Attention may now be turned to the evidence for trade between the stone age farmers of the northern deciduous forest and the Arctic hunter-fishers of the circumpolar zone.[47]

The main difficulty in any attempt at reconstructing this trade is the complete disappearance of all tangible traces of some of the most significant articles of merchandise. From this point of view it is fortunate that some of the chief exports from the south were objects fabricated from a material so imperishable as flint. Sources of this were not entirely lacking in the north—nodules are occasionally found in Norwegian beaches and the dolomitic flint of Finnmark was certainly used by early man—but there were sparse and the material

---

[40] J. Hawkes, 1937, 62–3.
[41] F. C. Bursch, 1936, 57 and aft. 43, 1.
[42] W. Buttler, 1938A, 29.
[43] op. cit., 30–33.
[44] G. Bersu, 1936, 229 f.
[45] Buttler and Haberey, 1936, 106–9.
[46] ibid., 142.
[47] J. G. D. Clark, 1948A.

deficient in size and quality.[48]   On the other hand the supplies of high-grade material found in its parent chalk in the district east of Malmö in Scania[49] and much more abundantly in surface spreads along the west coast of Sweden and in parts of Denmark,[50] supported the most splendid flint industry in Europe, and it was the surplus of this manufacture that found a ready market in the far north.

The objects of south Scandinavian flint found in the territories of the Arctic hunter-fishers comprise first and foremost gouges with hollow working-edges, axes and narrow chisels.   In other words they represent a further ramification of the " axe-trade," which as already stated had its roots away back in mesolithic times in Scandinavia.   This northern extension of trade was evidently carried on by the Swedish boat-axe people who controlled the source of flint in Scania, where their graves are liberally supplied with gouges, axes and chisels made from this material, and who, to judge from the distribution of boat-axes, actually traversed the main routes to the far north (Fig. 137).[51]   It is understandable that the southerners should have sought to obtain what they wanted of the Arctic hunter-fishers by developing a line of trade already established in the north, and it is most interesting to observe that nine-tenths of the flint celts are gouges resembling the stone ones which form an integral element in the circumpolar cultural zone.[52]   Evidently the boat-axe people found it easier to create a market in flint artifacts by reproducing forms already familiar to the natives of the northern territories.   Indeed, there is little doubt that the flint gouge was manufactured originally for the Arctic market and was taken into use in southern Sweden, Denmark and contiguous areas as a result of acculturation—a reminder that cultural borrowing no more flows in one direction than does trade itself.

The great majority of the flint gouges and axes are found in hoards, unused and even unpolished.   Nearly all the hoards are concentrated on or close to the old Litorina shore between Umeå and Piteå in Västerbotten, and more than half the single finds from northern Sweden come from the same area.   The chief locality, Bjurselet in the parish of Byske, has yielded in the course of the last hundred years or so a series of caches of unpolished flint gouges (Pl. XV, b), the largest comprising seventy specimens, and no less than four other localities in the same parish have produced single finds.[53]   Further south, a substantial collection of flints, including axes, chisels, scrapers, flakes and seventeen gouges, mostly

---

[48] e.g. the nodules of flint found in gravel of restricted occurrence in Norway are scarce and of poor quality (B. Hougen, 1934, 27) and the dolomitic flint of Finnmark, though used by early men rarely occurs in flawless lumps of substantial size and can readily be distinguished from the cretaceous variety by its coarser grain (J. Bøe, 1936, 134–5).

[49] This is illustrated, both by the presence of flint mines at Kvarnby and Tullstorp (N. O. Holst, 1906 ; B. Schnittger, 1911 ; Grimes Graves Rep., 1914, 237–53) and by the great wealth of flint implements in the area.   It is significant for example, that three-fifths of the flint " celts " associated with burials of the boat-axe culture occur in Scania, even though this province has yielded only one-fifth of the total number of boat-axes from Sweden.   See J. G. D. Clark, 1948A, 223–5.

[50] Clark, 1948A, 219.

[51] ibid., 227.

[52] ibid., 221 ; G. Gjessing (1944) has recently emphasized the importance of the stone gouge in the circumpolar zone.

[53] The finds include approximately 170 gouges, 2 thick-butted axes, 2 narrow chisels, 1 scraper and several flakes and nodules.   Stockholm (State Historical), Skelleftea and Uppsala Museums ; also see G. Hallström, 1925, 92 ff., 106 and J. G. D. Clark, 1948A, 229.

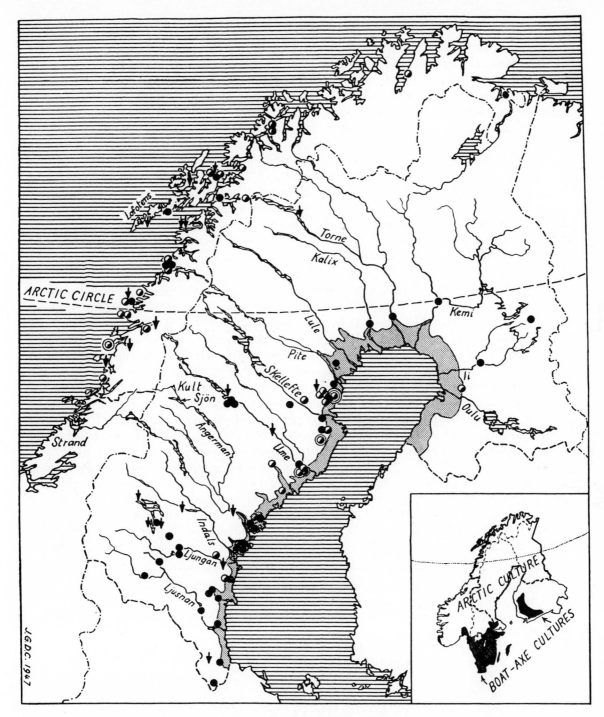

Fig. 137. Map showing distribution of objects of southern flint and of stone " boat-axes " in the northern provinces of Scandinavia.

◗ Flint gouge, chisel or axe.   ◉ Hoard of flint gouges, chisels or axes.

↓ Flint dagger.   ● Stone " boat-axe."

Note.—Areas covered by the Litorina Sea at its maximum extent are stippled.

unpolished, has been gathered from the shore of Kallbäcken in the parish of Burträsk,[54] and two hoards of gouges, one comprising five unpolished ones, have been found in the neighbourhood of Umeå.[55]   No counterpart to the Västerbotten finds exists in Norway, each of the two hoards known—three axes and a gouge found under a flat boulder at Alteren[56] and a gouge and a chisel from Skeid[57]—representing in all probability the kit of single individuals. Most of the Norwegian finds, and the one from northern Finland are single pieces and in at least two instances from Nordland there is evidence that these had not only been used, but worn out—viz. a portion of a polished flint axe reduced to a core by the removal of flakes from Bø, Rødøy,[58] and a stump of a thick-butted form found at Myrvold, Konsvik, Lurøy, together with three small flint scrapers and a slate arrowhead and knives of Arctic type.[59]   Further evidence that the flints were used by bearers of the Arctic culture is given by the finds at Erikstad, Trondenes, on Hinnøy, largest of the Vesterålen, where a partly polished flint axe of pointed-butt form occurred with a stone axe and slate knife of Arctic type,[60] and by the association at Fällfors, Byske, in Västerbotten of a thick-butted flint axe with a small slate chisel.[61]

It is evident from the distribution both of boat-axes and of the principal hoards of flint gouges that the chief bases were concentrated on the western shore of the gulf of Bothnia and that the trade passed northwards by the Torne and Ounas or Kemi rivers to Ofot and Varanger fjords, and north-westwards by the Pite and Skellefte rivers and their associated lakes to Salten fjord and by the Ljusnan, Ljungan and Indals rivers to the great fjord of Trondheim. The discovery of boat-axes and objects of south Scandinavian flint on the Lofotens and on Rødøy and Hinnøy shows that commerce flowed from the mouths of the Norwegian fjords up and down the coast and across to the islands. There is plenty of evidence from the Iron Age[62] and from the historical period that the mountains formed no barrier between the Bothnian and Arctic-Atlantic coasts of Scandinavia and that the Swedish rivers and the Norwegian fjords between them made the traffic comparatively easy. The prehistoric traders may well have used light boats like those favoured by the Finns when they crossed the mountains to raid the Northmen in the days of Ohthere,[63] but the hunter-fishers probably assembled their produce during the season of winter snows. Graphic evidence for traffic between the two coasts during the Stone Age is afforded by the stone plaque recently found mid-way between them on the shores of the Kultsjön in Jämtland, bearing on one face an engraving of a pilot-whale (Fig. 138), which recalls a rock-engraving at Strand on

---

[54] Stockholm (State Historical) and Umeå Museums. Also G. Hallström, 1925, 100–6 and 1929, 15 ; Clark, 1948A, 229.

[55] At Dalsjö (Umeå Mus. 1010 and 17013) and Overboda (Stockholm, State Hist. Mus., 20493, 1–5) ; Hallström, 1925, 102–3 ; Clark, 1948A, 229.

[56] Alteren, Alstahang, Nordland. Univ. Oldsaksamling, Oslo (Nos. 20562 and 20565). O. Nicolaissen, 1912–13, 46–50 and Clark, 1948A, 229.

[57] Skeid, Bodin, Nordland. Univ. Oldsaksamling, Oslo (Nos. 7502–3). G. Gjessing, 1942, Fig. 38A. Clark, 1948A, 228.

[58] Tromsø Mus. No. 2227. G. Gjessing, 1942, 79 ; Clark, 1948A, 229.

[59] Tromsø Mus. No. 4204. G. Gjessing, 1942, 79 and 283–4; Clark, 1948A, 222 and 229.

[60] Univ. Oldsaksamling, Oslo, N. C20005. G. Gjessing, 1942, 78, 324 ; Clark, 1948A, 222 and 228.

[61] Stockholm, State Hist. Mus. 17594. Clark, 1948A, 222 and 229.

[62] Slomann, 1950.

[63] . . . " the Cwenas (Finns) carry their boats over land into the meers, and thence make war on the Northmen. They have very little boats, and very light." A. S. C. Ross (edt.), 1940.

the coast of north-western Norway.[64] The hoards of east Baltic amber from Herø near Stadland and from Linnesə, an island some fifty miles north north-east of Trondheim, only serve to emphasize the same point.[65]

As already hinted, archæology has little to tell of the nature of the products obtained by the boat-axe traders, nor for that matter is there any reason to think that flint was the only material traded north—farming products may well have accompanied it to diversify the diet of the hunter-fishers. As regards southern exports, it is true that red Angerman slate was traded as far south as Östergötland, Blekinge and Västergötland,[66] but this was too insignificant to account for the facts. Evidently the principal exports from the north must have been primary products of hunter-fisher economy of a kind unlikely to leave many

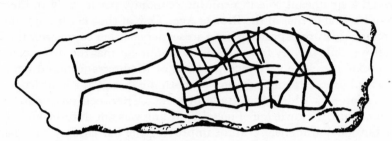

Fig. 138.   Engraving of a pilot-whale on a stone plaque (107 cm. l.) from the shore of the Kultsjön, Jämtland, in the heart of the Scandinavian Peninsula. (*After Bägge*).

traces. The most obvious materials, and the ones most often invoked, were furs, for which the northern parts of Scandinavia were famous when the region first came within the orbit of recorded history.[67] In parenthesis, it is worth noting that we need not despair of finding direct evidence of fur clothing from prehistoric times : for instance, the man buried in the second " dolmen " at Svobodnaya (Tsarskaya) in the north-western Caucasus, referred by Tallgren to the first half of the second millennium B.C., wore a black fur over two garments of vegetable fibre (the outer one downy, of camel colour and having a black criss-cross pattern, the nner one dyed purple and covered with red tassel-like threads).[68] It need not be assumed, though, that furs were the only northern products coveted by the farmers of the south. A vivid indication of the most desirable products of northern Norway may be found in Ohthere's account of the tribute paid to the Northmen by the Finns in the ninth century A.D., tribute which included, besides the skins of martens, bears, otters and reindeer, birds' feathers, whale-bone and ship-ropes made from the hides of whales and seals.[69] The importance of sea mammals as a source of wealth during the Stone Age needs no further emphasis, but it is worth noting that the Gulf of Bothnia, which since the time of Olaus Magnus (mid-sixteenth century) has been noted as a main centre of seal-hunting, was the focus of the old flint routes to the far north and that the coast of north-western Norway, where rock-engravings bear witness to the hunting of seals and small

[64] A. Bägge, 1943, 82–6 and Clark, 1948A, 228 and Fig. 3.

[65] A. W. Brøgger, 1909, 204–8 and 260; 1911.

[66] S. Lindqvist, 1934, 54. Clark, 1948A, 226.

[67] J. Ailio, 1920, 7 ; G. Hallström, 1925 and 1941, 190 ; S. Lindqvist, 1934, 54 ; G. Gjessing, 1942, 508.

[68] A. M. Tallgren, 1934, 24–9; Clark, 1948A, 226–7.

[69] J. Bosworth (edtn.), 1855, 44–5.

whales by men of the Arctic Stone Age, was a main terminus of the trade. Again, the number of finds on the Lofotens and the Vesterålen suggests the possibility that the trade in dried fish so characteristic of the area in later times may already have begun.

There is evidence that trade between the Arctic hunter-fishers and the southern farmers received a fresh impetus during the period of the Stone Cists, when flint daggers found their way as far north as the Vesterålen and far away to the south-east crossed the North Sea to lowland England.[70] Again, the spread of " Nordic " bronzes into the coastal strip of Nordland as far as Skellefte may well be interpreted as outposts of farming communities designed for trade with the aborigines.

If trade played a significant role in neolithic economy, particularly in the supply of axe blades, it was quite vital to that of the Bronze Age. One of the very finest schools of bronze-smithing in prehistoric Europe grew up in an area where neither copper nor tin were naturally available, and it was only in very few parts of the continent that the two metals were present in reasonable proximity. The very incorporation of Mediterranean and temperate Europe within the sphere of bronze technology implies both the spread of a knowledge of metallurgy and the organization of a widespread trade in metals. Between these two there is indeed an evident relationship. Knowledge of metal-smithing was not diffused among the neolithic peasantries of Europe out of sheer zeal for improving the barbarians, but as an out-growth from trade in such commodities as copper, tin and amber. It was through satisfying the needs of the more highly developed economies of the east Mediterranean that the European farmers worked their passage from the Stone Age to that of Bronze.

To attempt to justify this proposition for each part of Europe in the existing state of research in many of the most vital areas would be tedious. That the earliest metallurgical industries of central and south-western Europe arose in centres of mineral wealth and that the forms assumed by their products—and most significantly in some cases by their ingots—were inspired more or less directly by west Asiatic models is familiar doctrine,[71] when set out in sufficiently vague terms. To come to closer grips with the subject it would be better to consider an area, marginal to the ancient centres of metallurgy and which has been well studied from an archæological point of view, such as Denmark and contiguous zones of south Sweden and north Germany. Here at the core of the northern province of bronze metallurgy, one is confronted with an area into which, as Montelius long ago emphasized,[72] every scrap of copper and tin utilized in antiquity had to be imported. The problem is thus well defined. There can be no question of the Danes learning metallurgy for themselves because they had no metals to work upon. Beyond any doubt also the practice of metallurgy in this land was contingent on trade. The question is precisely how trade operated to draw the inhabitants of this territory within the range of bronze technology.

As de Navarro has recently stressed,[73] the mere importation of metal objects could never of itself have accomplished this. For instance, as stated in the last chapter, it is known that early in the middle neolithic stage of Denmark flat copper axes were imported in some numbers together with spiral arm-bands and at least one dagger, and that embossed plaques of copper were reaching the country even in the closing phase of the early neolithic; but there is no suggestion that this of itself brought the Danes any nearer towards the practice of metallurgy. During the period of the stone cists exotic bronzes were imported in much

[70] Clark, 1948A, 222 and 225–6.

[71] e.g. V. G. Childe, 1929, 221, 239 f.; and 1947, 115, 272 f., etc.

[72] O. Montelius, 1910, 272.

[73] J. M. de Navarro, 1949.

larger numbers and from at least two different provinces.[74] From the Aunjetitz province of central Germany came bulb-headed, loop-eyed and ring-headed pins, gold wire lock-rings, metal-hilted daggers and flanged axes, in return for amber; and from the Hiberno-British province came flat-flanged axes, sometimes with characteristic decoration, halberd blades and possibly some gold lunulæ or moon-shaped neck-ornaments of sheet gold with flattened terminals. Now, as de Navarro has pointed out,[75] there was a marked difference between the way in which the trade from the south and west was organized, a difference which affected profoundly the contributions each was destined to make to the genesis of the Northern Bronze Age. The presence of numerous hoards of finished and unused objects, some of them of great size—like that from Bennewitz, near Halle on the Saale, which alone contained more early flanged axes than the whole of Sweden[76]—shows that the central German trade was more highly organized than that of Britain, where the hoards of this period were comparatively few in number and small in size. Whereas the continental trade, which extended ultimately from the Baltic to the east Mediterranean, was carried on by middlemen, it may be supposed as a working hypothesis that the British trade was in the hands rather of merchant smiths, who brought their wares with them across the seas, but who were capable of making them on Danish soil from German metal if need be. This would help to explain among other things why, despite the weight of Aunjetitz material traded north, it was the Hiberno-British trade which exerted the greater influence upon—and indeed in Forssander's view[77] was actually responsible for—the origin of northern metallurgy. In so far as they were traded by middlemen, not themselves practising smiths, the Aunjetitz imports had no more effect than did the copper flat axes in earlier times. It was the travelling smith who was capable of teaching the natives how to copy imported bronzes.

More light will be thrown upon this when the actual working places of the early smiths are found and when their earliest products have been tested systematically for impurities to establish the sources of their parent ores.[78] What is already admitted, though, is that the leading product of the earliest metallurgical industry of the north, the Pile type of flanged axe, with its arc-shaped ribbing or grooving parallel to the cutting-edge, was essentially British in inspiration,[79] even though both the leading hoards—those from Pile in Scania[80] and Gallemose in Jutland[81]—contained massive penannular ingots of characteristically Aunjetitz type, indicating a central German source for the metal.

---

[74] J. E. Forssander, 1936, cap. III; H. C. Broholm, 1944.

[75] op. cit.

[76] Thus, the Bennewitz hoard contained 297 flanged axes af early type as against 244 for the whole of Sweden. See J. E. Forssander, 1936, 163–6.

[77] ibid., 178.

[78] It has already been shown, for instance, that the native Pile axes in the name-hoard were made from copper containing in one case 1.41 per cent nickel and 0.04 per cent tin and in another 0.27 nickel and 0.31 per cent tin, whereas a Hiberno-British axe proved to be of bronze (cu. 89.08 per cent, tin 10.87 per cent), the metallurgical analyses thus supporting the cultural indications of distinct origins. See J. E. Forssander, 1936. Again, objects of Hiberno-British type from Denmark are known to have been made from central German metal (H. C. Broholm, 1944, 25); but these are likely to have been Continental copies.

[79] The characteristic arc-shaped grooves or ribs parallel with the cutting-edge are met with on British axes (see Megaw and Hardy, 1938, 277 and n. 1). Again, the Pile type of axe is found precisely in those parts of Denmark and south Sweden where Hiberno-British imports occur (J. E. Forssander, 1936, 176).

[80] Forssander, 1936, 169 g., Taf. XXXV, XXXVI.   [81] ibid., 174 f.

This is a convenient point at which to say something about the form in which metal was traded during the Bronze Age. It is safe to assume that the movement of copper ore was kept to a bare minimum owing to the high proportion of waste involved, and in this respect it is significant that, as already stated (p. 191), ores were apparently smelted as close as possible to the outcrops or mines, from which they were won, even at the close of the Bronze Age. The same consideration, understandable enough when one remembers the conditions of transport prevailing at the time, had earlier determined that flint and stone should normally be traded in the form of finished or nearly finished articles. The over-riding need to reduce the bulk and weight of materials for transport worked itself out differently, though as between flint or stone and metal : whereas a flint tool could only be freed from its incubus of waste through the actual process of manufacture, in the case of copper this was accomplished at the intermediate stage of smelting, so that the metal could be traded with equal convenience as rough cakes from the furnace, as ingots or as finished objects.

There was scope for plenty of variation in the form of ingot used for trade or accumulation. For instance the type current in the east Mediterranean towards the end of the Bronze Age, the ox-hide form, was probably based on the primitive cattle standard of currency.[82] The earlier view that ox-hide ingots were necessarily of Cypriote copper[83] is no longer widely held, but whatever the source of the metal there is no doubt that the trade was in late Minoan or Mycenæan hands. This is supported by the distribution of the ingots (Fig. 139), which concentrate on Crete, but extend to Anatolia, Cyprus and the Greek mainland on the one hand and to Sicily and Sardinia on the other.[84] Again the well-known tomb painting at Thebes shows ox-hide ingots among the gifts being borne to Thothmes III, together with characteristically Minoan vases (Fig. 140)[85]; admittedly attempts have been made to derive the foreigners bearing the gifts from the Gulf of Issus or the mouth of the Orontes, but the consensus of opinion has favoured their identification with Minoans.[86]

In temperate Europe a number of well-defined types of ingot can be recognized, among them the double-axe form, having a perforation too small for a handle strong enough to support the weight of the head. These likewise were originally thought to represent a trade in Cypriote copper, which was conceived of by Lissauer as having been traded to central Germany by way of the south of France.[87] In this case some attempt has been made to settle the matter by applying scientific tests and, though even now only a few specimens have been submitted to spectrographic analysis, it is clear from the impurities contained in at least four of them, including up to $1\frac{1}{2}$ per cent of arsenic and traces of nickel, silver and antimony, that the metal contained in these particular ingots was obtained from central German ores, most probably from the Frankenwalde.[88] Thus, as Hawkes has recently

---

[82] P. Einzig, 1949, 228 f.; A. H. Quiggin, 1949. It is interesting that, according to Tacitus (*Annals*, IV, 72), Drusus imposed a tribute of ox-hides on the Frisians.

[83] O. Davies, 1932, 78.

[84] For a list, *ibid.*, 78–9.

[85] N. de G. Davies, 1935.

[86] G. A. Wainwright maintained that the Kft'iu came from Cilicia, but Pendlebury (1930, 4) supported their older identification as Cretans. Professor S. K. R. Glanville, to whom I am much indebted on this point, tells me that the identification of the gift-bearers is still an open one. V. G. Childe, 1947, 254, refers to such an ingot as " Cypro-Mycenaean." See also H. J. Kantor, 1947, 41–49.

[87] A. Lissauer, 1905, 525.   [88] W. Witter, 1938, I, 143.

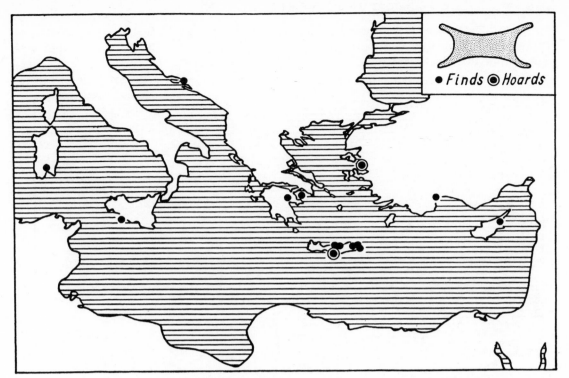

Fig. 139. Distribution of the Mycenaean copper ingots of ox-hide form.

Fig. 140. Theban tomb-painting, showing man
carrying ox-hide copper ingot on shoulder and
Minoan vase in right hand.

emphasized,[89] these ingots, although ultimately Mediterranean in form, so far from conveying copper to central Germany, serve in fact to define the routes whence copper was traded from this region westwards and south-westwards to the Middle Rhine, Switzerland and France (Fig. 141). Other types of ingot used in the Early Bronze Age of central

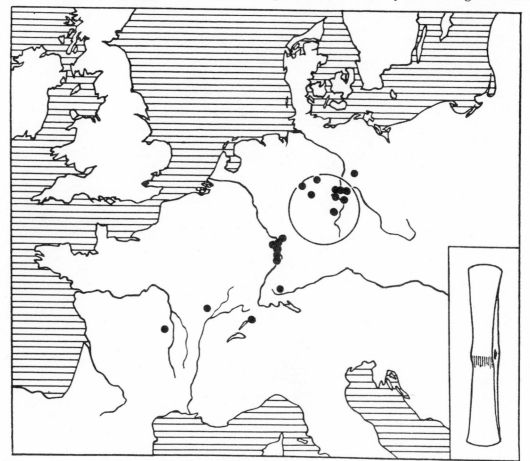

Fig. 141.   Map illustrating distribution of copper ingots of double axe form.   (*Based on Hawkes*)
The circle encloses the chief sources of copper ore in central Germany.

Europe included penannular torcs with tapered ends rolled back at the extremities, sometimes found in very large hoards,[90] and smaller, but much heavier and thicker penannular rings with abrupt terminals, like those exported to the northern area from central Germany and represented in the Gallemose and Pile hoards.[91]   Miniature bar ingots hammered

---

[89] C. F. C. Hawkes, 1940 b, 150 f.

[90] According to V. G. Childe (1929, 233), who cited a hoard from central Europe said to have contained 1,000 specimens, these " usually consist of almost pure copper," but W. Witter (1938, I, 143, and list Nos. 397–415) found that many yielded sufficiently high proportions of arsenic (mostly over 2 per cent), silver (0·9 to 1·7 per cent) and antimony (0·60–1·5 per cent), to make them unsuitable for tools.

[91] e.g. J. E. Forssander, 1936, Taf. XXXVI.   For a fine example in the Dieskau hoard : *ibid.*, Taf. XIV.   Also A. Oldeberg, 1942, I, Fig. 5.

flat and tapered at either end occur in large numbers in Bavarian hoards—325 from Thal, Hohenthann, Aibling and 245 from near Oberfahlheim, Neuulm—which probably date from the end of the Early Bronze Age,[92] but small bar ingots as a class are a feature of the Late Bronze Age from south Germany to Sweden.[93] Although, as Reinecke has shown,[94] metal had apparently begun to be traded in rough cakes from the smelter's furnace at a comparatively early stage of the Bronze Age in south Germany, this did not become general until later in the period and is presumably to be associated with the mass-production and cheapening of metal.

It has been argued that the lively trade, which ushered in and accompanied the spread of bronze technology in the temperate zone of Europe, arose in large measure under the stimulus of markets in the east Mediterranean. Material evidence for trade between the barbarians and the peoples of higher culture at this time may be seen first of all in importation to the east Mediterranean of northern amber. Amber of a kind is admittedly found in Iberia, south Italy, Sicily and Syria, but this can usually be distinguished by its relatively low content of succinic acid.[95] Analyses of amber beads from Mycenæan tombs has shown them to be of Baltic origin[96] and it is significant that amber was fashionable in prehistoric Greece only during the comparatively brief period when trade contacts with the north were close. The discovery of rectangular spacer and discoid beads in Shaft Grave VI at Mycenæ[97] shows that amber was already being imported into Greece during the sixteenth century B.C. at the transition from Middle to Late Helladic or Mycenæan times. Statistics relating to the finds of amber made durnig the excavation of *dromos* tombs at Mycenæ by Wace[98] strongly confirms Nilsson's view[99] that the hey-day of the trade fell in the opening phases of the Mycenæan period ; yet, as the finds from Metaxata on Kephallenia show,[99a] even in the latter phases it had not broken down completely.

---

[92] P. Reinecke, 1938, 5, Taf. 2, 2.

[93] A. Oldeberg, 1942, I, 34 f., Fig. 8; G. Kossinna, 1917–8, 165–171.

[94] P. Reinecke, 1938, 4–5.

[95] Spanish and Syrian amber is almost free of succinic acid and Italian and Sicilian hardly ever contains more than 0.4 per cent ; Galician and Rumanian amber may yield up to 1 or even 3 per cent. According to Helm, all amber yielding from 3 to 8 per cent must be of Baltic origin. The amber used in prehistoric Europe was mainly that found on the sea-shore, the richest amber coasts being those of West Jutland and Samland, but the whole coast from the Weser estuary to the Gulf of Riga, and those of Scania and eastern England yield lumps of amber. Amber is also found in tertiary and diluvial deposits in certain river valleys, particularly those of Poland and European Russia, and may sometimes be washed out of these. Mining for amber, such as has been carried on in Samland, is a development of historical times. See A. Götze in *Ebert*, I, 430–3.

[96] Thus, the disc and beads from the Tomb of the Double Axes were analysed by Professor O. Olshausen of Berlin and those from the Mycenaean shaft graves by Dr. Helm of Danzig, the determinations pointing to true succinite in each case (*Arch*. LXV. 42–3). The Kakovatos beads have also been shown to be of true succinite (K. Müller, 1909, 282) as have those from Argive Heraeum (C. Blegen, 1937, 286–7). On the other hand those claimed by Mosso for Kumasa, Crete, have been shown to be of some other resin (*Arch*. LXV, 44).

[97] G. Karo, 1930, 57, 69, 110 and 137.

[98] A. J. Wace, 1932, 204–5.

[99] M. P. Nilsson, 1927, 18–19.   [99a] N. Marinatos, *Arch. Eph*. 1933, 68–100

	Late Helladic I–II No. of beads		*Late Helladic III* No. of beads
Tombs		*Tombs*	
515	25	517	3 (plus 1 frag.)
518	c. 122	526	3
529	c. 40		

Amber has been recovered from several other cemeteries in the immediate neighbourhood of Mycenæ, at Dendra,[100] where tomb 10 yielded 75 beads, Argive Heræum,[101] Asine [102] and Nauplia,[103] as well as further afield at Menidi,[104] Delphi[105] and on the west coast of Elis at Pylos-Kakovatos.[106]

Detailed plotting of finds of amber from burials and hoards by de Navarro and others[107] has shown that the west Jutland deposits were those chiefly drawn upon during the Early and Middle Bronze Age and that supplies were brought across Germany mainly by way of rivers to the Brenner and so to the Po and the head of the Adriatic (Fig. 142). It was once argued by Nilsson,[108] on account of the comparative rarity of amber finds on the east Mediterranean islands—one group from Amira[109] and two beads and a disc from Isopata[110] on Crete, together with three pieces from a grave at Ialysos[111] on Rhodes, make up the total—that amber must have reached the mainland of Greece overland. The facts hardly necessitate this hard doctrine. The tradition that amber came from the north by way of the Adriatic was known to Pliny[112] and seems to find confirmation in the fact that the richest of all amber finds in Greece was that at Kakovatos on the west coast, where a single grave yielded some 500 complete beads or substantial fragments.[113]

How did the Mycenæans acquire their taste for northern amber? The attractions of the substance—its translucence and rich colour, its lightness and its mysterious powers of magnetism—are not of themselves sufficient to explain how and why lumps of this fossil resin should have found their way from the North Sea coast to the Peloponnese, some 1,300 miles as the crow flies, at this particular stage of prehistory. There can have been no

---

[100] A. W. Persson, 1931 and 1942.

[101] C. W. Blegen, 1937, 286–7.

[102] O. Frödin and A. W. Persson, 1938, 376 and 390.

[103] A. Furtwängler and G. Löschcke, 1886, 45.

[104] *ibid.*, 40.

[105] M. P. Nilsson, 1927, 401.

[106] K. Müller, 1909, 280–2.

[107] J. M. de Navarro, 1925.

[108] M. P. Nilsson, 1927, 18–9.

[109] A. Evans (*Palace*, II, 174, n. 2) speaks of " several amber beads " of disc and barrel form, M. P. Nilson (*op. cit.*) mentions one bead only.

[110] From the Tomb of the Double Axes, see A. Evans, 1914, 42–3. This find has recently been attributed to Zafer Papoura (e.g. V. G. Childe, 1948, 70), but Evans (1914, 43) goes out of his way to point out that no amber occurred at that site. The Tomb of the Double Axes is situated at Isopata

[111] From grave XIII. See M. P. Nilsson, 1927, 19.

[112] Pliny (Bk. III, cap. 30) repudiated the Greek idea that amber came from the islands of the Adriatic—in itself significant—and pointed out (Bk. XXXVII, cap. 11) that in reality it was " a product of the islands of the Northern Ocean . . . imported by the Germans into Pannonia, more particularly; from whence the Veneti, by the Greeks called Eneti, first brought it into general notice . . . From this it is evident how the story which connects it with the Padus first originated. . . ."

[113] K. Müller, *op. cit.*

question of prospecting over such a distance for a substance, for which there was previously no appreciation despite the occurrence of a closely similar substance in the homeland. Clearly enough the amber trade was conducted by middlemen, such as those who deposited the Dieskau hoard near Halle[114] and grew rich by exchanging metal objects or ingots of central German metal for northern amber, to be transmitted south to the Mediterranean and west to Britain.

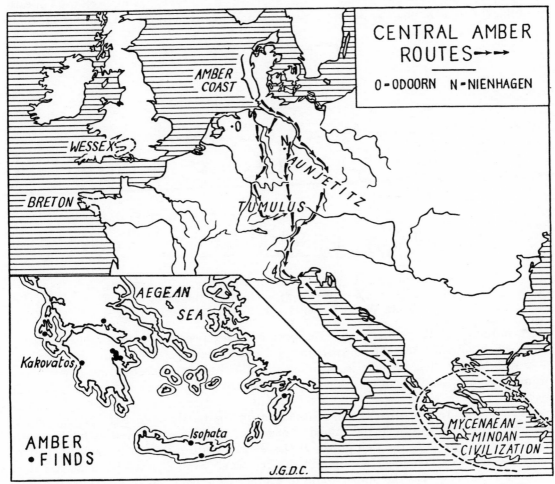

Fig. 142.   The main Central European amber routes and the distribution of finds in the East Mediterranean.

It was doubtless through contact with the Aunjetitz traders or some intermediaries that the east Mediterraneans first found out about northern amber, presumably in the course of acquiring some other substance already known to them, such as tin from the Vogtland (see p. 195).

Evidence for northern contracts at the transition from Middle to Late Helladic times is given by the bronze halberd blades from Shaft Grave VI at Mycenæ and from grave 25 at

---

[114] e.g. O'Riordain, 1936, 211–14.

Sesklo.[115] Although ultimately the type may be of Irish ancestry, the conical gold-capped rivets of the Mycenæan halberd suggested a northern origin to O'Riordain and one may imagine that this came to Greece by way of the amber route through Saxo-Thuringia. Even more striking are the parallels, to which von Merhart has drawn attention, between the intricate method of boring spacer beads observed on a specimen from cupola grave A at Kakovatos and on a number from tumulus burials in south Germany (Fig. 143).[116] The flat, laterally perforated spacer bead is of course an old type, having been used in early neolithic times in Denmark and reappearing in the Aunjetitz culture; but it was in the south

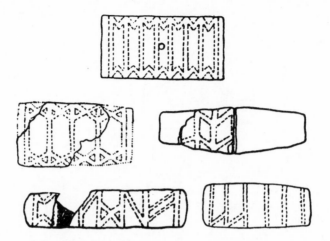

Fig. 143. Amber spacer beads with convergent perforations, from Kakovatos, Greece (No. 1) and from the tumulus culture of South West Germany (c. ½). (*After von Merhart*)

German tumulus culture that there first appeared large specimens having multiple string-holes which bifurcate near the point of emergence on either side. This feature is so remarkable that Merhart felt justified in claiming that the Kakovatos spacers must have come from the same school of craftsmen as that which produced those from the south German barrows.

There are many signs that at this particular time the inhabitants of central and south-western Germany controlled the diffusion of amber to the west as well as to the south. In his original study of the rich graves of the Wessex culture Piggott considered that the amber which they contained was imported direct from Scandinavia,[117] but he has since expressed the view that the amber route to southern England was in reality an off-shoot and a comparatively minor one of the main central German traffic.[118] A useful clue is given by the larger spacer beads from the amber necklace from Lake, Wilts.,[119] which exhibit, in addition to direct lateral string-holes, a number of converging ones like those seen on several of the south German and one of the Greek spacers. Several of the Wessex

---

[115] S. P. O'Riordain, 1936, 232–3.

[116] G. von Merhart, 1940.

[117] S. Piggott, 1938, 84.

[118] At the Exeter Conference of the Prehistoric Society, 1949.

[119] J. Thurnam, 1873, 505. Convergent perforations are present in jet examples from Burwell and Chippenham, Cambs., in the Univ. Mus. of Archæology and Ethnology.

graves[120] have yielded bronze pins of well-known Aunjetitz types including a bulb-headed pin from Camerton, Somerset and crutch-headed pins from Brigmerston, Normanton and Overton, Wilts.; in addition a multiple-ringed specimen from Everley resembles the tri-lobate type of central Europe. The well-known halberd pendants from three of the Wessex graves[121] point in the same direction : the transverse bands engraved on the sheet gold case of the handle of the Manton specimen and the four ribbed gold bands which encircle the amber handle of that from Wilsford leave no doubt that these are miniature reproductions of metal-shafted halberds; as O'Riordain has pointed out, the original focus of these lay in Saxo-Thuringia[122] the hub of the main amber routes, and a key source of metals at this time.

No doubt also it was by way of the central amber routes that the goldsmiths of Wessex gained their knowledge of Mycenæan techniques and usages.[123] Among these may be

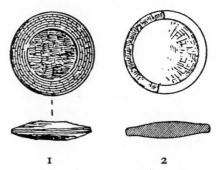

1   2

Fig. 144. Amber discs with gold casing from
Manton, Wiltshire (No. 1), and from the Tomb
of the Double Axes, Isopata, Crete (No. 2).

(*c.* $\frac{4}{5}$).

counted the use of gold *pointillé* ornament for dagger hafts, by which a pattern was built up from the heads of large numbers of gold pins or nails driven in flush with the surface, the practice of capping stone beads with gold and the manufacture of gold covered cones and of bi-conical ribbed beads of the same metal. Even more striking in some respects is the analogy between the amber discs with gold casing on the edges (Fig. 144) from Amesbury, Manton and Normanton, Wiltshire, and from the Tomb of the Double Axes at Isopata near Knossos.[124]

---

[120] S. Piggott, 1938, 85–7.

[121] *ibid.*, 84–5.

[122] S. P. O'Riordain, 1936, 300. In this connection the hoard from Dieskau, near Halle in Saxo-Thuringia, should be mentioned with its copper ingots, its amber, halberd blades and metal-shafted halberds and Hiberno-British decorated axe (see Forssander, 1936, Taf. XIV).

[123] S. Piggott, 1938, 95–6.

[124] First pointed out by Mrs M. E. Cunnington in 1925 (*Ant. J.* V, 68–70). Childe (1948, 70) has recently suggested that the Cretan disc may have been an import from the British Isles. His reason—that amber in Crete presumably came from the Baltic and that gold was plentiful in Eire— is unconvincing. The amber, whether in Wessex and Crete, came from a common source and gold is plentiful in Greece as well as in Eire. An analogy possibly worth pointing out is between the gold-bound amber discs and the bronze-bound one with a handle from Denmark tentatively attributed to the Northern Early Bronze Age by Brøndsted (1938, II, 147, and Fig. 142).

It would seem also that a certain amount of amber was traded off the central route to Brittany by way of the route followed earlier by the double-axe ingots of copper. The hafts of the metal daggers from the Breton graves[125] were commonly decorated in the gold *pointillé* technique and amber beads, including spacers from Lesconil, are also present.[126]

The only objects of east Mediterranean manufacture[127] at all widely diffused in bronze age Europe are segmented beads made from faience (Fig. 145), a composite material consisting of a core of " finely ground quartz grains cemented together by means of some other material " and a glaze resembling glass and commonly coloured blue by copper compounds.[128] When Beck and Stone examined in detail the specimens from the British Bronze Age, they found evidence of no less than a hundred and twenty-one beads of this type from thirty-six different burials.[129] It is a striking fact that twenty-five of these belong to the Wessex culture and that indeed segmented faience beads with a surface glaze occurred in just over a quarter of the graves from this culture listed by Piggott.[130] At Upton Lovell in Wiltshire as many as sixteen beads were found together, but as a rule only one, two or three beads accompanied the dead, an indication of the high value placed upon them. Outside Britain the only certain records of beads of this particular type in prehistoric Europe quoted by Beck and Stone[131] were a single specimen from Parc Guren, Carnac, eight from a burial of the Argaric bronze age at Fuente Alamo in Almeria, and four discovered by a peat-digger at Odoorn, near Exloo in north Holland, together with fourteen amber beads and twenty-five segmented beads made from tin.

It has since been appreciated that segmented faience beads were represented in burials of no less than five distinct cultural groups dating from the Early Bronze Age of east central Europe, namely the Perjamos culture of Hungary,[132] the Wieselburg culture of Lower Austria,[133] the Moravian province of the Aunjetitz culture,[134] the Tomaszow culture of the loess belt north of the Vistula[135] and the tumulus culture of south-eastern Poland.[136]

---

[125] C. D. Forde, 1930, 89.

[126] The occurrence of amber in the chalk-cut grottoes of the Marne (T. D. Kendrick, 1925, 60), would appear to indicate that amber was already reaching this part of France during neolithic times, presumably as a result of the penetration of the Seine-Marne-Oise culture into Westphalia and Thuringia, where it was in full use at this time. Further south amber is found in the megalithic tombs of the Pyrenean area (*Ebert* IV, 30) and in the passage graves of Los Millares, Llano de la Tja and Alcalá. Analysis of amber from the Iberian tombs showed that the material was definitely of Baltic origin (Leisner, 1943, 476).

[127] Discussion is advisedly confined to segmented faience beads of the kind designated " normal " by Beck and Stone (1936, 205). The crude examples found in Scotland were formed according to our authorities by crimping an unfired or semi-molten tube and, like the other type of faience beads from North Britain and Ireland, are distinguished by the fact that the glaze, instead of forming a distinct outer layer, permeates the inner core. It is conceivable that these may prove to be of local manufacture.

[128] *ibid.*, 207 f.

[129] *ibid.*, 231 and 234 ff.

[130] S. Piggott, 1938, Appendix VII.

[131] *op. cit.*, 242–3.

[132] e.g. four graves at S zöreg and one at Oszentivan in the Szeged area, C. F. C. Hawkes, 1940, 435.

[133] e.g. Leopoldsdorf, *ibid.*

[134] e.g. graves at Němčice and Jirikovice, *ibid.*

[135] T. Sulimirski, 1948.

[136] *ibid.*

A single grave of the last-mentioned group at Kolpiec near Drohobycz, south-west of Lwow, yielded no less than 43 beads of faience, including rounded and flattened as well as segmented forms. The appearance of segmented faience beads in so many distinct cultures more or less contemporaneously suggests that they must have arrived by trade during a comparatively short period of time.

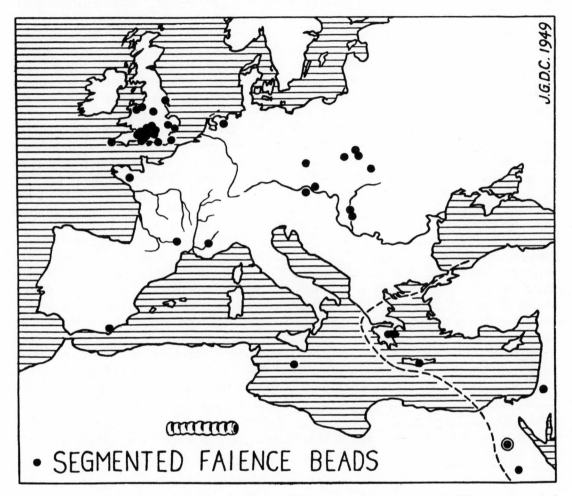

Fig. 145. Trade in segmented faience beads. The metropolitan area in the Mycenæan period is enclosed by a broken line.

There can be little doubt that segmented faience beads were first made either in Mesopotamia, or in Egypt, where they had already appeared by the VIth dynasty.[137] Equally though, it is important to remember that faience manufactures were established in Crete already by the end of Middle Minoan times under Egyptian influence and that during the XVIIIth dynasty, when the production of segmented faience beads reached its peak in Egypt and when trade relations with the Aegæan were at their liveliest, beads of Egyptian

---

[137] Beck and Stone, 1936, 222 f.

manufacture found their way to the Greek mainland and were there imitated.[138] It cannot be said that the segmented form was ever common in Crete, though some faience ones occurred in the Temple Repositories at Knossos[139] and vitreous paste copies have been found in Late Minoan III deposits at Isopata[140] and Phaistos.[141] On the mainland spherical melon, gadrooned and disc faience beads are common ;[142] segmented forms occurred in no less than eight of the Mycenæan tombs at Prosymna, predecessor of Argive Heræum ;[143] and Wace found nineteen segmented beads of greenish glass paste in the Tomb of Clytemnestra at Mycenæ.[144] The rarity of segmented faience beads, as of amber finds, in Crete suggests that during the Mycenæan period the mainland power played the chief part in trade with the north and west, as well as according to Miss Kantor[144a] it did with the east.

Until detailed and systematic analyses have been made of the material of segmented faience beads over the whole area of their distribution, discussion of the relationships of the different groups is bound to be attended with a good deal of uncertainty but in the last resort the interpretation of the evidence is a matter for archæology. In the postscript to their classic paper Beck and Stone were able to report that spectrographic analysis had shown that a Wiltshire bead resembled one from Tell el Amarna (1380–50 B.C.) so closely as to leave " little doubt that both were made in Egypt and are roughly of the same date."[145] Since then, though, Blegen has stated his view that some at least of those from Mycenæan tombs of Prosymna were of Egyptian manufacture[146] and Persson has published an analysis of faience from a tholos tomb at Dendra which shows it to be definitely Egyptian.[147] The evidence is consistent with the view that segmented faience beads of Egyptian manufacture, together, it may be, with some of Mycenæan origin, were traded to barbarian Europe in the course of Mycenæan trade. The occurrence of the type in Malta[148] and the south of France,[149] as well as in Almeria, suggests that segmented faience beads found their way, though apparently in small numbers, by the trade currents which are known to have passed at this time from the east to the west Mediterranean. It is not improbable that they reached Wessex from there by way of the Narbonne-Garonne route, later followed by the Greek tin trade. Alternatively the beads may have travelled from the east Mediterranean by the central amber routes and been distributed east and west by the middlemen who controlled them. Such an explanation has the merit of accounting for both the main

---

[138] According to C. W. Blegen, 1937, 306–7, the majority of the faience beads, including segmented ones, from the Prosymna graves were of local manufacture, only a few being admitted as imports from Egypt.

[139] A. Evans, *Palace*, I, 490–3.

[140] A. Evans, 1914, 18.

[141] *Monumenti Antichi*, XIV, 632–3, Fig. 102.

[142] e.g. A. W. Persson, 1942, 86, records, 315 melon-shaped, 97 long, gadrooned and 98 small black beads of faience from tholos 10 at Dendra. Considerable numbers are recorded from Prosymna by Blegen, 1937, 306 ff., and by Wace from Mycenae (1937, 205).

[143] Blegen, 1937, 310–1.

[144] *Ann. Brit. School at Athens*, XXV, 372.

[144a] H. J. Kantor, 1947, 49 and 103.

[145] Beck and Stone, 1936, 252.

[146] Blegen, 1937, 306.

[147] Persson, 1942, 197 f.

[148] Information from Dr. J. F. S. Stone.

[149] e.g. " Dolmen " of Tourine, arr. St. Affrique, Aveyron, (E. Cartailhac, 1868, Pl. 1, No. 18) and Grotte du Ruisseau, Monges (Childe, 1947, 300).

distributions at once. So far as the " normal " segmented beads of Britain are concerned, their concentration in graves of the Wessex culture has already been noted, but it is worth adding that out of the twenty-five graves of this culture to yield them no less than seventeen produced amber,[150] including one with a gold mounted disc resembling that from Isopata. If the Wessex amber was derived from the central amber route, there would be no difficulty in bringing the segmented faience beads by the same way. At this stage it has to be admitted that so far neither the rich hoards and burials of the Saxo-Thuringian area of the Aunjetitz culture nor those of the south German tumulus culture have so far yielded segmented faience beads; but this is not necessarily fatal, since it is conceivable that middlemen might handle a trade line without necessarily modifying their own taste in jewellery. A point of some relevance here is that gold earrings of Irish type were found in graves of each of the Polish cultures to import segmented faience beads,[151] a link with the far west which once again must have been maintained by those who controlled the central amber routes. Whatever light future research may throw on the machinery of the trade in segmented faience beads, their adoption by so many different cultural groups in barbarian Europe only serves to emphasize the essentially inferior status of these peoples in relation to the comparatively civilized inhabitants of the east Mediterranean area in the Mycenæan Age.

If the requirements of the east Mediterranean market had much to do with the rise of European metallurgy, it is also arguable that before the Mycenæan world sank into decline it played a large part in the genesis of the late bronze age in central Europe. Whatever becomes of Childe's hypothesis that copper mines were opened up in the Eastern Alps to provide metal for the Aegæan world[152]—and systematic analysis of late Mycenæan bronzes might settle this question—it is certain that the notable advances were made in smithing at this time under east Mediterranean inspiration. The products of the central European smiths, particularly vessels of hammered bronze, were widely traded both to northern and eastern Europe.

The course and extent of this trade can best be illustrated by considering the class of small handled cups, of which three main varieties have been distinguished: the earliest type, which appeared early in the Late Bronze Age in period D2,[153] the Friedrichsruhe type, after the finding-place in Mecklenburg, betrays east Mediterranean inspiration in its shape; the Fuchsstadt type, after the site in Unterfranken, which developed rather later and survived into period E, diverged more widely from the prototype; and lastly in period E, came the Jenšovice cups, distinguished by embossed decoration and named after the Bohemian site which yielded a hoard of thirteen together with numerous objects of adornment and other things. Although, to judge from their main geographical concentrations the different types of handled cup were manufactured over slightly different areas, the Fuchsstadt cups centring for instance on south Germany and the Jenšovice ones on Bohemia and the middle Danube area, they appear to have been traded over much the same territories. The first point brought out by the maps (Fig. 146) prepared by Sprockhoff[154] and brought up to date by Childe[155] is that, although extensive, the area served by this

---

[150] Piggott, 1938, Appendix VII.

[151] T. Sulimirski, 1948.

[152] V. G. Childe, 1948A, 189 f.

[153] The periods of the central European bronze age referred to here are those agreed by Professors Childe and Hawkes and set out in the table published in *Proc. Prehist. Soc.*, 1948, 216.

[154] E. Sprockhoff, 1930. For map of Friedrichsruhe cups, see Taf. 14.

[155] V. G. Childe, 1948A, gives distributions of Fuchsstadt and Jensovice cups on the same map, Fig. 8.

trade was limited fairly definitely by the Alps to the south and by the Swiss lakes and the Rhineland to the west. Only the youngest form, the Jenšovice cup, spread beyond these limits and then only rarely and sporadically, as shown by finds at Coste Merano in Latium or Hauterives in the Drôme. All three found their way north, Friedrichsruhe cups extending to north Jutland and Scania and a Fuchsstadt vessel even reaching the neighbourhood of

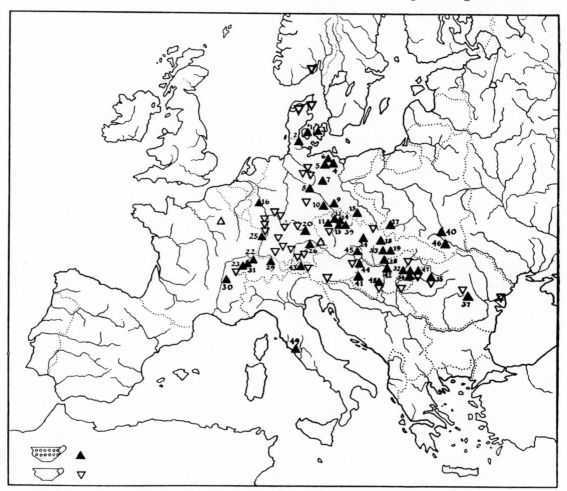

Fig. 146. Late Bronze Age trade. Distribution of ▲ Jenšovice and ▽ Fuchstadt cups.
(*After Childe*).

Skien in south-east Norway. Both the younger types, moreover, spread along the margin of the western Alps to lake Neuchâtel and in much larger numbers eastwards to Roumania, Fuchsstadt cups reaching even the mouth of the Danube and Jenšovice ones penetrating Galicia to the Dniester. It is significant of the reality of these trade routes that the bronze cauldrons with T-shaped handle-attachments, studied by Sprockhoff[156] and which began to be made in period E, spread over a closely similar territory. On the other hand, the impression should not be given that even in this part of Europe the pattern of trade in

[156] E. Sprockhoff, 1930, Taf. 33.

bronze manufactures, let alone other commodities, was a simple one of exports from central Europe. One need only recall the well-known belt-case and fibula of northern type from the Swiss lake-settlement of Corcelettes on lake Neuchâtel, the pieces of a belt-case from Bourges in central France, or the famous bronze tutulus from Pfeffingen in Wurttemburg, all cited in the classic paper on prehistoric trade by Montelius,[157] to appreciate that finished bronzes sometimes flowed south, particularly on the western margin of the main field of central European activity, though whether these need imply trade is doubtful.

To turn to quite another area, one meets with plenty of evidence in the extreme south-west of the continent for widespread and this time largely sea-borne trade. The famous hoard dredged in 1923 from the harbour of Huelva[158] at the mouth of the Rio Tinto, which flows down from the copper region of the Sierra Morena, contained bronzes of Hiberno-British, Biscayan French and west Mediterranean affinities, and without accepting is naïvely as part of the cargo of a ship plying between Ireland and Sicily,[159] the catholicity of the objects which compose it is most easily interpreted in terms of trade activity, embracing at one time or another both the Atlantic and west Mediterranean routes. More reliable because built up from so large a number of finds, is the picture given by the distribution of the double looped palstave (Fig. 147). The concentration of hoards and of specimens still retaining the jet at the heart of the north-western province of the Atlantic bronze age of Iberia[160] shows pretty clearly that these objects were a product of local industry based on exploitation of Asturian copper and Galician tin. It is reasonable therefore to interpret at least a large proportion of the stray finds from other parts of Europe as due to some form of trade. Once again these are indications of trade by each of the two main sea routes, though in view of the more northerly focus of the industry it is hardly surprising to find that the Atlantic is now even more predominant. The presence of double-looped palstaves in the Monte sa' Idda[161] and Monte Arrubbiu hoards in southern Sardinia shows that objects from the north-western province of the Atlantic bronze age penetrated the western Mediterranean, as did those of the south-west, but the main flow of trade was undoubtedly northwards along the sea ways to Britain[162] and up the rivers en route into France, Belgium and north-west Germany, a single specimen apparently travelling as far as Östergötland.[163]

---

[157] O. Montelius, 1910, 265.

[158] *Antiquity*, 1927, 106–7.

[159] H. N. Savory, 1949, 140–1, goes so far as to doubt whether the fibulae of Siculan type in the Huelva hoard were in fact made in Sicily at all. Since, though, his alternative place of manufacture is north-eastern Spain, this does not destroy the notion of a trade route penetrating the western Mediterranean.

[160] The map given by our Fig. 147 is based so far as those outside Iberia are concerned on that published by V. G. Childe, 1939, Fig. 1; for Iberia the more detailed map published by H. N. Savory, 1949, Fig. 3, has been used.

[161] See *Bull. d. Paleontologia It.* XLIV, 218, Pl. IX.

[162] The Irish cauldron from Cabarceno, Santander, is one reflex of this trade (H. N. Savory, 1949, 135). According to Savory fragments of what may have been a similar cauldron were found in the Huelva hoard, as well as the Irish type of bronze spearhead with lunate openings in the wings.

[163] It should be noted, though, that this specimen from the neighbourhood of Lake Tåkern Svanshals, Östergötland, came from the collection of a farmer, who was also a keen collector and that details were only obtained from his grand-daughter some years after his death. The circumstances are set out in detail by A. Nordén, 1925, 18–19.

During the final stage in the prehistory of temperate Europe, trade continued to develop and flourish among the various barbarian peoples, but inevitably it is the trade between these and the civilized peoples of the Mediterranean which claims the chief interest. The settlement on the west coast of Italy of the Etruscans, followed shortly after by Greek traders and colonists in southern Italy, began a process which led within two or three

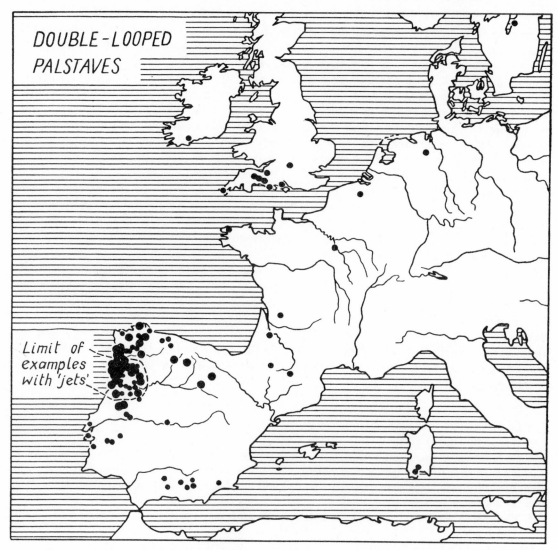

DOUBLE-LOOPED
PALSTAVES

Limit of
examples
with 'jets'

Fig. 147. Trade in double-looped bronze palstaves. (*Based on Childe and Savory*).

centuries to the incorporation of the whole littoral of Mediterranean Europe within the sphere of literate civilization. The arrival in Italy of Etruscans and Greeks inevitably led to a rise in the standards of metal-working among the indigenous smiths and it was this which made it possible to penetrate central European markets during the final stage of the Bronze Age in that area. Indeed the trade flowed on up the old routes from central Europe to the north, as shown by the amphoræ and cauldrons of beaten bronze decorated in the superior embossed style of the Villanovan workshops found on Danish and Scanian soil.[164]

The spread of Greek colonization to the south of France greatly extended the frontier between the barbarian and civilized worlds. By the sixth century B.C. virtually the whole Mediterranean coastal zone had been incorporated into the sphere of civilization, so that trade between barbarian and Greek in effect flowed across a major ecological boundary. This makes it all the more significant that it was wine, one of the leading products of the Mediterranean region, and the appurtenances of wine-drinking, which played the leading part in the trade. Celtic society at the time of the Hallstatt culture was indeed well attuned to such a trade, since wealth was concentrated in the hands of princes who found in exotic

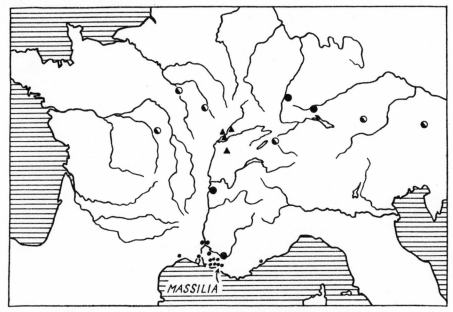

Fig. 148. Greek exports to the Celtic people during the Hallstatt D period (6th cent. B.C.)
(*Based largely on Jacobsthal*).

| • Ionian pottery. | ● Rhodian wine-flagons. |
| ▲ Greek amphorae. | ◑ Various bronzes. |

purchases a convenient outlet for conspicuous consumption. The indications are that much of this early trade passed through the Greek colony of Massilia, up the Rhône and the Saône into central France and by way of the Belfort gap to the upper Rhine (Fig. 148). Particularly significant from this point of view are the Ionian wine amphoræ of sixth century type, which cluster in the Jura and in the upper Saône valley,[165] and the trail of bronze wine flagons of Rhodian type from Pertuis on the Durance in Provence, to the neighbourhood of Vienne in the Rhône valley, the upper Rhine and the upper Danube.[166]

---

[164] e.g. the often-cited amphorae from Scania (Montelius, 1910, abb. 16) and from Lavinds-gaard Mose, Fyen (C. F. C. Hawkes, 1948, Pl. XXI) or the cauldron from Siem, Himmerland, Jutland (Brøndsted, 1938, II, 190).

[165] e.g. Mercey-sur-Saône ; Mantoche (several) ; Camp de Château-sur-Salins, Jura (with red and black figured Attic vases); Mont Guèrin (sherds from Late Hallstatt levels). See M. Piroutet 1918; J. M. de Navarro, 1928, 426–7; Jacobsthal and Neuffer, 1933, 63–4; P. Jacobsthal, 1934, 18.

[166] Jacobsthal, 1929.

The source of the wine traded to the Hallstatt world during the sixth and fifth centuries B.C. is unlikely to have been Italian, since down to the middle of the second century B.C. much of the wine consumed in the peninsula itself was imported from Greece.[167] While it is known that viticulture was introduced to Gaul by the colonists of Massilia, in the neighbourhood of which it was confined down to about 120 B.C., it is uncertain to what extent the wine they exported northwards was brought from Greece or to what extent, if at all, it was grown in Provence. In any event the bronze flagons, considered by Jacobsthal[168] to have been made in all probability in Rhodes and which were traded to Asia Minor and Syria, as well as westwards to Sicily, western Italy and the south of France, emphasize the Mediterranean origin of the whole ritual of wine drinking, as it was transmitted to the Celts. Apart from the flagons, several other bronzes of Greek or Etruscan character were imported into the Celtic territories at this time. These included not only a number of finds from central France—notably a bronze tripod and bowl with griffon's heads from La Garenne,[169] a griffon's head from Sens[170] and a hydria handle from Bourges,[171]—but also the splendid hydria from Grachwyl, canton Bern,[172] the lathe-turned wooden cup, mentioned in a previous chapter (p. 216), from Uffing in Bavaria, and a bronze basin of Etruscan affinities from cremation grave 682 at Hallstatt[173] in Lower Austria. The extension of these finds round the northern margin of the Alps and the Etruscan character of certain pieces suggests that some of them may have reached the Hallstatt area by way of the Brenner Pass. The effect of the penetration of Mediterranean trade into Celtic territory was not great during Hallstatt times : as an art historian Jacobsthal could write[174] of the classical imports that " these forms were foreign bodies in the otherwise still rigid geometric style "; it was not until the late fifth and fourth centuries that classical influence transformed Celtic society, stimulating the art distinctive of La Tène culture and introducing in due course a whole series of technological changes, including a much more extended use of iron for tools and such devices as rotary lathes and querns.

During the life of the La Tène culture trade between the central Celtic areas and the Mediterranean passed under Etruscan control and followed routes over the Alpine passes.[175] Exports from the south, though including such things as coral,[176] ivory and glass, continued to comprise for the most part wine and the vessels of pottery or bronze connected with " carrying, storing, mixing and drinking " it.[177] The most numerous traces of this trade are the bronze flagons with beaked spouts (*Schnabelkannen*) made in an Etruscan workshop

---

[167] R. Billiard, 1913, 436.

[168] Jacobsthal, 1929, 220. Some specimens, e.g. those from Carthage, he regards as either of Phoenician manufacture or as made for the Phoenician market.

[169] Déchelette, III (1927), 273–4.

[170] Déchelette, II (1914), 1598.

[171] Jacobsthal, 1944, 158 n. 1.

[172] Déchelette, III (1927), 270 f.; de Navarro, 1928, Pl. 1.

[173] Jacobsthal, 1944, 158, n. 1.

[174] Jacobsthal, 1944, 158–9.

[175] Jacobsthal, 1944, 142 and 158–9.

[176] The use of coral incrustation as a decoration was a Celtic invention. The material itself was imported from the Mediterranean, though its precise source is unknown (Jacobsthal, 1944, 133) Pliny (*Hist. Nat.* XXXII, 21) mentions coral from the Stoichades (Iles dé Hyères); Drepranum, Sicily; Naples; Graviscae, Etruria; and the Aeolian islands (Lipari).

[177] Déchelette (II (1914), 1429–1430) and de Navarro (1928, 434–6) among others, have emphasized the importance of the wine trade.

as yet unidentified,[178] and traded over an extensive area north of the Alps from central France to the middle Rhineland and the headwaters of the Elbe (Fig. 149). It is particularly

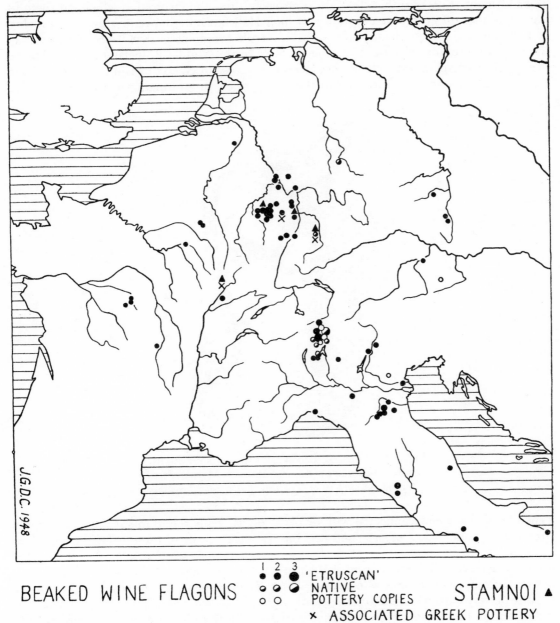

BEAKED WINE FLAGONS

1 2 3 'ETRUSCAN'
NATIVE
POTTERY COPIES
× ASSOCIATED GREEK POTTERY

STAMNOI ▲

J.G.D.C. 1948

Fig. 149. Greek exports to the Celtic peoples during the La Tène A period (5th cent. B.C.). *(Based on Jacobsthal and Langsdorff).*

to be noted that these Etruscan vessels were imitated in at least two distinct workshops north of the Alps, as well as being reproduced in pottery, a sign that southern imports

---

[178] Jacobsthal and Langsdorff, 1929, 63.

were no longer received passively, but served rather to stimulate the latent capacities of the Celtic craftsmen. It was largely from the rich designs of the handle-attachments of beaked flagons (Fig. 150) that the Celtic craftsmen drew the inspiration which led them to transmute the stiff geometric decoration of their Hallstatt inheritance into the living reality of La Tène art, a fact which justifies de Navarro's comment[179] that "La Tène art may largely have owed its existence to Celtic thirst." In the Middle Rhineland and the Marne these beaked flagons commonly accompanied the burials of chieftains laid to rest with their chariots and horse-gear, a sure sign of the place which wine-drinking had assumed in La

Fig. 150. Beaked flagon of bronze, showing rich handle attachment; Somme Bionne, Marne, France (c. ¼). (*Courtesy of Trustees of British Museum*).

Tène life. Other items connected with drinking occasionally found in such burials include large bronze containers (*stamnoi*) and it is interesting that one of these from Weisskirchen contained a residue of pitch, such as the ancients used for seasoning their wine and for preparing vessels used for storing it.[180] In several instances, also, wine cups of Attic pottery accompanied bronze wine vessels. At Klein Aspergle,[181] for example, a couple of Attic pottery cups were found buried with a bronze *stamnos* and a Celtic copy of a beaked flagon, and in the Somme Bionne chariot-burial a kylix in red-figure ware was placed, side by side with a bronze beaked flagon, at the chieftain's feet.[182]

---

[179] de Navarro, 1928, 436.

[180] cf. Pliny, *Hist. Nat.* XIV, 24–5; Jacobsthal, 1944, 142.

[181] Déchelette, II (1914), 1599–1600.

[182] *British Museum Guide to the Iron Age Collections*, 55 f.

Even if the wine itself, like so many of the most important trade commodities, has disappeared completely leaving only a residue of pitch behind, the importation of Greek and Etruscan manufactures into the Celtic world is sufficiently attested by the bronze and clay fictiles already mentioned. In the case of exports archæology is less helpful, since these mainly took the form of raw materials like those described by Strabo. Among such, animal hides would have been of particular importance to Mediterraneans owing to the poor conditions for cattle-raising in their homeland, but for the existence of this trade it would be too much to expect direct archæological evidence. More promising from this point of view are metals, of which the Mediterraneans particularly coveted silver and tin. It is indeed generally accepted that tin was the chief attraction to Greek commercial enterprise in the west. To begin with Galicia was the chief source, but the blockade of the Straits of Gibraltar by the Carthaginians from towards the end of the sixth century B.C. until the Roman conquest of 206 B.C. led the Greek traders to concentrate on Cornish supplies, knowledge of which was reputedly brought home by Pytheas on his blockade-running voyage up the Atlantic coast around 325 B.C. Of the three main routes by which Greek trade may have reached Britain, one passed through Narbonne and the Carcassonne gap to the Garonne and the Gironde; a second led from the Rhône to the Loire and down to the native port of Corbilo; and a third followed the route from the Saône to the Marne, already marked out by the wine trade, and on to the Seine.[183] Stray finds from tin-streams and indications of tin-working at Chûn Castle and elsewhere show that tin was being won in parts of Cornwall during the Pre-Roman Iron Age and a few finds of exotic objects, like the sherds of wine amphoræ from Chûn, bear witness to foreign interest.[184] On the whole, though, the literary evidence discussed by Hencken[185] is a good deal more impressive, even if in places ambiguous, and there is little doubt that a vigorous trade in tin was carried on between Cornwall, the mouths of the Loire and the Gironde, and ultimately the Greek consumers of the metal. It is possible, also, that lead or silver from Mendip was traded during the Early Iron Age and that this may explain the concentration of autonomous Greek bronze coins, dating mainly from the second quarter of the third until well into the second century B.C., found on the main routes from this area as they converge on Poole Harbour[186]; we know from Caesar[187] that southern Britain at least was importing copper in his time and it may well be that in preceding centuries bronze coins were imported as so many ingots.

The conquest of Gaul by Julius Caesar brought the frontier of the classical world right up to the shores of the English Channel and it becomes possible to study the interplay of barbarian and civilized economy at closer range. The pattern of trade between the two revealed in Strabo's description[188] is sufficiently familiar; on the one hand primary commodities, like corn, cattle, gold, silver, iron, skins, slaves and hunting-dogs; on the other foreign luxuries and manufactures, such as the " ivory bracelets, necklaces, amber, vessels of glass, and small wares " detailed by the ancient historian. Archæological evidence shows that the Belgic aristocracy of the south-east was importing oil and wine in amphoræ of Mediterranean type, together with such manufactures as silver cups, bronzes, glass and

---

[183] M. Cary, 1924, 166.

[184] H. O'N. Hencken, 1932, 160, 166 f.

[185] *ibid.*, 167–86.

[186] J. G. Milne, 1948.

[187] *De Bello Gallico*, V, 12.

[188] Strabo, IV, 5, 2–3. Hamilton and Falconer's trans., 1852.

red-glazed Arretine ware mainly from Arretium and other localities in Italy.[189] During the last century or so of independence the upper strata of Belgic society were thus to some degree Romanized in taste through the mechanism of trade.

This permeation of barbarian society by classical influences extended hundreds of miles beyond the frontiers of the Empire and affected communities up to the northern limits of the temperate zone. Indeed, Scandinavian archæologists have been accustomed to designate the first four centuries of the Christian era the " Roman Iron Age " on the ground that " the whole cultural development of northern Europe was subject during that time to the dominating influence of Roman culture."[190] Trade was not by any means the only factor involved—the return of men from service in the Empire must have been one of the most potent influences—but it was certainly persistent and helped to render more permanent the effect of contacts of a more personal and fleeting kind. It is particularly striking to note how even the bronze accessories of wine-drinking, whether manufactured in Italy, or, as later, in Gaul or the Rhineland, spread right up into Scandinavia to the very limits of the farming zone. To quote just one of the many instances collected by Ekholm[191] and others, no less than a hundred sieved wine ladles, dating from the second to the fourth centuries A.D. and of provincial manufacture, have been found in the north, seventy-five from Denmark, seventeen from Sweden and eight from Norway up to beyond Trondheim (Fig. 151). It was only into the circumpolar zone that classical impulses failed to penetrate. Yet it may be surmised that the trappers and fishermen of these northernmost territories provided at least some of the commodities which entered into trade with the south.

It is scarcely necessary to state that trade in prehistoric Europe was primitive in character in the sense that it was mainly conducted by barter. Coinage appeared only in the last generations of the prehistoric period and then only in territories in close contact with civilization. The native coinage, which developed in central Gaul during the closing years of the second century B.C., was modelled on gold staters of Philip II of Macedon captured in the Macedonian and Syrian wars earlier in the century, taken into currency by Rome and introduced to Gaul as a direct consequence of the defeat of the Arverni by Ahenobarbus in 121 B.C. The coinage introduced to Britain by the Belgæ during the second quarter of the first century B.C. stemmed from the same pedigree (Fig. 152).[192]

How far trade was conducted in prehistoric Europe on a basis of pure barter, under which commodities were exchanged for direct consumption only, and how far and when the use of one particular object of barter became so regularized as to become a medium of exchange,[193] are questions to which satisfactory answers can hardly be given. One is free to imagine, without much prospect of proof, that in exchanges between hunter-fishers and agriculturalists furs may have served as currency already during the Stone Age, as they did in medieval Europe and more recently in the territories of the Hudson's Bay Company.[194] It has been hinted earlier in the present chapter (see p. 258), that metal ingots may

---

[189] A. J. Evans, 1891 ; Fox, 1923, 99–102 and 1933, 160 and Fig. 6c ; Hawkes and Hull, 1947, 28–9 and 289.

[190] H. Shetelig and H. Falk, 1937, 192. Olwen Brogan (1936) gives a good account of trade between the Roman Empire and the free Germans. For a general account of trade in the Roman world, see M. P. Charlesworth, 1926.

[191] G. Ekholm, 1935 and refs.

[192] Sir J. Evans, 1864 and 1890; but for modern work, see G. C. Brooke, 1933, and D. Allen 1944.

[193] On this see P. Einzig, 1949, 353 f.

[194] ibid., 175, 259, 274, 278–80.

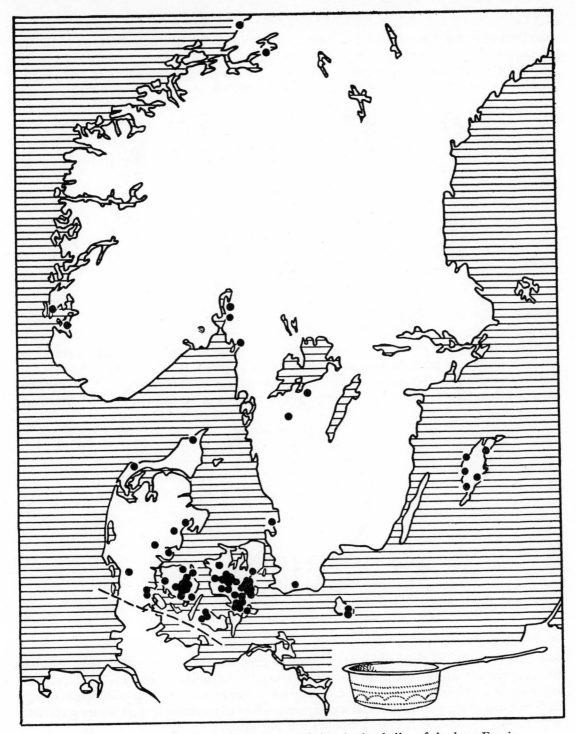

Fig. 151.   The distribution in Scandinavia of sieved wine ladles of the later Empire.
(*Based on Ekholm*).

279

have served as currency during prehistoric times and in this connection the ox-hide form of copper ingots current in the Mediterranean during Mycenæan times was noted as particularly significant. Again, it is instructive to compare the metal cakes and roughly moulded ingots from bronze age hoards with the *æs rude* and *æs signatum* which preceded

Fig. 152. British coins; degeneration series from Greek protoype.

the earliest copper coinage of Italy.[195]   The large numbers and uniform size in which copper ingots and iron bars (see p. 260) sometimes occur is consistent with their use as currency or as stores of value, though of course it by no means proves that they were so used. Equally it is possible, though hardly capable of proof, that ring-money was used in bronze age Europe, whether in comparatively rude state like the gold ring with smaller ones attached from Grunty Fen, Cambridgeshire (Fig. 153), or in the form of finished ornaments

Fig. 153. Gold ring money from Grunty Fen, Cambs. (*c*. ⅔). (*After Quiggin*).

like " ingot torcs " or the bronze bracelets with expanded terminals, which have so often been compared with West African manilla currency.[196] In judging such, it is worth pondering what one authority on primitive currency has recently written : " It is difficult enough to discriminate between ornamental and currency rings in recent or contemporary material ; with prehistoric or early historic examples it is impossible."[197]

---

[195] *ibid.*, 234–9; also A. H. Quiggin, 1949, Chap. VIII.
[196] e.g. A. H. Quiggin, 1949, 288–9 and Fig. 26.
[197] *ibid.*, 280.

The attempt to detect weight ratios between different specimens of the same class of ingot offers a more objective line of approach, especially when comparatively well preserved objects are in question. In the case of the iron " currency bars " the attempt to detect units has been laboured and little more can be said than that some approximate standard was aimed at.[198] Rather more convincing results have been obtained for the double-axe copper ingots of France and Germany which appear to have been made in some cases in multiples of a unit of between five and six hundred grammes.[199] It may be added that the question of the weights used in prehistoric Europe is an extremely difficult one, on which little work of value has been done.[200] It seems reasonably certain, though, that some form of weights and weighing apparatus must have been available for standard bronze to have been made and for trade in precious minerals like gold and tin to have been carried on, and there is positive evidence that scales were used at least by Mycenæan times in Greece.[201]

---

[198] cf. Sir Cyril Fox, 1945, 33.

[199] C. F. C. Hawkes, 1940b, 150 f.

[200] It may be noted, for example, that weights from Swiss lake-villages of the Late Bronze Age approximate closely to the Phoenician mine of 0.727 gr. : thus lead weights from Wollishofen weigh 0·727 gr. and 0·735 gr. and lead and tin ones from Auvernier respectively 0·730 gr. and 0·735 gr. Déchelette, II (1924), 400 f.

[201] Golden scales, symbolizing the Egyptian conception of weighing the soul, were found in Shaft Grave III at Mycenae (G. Karo, 1930, Pl. XXXIV) and bronze scale-pans occurred in the *dromos* of tomb 515 and in the chamber of tomb 529 at Mycenae (A. J. Wace, 1932, 190).

CHAPTER X

TRAVEL AND TRANSPORT

NAVIGATION : INLAND WATERS AND THE SEA

EXCEPT in the circumpolar zone, where during the season of snow it was possible to cover long distances by sledge and ski, travel and transport were mainly carried on by water during the prehistoric period, as indeed they continued to be down to comparatively modern times. The importance of rivers as arteries of prehistoric trade is frequently reflected in the archæological evidence as with that for the transcontinental amber routes or the Grand-Pressigny flint trade. Equally revealing is the interest in rivers displayed by ancient geographers, as when Strabo[1] wrote of Gaul that

> " the course of the rivers is so happily disposed in relation to each other that you may travel from one sea to the other carrying the merchandise only a short distance, and that easily across the plains; but for the most part by the rivers, ascending some, and descending others."

If rivers were the main vehicles of internal trade—and one should not forget that their valleys afforded easy lines of movement by foot or pack-horse—it was the sea that linked the different territories of prehistoric Europe and often, where rivers were awkward or mountains difficult, different parts of the same country. It is impossible not to be impressed, for example, by the ease with which stone axe blades were distributed by neolithic traders from Ireland to Britain or from England to the Isle of Man or the Channel Isles. Again, as Montelius emphasized in his classic paper on prehistoric trade,[2] the importance of islands is one of the most striking facts of antiquity. This applies not only to the British and neighbouring islands, but to those of the Baltic, including the Danish islands with Bornholm, Gotland, Öland and the Aaland Islands, and even more forcibly to the Mediterranean—to Crete, Cyprus and the Aegean Islands, to Malta, Sicily, Sardinia and the Balearics. The sea was a highway, indeed, for those capable of navigation.

Precisely at what stage of prehistory boats were first brought into use is still an open question, but at the moment there is no evidence that this happened during palæolithic times. The low sea-levels, which prevailed in the late glacial period, make it hard to estimate how far upper palæolithic man was able to cross open water. There is no evidence that fish were caught off-shore at this time, though, nor are boats depicted in any of the several groups of upper palæolithic art. On the other hand, the distribution of mesolithic settlements and the indications afforded by fish-bones from mesolithic middens (see p. 84) points to the use of boats comparatively early in the post-glacial period; and the truth of

---

[1] Strabo, IV, 1, 22. Hamilton and Falconer, transl., 1852.
[2] O. Montelius, 1910, 277.

this is indeed established by the recovery of wooden paddles from Maglemosian sites in Duvensee, near Lübeck, and at Holmegaard on Sjaeland.[3]

Although the only boat which can possibly be claimed as mesolithic in age—the one found many years ago under carse clay at Friarton brick-works, near Perth[4]—was a dug-out canoe, it is highly probable that the vessels used by the Larnians and Obanians of northern Ireland and Scotland on the open sea were made from skins stretched over a light frame. As Gjessing has recently emphasized,[5] boats of basic *umiak* type still exist " in a fairly homogeneous form throughout the arctic regions, from western Siberia to Greenland," and during the Stone Age extended certainly to west Norway and probably to the British Isles. A significant pointer is the survival of the tradition of skin-boat construction in the highland zone of Britain. For descriptions of the coracles, which existed during modern times over most of the region and which still survive locally on certain rivers of Wales and the Marches and on the Boyne near Oldbridge, the reader is referred to the published works of James Hornell.[6] The same author has given an admirable account of the sea-going curraghs, which survive, though no longer covered with skins of seal or even of ox, on the cost of Ireland from Donegal to Kerry. There is no doubt from the well-known references in classical authors[7] that keeled, skin-covered boats were used during pre-Roman times in connection with the Cornish tin-trade, and, as they continued to be in the days of the Saints, for passages between Ireland and Britain. Archæological indications of such frail craft are likely to be rare, but it is worth mentioning that around 1926 a contracted human skeleton was found in an oval basket in the clay of the Ancholme estuary; this may conceivably have been a coracle-burial.[8] The presence of sewn wooden boats in both Britain and Scandinavia during the prehistoric Iron Age (see p. 289), also points to a former widespread distribution of skin boats in the north. Most conclusively, as Gjessing recognized,[9] skin-boats are depicted on at least three groups of rock-engravings from the Arctic art-group of north-western Norway, at Forselv and Rødøy on the coast of Nordland and at Evenhus near Trondheim : the straightness of the keels and gunwales, the steepness of the prows and sterns and in particular the projecting ends of the top of the frame, clearly visible in profile on the Rødøy engraving (Pl. IV, b), confirm beyond reasonable doubt that skin-boats of basic *umiak* type were used during the Stone Age of the circumpolar zone of Europe.

The keeled skin-covered boat represents in effect a perfect adjustment in the sphere of sea-transport between an economy based to some extent on the pursuit of sea mammals and an ecology deficient in trees capable of providing the timber needed for solid dug-out canoes. The lightness of the boats and the ease with which they could be manœuvred, combined with their toughness and resistance to floating ice, made them ideal for hunting and there is no doubt that they were evolved primarily for pursuing seals and small whales. In this connection it is worth noting that on each of the three occasions, on which boats are

---

[3] J. G. D. Clark, 1936, 107 and Fig. 39. A paddle, with symmetrical blade, dated by pollen-analysis to a period contemporary with the middle Swedish dwelling-place culture, was found at Åkermyra, Hedemora parish, Dalarna (G. Lundquist, 1929).

[4] J. Geikie, 1879.

[5] G. Gjessing, 1942, 493–4.

[6] J. Hornell, 1946, and references.

[7] *op. cit.*, 112–16.

[8] Information from Mr C. W. Phillips. The object was destroyed by enemy action while in Hull Museum.   [9] G. Gjessing, 1936, 197.

depicted in the arctic art, whales are also shown and that on the Rödöy engraving seals are also represented.

Whether the boats reported by Ohthere to have been carried by the Finns " over land into the meers . . . then (to) make war on the Northmen " were of skin or bark, he does not say : we only know that they were " very little boats, and very light."[10] Although birch-bark was plentiful in the northern territories of Scandinavia and was admirably adapted for making boats, there is no indication that it was so used in this region either in ancient or modern times. Indeed, the only evidence one can cite for an early bark boat from Europe comes from Istorp in Västergotland,[11] well within the temperate zone. Some have hesitated to accept this as prehistoric, partly on account of its uniqueness and partly because of its state of preservation, but the vessel would be far more out of place in a recent or even in an early historical context than it would be in a prehistoric one and its survival is no more remarkable than the certainly older bark flooring, associated with Maglemosian material, in Aamosen, Denmark.[12] The vessel has been made from a single sheet of bark, described in the report as of beech or elm, but later identified as of spruce,[13] and a wooden framework of which the members were of blunted triangular section. The bark hull was sewn to the frame by thongs described as of juniper and leather slips had been inserted between them to prevent chafing.

The only class of boat to survive in any number from prehistoric Europe is the wooden dug-out canoe and specifically the primitive, trough-like (*trogförming*) kind hollowed out of a solid tree trunk. Such boats have come down to us so commonly partly because of their solidity, partly because they were used so largely on inland waters or estuaries and partly because of the long period over which they continued in use. Technically the dug-out became feasible with the appearance, during mesolithic times, of stone or flint-bladed axes capable of hollowing out and shaping tree trunks. The canoe, which according to Geikie came from under carse clay in the neighbourhood of Perth, and should therefore date from mesolithic times, was hollowed out from a pine stem. It is significant that the primitive type of dug-out extended during later times over much of the coniferous forest as well as abounding in the deciduous zone (Fig. 154). To the south the position is less definite, since physical conditions in the Mediterranean zone are not commonly favourable to the survival of early wooden boats. Dug-outs are mentioned by Strabo as being in use on the upper reaches of the Guadalquivir and in Lusitania,[14] and the Roman army, as depicted on Trajan's column, used them for pontoons,[15] but it does not appear probable that they were employed to anything like the same extent in this as in the temperate zone, the all-pervasive forests of which were rich in the most suitable kinds of tree.

In his survey of dug-out canoes in England and Wales, Fox observed that " the wood of which the canoes were hewn seems to have been almost invariably oak "[16] and Paret noted that out of sixty-two European examples, of which the material was identified, no less than fifty-eight were of oak, one each being of elm, poplar, Scottish fir and spruce or silver fir.[17]

---

[10] A. S. C. Ross, edtn. 1940.

[11] P. Humbla and L. von Post, 1937, 11.

[12] Demonstrated to the author in the field by Dr. Mathiassen in the summer of 1947.

[13] For this correction I have to thank Dr. N. Niklasson of Göteborg in answer to my queries.

[14] Strabo, III.2.3 and III.3.7.

[15] I. A. Richmond, 1935, 28.

[16] C. Fox, 1926, 131.

[17] O. Paret, 1930. For Finnish dug-outs see T. I. Itkonen, 1941.

But, as Troels-Smith has recently pointed out,[18] one should remember that such figures relate mainly to specimens preserved in museums, and these comprise examples chosen

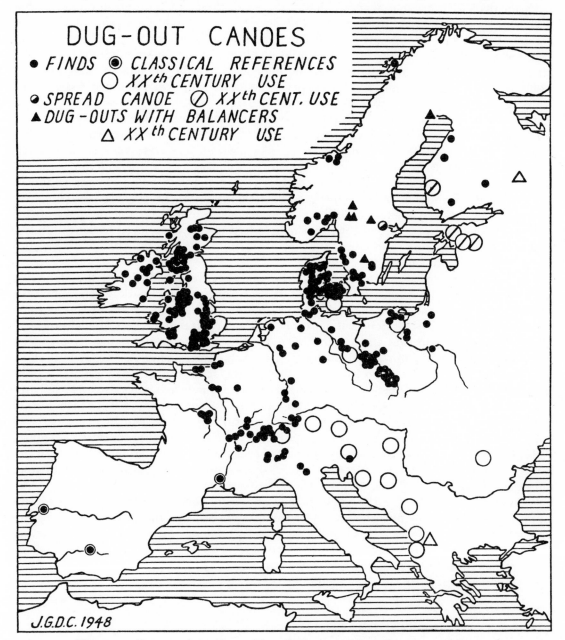

Fig. 154. Dug-out boats in prehistoric Europe with some recent survivals.

from a vastly greater number of discoveries; since on the whole they represent those which have survived most completely and offer the best chance of successful preservation, it

[18] J. Troels-Smith, 1946, 18.

stands to reason that most of them are of oak rather than of more perishable trees. It is notable, for instance, that of the fifteen dug-outs recovered from Aamosen in Sjælland between 1938–45 every one of those identified proved to be of alder, which though not so enduring was certainly easier to work. The essential fact remains, though, that dug-out canoes of the primitive type are normally hollowed out of substantial trunks of deciduous trees, which, growing as they did under wild conditions, were commonly of a length and straightness far beyond anything to be found in open parklands: the famous Brigg boat, for example, was 48 ft. 8 in. long and between 4 ft. and 5 ft. wide when found and showed no signs of side branches other than two or three small ones near the bows.[19]

By contrast the pod-like (*schotenförming*) dug-out with thin, spread walls, originally forced apart by wedges while filled with water and heated by fire, and supported against the external pressure of water by cross-pieces or ribs sewn on to cleats, were cut from comparatively slender trees like aspen and poplar.[20] Such canoes are found to-day in the northern parts of the deciduous forest, particularly in the east Baltic territories and in north-west Russia, among such peoples as the Esthonians, the Finno-Ougrians (Pl. XVI, a, b) and the Ostjaks. There is no direct archæological evidence for the antiquity of this type in Europe, but part of one cut from fir, and having cracks repaired by long splinters sewn on in the same way as in one of the North Ferriby boats, has been found on Swedish soil at Fiholm, Västmanland.[21]

The best evidence that dug-out canoes of the solid type were made during the Stone Age is the assemblage from Aamosen (Pl. XVI, c, d) each one of which has been referred on the evidence of pollen-analysis to the early or early-middle neolithic of Denmark.[22] Dug-outs have been recovered from stone age locations in the Federseemoor, in south Germany,[23] and from neolithic lakeside stations in Switzerland[24]; some of which latter have yielded wooden paddles with symmetrical blades.[25] Dug-outs found many years ago, but which may have been neolithic, came from a depth of 25 ft. at St. Enoch's Church, Glasgow[26] and from Erith marshes, Kent[27]; the former contained a polished stone axe and the latter a polished flint axe and flint scraper. The dug-out boat was one of those types which, having once come into existence, persisted throughout prehistoric times, and in many parts of northern, central and south-eastern Europe it survived down to the twentieth century. Indeed, as Mitzka has pointed out in the case of Germany, when dug-outs were given up, it was not because they were ineffective, but simply that under modern conditions they were too expensive to replace[28] by their own kind.

Even from the Stone Age the prows of dug-outs were sometimes carefully shaped and tapered, as illustrated by neolithic examples from Aamosen[29] and the Federsee.[30] A feature

---

[19] T. Sheppard, 1910, 36.

[20] I. Manninen, 1927, 11 ff. and 1932, 136–7 and 357–9; E. Nikkilä, 1947, 33–46.

[21] I. Manninen, 1927, 15.

[22] J. Troels-Smith, 1946, 16.

[23] O. Paret, 1930, 112.

[24] e.g. an example from Robenhausen, unfortunately not closely dated.

[25] e.g. from Egolzwil, Luzern (Luzern Mus.) and from St. Aubin, Bouldry, Neuchâtel (Neuchâtel Mus.).

[26] D. Wilson, 1863, 52–3.

[27] C. Fox, 1926, 127.

[28] W. Mitzka, 1933, 12.

[29] e.g. J. Troels-Smith, 1946, Fig. 1.

[30] O. Paret, 1930, 112.

which seems first to have appeared, at least in a developed form, during the Late Bronze Age, at a time when the increasing range and cheapness of metal tools were leading to comparable developments in the sphere of coopering, was the separate stern-board set into a groove in the hull. The device, which is admirably seen in the Brigg boat, is also present on examples from the Federsee[31] and from Clifton on the Trent (Pl. I, e),[32] both dated more or less securely to this time. Another feature seen on the Clifton and on many other British and continental dug-outs is the presence of ridges left in the solid at intervals along the floor of the hull. As both Paret and Hornell[33] have pointed out, these can hardly have reinforced the hulls to any worthwhile extent, since they cross the grain of the wood. Hornell's idea that these ridges recapitulate the ribs of the framework of the bark canoes, from which, largely on account of the ridges themselves, the dug-outs are held to be descended, loses much of its force from the fact that the ridges on the prehistoric boats from Europe are confined to the floor. It seems more likely that the ridges were left to provide foot-holds for the paddlers and others who used the craft or to give clearance to floor planks.

As regards the uses to which dug-outs were put in prehistoric Europe, it is noteworthy that where they have survived up till modern times on the lakes of central Europe—on the Bavarian Ammersee and Starnbergersee, the Swiss Aegerisee, the Austrian Attersee and Mondsee and the Hungarian Plattensee, for example[34]—it has normally been for fishing and particularly for net-fishing. On the other hand, where settlements were sited on the margins of lakes or on small islands, artificial or natural, dug-outs must also have been vital for communication. Thus, around a dozen were found within the late bronze age limits of the Federsee, including three within the outer palisade of the Wasserburg Buchau (see Fig. 84). Again, most of those recorded by Robert Munro from Scotland were found in more or less close association with iron age crannogs and it is certain that vessels of this kind were used to carry the stones and other materials from which these artificial islands were actually constructed.[35] Some of the finest and largest dug-outs have been recovered from the beds of flood-plains of rivers like the Thames, the Severn, the Trent or the Clyde, to mention only some from Britain. Many of these, it is reasonable to assume, served for long distance transport up and down the rivers, which were main arteries of internal trade at the time.

In the absence of bridges, others may have served as ferries at points where important lines of movement crossed the courses of rivers too deep to ford. In this connection it is significant that the Brigg boat was found close to the point where the flood plain of the Ancholme was crossed by a timber trackway.[36] The boats from North Ferriby indicate pretty certainly a ferry across the Humber estuary between the Lincolnshire Edge and the Yorkshire Wolds towards the end of the Early Iron Age, though these were of sewn plank construction. Especially when draft animals had begun to come into use for transport, the need for something more stable than a single dug-out hull must have been felt. In parts of eastern Europe from Russia[37] to Albania[38] one could see until recently how this

[31] *ibid.*, abb. 5, No. 2.
[32] C. W. Phillips, 1941.
[33] O. Paret, 1930, 113–14 and J. Hornell, 1946, 187.
[34] W. Mitzka, 1933, 60; K. Brunner, 1903, 1 and 10–11; L. Rütimeyer, 1924, 307.
[35] R. Munro, 1882, *passim*.
[36] E. V. and C. W. Wright, 1947, 128 and map (Fig. 1).
[37] D. Zelenin, 1927, 143 and abb. 89.
[38] P. Traeger, 1904, 28 and Fig. 7.

was achieved by using pairs of dug-outs. These were joined with a space between by driving crossbars into holes cut through projections from the stern and sometimes through the solid prow or by fixing cross-timbers to the upper surfaces of either end of the dug-out. In such a craft one could, for example, ferry horses, with the forelegs in one hull and the hind ones in the other. Paired dug-outs certainly existed in Sweden—a hull with a laterally perforated stern-projection has been found in Västergotland[39] and one with a slot cut across the stern to hold a cross-piece comes from Ocklebo, Gästrikland[40]—and several examples with slots of this type, clearly distinguished from those designed to hold stern-boards, which were set into the floor of the hull, have been recovered from Kosel on the Oder in Silesia.[41] It is possible that the pair of dug-outs recently found side by side in the Trent near Clifton and probably of late bronze age date[42] may once have been joined to form a ferry.

Archæology can throw no direct light on the question how far dug-out boats were used at sea, since the vessels which have survived are naturally those which plied on inland waters. It has been claimed, though, that the bronze age rock-engravings of south Sweden depict large dug-outs with outrigger attachments, which would make them seaworthy. Elgström and Kaudern each argue that what is usually interpreted as a projecting keel is really a representation of an outrigger and its attachments seen in silhouette.[43] While admitting that this offers one possible interpretation of selected examples of these schematic, and from many points of view, enigmatic engravings, one may urge first that outriggers are notably absent from the folk tradition of Europe or of contiguous parts of Africa or Asia, despite the intense conservatism of boat-construction. Examples cited by Hallström[44] are no more than stabilizers, timbers pegged directly to the side of the hull, which is always small and narrow, suitable for one or two men: such stabilizers or balancers were made necessary by the use of narrow timbers and the type is characteristically found on the margins of the deciduous forest, as on Lake Ochrida[45] near the junction of Albania, Yugoslavia and Greece and in middle Sweden,[46] or beyond, like the outlier at Raneå in Norbotten.[47] Again, more positively, it may be emphasized that the projecting keel is on the contrary well established as a feature of European boat-construction in early times. Not only had it been adopted by the Cretans by Early and Middle Minoan times[48]—presumably to lessen the shock to the hull incurred by rowing boats hard on to the shore, as was the practice in Homeric times—but, even more to the point, the Hjortspring boat shows that the projecting keel was known to the boat-builders of the west Baltic area at least by the Pre-Roman Iron Age.

---

[39] Humbla and von Post, 1937, Fig. 5B.

[40] *ibid.*, Fig. 4.

[41] O. Paret, 1930, abb. 19, 4.

[42] According to C. W. Phillips, 1941, 133–4, the dredger cut through many wooden stakes jokingly referred to as a " skittle alley "! This could as well have been part of a staithe as of a dwelling. Although the prows were damaged the boats were of approximately equal length (*c.* 28 or 30 feet).

[43] O. Elgström, 1924; W. Kaudern, 1924.

[44] G. Hallström, 1925.

[45] P. Traeger, 1904, Figs. 13–14.

[46] *ibid.*, Figs. 46, 47 and 51, etc.; P. Humbla, 1937, 14 and Fig. 3.

[47] G. Hallström, 1925A, 60–2, Fig. 51. State Hist. Mus. No. 17652.

[48] S. Marinatos, 1933, 215–16.

To judge from its cargo of shields and weapons, the boat deposited in the Hjortspring bog on the Danish island of Als was a war canoe.[49] Of light construction and narrow form —10 m. long within the hull and less than 2 m. wide—it was evidently built for speed. The bottom plank had no keel, but was slightly concave admidships. At either end it tapered, the concavity passing into a deep and narrowing groove, which ultimately disappeared in ram-like projections extending beyond the hull at stern and prow. Although it is perfectly true that the precise extent and character of these projections is not certainly known, their relevance to the rock-engravings (Fig. 155) must surely be accepted, despite Althin's demur.[50] The five thin lime planks, one for the floor and two for each wall, over-sailed one another clinker-fashion and were sewn together by bast cords, the interstices being caulked with resin. (Pl. I, d). Ten rows of raised cleats were left standing on the inner face of the planks and to them transverse ribs, forming an inserted frame, were secured by means of bast cords. The lack of any provision for holding oars in position on the gunwales argues for the use of paddles and further emphasizes the canoe-like character of the vessel. There

Fig. 155. Rock-engravings of boats with projecting keels : South Sweden.

can be no doubt that the Hjortspring boat was inspired by the skin boats, which since the Stone Age had provided the chief indigenous means of transport over the open seas of northern and north-western Europe.

On the other hand, there are indications that boats of considerable beam, and presumably of timber plank construction, had come into use in northern waters already before the end of the Bronze Age. The most striking evidence of this is to be found in the stone grave-settings in the form of broad, beamy vessels which first appeared in Gotland and Halland during the Late Bronze Age (per. V) and continued into the beginning of the Iron Age.[51] Closely similar proportions are shown by the small votive models of boats made from thin

[49] G. Rosenberg, 1937; Shetelig and Falk, 1937, 346–7; Brøndsted, 1938, III, 30–7.

[50] C.-A. Althin, 1945, 49.

[51] B. Schnittger, 1920; Shetelig and Falk, 1937, 151 and Pl. 24; C. -A. Althin, 1945, 49 f.

gold sheet (Fig. 156), a hundred or so of which were found in a pot under a stone at Nors in northern Thy.[52]

The earliest vessel of this class to survive at all completely[53] is the famous boat from Nydam in south Jutland dating from the fourth century A.D.[54]   It was substantially larger and beamier than the Hjortspring canoe and was propelled by fifteen pairs of oars instead of by paddles. Structurally it stands between the Hjortspring canoe and the sailing ships of the Viking age. The medial plank shows only an incipient keel and must have remained a weak feature. The side strakes, now increased to five in number, were built up in clinker

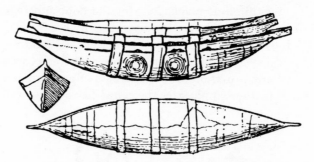

Fig. 156.   Small votive models of boats made from gold sheet :
Nors, Thy, Denmark (c. $\frac{2}{3}$)

fashion, but were fastened to one another by iron rivets instead of being sewn. On the other hand the frame, comprising ribs joined by cross-thwarts, continued to be sewn to cleats, now reduced to two on each strake instead of three, in conformity with the narrowing of the planks. Later progress in the north cannot be treated here, but it is worth emphasizing that the clinker tradition in which Scandinavian shipwrights continued to work originated among the prehistoric peoples of the north.

Another group of sewn plank boats, quite distinct because carvel-built, has recently been recognized in eastern England. It comprises two examples from the foreshore at North Ferriby, evidently used as ferries across the Humber estuary, and another near the Brigg dug-out in the Ancholme valley.[55] The better preserved of the Ferriby boats is estimated to have been approximately 15·35 m. long by 2.60 m. broad (Fig. 157). The bottom was made of three stout oak planks, one of which, though about twice as thick as the others, showed no sign of a projecting middle keel ; this middle plank was made up of two pieces joined together by a short scarf amidships and one of the side ones had a piece inserted along one edge (Fig. 158). The planks were presumably first sewn together by the yew withes, remains of which were found in the ingeniously and accurately con-trived holes; then the holes were plugged by pounded wood and the seams caulked with moss, and, lastly, oak laths were pushed under the stitches to tighten these and seal the seams.

---

[52] Brøndsted (1938, II, 173–4) includes these in the Late Bronze Age. It has been suggested that they ought to be referred to a later period on account of the type of boat, but the recognition that stone-settings of the same form go back to the Late Bronze Age in Sweden has destroyed the basis of this criticism.

[53] Undated fragments of a boat of similar type, but with the strakes still sewn by cords, were found at Halsnø near Bergen (*Bergens Mus. Aarb.* 1903).

[54] Shetelig and Johannessen, 1930; Shetelig and Falk, 1937, 353 f.

[55] E. V. and C. W. Wright, 1947.

Only part of one of the side planks survived, but from the number and disposition of the stitch-holes on the upturned ends of the keel-plank it is evident that originally there must have been three on each side. The method of fitting the planks together must, when allowance is made for the swelling of the timbers in water, have made the hull at once watertight and resilient. The problem is rather to see how the builders secured the bracing necessary for so large a vessel. The floor planks were apparently stiffened in four places by pairs of bars passed transversely through raised and laterally-perforated cleats, but the

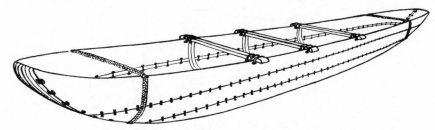

Fig. 157. Reconstruction of boat from North Ferriby, Yorkshire.
(*After E. V. and C. W. Wright*)

a   b

Fig. 158. Seams of boat I, North Ferriby, Yorkshire.
(*a*) Outer bottom plank and side-strake.
(*b*) Keel plank and outer bottom plank.
(*After E. V. and C. W. Wright*).

cross-thwarts shown in the reconstruction (Fig. 159) are to a large extent speculative. The high standard of craftsmanship exhibited by these ferry-boats shows that there must have been a school of shipwrights in eastern Britain during the latter part of the Pre-Roman Iron Age rivalling those of Scandinavia.

It is noteworthy, though, that from neither of these centres of maritime activity is there sound evidence for the use of sails during prehistoric times. In the Mediterranean region the sail was of great antiquity. Sailing vessels, for instance, plied on the Nile during the Predynastic period of Egypt. The ships which carried the trade of Minoans and Mycenæans also used sails, but it should be remembered that, since early navigators were unable to tack or sail close to the wind, they were compelled to rely mainly on oars. Since our main sources of information about the boats of the second millenium in the Mediterranean are representations on such objects as gems or seals, or small and imperfect models, extremely little is known about the details of their construction.[56] There is no question, though, that at favourable times of the year ships from the east Mediterranean were able to visit the islands and shores of the western basin. Indeed, the distribution of the most elaborate types of passage-grave at intervals along the sea ways to France and Britain suggests that wooden ships of comparatively advanced type passed through the Straits of Gibraltar and explored the Atlantic coasts of western Europe. Engravings on the stones of Manélud,

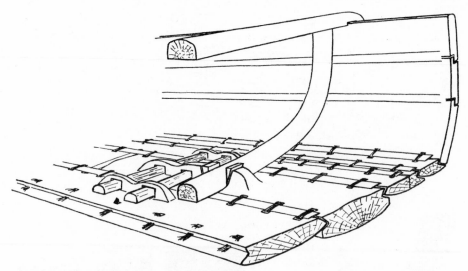

Fig. 159. Reconstruction showing possible method of bracing the hull of boat I from North Ferriby, Yorkshire. (*After E. V. and C. W. Wright*).

Locmariaquer, Morbihan, have indeed been treated as representations of ships and Ekholm has gone so far as to accept them as prototypes of those found on the Swedish rock-engravings; but such signs are enigmatic and should be treated with the caution and reserve accorded them by Déchelette.[57] This only serves to emphasize how little is known about the sea-going ships of the western seas during the second or even the first millenium B.C., active though these must have been. Some of the few seagoing vessels of the Atlantic coasts of which there is certain knowledge are those of the Veneti, mariners of the Vannes region, who may well have controlled the tin trade with Cornwall and were defeated by Caesar for disputing his passage to Britain. Their vessels were constructed, so we are told by Strabo.[58]

" with broad bottoms and high poops and prows, on account of the tides. They are built of the wood of the oak, of which there is great abundance. On this account, instead of of fitting the planks close together, they leave interstices between them; these they fill with seaweed to prevent the wood from drying up in dock for want of moisture; for the seaweed is damp by nature, but the oak dry and arid. . . . The sails are made of leather to resist the violence of the winds, and managed by chains instead of cables.''

[56] S. Marinatos, 1933.
[57] G. Ekholm, 1916; Déchelette, I (1924), 610 f.; C. -A. Althin, 1945, 156 ff., abb. 85.
[58] Strabo, IV.4.1. Hamilton and Falconers' transl., 1852.

MOVEMENT OVER SNOW : CIRCUMPOLAR ZONE

During prehistoric times the margins of the temperate deciduous forest and of the farming economy that went with it formed an important divide in the realm of land transport. Wheeled vehicles, like agriculture, first began to penetrate favoured parts of the coniferous zone during the historical period. Over vast territories of tundra and birch and pine forest from northern Scandinavia across into Russia the only means of travel or transport over land were sliding devices such as sledges and skis. These were adapted at the same time to an economy based on hunting and seasonal movement and to a climate in which snow covered the ground for an appreciable part of the year. It will be seen from the map (Fig. 160) that the distribution of sledge-runners and skis dating from the period before the middle of the first millenium A.D. is confined to the coniferous zone and with few exceptions to territories having a period of snow-cover of upwards of 150 days during the year. A further point of interest is that the woods of this zone provided materials particularly well suited for making such devices. This applies especially to skis, for which the compression wood of pine from the outer curve of crooked trees was particularly favourable.[59] Except for the two most southerly Norwegian skis, those from Øvrebø and Finsland in Vest Agder, both of which were made from oak,[60] all the prehistoric skis of northern Europe appear to have been of pine wood.

Before describing the winter travelling gear of the Arctic hunter-fishers, a word may be said about the nature of the evidence. Apart from a limited number of rock-engravings, this comprises in the main the runners of sledges and skis discarded in bogs and preserved owing to the dampness of the deposits in which they were found. The degrees to which they have survived varied no doubt according to local conditions and it must be remembered that most were probably damaged before being abandoned. Moreover, the fact that as a rule only runners were discarded in localities where they would be likely to survive means that in the case of sledges the character of the superstructure is generally a matter for conjecture. Again, so far as the early undecorated runners are concerned, the possibility of dating them rests almost entirely upon pollen-analysis. Fortunately they generally occur in localities where fossil pollen is well preserved and the fact that they are light in weight and found their way into the bogs casually means that they are likely to be discovered at their true level in the sequence of natural deposits. Again, it is fortunate that Scandinavians have been pioneers in the application of pollen-analysis and that great trouble has been taken to verify the levels of objects, which in the nature of things are almost invariably found by chance. Their consistency engenders confidence in the results obtained by palæo-botanists in this field, though it should be remembered that the archæological correlations in the literature are nearly always those obtained in the zone of farming economy in southern Scandinavia and care must be used in applying these to the northern territories.

Dealing first with sledges, to judge from the runners three main types were used in prehistoric Europe. The oldest is represented by a small number of heavy runners from Finland, hollowed out along the whole or the greater part of their length and with the side walls perforated at intervals in opposite pairs. Those which could be dated were both

---

[59] Berg *et al.*, 1941, 44 f.

[60] Øvrebø : N. Lid, 1930 and G. Berg *et al.*, 1941, 26 and Fig. 9 : Finsland (Hoenemyr) ; N. Lid, 1937, 19–21.

mesolithic, that from Heinola (Fig. 161)[61] being referred to the time of the Ancylus lake and that from Saarijärvi[62] to that of the early Litorina sea. A modified version from Alatornio,[63] in which the sides were cut away between the perforations, leaving a series of ears at intervals along either edge, has been dated to the latter half of the second millenium B.C. There has been some debate about the function of these runners. U. T. Sirelius and Gosta Berg,[64] indeed, interpreted them as the keels of single-runner sledges with the sides built up boat-wise by planks, like those used by the ski-shod Lapps of modern times for winter travel and hunting. More recently, though, Itkonen[65] has argued convincingly in favour of their having belonged to sledges with two runners and platforms raised above the slush and snow on supports, and it is a fact that so far no skis have yet been found from the time of the Heinola and Saarijärvi runners.

The second type of built-up sledge, Berg's Gråträsk and Itkonen's Kuortane type, is represented by a substantial number of finds and is altogether better documented. The runners are easily distinguished by their medial groove and by the complex series of holes on the upper surface, in which the wooden uprights of the platform were set and through which the bracing cords were passed (Fig. 162). An excellent idea of the appearance of these sledges is given by Itkonen's reconstruction, though it is certain that the side posts were sometimes taller than he allows, since those found with a runner at Gorbunowa,

---

SCHEDULE OF FINDS SHOWN ON FIG. 160.

Skis

A. Pudasjärvi (Itkonen, 1936, 71; 1941, 41); B. Muhos (Itkonen, 1938, 13; 1941, 41); C. Viitasaari (Itkonen, 1937, 72-4; Okkola, 1945, 258-61); D. Hämeenkyröl (Itkonen, 1937, 74); E. Riihimäki (Auer, 1928, 86-8; Itkonen, 1937, 72); F. Bodan, Norsjö; G. Arvträsk, Lycksele; H. Åmsele, Degerfors; I. Kalvträsk, Burträsk; J. Fäbodtjälen, Burträsk; K. Anumark, Umeå; L. Brattsbacka, Nordmaling (F-L, Berg et al., 1941); M. Lomsjökullen, Vilhelmina (Manker, 1946 and 1947); N. Storbäck, Dorotea; O. Hoting, Tåsjö; P. Sörviken, Sundsjö; Q. Arnäs, Älvdalen; R. Färnäs, Mora (N-R, Berg et al., 1941); S. Steinhaugmo, Hemnes (Lid inf.); T. Kveberg, Alvadal (Lid, 1937, 15 f.); U. Furnes (Lid, 1937, 13 and 1938); V. Øvrebø (Lid, 1930 and 1937, 19); W. Heonemyr, Finland (Lid, 1937, 20-1).

Sledge-runners

1. Salla (Itkonen, 1938, 21; 1941, 42); 2. Alatornio (Itkonen, 1936, 77; 1941, 42); 3. Kuusamo (Itkonen, 1936, 78; 1941, 42); 4. Evijärvi (Itkonen, 1931-2); 5. Pielavesi (Luho, 1945; Okkola, 1945, 266); 6. Ylistaro (Sirelius, 1913, 14 and 1928, 949; Itkonen, 1931-2, 62); 7. Kuortane (Itkonen, 1931-2); 8. Saarijärvi (Itkonen, 1938, 25); 9. Heinola (Itkonen, 1934, 10; Aario, 1934); 10. Gråträsk; 11. Storholmen, Stensele; 12. Malgonäset, Vilhelmina; 13. Siksele, Lycksele; 14. Botesflon, Hammerdal; 15. Ragunda; 16. Delsbo (10-16, Berg, 1935, 36, n. 2 et passim); 17. V. Nyasen, Ovanaker (Berg. inf.).

---

[61] T. I. Itkonen, 1934, 10, Fig. 5A; L. Aario, 1934.
[62] Itkonen, 1938, 25 f., Fig. 6.
[63] Itkonen, 1936, 77 f., Fig. 5A; 1941, 42.
[64] U. T. Sirelius, 1913, 14 and 1928, 949; G. Berg, 1935, 15-18 and 34.
[65] Itkonen, 1938, 26 ff.

Fig. 160. Prehistoric skis and sledge-runners from Norway, Finland and Sweden.

Only specimens dated by pollen-analysis to a period earlier than 500 A.D. are shown. Examples dated to a period contemporary with the Stone Age in southern Scandinavia are marked by an oblique stroke.

NOTE. The zone of temperate deciduous forest is shaded obliquely. The stippled line marks the southern margin of the territory having 150 days or more of snow cover during the year.

west of Tobolsk,[66] were as much as 52.5 cm. long.   The sledges are so substantial—the Kuortane runner, for instance, was over 10 feet (317·5 cm.) long—that Sirelius at one time

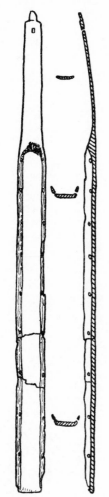

Fig. 161.   Stone Age Sledge Runner from Heinola, Finland. (*After Itkonen*). (l. 3.8 metres)

maintained that they must have been drawn by reindeer. Apart, though, from the lack of evidence that reindeer had been tamed for traction so early as this, Kai Donner has since pointed out that in the Urals equally heavy loads are drawn by dogs and Sirelius has latterly accepted that the Kuortane sledges were probably dog-drawn.[67]   The oldest representative of the type is the forepart of a runner from Ylistaro[68] in Finland found in clay dating from an early part of the Litorina stage of the Baltic, but there are a fair number which can be referred to the Arctic Stone Age.   These include finds from Gråträsk and Ragunda[69] in Norbotten and Jämtland and from Kuortane[70] and Evijärvi[71] in Finland. Geographically the range of the type extends to the Tagil district of the Urals, where it is associated with pottery from the beginning of the local Bronze Age,[72] and beyond to Gorbunowa between Yekaterinenburg and Tjumen, west of Tobolsk.[73]   The distribution of this particular type of sledge is only one of many lines of evidence serving to emphasize the unity of the Arctic Stone Age over its extensive territory,[74] of which indeed the sledges themselves were a main condition, permitting as they did a wide range of winter movement.

In the third and most recent type of built-up sledge from prehistoric Europe, the Swedish Morjärv type,[75] the runners and the horizontal side-rails of the platform formed the main structural elements and the vertical side-posts were few in number and comparatively unimportant (Fig. 163).   Sledges of this kind were light and were intended to be hauled by a line attached to a harness over the left shoulder of a man shod with skis.   As a rule the runners are narrower than those of the Gråträsk type and are convex on the under face.   The results of pollen-analysis show that the Morjärv type first came into use at the transition from the Late Bronze to the Early Iron Ages, as witness finds from Lycksele in north Sweden and Pielavesi in Finland[76]; on the other hand, the majority of the dated finds belong to the first millenium A.D.

As regards the keel-planks of the single-runner sledges or *ackjas* of the kind used by ski-shod hunters, the earliest examples of these, if we agree to exclude the heavy runners discussed in our first

[66] G. Berg, 1935, 39.   [67] Sirelius, 1916, 14–18, 35 and 1928, 953.

[68] Sirelius, 1913, 14, Fig. 2; 1928, 949.

[69] G. Berg, 1935, Chap. II.

[70] Itkonen, 1930, Fig. 2A2.

[71] Itkonen, 1932, Fig. 2B.

[72] Itkonen, 1932, 62.   [73] Berg, 1935, 39.

[74] Pointed out by G. Gjessing (1944), who however neglected snow sliding equipment as a factor in maintaining this.

[75] Berg, 1935, 44 f.

[76] Lycksele : Berg, 1935, 46. Pielavesi (Joutsenniemi) ; T. Okkola, 1945, 266 and V. Luho, 1945.

group, is that from Lappajärvi in south Österbotten,[77] which dates from the period of the Bronze Age in south-west Finland. A specimen from Haapavesi,[78] also in Finland, probably belongs to the historical period.

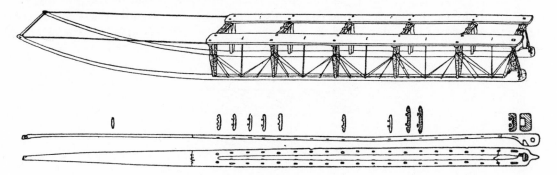

Fig. 162. Runner from Kuortane, Finland, and reconstruction of Gråträsk-Kuortane type sledge. (*After Itkonen*).

(l. 3.17 metres).

The skis recovered from the northern bogs[79] belong to several different types and these can be distinguished most easily in the first instance by noting the manner of securing the

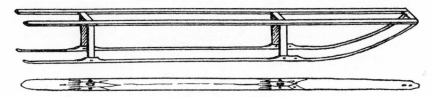

Fig. 163. Runner from Morjärv, Sweden, and reconstruction of sledge.
(*After Berg*).

(l. 1.86 metres)

skier's foot. The chief division is that between the more primitive types (Fig. 164, Nos. 1 and 2) and those with a raised foot-rest laterally perforated for the straps (Nos. 3–7). The Swedish investigator K. B. Wiklund[80] distinguished two main classes of primitive ski, the " Southern " ski, in which the foot rests in a hollow between two raised side-pieces, and the " Arctic " or " Northern " ski, to which the foot was secured by loops passed through the thickness of the runner itself.

The Arctic ski, short and broad and generally tapered in front and squared behind, has been used in modern times over a vast territory from Finnmark in northern Norway right

[77] Okkola, 1945, 266–7.

[78] Itkonen, 1938, 3 and 1941, 42.

[79] The leading references are G. Berg *et al.*, 1941 (Sweden), N. Lid, 1937 (Norway) and T. I. Itkonen, 1937 (Finland). For further references see footnotes 80–96 and the legend to Fig. 160. More general references include F. Nansen, 1890, Vol. I, Chap. III, and O. T. Mason, 1894.

[80] K. B. Wiklund, 1931.

across northern Eurasia to Behring Strait, among such folk as Lapps, Ostiaks, Woguls and even the Ainu of Japan. It is primarily a hunting-ski and to make it slide as noiselessly as possible, the under surface is often covered by hairy skin, a reminder, as the Norwegian, Nils Lid, has pionted out,[81] of a possible origin in the fur-shoe. Proof that skis of this type were already in use during the Stone Age of northern Europe is given by the discovery of a pair, one of them fragmentary, and an accompanying stick at Kalvträsk in Västerbotten,

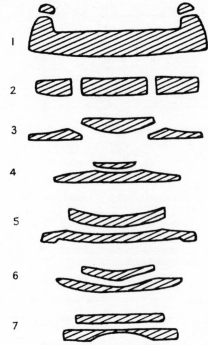

Fig. 164. Sections of main ski-types from circumpolar Europe. (*After Berg*).

north Sweden, which can be referred to this period on the evidence of pollen-analysis.[82] A detail worth noting in the better preserved ski (Fig. 165, No. 2) is that the tapered end shows signs of having split and been repaired in antiquity. The main function of the stick was, of course, to help steer, but to judge from Lapp analogies the spatulate end was designed for such purposes as scooping melted snow from a rill for drinking or removing frozen lumps from travelling gear. Additional evidence for the early use of skis, almost certainly of this type, among the stone age people of the far north is provided by the rock-engravings. At Zalavrouga on the river Vyg, which flows into the White Sea, phallic figures are depicted mounted on skis and grasping sticks and a bowman, also on skis, is shown apparently in pursuit of an elk (Fig. 166).[83] Again, Gjessing[84] was almost certainly right in interpreting

[81] N. Lid, 1937, 7.
[82] Berg *et al.*, 1941, 19–20, No. 21.
[83] W. J. Raudonikas, 1938, Pl. 4, Nos. 28–30; Pl. 5, Nos. 14, 15; Pl. 12, Nos. 169–172.
[84] G. Gjessing, 1936, 5–10.

some engravings at Rödöy on the coast of north-west Norway as skiers, although Hallström has argued[85] that they portray paddlers standing in canoes.

Whereas the Arctic ski is adapted for use where hardened snow lies long on the ground, the Southern type is particularly suitable for loose heavy snow, such as is commonly experienced in regions with a shorter period of snow-cover. It remains in use, or was in comparatively recent use, over a broad belt of Russia from a line between the upper Pechora river and the gulf of Finland in the north to the middle Volga and the Dnieper in the south; in the East Baltic countries, especially Latvia and mainland Esthonia; in south

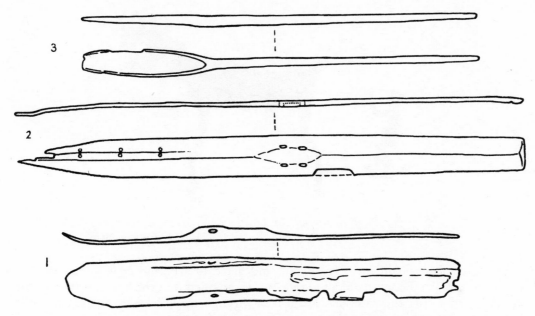

Fig. 165. Stone Age ski-ing gear from circumpolar Europe ($\frac{1}{10}$).

No. 1. " Southern " ski from Riihimaki, South Tavastland, Finland. (*After Itkonen*)

Nos. 2, 3. " Arctic," ski and stick from Kalvträsk, Burträsk, Västerbotten, Sweden.

(*After Berg*).

Sweden as far north as the boundary between Göta- and Svea-land; and in the warm coastal tract of north-west Norway. The survival of this primitive type in south Sweden is no doubt due to the subsidiary role played by skis in this area: they are used mainly for crossing from one building to another and served rather like highly specialized clogs; in origin, indeed, it is held by Nils Lid[86] that " they actually bear the same relation to wooden shoes as the Northern fur-covered ski-type does to fur shoes." The Southern ski can likewise be traced back to the Late Stone Age, though so far examples from early deposits have only been recovered from Finland. The classic find is the damaged ski from Riihimäki in southern Finland (Fig. 165, No. 1),[87] dated by pollen-analysis to a slightly later period than the Kalvträsk find, though still within the Stone Age of the region.

---

[85] G. Hallström, 1938, 184–91.

[86] N. Lid, 1937, 8.

[87] V. Auer, 1928, 86–8; Itkonen, 1937, 72.

The first skis with built-up foot-rests were those with flat sliding-surfaces (Fig. 164, No. 4), characteristic of the northernmost provinces of Finland and Sweden. The oldest specimen, a fragment from Hoting in Angermanland, has been referred to a period equivalent to that of the passage-graves in southern Scandinavia[88]; and two at least from each country have been dated to the period of the Bronze Age, namely those from Hämeenkyrö[89] and Muhos[90] in Finland, and from Storbäck and Fäbodtjälen in north Sweden.[91] What may represent either an evolutionary link between this and the Arctic ski or alternatively a product of contact between users of the two, is the specimen recently published by

Fig. 166. Rock-engraving of bowman mounted on skis and pursuing elk : Zalavrouga, N.W. Russia (c. $\frac{1}{9}$) (*After Raudonikas*).

Manker[92] from Lomsjökullen in Lappland, and dated to a period contemporary with the Early Bronze Age in the south : a raised foot-rest is provided, but the holes for the toe-straps, instead of perforating this laterally, are driven through the thickness of the runner from either side of the rest (Fig. 164, No. 3).

The Bothnic type proper, as defined by Berg, with slightly concave foot-rest and definitely convex sliding-surface (Fig. 164, No. 6), does not appear on present evidence to have come into use until early in the present era. Finds from the first part of the first millenium A.D. include a damaged pair of skis from Arvträsk in Lappland and a fragment from Bodan in Västerbotten.[93] Like the type with flat sliding-surfaces, which it otherwise closely resembles, the Bothnic ski is characteristic of the most northerly provinces of Finland and Sweden.

Further south is the territory of Gosta Berg's Scandic type, with foot-rest and lists on either edge of the under surface of the runner, designed probably to make it easier to stem on slopes and to assist in steering (Fig. 164, No. 5). To judge from the pollen-dating of fragments from Arnäs in Darlarna and from Sörviken in Jämtland,[94] this type of ski had already come into use by the time of the Bronze Age in south Scandinavia. A damaged ski

---

[88] Berg *et al.*, 1941, No. 25.

[89] Itkonen, 1937, 74.

[90] Itkonen, 1938, 13.

[91] Berg *et al.*, 1941, Nos. 10 and 20.

[92] E. Manker, 1946.

[93] Berg *et al.*, 1941, Nos. 9 and 19.

[94] *ibid.*, Nos. 34 and 32.

dating from the last centuries before Christ has the grooves characteristic of the Scandic with the foot attachments typical of the Southern type of ski and may indicate contact between users of the two kinds. It has sometimes been argued, and Nils Lid regards it as evident,[95] that the Scandic type gave rise, through a reduction in the width of the runner and a coalescing of the edge grooves, to the ski with strong steering groove in the middle of the under surface (Fig. 164, No. 7). The chronological evidence is certainly consistent with this view, since grooved skis as a group come latest in the series: indeed, with the exception of the front part of a runner from Övrebö in south-west Norway, referred to the Late Bronze Age on the evidence of pollen-analysis,[96] no examples appear to have survived from before the early medieval period.

The earliest skates[97] were made from long bones—most commonly the metacarpals of horse and ox—smoothed on the under-surface and cut away on the upper. Sometimes they were perforated at either end to secure thongs for the feet, but this was not always done. The up-turned end of the foot-rest must have given some purchase to a skilled user and it should be remembered that, to judge from Olaus Magnus' illustration, iron-shod staves were a material aid whether passed between the legs or pressed to one side of the skater. It was once claimed that bone skates were used as early as the Late Stone Age, but Robert Munro's rejection of these has been confirmed by the results of scientific excavation. The exploration of sites like Birka has shown that they had come into use by the Viking period and it would seem that during medieval times they spread over a wide extent of northern Europe, in the folk culture of which they survived down to the recent past.

OVERLAND TRAFFIC : MEDITERRANEAN AND TEMPERATE ZONES

How far sleds of the type still found in mountainous parts of the continent were used in Mediterranean and temperate Europe during the prehistoric period it is not easy to say. No actual traces of such appear to have been recognized, but it is possible that the barred triangles depicted in " chalcolithic " rock-paintings in the Spanish province of Badajoz were intended, as Breuil has supposed, to represent sliding vehicles.[98] However this may be, the most striking developments in these zones were the introduction and adoption of wheeled-vehicles and of horse-riding. The archæological evidence for each of these is both slight and difficult to interpret. It is slight because objects connected with land transport, though in special cases, such as chariots, they might be buried with the dead, did not survive in the ordinary way like dug-out canoes in lacustrine or riverine deposits; and difficult to interpret because the metal parts, the only ones as a rule to come down to us, mostly belong to vehicles especially concerned with war or cult. Indeed, it is precisely the vehicles of daily use which disappear most completely. A main problem is to know how much can legitimately be deduced about these from the vehicles or parts of vehicles of different status, which survive. As a working rule it seems legitimate to infer a knowledge of wheeled vehicles among communities in which waggons or wheeled models featured in cults, since such a cult would hardly have spread among people without this any more than it could originally have developed among such. Again, it is reasonable to think that a people addicted to the use of the chariot in war would have maintained wheelwrights of

---

[95] N. Lid, 1937, 15.
[96] N. Lid, 1930.
[97] R. Munro, 1894; H. Vilppula, 1940.
[98] H. Breuil, 1917.

their own. On the other hand, mere knowledge of how to make wheeled vehicles would not have ensured the adoption of such in daily life unless general economic conditions were favourable for their use and the problem remains how to decide the extent to which this in fact occurred. Even more difficult is it to estimate the importance of wheeled vehicles in the day-to-day life of societies, in which they were used neither for cult nor for war and from the surviving material equipment of which they might in consequence have vanished completely.

It is generally accepted that oxen were yoked to ploughs before they were used to draw vehicles by the same means, and as already stated, it is doubtful whether the traction plough came into use in any part of Europe before the Bronze Age. On the other hand, it has been claimed that the corded-ware people, whose migrations were a feature of the late neolithic period in parts of central and northern Europe, owed their mobility in some measure to the use of the horse. There can be no doubt that among many groups of these people the horse had been domesticated, but it by no means follows that they used horses for transport; their mobility by contrast with more settled agriculturalists was, after all, only comparative and need not imply a speed of movement more rapid than walking; again, they may well have kept horses for milk and meat, and in this connection it is surely significant that the Złota group of Poland gave precisely the same form of burial to cattle, sheep and pig as they did to horses.[99]

If, then, it is at best doubtful whether the corded-ware people used horses for transport at all, it might be thought hardly worth discussing more precisely how they might have used them. To do so, though, may help to illustrate how open this question must remain in the existing state of knowledge. Even if the use of wheeled vehicles is ruled out, there remain a number of alternatives, none of which could reasonably be excluded in the existing state of research for lack of positive evidence. For instance, it might be argued that these people used horses to draw simple sliding vehicles of the kind already mentioned. Again, it is not out of the question that they rode horses. Ridgeway's dictum[100] that chariot-driving preceded horse-riding as a mode of fighting is true enough whether applied to the higher civilizations of Western Asia, of Mediterranean Europe, or of China, but it is significant that he was careful to exclude the Turko-Tartaric peoples from his generalization. Among the Scythians and kindred peoples horses were ridden, but, as Herodotus reported, oxen were used for drawing waggons. Ridgeway held[101] that the fact that these peoples and their descendants " preferred and still prefer mare's milk to that of the cow naturally suggests that (they) had domesticated the horse before they possessed the ox, and that they tamed the former not for locomotion, but rather as a means of subsistence." Riding in fact was ancillary in this case to herding and so it may have been among earlier peoples of south Russia and contiguous territories. The Scythians, living when they did, acquired bridles with cheek-pieces, but it is possible to control a horse sufficiently for riding, if not for fighting by means of halters or headstalls made from highly perishable materials, like the rush bridles reported by Strabo for Libya or the straw halters cited by Ridgeway himself for the remoter parts of Ireland.[102] If it is conceded that the corded-ware people, whose connections with south Russia are undoubted, even if the significance of these is debated, kept

---

[99] O. Rydbeck, 1934 ; J. Zurowski, 1930, abb. 13 ; cf J.-E. Forssander, 1933, 212. The remains of a horse were buried with a man accompanied by a Corded Beaker under a round barrow at Emst, Gelderland, see J. H. Holwerda, 1912, Taf. 32, 2.

[100] Sir William Ridgeway, 1905, 481–2.

[101] ibid., 127–8.   [102] ibid., 240.

herds of horses, the absence of cheek-pieces or other harness fittings from their sites does not dispose of the possibility that they may have ridden horses in a primitive fashion.

Direct evidence about draft animals and their harnessing has a greater chance of surviving for horses than for oxen. For one thing, warlike or ceremonial activities are much more likely to be recorded in the form of representations than are the more hum-drum ones of daily life, and for such high activities horses were employed rather than oxen. Again, though dung carts may be able to tell more of economic life than chariots or hearses, it is only too evident which would be preferred to accompany chieftains to their graves. Then, the more deliberate harnessing used for horses involved such things as bits and cheek-pieces, which have a much greater chance of surviving, especially when made of metal, than the homely headstall which sufficed for the ox.

How far oxen were used for drawing vehicles in prehistoric Europe remains an open question, but it is worth emphasizing that for heavy draft work the ox has many advantages over the horse. For one thing it is notably the steadier and this characteristic is especially important when the going is poor, as it must nearly always have been during much of the year in temperate Europe down to quite modern times. Daniel Defoe has left it on record[103] how, not far from Lewes, he saw " an ancient lady . . . drawn to church in her coach with six oxen; nor was it done in frolic or humour, but mear necessity, the way being so stiff and deep, that no horses could go in it." Moreover, as Lefebvre des Nöettes has shown,[104] the method of harnessing in vogue down to the early middle ages, while admirably adapted to the physiology of the ox, was hardly suited to the horse, since the collar or neckband, by which the whole tractive power of the beast was transmitted to the yoke and so to the shaft of the vehicle, pressed on the windpipe and trancheal artery. Thus, the horse was unable to put out the superior energy which he undoubtedly possessed, when the load was at all heavy. When it is remembered that horses were substantially more expensive to maintain—they needed more attention and grooming and cost more to feed during the winter[105]—it is not difficult to see why cattle would have been the more economic for heavy work about the farm. Yet if we omit the enigmatic signs on a German port-holed gallery-grave at Züschen,[106] the only certain indication of ox-drawn vehicles are representations among the south Swedish rock-engravings which date in the main from periods V and VI of the Northern Bronze Age. The waggons are of primitive type with beam, forked at the rear and apparently fixed directly to the axles, and in the case of one from Långön, Tossene, Bohuslän, the shaft was also forked as it joined the front axle.[107] It is interesting to note that ox-drawn waggons of fundamentally the same type survived down to modern times in the folk-culture of a large part of central Europe.[108]

The use of wheeled vehicles began in western Asia long before the earliest dynasties, as far back as the Halafian culture, but neither in Greece nor in Crete is there evidence that

---

[103] Daniel Defoe (Everyman Edtn., 1928, I, 129).

[104] L. des Nöettes, 1926.

[105] Walter of Henley reckoned the cost of winter feed for an ox at only a quarter that of a horse.

[106] E. Whale, *Deutsche Vorzeit*, abb. 15. Leipzig, 1932.

[107] G. Berg, 1935, Pl. XXVII, 1 and 2.

[108] Berg, *op. cit.*, Chap. VIII, states that the four-wheeled waggon was formerly distributed from Holland to the Urals and from Västergotland and the Åland islands to Bavaria and Bulgaria. The type probably did not reach Britain from the Low Countries until the sixteenth century (cf. J. Parkes 1925, 7, n. 1). It would appear that in prehistoric times the four-wheeled waggon existed in the Mediterranean zone.

they played a part of any importance until Mycenæan times and then mainly for war or hunting. One of the few signs of wheeled transport in this area from an earlier period is the clay model of a waggon with two pairs of solid wheels from Palaikastro, dating from Middle Minoan Ia times.[109]   Among the vehicles which appeared in Crete in Late Minoan times, one, depicted on a tablet from Talyssos, evidently had four wheels, of which the front ones were spoked in the usual way and the rear ones solid.[110]   On the mainland chariots with a single pair of four-spoked wheels are represented already from the period of the Shaft-Graves[111] and from a later stage at Mycenæ comes a bronze bit with cross-bar broken in the middle and cheek-pieces having spikes on the inner faces.[112]   Such light chariots drawn by a pair of yoked and bridled horses were used for hunting, as well as fighting, and if Homeric practice is any guide also for travelling. Evidence for wheeled vehicles among the bronze age peoples of the Mediterranean zone outside the Mycenæan world is scanty, though there is an important series of rock-paintings, in south-west Iberia, conventionally referred to as "chalcolithic," at Los Buitres near Penalsordo in the province of Badajoz.[113] Here are shown (Fig. 167), two-wheeled carts and at least one four-wheeled waggon, together with the triangular signs interpreted by Breuil as sliding vehicles. It is particularly

Fig. 167.   Chalcolithic rock-paintings showing wheeled vehicles, Los Buitres, Penalsordo, Badajoz. (*After Breuil*).

interesting to note that, although some of the wheels are shown with four spokes, others appear to have been of the disc type made from two pieces dowelled together by cross-ties.

The evidence for wheeled vehicles is much fuller for parts of temperate Europe, though nearly all of this relates to hearses, cult-vehicles, or chariots. Four-wheeled hearses, like those excavated by Woolley from the royal cemetery at Ur,[114] are indeed among the earliest wheeled vehicles for which actual traces have survived in Mesopotamia. Doubtless it was ultimately from western Asia that the idea spread into central Europe by way of south Russia. Childe is surely right in supposing that the four-wheeled vehicles, in this case, horse-drawn, buried with leaders of Late Hallstatt and early La Tène society, were used to convey the dead to their place of burial.[115]   Exact details of these are lacking, but the

---

[109] Evans, *Palace*, II, 156 and Fig. 78.

[110] *ibid.*, IV, 796 and Fig. 769.

[111] e.g. a gold seal ring from shaft-grave IV shows a bowman shooting at a deer from a chariot mounted on four-spoked wheels, drawn by two horses and provided with a driver. (G. Karo, 1930. No. 240, Taf. XXIV).

[112] W. von Reichel, 1901, 142, Fig. 90.

[113] H. Breuil, 1933–5, II, 64–5, Fig. 20, Pl. XIV, XVIII, XIX.

[114] *Ant. J.*, VIII, 436

[115] V. G. Childe, *Prehistoric Migrations in Europe*, 222. Oslo, 1950.

splendid 'cult waggon' (Fig. 168) from the Dejbjerg bog, near Ringkøbing, Jutland,[116] gives a fair idea of what they may have been like.

Similar hearses were apparently used to bring cremated remains to the place of burial. What is evidently a funeral cortège is depicted on the surface of a pottery cinerary urn of

Fig. 168.   Four-wheeled waggon from Dejbjerg Bog, Ringkøbing, Jutland.   (*After Sophus Müller*)

Hallstatt character from Ödenburg in Hungary[117] (Fig. 169). The urn containing the ashes is shown resting on a platform mounted on spoked wheels and drawn by two horses yoked

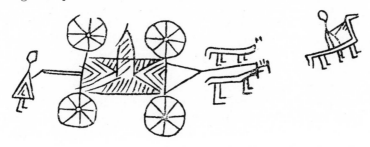

Fig. 169.   Representation of horse-drawn waggon in procession on a sherd from
Ödenburg, Hungary (*c.* ⅓).   (*After Déchelette*).

to a central shaft. A third horse, probably the dead man's charger, is represented as if being led by a groom at the head of the procession, a feature of special interest in view of the occurrence in burials of a third bit indicating the presence of a horse additional to those

---

[116] H. Petersen, 1888 ; Shetelig and Falk, 1937, 187 and Fig. 10 ; Brøndsted, 1938, III, 52 f. For an oblique rear view showing the forked beam, see Berg, 1935, Pl. XXVII, 3.

[117] Déchelette, III (1927), Fig. 232.

actually harnessed to the hearse.   Four-wheeled vehicles, drawn by pairs of horses and sometimes preceded by others, are also found incised on a number of cinerary urns dating from the Early Iron Age in the territory between the Oder and the Vistula.[118] Actual remains of four-wheeled carriers for cinerary urns have been found fairly commonly. Bronze cinerary urns of Hallstatt type found at Stade, Hanover, and at La Côte-Saint-André in southern France were set on wooden platforms mounted on two pairs of bronze spoked wheels of rather special type having wooden felloes set in grooved rims.   Closely similar wheels are distributed widely over Hallstatt territory from the south of France to Hungary.[119]

It may well be that fundamentally the same idea underlay the mounting of bronze globular ' cauldrons ' on wheeled chassis, which appeared as far back as the Late Bronze Age in central Europe and which reached Denmark and south Sweden by Period III of the Northern Bronze Age.[120] Additional evidence that wheeled vehicles had reached northern Europe by this time is provided by the horse-drawn sun-disc of Trundholm[121] and by the engraving of a chariot of Mycenæan type (Fig. 170) on a slab of the Kivik burial chamber in south Sweden.[122]

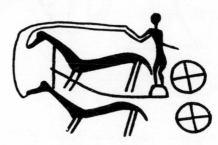

Fig. 170.   Engraving of horse-drawn chariot on slab of burial chamber, Kivik, Scania, South Sweden. (*After Althin*).

Direct evidence that horses were harnessed, presumably for drawing vehicles, already by the Late Bronze Age in parts of Europe, is given by finds of bridle cheek-pieces made from the tips of antler tines perforated to receive the reins and the cross-piece of the bit (Fig. 171, a, b). As Hermes[123] has so well shown, the dates assigned to some of these finds in the early literature can hardly any longer be accepted.   The earliest examples are probably those from Hungary, but the single specimen cited by Childe[124] from level B in the tell of Tószeg, on the margin of the flood-plain of the Theiss, can hardly of itself form the basis of much argument, especially as other examples were found in upper levels of the tell. Before the close of the Bronze Age similar cheek-pieces appeared with other elements of the urnfield culture in Italy, the Alpine areas, the Rhine Valley and Britain, as well as in

---

[118] W. La Baume, 1928.

[119] K. H. Jacob-Friesen, 1927; Déchelette, II (1924), 291–5.

[120] e.g. Déchelette, II (1924), Figs. 107 & 170 ; Brøndsted, II, Fig. 108.

[121] Brøndsted, 1938, II, 88 f., Fig. 81.

[122] C.-A. Althin, 1945, 60–71.

[123] G. Hermes (1935) attacked and effectively demolished the scheme advanced by R. Forrer and R. Zschille (1893), by which the evolution of bits was traced back to neolithic origins.

[124] V. G. Childe, 1929, 263.

much of Germany, Denmark and south Sweden and eastwards in the Caucasus.[125] It is interesting to note that when metal bits spread (Fig. 171C), during the final stage of the Bronze Age and during the Early Iron Age, they did not replace so much as supplement the older and simpler type, which thus occurred alongside the other, not only at late

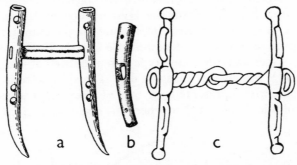

Fig. 171. Bits and cheek pieces of antler and bronze from late bronze age sites in Switzerland : (*a*) Corcelettes ; (*b, c*) Mörigen
a and *b* ($\frac{1}{5}$) ; *c* ($\frac{1}{3}$).

bronze age settlements in Hungary[126] and Switzerland[127] but also down to the end of the prehistoric period, as at Glastonbury.[128] It is tempting to interpret the survival of this primitive form over so many centuries and among so many communities as due to its use for cart or waggon harness in distinction to the more costly and rapidly changing chariot harness, and it is significant that the antler cheek-piece is pre-eminently a type found on settlement sites.

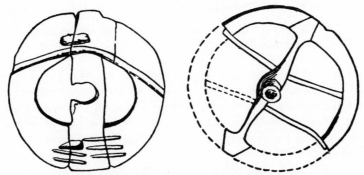

Fig. 172. Wooden three-piece wheels from Mercurago, near Ancona, Italy (*c*. $\frac{1}{14}$). (*After Déchelette*).

In addition to numerous antler cheek-pieces, the terremare settlements of north Italy have yielded at least three wooden wheels. The two from Mercurago, near Ancona,[129] were each made from three members dowelled by cross-ties, (Fig. 172) one being of disc

---

[125] *ibid.*, 263–4.
[126] e.g. Tószeg, D. and Füzesabony (von Tompa, 1937, Pl. 41, Nos. 11, 17 and Pl. 42, Nos. 21-2).
[127] e.g. Zürich-Alpenquai, Mörigen and Corcelettes.
[128] The lake-village yielded 4 iron bridle-bits and 45 antler cheek-pieces. See Bulleid and Gray 1911, *passim*.
[129] Déchelette, II (1924), 289–90.

form with no more than lunate openings cut from the inner edges of the outer timbers, the other much more open with the middle member reduced to spoke-like proportions and the side ones down to mere felloes, the cross-ties surviving as struts. Another wheel from Castione, Parma,[130] resembled the disc one from Mercurago. Two disc wheels made from three pieces dowelled together come from northern bogs,[131] one from the boundary of Oldenburg and Hanover, the other from the Dystrup bog in Jutland. Neither of these can be dated, but the Dystrup specimen is interesting for the complexity of the dowelling, the oak pegs or slats being set into either face and also into the thickness of the alder timbers composing the wheel. Essentially the same type is represented at the great Polish iron age settlement of Biskupin,[132] but in this case the disc is made up from two instead of three members, a type apparently represented on one of the rock-paintings of Los Buitres, supposedly of " chalcolithic " age. A disc wheel cut out of a single piece, but with lunate

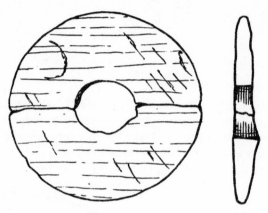

Fig. 173. Wooden disc wheel from a bog at Beckdorf near Stade, Hanover, Germany ($\frac{1}{13}$). (*After Cassau*).

openings on either side of the axle-hole from Tindbaek bog, Viborg, Jutland,[133] is unfortunately not dated. The only plain disc wheel from an archæologically dated site seems to be that from the Glastonbury lake-village,[134] cut from solid oak with a slightly biconical section, but one of alder found loose at a depth of 2 m. in a bog at Beckdorf, nr. Stade, Hanover, has been referred to an early stage of the Northern Bronze Age on the strength of pollen-analysis (Fig. 173).[135]

In origin, disc-wheels, including those made up by three members with cross-ties, are substantially older than spoked wheels, but whether they spread into Europe in advance of the more sophisticated type can hardly be determined. What is certain, though, is that disc-wheels continued to be used alongside spoked ones in Europe, and indeed survived down to the present day over a broad territory from Ireland to Russia and from Scandinavia

---

[130] G. Säflund, 1939, 105, Taf. 98, 4.

[131] S. Müller, 1907, 75–9.

[132] J. Kostrzewski, 1936, 40 and Tab. XLVI, 7.

[133] Brøndsted, 1938, I, Fig. 93.

[134] Bulleid and Gray, 1911, Fig. 84.

[135] A. Cassau, 1938. From S. Schneider's pollen diagrams, it is evident that the level at which the wheel was found, if not the object itself, was older than the *Grenzhorizont* but younger than the Wiepenkathen flint dagger dating from the period of the Stone Cists.

to Iberia.[136]   The question arises, as it did with the bits, whether the survival in use of the cruder, more primitive form does not argue the existence of more homely vehicles, whether two- or four-wheeled, alongside chariots and cult-waggons. It should be remembered, though, that the earliest chariots moved on disc-wheels and that, conversely, as shown by the Swedish rock-engravings, spoked wheels were already used before the end of the Northern Bronze Age for ox-drawn waggons.

While there seems no doubt that horse-drawn vehicles, mainly in the form of hearses and chariots, first appeared in central Europe during the Late Bronze Age, the spread of higher culture to Italy gave a further impetus to the adoption of wheeled transport in temperate Europe. The spread of the custom of burying chieftains with their chariots contributed greatly to the evidence available about this type of vehicle during the Early Iron Age, though as a rule the only parts to survive are such things as metal tyres, nave-bands, linch-pins, horn-caps, rein-terrets and bits.[137] As a rule it is only from votive-offerings or settlements in bogs or on lake margins, or from wells or similar wet places that one can expect to find the wooden parts of vehicles. Such finds show clearly enough the effect of the spread of the rotary lathe among the Celtic artificers, particularly in the turning of axle-hubs and spokes. The available wheels, whether from prehistoric sites like La Tène[138] and Glastonbury,[139] or native products from Roman military stations, such as Bar Hill[140] or Newstead[141] in Scotland, reflect a remarkably high standard of workmanship and a well-established tradition.   Among notable features of the spoked wheels of this period are the multiplication of spokes, commonly ten or twelve for chariots or carts and as many as fourteen for the Dejbjerg waggon; the method of mortising the spokes into the hubs, noted both in the north and south-west of Britain, by which they are set in circular dowel-holes prolonged into oblong tenons (Fig. 174)[142]; the method of making felloes from single pieces of wood bent round and held fast by iron cramps; and the fitting of iron tyres, which, from the absence of nails, must presumably have been sweated on to the wheel, as they are to-day, while still red hot and expanded.[143] The discovery of a roughed-out axle-hub at the Glastonbury lake-village[144] suggests that by the end of the prehistoric period at least in the area of La Tène culture, the wheelwright was an established member of the village community.   The most likely explanation is that the wheels belonged to carts or waggons, such as would be needed during the period of settled agriculture for work about the farm, notably for distributing manure.

Another item to survive in water-logged sites is the wooden yoke (Fig. 175), used alike for oxen and horses and for ploughing as well as transport. Although depicted in early bronze-age plough scenes, the earliest actual specimens obtained from modern controlled excavations date from the prehistoric Iron Age.[145] The most shapely examples of prehistoric

---

[136] Berg, 1935, 114–16.

[137] For a most valuable discussion with references, see Sir Cyril Fox, 1945, 12–30.

[138] P. Vouga, 1923, 91–4, Fig. 9 and Pl. XXX, 6.

[139] Bulleid and Gray, 1911, 321 ff., Figs. 99, 112–13.

[140] Macdonald and Park, 1906, 92–9.

[141] J. Curle, 1911, 292–4, Pl. LXIX.

[142] This has been brought out by Professor Stuart Piggott in *Proc. Prehist. Soc.*, 1949, 191.

[143] cf. Sir Cyril Fox, 1945, 13.

[144] Bulleid and Gray, 1911, Fig. 110.

[145] An example from a bog at Petersfehn, Oldenburg, has been referred to as neolithic on the evidence of pollen-analysis (E. Sprockoff, 1938, 136, Fig. 91), and one was obtained during early explorations at the lake-settlement of Vinelz on the Bielersee (T. Ischer, 1928, 43–4, Taf. VII), which has yielded material dating from the final neolithic period of Switzerland.

age are those from La Tène and from an unidentified site in Ulster. Piggott[146] has compared the full, curvilinear character of these with the leaner, more angular form of others from the Teutonic area, in particular from a stratum of La Tène age in the north Dutch

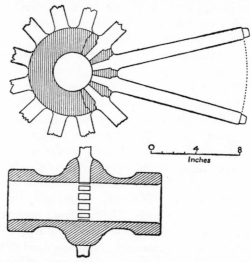

Fig. 174. Lathe-turned wheel hub showing method
of inserting spokes, Glastonbury marsh-village.

settlement mound (*terp*) of Ezinge[147] and from iron age levels in a number of Danish bogs,[148] including one find close to the Dejbjerg waggons. This is a useful reminder of the

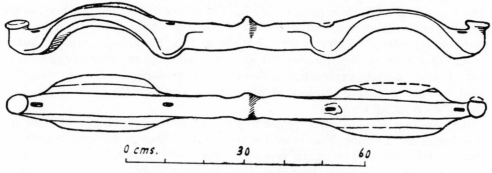

Fig. 175. Wooden yoke from La Tène.

influence of æsthetic considerations on the form of even such functional objects as animal yokes and serves to emphasize the danger of deducing on purely subjective grounds the specific use of individual examples.[149]

---

[146] *Proc. Prehist. Soc.*, 1949, 193.

[147] A. E. van Giffen, 1936, 40.

[148] Yokes have been found at Dejbjerg, from a bog near Finderup, Jutland, and from Jordrup and Sevel (S. Müller, 1907). For a recent and accessible photograph, see *Proc. Prehist. Soc.*, 1949, Pl. XXVII.

[149] As when, for example, P. Vouga (1923, 96) suggests interpreting one of the yokes from La Tène as horse, another as ox harness.

If the extent to which wheeled vehicles were used for normal economic purposes in prehistoric Europe must remain for the present an open question, it is even more difficult to trace the rise of horse-riding. It is possible, as already suggested, that riding of a primitive kind may have been introduced to central Europe from south Russia already before the end of the Stone Age. That it was certainly carried on there at the opening of the Early Iron Age is shown by representations in Hallstatt style, like the mounted warriors on the model cult waggon from Strettweg, Styria, or the riding figure set on the shoulder of an urn from Gemeinlebarn in Lower Austria.[150] The earliest item of specialized riding equipment likely to survive was the prick-spur (Fig. 176), which seems to have been introduced by the La Tène I period, to judge from a broken specimen of bronze from a

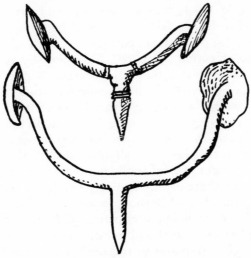

Fig. 176. Early iron age prick-spurs ($\frac{1}{1}$).
Upper : Bronze from Stradonitz, Bohemia. (*After Déchelette*).
Lower : Iron from La Tène (*After Vouga*).

warrior's burial at Trugny, Aisne.[151] The fact that only two specimens, both of iron and with buttons for attachment, were found at a site yielding as much military equipment as La Tène[152] suggests that spurs were not in common use at the time, and it was noted by Déchelette that spurs were worn singly during the La Tène period, as they still were in Merovingian times.[153] Metal stirrups, which originated from the rope or strap attachment used by the Scythians[154] and presumably by kindred people as an aid to mounting, were invented by the nomads of central Asia and were apparently first introduced both to western Europe and to China by the Huns. Riding saddles, as distinct from mere cloths, were also an invention of a later time.[155]

---

[150] M. Hoerness, 1898, Pl. VIII, Fig. 14 and Pl. XIX, Fig. 13.

[151] Déchelette, III (1914), 1202–4, Fig. 514, 5. Rowel-spurs were a medieval invention.

[152] P. Vouga, 1923, 102, Pl. XXXI, Fig. 15–16.

[153] *op. cit.*, 1204.

[154] Depicted, for example, on the Chertomlyk vase, Minns, 1913, Fig. 48 ; cf. Ridgway, 1905, 498–9.

[155] Ridgeway, *op. cit.*, 497–8.

Where goods were carried overland for any considerable distance, it is likely that at least since the introduction of horse-riding pack-horses were used. Diodorus Siculus,[156] indeed, says that waggons were used to transport tin for the short journey along the causeway, which joined Ictis to the mainland at low water, but that for the long traverse of Gaul the metal was carried on horses. Another vivid picture of the use of pack-horses under conditions which must have been much like those in parts of prehistoric Europe, is found in the Icelandic saga of Grettir, in the passage telling how the bondi Atli went with two companions to Snaefellsnes towards the end of summer to fetch dried fish for the winter and how they " bought much fish and carried it away on seven horses."[157] In Britain pack-horses continued to provide the main means of transporting goods, particularly textiles, overland down to modern times: Daniel Defoe notes that " droves of pack horses " were sent out by the clothiers of Leeds " to all the fairs and market-towns over the whole island " and says that at Sturbridge fair there would be " near a thousand horse-packs " of " Yorkshire cloths, kerseys, permistone, cottons, etc. with all sorts of Manchester ware, fustians and things made of cotton wool."[158] Transport by pack-horse, though, is one of those activities, which, however real, find little reflection in purely archæological evidence. Nevertheless, the site of La Tène yielded what is commonly interpreted as the wooden frame of a horse-pack[159] and it seems a fair guess that bales of wool like the one reproduced in the votive model (Fig. 177) of a Roman merchant found in the broch of Dunanlardhard, Skye,[160] were carried south on the backs of small Celtic horses.

In temperate Europe with its heavy rainfall and substantial areas of heavy soils one of the best indicators of the weight of land traffic is the state of the roads. Among the few traces of metalled roadways of prehistoric age may be cited a stone-laid causeway linking a defended island in the Jutish bog of Borremose with the solid land only sixty-five metres distant, or those noted from the Belgic occupation of Maiden Castle, Dorset; both date from the close of the prehistoric period and neither rank as cross-country routes.[161] The nailed-on horseshoe, though a response to metalled roads, was not used by the classical Italians, but was evidently a provincial invention, which probably occurred in Gaul at an early stage of the occupation, whence it reached southern England. It is significant that this device first appeared in Britain, at Colchester, in the period immediately before the Roman Conquest.[162] Early horseshoes of the type used in the northern provinces of the Empire had a characteristically wavy profile, the outer edge bulging at each perforation (Fig. 178).

For movement across country it would seem that the peoples of prehistoric Europe had to content themselves with natural routes. These were not always well defined, but generally followed the belts of lighter soils which were among the first to be cleared for farming and settlement. Among such may be mentioned the Jurassic formation, which formed a corridor from the Cotswolds to the wolds of the East Riding ranging in width

---

[156] V.2.

[157] Everyman Edtn., 1913, p. 114.

[158] Daniel Defoe, *A Tour Through England*, I, 82. Everyman Edtn., 1928. See also Dr G. B. Grundy, *Arch.J.* LXXIV, 83 f.

[159] P. Vouga, 1923, Fig. 10.

[160] V. G. Childe, 1946, 84, Fig. 20.

[161] R. E. M. Wheeler, 1943, 58, 116. Brønsted, III, 60-1, Fig. 46.

[162] Hawkes and Hull, 1947, 342, Fig. 64, Nos. 2, 3. On early horseshoes, see also Ward-Perkins, 1941, and Gordon Ward, 1938 and 1941.

from four to twenty-four miles; no estimate can be formed about the density of traffic on this route but the archaeological evidence leaves no doubt that it formed an actual line of movement, at least during the Early Iron Age.[163] Or, again, one might point to the ridge-ways which crossed the chalk country from Wessex to the coasts of Kent and Norfolk.[164]

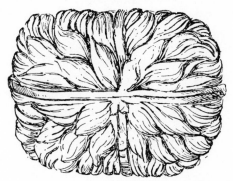

Fig. 177. Votive model of a bale of wool from Dunanlardhard Broch, Skye (⅟).

As Sophus Müller was the first to point out, the long winding lines of bronze age round barrows strung out along the margins of the morainic soils of Jutland are most easily explained as marking the courses of ancient lines of communication, along which, on may suppose, apart from the other traffic, funeral parties bore corpses to their burial.[165]

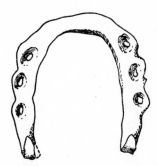

Fig. 178. Iron horseshoe from Pre-Roman level, Camulodunum (½).

Where soft ground had to be crossed, timber or brushwood might be laid down to give foothold or even to bear the weight of wheeled vehicles. Like dug-out boats, timber track-ways were essentially products of the forest regions. Present indications are that within this zone they began to be built during the Late Bronze Age : no examples of earlier date have been recorded,[166] but, thanks to pollen analysis, one can point to examples of this

---

[163] C. Fox, 1927, 94–100.

[164] J. G. D. Clark, 1940, 72 ff.

[165] S. Müller, 1904. See also T. Mathiassen, 1948, 142–3.

[166] H. Reinerth (1926, 216, abb. 88) included the Ödenbühl track as a neolithic feature, but see the same author 1936, 146–7.

age in the Cambridgeshire[167] and Somerset Fens[168] and in north-western[169] and southern-Germany.[170] It is likely that the heavy rainfall, which preceded the Sub-atlantic deterioration of climate, at once stimulated the construction of these causeways and ensured their preservation through the rapid growth of Sphagnum peat.

One of their uses was to traverse river valleys to fords or ferries, as is illustrated by the example near Brigg, already referred to (p. 287), or by those, respectively 640 m. and 1,230 m. long, which crossed the valley of the Sorge above Elbing in East Prussia.[171] Another function was to link islands of habitable ground in low-lying areas with the surrounding dry land, as with those joining the area of Stuntney with the isle of Ely[172] or the network of tracks of different types now coming to light in the Somerset levels, by which Meare is linked with the Wedmore Ridge and the Poldens on the north and south and with Catcott Burtle on the west.[173] Timber tracks are commonly found traversing the silted-up beds of

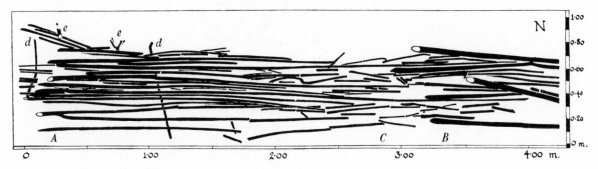

Fig. 179.   Blakeway Farm trackway, Somerset.   (*After Clapham and Godwin*).

old lakes, running from the outer margin of the bog to the contemporary strand, like the well-known one at Ödenbühl in the basin of the Federsee.[174]   Again, it should not be forgotten that corduroy tracks were sometimes used in prehistoric, as they were later in early historic, times to pave the streets of settlements, such as is well seen at the defended village of Biskupin in Poland, dating from the Early Iron Age.[175]

Structurally, the tracks fall into two main classes, according as the majority of the timbers were laid lengthwise or transversely, but a wide range of variation is met with both in the build and in the devices used to hold the structures together. It is difficult to say much at present about the traffic they were designed to carry except that many, especially those with longitudinal timbers, were too narrow to have served for more than foot or horse traffic. Some of the narrow foot-paths were excessively slight, like that recently explored on Blakeway Farm, on the border of Westhay and Mudgley in Somerset, which was made from rods of hazel, not more than $1\frac{1}{2}$ inches across at the butt ends, laid down in lengths of 10 to 13

[167] Clark and Godwin, 1940, 52–3.
[168] Clapham and Godwin, 1948, 249–73.
[169] H. Krüger, 1936.
[170] Reinerth, 1936, 146–7.
[171] H. Conwentz, 1897.
[172] T. C. Lethbridge, 1934.
[173] Clapham and Godwin, 1948, Fig. 13.
[174] Reinerth, 1936, Taf. XLII.
[175] J. Kostrzewski, 1938, Pl. II–IV.

feet on a width of no more than 2 feet (Fig. 179). On the other hand one meets with structures like that at Meare Heath a mile and a half long, made up of cross-timbers, 6 to 8 feet
long, mostly of oak, set at irregular intervals, overlying and packed between by alder and
birch brushwood, and pegged down by mortised stakes, which also held in position the
long stringers serving as margins to the track; from its dimensions such could have carried
wheeled vehicles and the wooden margins support the idea that it was so used. The commonest build for corduroy tracks with transverse timbers was to lay these across parallel

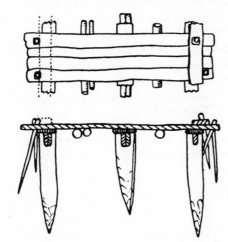

Fig. 180. Trackway with transverse timbers,
Diepholz Moor, North West Germany.
(*After Krüger*).

runners to spread the weight, as in the one at Ödenbühl. Much more elaborate methods
were sometimes used, though, doubtless in response to widely ranging differences in local
conditions, as shown by one of those explored in Diepholz Moor on the borders of Oldenburg and Hanover,[176] in which the cross-timbers have been laid on three rows of stout
piles with lengthwise sleeper timbers laid between (Fig. 180). These timber trackways offer
a fascinating and much too little explored field of research, but already they may serve to
warn us against depreciating unduly the volume of traffic which flowed overland across the
temperate zone of Europe during the closing stages of the prehistoric period.

---

[176] This track (No. III) is dated to the period immediately preceding the climatic deterioration :
see H. Krüger, 1936, 493, Fig. 17.

WORKS TO WHICH REFERENCE IS MADE IN THE TEXT*

ABBREVIATIONS

Ant. J. = *The Antiquaries Journal.* London.
Arch. = *Archaeologia.* London.
Arch. J. = *The Archaeological Journal.* London.
J.R.A.I. = *Journal of the Royal Anthropological Institute.* London.
P.P.S. = *Proceedings of the Prehistoric Society.* Cambridge.
P.R.I.A. = *Proceedings of the Royal Irish Academy.* Dublin.
P.S.A.S. = *Proceedings of the Society of Antiquaries of Scotland.* Edinburgh.

AARIO L. [1934]. 'Heinolan pitäjän Viikinä-isistä löydetyn reenjalaksen turvegeologinen iänmääräys,' *Suomen Museo*, XLI, 22–7.

ACERBI, J. [1802]. *Travels through Sweden, Finland and Lapland to the North Cape in the years 1798 and 1799*, 2 vols. London.

AILIO, J. [1909]. *Die steinzeitlichen Wohn-platz-funde in Finland*, I, II. Helsingfors.

AILIO, J. [1920]. 'Om handeln mellan Finland och andra länder under Stenåldern,' *Rig*, bd. 3, 1–7. Stockholm.

AILIO, J. [1922]. 'Fragen der russischen Steinzeit,' *Finska fornm.-fören. tidskr.*, XXIX, 3–14.

ALBRECTSEN, E. [1946]. 'Fyns bebyggelse i den aeldre jernalder,' *Aarbøger*, 1–71.

ALIN, J., NIKLASSON, N. and THOMASSON, H. [1934]. *Stenåldersboplatsen på Sandarna vid Göteborg*, Göteborgs Kungl., Vet. och Vitt. Handl.

ALLEN, D. [1944]. 'The Belgic Dynasties of Britain and their Coins,' *Arch.*, XC, 1–46.

ALTHIN, C.-A. [1945]. *Studien zu den bronze-zeitlichen Felszeichnungen von Skåne* 1–11. Lund.

ALTHIN, C.-A. with B. BRORSON-CHRISTENSEN and H. BERLIN [1949]. 'Renfyndet från Nebbe Mosse och Sveriges Senglaciala Bebyggelse,' *Bull. Soc. Roy. des Lettres de Lund*, 1948–9, 114–46.

AMSCHLER, J. W. [1949]. 'Ur- und Frühge-schichtliche Haustierfunde aus Österreich,' *Archaeologia Austriaca*, hft. 3. Wien.

ANDERSON, A. B. [1948]. 'Et forhistorisk pålebyggverk fra Kylles i Høyland,' *Stav-anger Museums Årbok*, 77–98.

ANDERSON, J. [1883]. *Scotland in Pagan Times: The Iron Age.* Edinburgh.

ANDREE, J. [1922]. *Bergbau in der Vorzeit.* Leipzig.

ANDREE, J. [1939]. *Der eiszeitliche Mensch in Deutschland und seine Kulturen.* Stuttgart.

ANNANDALE, N. [1905]. *The Farœs and Ice-land.* Oxford.

ARMSTRONG, A. L. [1926]. 'The Grimes Graves Problem in the Light of Recent Researches,' *P.P.S., East Anglia*, V., 91–136.

AUER, V. [1924]. 'Die postglaziale Geschichte des Vanajavesisees,' *Communicationes ex Instituto quaestionum forestalium Finlandiae editae*, 8. Helsinki.

AUER, V. [1928]. 'Rühimäen Herajoen suk-silöydön turvegeologinen ikämääräys, *Suo-men Museo*, XXXV, 86–8.

BÄGGE, A. [1943]. 'Nya märkliga stenålders-fynd från Västerbotten lappmarker,' *Väster-bottens läns Hembygdsföreningens Årsbok*, 77–94.

BALTZER, L. [1919]. *Schwedische Felsbilder von Göteborg bis Strömstad.* Hagen i. W.

BANDI, H.-G. [1947]. *Die Schweiz zur Ren-iterzeit.* Frauenfeld.

BANNER, J. [1929]. 'Beiträge zur frage des neolithischen Wohnhauses,' *Dolgozatok*, V, 126–31.

* It should be emphasised that this is not intended as a bibliography. Fuller references to the literature may be found in some of the present author's articles and in monographs and papers dealing with special topics, such as Oldeberg's book on metal working or Vogt's on textiles.

BANNER, J. [1930]. 'Die neolithische Ansiedelung von Kökénydomb,' *Dolgozatok*, VI, 107–58.

BAYE, J. DE [1874]. 'Grottes de Baye. Pointes de flèches en silex à tranchant transversal,' *Rev. archéologique*, N.S. XXVII, 401–8. Paris.

BECK, H. C. and STONE, J. F. S. [1936]. 'Faience Beads of the British Bronze Age,' *Arch.*, LXXXV, 203–52.

BECKER, C. J. [1939]. 'En Stenalderboplads paa Ordrup Næs i Nordvestsjælland,' *Aarbøger*, 199–280.

BECKER, C. J. [1941]. 'Fund af Ruser fra Danmarks Stenalder,' *Aarbøger*, 131–41.

BECKER, C. J. [1943]. 'Et 6000—aarigt Fiskeredskap', *Fra det gamle Gilleleje*, 1943, 70–87.

BECKER, C. J. [1945]. 'En 8000—aarig Stenalderboplads i Holmegaards Mose', *Fra Nationalmuseets Arbejdsmark*, 1945, 61–72.

BECKER, C. J. [1947]. 'Mosefundne Lerkar fra yngre Stenalder,' *Aarbøger*, 1947, 1–313.

BEHRENS, G. [1926]. 'Neue Hausgrundrisse vorrömischer Zeit aus Rheinhessen,' *Germania*, X, 1–10.

BERG, G. and SVENSSON, S. [1934]. *Svensk Bondekultur*. Stockholm.

BERG, G. [1935]. *Sledges and Wheeled Vehicles. Ethnological Studies from the view-point of Sweden*. Stockholm.

BERG, G. with LUNDQVIST, G., ZETTERSTEN, A. and GRANLUND, E. [1941]. *Finds of Skis from prehistoric time in Swedish bogs and marshes*. Stockholm.

BERLIN, H. [1941]. 'Benfynden från stenåldersboplatsen i Gualöv,' *Medd. Lunds univ. hist. mus.*, 1940–1, 151–2.

BERSU, G. and GOESSLER, P. [1924]. 'Der Lochenstein bei Balingen,' *Fundberichte aus Schwaben*, N.F. II, 1924, 73–103.

BERSU, G. [1930]. 'Fünf Mittel-la-Tène Häuser vom Goldberg,' *Schumacher Festschrift*, 156–59, tf. XV. Mainz.

BERSU, G. [1936]. 'Rössener Wohnhäuser vom Goldberg, O.A., Neresheim, Württemberg,' *Germania*, 1936, 229–43.

BERSU, G. [1937]. 'Altheimer Wohnhäuser vom Goldberg, O.A., Neresheim, Württemberg,' *Germania*, 1937, 149–58.

BERSU, G. [1940]. 'Excavations at Little Woodbury, Wiltshire: Part I,' *P.P.S.*, 1940, 30–111.

BERSU, G. [1946]. 'Celtic Homesteads in the Isle of Man,' *Journal of the Manx Museum*, Vol. V, 177–82.

BERTSCH, K. [1932]. 'Die Pflanzenreste der Pfahlbauten von Sipplingen und Langenrain im Bodensee,' *Badische Fundber.*, bd. 2, hft. 9.

BERTSCH, F. [1939]. 'Herkunst und Entwicklung unserer Getreide,' *Mannus Z.*, 1939, 171–224.

BERTSCH, K. [1941]. 'Die spätglaziale Waldentwicklung,' *Ber. d. deutschen bot. Ges.* LIX, hft. 3, 99–103.

BICKNELL, C. [1913]. *A Guide to the Prehistoric Rock Engravings in the Italian Maritime Alps*. Bordighera.

BILLIARD, R. [1913]. *La Vigne dans l'antiquité*. Lyon.

BIRKET-SMITH, K. [1929]. *The Caribou Eskimos*. Vols. I, II. Copenhagen.

BIRKET-SMITH, K. [1936]. *The Eskimos* (Trans.) London.

BLANC, A. C. [1939]. 'Les " Microburins " dans les niveaux à faune glaciaire de la Grotte Romanelli en Terre d'Otrante (Italie),' *Bull. Soc. Préhist. Française*, 1939, No. 2.

BLANC, G. A. [1920]. 'Grotta Romanelli,' *Archiv. per l'Antrop. e la Etnologia*, L, 65–103.

BLEGEN, C. W. [1937]. *Prosymna, the Helladic Settlement preceding the Argive Heraeum*. Cambridge.

BLINKENBERG, C. [1925]. 'Le Pays Natal du Fer,' *Mém. Soc. Roy. Antiqu. du Nord*, 1925, 191–206.

BLOCH, M. [1931]. *Les Caractères Originaux de l'histoire rurale française*. Inst. for sammenlignende Kulturforskning. Series B, XIX, Oslo.

BOAS, F. [1888]. 'The Central Eskimo,' *Sixth Annual Report Bureau of Ethnology*, 401–669. Washington.

BØE, J. [1934]. 'Boplassen i Skipshelleren,' *Bergens Mus. Skr.* Nr. 17.

BØE, J. and NUMMEDAL, A. [1936]. *Le Finnmarkien. Les Origins de la Civilisation dans l'Extrême-Nord de l'Europe*. Oslo, 1936.

BOLIN, Prof. Store [1941]. 'Medieval Agrarian Society in its Prime: Scandinavia,' *The Camb. Econ. History of Europe*, vol. I, 467–492. Cambridge.

BOLZ, M. [1914]. 'Das neolithische Gräberfeld von Küvisaare in Livland,' *Baltische Studien zur Archäologie und Geschichte*. XVI. Arch. Kongr. in Pleskau, 1914. Berlin. S.15–32.

BORLASE, W. C. [1897]. *Tin-mining in Spain, past and present*. London.

BOSANQUET, A. C. [1904]. 'The Obsidian Trade,' in EDGAR, 1904, 216–233. London.

BOSCH, R. [1924]. 'Uber des Moordorf Riesi am Hallwilersee,' *Anz. für schweiz. altertum.*, XXVI (1924), 73–83.

BOSCH, R. (Festschrift) [1947]. *Beiträge zur Kulturgeschichte*. Aarau.

BOSWORTH, Rev. J. [1855]. *A literal English translation of King Alfred's Anglo-Saxon version of the Compendious History of the World by Orosius.* London.

BOULE, M. and VILLENEUVE, L. DE [1927]. *La Grotte de l'Observatoire à Monaco.* Arch. Inst. Paléont. Mus. Paris, Mém. 1.

BRADFORD, J. S. P. [1949]. '"Buried Landscapes" in Southern Italy,' *Antiquity*, XXIII, 58–72.

BREA, L. B. [1946]. *Gli scavi nella Caverna delle Arene Candide. Parte I. Gli strati con ceramiche.* Coll. monogr. preistoriche ed Archeol. Inst. d. studi Liguri, Bordighera.

BREUIL, H. [1910]. *La Caverne de Font-de-Gaume.* Monaco.

BREUIL, H. et al. [1911]. *Les Cavernes de la région Cantabrique.* Monaco.

BREUIL, H. [1912, 1937]. 'Les subdivisions du Paléolithique Supérieur et leur signification,' *C.R. Congr. Int. d'Anthrop. et d'Arch. Préhist., Geneva*, 1912. 2ᵉ Edition, 1937.

BREUIL, H. [1917]. 'Le char et le traineau dans l'art rupestre d'Estramadure,' *Terra portuguesa*, 1917, nr. 15–16. Lisbon.

BREUIL, H. [1933–5]. *Les Peintures Rupestres Schématiques de la Péninsule Ibérique.* T. I–IV. Lagny.

BREUIL, H. and DE SAINT-PÉRIER, R. [1937]. *Les Poissons, les Batraciens et les Reptiles dans l'art quaternaire.* Archives de l'Inst. de Paléont. Hum. Mém. 2. Paris.

BRIART, A. (with CORNET, F. and DE LEHAIE, A. H.) [1868]. 'Rapport sur les découvertes géologiques et archéologiques faites à Spiennes en 1867,' *Mém. et publications de la Soc. des Sciences, des Arts et des Lettres du Hainaut*, 3rd ser., vol. II.

BRIART, A. (with CORNET, F. L.) [1872]. 'Sur l'âge de la pierre polie et les exploitations préhistoriques de Silex dans la province de Hainaut,' *Congr. int. d'anthr. et d'arch. préhistoriques, C.r. 6ᵉ sess. Bruxelles*, 1872, 279–99. cf. *C.r. 10ᵉ sess. Paris*, 1889, 569–612.

BRINKMANN, A. and SHETELIG, H. [1920]. 'Ruskenesset. En stenalders jagtplass,' *Norske Oldfund*, III. Christiania.

BRITISH MUSEUM [1920]. *British Museum Guide to the Antiquities of the Bronze Age.* 2nd ed. London.

BRITISH MUSEUM [1925]. *British Museum Guide to Early Iron-Age Antiquities.* 2nd ed. London.

BRITISH MUSEUM [1926]. *British Museum Guide to Antiquities of the Stone Age.* 3rd ed. London.

BROCKMANN-JEROSCH, H. [1917]. 'Die ältesten Nutz- und Kulturpflanzen,' *Vierteljahrsschrift d. Naturforsch. Ges. in Zürich*, Jg. 62, 80–102.

BRODAR, S. [1938]. 'Das Paläolithikum in Jugoslawien,' *Quartär*, I, 1938, 140–72.

BROGAN, O. [1936]. 'Trade between the Roman Empire and the Free Germans,' *J. Roman Studies*, XXVI, 195–222.

BRØGGER, A. W. [1908]. *Vistefundet. En ældre stenalders Kjøkkenmødding fra Jæderen.* Stavanger.

BRØGGER, A. W. [1909]. *Den arktiske stenalder i Norge*, Videnskabs-selskabets Skrifter, II. Hist.-Filos. kl. 1909, nr. 1. Christiania.

BRØGGER, A. W. [1911]. 'Et norsk ravfund fra stenalderen,' *Bergen Museums Årbok*, 1911, no. 11.

BRØGGER, A. W. [1926]. *Kulturgeschichte des Norwegischen Altertums.* Oslo.

BRØGGER, A. W. [1932]. 'The Prehistoric Settlement of Northern Norway,' *Bergens Museums Årbok*, 1932, Hist.-antik. r., no. 2.

BRØGGER, A. W. [1940]. 'From the Stone Age to the Motor Age,' *Antiquity*, 1940, 163–81.

BROHOLM, H. C. [1931]. 'Nouvelles trouvailles du plus ancien âge de la pierre. Les trouvailles de Holmegaard et de Svaerdborg,' *Mém. de la Soc. Roy. des Antiqu. du Nord*, 1926–31, 1–128.

BROHOLM, H. C. and RASMUSSEN, J. P. [1931]. 'Ein steinzeitlicher Hausgrund bei Strandegaard, Ostseeland,' *Acta Arch.*, II, 1931, 265–78.

BROHOLM, H. C. and HALD, M. [1935]. 'Danske Bronzealders Dragter,' *Nordiske Fortidsminder*, II bd., 5/6 hft. Copenhagen.

BROHOLM, H. C. [1938]. 'Nye Fund fra den Aeldste Bronzealder,' *Aarbøger*, 1938, 65–85.

BROHOLM, H. C. and HALD, M. [1939]. *Skrydstrupfundet.* Nordiske Fortidsminder III. 2, Copenhagen.

BROHOLM, H. C. [1943–4]. *Danmarks Bronzealder*, bd. 1 (1943), bd. 2 (1944). Copenhagen.

BRØNDSTED, J. [1934]. 'Danmarks handelsliv i oltiden,' *Nordisk Kultur*, XVI, Handel og Samfaerdsal, 6–26.

BRØNDSTED, J. [1938]. *Danmarks Oldtid.* 3 vols. Copenhagen.

BROOKE, G. C. [1933]. 'The distribution of Gaulish and Roman Coins in Britain,' *Antiquity*, 1933, 268–89. See also *Numismatic Chron.*, 1933, 5th Ser., vol. XIII, 88–138.

BRUCE, J. R., and MEGAW, E. M. and B.R.S. [1947]. 'A Neolithic Site at Ronaldsway, Isle of Man,' *P.P.S.*, 1947, 139–60.

BRUNHES, J. [1925]. *La Géographie humaine.* 3rd ed. 2 vols. Paris.

BRUNN, W. A. VON [1939]. 'Untersuchung von Kulturschichten mit Briquetage in Halle Aiebichenstein,' *Nach. für Deutsche Vorzeit*, 1939, 92–7.

BRUNNER, K. [1903]. 'Zur Forschung über alte Schiffstypen auf den Binnengewässern und an den Küsten Deutschlands und der angrenzenden Länder,' *Correspondenz-Blatt d. deutschen Ges. f. Anthrop. Ethnologie u. Urgeschichte*, XXXIV (1903), 1–13.

BRUNTON, G. [1928]. *The Badarian Civilization.* London.

BUCH, L. VON [1813]. *Travels through Norway and Lapland during the years* 1806, 1807, *and* 1808. London.

BUCKLEY, T. E. and HARVIE-BROWN, J. A. [1888]. *A vertebrate fauna of the Outer Hebrides.* Edinburgh.

BUCKLEY, T. E. and HARVIE-BROWN, J. A. [1891]. *A vertebrate fauna of the Orkney Islands.* Edinburgh.

BULLEID, A. and GRAY, H. ST. G. [1911]. *The Glastonbury Lake Village.* Glastonbury.

BULLEID, A. [1933]. 'Ancient Trackway in Meare Heath, Somerset,' *Proc. Som. A. and N.H.S.*, LIX (1933), 19–29.

BUNCH, B (with FELL, C. I.) [1949]. 'A Stone-axe Factory at Pike of Stickle, Great Langdale, Westmorland,' *P.P.S.*, 1949, 1–20.

BURKART, W. [1946]. *Eine bronzezeitliche hügelsiedlung bei Surin im Lugnez.* Basel.

BURKITT, M. C. [1925]. *Prehistory*, 2nd ed. Cambridge.

BURSCH, F. C. [1928]. 'Silex du Grand-Pressigny en Hollande,' *Bull. Soc. Anthr. Brux..*, vol. 43, 173 ff.

BURSCH, F. C. [1936]. 'Grafvormen van het Noorden,' *Oudheidkundige Mededeelingen*, N.R. XVII, 53–72.

BUTTLER, W. (and HABEREY, W.) [1936]. Die Bandkeramische Ansiedlung bei Köln-Lindenthal. Leipzig.

BUTTLER, W. [1936]. 'Pits and Pit-dwellings in Southeast Europe,' *Antiquity*, 1936, 25–36.

BUTTLER, W. [1938]. *Der donauländische und der westische Kulturkreis der jüngeren Steinzeit.* Berlin.

BUTTLER, W. [1938a]. 'Beiträge zur Frage des jungsteinzeitlichen Handels,' *Marburger studien.* Darmstadt, 26–33.

CALLENDER, J. G. [1917]. 'A flint workshop on the hill of Skares, Aberdeenshire,' *P.S.A.S.*, LI, 117–27

CARTAILHAC, E. [1868]. 'Monuments mégalithiques du département de l'Aveyron,' *Trans. Int. Congr. of Prehistoric Archaeology*, 3rd Sess., Norwich. 1868, pp. 351–358.

CARY, M. [1924]. 'The Greeks and Ancient Trade with the Atlantic,' *J. Hellenic Studies*, 1924, 166–79.

CASSAU, A. [1935]. 'Ein Feuersteindolch mit Holzgriff und Lederscheide aus Wiepenkathen, Kreis Stade,' *Mannus Z.*, 1935, 199.

CASSAU, A. [1938]. 'Ein frühbronzezeitlicher oder endsteinzeitlicher Wagenradfund in Beckdorf, Kr. Stade,' *Nachr. aus Niedersachsens Urgeschichte*, nr. 12, 63–71. Hildesheim.

CATON-THOMPSON, G. [1935]. *The Desert Fayum.* London.

CHAPPLE, E. D. and COON, C. S. [1947]. *Principles of Anthropology.* London.

CHARLESWORTH, M. P. [1926]. *Trade-routes and Commerce of the Roman Empire.* 2nd ed. Cambridge.

CHILDE, V. G. [1929]. *The Danube in Prehistory.* Oxford.

CHILDE, V. G. [1931]. *Skara Brae, a Pictish Village in Orkney.* London.

CHILDE, V. G. [1931a]. 'The Continental Affinities of British Neolithic Pottery,' *Arch. J.*, LXXXVIII, 37–66.

CHILDE, V. G. [1935]. *The Prehistory of Scotland.* Edinburgh.

CHILDE, V. G. and GRANT, W. G. [1939]. 'A Stone-Age Settlement at the Braes of Rinyo, Rousay, Orkney (First Report),' *P.S.A.S.*, LXXIII, 6–31. [1947] (Second Report), *P.S.A.S.*, LXXXI, 16–42.

CHILDE, V. G. [1939]. 'Double-looped palstaves in Britain,' *Ant. J..*, XIX, 320–3.

CHILDE, V. G. [1940]. *Prehistoric Communities of the British Isles.* London.

CHILDE, V. G. [1943]. 'Rotary Querns on the Continent and in the Mediterranean Basin,' *Antiquity*, 1943, 19–26.

CHILDE, V. G. [1944]. 'Archæological Ages as Technological Stages,' *J.R.A.I.*, LXXIV, 1–19.

CHILDE, V. G. [1946]. 'A bronze-worker's anvil and other tools . . .,' *P.S.A.S.*, vol. LXXX, 8–11.

CHILDE, V. G. [1947]. *The Dawn of European Civilization.* 4th ed. London.

CHILDE, V. G. [1948]. 'Cross-dating in the European Bronze Age,' *Festschrift für Otto Tschumi*, 70–6. Frauenfeld.

CHILDE, V. G. [1948a]. 'The Final Bronze Age in the Near East and in Temperate Europe,' *P.P.S.*, XIV, 177–95.

CHILDE, V. G. [1949]. 'Neolithic House-types in Temperate Europe,' *P.P.S.*, 1949, 77–86.

CLAPHAM, A. R. and GODWIN, H. [1948].
'Studies of the Post-glacial History of
British Vegetation. VIII, Swamping surfaces
in peats of the Somerset levels. IX, Prehistoric trackways in the Somerset levels.'
Phil. Trans. Roy. Soc. London. Ser. B., vol.
233, pp. 233–73.

CLARK, J. G. D. [1932]. 'The curved sickle
blades of Britain,' *P.P.S.E.A.*, VII, 67–81.

CLARK, J. G. D. (and PIGGOTT, S.) [1933].
'The Age of the British Flint Mines,'
Antiquity, 1933, 166–83.

CLARK, J. G. D. (and GODWIN, H. and M. E.,
and CLIFFORD, M. H.) [1935]. 'Report on
Recent Excavations at Peacock's Farm,
Shippea Hill, Cambridgeshire,' *Ant. J.*, XV
(1935), 284–319.

CLARK, J. G. D. [1936]. *The Mesolithic Settlement of Northern Europe.* Cambridge.

CLARK, J. G. D. [1936a]. 'Early Navigation in
North-western Europe,' *P.P.S.*, 1936, 146.

CLARK, J. G. D. [1938]. 'The Reindeer-
Hunting Tribes of Northern Europe,' *Antiquity*, 1938, 154–71.

CLARK, J. G. D. [1939]. *Archaeology and Society.* London.

CLARK, J. G. D. and RANKINE, W. F. [1939].
'Excavations at Farnham, Surrey (1937–38);
the Horsham Culture and the Question of
Mesolithic Dwellings,' *P.P.S.* V (1939),
61–118.

CLARK, J. G. D. and GODWIN, H. [1940]. 'A
Late Bronze Age find near Stuntney, Isle of
Ely,' *Ant. J.*, XX, 52–71.

CLARK, J. G. D. [1940]. *Prehistoric England.*
London, 1940, 1941, 1944, 1948.

CLARK, J. G. D. [1942]. 'Bees in Antiquity,'
Antiquity, 1942, 208–15.

CLARK, J. G. D. [1944]. 'Water in Antiquity,'
Antiquity, 1944, 1–15.

CLARK, J. G. D. [1945]. 'Farmers and forests
in Neolithic Europe,' *Antiquity*, 1945, 57–71.

CLARK, J. G. D. [1945a]. 'Man and nature in
prehistory, with special reference to neolithic settlement in northern Europe,'
Occasional Paper No. 6, 20–28. Univ. of
London Inst. of Archæology.

CLARK, J. G. D. [1946]. 'Seal-hunting in the
Stone Age of north-western Europe: a study
in economic prehistory,' *P.P.S.*, 1946, 12–48.

CLARK, J. G. D. [1947]. 'Whales as an economic factor in Prehistoric Europe,' *Antiquity*, 1947, 84–104.

CLARK, J. G. D. [1947a]. 'Forest Clearance
and Prehistoric Farming,' *Economic History
Review*, XVII, 45–51.

CLARK, J. G. D. [1947b]. 'Sheep and Swine in
the Husbandry of Prehistoric Europe,'
Antiquity, 1947, 122–36.

CLARK, J. G. D. [1948]. 'The development of
fishing in prehistoric Europe,' *Ant. J.*,
XXVIII, 45–85.

CLARK, J. G. D. [1948a]. 'Objects of South
Scandinavian Flint in the Northernmost
Provinces of Norway, Sweden and Finland,'
P.P.S., 1948, 219–232.

CLARK, J. G. D. [1948b], 'Fowling in Prehistoric Europe,' *Antiquity*, 1948, 116–30.

CLARK, J. G. D. (with H. GODWIN, F. C. FRASER
and J. E. KING) [1949]. 'A Preliminary
Report on Excavations at Star Carr, Seamer,
Scarborough, Yorkshire, 1949,' *P.P.S.*, 1949,
52–69.

CLARK, J. G. D. [1951]. 'Folk-culture and
the study of European Prehistory,' in *Aspects
of Archaeology in Britain and Beyond*
(O. G. S. Crawford vol. 49–65). London.

CLOWES, G. S. Laird [1930]. *Sailing Ships,
Their History and Development.* Science
Museum, London.

COFFEY, G. [1907]. 'Two Finds of Late Bronze
Age Objects,' *P.R.I.A.*, XXVI, 119–24.

COFFEY, G. [1913]. *The Bronze Age in Ireland.*
Dublin.

COLE, G. A. J. [1922]. *Memoir and Map of
Localities of Minerals of Economic Importance
and Metalliferous Mines in Ireland.* Memoirs
of the Geological Survey of Ireland, Dublin,
1922.

COLLETT, R. [1881]. 'On *Halichœrus grypus*
and its Breeding on the Fro Islands off
Throndhjems-fjord in Norway,' *Proc. Zool.
Soc. London*, 1881, 380–387.

COLLINS, A. L. [1893]. 'Fire-setting, the art
of mining by fire,' *Trans. of the Federated
Inst. of Mining Engineers*, vol. V, 82–92.

CONWENTZ, H. [1897]. 'Die Moorbrücken im
Tal der Sorge,' *Abh. z. Landesk. d. Prov.
Westpr.* Hft. X. Danzig, 1897.

CRAWFORD, O. G. S., and WHEELER, R. E. M.
[1921]. 'The Llynfawr and other Hoards of
the Bronze Age,' *Arch.* LXXI, 133 ff.

CRAWFORD, O. G. S. [1925]. *Long Barrows of
the Cotswolds.* Gloucester.

CRAWFORD, O. G. S. and KEILLER, A. [1928].
Wessex from the Air. Oxford.

CROWFOOT, G. M. [1938]. 'Mat impressions
on pot bases,' *Liv. Ann. Arch. and Anthr.*,
XXV, 3–11.

CROWFOOT, G. M. [1939]. 'The Tablet-
woven Braids from the Vestments of St.
Cuthbert at Durham,' *Ant. J.*, XIX, 57.

CUNNINGTON, M. E. [1923]. *The Early Iron Age Inhabited Site at All Cannings Cross Farm, Wiltshire.* Devizes.

CUNNINGTON, M. E. [1931]. 'The "Sanctuary" on Overton Hill, near Avebury,' *Wilts. Arch. Mag.*, XLV, 300–35.

CURLE, A. O. [1932]. 'Interim Report on the Excavation of a Bronze Age Dwelling at Jarlshof, Shetland in 1931,' *P.S.A.S.*, LXVI, 113–28. [1933]. 'II. Account of Further Excavations . . .' *P.S.A.S*, LXVII, 82–136. [1934]. 'III. An Account of Further Excavations . . .' *P.S.A.S*, LXVIII, 224–319.

CURLE, J. [1911]. *A Roman Frontier Post and its People. The Fort of Newstead.* Glasgow.

CURWEN, E. C. [1930]. 'Neolithic Camps,' *Antiquity*, 1930, 22–54.

CURWEN, E. C. [1937]. *The Archaeology of Sussex.* London.

CURWEN, E. C. [1937a]. 'Querns,' *Antiquity*, 1937, 133–51.

CURWEN, E. C. [1938]. 'The Early Development of Agriculture in Britain,' *P.P.S.* IV (1938), 27–51.

CURWEN, E. C. [1938a]. *Air Photography and the Evolution of the Corn-field.* Economic History Society Pamphlet, No. 2. London School of Economics.

CURWEN, E. C. [1941]. 'Some Food-gathering Implements,' *Antiquity*, 1941, 320–36.

CURWEN, E. C. [1941a]. 'More about Querns,' *Antiquity*, 1941, 15.

CURWEN, E. C. [1946]. *Plough and Pasture.* London.

CZAPLICKA, M. A. [1914]. *Aboriginal Siberia.* Oxford.

DANIEL, G. E. and POWELL, T. G. E. [1949]. 'The Distribution and Date of the Passage-Graves of the British Isles,' *P.P.S.*, 1949, 169–187.

DARBY, H. C. [1934]. 'Domesday Woodland in East Anglia,' *Antiquity*, 1934, 211–15.

DARBY, H. C. [1940]. *The Draining of the Fens.* Cambridge.

DAVIES, H. [1937]. 'The Shale-industries at Kimmeridge, Dorset,' *Arch. J.*, XCIII, 200–219.

DAVIES, N. DE G. [1920]. *The Tomb of Antefoker.* London.

DAVIES, N. DE. G. [1935]. *Paintings from the Tomb of Rekhmire.* New York.

DAVIES, O. [1929]. 'Two North Greek Mining Towns,' *J. Hellenic Studies*, vol. XLIX, 89–99.

DAVIES, O. [1932]. 'The Copper Mines of Cyprus,' *Annual of the British School at Athens*, No. XXX, 74–85. London.

DAVIES, O. [1935]. *Roman Mines in Europe.* Oxford.

DEBES, L. J. [1676]. *Færoœ et Fœroa reserata*: that is a Description of the Islands and Inhabitants of Fœrœ (Transl. from the Danish). London.

DEFOE, D. [1724/6]. *A Tour through England and Wales.* Everyman Ed. London, 1928, 2 vols.

DEGERBØL, M. [1933]. 'Danmarks Pattedyr i Fortiden i Sammenligning med recente Former,' *Vidensk. Medd. naturhist. Foren. København.* Bd. 96.

DEGERBØL, M. et al. [1935]. *Danmarks Pattedyr.* Copenhagen.

DEGERBØL, M. [1945]. 'Subfossile Fisk fra Kvartærtiden i Danmark,' *Vidensk. Medd. naturhist. Foren, København.* Bd. 108, 1945, 103–60.

DIKAIOS, P. [1933]. 'Ploughing in Cyprus in the Early Bronze Age,' *Man*, 1933, No. 134. Cf. *Arch.*, LXXXVIII, 127–9.

DIXON, Pierson [1940]. *The Iberians of Spain and their relations with the Aegean World.* Oxford.

DUNBABIN, T. J. [1948]. *The Western Greeks.* Oxford.

DURSIN, L. [1931]. 'La question tardenoisième en Belgique et aux Pays-Bas,' *Inst. Intern. d'Anthr.*, Sess. de Paris, 1931, 389–400.

DYAKOWSKA, J. [1936]. 'Pollenanalyse des an einer vorgeschichtlichen Matte aus Łączyńska Huta, Kr. Kartuzy, haftenden Torfes,' *Wiadomósci Archeologiczne*, t. XIV, 92–95. Warsaw.

EBERT'S *Reallexikon der Vorgeschichte.* Berlin, 1924–32.

EDGAR, C. C. (editor) [1904]. *Excavations at Phylakopi in Melos.* London.

EINZIG, P. [1949]. *Primitive Money in its Ethnological, Historical and Economic Aspects.* London.

EKHOLM, G. [1935]. 'Zur Geschichte des Römisch-Germanischen Handels,' *Acta Arch.*, 1935, 49–98.

EKMAN, S. [1910]. *Norrlands jakt och fiske.* Uppsala.

EKMAN, S. [1933]. 'Die biologische Geschichte der Nord- und Ostsee,' *Die Tierwelt der Nord- und Ostsee* (Ed. G. Grimpe), Lief. XXIII, teil 1b, 1–40. Leipzig.

EKMAN, S. [1935]. *Tiergeographie des Meeres.* Leipzig, 1935.

ELGEE, FRANK [1930]. *Early Man in North-East Yorkshire.* Gloucester.

ELGSTRÖM, O. [1924]. 'De bohuslänska hallristningarnas skeppsbilder,' *Fornvännen*, 1924, 281–97.

ENGLEHARDT, C. [1866]. *Denmark in the Early Iron Age*. Copenhagen. [1869]. *Vimose Fundet*. Copenhagen.

ENGELSTAD, E. S. [1934]. *Østnorske Ristninger og Malinger av den Arktiske Gruppe*. Oslo.

ERIXON, S. [1937]. 'Regional European Ethnology. I. Main Principles and Aims with Special Reference to Nordic Ethnology,' *Folkliv*, 1937, 89–108. Stockholm.

ERMAN, A. [1848]. *Travels in Siberia*. London. 2 vols.

ESCHRICHT, D. F. [1849]. *Untersuchungen über die nordischen Wallthiere*. Leipzig.

EVANS, A. J. [1891]. 'On a late-Celtic urn-field at Aylesford, Kent, and on the Gaulish Illyro-Italic, and Classical Connexions of the forms of pottery and bronze-work there discovered,' *Arch.*, LII, 315–88.

EVANS, Sir A. [1914]. 'The "Tomb of the Double Axes" and Associated Group, and the Pillar Rooms and Ritual Vessels of the "Little Palace" at Knossos,' *Arch.*, LXV, 1–94.

EVANS, Sir A. [1921–8]. *The Palace of Minos at Knossos*. London.

EVANS, A. J. [1909]. *Scripta Minoa*, I, Oxford.

EVANS, E. E. [1939]. 'Donegal Survivals,' *Antiquity*, 1939, 207–22.

EVANS, E. E. [1942]. *Irish Heritage. The Landscape, the People and their Work*. Dundalk.

EVANS, Sir J. [1864, 1890]. *The Coins of the Ancient Britons*. London, 1864. *Supplement*. London, 1890.

EVANS, Sir J. [1881]. *Ancient Bronze Implements of Great Britain and Ireland*. London.

EVANS, Sir J. [1897]. *Ancient Stone Implements of Great Britain*. 2nd ed. London.

EVANS-PRITCHARD, E. [1940]. *The Nuer*. Oxford.

EWART, J. C. [1911]. 'On Skulls of Oxen from the Roman Military Station at Newstead, Melrose,' *Proc. Zool. Soc.*, 1911, 249–82. London.

FAEGRI, KNUT [1943]. *Studies on the Pleistocene of Western Norway. III Bømlo*. Bergens Museums Årbok 1943. Naturvit. rk. Nr. 8.

FAEGRI, K. [1944]. 'On the Introduction of Agriculture in western Norway,' *Geol. Fören. Förhandl.* bd. 66, h. 3, 1944, 449–62.

FELL, C. I. [1937]. 'The Hunsbury Hill-fort, Northants: a new survey of the material, *Arch. J.*, XCIII, 57–100.

FERNHOLM, H. [1942]. 'Ljusterfiske. En översikt över redskap och metoder,' *Folk-Liv*, 1942, t. VI, 50–72.

FIRBAS, F. [1935]. 'Die Vegetationsentwicklung und Klimawandel in der mittel-europäischen Spätglazials,' *Bibliotheca Botanica*, hft. 112.

FIRBAS, F. [1949]. *Spät- und nacheiszeitliche Waldgeschichte Mitteleuropas nördlich der Alpen*. Jena.

FISCHER, P. [1881]. 'Cétacés du Sud-Ouest de la France,' *Actes Soc. Linn. Bordeaux*, XXXV (4ᵗʳ Sér., V), 5–219.

FISCHER, T. [1904]. 'Der Ölbaum. Seine geographische Verbreitung, seine wirtschaftliche und Kulturhistorische Bedeutung' *Petermann's Mitteilungen*. Erganzungsheft No. 147, 1–87. Gotha.

FORDE, C. DARYLL [1930]. 'On the use of Greenstone in the Megalithic Culture of Brittany,' *J.R.A.I.*, LX, 211–234.

FORRER, R. and ZSCHILLE, R.'[1893]. *Die Pferdetrense in ihrer Form-Entwicklung*. Berlin.

FORSSANDER, J. E. [1933]. *Die Schwedische Bootaxtkultur*. Lund.

FORSSANDER, J. E. [1936]. *Der ostskandinavische Norden während der ältesten Metallzeit Europas*. Lund.

FORSSANDER, J. E. [1941]. 'Den sydsvenska boplatskulturen,' *Medd. Lunds univ. hist. mus.*, 1940–1, 128-50. Cf. H. BERLIN, 1941.

FOX, Sir CYRIL [1923]. *The Archaeology of the Cambridge Region*. Cambridge, 1923.

FOX, C. [1926]. 'A Dug-out Canoe from South Wales . . .,' *Ant. J.*, VI, 121–51.

FOX, C. [1927]. 'A La Tène Brooch from Wales,' *Arch. Camb.*, 1927, 67–112.

FOX, C. [1933]. 'The Distribution of Man in East Anglia,' *P.P.S.E.A.*, VII, 149–64.

FOX, C. [1932]. *The Personality of Britain*. Cardiff, 1932, 1938 and 1943.

FOX, Sir CYRIL and HYDE, H. A. [1939]. 'A Second Cauldron and an Iron Sword from the Llyn Fawr Hoard, Rhigos, Glamorganshire,' *Ant. J..*, XIX, 369–404.

FOX, C. [1940]. 'The Distribution of Currency Bars,' *Antiquity*, 1940, 427–33.

FOX, Sir CYRIL [1945]. *A Find of the Early Iron Age from Llyn Cerrig Bach, Anglesey*. Cardiff.

FOX, Sir CYRIL and DICKINS, BRUCE (editors), [1950]. *The Early Cultures of North-West Europe*. Cambridge.

FRANZ, L. [1929]. *Vorgeschichtliches Leben in den Alpen*. Vienna.

FREDSJÖ, A. [1943]. 'En fiskescen på en bohuslänsk hällristning,' *Göteborgs och Bohusläns Fornminnesförenings Tidskrift*, 1943, 61–71.

FRIIS JOHANSEN, K. [1920]. 'Une station du plus ancien âge de la pierre dans la tourbière de Svaerdborg,' *Mém. de la Soc. Roy. des Antiqu. du Nord*, 1918–19, 241–359.

FRÖDIN, O. [1906]. 'En svensk kjökkenmödding,' *Ymer*, 1906, 17–35.

FRÖDIN, O. [1910] 'En svensk pålbyggnad från stenåldern,' *Fornvännen*, 1910, 29 f.

FRÖDIN, O. and PERSSON, A. W. [1938]. *Asine*. Stockholm.

FURTWÄNGLER, A. and LÖSCHCKE, G. [1886]. *Mykenischen Vasen*. Berlin.

FURTWÄNGLER, A. [1893]. *Meisterwerke der Greichischen Plastik*. Berlin.

GALLUS, SÁNDOR [1934]. 'Die Figuralverzierten Urnen von Soproner Burgstall,' *Archaeologia Hungarica*, XIII. Budapest, 1934.

GARCÍA, L. PERICOT [1942]. *La Cueva del Parpalló (Gandía)*. Madrid.

GARNETT, A. [1945]. 'The Loess Regions of Central Europe in prehistoric times,' *Geogr, J.*, CVI, 132–43.

GARROD, D. A. E. [1926]. *The Upper Palæolithic Age in Britain*. Oxford.

GARROD, D. A. E. *et al* [1928]. 'Excavation of a Mousterian Rock-Shelter at Devil's Tower, Gibraltar,' *J.R.A.I.*, LVIII, 33–113.

GARROD, D. A. E. and BATE, D. M. A. [1937]. *The Stone Age of Mount Carmel*, vol I. Oxford.

GARROD, D. A. E. [1938]. 'The Upper Palæolithic in the Light of Recent Discovery,' *P.P.S.*, 1938, 1–26.

GAUL, J. H. [1948]. *The Neolithic Period in Bulgaria*. Am. School of Prehistoric Research, Bull. 16. Cambridge, Mass.

GEIJER, A. and LJUNGH, H. [1937]. 'Die Kleider der Dänischen Bronzezeit,' *Acta Arch.*, VIII, 266–75.

GEIKIE, JAMES [1879]. 'Discovery of an Ancient Canoe in the Old Alluvium of the Tay at Perth,' *Scottish Naturalist*, V, 1–7.

GELLERT, J. F. and GARSCHA, Fr. [1930]. 'Prähistorisches aus dem östlichen Tafelbalkan, insbesondere Muschelringe,' *Prähist. Z.*, XXI, 269–71.

GEORGE, P. [1933]. 'Les sols et les forêts en région méditerranéenne, d'après quelques travaux récents,' *Annales de Géogr.*, XLII, 194–99.

GIESSLER, R. [1948]. 'Eine Lanzenspitze aus Pressigny-Feuerstein von Kork, Ldkrs. Kehl,' *Badische Fundberichte*, 17, 138–43.

GIFFEN, A. E. VAN [1914]. 'Die Fauna der Wurten,' *Tijdschrift der Nederlandsche Dierkundige Vereeniging*, 2e serie, diel 13, 1914. 1–166. Leiden.

GIFFEN, A. E. VAN [1928]. 'Prehistoric Fields in Holland,' *Antiquity*, 1928, 85–7.

GIFFEN, A. E. VAN [1930]. *Die Bauart der Einzelgräber*. Leipzig.

GIFFEN, A. E. [1936]. 'Der Warf in Ezinge, Provinz Groningen, Holland, und seine westgermanischen Häuser,' *Germania*, 1936, 40–47.

GIFFEN, A. E. VAN [1944]. 'Grafheuvels te Zwaagdijk, Gem. Werveshoof (N.H.),' *West-Friesland's Oud en Nieuw*, XVII, 121 ff.

GJESSING, G. [1932]. *Arktiske Helleristninger i Nord-Norge*. Oslo.

GJESSING, G. [1936]. *Nordenfjelske Ristninger og Malinger av den arktiske gruppe*. Oslo.

GJESSING, G. [1942]. *Yngre Steinalder i Nord-Norge*. Oslo.

GJESSING, G. [1943]. *Traen-Funnene*. Inst. f. Sammenl. Kulturforsk. Ser. B, Skr. XLI. Oslo.

GJESSING, G. [1944]. 'Circumpolar Stone Age,' *Acta Arctica*, fasc. II. Copenhagen.

GJESSING, G. [1945]. *Norges Steinalder*. Oslo.

GJESSING, H. [1920]. *Rogalands Stenalder*. Stavanger.

GLENN, T. A. [1935]. 'Distribution of the Graig Lwyd Axe and its Associated Cultures,' *Arch. Cambr.* XC, 189–218.

GLØB, P. V. [1939]. 'Norske Skiferøkser i Danske Fund,' *Aarbøger*, 1939, 296–301.

GLØB, P. V. [1942]. 'Pflüge vom Walle-typus aus Dänemark,' *Acta Arch.*, XIII (1942), 258–69.

GLØB, P. V. [1949]. 'Barkær, Danmarks ældste landsby,' *Fra Nationalmuseets Arbejds, mark*, 1949, 5–16.

GODWIN, H. and CLIFFORD, M. H. [1938]. 'Studies of the Post-glacial History of British Vegetation,' *Phil. Trans. Roy. Soc.*, ser. B, vol. 229, 323–406.

GODWIN, H. [1944]. 'Age and Origin of the "Breckland" Heaths of East Anglia,' *Nature*, vol. 154, p. 6 f.

GODWIN, H. [1947]. 'The Late-Glacial Period,' *Science Progress*, vol. 138, 185.

GOLOMSHTOK, EUGENE A. [1938]. 'The Old Stone Age in European Russia,' *Trans. Am. Phil. Soc.* N.S. vol. XXIX, pt. II, March 1938, pp. 191–468. Philadelphia.

GÓNGORA Y MARTINEZ, M. DE [1868]. *Antigüedades prehistóricas de Andulacía*. Madrid.

GONZENBACH, V. VON [1949]. *Die Cortaillod-kultur in der Schweiz*. Basel.

GOODCHILD, R. G. [1943]. 'T-shaped Corn-drying Ovens in Roman Britain,' *Ant. J.*, XXII, 148–53.

GÖRZ, G. [1928]. 'Über den vorgeschichtlichen Pflug von Georgsfeld,' *Jahb. der Preuss. Geolog. Landesanstalt*, Bd. 49, 592–601.

GOULD, S. BARING et al. [1894]. 'The Exploration of Grimspound. First Report of the Dartmoor Exploration Committee,' *Trans. Devon Assoc.* XXVI, 101–21.

GOW, A. S. F. [1914]. 'The Ancient Plough,' *J. Hellenic Soc.*, XXXIV, 1914.

GOWLAND, W. [1912]. 'Copper and its Alloys in Early Times,' *J. Inst. Metals*, VII (1912), 23–49. London.

GRAM, B. [1891]. 'Undersögelser af archæologisk materiale udförte i Prof. Steins laboratorium,' *Aarbøger*, 1891, 97–123.

GRANLUND, J. [1939]. 'Hartstätningar till Svepta Kärl under Äldre Järnålder,' *Fornvännen*, 1939, 257–87.

GRANLUND, J. [1940]. 'Styggberget—en älgstupa,' *Folk-Liv*, 1940, t. IV., 5–9.

GRANLUND, J. [1943–4]. 'Lindbast och träbast,' *Folk-Liv*, 1943–44, t. VII–VIII, 166–99.

GRIEG, S. [1934]. *Jernaldershus på Lista*. Oslo.

GRIEVE, SYMINGTON [1885]. *The Great Auk, or Garefowl. Its History, Archaeology and Remains*. London.

GRIMES, W. F. [1939]. *Guide to the Collection illustrating the Prehistory of Wales*. Cardiff.

GRIMES GRAVES: *Report on the Excavations. March–May*, 1914. Prehistoric Society of East Anglia. London, 1915.

GROSS, H. [1938]. 'Auf den ältesten Spuren des Menschen in Altpreussen,' *Prussia*, bd. 32 (1938), 84–139.

GROSS, H. [1940]. Die Renntierjäger-kulturen Ostpreussens, *Prähist. Z.*, bd. 30/1, 39–67.

HALD, M. [1932]. *Brikvævning*. Copenhagen.

HALD, M. [1934]. 'Le tissage aux plaques dans les trouvailles préhistoriques du Danemark,' *Mém. des antiqu. du Nord*, 1926–34, 389–416.

HALD, M. [1942]. 'The Nettle as a Culture Plant,' *Folk-Liv*, 1942, t. VI, 28–49.

HALLSTRÖM, G. [1925]. 'En importvara till Västerbotten för 4,000 år sedan,' *Västerbottens läns hembygdsförenings årsbok*, 1924/25, 88–109. Umeå.

HALLSTRÖM, G. [1925a]. 'Utriggade Kanoter i Sverige,' *Fornvännen*, 1925, 50–70.

HALLSTRÖM, G. [1929]. 'Ur fjälltrakternas förhistoria,' *Till fjälls*, 1929, 10–19.

HALLSTRÖM, G. [1938]. *Monumental Art of Northern Europe from the Stone Age*. Stockholm.

HALLSTRÖM, G. [1941]. 'Bronsåldersfyndet från Flarken i Nysätra Socken,' *Västerbottens läns Hembygdsföreningens Årsbok*, 1941, 180–196. Umeå.

HARLÉ, E. [1908]. 'Ossements de renne en Espagne,' *L'Anthropologie*, XIX, 573–7.

HARLÉ, E. [1913]. 'Lagomys de la grotte de la Madeleine et Phoque de l'abri Castanet (Dordogne),' *Bull. Soc. Géol. de France*, 4th sér. XIII, 1913, 342–351.

HARMER, Sir S. F. [1927]. *Report on Cetacea stranded on the British Coasts from 1913 to 1926*. B.M. (Nat. Hist.), London.

HARTMANN, F. [1923]. *L'Agriculture dans l'ancienne Égypte*. Paris.

HARTZ, N. and WINGE, H. [1906]. 'Om Uroxen fra Vig, saaret og dræbt med Flintvaaben,' *Aarbøger*, bd. 21.

HATT, G. [1928]. 'To Bopladsfund fra den ældre Jernalder,' *Aarbøger*, 1928, 219–60.

HATT, G. [1930]. 'En Brandtomt af et Jernalderhus paa Mors,' *Aarbøger*, 1930, 83–118.

HATT, G. [1931]. 'Prehistoric Fields in Jutland,' *Acta Arch.*, II. 1931, 1.

HATT, G. [1935]. 'Jernaldersbopladsen ved Ginderup i Thy,' *Fra Nationalmuseets Arbejdsmark*, 1935. [1935a]. 'En Jernaldershustomt i Troldtoft,' *Aarbøger*, 1935.

HATT, G. [1936]. 'Nye Iagttagelser vedrørende oldtidens Jernudvinding i Jylland,' *Aarbøger*, 1936, 19–45.

HATT, G. [1937]. *Landbrug i Danmarks Oldtid*. Copenhagen.

HATT, G. [1937a]. 'Dwelling-houses in Jutland in the Iron Age,' *Antiquity*, 1937, 162–73.

HATT, G. [1938]. 'Jernalders Bopladser i Himmerland,' *Aarbøger*, 1938, 119–266.

HATT, G. [1939]. 'The Ownership of Cultivated Land,' *Det. Kgl. Danske Videnskab. Selskab. Hist.-Filolog. Medd.*, XXVI, 6, 1–22.

HATT, G. [1941]. 'Forhistoriske Plovfurer i Jylland,' *Aarbøger*, 1941, 155–65.

HATT, G. [1949]. *Oldtidsagre*. Kong. Danske Vidensk. Selsk. Ark.-Kunsthist. Skr., bd. II, nr. 1. Copenhagen.

HAUGE, T. D. [1946]. *Blesterbruk og Myrjern*. Univ. Oldsaks. Skr., bd. III. Oslo.

HAWKES, C. F. C. and DUNNING, G. C. [1930]. 'The Belgæ of Gaul and Britain,' *Arch. J.*, LXXXVII (1930), 150–335.

HAWKES, C. F. C. [1940]. *The Prehistoric Foundations of Europe to the Mycenaean Age*. London.

HAWKES, C. F. C. [1940a]. 'The Double Axe in Prehistoric Europe,' *British School at Athens Annual*, XXXVII, 140–59.

HAWKES, C. F. C. and HULL, M. R. [1947]. *Camulodunum. First Report on the Excavations at Colchester, 1930–39.* Soc. Ant. London.

HAWKES, J. [1937]. *The Archaeology of the Channel Islands*, vol. II. *The Bailiwick of Jersey.* Jersey.

HEER, O. [1866]. *Die Pflanzen der Pfahlbauten.* Zürich.

HEIERLI, J. and SCHERER, P. E. [1924]. 'Die neolithischen Pfahlbauten im Gebiete des ehemaligen Wauwiler Sees,' *Mitt. d. Naturf. Ges. Luzern*, IX, 1924.

HELL, M. [1927]. 'Der Götschenberg bei Bischofshofen in Salzburg und seine Beziehung zum Beginne des alpinen Kupferbergbaues,' *Wiener Prähist. Z.*, XLV, 8–23.

HENCKEN, H. O'N. [1932]. *The Archaeology of Cornwall and Scilly.* London.

HENCKEN, H. O'N. [1933]. 'An Excavation by H.M. Office of Works at Chysauster, Cornwall, 1931,' *Arch.*, LXXXIII, 237–84.

HENCKEN, H. O'N. [1942]. 'Ballinderry Crannog No. 2,' *P.R.I.A.*, vol. XLVII, Sect. C, No. 1, pp. 1–76.

HENTSCHEL, E. [1937]. *Naturgeschichte der nordatlantischen Wale und Robben.* Handbuch der Seefischerie Nordueropas, vol. III, hft. 1. Suttgart.

HERMES, G. [1935]. 'Das gezähmte Pferd im neolithischen und früh bronzezeitlichen Europa,' *Anthropos*, XXX, 803–23. [1936]. *ibid.*, XXXI, 115–29.

HESCHELER, K. [1920]. 'Beiträge zur kenntnis der Pfahlbaufauna des Neolithikums. (Die Fauna der Pfahlbauten im Wauwylersee),' *Vierteljahrs. Naturf. Ges. Zürich*, Jhg., LXV, 1920, 248–322.

HESCHELER, K. [1924]. 'Die Tierwelt der schweizerischen Pfahlbauten,' *Pfahlbauten Zehnter Bericht.* Zürich, 1924, s. 98–108.

HESCHELER, K. [1933]. 'Die fauna der neolithischen Pfahlbauten der Schweiz und des deutschen Bodenseegebietes nach neueren Forschungen, *Vierteljahrsschrift d. Naturf. Ges. Zürich*, Jahrg. 87, 1933, 198–231.

HESCHELER, K. and RÜEGER, J. [1939]. 'Die Wirbeltierreste aus dem neolithischen Pfahlbaudorf Egolzwil 2 (Wauwilersee) nach den Grabungen von 1932 bis 1934,' *Vierteljahrsschrift d. Naturf. Ges. Zürich*, Jahrg. 84, 1939, 307–30.

HEURTLEY, A. W. [1939]. *Prehistoric Macedonia.* Cambridge.

HILLEBRAND, J. [1928]. 'A nyirlugosi obsidiannucleus depotleletröl (Der Obsidian-Nucleus-Verwahrfund von Nyirlugos),' *Archaeologiai Értesitö*, 42, 39 ff. and 301–3. SA.

HILZHEIMER, M. [1936]. 'Sheep,' *Antiquity*, 1936, 195–206.

HJORT, J. [1896]. *Hydrographic-Biological Studies of the Norwegian Fisheries.* Christiania.

HOERNES, M. [1898]. *Urgeschichte der Bildenden Kunst in Europa.* Vienna.

HOGG, A. H. A. [1943]. 'Native Settlements of Northumberland,' *Antiquity*, 1943, 136–147.

HOLLEYMAN, G. A. and CURWEN, E. C. [1935]. 'Late Bronze-Age Lynchet-Settlements on Plumpton Plain, Sussex,' *P.P.S.*, I, 16–38.

HOLMBOE, J. [1927]. 'Nytteplanter og Ugræs,' *Osebergfundet*, V, 5–78. Oslo.

HOLST, N. O. [1906]. 'Flintgrufvor och flintgräfvare i Tullstorpstrakten,' *Ymer*, 1906, 139–174.

HOOPS, J. [1905]. *Waldbäume und Kulturpflanzen im germanischen Altertum.* Strassburg.

HORNELL, J. [1946]. *Water Transport. Origins and Early Evolution.* Cambridge.

HOUGEN, B. [1934]. 'Handelsforbindelser i Norge inntil tiden omkring 600 e. kr.', *Nordisk Kultur*, XVI, *Handel og Samfærdsel*, 27–38.

HOWITT, A. W. [1904]. *The Native Tribes of South-East Australia.* London.

HULME, E. W. [1933]. 'Currency Bars and Water-Clocks,' *Antiquity*, 1933, 61–72, and 210 f.

HUMBLA, P. and POST, L. VON [1937]. *Galtabäcksbåten och tidigt båtbyggeri i Norden.* Gothenburg. Göteborgs kungl. Vetenskaps. och Vitterhets-Samhälles Handl.

INDREKO, R. [1937]. *Über die vorgeschichtliche Fischerei in Estland.* Abhandl. der Fischereikammer, nr. 2. Tallinn.

INDREKO, R. [1948]. *Die Mittlere Steinzeit in Estland.* Kungl. Vitt. Hist. och Antik. Akad. Handl., Stockholm.

ISBERG, O. [1930]. 'Das Vorkommen des Renntiers (*Rangifer tarandus* L.) in Schweden während der postglacialen Zeit,' *Arkiv f. Zoologi*, 1930, 1–26. Cf. *Ymer*, 1930, 381–402.

ISCHER, TH. [1928]. *Die Pfahlbauten des Bielersees.* Biel.

ITKONEN, T. I. [1930]. 'Muinaissuksia jajalaksia,' *Suomen Museo*, XXXVII, 82–90. Also *S.M.*, XXXVIII–IX (1932), 50–63; XLI (1934), 1–21; XLIII (1936), 68–83; XLV (1938), 13–34; XLVIII (1941), 31–43; LIII (1946), 47–56.

ITKONEN, T. I. [1937]. 'Finlands fornskidor,' *På Skidor*, 1937, 71–89.

ITKONEN, T. I. [1941]. *Suomen Ruuhet.* Helsingfors.

ITKONEN, T. I. [1942]. 'Temmeksen muinais-jalas,' *Suomen Museo*, XLIX, 28–30.

IVERSEN, J. [1941]. 'Land Occupation in Denmark's Stone Age,' *Danmarks Geologiske Undersøgelse*. II. Raekke. Nr. 66. Copenhagen, 1941.

IVERSEN, J. and DEGERBØL, M. [1945]. *The Bison in Denmark. A Zoological and Geological Investigation of the Finds in Danish Pleistocene Deposits.* D. G. U. 11 R. Nr. 73. Copenhagen.

IVERSEN, J. [1946]. 'Geologisk Datering af Boplads ved Bromme,' *Aarbøger*, 1946, 198–231.

JACKSON, J. W. [1917]. *Shells as Evidence of the Migrations of Early Culture.* Manchester.

JACOB-FRIESEN, K. H. [1927]. 'Der Bronzeräderfund von Stade,' *Prähist. Z.*, 1927, XVIII, 154–86.

JACOB-FRIESEN, K. H. [1934]. 'Die älteste Pflug der Welt,' *Natur und Volk*, LXIV, 1934, 83–91.

JACOBI, A. [1931]. *Das Rentier. Eine zoologische monographie der Gattung Rangifer.* (Ergbd. z bd. 96, Zoologischer Anz.). Leipzig.

JACOBI, L. [1897]. *Das Römerkastell Saalburg.*

JACOBSTHAL, P. [1929]. 'Rhodische Bronzekannen aus Hallstattgräbern,' *Jhb. d. deutschen Arch. Inst.*, 44, hft. 3/4, 198–228.

JACOBSTHAL, P. and LANGSDORFF, A. [1929]. *Die Bronzeschnabelkannen. Ein beitrag zur Geschichte des Vorrömischen imports nördlich der Alpen.* Berlin.

JACOBSTHAL, P. and NEUFFER, E. [1933]. 'Gallia Græca. Recherches sur l'hellénisation de la Province,' *Préhistoire*, t. II, fasc. 1, 1–64. Paris, 1933.

JACOBSTHAL, P. [1934]. 'Bodenfunde grieschischer Vasen nördlich der Alpen,' *Germania*, Jhg. 18 14–19.

JACOBSTHAL, P. [1944]. *Early Celtic Art.* Oxford.

JANKÓ, JANOS [1900]. *Herkunst der magyarischen Fischerei. Dritte asiatische Forschungsreise des Grafen Eugen Zichy*, bd. 1. Budapest.

JAPHA, A. [1909]. 'Zusammenstellung der in der Ostsee bisher beobachteten Wale,' *Schr. Phys.-ökonom. Ges. Königsberg*, XLIX Jhg., 119–89.

JAŻDŻEWSKI, K. [1938]. 'Gräberfelder der bandkeramischen kultur und die mit ihnen verbundenen siedlungspuren in Brześć Kujawski,' *Wiadomości Archeologiczne*, t. XV, 1–105.

JESSEN, K. and HELBAEK, [1944]. *Cereals in Great Britain and Ireland in Prehistoric and Early Historic Times.* Det Kong. Danske Vidensk. Selsk. Biol. Skr. bd. III, nr. 2. Copenhagen.

JESSEN, K. [1949]. 'Studies in Late Quaternery Deposits and Flora-History of Ireland,' *P.R.I.A.*, vol. 52, sect. B, no. 6. Dublin.

JOCHELSON, W. [1928]. *Peoples of Asiatic Russia.* New York.

JOCHELSON, W. [1933]. *History, Ethnology and Anthropology of the Aleut.* Carnegie Institution of Washington, Pub. 432.

KANE, Robert [1845]. *The Industrial Resources of Ireland.* 2nd ed. Dublin.

KANTOR, H. J. [1947]. *The Aegean and the Orient in the Second Millennium B.C.* Arch. Inst. Am., Monographs on Arch. and Fine Arts, no. 14.

KARO, G. H. [1930]. *Die Schachtgräber von Mykenai.* Munich.

KARSLAKE, J. B. P. [1933]. 'Plough Coulters from Silchester,' *Ant. J.*, XIII, 455–63.

KAUDERN, W. [1924]. 'Om infödingsbåtar i Nederländska Ost-Indien och hällristningsbåtar i Sverige,' *Göteborgs sjöfartsmuseums Årsbok*, 1924.

KEILLER, A. [1936]. 'Two Axes of Presely Stone from Ireland,' *Antiquity*, 1936, 220–1.

KELLER, F. [1866–78]. *The Lake Dwellings of Switzerland and other parts of Europe.* London.

KELLER, O. [1909–13]. *Die antike Tierwelt.* 2 bd. Leipzig.

KENDRICK, T. D. [1925]. *The Axe Age.* London.

KENDRICK, T. D. and HAWKES, C. F. C. [1932]. *Archaeology in England and Wales, 1914–31.*

KERSTEN, K. [1936]. *Zur älteren nordischen Bronzezeit.* Kiel.

KERSTEN, K. [1936a]. 'Das Totenhaus von Grünhof-Tesperhude, Kreis Herzogtum Lauenburg,' *Offa*, 1936, 56–87. Kiel.

KIEKEBUSCH, A. [1911]. 'Ein Dorf aus der Bronzezeit bei Hasenfelde, Kr. Lebus,' *Prähist. Z.*, III, 1911, 287–96.

KIEKEBUSCH, A. [1923]. *Die Ausgrabung des bronzezeitlichen Dorfes Buch bei Berlin.* Berlin.

KJAER, H. [1928]. 'Oldtidshuse ved Ginderup i Thy,' *Fra Nationalmuseets Arbejdsmark*, 1928. [1930]. 'En ny Hustomt fra oldtidsbopladsen ved Ginderup,' *ibid*, 1930.

KLOSE, O. [1926]. 'Ein buntes Gewebe aus dem prähistorischen Salzbergwerke auf dem Dürrnberge bei Hallein,' *Mitt. Ant. Ges. Wien*, LVI, 346–50. Vienna.

KNOWLES, W. J. [1903]. 'Stone-Axe Factories near Cushendall, County Antrim,' *J.R.A.I.*, XXXIII (1903), 360–6. [1906] 'Stone-Axe Factories near Cushendall," *J.R.S., Ant. Ireland*, XVI (1906), 283–94.

KØIE, M. [1943]. 'Töj fra Yngre Bronzealder fremstillet af nælde (*Urtica dioica* L.), *Aarbøger*, 1943, 98–102.

KOSSINNA, G. [1915]. 'Zu den vorgeschichtlichen Eisenbarren,' *Mannus Z.*, 1915.

KOSSINNA, G. [1917–18]. 'Meine Reise nach West- und Ostpreussen und meine Berufung zu Generalfeld-marschall v. Hindenburg im August 1915,' *Mannus Z.*, IX, 119–95. Also X, 202–6 and taf. IV (map.) (1918).

KOSTRZEWSKI, J. [1936]. *Osada bagienna w Biskupinie w. pow. żnińskim.* Poznán.

KOSTRZEWSKI, J. [1938]. 'Biskupin. An Early Iron Age Village in Western Poland,' *Antiquity*, 1938, 311–17.

KOSTRZEWSKI, J. (Ed.) [1939]. *Gniezno.* Biblioteka prehistoryczna t. IV. Poznán.

KRASHENINNIKOV, S. [1764]. *History of Kamtschatka and the Kurilski Islands, with Countries Adjacent.* (J. Grieve's transl.). Gloucester.

KRAUSE, E. [1904]. 'Vorgeschichtliche Fischereigeräte und neuere Vergleichsstücke,' *Z. für Fischerei*, bd. XI, s. 133–300. Berlin.

KRIČEVSKIJ, E. [1940]. 'Les "Plateformes" de Tripolje,' *Sovyetskaya Archeologia*, VI, 20–45.

KRÜGER, H. [1936]. 'Zur Geschichte der Bohlenweg-Forschung in Nordwestdeutschland,' *Mannus Z.*, 28, 463–95. Leipzig.

KUHN, E. [1932]. Beiträge zur Kenntnis der Säugetierfauna der Schweiz seit dem Neolithikum,' *Revue suisse de zoologie*, t. 39, no. 18, 531–768.

KUHN, E. [1935]. 'Die Fauna des Pfahlbaues Obermeilen am Zürichsee,' *Vierteljahrsschrift Naturf. Ges. in Zürich*, Jhg. LXXX, 1935, 241–330.

KUHN, E. [1947]. 'Paläontologie und Prähistorie,' *Bosch Festschrift*, 27–43. Aarau.

KUJALA, V. [1948]. 'Antrean Korpilahden kivikautisen verkon kuituaines,' *Suomen Museo*, LIV–LV (1947–8), 24–7.

KYRLE, G. [1912]. 'Die zeitliche Stellung der prähistorischen Kupfergruben auf dem Mitterberge bei Bischofshofen,' *Mitt. Ant. Ges. Wien*, XLII, 1912, 196–208. Vienna.

KYRLE, G. [1916]. Der prähistorische Bergbaubetrieb in den Salzburger Alpen,' *Österreichische Kunsttopographie*, bd. XVII, 1–70. Vienna.

KYRLE, G. [1924]. 'Bergbau,' *Ebert's Reallexikon*, I, 409–25.

KYRLE, G. [1932]. 'Die Höttinger Kultur in ihrer Beziehung zu den endbronzezeitlichen kupferbergwerken der nördlichen Ostalpen,' *Wiener Prähist. Z.*, XIX, 9–24. Vienna.

LA BAUME, W. [1928]. 'Bildliche darstellungen auf ostgermanischen tongefässen der frühen Eisenzeit,' *IPEK*, 1928, 25–48.

LARTET, E. and CHRISTY, H. [1865–75]. *Reliquiae Aquitanicae, being Contributions to the Archaeology and Palaeontology of Périgord and the adjoining Provinces of southern France.* London.

LECHLER, G. [1945]. 'Nutrition of Paleolithic Man,' *Papers of the Michigan Academy of Science, Arts and Letters*, XXX, 499–510.

LEHMAN-FILHÉS, M. [1901]. *Über Brettchenweberei.* Berlin.

LEINBOCK, F. [1932]. *Die materielle kultur der Esten.* Tartu.

LEISNER, G. and V. [1943]. *Die megalithgräber der Iberische halbinsel.* 2 vols. Berlin.

LEPPÄAHO, J. et al. [1936]. 'Närpiön ja Oulujoen kivikauden hyljelöydöt,' *Suomen Museo*, XLIII, 1–37. Helsinki.

LESER, P. [1931]. *Entstehung und verbreitung des Pfluges.* Münster.

LETHBRIDGE, T. C. [1934]. 'Investigation of the Ancient Causeway in the Fen between Fordy and Little Thetford, Cambridgeshire,' *Proc. Camb. Ant. S.*, XXXV, 86–9.

LID, N. [1930]. 'Skifundet fra Övrebö,' *Univ. oldsaksam., Årbok*, 152–78. Oslo.

LID, N. [1937]. *On the History of Norwegian Skis.* Oslo.

LID, N. [1938]. *Skifundet frå Furnes.* Oslo.

LIDDELL, D. M. [1929]. 'New Light on an Old Problem,' *Antiquity*, 1929, 283–91.

LINDNER, K. [1937]. *Die Jagd der Vorzeit.* Berlin.

LINDQUIST, S. [1924]. 'Båten från Fiholm, Västmanland,' *Fornvännen*, 1924, 224 f.

LINDQVIST, S. [1934]. 'Sveriges handel och samfärdsel under forntiden,' *Nordisk Kultur*, XVI, *Handel og Samfaerdsel*, 49–67.

LINKOLA, K. [1916, 1921]. 'Studien über den Einfluss der Kultur auf die Flora in den Gegenden nördlich vom Ladogasee,' *Acta Soc. Fauna et Flora Fennica*, 45: 1 (1916) and 45: 2 (1921).

LINNAEUS, C. v. [1745]. *Öländska och Gothländska Resa.* Stockholm and Uppsala.

LISSAUER, A. [1905]. 'Die Doppeläxte der Kupferzeit im westlichen Europa,' *Z. f. Ethnologie*, XXXVII, 519–25. Berlin.

LITHBERG, N. [1914]. *Gotlands Stenålder.* Stockholm.

Loë, Baron A. DE and MUNCK, E. DE [1889]. 'Notice sur des fouilles pratiquées récemment sur l'emplacement du vaste atelier néolithique de Spiennes (Hainaut),' *Congr. int. d'anthr. et d'arch. préhistoriques, C. r. 10ᵉ. Sess. Paris*, 1889, 569–602.

Loë, Baron A. DE [1928]. *Belgique ancienne*. I. Brussels.

LÖNNBERG, E. [1908]. 'Om några fynd i Litorinalera i Norrköping, 1907, *Arkiv. f. Zoologi*, bd. 4, no. 22, pp. 1–27. Stockholm.

LORD, J. K. [1866]. *The Naturalist in Vancouver Island and British Columbia*. 2 vols. London.

LOUIS, M., PEYROLLE, D. and ARNALL, J. [1947]. 'Les fonds de cabanes énéolithiques de Fontbouïsse,' *Gallia*, V, 1947, 235–57.

LUCAS, A [1948]. *Ancient Egyptian Materials and Industries*. 3rd ed. London.

LUHO, V. [1945]. 'Das Alter der Schlittenkufe aus Pielavesi,' *Suomen Museo*, LII, 82–4.

LUNDQVIST, G. [1929]. 'En förhistorisk paddel från Dalarna,' *Geol. För. Förh.*, LI, 367–81. Stockholm.

LUNG, W. [1942]. 'Hüttenreste der Mittelsteinzeit im Königsforst, Bezirk Köln,' *Germania*, bd. 26, 79–84.

LYDEKKER, R. [1912]. *The Sheep and its Cousins*. London.

MACDONALD, G. and PARK, A. [1906]. *The Roman Forts on the Bar Hill, Dumbartonshire*. Glasgow.

MACGREGOR, M., LEE, G. W. and WILSON, G. V. [1920]. *The Iron Ores of Scotland. Special Reports on the Mineral Resources of Great Britain*. Vol. XI, *Iron Ores (cont.)*. Mem. Geological Survey, Scotland.

MACPHERSON, H. A. [1897]. *A History of Fowling, being an Account of the many curious devices by which wild birds are or have been captured in different parts of the world*. Edinburgh.

MADSEN, A. P. (MÜLLER, S., NEERGAARD, C., PETERSEN, C. G. J., ROSTRUP, E., STEENSTRUP, K. J. V., and WINGE, H) [1900]. *Affaldsdynger fra Stenalderen i Danmark*. Copenhagen.

MAHR, A. [1937]. 'New Aspects and Problems in Irish Prehistory,' *P.P.S.*, III (1937), 262–436.

MANKER, E. [1946]. 'Ett förhistoriskt skidfynd,' *Fataburen*, 1946, 195–200.

MANKER, E. [1947]. 'Lomsjökulleskidan,' *På skidor*, 1947, 167–73.

MANNINEN, I. [1927]. 'Zur Ethnologie des Einbaumes,' *Eurasia Septentrionalis Antiqua* I, 4–17. Helsingfors.

MANNINEN, I. [1932]. *Die Finnisch-Ugrischen Völker*. Leipzig, 1932.

MARINATOS, SP. [1933]. 'La marine Créto-Mycénienne,' *Bull. de Correspondance Hellénique*, 1933, 170–235.

MARTIN, Martin [1934]. (a) *A Description of the Western Islands of Scotland*, pp. 1–391. Orig. publ. London, 1703. (b) *A Late Voyage to St. Kilda*, pp. 394–476. Orig. publ. London, 1698. 1934 edition, Stirling.

MARYON, H. [1936]. 'Soldering and Welding in the Bronze and Early Iron Ages,' *Technical Studies in the Field of the Fine Arts*, 5: 2, 1936, 75–108.

MARYON, H. [1938]. 'The Technical Methods of the Irish Smiths in the Bronze and Early Iron Ages,' *P.R.I.A.*, XLIV, C. 7 (1938), 181–228.

MARYON, H. [1938a]. 'Some Prehistoric Metalworkers' Tools,' *Ant. J.*, XVIII (1938), 243–50.

MASON, O. T. [1893]. 'North American Bows, Arrows, and Quivers,' *Ann. Rep. Smithsonian Inst.*, 1893, 631–79.

MASON, O. T. [1899]. 'Amerindian Arrow Feathering,' *Am. Anthrop.*, 1899, 583–5.

MASON, O. T. [1894]. 'Primitive Travel and Transportation,' *Rep. U.S. Nat. Museum for* 1894, 237–593. Washington.

MASON, O. T. [1904]. 'Aboriginal American Basketry: studies in a textile art without machinery,' *Rep. U.S. National Museum for* 1902, pp. 171–548. Washington.

MATHIASSEN, T. [1934]. 'Flinthandel i Stenalderen,' *Nationalmuseets Arbejdsmark*, 1934, 18–22.

MATHIASSEN, T. [1935]. 'Blubber Lamps in the Ertebølle Culture,' *Acta Arch.*, vol. VI, 1935, 139–52.

MATHIASSEN, T. [1938]. 'Some recently found reindeer antler implements in Denmark,' *Acta Arch.*, IX, 173–5.

MATHIASSEN, T. [1938a]. 'Some Unusual Danish Harpoons,' *Acta Arch.* IX, 224–8.

MATHIASSEN, T. (with JESSEN, K. and DEGERBØL, M.) [1939]. 'Bundsø, en yngre stenalders boplads paa Aals,' *Aarbøger*, 1939, 1–55.

MATHIASSEN, T. [1940] 'Havnelev-Strandegaard. Et Bidrag til Diskussionen om den yngre Stenalders Begyndelse i Danmark,' *Aarbøger*, 1940.

MATHIASSEN, T. [1941]. 'Two new Danish Implements of Reindeer Antler,' *Acta Arch.*, 1941, XII, 125 ff. Also cf. TROELS-SMITH, J. [1941]. 'Geological Dating of Reindeer Antler Hammer from Vedbaek,' *ibid.*, 135–44.

MATHIASSEN, T., DEGERBØL, M. and TROELS-SMITH, J. [1942]. *Dyrholmen. En sten-alderboplads paa Djursland.* Klg. Danske Videnskab. Selskab Ark-Kunsthist. Skr., Bd. 1, Nr. 1. Copenhagen.

MATHIASSEN, T. *et al.* [1943]. *Stenalder-bopladser i Aamosen.* Nordiske Fortids-minder, III, 3. Copenhagen.

MATHIASSEN, T. [1948]. *Studier over Vestjyl-lands Oldtidsbebyggelse.* Nationalmuseets Skr. Ark.-Hist. R.II. Copenhagen.

MAURIZIO, A. [1927]. *Die Geschichte unserer pflanzennahrung von den Urzeiten bis zur Gegenwart.* Berlin.

MAYET, L. and PISSOT, J. [1915]. *Abri-sous-roche préhistorique de la Colombière.* Lyon.

MEGAW, B. R. S. and HARDY, E. M. [1938]. 'British Decorated Axes and their Diffusion during the Earlier Part of the Bronze Age,' *P.P.S.*, IV, 272–307.

MERHART, G. VON [1940]. 'Die Bernstein-schieber von Kakovatos,' *Germania*, bd. 24, 1940, 99–102.

MIKOV, V. [1933]. *Stations et trouvailles pré-historiques en Bulgarie.* Sofia.

MILNE, J. G. [1948]. *Finds of Greek Coins in the British Isles.* Ashmolean, Oxford.

MINNS, E. H. [1913]. *Scythians and Greeks.* Cambridge.

MISKE, K. VON [1908]. *Die prähistorische Ansiedelung Velem St. Vid.* Bd. 1. Vienna.

MITCHELL, G. F. [1941]. 'Studies in Irish Quaternary Deposits, No. 3—The Reindeer in Ireland,' *P.R.I.A.*, vol. XLVI, sect. B., no. 14.

MITCHELL, G. F. [1945]. 'The Relative Ages of Archæological Objects recently found in bogs in Ireland,' *P.R.I.A.*, vol. L, sect. C, no. 1.

MITCHELL, G. F. and PARKES, H. M. [1949]. 'The Giant Deer in Ireland,' *P.R.I.A.*, LII, Sect. B., no. 7, 291–314.

MITCHELL, J. M. [1864]. *The Herring. Its Natural History and National Importance.* Edinburgh.

MITZKA, W. [1933]. *Deutsche Bauern- und Fischerboote.* Wörter und Sachen, beiheft 6. Heidleberg.

MONTELIUS, O. [1910]. 'Der Handel in der Vorzeit,' *Prähist. Z.*, II, 249–91.

MORTIMER, J. R. [1905]. *Forty Years' Re-searches in British and Saxon Burial-Mounds of East Yorkshire.* London.

MORTON, F. [1942]. 'Zwei hallstattzeitliche Kopfbedeckungen,' *Germania*, bd. 26, 115–6.

MOVIUS, H. L. [1936]. 'A Neolithic Site on the River Bann,' *P.R.I.A.*, XLIII, C., 17–40.

MOVIUS, H. J. [1942]. *The Irish Stone Age.* Cambridge.

MUCH, M. [1893]. *Die Kupferzeit in Europa.* 2nd ed. Jena.

MÜLLER, K. [1909]. 'Die Funde aus den Kuppelgräbern von Kakovatos,' *Athenische Mitt.*, XXXIV, 1909, 269–328.

MÜLLER, S. [1904]. 'Vej og Bygd i Sten- og Bronzealderen,' *Aarbøger*, 1904.

MULLER, S. [1907]. 'Charrue, joug et mors,' *Mém. de la Soc. Roy. des Antiqu. du Nord*, 1902–7, 55–59.

MUNRO, R. [1882]. *Ancient Scottish Lake-dwellings.* Edinburgh.

MUNRO, R. [1894]. 'Notes on Ancient Bone Skates,' *P.S.A.S.*, XXVIII, 185–97.

MUNRO, R. [1897]. *Prehistoric Problems.* Edinburgh and London.

MUNRO, R. [1912]. *Palaeolithic Man and Terra-mara Settlements in Europe.* Edinburgh.

MUNRO, R. and GILLESPIE, P. [1918–9]. 'Fur-ther notes on ancient wooden traps—the so-called otter and beaver traps,' *P.S.A.S.*, LIII, 162–7.

MUNTHE, H. [1940]. *Om Nordens främst Balti-kums, senkvartära Utveckling och Stenålders-bebyggelse*, Kungl. Sv. Vet. Akad.Handl., bd. 19, no. 1. Stockholm 1940.

MURDOCH, J. [1892]. *Ethnological Results of the Point Barrow Expedition*, 1881–83. IXth Ann. Rep. Smithsonian Institution. Washington.

MYRES, J. L. [1930]. *Who were the Greeks?* Berkeley, California.

MYRES, Sir JOHN [1943]. *Mediterranean Cul-ture.* (Frazer Lecture.) Cambridge.

NANSEN, F. [1890] *First Crossing of Greenland.* London, 1890.

NAUE, J. [1887]. *Die Hügelgräber zwischen Ammer- und Staffelsee.* Stuttgart.

NAVARRO, J. M. DE [1925]. 'Prehistoric Routes between Northern Europe and Italy defined by the Amber Trade,' *Geogr. J.*, 66, 481–507.

NAVARRO, J. M. DE [1928]. 'Massilia and Early Celtic Culture,' *Antiquity*, 1928, 423–440. Cf. Review of Jacobsthal and Langs-dorf in *Antiquity*, 1930, 130–2.

NAVARRO, J. M. DE [1950]. 'The British Isles and the Beginning of the Northern Early Bronze Age,' in FOX and DICKINS (1950), 75–106.

NETOLITZKY, F. [1931]. 'Unser Wissen von den alten Kulturpflanzen Mitteleuropas,' XX *Ber. d. Römisch-German. Komm.*, 14–76.

NEUWEILER, E. [1905]. 'Die prähistorischen Pflanzenreste Mitteleuropas mit besonderer Berücksichtigung der schweizerischeu Funde' *Vierteljahrschr. d. naturf. Ges. in Zürich*, bd. L, 1905, 23–111.

NEUWEILER, E. [1919]. 'Die Pflanzenreste aus den Pfahlbauten am Alpenquai in Zürich und von Wollishofen,' *ibid.*, bd. LXIV, 1919, 617–46.

NEUWEILER, E. [1924]. 'Die Tierwelt der schweizerischen Pfahlbauten,' in VIOLLIER, D. *et. al.* 1924, 109–20.

NEUWEILER, E. [1935]. 'Nachträge urgeschichtlicher Pflanzen,' *Vierteljahreschrift d. Naturf. Ges. in Zürich*, Jhg. 80. [1946]. 'Nachträge II . . .', *ibid.*, Jhg. 91.

NEWALL, R. S. [1929]. 'Two Shale Cups of the Early Bronze Age and Other Similar Cups,' *Wilts. Arch. Mag.*, XLIV (1929), 111–17.

NICOLOAISSEN, O. [1912–13]. 'Flintredskaper fra det nordlige Norges stenalder,' *Tromsø Museums Aarshefter*, 35–36, 1912–13, 44–52. Kristiania.

NIELSEN, N. [1925]. 'La Production du fer en Jutland Septentrional dans les temps préhistoriques et au moyen âge,' *Mém. d. Antiqu. du Nord*, 1920–5, 337–440.

NIETSCH, H. [1939]. *Wald und Siedlung im Vorgesch. Mitteleuropa*. Mannus Biblio. 64.

NIHLÉN, J. [1927]. *Gotlands Stenåldersboplatser*. Stockholm.

NIHLÉN, J. and BOËTHIUS, G. [1933]. *Gotländska gårdar och byar under äldre järnåldern*. Stockholm.

NILSSON, M. P. [1927]. *The Minoan-Mycenæan Religion and its Survival in Greek Religion*. Lund.

NILSSON, SVEN [1838/43]. *Skandinaviska Nordens Urinvånare. Ett försök i Komparativa Ethnografien och ett bidrag till menniskoslägtets utvecklingshistoria*. Lund, 1838–43.

NOËTTES, L. DE [1926]. 'La force motrice animale à travers les âges et la question de l'esclavage,' *L'Anthropologie*, XXXVI, 297–308.

NORDÉN, A. [1925]. *Östergötlands Bronsålder*. Linköping.

NORDÉN, A. [1926]. *Kiviksgraven*. 2nd ed. Stockholm.

NORDENSKIÖLD, A. E. [1881]. *The Voyage of the Vega round Asia and Europe*. (Transl.) London.

NORDGAARD, O. [1908]. 'Træk av fiskeriets utvikling i Norge,' *Kgl. norske Videns. Selsk. Skr.*, 1908, no. 1, pp. 1–116. Trondheim.

NORDHAGEN, R. [1933]. *De Senkvartære Klimavekslinger i Nordeuropa og deres Betydning for Kulturforskningen*. Oslo.

NORDMANN, C. A. [1935]. 'The Megalithic Culture of Northern Europe,' *Suomen Muin. Aik.*, XXXIX, 1935. Helsingfors.

NORDMANN, V. [1936]. *Menneskets Indvandring til Norden*. Danmarks Geolog. Unders. III R., nr. 27. Copenhagen.

NORDQVIST, O. [1899]. 'Beitrag zur Kenntniss der isolirten Formen der Ringelrobbe (*Phoca fœtida* Fabr.),' *Acta Societatis pro Fauna et Flora Fennica*, XV, no. 7, pp. 1–43. Helsingfors.

NØRLUND, P. [1948]. *Trelleborg*. Nordiska Fortidsminder, IV bd., 1 hft. Copenhagen.

NORTH, F. J. [1937]. *Finland in Summer*. Cambridge.

NUMMEDAL, A. [1912]. 'Björneremsfundet forhistoriske hulefund fra Mien i Romsdalen,' *Det Kgl. Norske Vidensk. Selsk. Skr.*, 1912, nr. 12. Trondhjem.

NUMMEDAL, A. [1919]. 'Bopladsfund paa Halmöy og Dönna,' *Det Kgl. Norske Vidensk. Selsk. Skr.*, 1919, nr. 5. Trondhjem.

OBERMAIER, H. [1925]. *Fossil Man in Spain*. New Haven. Also Spanish edition.

OELMANN, F. [1927]. *Haus und hof in altertum*. Berlin and Leipzig.

OELMANN, F. [1929]. 'Hausurnen oder Speicherurnen,' *Bonner Jahrbücher*, hft. 134 (1929), 1–39.

OKEY, T. [1932]. *An Introduction to the Art of Basket-Making*. London.

OKKOLA, T. [1945]. 'Einige vorgeschichtliche Skier und Schlittenkufen, *Finska Fornminnesföreningens Tidskrift*, XLV, 258–67.

OLAUS, MAGNUS [1555]. *Historia de gentibus septentrionalibus*. Rome.

OLDEBERG, A. [1932]. 'Some contributions to the earliest history of the Sickle,' *Acta Arch.*, III, 209–30.

OLDEBERG, A. [1942, 1943]. *Metallteknik under Förhistorisk Tid*. Del. I, II. Lund.

OLSSON, A. [1938]. 'Den extensiva foderfångsten i Ytterbergs by i Härjedalen,' *Rig*, 1938, 177–206. Stockholm.

O'NEIL, B. H. ST. J. [1936]. Excavations at Caerau Ancient Village, Clynnog, Caernarvonshire, 1933 and 1934,' *Ant., J.*, 1936, 295–320.

O'RÍORDÁIN [1936]. 'The Halberd in Bronze Age Europe,' *Arch.*, LXXXVI, 195–321.

O'RÍORDÁIN, S. P. [1946]. 'Prehistory in Ireland, 1937–46, *P.P.S.*, 1946, 142–71.

ORWIN, C. S. [1938]. *The Open Fields*. Oxford.

PALMER, L. J. [1926]. *Progress of Reindeer Grazing Investigations in Alaska.* U.S. Dept. of Agriculture, Dept. Bulletin, No. 1423. Washington.

PÄLSI, S. [1912]. ' Über steinzeitliche Hakenfischgeräte in Finland,' *Finska Fornm. Tidskr.* XXVI, 195–204.

PÄLSI, S. [1920]. ' Ein steinzeitlicher Moorfund bei Korpilahti im Kirchspiel Antrea, Län Wiborg,' *Finska Fornm. Tidskr.*, XXVIII, no. 2.

PARAIN, Prof. CHARLES [1941]. ' The Evolution of Agricultural Technique,' *The Cambr. Econ. Hist. of Europe*, I, 118–68. Cambridge.

PARET, O. [1930]. ' Die einbäume im Federseeried und im übrigen Europa,' *Prähist. Z.*, XXI, 76–116.

PARET, O. [1942]. ' Vorgeschichtliche Wohngruben,' *Germania*, bd. 26 (1942), 84–103.

PARET, O. [1946]. *Das Neue Bild Vorgeschichte.* Stuttgart.

PARKES, JOAN [1925]. *Travel in England in the Seventeenth Century.* Oxford.

PASSEMARD, E. [1922]. ' La caverne d'Isturitz (Basses-Pyrénées),' *Rev. archéologique*, t. XV, 1–45.

PAYNE, F. G. [1948]. ' The Plough in Ancient Britain,' *Arch. J.*, CIV, 82–111.

PEACH, MABEL W. [1934]. *Tablet Weaving.* The Dryad Press, Leicester.

PENDLEBURY, J. D. S. [1930]. *Aegyptiaca.*

PENDLEBURY, J. D. S. [1939]. *The Archaeology of Crete.* London.

PÉQUART, M. and S.-J. [1937]. *Téviec. Station-nécropole mésolithique du Morbihan.* Arch. Inst. Pal. Humaine, Mém. 18. Paris.

PERCIVAL, JOHN [1943]. *Wheat in Great Britain.* 2nd ed. London.

PERSSON, A. W. [1931]. *The Royal Tombs at Dendra near Midea.* Lund. [1942]. *New Tombs at Dendra near Midea.* Lund.

PETERS, E. [1930]. *Die altsteinzeitliche kulturstätte Petersfels.* Augsburg.

PETERS, E. and TOEPFER, V. [1932]. ' Der Abschluss der Grabungen am Petersfels bei Engen im badischen Hegau,' *Prähist. Z.*, XXIII, 155–99.

PETERSEN, H. [1888]. *Vognfundene i Dejbjerg Prestegaardsmose.* Copenhagen.

PETERSEN, JAN [1933]. *Gamle gårdsanlegg i Rogaland*, I. Inst. for Sammenlign. Kulturforskn. Ser. B, XXIII. Oslo. [1936], *ibid.*, II. *ibid.* Ser. B, XXXI.

PETERSEN, T. [1940]. ' Hestneshulen,' *Det. Kgl. norske vidensk, selsk. Skr. Trondheim*, 1910, nr. 2.

PETERSEN, T. [1916]. ' Haugshulen paa Leka. Et nyt hulefund fra aeldre jernalder,' *Det. Kgl. Norske Vidensk. Selsk. Skr.*, 1916, nr. 4. Trondhjem.

PETRIE, G. [1866–7]. ' Notice of Ruins of Ancient Dwellings at Skara, Bay of Skaill, in the Parish of Sandwick, Orkney, recently excavated,' *P.S.A.S.*, VII, 201–219.

PETRIE, W. M. FLINDERS [1917]. *Tools and Weapons.* London.

PHILLIPS, C. W. [1940]. ' The Excavation of the Sutton Hoo Ship-burial,' *Ant. J.*, XX (1940), 149–202.

PHILLIPS, C. W. [1941]. ' Some Recent Finds from the Trent near Nottingham,' *Ant. J.*, 1941, 133–43.

PJESKER, H. [1937]. ' Ein mittelsteinzeitlicher Hüttengrundriss von Bockum, Landkreis Lüneburg,' *Nachr. f. Deutsche Vorzeit*, 1937, 37–51.

PIETTE, E. [1895]. ' Études d'ethnographie préhistorique,' *L'Anthropologie*, t. VI, 276–92.

PIGGOTT, S. [1931]. ' The Neolithic Pottery of the British Isles,' *Arch. J..*, LXXXVIII (1931), 67–158.

PIGGOTT, S. [1938]. ' The Early Bronze Age in Wessex,' *P.P.S.*, IV (1938), 52–106.

PIRA, A. [1909]. ' Studien zur Geschichte der Schweinerassen, insbesondere derjenigen Schwedens,' *Zoologische Jahrbücher*, Suppl. 10, 233–426. Jena.

PIRA, A. [1926]. ' On Bone Deposits in the Cave " Stora Förvar," on the Isle of Stora Karlsö, Sweden,' *Acta Zoologica*, bd. 7, pp. 123–217. Stockholm.

PITT-RIVERS, Gen. A. [1887–98]. *Excavations in Cranborne Chase*, vols. I–IV.

PREUSCHEN, E. and PITTIONI, R. [1937]. ' Untersuchungen im Bergbaugebiete Kelchalpe bei Kitzbühel, Tirol. Erster Bericht (1931–6), *Mitt. d. Prähistorischen Komm. d. Akademie d. Wissen*, VI bd., nr. 1–3, Vienna.

PITTIONI, R. [1947]. ' Untersuchungen im Bergbaugebiete Kelchalpe bei Kitzbühel, Tirol. Zweiter Bericht (1937–8),' *Mitt. d. Prähist. Komm. d. Akad. d. Wissen*, V bd., nr. 2–3. Vienna.

PRICHARD, H. Hesketh [1936]. *Sport in Wildest Britain.* 1936 ed. London.

PUMPELLY, R. [1904]. *Explorations in Turkestan.* Washington.

PUYDT, M. DE., HAMAL-NANDRIN, J. and SERVAIS, J. [N.D.]. *Mélanges d'Archéologie préhistorique.* Liège.

QUIGGIN, A. H. [1949]. *A Survey of Primitive Money.* London.

RANKINE, W. F. [1949]. ' Stone " Maceheads " with Mesolithic Associations from South-Eastern England,' *P.P.S.*, 1949, 70–76.

RASMUSSEN, H. [1940]. ' Dyrefælder fra Broncealderen,' in *Fra Danmarks Ungtid.*, 112–28. Copenhagen.

RAU, C. [1884]. *Prehistoric Fishing in Europe and North America*, Smithsonian Contributions to Knowledge, vol. 25. Washington.

RAUDONIKAS, W. J. [1938]. *Les gravures rupestres des bords du lac Onéga et de la mer Blanche.* Moscow.

RAUSING, G. [1949]. ' Three Bronze Age Mounds at Barkåkra in Skane,' *Medd. Lunds Univ. Hist. Mus.*, 1949, 147–82.

READER, F. W. [1908]. ' Report of the Red Hills Exploration Committee, 1906–7,' *Proc. Soc. Ant.*, XXII, 164–207. [1910]. *ibid.* 1908–9, *P.S.A.*, XXIII, 66–96.

REESEMA, E. S. VAN [1926]. *Contribution to the Early History of Textile Technics.* Verh. d. kon. Akad. v. Wetenschappen Amsterdam. Afd. Letterkunde. N.R., d. XXVI, no. 2.

REICHEL, W. VON [1901]. *Homerische Waffen.* 2nd ed. Vienna.

REID, R. W. [1922]. ' Ancient Wooden Trap from the Moss of Auquharney,' *P.S.A.S.*, LVI, 282–7.

REINECKE, P. [1930]. ' Die Bedeutung der Kupferbergwerke der Ostalpen für die Bronzezeit Mitteleuropas,' *Schumacher-Festschrift*, 107–115. Mainz.

REINECKE, P. [1933]. ' Kyprische Dolche aus Mitteleuropa,' *Germania*, bd. 17, 256–59.

REINECKE, P. [1938]. ' Neue frühbronzezeitliche Hortfunde aus Südbayern,' *Germania*, bd. 22, 4–7.

REINERTH, H. [1926]. *Die Jüngere Steinzeit der Schweiz.* Augsburg.

REINERTH, H. [1928]. ' Die schnurkeramischen Totenhäuser von Sarmenstorf,' *Mannus*, *Erg..-Bd.* 6.

REINERTH, H. [1929 and 1936]. *Das Federseemoor.* Leipzig.

REINERTH, H. [1938]. *Das Pfahldorf Sipplingen.* Leipzig.

RETZIUS, G. [1885]. *Finnland, Schilderungen aus seiner Natur, seiner alten kultur und seinem heutigen Volksleben.* Berlin.

REVERDIN, L. [1922]. La Faune néolithique de la station de St.-Aubin (Port-Conty, lac de Neuchâtel), *Archives suisses d'Anthropologie générale*, t. IV, 1920–2, 251–4.

REVERDIN, L. [1931]. ' Sur la faune du Kjökkenmödding morbihannais, Er Yoh, et ses rapports avec celle des stations néolithiques lacustres de la Suisse,' *Archives suisses d'Anthropologie générale*, t. VI, 1930–1, 79–86.

REVERDIN, L. [1932]. ' Sur la faune du néolithique ancien et moyen des stations lacustres,' *Archives suisses d'Anthropologie générale*, t. V, 1928–31, 41–6.

RICHARDS, AUDREY I. [1939]. *Land, Labour and Diet in Northern Rhodesia. An Economic Study of the Bemba Tribe.* London.

RICHMOND, I. A. [1935]. ' Trajan's Army on Trajan's Column,' *Papers of the British School at Rome*, vol. XIII, 1–40.

RICKARD, T. A. [1932]. *Man and Metals.* 2 vols. New York.

RICKARD, T. A. [1941]. ' The Use of Meteoric Iron,' *J.R.A.I.*, LXXI, 55–66.

RIDGEWAY, Sir W. [1905]. *The Origin and Influence of the Thoroughbred Horse.* Cambridge.

RIETH, A. [1941]. ' Zur Tecknik antiker und prähistorischer Kunst, das Holzdrechseln,' *IPEK*, bd. 13–14, 85–107. Berlin.

RIKLI, M. [1943]. *Das Pflanzenkleid der Mittelmeerländer*, bd. I. [1946]. bd. II.

RIVIÈRE, E. [1886]. ' Des Reptiles et des Poissons trouvés dans les grottes de Menton (Italie),' *C. r. de l'Ac. des Sc.* 1886, t. CIII, 1211–3. Paris.

ROBERTSON, A. J. [1939]. *Anglo-Saxon Charters.* Cambridge.

ROEDER, C. [1901]. ' Prehistoric and Subsequent Mining at Alderley Edge, with a Sketch of the Archæological Features of the Neighbourhood,' *Lancs. and Chesh. Ant. Soc.*, XIX, 77–118.

ROSENBERG, G. [1937]. *Hjortspringfundet.* Copenhagen.

ROSS, ALAN S. C. [1940]. *The Terfinnas and Beormas of Ohthere.* Leeds.

ROSTOVTZEFF, M. [1922]. *Iranians and Greeks.* Oxford.

ROTH, H. LING [1918]. *Studies in Primitive Looms.* Halifax.

ROUSSELL, Aage [1934]. *Norse Building Customs in the Scottish Isles.* London.

ROUSSELL, A. [1943]. ' Det nordiske hus i Vikingetid,' in Stenberger, ed., 1943, pp. 193–200.

RUST, A. [1937]. *Das Altsteinzeitliche Rentierjägerlager Meiendorf.* Neumünster, 1937.

RUST, A. [1938]. ' Die früh- und mittelmesolithischen Hüttengrundrisse auf dem Pinnberg bei Ahrensburg,' *Offa*, 1938, 1–17.

RUST, A. [1943]. *Die alt- und mittelsteinzeitlichen Funde von Stellmoor.* Neumünster.

RÜTIMEYER, L. [1862]. ' Die Fauna der Pfahlbauten der Schweiz,' *Neue Deutschr. d. allgem-schweiz. Ges. f. d. ges. Naturwiss.* Bd. 19. Zürich.

RÜTIMEYER, L. [1924]. *Ur-ethnographie der Schweiz.* Basel.

RYDBECK, O. [1934]. 'Aktuelle Steinzeitprobleme. II. Das Pferd als Transport—und Kampfmittel in den Völkerwanderungen der Gangräberzeit,' *Medd. Lunds Univ. hist. Mus.* 1933–4, 77–98.

RYDH, H. [1931]. *Stora Karlsö under Forntiden* Stockholm.

RYTZ, W. [1935]. 'Der älteste Pflug der Welt: in Deutschland,' *Ber. der Deutschen Botan. Ges.* Jahrg. 1935, Bd. LIII, s. 811–818.

SÄFLUND, G. [1939]. *Le Terremare delle province di Modena, Reggio Emilia, Parma, Piacenza.* Lund and Leipzig.

SAINT-PÉRIER, R. DE [1920]. 'Les migrations des Tribus magdaléniennes des Pyrénées,' *Rev. anthropol.*, t. xxx, 136.

SAINT-PÉRIER, R. DE [1936]. *La Grotte d'Isturitz II. Le Magdalénien de la Grande Salle.* Arch. de l'Inst. de Paléont. hum., Mém. no. 17. Paris.

SAINT-VENANT, J. DE [1911]. *Tailleries de silex du sud de la Touraine. Inventaire des produits exportés aux temps préhistoriques et carte de leur aire de diffusion,* pp. 46. Le Mans, 1911.

SANDARS, H. W. [1910]. 'On the Use of the Deer-horn Pick in the Mining Operations of the Ancients,' *Arch.* LXII, 101–24.

SANDKLEFF, A. [1934]. 'Are Scandinavian Flint-Saws to be Considered as Leaf Knives?' *Acta Arch..,* v, 1934, 284–90.

SANGMEISTER, E. [1937]. 'Eine bandkeramische Siedlung bei Arnsbach im Regierungsbezirk Kassel,' *Germania,* 21 (1937), 213–17.

SANTA-OLALLA, J. M. [1946]. *Esquema Paletnológico de la Peninsula Hispánica.* Madrid.

SARAUW, G. F. L. [1898]. 'Lyngheden i Oldtiden. Jagttagelser fra Gravhøie,' *Aarbøger,* 1898, 69–124. Cf. *Mém. Soc. Roy. Antiqu. du Nord,* N.S. 1896–1901, 199–228.

SARAUW, G. F. L. *et al.* [1903]. 'En Stenalders Boplads i Maglemose ved Mullerup,' *Aarbøger,* 1903, 148–315.

SAURAMO, M. [1938]. 'Ein harpunierter Seehund aus dem Litorina- ton Nordfinnlands,' *Quartär,* I, 26–35.

SAVORY, H. N. [1949]. 'The Atlantic Bronze Age in South-west Europe,' *P.P.S.,* 1949, 128–155.

SCHEFFER, J. [1674]. *The History of Lappland* (Transl.). Oxford.

SHETELIG, H. and JOHANNESSEN, F. 'Das Nydamschiff,' *Acta Archaeologica,* I, 1–30. Copenhagen.

SCHLABOW, K. [1939]. 'Das Spinngut des bronzezeitlichen Webers,' *Offa,* 1939, 109–27.

SCHMIDL, M. [1928]. 'Altägyptische Techniken an afrikanischen Spiralwulstkörben,' *Festschrift. P.W. Schmidt,* 645–654. Vienna.

SCHMIDT, R. R. [1912]. *Die diluviale Vorzeit Deutschlands.* Stuttgart.

SCHMIDT, R. R. [1930–6]. *Jungsteinzeit-Siedlungen in Federseemoor.* Stuttgart.

SCHNITTGER, B. [1911]. 'Förhistoriska flintgrufvor och Kulturlager vid Kvarnby och S. Sallerup i Skåne,' *Antikvarisk Tidskrift för Sverige,* 19, 1. Stockholm.

SCHNITTGER, B. [1920]. 'Göttlandska skäppssätningar från bronsålderns slut och järnålderns början, *Aarbøger,* 1920, 43.

SCHNITTGER, B. and RYDH, H. [1940]. *Grottan Stora Förvar på Stora Karlsö.* Kgl. Vitt. Hist. och Ant. Akademien. Stockholm.

SCHOTT, C. [1935]. 'Urlandschaft und rodung. Vergleichende betrachtungen aus Europa und Kanada,' *Z.d. Ges. f. Erdkunde zu Berlin,* 1935, 81–102.

SCHREINER, K. E. [1927]. In *Osebergfundet,* bd. v, 301–4. Oslo.

SCHUCHHARDT, C. [1909–10]. 'Das technische Ornament in den Anfängen der Kunst,' *Prähist. Zeit.,* bd. I (1909), 37–54 and 351–69; bd. II (1910), 145–62.

SCHWABEDISSEN, H. [1937]. 'Die Hamburger Stufe in nordwestlichen Deutschland,' *Offa,* 2 (1937), 1–30.

SCHWANTES, G. [1928]. 'Nordisches Paläolithikum und Mesolithikum,' *Mitt Mus. Volkerk. Hamburg,* XIII, 159 ff.

SCHWANTES, G. [1939]. *Geschichte Schleswig-Holsteins.* Bd. I. *Vorgeschichte.* Lief. 1–7. Neumünster.

SCOTT, Sir LINDSAY [1947]. 'The problem of the brochs,' *P.P.S.,* 1947, 1–36.

SCOTT, Sir LINDSAY [1948]. 'Gallo-British Colonies. The Aisled Round-House Culture in the North,' *P.P.S.,* 1948, 46–125.

SEMPLE, E. C. [1932]. *Geography of the Mediterranean Region.* London.

SHEPPARD, T. [1910]. 'The Prehistoric Boat from Brigg (Lincs.),' *Trans. E. Riding, Ant. Soc..,* XVII, 33–60.

SHETELIG, H. [1909]. 'En ældre jernalders gaard paa Jäderen,' *Bergens Museums Aarbog,* 1909.

SHETELIG, H. and FALK, H. [1937]. *Scandinavian Archaeology.* Oxford.

SIBLY, T. FRANKLIN [1919]. *The Haematites of of the Forest of Dean and South Wales. Special Reports on the Mineral Resources of Great Britain. Vol. x. Iron Ores (cont.).* Mem. Geological Survey.

SIRELIUS, U. T. [1913]. 'Über einige prototype des schlittens,' *J. Soc. Finno-Ougrienne,* XXX, no. 32.

SIRELIUS, U. T. [1916]. 'Über die Art and Zeit der Zähmung des Renntiers,' *J. Soc. Finno-Ougrienne*, XXXIII, no. 2.

SIRELIUS, U. T. [1928]. 'Zur Geschichte des prähistorischen Schlittens,' *P.W. Schmidt Festschrift*, 949–53.

SIRELIUS, U. T. [1934]. *Die Volkskultur Finnlands. I. Jagd und Fischerei.* (Transl.). Berlin and Leipzig.

SIRET, L. [1887]. *Les premiers ages du métal dans le sud-est de l'Espagne.* Brussels.

SJÖBECK, M. [1932]. 'Löväng och trädgård,' *Fataburen*, 1932, 59–74.

SJÖBECK, M. [1933]. 'Lövängskulturen i Sydsverige,' *Ymer*, 1933, 33–66.

SLOMANN, W. [1950]. *Medelpad og Jämtland i eldre jernalder.* Univ. Bergen Årbok, 1948. Hist.-antikv. r. Nr. 2.

SMITH, H. T. U. [1949]. 'Physical Effects of Pleistocene Climatic Changes in Nonglaciated Areas,' *Bull. Geol. Soc. America*, vol. 60, 1485–1515.

SMITH, J. A. [1869]. 'Notice of the Remains of the Reindeer, *Cervus tarandus*, found in Ross-shire, Sutherland, and Caithness, with notes of its occurrence throughout Scotland,' *P.S.A.S.*, VIII, 186–222.

SMITH, R. A. and GOWLAND, W. [1905]. 'Ancient British Iron Currency,' *Proc. Soc. Antiq.*, 2nd S., XX, 179–94.

SMITH, R. A. [1912]. 'Date of Grimes' Graves and Cissbury,' *Arch.*, LXIII, 109.

SMITH, R. A. [1918]. 'The Essex Red Hills as Salt-Works,' *Proc. Soc. Antiq.*, XXX, 36–53.

SOLBERG, O. [1910]. 'Eisenzeitfunde aus Ostfinmarken. Lappländische Studien,' *Videnskabsselskabets skrifter*. II. Hist.-Filos. Kl. 1909. Kristiania. [1911]. 'Ein neuer eisenzeitlicher Fund aus Ost-Finmarken in Norwegen,' *P.Z.* III, 347–355. Leipzig.

SPROCKHOFF, E. [1930]. *Zur Handelsgeschichte der germanischen Bronzezeit.* Vorgeschichtliche Forschungen, (Ebert), hft. 7. Berlin.

SPROCKHOFF, E. [1938]. *Die nordische Megalithkultur.* Berlin.

STAMPFUSS, R. [1938]. 'Ausgrabungen am Niederrhein. 1. Das germanische Haus von Bruckhausen, Kr. Dinslaken,' *Bonner Jahrbücher*, hft. 143/4, 221–38.

STEENSBERG, A. [1936]. 'En Muldfjaelsplov fra Førromersk Jernalder,' *Aarbøger*, 1936, 130–44.

STEENSBERG, A. [1936a]. 'North-West European Plough-Types of Prehistoric Times and the Middle Ages,' *Acta Arch.*, vol. VII, 1936, 244–80.

STEENSBERG, A. [1943]. *Ancient Harvesting Implements.* Nationalmuseets Skr. Ark.-Hist. R. I. Copenhagen.

STEENSBERG, A. [1945]. 'The Vebbestrup Plough. An Iron Age Plough of the Crook-Ard Type from a Jutland Bog,' *Acta Arch.*, 1945, 57–66.

STEINDORFF, G. [1913]. *Das Grab des Ti.* Leipzig.

STENBERGER, M. [1931]. 'Remnants of Iron Age Houses on Öland,' *Acta Arch.*, II, 93–104.

STENBERGER, M. [1933]. *Öland under äldre Järnåldern.* Stockholm.

STENBERGER, M. (editor) [1943]. *Forntida Gårdar i Island.* Copenhagen.

STENBERGER, M., DAHR, E. and MUNTHE, H. [1943]. *Das Grabfeld von Västerbjers auf Gotland.* Kungl. Vitt. Hist. och Antik. Akad. Stockholm.

STEVENS, C. E. [1941]. 'Agriculture and Rural Life in the Later Roman Empire,' *The Cambridge Economic History*, vol. I, chap. 2.

STIEREN, A. [1935]. 'Vorgeschichtliche Eisenhütting in Südwestfalen,' *Germania*, bd. 19, 12–20.

STIMMING, R. [1928]. 'Die Ancyluszeit in der märkischen Havelgegend,' *Archiv. f. Anthrop.*, XXI, 109–21.

STOCKAR, W. VON [1938]. *Spinnen und Weben bei den Germanen.* Mannus-Büch. nr. 59. Leipzig.

STONE, J. F. S. [1931, 1933, 1935]. 'Easton Down, Winterslow, S. Wilts., Flint Mine Excavation, 1930 and a Settlement Site of the Beaker Period . . .' *Wilts. Arch. Mag.*, XLV, 350–72. Also XLVI, 225–42 and XLVII, 68–80.

STRAKER, E. [1931]. *Wealden Iron.* London.

STRÖBEL, R. [1939]. *Die Feuersteingeräte der Pfahlbaukultur.* Mannus—Bücherei, nr. 66. Leipzig.

STUART, J. D. M. and BIRKBECK, J. M. 'A Celtic Village on Twyford Down,' *Proc. Hants. F.C.* XIII, 188–207.

SULIMIRSKI, T. [1948]. 'Faience Beads in the Polish Bronze Age,' *Man*, 1948, no. 139.

SULZBERGER, R. [1924]. 'Das Moorbautendorf "Weiher" bei Thayngen,' *Mitt. d. Antiqu. Ges. Zürich*, XXIX, 1924, 163 f.

SUNDELIN, U. [1920]. 'Stenåldersfolket och sjönöten,' *Ymer*, 1920, 131–95. [1924]. 'Boplatsspår från stenåldern inom Ätrans vattenområde,' *Ymer*, 1924, 346–60.

TACKENBERG, K. [1937]. 'Eine bandkeramische Siedlung in der Harth, Gemeinde Zwenkau,' *Germania*, 21 (1937), 217–220.

TALLGREN, A. M. [1934]. 'Sur les monuments mégalithiques du Caucase occidental,' *Eurasia Sept. Ant.*, IX, 1–45. Helsingfors.

TALLGREN, A. M. [1937]. 'The Arctic Bronze Age,' *Eurasia Sept. Ant.*, XI.

TANSLEY, A. G. [1939]. *The British Islands and Their Vegetation.* Cambridge.

TANSLEY, A. G. [1946]. *Introduction to Plant Ecology.* London.

TARAMELLI, A. [1916]. 'Gonnesa. Indagini nella Cittadella Nuragiea di Serrucci,' *Monumenti Antichi*, XXIV, 633–92. Milano.

THOMAS, H. H. [1923]. 'The Source of the Stones of Stonehenge,' *Ant. J.*, III, 239 ff.

THOMSEN, T. [1900]. 'Vævede stoffer fra Jernalderen,' *Aarbøger*, 1900, 257–78.

THOMSEN, T. [1929]. *Egekistfundet fra Egtved, fra den Aeldre Bronzealder.* Nordiske Fortidsminder, II, 4. Copenhagen.

THURNAM, J. [1873]. 'On ancient British barrows, especially those of Wiltshire and the adjoining counties,' *Arch.* XLII, 161–244; XLIII, 285–552.

THURNWALD, R. [1932]. *Economics in Primitive Communities.* Oxford.

TOMPA, F. VON [1937]. '25 Jahre Urgeschichtsforschung in Ungarn, 1912–1936,' 24/25 *Ber. Röm.-Germ. Komm.*, 27–127.

TOPELIUS, G. [1912]. 'Ett fiskstängsel från stenåldern,' *Finska Fornm. Tidskr.* XXVI, 227–32.

TRAEGER, P. [1904]. 'Zur Forschung über alte Schiffstypen. Schiffsfahrzeuge in Albanien u. Macedonien,' *Correspondenz-Blatt der deutschen Gesellschaft für Anthropologie, Ethnologie und Urgeschichte*, XXXV, 25–38.

TROELS-SMITH, J. [1942]. 'Pollenanalytische datierung zweier pflüge vom Walletypus,' *Acta Arch.*, XIII (1942), 269–72.

TROELS-SMITH, J. [1946]. 'Stammebaade fra Aamosen,' *Fra Nationalmuseets Abejdsmark*, 1946, 15–23.

TSCHUMI, O. [1940]. *Die ur- und frühgeschichtliche Fundstelle von Port im Amt Nidau.* Biel.

TURVILLE-PETRE, F. [1932]. 'Excavations in the Mugharet el-Kebarah,' *J.R.A.I.*, LXII, 271.

TÜXEN, R. [1931]. 'Die Grundlagen der Urlandschaftsforschung. Ein Beitrag zur Erforschung der Geschichte der anthropogenen Beeinflussung der Vegetation Mitteleuropas,' *Nachr. aus Niedersachsens Urgeschichte*, 1931, s. 59–105.

VASSITS, M. [1910]. 'Die Hauptergebnisse der prähistorischen Ausgrabung in Vinča im ahre 1908,' *Prähist. Z.* bd. 2, 1910, 23–9.

VASIĆ (VASSITS) M. M. [1932]. *Preistorijska Vinča.* 4 vols. Belgrade.

VAYSON, A. [1920]. 'Faucille préhistorique de Solférino,' *L'Anthropologie*, XXIX, 393–422.

VILARÓ, J. SERRA [1923]. 'Mina i fundició d'aram del primer período de l'Edat del bronze de Riner,' *Anuari de l'Institut d'Estudis Catalans*, vol. VI (1915–20), 535–38. Barcelona.

VILPPULA, H. [1940]. 'Luuluistimista,' *Suomen Museo*, XLVII, 51–58.

VIOLLIER, D. et al. [1924]. 'Pfahlbauten. Zehnter Bericht,' *Mitt. d. Antiqu. Ges. in Zürich*, bd. XXIX, h.4. Zürich.

VOGT, E. [1937]. *Geflechte und Gewebe der Steinzeit.* Basel.

VOGT, E. [1947]. 'Basketry and Woven Fabrics of the European Stone and Bronze Ages,' *Ciba Review*, no. 54, 1938–64. Basel.

VOGT, E. [1947]. 'Zum Problem des urgeschichtlich-völkerkundlichen Vergleichs,' *Bosch Festschrift*, 44–57.

VOGT, E. [1949]. 'The Birch as a Source of Raw Material during the Stone Age,' *P.P.S.*, 1949, 50–1.

VOUGA, P. [1923]. *La Tène.* Leipzig.

VOUGA, P. [1929]. *Classification du néolithique lacustre Suisse.* Neuchâtel.

VOUGA, P. [1934]. 'Le néolithique lacustre ancien,' *Recueil de travaux publiés par le Faculté des lettres, Univ. de Neuchâtel*, 1934, fasc. 17.

WACE, A. J. B. and THOMPSON, M. S. [1912]. *Prehistoric Thessaly.* Cambridge.

WACE, A. J. B. [1932]. *Chamber tombs at Mycenae.* (*Arch.*, vol. LXXXII). London.

WAGNER, K. H. [1938]. 'Steinzeitliche Pfostenhütten bei Mayen,' *Marburger Studien*, 254–8.

WAHLE, E. [1918]. *Ostdeutschland in jungneolithischer Zeit ein prähistorisch-geographischer Versuch.* Mannus-biblio., no. 15. Würzburg.

WAINWRIGHT, G. A. [1936]. 'The Coming of Iron,' *Antiquity*, 1936, 5–24.

WAKARELSKI, C. [1939]. 'Brunnen und wasserleitungen in Bulgarien,' *Folk-Liv*, 1939, 5–43.

WARD, GORDON [1941]. 'The Iron-Age Horseshoe and its derivatives,' *Ant. J.*, XXI, 9–27.

WARD-PERKINS, J. B. [1941]. 'The Iron-Age Horseshoe,' *Ant. J.*, 1941, 144–9.

WARREN, S. HAZZLEDINE [1911]. 'On a prehistoric Interment near Walton-on-Naze,' *Essex Naturalist*, XVI, 198–208.

WARREN, S. H. [1919]. 'A Stone-Axe Factory at Graig-Lwyd, Penmænmawr,' *J.R.A.I.*, XLIX (1919), 342–65. [1921] 'Excavations at the Stone-Axe Factory of Graig-Lwyd, Penmænmawr,' *J.R.A.I.*, LI (1921), 165–99. [1922] 'The Neolithic Stone Axes of Graig-Lwyd, Penmænmawr,' *Arch. Camb.*, II (1922), 7th Ser., 1–36.

WEIERSHAUSEN, P. [1939]. *Vorgeschichtliche Eisenhütten Deutschlands. Mannus Buch.*, bd. 65. Leipzig.

WERTH, E. [1932]. 'Die wilde Feige im östlichen Mittelmeergebiet und die Herkunst der Feigenkultur.' *Ber. der Deutschen Bot. Ges.* Bd. 50 (1932), 539 ff.

WERTH, E. [1937]. 'Zur Geographie und Geschichte der Hirsen,' *Angewandte Botanik*, bd. 19 (1937), 42 ff.

WESTERBY, E. [1927]. *Stenalderbopladser ved Klampenborg*. Copenhagen.

WHEELER, R. E. M. [1936]. *Verulamium. A Belgic and Two Roman Cities.* Soc. of Antiquaries London, Research Rep. no. XI.

WHEELER, R. E. M. [1943]. *Maiden Castle, Dorset.* Soc. of Antiquaries London, Research Rep. no. XII.

WIKLUND, K. B. [1931]. 'Den nordiska skidan, den södra och den arktiska,' *På skidor*, 5–50.

WILDE, W. R. [1857–62]. *A Descriptive Catalogue of the Antiquities . . . in the Museum of the Royal Irish Academy.* Dublin.

WILLIAMSON, K. [1948]. *The Atlantic Islands.* London.

WILLOCK, E. H. [1937]. 'A Neolithic Site on Haldon,' *Proc. Devon Arch. E.S.*, II, 244 ff.

WILSON, DANIEL [1863]. *Prehistoric Annals of Scotland.* 2 vols. London and Cambridge. 2nd ed.

WINGE, H. [1903]. 'Om jordfundne Fugle fra Danmark,' *Vidensk. Medd naturhist. For. København*, 1903, 61–109.

WINGE, H. [1904]. 'Om jordfundne Pattedyr fra Danmark,' *Vidensk. Medd. naturhist. For. København*, 1904, 193–304.

WINGE, H. [1919]. 'Dyreknogler fra Bronzealders Bopladser,' *Aarbøger*, 1919, 93–101.

WINKLER, H. [1938]. *Rock-Drawings of Southern Upper Egypt*, 1. London.

WINTHER, J. [1935]. *Troldebjerg*. Rudkøbing.

WITTER, W. [1936]. 'Woher kam das Zinn in der Frühen Bronzezeit? Ein Beitrag zur Herkunst der Bronze,' *Mannus Z.*, bd. 28, 446–56.

WITTER, W. [1938]. *Die älteste Erzgewinnung im nordisch-germanischen Lebenskreis.* Bd. I–II. Leipzig. Mannus-Büch. bd. 60, 63.

WOOLDRIDGE, S. W. and LINTON, D. L. [1933] 'The Loam-Terrains of South-East England and their Relation to its Early History,' *Antiquity*, 1933, 297–310.

WOLFF, G. [1917]. 'Eine neolithische Hüttengrube mit Pfostenlöchern und Brandgrab am Frauenberg bei Marburg,' *Germania*, I (1917), 19–26.

WRIGHT, E. V. and C. W. [1947]. 'Prehistoric Boats from North Ferriby, East Yorkshire,' *P.P.S.*, 1947, 114–38.

ZAMBOTTI, P. LAVIOSA [1939]. 'Civiltà palafitticola lombarda e civiltà di Golasecca,' *Rivista archeologica dell'antica provincia e diocesi di Como*, XVII (1939), 5–239. Cf. *Bull. Pal. Italiana*, 1939, 1–34.

ZAMIATNINE, S. [1934]. 'Gagarino,' *Bull. Acad. de Hist. de la Culture Matérielle*, fasc. 88.

ZAMMIT, T. [1930]. *Prehistoric Malta. The Tarxien Temples.* Oxford.

ZELENIN, D. [1927]. *Russische (Ostslavische) Volkskunde.* Berlin and Leipzig.

ZEUNER, F. E. [1950]. *Dating the Past. An Introduction to Geochronology.* 2nd edition. London.

ZSCHOCKE, K. and PREUSCHEN, E. [1932]. *Das urzeitliche Bergbaugebiet von Mühlbach-Bischofshofen.* Materialen zur Urgeschichte Österreichs, Heft. VI. Wien.

ZUROWSKI, J. [1930]. 'Neue Ergebnisse der neolithischen Forschung im südwestpolnischen Lössgebiet, *Prähist. Z.*, XXI, 2–20.

INDEX